CAMBRIDGE LIBRARY CO

Books of enduring scholarly valu

Literary Studies

This series provides a high-quality selection of early printings of literary works, textual editions, anthologies and literary criticism which are of lasting scholarly interest. Ranging from Old English to Shakespeare to early twentieth-century work from around the world, these books offer a valuable resource for scholars in reception history, textual editing, and literary studies.

Letters and Journals of Lord Byron

George Gordon Noel Byron, 6th Baron Byron of Rochdale (1788–1824) is one of the central writers of British Romanticism and his 'Byronic' hero – the charming, dashing, rebellious outsider – remains a literary archetype. But to what extent is this character a portrayal of the author himself? Byron was known for his extremely unconventional, eccentric character and his extravagant and flamboyant lifestyle: he had numerous scandalous love affairs, including a suspiciously close relationship with his half-sister Augusta Leigh. Lady Caroline Lamb, one of his lovers, famously described him as 'mad, bad and dangerous to know'. This two-volume work, compiled by his friend Thomas Moore, to whom Byron had given his manuscript memoirs (which he later burnt), was published in 1830. Volume 1 gives an account of Byron's early life, including his time as a star of the literary scene in London, and ends with his departure from the country in 1816.

Cambridge University Press has long been a pioneer in the reissuing of out-of-print titles from its own backlist, producing digital reprints of books that are still sought after by scholars and students but could not be reprinted economically using traditional technology. The Cambridge Library Collection extends this activity to a wider range of books which are still of importance to researchers and professionals, either for the source material they contain, or as landmarks in the history of their academic discipline.

Drawing from the world-renowned collections in the Cambridge University Library and other partner libraries, and guided by the advice of experts in each subject area, Cambridge University Press is using state-of-the-art scanning machines in its own Printing House to capture the content of each book selected for inclusion. The files are processed to give a consistently clear, crisp image, and the books finished to the high quality standard for which the Press is recognised around the world. The latest print-on-demand technology ensures that the books will remain available indefinitely, and that orders for single or multiple copies can quickly be supplied.

The Cambridge Library Collection brings back to life books of enduring scholarly value (including out-of-copyright works originally issued by other publishers) across a wide range of disciplines in the humanities and social sciences and in science and technology.

Letters and Journals of Lord Byron

VOLUME 1

EDITED BY THOMAS MOORE

CAMBRIDGE
UNIVERSITY PRESS

CAMBRIDGE UNIVERSITY PRESS

Cambridge, New York, Melbourne, Madrid, Cape Town,
Singapore, São Paolo, Delhi, Mexico City

Published in the United States of America by Cambridge University Press, New York

www.cambridge.org
Information on this title: www.cambridge.org/9781108047128

© in this compilation Cambridge University Press 2012

This edition first published
This digitally printed version 2012

ISBN 978-1-108-04712-8 Paperback

LETTERS

JOURNALS OF LORD BYRON:

WITH

NOTICES OF HIS LIFE,

BY

THOMAS MOORE.

IN TWO VOLUMES.

VOL. I.

LONDON:

JOHN MURRAY, ALBEMARLE-STREE

MDCCCXXX.

TO

SIR WALTER SCOTT, BARONET,

THESE VOLUMES

ARE INSCRIBED,

BY HIS AFFECTIONATE FRIEND,

THOMAS MOORE.

December, 1829.

PREFACE.

In presenting these volumes to the public I should have felt, I own, considerable diffidence, from a sincere distrust in my own powers of doing justice to such a task, were I not well convinced that there is in the subject itself, and in the rich variety of materials here brought to illustrate it, a degree of attraction and interest which it would be difficult, even for hands the most unskilful, to extinguish. However lamentable were the circumstances under which Lord Byron became estranged from his country, to his long absence from England, during the most brilliant period of his powers, we are indebted for all those interesting letters which compose the greater part of the Second Volume of this work, and which will be found equal, if not superior, in point of vigour, variety and liveliness, to any that have yet adorned this branch of our literature.

What has been said of Petrarch, that "his correspondence and verses together afford the progressive interest of a narrative in which the poet is always identified with the man," will be found applicable, in a far greater degree, to Lord Byron, in whom the literary and the personal character were so closely interwoven that to have left his works without the instructive commentary which his Life and Correspondence afford, would have been equally an injustice both to himself and to the world.

ERRATUM.

Page 114, line 3, *for* Huntingdon, *read* Hartington.

NOTICES

LIFE OF LORD BYRON.

It has been said of Lord Byron, that "he was prouder of being a descendant of those Byrons of Normandy, who accompanied William the Conqueror into England, than of having been the author of Childe Harold and Manfred." This remark is not altogether unfounded in truth. In the character of the noble poet the pride of ancestry was undoubtedly one of the most decided features; and, as far as antiquity alone gives lustre to descent, he had every reason to boast of the claims of his race. In Doomsday-book, the name of Ralph de Burun ranks high among the tenants of land in Nottinghamshire; and in the succeeding reigns, under the title of Lords of Horestan Castle*, we find his descendants holding considerable possessions in Derbyshire, to which afterwards, in the time of Edward I., were added the lands of Rochdale in Lancashire. So extensive, indeed, in those early times was the landed wealth of the family, that the partition of their property, in Nottinghamshire alone, has been sufficient to establish some of the first families of the county.

Its antiquity, however, was not the only distinction by which the

---

* " In the park of Horseley (says Thoroton) there was a castle, some of the ruins whereof are yet visible, called Horestan Castle, which was the chief mansion of his (Ralph de Burun's) successors."

VOL. I.   B

name of Byron came recommended to its inheritor; those personal merits
and accomplishments, which form the best ornament of a genealogy, seem
to have been displayed in no ordinary degree by some of his ancestors.
In one of his own early poems, alluding to the achievements of his race,
he commemorates, with much satisfaction, those "mail-cover'd barons"
among them,

> " who proudly to battle
> Led their vassals from Europe to Palestine's plain."

Adding,

> " Near Askalon's towers John of Horiston slumbers,
> Unnerved is the hand of his minstrel by death."

As there is no record, however, as far as I can discover, of any of
his ancestors having been engaged in the Holy Wars, it is possible that
he may have had no other authority for this notion than the tradition
which he found connected with certain strange groups of heads, which
are represented on the old panel-work in some of the chambers at Newstead.   In one of these groups, consisting of three heads, strongly carved
and projecting from the panel, the centre figure evidently represents a
Saracen or Moor, with an European female on one side of him, and a
Christian soldier on the other.   In a second group, which is in one of
the bedrooms, the female occupies the centre, while on each side is the
head of a Saracen, with the eyes fixed earnestly upon her.   Of the exact
meaning of these figures there is nothing certain known; but the tradition is, I understand, that they refer to some love-adventure, in which
one of those crusaders, of whom the young poet speaks, was engaged.

Of the more certain, or, at least, better known exploits of the family,
it is sufficient, perhaps, to say, that, at the siege of Calais under Edward
III., and on the fields, memorable in their respective eras, of Cressy,
Bosworth, and Marston Moor, the name of the Byrons reaped honours,
both of rank and fame, of which their young descendant has, in the verses
just cited, shown himself proudly conscious.

It was in the reign of Henry VIII., on the dissolution of the monasteries, that, by a royal grant, the church and priory of Newstead, with
the lands adjoining, were added to the other possessions of the Byron

family*. The favourite, upon whom these spoils of the ancient religion were conferred, was the grand-nephew of the gallant soldier who fought by the side of Richmond at Bosworth, and is distinguished from the other knights of the same christian name, in the family, by the title of "Sir John Byron the Little with the great beard." A portrait of this personage was one of the few family pictures with which the walls of the abbey, while in the possession of the noble poet, were decorated.

At the coronation of James I. we find another representative of the family selected as an object of royal favour,—the grandson of Sir John Byron the Little, being, on this occasion, made a Knight of the Bath. There is a letter to this personage, preserved in Lodge's Illustrations, from which it appears that, notwithstanding all these apparent indications of prosperity, the inroads of pecuniary embarrassment had already begun to be experienced by this ancient house. After counselling the new heir as to the best mode of getting free of his debts, " I do therefore advise you," continues the writer†, " that so soon as you have, in such sort as shall be fit, finished your father's funerals, to dispose and disperse that great household, reducing them to the number of forty or fifty, at the most, of all sorts; and, in my opinion, it will be far better for you to live for a time in Lancashire rather than in Notts for many good reasons that I can tell you when we meet, fitter for words than writing."

---

* The priory of Newstead had been founded and dedicated to God and the Virgin, by Henry II.:—and its monks, who were canons regular of the Order of St. Augustine, appear to have been peculiarly the objects of royal favour, no less in spiritual than in temporal concerns. During the lifetime of the fifth Lord Byron, there was found in the Lake at Newstead,—where it is supposed to have been thrown for concealment by the monks,—a large brass eagle, in the body of which, on its being sent to be cleaned, was discovered a secret aperture, concealing within it a number of old legal papers connected with the rights and privileges of the foundation. At the sale of the old lord's effects in 1776-7, this eagle, together with three candelabra, found at the same time, was purchased by a watchmaker of Nottingham (by whom the concealed manuscripts were discovered), and having from his hands passed into those of Sir Richard Kaye, a prebendary of Southwell, forms at present a very remarkable ornament of the cathedral of that place. A curious document, said to have been among those found in the eagle, is now in the possession of Colonel Wildman, containing a grant of full pardon from Henry V., of every possible crime (and there is a tolerably long catalogue enumerated) which the monks might have committed previous to the 8th of December preceding:—" *murdris* per ipsos *post decimum nonum diem Novembris* ultimo præteritum perpetratis, si quæ fuerint, *exceptis.*"

† The Earl of Shrewsbury.

From the following reign (Charles I.) the nobility of the family dates its origin. In the year 1643, Sir John Byron, great grandson of him who succeeded to the rich domains of Newstead, was created Baron Byron of Rochdale in the county of Lancaster; and seldom has a title been bestowed for such high and honourable services as those by which this nobleman deserved the gratitude of his royal master. Through almost every page of the History of the Civil Wars, we trace his name in connexion with the varying fortunes of the king, and find him faithful, persevering, and disinterested to the last. " Sir John Biron (says the writer of Colonel Hutchinson's Memoirs), afterwards Lord Biron, and all his brothers, bred up in arms and valiant men in their own persons, were all passionately the king's." There is also, in the answer which Colonel Hutchinson, when governor of Nottingham, returned, on one occasion, to his cousin-german, Sir Richard Biron, a noble tribute to the valour and fidelity of the family Sir Richard, having sent to prevail on his relative to surrender the castle, received for answer, that, " except he found his own heart prone to such treachery, he might consider there was, if nothing else, so much of a Biron's blood in him, that he should very much scorn to betray or quit a trust he had undertaken."

Such are a few of the gallant and distinguished personages, through whom the name and honours of this noble house have been transmitted. By the maternal side also Lord Byron had to pride himself on a line of ancestry as illustrious as any that Scotland can boast,—his mother, who was one of the Gordons of Gight, having been a descendant of that Sir William Gordon, who was the third son of the Earl of Huntley by the daughter of James I.

After the eventful period of the Civil Wars, when so many individuals of the house of Byron distinguished themselves—there having been no less than seven brothers of that family on the field at Edgehill—the celebrity of the name appears to have died away for near a century. It was about the year 1750, that the shipwreck and sufferings of Mr. Byron* (the grandfather of the illustrious subject of these pages), awakened in no small degree the attention and sympathy of the public. Not long after, a less innocent sort of notoriety attached itself to two

---

* Afterwards Admiral.

other members of the family,—one, the grand-uncle of the poet, and the other, his father. The former, in the year 1765, stood his trial before the House of Peers for killing, in a duel, or rather scuffle, his relation and neighbour Mr. Chaworth; and the latter, having carried off to the continent the wife of Lord Carmarthen, on the noble marquis obtaining a divorce from the lady, married her. Of this short union one daughter only was the issue, the honourable Augusta Byron, now the wife of Colonel Leigh.

In reviewing thus cursorily the ancestors, both near and remote, of Lord Byron, it cannot fail to be remarked how strikingly he combined in his own nature some of the best and, perhaps, worst qualities that lie scattered through the various characters of his predecessors,—the generosity, the love of enterprise, the high-mindedness of some of the better spirits of his race, with the irregular passions, the eccentricity, and daring recklessness of the world's opinion, that so much characterized others.

The first wife of the father of the poet having died in 1784, he, in the following year, married Miss Catharine Gordon, only child and heiress of George Gordon, Esq. of Gight. In addition to the estate of Gight, which had, however, in former times, been much more extensive, this lady possessed, in ready money, Bank shares, &c. no inconsiderable property; and it was known to be solely with a view of relieving himself from his debts that Mr. Byron paid his addresses to her. A circumstance related, as having taken place before the marriage of this lady, not only shows the extreme quickness and vehemence of her feelings, but, if it be true that she had never at the time seen Captain Byron, is not a little striking. Being at the Edinburgh Theatre one night when the character of Isabella was performed by Mrs. Siddons, so affected was she by the powers of this great actress, that, towards the conclusion of the play, she fell into violent fits, and was carried out of the theatre, screaming loudly, " Oh my Biron, my Biron."

On the occasion of her marriage there appeared a ballad by some Scotch rhymer, which has been lately reprinted in a collection of the " Ancient Ballads and Songs of the North of Scotland;" and as it bears testimony both to the reputation of the lady for wealth, and that of her husband for rakery and extravagance, it may be worth extracting:—

MISS GORDON OF GIGHT.

O whare are ye gaen, bonny Miss Gordon?
  O whare are ye gaen, sae bonny an' braw?
Ye 've married, ye 've married wi' Johnny Byron,
  To squander the lands o' Gight awa'.

This youth is a rake, frae England he 's come;
  The Scots dinna ken his extraction ava;
He keeps up his misses, his landlord he duns,
  That 's fast drawen' the lands o' Gight awa'.
                     O whare are ye gaen', &c.

The shooten' o' guns, an' rattlin' o' drums,
  The bugle in woods, the pipes i' the ha',
The beagles a howlin', the hounds a growlin';
  These soundings will soon gar Gight gang awa'.
                     O whare are ye gaen', &c.

Soon after the marriage, which took place, I believe, at Bath, Mr.
Byron and his lady removed to their estate in Scotland; and it was not
long before the prognostics of this ballad-maker began to be realized. The
extent of that chasm of debt, in which her fortune was to be swallowed up,
now opened upon the eyes of the ill-fated heiress. The creditors of Mr.
Byron lost no time in pressing their demands, and not only was the whole
of her ready money, Bank shares, fisheries, &c. sacrificed to satisfy them,
but a large sum raised by mortgage on the estate for the same purpose.
In the summer of 1786, she and her husband left Scotland, to proceed to
France; and in the following year the estate of Gight itself was sold,
and the whole of the purchase-money applied to the further payment of
debts,—with the exception of a small sum vested in trustees for the use
of Mrs. Byron, who thus found herself, within the short space of two
years, reduced from competence to a pittance of £150 per annum*.

---

* The following particulars respecting the amount of Mrs. Byron's fortune before marriage,
and its rapid disappearance afterwards, are, I have every reason to think, from the authentic
source to which I am indebted for them, strictly correct:

"At the time of the marriage Miss Gordon was possessed of about £3000 in money, two
shares of the Aberdeen Banking Company, the estates of Gight and Monkshill, and the Superiority of two Salmon Fishings on Dee. Soon after the arrival of Mr. and Mrs. Byron Gordon

From France Mrs. Byron returned to England at the close of the year 1787, and on the 22d of January, 1788, gave birth, in Holles-street, London, to her first and only child, George Gordon Byron. The name of Gordon was added in compliance with a condition imposed by will on whoever should become husband of the heiress of Gight; and at the baptism of the child, the Duke of Gordon, and Colonel Duff of Fetteresso, stood godfathers.

In reference to the circumstance of his being an only child, Lord Byron, in one of his journals, mentions some curious coincidences in his family, which to a mind disposed as his was to regard every thing connected with himself as out of the ordinary course of events, would naturally appear even more strange and singular than they are. " I have been thinking," he says, " of an odd circumstance. My daughter (1), my wife (2), my half-sister (3), my mother (4), my sister's mother (5), my natural daughter (6), and myself (7), are, or were, all *only* children. My sister's mother (Lady Conyers) had only my half-sister by that second marriage (herself, too, an only child), and my father had only me, an only child, by his second marriage with my mother, an only child too. Such a compli-

in Scotland, it appeared that Mr. Byron had involved himself very deeply in debt, and his creditors commenced legal proceedings for the recovery of their money. The cash in hand was soon paid away,—the Bank shares were disposed of at £600 (now worth £5000)—timber on the estate was cut down and sold to the amount of £1500—the farm of Monkshill and Superiority of the Fishings, affording a freehold qualification, were disposed at £480; and, in addition to these sales, within a year after the marriage, £8000 was borrowed on a mortgage upon the estate, granted by Mrs. Byron Gordon to the person who lent the money.

" In March 1786 a contract of marriage in the Scotch form was drawn up and signed by the parties. In the course of the summer of that year Mr. and Mrs. Byron left Gight, and never returned to it; the estate being, in the following year, sold to Lord Haddo for the sum of £17,850, the whole of which was applied to the payment of Mr. Byron's debts, with the exception of £1122, which remained as a burden on the estate (the interest to be applied to paying a jointure of £55. 11s. 1d. to Mrs. Byron's grandmother, the principal reverting, at her death, to Mrs. Byron), and £3000, vested in Trustees for Mrs. Byron's separate use, which was lent to Mr. Carswell of Ratharllet in Fifeshire."

" A strange occurrence" (says another of my informants) " took place previous to the sale of the lands. All the doves left the house of Gight and came to Lord Haddo's, and so did a number of herons, which had built their nests for many years in a wood on the banks of a large loch, called the Hagberry Pot. When this was told to Lord Haddo, he pertinently replied, ' Let the birds come, and do them no harm, for the land will soon follow;' which it actually did."

cation of *only* children, all tending to *one* family, is singular enough, and looks like fatality almost." He then adds, characteristically, "But the fiercest animals have the fewest numbers in their litters, as lions, tigers and even elephants, which are mild in comparison."

From London Mrs. Byron proceeded with her infant to Scotland and, in the year 1790, took up her residence in Aberdeen, where she was soon after joined by Captain Byron. Here for a short time they lived together in lodgings at the house of a person named Anderson, in Queen-street. But their union being by no means happy, a separation took place between them, and Mrs. Byron removed to lodgings at the other end of the street* Notwithstanding this schism, they for some time continued to visit, and even to drink tea with each other; but the elements of discord were strong on both sides, and their separation was, at last, complete and final. He would frequently, however, accost the nurse and his son in their walks, and expressed a strong wish to have the child for a day or two, on a visit with him. To this request Mrs. Byron was, at first, not very willing to accede, but, on the representation of the nurse, that "if he kept the boy one night, he would not do so another," she consented. The event proved as the nurse had predicted; on inquiring next morning after the child, she was told by Captain Byron that he had had quite enough of his young visitor, and she might take him home again.

It should be observed, however, that Mrs. Byron, at this period, was unable to keep more than one servant, and that, sent as the boy was on this occasion to encounter the trial of a visit, without the accustomed superintendence of his nurse, it is not so wonderful that he should have been found, under such circumstances, rather an unmanageable guest. That, as a child, his temper was violent, or rather sullenly passionate, is certain. Even when in petticoats, he showed the same uncontrollable spirit with his nurse, which he afterwards exhibited, when an author, with his critics. Being angrily reprimanded by her, one day, for having soiled or torn a new frock in which he had been just dressed, he got into one of his " silent rages" (as he himself has described them), seized the

---

* It appears that she several times changed her residence during her stay at Aberdeen, as there are two other houses pointed out, where she lodged for some time; one, situated in Virginia-street, and the other, the house of a Mr. Leslie, I think, in Broad-street.

frock with both his hands, rent it from top to bottom, and stood in sullen stillness, setting his censurer and her wrath at defiance.

But, notwithstanding this, and other such unruly outbreaks—in which he was but too much encouraged by the example of his mother, who frequently, it is said, proceeded to the same extremities with her caps, gowns, &c.—there was in his disposition, as appears from the concurrent testimony of nurses, tutors, and all who were employed about him, a mixture of affectionate sweetness and playfulness, by which it was impossible not to be attached; and which rendered him then, as in his riper years, easily manageable, by those who loved and understood him sufficiently to be at once gentle and firm enough for the task. The female attendant of whom we have spoken, as well as her sister, May Gray, who succeeded her, gained an influence over his mind against which he very rarely rebelled; while his mother, whose capricious excesses, both of anger and of fondness, left her little hold on either his respect or affection, was indebted solely to his sense of filial duty for any small portion of authority she was ever able to acquire over him.

By an accident which, it is said, occurred at the time of his birth, one of his feet was twisted out of its natural position, and this defect (chiefly from the contrivances employed to remedy it) was a source of much pain and inconvenience to him during his early years. The expedients used at this period to restore the limb to shape were adopted by the advice, and under the direction, of the celebrated John Hunter, with whom Doctor Livingstone of Aberdeen corresponded on the subject; and his nurse, to whom fell the task of putting on these machines or bandages, at bedtime, would often, as she herself told my informant, sing him to sleep, or tell him stories and legends, in which, like most other children, he took great delight. She also taught him, while yet an infant, to repeat a great number of the Psalms; and the first and twenty-third Psalms were among the earliest that he committed to memory. It is a remarkable fact, indeed, that through the care of this respectable woman, who was herself of a very religious disposition, he attained a far earlier and more intimate acquaintance with the Sacred Writings than falls to the lot of most young people. In a letter which he wrote to Mr. Murray, from Italy, in 1821, after requesting of that gentleman to send him, by the first opportunity, a Bible, he adds—" Don't forget this, for I am a great reader and admirer of those books, and had read them through and through before I was eight years old,—that is to say, the Old Testament, for the New struck me as a task, but the other as a pleasure. I speak, as a boy, from the recollected impression of that period at Aberdeen, in 1796."

The malformation of his foot was, even at this childish age, a subject on which he showed peculiar sensitiveness. I have been told by a gentleman of Glasgow, that the person who nursed his wife, and who still lives in his family, used often to join the nurse of Byron when they were out with their respective charges, and one day said to her, as they walked together, " What a pretty boy Byron is! what a pity he has such a leg!" On hearing this allusion to his infirmity, the child's eyes flashed with anger, and striking at her with a little whip which he held in his hand, he exclaimed impatiently, " Dinna speak of it!" Sometimes, however, as in after life, he could talk indifferently and even jestingly of this lameness; and there being another little boy in the neighbourhood, who had a similar defect in one of his feet, Byron would say, laughingly, " Come and see the twa laddies with the twa club feet going up the Broadstreet."

Among many instances of his quickness and energy at this age, his nurse mentioned a little incident that one night occurred, on her taking him to the theatre to see the Taming of the Shrew. He had attended to the performance, for some time, with silent interest; but, in the scene between Catherine and Petruchio, where the following dialogue takes place,—

> " *Cath.* I know it is the moon.
> *Pet.* Nay, then, you lie,—it is the blessed sun,"—

little Geordie (as they called the child), starting from his seat, cried out boldly, " But I say it is the moon, sir."

The short visit of Captain Byron to Aberdeen has already been mentioned, and he again passed two or three months in that city, before his last departure for France. On both occasions, his chief object was to extract still more money, if possible, from the unfortunate woman whom he had beggared; and so far was he successful, that, during his last visit, narrow as were her means, she contrived to furnish him with the money necessary for his journey to Valenciennes*, where, in the following year, 1791, he died. Though latterly Mrs. Byron would not see her husband, she entertained, it is said, a strong affection for him to the last, and on those occasions, when the nurse used to meet him in her walks, would inquire of her with the tenderest anxiety as to his health and looks. When the intelligence of his death, too, arrived, her grief, according to the account of this same attendant, bordered on distraction, and her shrieks were so loud as to be heard in the street. She was, indeed, a woman full of the most passionate extremes, and her grief and affection were bursts as much of temper as of feeling. To mourn at all, however, for such a husband was, it must be allowed, a most gratuitous stretch of generosity. Having married her, as he openly avowed, for her fortune alone, he soon dissipated this, the solitary, charm she possessed for him, and was then unmanful enough to taunt her with the inconveniences of that penury which his own extravagance had occasioned.

When not quite five years old, young Byron was sent to a day-school at Aberdeen, taught by Mr. Bowers†, and remained there, with some interruptions, during a twelvemonth, as appears by the following extract from the day-book of the school:

> " George Gordon Byron.
> 19th November, 1792.
> 19th November, 1793—paid one guinea."

The terms of this school for reading were only five shillings a quarter, and it was evidently less with a view to the boy's advance in learning than as a cheap mode of keeping him quiet that his mother had sent him

---

* By her advances of money to Mr. Byron (says an authority I have already cited) on the two occasions when he visited Aberdeen, as well as by the expenses incurred in furnishing the floor occupied by her, after his death, in Broad-street, she got in debt to the amount of £300, by paying the interest on which her income was reduced to £135. On this, however, she contrived to live without increasing her debt, and on the death of her grandmother, when she received the £1122 set apart for that lady's annuity, discharged the whole.

† In Long Acre. The present master of this school is Mr. David Grant, the ingenious editor of a collection of " Battles and War-Pieces," and of a work of much utility entitled " Class-Book of Modern Poetry."

to it.   Of the progress of his infantine studies at Aberdeen, as well under
Mr. Bowers as under the various other persons that instructed him, we
have the following interesting particulars communicated by himself, in a
sort of journal which he once began, under the title of " My Dictionary,"
and which is preserved in one of his manuscript books.

" For several years of my earliest childhood, I was in that city, but
have never revisited it since I was ten years old.   I was sent, at five
years old, or earlier, to a school kept by a Mr. Bowers, who was called
' *Bodsy* Bowers,' by reason of his dapperness.   It was a school for both
sexes.   I learned little there except to repeat by rote the first lesson of
monosyllables (' God made man'—' Let us love him') by hearing it often
repeated, without acquiring a letter.   Whenever proof was made of my
progress at home, I repeated these words with the most rapid fluency;
but on turning over a new leaf, I continued to repeat them, so that the
narrow boundaries of my first year's accomplishments were detected, my
ears boxed (which they did not deserve, seeing it was by ear only that I
had acquired my letters), and my intellects consigned to a new preceptor.
He was a very devout, clever little clergyman, named Ross, afterwards
minister of one of the kirks (*East*, I think).   Under him I made astonishing progress, and I recollect to this day his mild manners and good-
natured pains-taking.   The moment I could read, my grand passion was
history, and, why I know not, but I was particularly taken with the
battle near the Lake Regillus in the Roman History, put into my hands
the first.   Four years ago, when standing on the heights of Tusculum,
and looking down upon the little round lake that was once Regillus, and
which dots the immense expanse below, I remembered my young enthusiasm and my old instructor.   Afterwards I had a very serious, saturnine,
but kind young man, named Paterson, for a tutor.   He was the son of
my shoemaker, but a good scholar, as is common with the Scotch.   He
was a rigid presbyterian also.   With him I begun Latin in Ruddiman's
grammar, and continued till I went to the ' Grammar School' (*Scoticè*,
' Schule;' *Aberdonicè*, ' Squeel') where I threaded all the classes to the
fourth, when I was recalled to England (where I had been hatched) by
the demise of my uncle.   I acquired this handwriting, which I can
hardly read myself, under the fair copies of Mr. Duncan of the same

city: I don't think he would plume himself much upon my progress. However, I wrote much better then than I have ever done since. Haste and agitation of one kind or another have quite spoilt as pretty a scrawl as ever scratched over a frank. The grammar-school might consist of a hundred and fifty of all ages under age. It was divided into five classes taught by four masters, the chief teaching the fourth and fifth himself. As in England, the fifth, sixth forms, and monitors, are heard by the head masters."

Of his class-fellows at the grammar-school there are many, of course, still alive, by whom he is well remembered*; and the general impression they retain of him is, that he was a lively, warm-hearted, and high-spirited boy—passionate and resentful, but affectionate and companionable with his schoolfellows—to a remarkable degree venturous and fearless, and (as one of them significantly expressed it) " always more ready to give a blow than take one." Among many anecdotes illustrative of this spirit, it is related that once, in returning home from school, he fell in with a boy who had on some former occasion insulted him, but had then got off unpunished—little Byron, however, at the time, promising to " pay him off" whenever they should meet again. Accordingly, on this second encounter, though there were some other boys to take his opponent's part, he succeeded in inflicting upon him a hearty beating. On his return home, breathless, the servant inquired what he had been about, and was answered by him, with a mixture of rage and humour, that he had been paying a debt, by beating a boy according to promise; for that he was a Byron, and would never belie his motto, " *Trust Byron.*"

He was, indeed, much more anxious to distinguish himself among his schoolfellows by prowess in all sports† and exercises, than by advancement in learning. Though quick, when he could be persuaded to attend, or had any study that pleased him, he was in general very low in the class, nor seemed ambitious of being promoted any higher. It is the

* The old Porter, too, at the College, "minds weel" the little boy, with the red jacket and nankeen trowsers, whom he has so often turned out of the College court-yard.

† " He was," says one of my informants, " a good hand at marbles, and could drive one farther than most boys. He also excelled at ' Bases,' a game which requires considerable swiftness of foot."

custom, it seems, in this seminary, to invert, now and then, the order of the class, so as to make the highest and lowest boys change places,—with a view, no doubt, of piquing the ambition of both. On these occasions, and only these, Byron was sometimes at the head, and the master, to banter him, would say, " Now, George, man, let me see how soon you 'll be at the foot again*."

During this period, his mother and he made, occasionally, visits among their friends, passing some time at Fetteresso, the seat of his godfather, Colonel Duff (where the child's delight with a humorous old butler, named Ernest Fidler, is still remembered), and also at Banff, where some near connexions of Mrs. Byron resided.

In the summer of the year 1796, after an attack of scarlet-fever, he was removed by his mother for change of air into the Highlands; and it was either at this time, or in the following year, that they took up their residence at a farm-house in the neighbourhood of Ballater, a favourite summer resort for health and gaiety, about forty miles up the Dee from Aberdeen. Though this house, where they still show with much pride the bed in which young Byron slept, has become naturally a place of pilgrimage for the worshippers of genius, neither its own appearance, nor that of the small, bleak valley, in which it stands, is at all worthy of being associated with the memory of a poet. Within a short distance of it, however, all those features of wildness and beauty, which mark the course of the Dee through the Highlands, may be commanded. Here the dark summit of Lachin-y-gair stood towering before the eyes of the future bard; and the verses in which, not many years afterwards, he commemorated this sublime object, show that, young as he was, at the time, its " frowning glories" were not unnoticed by him†.

---

* On examining the quarterly lists kept at the grammar-school of Aberdeen, in which the names of the boys are set down according to the station each holds in his class, it appears that in April of the year 1794, the name of Byron, then in the second class, stands twenty-third in a list of thirty-eight boys. In the April of 1798, however, he had risen to be fifth in the fourth class, consisting of twenty-seven boys, and had got ahead of several of his contemporaries, who had, previously, always stood before him.

† Notwithstanding the lively recollections expressed in this poem, it is pretty certain, from the testimony of his nurse, that he never was at the mountain itself, which stood some miles distant from his residence, more than twice.

" Ah, there my young footsteps in infancy wander'd,
  My cap was the bonnet, my cloak was the plaid;
On chieftains long perish'd my memory ponder'd,
  As daily I strode through the pine-cover'd glade.
I sought not my home till the day's dying glory
  Gave place to the rays of the bright polar-star;
For Fancy was cheer'd by traditional glory,
  Disclosed by the natives of dark Loch-na-gar."

To the wildness and grandeur of the scenes, among which his child-hood was passed, it is not unusual to trace the first awakening of his poetic talent. But it may be questioned whether this faculty was ever so produced. That the charm of scenery, which derives its chief power from fancy and association, should be much felt at an age when fancy is yet hardly awake, and associations but few, can with difficulty, even making every allowance for the prematurity of genius, be conceived. The light which the poet sees around the forms of nature is not so much in the objects themselves as in the eye that contemplates them; and Imagination must first be able to lend a glory to such scenes, before she can derive inspiration *from* them. As materials, indeed, for the poetic faculty, when developed, to work upon, these impressions of the new and wonderful retained from childhood, and retained with all the vividness of recollection which belongs to genius, may form, it is true, the purest and most pre-cious part of that aliment, with which the memory of the poet feeds his imagination. But still, it is the newly awakened power within him that is the source of the charm;—it is the force of fancy alone that, acting upon his recollections, impregnates, as it were, all the past with poesy. In this respect, such impressions of natural scenery as Lord Byron received in his childhood, must be classed with the various other remembrances which that period leaves behind—of its innocence, its sports, its first hopes and affections—all of them reminiscences which the poet afterwards converts to his use, but which no more *make* the poet than—to apply an illustration of Byron's own—the honey can be said to make the bee that treasures it.

When it happens—as was the case with Lord Byron in Greece—that the same peculiar features of nature, over which Memory has shed this reflective charm, are reproduced before the eyes under new and inspiring circumstances, and with all the accessories which an imagination, in its full vigour and wealth, can lend them, then, indeed, do both the past and present combine to make the enchantment complete; and never was there a heart more borne away by this confluence of feelings than that of Byron. In a poem, written about a year or two before his death*, he traces all his enjoyment of mountain scenery to the impressions received during his residence in the Highlands; and even attributes the pleasure which he experienced in gazing upon Ida and Parnassus, far less to classic remembrances, than to those fond and deep-felt associations by which they brought back the memory of his boyhood and Lachin-y-gair.

> " He who first met the Highland's swelling blue,
>   Will love each peak that shows a kindred hue,
>   Hail in each crag a friend's familiar face,
>   And clasp the mountain in his mind's embrace.
>   Long have I roam'd through lands which are not mine,
>   Adored the Alp, and loved the Apennine,
>   Revered Parnassus, and beheld the steep
>   Jove's Ida and Olympus crown the deep:
>   But 'twas not all long ages' lore, nor all
>   Their nature held me in their thrilling thrall;
>   The infant rapture still survived the boy,
>   And Loch-na-gar with Ida look'd o'er Troy,
>   Mix'd Celtic memories with the Phrygian mount,
>   And Highland linns with Castalie's clear fount."

In a note appended to this passage, we find him falling into that sort of anachronism in the history of his own feelings, which I have above adverted to as not uncommon, and referring to childhood itself that love of mountain prospects, which was but the after result of his imaginative recollections of that period.

" From this period" (the time of his residence in the Highlands) " I date my love of mountainous countries. I can never forget the effect, a few years afterwards in England, of the only thing I had long

* The Island.

seen, even in miniature, of a mountain, in the Malvern Hills. After I returned to Cheltenham, I used to watch them every afternoon at sunset, with a sensation which I cannot describe."

His love of solitary rambles, and his taste for exploring in all directions, led him not unfrequently so far as to excite serious apprehensions for his safety. While at Aberdeen, he used often to steal from home unperceived;—sometimes he would find his way to the seaside; and once, after a long and anxious search, they found the adventurous little rover struggling in a sort of morass or marsh, from which he was unable to extricate himself.

In the course of one of his summer excursions up Dee-side, he had an opportunity of seeing still more of the wild beauties of the Highlands than even the neighbourhood of their residence at Ballatrech afforded,—having been taken by his mother through the romantic passes that lead to Invercauld, and as far up as the small waterfall, called the Linn of Dee. Here his love of adventure had nearly cost him his life. As he was scrambling along a declivity that overhung the fall, some heather caught his lame foot and he fell. Already he was rolling downward when the attendant luckily caught hold of him, and was but just in time to save him from being killed.

It was about this period, when he was not quite eight years old, that a feeling partaking more of the nature of love than it is easy to believe possible in so young a child, took, according to his own account, entire possession of his thoughts, and showed how early, in this passion, as in most others, the sensibilities of his nature were awakened *. The name of the object of this attachment was Mary Duff; and the following passage from a Journal, kept by him in 1813, will show how freshly, after an interval of seventeen years, all the circumstances of this early love still lived in his memory.

---

* Dante, we know, was but nine years old when, at a May-day festival, he saw and fell in love with Beatrice; and Alfieri, who was himself a precocious lover, considers such early sensibility to be an unerring sign of a soul formed for the fine arts:—" Effetti (he says, in describing the feelings of his own first love) che poche persone intendono, e pochissime provano: ma a quei soli pochissimi è concesso l'uscir dalla folla volgare in tutte le umane arti." Canova used to say, that he perfectly well remembered having been in love when but five years old.

" I have been thinking lately a good deal of Mary Duff. How very odd that I should have been so utterly, devotedly fond of that girl at an age when I could neither feel passion, nor know the meaning of the word. And the effect!—My mother used always to rally me about this childish amour; and, at last, many years after, when I was sixteen, she told me one day, 'Oh, Byron, I have had a letter from Edinburgh, from Miss Abercromby, and your old sweetheart Mary Duff is married to a Mr. Co⁰.' And what was my answer? I really cannot explain or account for my feelings at that moment; but they nearly threw me into convulsions, and alarmed my mother so much, that, after I grew better, she generally avoided the subject—to *me*—and contented herself with telling it to all her acquaintance. Now, what could this be? I had never seen her since her mother's faux-pas at Aberdeen had been the cause of her removal to her grandmother's at Banff; we were both the merest children. I had and have been attached fifty times since that period; yet I recollect all we said to each other, all our caresses, her features, my restlessness, sleeplessness, my tormenting my mother's maid to write for me to her, which she at last did, to quiet me. Poor Nancy thought I was wild, and, as I could not write for myself, became my secretary. I remember, too, our walks, and the happiness of sitting by Mary, in the children's apartment, at their house not far from the Plainstones at Aberdeen, while her lesser sister Helen played with the doll, and we sate gravely making love, in our way.

" How the deuce did all this occur so early? where could it originate? I certainly had no sexual ideas for years afterwards; and yet my misery, my love for that girl were so violent, that I sometimes doubt if I have ever been really attached since. Be that as it may, hearing of her marriage several years after was like a thunder-stroke—it nearly choked me —to the horror of my mother and the astonishment and almost incredulity of every body. And it is a phenomenon in my existence (for I was not eight years old) which has puzzled, and will puzzle me to the latest hour of it; and lately, I know not why, the *recollection* (*not* the attachment) has recurred as forcibly as ever. I wonder if she can have the least remembrance of it or me? or remember her pitying sister Helen for not having an admirer too? How very pretty is the perfect image of

her in my memory—her brown, dark hair, and hazel eyes; her very dress!
I should be quite grieved to see *her now*; the reality, however beautiful,
would destroy, or at least confuse, the features of the lovely Peri which
then existed in her, and still lives in my imagination, at the distance of
more than sixteen years.   I am now twenty-five and odd months. . . . .

" I think my mother told the circumstances (on my hearing of her
marriage) to the Parkynses, and certainly to the Pigot family, and probably mentioned it in her answer to Miss A., who was well acquainted
with my childish *penchant*, and had sent the news on purpose for *me*,—
and, thanks to her!

" Next to the beginning, the conclusion has often occupied my reflections, in the way of investigation.   That the facts are thus, others
know as well as I, and my memory yet tells me so, in more than a
whisper.   But, the more I reflect, the more I am bewildered to assign
any cause for this precocity of affection."

Though the chance of his succession to the title of his ancestors was
for some time altogether uncertain—there being, so late as the year 1794,
a grandson of the fifth lord still alive—his mother had, from his very
birth, cherished a strong persuasion that he was destined not only to be a
lord, but " a great man."   One of the circumstances on which she founded
this belief was, singularly enough, his lameness;—for what reason it is
difficult to conceive, except that, possibly (having a mind of the most
superstitious cast), she had consulted on the subject some village fortune-
teller, who, to ennoble this infirmity in her eyes, had linked the future
destiny of the child with it.

By the death of the grandson of the old lord at Corsica in 1794, the
only claimant, that had hitherto stood between little George and the
immediate succession to the peerage, was removed; and the increased
importance which this event conferred upon them was felt not only by
Mrs. Byron, but by the young future Baron of Newstead himself.   In
the winter of 1797, his mother having chanced, one day, to read part of a
speech spoken in the House of Commons, a friend who was present said
to the boy, " We shall have the pleasure, some time or other, of reading
your speeches in the House of Commons."   " I hope not," was his answer;
"if you read any speeches of mine, it will be in the House of Lords."

The title, of which he thus early anticipated the enjoyment, devolved
to him but too soon. Had he been left to struggle on for ten years longer
as plain George Byron, there can be little doubt that his character would
have been, in many respects, the better for it. In the following year
his grand-uncle, the fifth Lord Byron, died at Newstead Abbey, having
passed the latter years of his strange life in a state of austere and almost
savage seclusion. It is said, that the day after little Byron's accession to
the title, he ran up to his mother and asked her, " whether she perceived
any difference in him since he had been made a lord, as he perceived none
himself:"—a quick and natural thought; but the child little knew what
a total and talismanic change had been wrought in all his future relations
with society, by the simple addition of that word before his name. That
the event, as a crisis in his life, affected him, even at that time, may be
collected from the agitation which he is said to have manifested on the
important morning, when his name was first called out in school with
the title of " Dominus" prefixed to it. Unable to give utterance to the
usual answer " adsum," he stood silent amid the general stare of his
schoolfellows, and, at last, burst into tears.

The cloud, which, to a certain degree, undeservedly, his unfortunate
affray with Mr. Chaworth had thrown upon the character of the late
Lord Byron, was deepened and confirmed by what it, in a great measure,
produced,—the eccentric and unsocial course of life to which he afterwards betook himself. Of his cruelty to Lady Byron, before her separation from him, the most exaggerated stories are still current in the
neighbourhood; and it is even believed that, in one of his fits of fury, he
flung her into the pond at Newstead. On another occasion, it is said,
having shot his coachman for some disobedience of orders, he threw the
corpse into the carriage to his lady, and, mounting the box, drove off
himself. These stories are, no doubt, as gross fictions as some of those
which his illustrious successor was afterwards made the victim of; and a
female servant of the old lord, still alive, in contradicting both tales as
scandalous fabrications, supposes the first to have had its origin in the
following circumstance. A young lady, of the name of Booth, who was
on a visit at Newstead, being one evening with a party who were diverting
themselves in front of the abbey, Lord Byron, by accident, pushed her

into the basin which receives the cascades; and out of this little incident, as my informant very plausibly conjectures, the tale of his attempting to drown Lady Byron may have been fabricated.

After his lady had separated from him, the entire seclusion in which he lived gave full scope to the inventive faculties of his neighbours. There was no deed, however dark or desperate, that the village gossips were not ready to impute to him; and two grim images of satyrs, which stood in his gloomy garden, were, by the fears of those who had caught a glimpse of them, dignified with the name of " the old lord's devils." He was known always to go armed; and it is related that, on some particular occasion, when his neighbour, the late Sir John Warren, was admitted to dine with him, there was a case of pistols placed, as if forming a customary part of the dinner service, on the table.

During his latter years, the only companions of his solitude—besides that colony of crickets, which he is said to have amused himself with rearing and feeding*—were old Murray, afterwards the favourite servant of his successor, and the female domestic, whose authority I have just quoted, and who, from the station she was suspected of being promoted to by her noble master, received generally through the neighbourhood the appellation of " Lady Betty."

Though living in this sordid and solitary style, he was frequently, as it appears, much distressed for money; and one of the most serious of the injuries inflicted by him upon the property was his sale of the family estate of Rochdale in Lancashire, of which the mineral produce was accounted very valuable. He well knew, it is said, at the time of the sale, his inability to make out a legal title; nor is it supposed that the purchasers themselves were unacquainted with the defect of the con- veyance. But they contemplated, and, it seems, actually did realize, an indemnity from any pecuniary loss, before they could, in the ordinary course of events, be dispossessed of the property. During the young lord's minority, proceedings were instituted for the recovery of this estate, and, as the reader will learn hereafter, with success.

---

* To this Lord Byron used to add, on the authority of old servants of the family, that on the day of their patron's death, these crickets all left the house simultaneously, and in such numbers that it was impossible to cross the hall without treading on them.

At Newstead, both the mansion and the grounds around it were suffered to fall helplessly into decay; and among the few monuments of either care or expenditure which their lord left behind, were some masses of rockwork, on which much cost had been thrown away, and a few castellated buildings on the banks of the lake and in the woods. The forts upon the lake were designed to give a naval appearance to its waters and frequently, in his more social days, he used to amuse himself with sham fights,—his vessels attacking the forts, and being cannonaded by them in return. The largest of these vessels had been built for him at some seaport on the eastern coast, and, being conveyed on wheels over the Forest to Newstead, was supposed to have fulfilled one of the prophecies of Mother Shipton, which declared that "when a ship laden with *ling* should cross over Sherwood Forest, the Newstead Estate would pass from the Byron family." In Nottinghamshire, "ling" is the term used for *heather*; and, in order to bear out Mother Shipton and spite the old lord, the country people, it is said, ran along by the side of the vessel, heaping it with heather all the way.

This eccentric peer, it is evident, cared but little about the fate of his descendants. With his young heir in Scotland he held no communication whatever; and if at any time he happened to mention him, which but rarely occurred, it was never under any other designation than that of " the little boy who lives at Aberdeen."

On the death of his grand-uncle, Lord Byron having become a ward of chancery, the Earl of Carlisle, who was in some degree connected with the family, being the son of the deceased lord's sister, was appointed his guardian; and in the autumn of 1798, Mrs. Byron and her son, attended by their faithful May Gray, left Aberdeen for Newstead. Previously to their departure, the furniture of the humble lodgings which they had occupied was—with the exception of the plate and linen, which Mrs. Byron took with her—sold, and the whole sum, that the effects of the mother of the Lord of Newstead yielded, was £74. 17s. 7d.

From the early age at which Byron was taken to Scotland, as well as from the circumstance of his mother being a native of that country, he had every reason to consider himself—as, indeed, he boasts in Don Juan—" half a Scot by birth and bred a whole one." We have already seen how warmly he preserved through life his recollection of the mountain scenery in which he was brought up; and in the passage of Don Juan, to which I have just referred, his allusion to the romantic bridge of Don, and to other localities of Aberdeen, shows an equal fidelity and fondness of retrospect:

> " As Auld Lang Syne brings Scotland, one and all,
>> Scotch plaids, Scotch snoods, the blue hills and clear streams,
> The Dee, the Don, Balgounie's brig's black wall,
>> All my boy feelings, all my gentler dreams
> Of what I *then dreamt*, clothed in their own pall,
>> Like Banquo's offspring;—floating past me seems
> My childhood in this childishness of mine;—
> I care not—'tis a glimpse of ' Auld Lang Syne.' "

He adds in a note, " The Brig of Don, near the ' auld town' of Aberdeen, with its one arch and its black deep salmon stream, is in my memory as yesterday. I still remember, though perhaps I may misquote the awful proverb which made me pause to cross it, and yet lean over it with a childish delight, being an only son, at least by the mother's side. The saying, as recollected by me, was this, but I have never heard or seen it since I was nine years of age:

> " Brig of Balgounie, *black*'s your wa',
>> Wi' a wife's *ae son*, and a mear's ae foal,
> Down ye shall fa' * "

To meet with an Aberdonian was, at all times, a delight to him; and when the late Mr. Scott, who was a native of Aberdeen, paid him a visit at Venice in the year 1819, in talking of the haunts of his childhood, one of the places he particularly mentioned was Wallace-nook, a spot where there is a rude statue of the Scottish chief still standing. From first to last, indeed, these recollections of the country of his youth never forsook him. In his early voyage into Greece, not only the shapes of the moun-

---

* The correct reading of this legend is, I understand, as follows:

> " Brig o' Balgounie, *wight* (strong) is thy wa',
>> Wi' a wife's ae son on a mare's ae foal,
> Down shalt thou fa'."

tains, but the kilts and hardy forms of the Albanese,—all, as he says
" carried him back to Morven;" and, in his last fatal expedition, the dres.
which he himself chiefly wore at Cephalonia was a tartan jacket.

Cordial, however, and deep as were the impressions which he retained
of Scotland, he would sometimes in this, as in all his other amiable feelings
endeavour perversely to belie his own better nature, and, when under the
excitement of anger or ridicule, persuade not only others, but even himself, that the whole current of his feelings ran directly otherwise.   The
abuse with which, in his anger against the Edinburgh Review, he overwhelmed every thing Scotch, is an instance of this temporary triumph of
wilfulness; and, at any time, the least association of ridicule with the
country or its inhabitants was sufficient, for the moment, to put all his
sentiment to flight.   A friend of his once described to me the half playful
rage, into which she saw him thrown, one day, by a heedless girl, who
remarked that she thought he had a little of the Scotch accent.   " Good
God, I hope not !" he exclaimed.   " I'm sure I have n't.   I would rather
the whole d—d country was sunk in the sea—I, the Scotch accent !"

To such sallies, however, whether in writing or conversation, but
little weight is to be allowed.—particularly, in comparison with those
strong testimonies which he has left on record of his fondness for his early
home; and while, on his side, this feeling so indelibly existed, there is,
on the part of the people of Aberdeen, who consider him as almost their
fellow-townsman, a correspondent warmth of affection for his memory
and name.   The various houses where he resided in his youth are pointed
out to the traveller; to have seen him but once is a recollection boasted
of with pride; and the Brig of Don, beautiful in itself, is invested, by
his mere mention of it, with an additional charm.   Two or three years
since, the sum of five pounds was offered to a person in Aberdeen for a
letter which he had in his possession, written by Captain Byron a few
days before his death; and, among the memorials of the young poet,
which are treasured up by individuals of that place, there is one which it
would have not a little amused himself to hear of, being no less characteristic a relic than an old china saucer, out of which he had bitten a large
piece, in a fit of passion, when a child.

It was in the summer of 1798, as I have already said, that Lord

Byron, then in his eleventh year, left Scotland with his mother and nurse, to take possession of the ancient seat of his ancestors. In one of his latest letters, referring to this journey, he says, " I recollect Loch Leven as it were but yesterday—I saw it in my way to England in 1798." They had already arrived at the Newstead toll-bar, and saw the woods of the Abbey stretching out to receive them, when Mrs. Byron, affecting to be ignorant of the place, asked the woman of the toll-house—to whom that seat belonged? She was told that the owner of it, Lord Byron, had been some months dead. " And who is the next heir?" asked the proud and happy mother. " They say," answered the woman, " it is a little boy who lives at Aberdeen."—" And this is he, bless him!" exclaimed the nurse, no longer able to contain herself, and turning to kiss with delight the young lord who was seated on her lap.

Even under the most favourable circumstances, such an early eleva-tion to rank would be but too likely to have a dangerous influence on the character; and the guidance under which young Byron entered upon his new station was, of all others, the least likely to lead him safely through its perils and temptations. His mother, without judgment or self-command, alternately spoiled him by indulgence, and irritated, or —what was still worse,—amused him by her violence. That strong sense of the ridiculous, for which he was afterwards so remarkable, and which showed itself thus early, got the better even of his fear of her; and when Mrs. Byron, who was a short and corpulent person, and rolled con-siderably in her gait, would, in a rage, endeavour to catch him, for the purpose of inflicting punishment, the young urchin, proud of being able to outstrip her, notwithstanding his lameness, would run round the room, laughing like a little Puck, and mocking at all her menaces. In the few anecdotes of his early life which he related in his " Memoranda," though the name of his mother was never mentioned but with respect, it was not difficult to perceive that the recollections she had left behind—at least, those that had made the deepest impression—were of a painful nature. One of the most striking passages, indeed, in the few pages of that Memoir which related to his early days, was where, in speaking of his own sensitiveness, on the subject of his deformed foot, he described the feeling of horror and humiliation that came over him, when his mother, in one of her fits of passion, called him " a lame brat." As all that he had felt strongly through life was, in some shape or other reproduced in his poetry, it was not likely that an expression such as this should fail of being recorded. Accordingly we find, in the opening of his drama, " The Deformed Transformed,"

> " *Bertha.* Out, hunchback !
> *Arnold.* I was born so, mother !"

It may be questioned, indeed, whether that whole drama was not indebted for its origin to this single recollection.

While such was the character of the person under whose immediate eye his youth was passed, the counteraction which a kind and watchful guardian might have opposed to such example and influence was almost wholly lost to him. Connected but remotely with the family, and never having had any opportunity of knowing the boy, it was with much reluctance that Lord Carlisle originally undertook the trust; nor can we wonder that, when his duties as a guardian brought him acquainted with Mrs. Byron, he should be deterred from interfering more than was absolutely necessary for the child by his fear of coming into collision with the violence and caprice of the mother.

Had even the character which the last lord left behind been sufficiently popular to pique his young successor into an emulation of his good name, such a salutary rivalry of the dead would have supplied the place of living examples; and there is no mind in which such an ambition would have been more likely to spring up than that of Byron. But unluckily, as we have seen, this was not the case; and not only was so fair a stimulus to good conduct wanting, but a rivalry of a very different nature substituted in its place. The strange anecdotes told of the last lord by the country people, among whom his fierce and solitary habits had procured for him a sort of fearful renown, were of a nature livelily to arrest the fancy of the young poet, and even to waken in his mind a sort of boyish admiration for singularities which he found thus elevated into matters of wonder and record. By some it has been even supposed that in these stories of his eccentric relative his imagination found the first dark outlines of that ideal character, which he afterwards embodied in so many different shapes, and ennobled by his genius. But however this may be, it is at least far from improbable that, destitute as he was of other and better models, the peculiarities of his immediate predecessor should, in a considerable degree, have influenced his fancy and tastes. One habit, which he seems early to have derived from this spirit of imitation, and which he retained through life, was that of constantly having arms of some description about or near him—it being his practice, when quite a boy, to carry, at all times, small loaded pistols in his waistcoat pockets. The affray, indeed, of the late lord with Mr. Chaworth had, at a very early age, by connecting duelling in his mind with the name of his race, led him to turn his attention to this mode of arbitrament; and the mortification which he had, for some time, to endure at school, from insults, as he imagined, hazarded on the presumption of his physical inferiority, found consolation in the thought that a day would yet arrive when the law of the pistol would place him on a level with the strongest.

On their arrival from Scotland, Mrs. Byron, with the hope of having his lameness removed, placed her son under the care of a person, who professed the cure of such cases, at Nottingham. The name of this man, who appears to have been a mere empirical pretender, was Lavender; and the manner in which he is said to have proceeded was by first rubbing the foot over, for a considerable time, with handfuls of oil, and then twisting the limb forcibly round, and screwing it up in a wooden machine. That the boy might not lose ground in his education during this interval, he received lessons in Latin from a respectable schoolmaster, Mr. Rogers, who read parts of Virgil and Cicero with him, and represents his proficiency to have been, for his age, considerable. He was often, during his lessons, in violent pain, from the torturing position in which his foot was kept; and Mr. Rogers one day said to him, " It makes me uncomfortable, my lord, to see you sitting there in such pain as I *know* you must be suffering." " Never mind, Mr. Rogers," answered the boy; " you shall not see any signs of it in *me*."

This gentleman, who speaks with the most affectionate remembrance of his pupil, mentions several instances of the gaiety of spirit with which he used to take revenge on his tormentor, Lavender, by exposing and laughing at his pompous ignorance. Among other tricks, he one day scribbled down on a sheet of paper all the letters of the alphabet, put together at random, but in the form of words and sentences, and, placing them before this all-pretending person, asked him gravely what language it was. The quack, unwilling to own his ignorance, answered confidently " Italian,"—to the infinite delight, as it may be supposed, of the little satirist in embryo, who burst into a loud, triumphant laugh at the success of the trap which he had thus laid for imposture.

With that mindfulness towards all who had been about him in his youth, which was so distinguishing a trait in his character, he, many years after, when in the neighbourhood of Nottingham, sent a message, full of kindness, to his old instructor, and bid the bearer of it tell him, that, beginning from a certain line in Virgil which he mentioned, he could recite twenty verses on, which he well remembered having read with this gentleman, when suffering all the time the most dreadful pain.

It was about this period, according to his nurse, May Gray, that the first symptom of any tendency towards rhyming showed itself in him; and the occasion which she represented as having given rise to this childish effort was as follows. An elderly lady, who was in the habit of visiting his mother, had made use of some expression that very much affronted him, and these slights, his nurse said, he generally resented violently and implacably. The old lady had some curious notions respecting the soul, which, she imagined, took its flight to the moon after death, as a preliminary essay before it proceeded further. One day, after a repetition, it is supposed, of her original insult to the boy, he appeared before his nurse in a violent rage. " Well, my little hero," she asked, " what's the matter with you now?" Upon which the child answered, that " this old woman had put him in a most terrible passion—that he could not bear the sight of her," &c. &c.—and then broke out into the following doggerel, which he repeated over and over, as if delighted with the vent he had found for his rage :—

> " In Nottingham county there lives at Swan Green,
>   As curst an old lady as ever was seen;
>   And when she does die, which I hope will be soon,
>   She firmly believes she will go to the moon."

It is possible that these rhymes may have been caught up at second-hand; and he himself, as will presently be seen, dated his "first dash into poetry," as he calls it, a year later:—but the anecdote altogether, as containing some early dawnings of character, appeared to me worth preserving.

The small income of Mrs. Byron received at this time the addition,—most seasonable, no doubt, though on what grounds accorded, I know not —of a pension, on the Civil List, of £300 a year. The following is a copy of the King's Warrant for the grant:—

(Signed)
" GEORGE R.

" WHEREAS we are graciously pleased to grant unto Catharine Gordon Byron, widow, an annuity of £300, to commence from 5th July, 1799, and to continue during pleasure: our will and pleasure is, that, by virtue of our general letters of Privy Seal, bearing date 5th November, 1760, you do issue and pay out of our treasure, or revenue in the receipt of the Exchequer, applicable to the uses of our civil government, unto the said Catharine Gordon Byron, widow, or her assignees, the said annuity, to commence from 5th July, 1799, and to be paid quarterly, or otherwise, as the same shall become due, and to continue during our pleasure; and for so doing this shall be your warrant. Given at our Court of St. James, 2d October, 1799, 39th year of our reign.

" By His Majesty's command.

(Signed)   " W. PITT.
                " S. DOUGLAS.

" Edwd. Roberts, Dep. Cler^us. Pellium."

Finding but little benefit from the Nottingham practitioner, Mrs. Byron, in the summer of the year 1799, thought it right to remove her boy to London, where, at the suggestion of Lord Carlisle, he was put under the care of Dr. Baillie. It being an object, too, to place him at some quiet school, where the means adopted for the cure of his infirmity might be more easily attended to, the establishment of the late Dr. Glennie, at Dulwich, was chosen for that purpose; and, as it was thought

advisable that he should have a separate apartment to sleep in, Docto
Glennie had a bed put up for him in his own study.　Mrs. Byron, wh
had remained a short time behind him at Newstead, on her arrival in tow
took a house upon Sloane Terrace; and, under the direction of Dr. Bailli
one of the Messrs. Sheldrake* was employed to construct an instrumer
for the purpose of straightening the limb of the child.　Moderation in a
athletic exercises was, of course, prescribed; but Dr. Glennie found it b
no means easy to enforce compliance with this rule, as, though sufficientl
quiet when along with him in his study, no sooner was the boy release
for play, than he showed as much ambition to excel in all exercises as th
most robust youth of the school;—" an ambition," adds Dr. Glennie, i
the communication with which he favoured me a short time before hi
death, " which I have remarked to prevail in general in young person
labouring under similar defects of nature†."

Having been instructed in the elements of Latin grammar according
to the mode of teaching adopted at Aberdeen, the young student had
now unluckily to retrace his steps, and was, as is too often the case, re
tarded in his studies and perplexed in his recollections, by the necessity
of toiling through the rudiments again in one of the forms prescribed by
the English schools.　" I found him enter upon his tasks," says Dr. Glennie
" with alacrity and success.　He was playful, good-humoured, and beloved
by his companions.　His reading in history and poetry was far beyond the
usual standard of his age, and in my study he found many books open to
him, both to please his taste and gratify his curiosity; among others, a
set of our poets, from Chaucer to Churchill, which I am almost tempted

---

* In a letter, addressed lately by Mr. Sheldrake to the Editor of a Medical Journal, it is
stated that the person of the same name who attended Lord Byron at Dulwich owed the honour
of being called in to a mistake, and effected nothing towards the remedy of the limb.　The writer
of the letter adds that he was himself consulted by Lord Byron four or five years afterwards,
and though unable to undertake the cure of the defect, from the unwillingness of his noble
patient to submit to restraint or confinement, was successful in constructing a sort of shoe for
the foot, which, in some degree, alleviated the inconvenience under which he laboured.

† " Quoique," says Alfieri, speaking of his school-days, " je fusse le plus petit de tous les
grands qui se trouvaient au second appartement où j'étais descendu, c'était précisément mon
inferiorité de taille, d'age, et de force, qui me donnait plus de courage, et m'engageait à me
distinguer."

to say he had more than once perused from beginning to end. He showed at this age an intimate acquaintance with the historical parts of the Holy Scriptures, upon which he seemed delighted to converse with me, especially after our religious exercises of a Sunday evening; when he would reason upon the facts contained in the Sacred Volume, with every appearance of belief in the divine truths which they unfold. That the impressions," adds the writer, " thus imbibed in his boyhood, had, notwithstanding the irregularities of his after life, sunk deep into his mind, will appear, I think, to every impartial reader of his works in general; and I never have been able to divest myself of the persuasion that, in the strange aberrations which so unfortunately marked his subsequent career, he must have found it difficult to violate the better principles early instilled into him."

It should have been mentioned, among the traits which I have recorded of his still earlier years, that, according to the character given of him by his first nurse's husband, he was, when a mere child, "particularly inquisitive and puzzling about religion."

It was not long before Dr. Glennie began to discover—what instructors of youth must too often experience—that the parent was a much more difficult subject to deal with than the child. Though professing entire acquiescence in the representations of this gentleman, as to the propriety of leaving her son to pursue his studies without interruption, Mrs. Byron had neither sense nor self-denial enough to act up to these professions; but, in spite of the remonstrances of Dr. Glennie, and the injunctions of Lord Carlisle, continued to interfere with and thwart the progress of the boy's education in every way that a fond, wrong-headed, and self-willed mother could devise. In vain was it stated to her that, in all the elemental parts of learning which are requisite for a youth destined to a great public school, young Byron was much behind other youths of his age, and that, to retrieve this deficiency, the undivided application of his whole time would be necessary. Though appearing to be sensible of the truth of these suggestions, she not the less embarrassed and obstructed the teacher in his task. Not content with the interval between Saturday and Monday, which, contrary to Dr. Glennie's wish, the boy generally passed at Sloane Terrace, she would frequently keep him at home a week beyond this time, and, still further to add to the distraction of such inter ruptions, collected around him a numerous circle of young acquaintance without exercising, as may be supposed, much discrimination in he choice. "How indeed could she?" asks Dr. Glennie—"Mrs. Byron wa a total stranger to English society and English manners; with an exteric far from prepossessing, an understanding where nature had not been mor bountiful, a mind almost wholly without cultivation, and the peculiaritic of northern opinions, northern habits, and northern accent, I trust I do n great prejudice to the memory of my countrywoman, if I say Mrs. Byro was not a Madame de Lambert, endowed with powers to retrieve th fortune, and form the character and manners of a young nobleman, he son."

The interposition of Lord Carlisle, to whose authority it was foun necessary to appeal, had more than once given a check to these disturbing indulgences. Sanctioned by such support, Dr. Glennie even ventured t oppose himself to the privilege, so often abused, of the usual visits on ? Saturday; and the scenes which he had to encounter on each new case o refusal were such as would have wearied out the patience of any les? zealous and conscientious schoolmaster. Mrs. Byron, whose paroxysm? of passion were not, like those of her son, "silent rages," would, on al these occasions, break out into such audible fits of temper as it wa? impossible to keep from reaching the ears of the scholars and the servants; and Dr. Glennie had, one day, the pain of overhearing a schoolfellow of his noble pupil say to him, "Byron, your mother is a fool;" to which the other answered gloomily, "I know it." In conse- quence of all this violence and impracticability of temper, Lord Carlisle at length ceased to have any intercourse with the mother of his ward, and on a further application from the instructor, for the exertion of his influence, said, "I can have nothing more to do with Mrs. Byron,—you must now manage her as you can."

Among the books that lay accessible to the boys in Doctor Glennie's study was a pamphlet written by the brother of one of his most intimate friends, entitled "Narrative of the Shipwreck of the Juno on the coast of Arracan, in the year 1795." The writer had been the second officer of the ship, and the account which he had sent home to his friends of the sufferings of himself and his fellow-passengers had appeared to them so touching and strange, that they determined to publish it. The pamphlet attracted but little, it seems, of public attention, but among the young students of Dulwich Grove it was a favourite study; and the impression which it left on the retentive mind of Byron may have had some share, perhaps, in suggesting that curious research, through all the various Accounts of Shipwrecks upon record, by which he prepared himself to depict with such power a scene of the same description in Don Juan. The following affecting incident, mentioned by the author of this pamphlet, has been adopted, it will be seen, with but little change either of phrase or circumstance, by the poet :—

"Of those who were not immediately near me I knew little, unless by their cries. Some struggled hard, and died in great agony; but it was not always those whose strength was most impaired that died the easiest, though, in some cases, it might have been so. I particularly remember the following instances. Mr. Wade's servant, a stout and healthy boy, died early and almost without a groan; while another of the same age, but of a less promising appearance, held out much longer. The fate of these unfortunate boys differed also in another respect highly deserving of notice. Their fathers were both in the fore-top when the lads were taken ill. The father of Mr. Wade's boy hearing of his son's illness, answered with indifference, 'that he could do nothing for him,' and left him to his fate. The other, when the accounts reached him, hurried down, and watching for a favourable moment, crawled on all fours along the weather gunwale to his son, who was in the mizen rigging. By that time, only three or four planks of the quarter-deck remained, just over the weather-quarter gallery; and to this spot the unhappy man led his son, making him fast to the rail to prevent his being washed away. Whenever the boy was seized with a fit of retching, the father lifted him up and wiped the foam from his lips; and, if a shower came, he made him open his mouth to receive the drops, or gently squeezed them into it from a rag. In this affecting situation both remained four or five days, till the boy expired. The unfortunate parent, as if unwilling to believe the fact, then raised the body, gazed wistfully at it, and, when he could no longer entertain any doubt, watched

it in silence till it was carried off by the sea; then, wrapping himself
a piece of canvas, sunk down and rose no more; though he must hav
lived two days longer, as we judged from the quivering of his limbs, whe
a wave broke over him *."

* The following is Lord Byron's version of this touching narrative, and it will be felt,
think, by every reader, that this is one of the instances in which poetry must be content to yie
the palm to prose.   There is a pathos in the last sentences of the seaman's recital, which t
artifices of metre and rhyme were sure to disturb, and which, indeed, no verses, howev
beautiful, could half so naturally and powerfully express.

> " There were two fathers in this ghastly crew,
>   And with them their two sons, of whom the one
> Was more robust and hardy to the view,
>   But he died early; and when he was gone,
> His nearest messmate told his sire, who threw
>   One glance on him, and said, ' Heaven's will be done
> I can do nothing,' and he saw him thrown
> Into the deep without a tear or groan.
>
> " The other father had a weaklier child,
>   Of a soft cheek, and aspect delicate;
> But the boy bore up long, and with a mild
>   And patient spirit held aloof his fate;
> Little he said, and now and then he smiled,
>   As if to win a part from off the weight
> He saw increasing on his father's heart,
> With the deep, deadly thought, that they must part.
>
> " And o'er him bent his sire, and never raised
>   His eyes from off his face, but wiped the foam
> From his pale lips, and ever on him gazed,
>   And when the wish'd-for shower at length was come,
> And the boy's eyes, which the dull film half glazed,
>   Brighten'd, and for a moment seem'd to roam,
> He squeezed from out a rag some drops of rain
> Into his dying child's mouth—but in vain.
>
> " The boy expired—the father held the clay,
>   And look'd upon it long, and when at last
> Death left no doubt, and the dead burthen lay
>   Stiff on his heart, and pulse and hope were past,
> He watch'd it wistfully, until away
>   'Twas borne by the rude wave wherein 'twas cast;

It was probably during one of the vacations of this year, that the boyish love for his young cousin, Miss Parker, to which he attributes the glory of having first inspired him with poetry, took possession of his fancy. " My first dash into poetry (he says) was as early as 1800. It was the ebullition of a passion for my first cousin, Margaret Parker (daughter and granddaughter of the two Admirals Parker), one of the most beautiful of evanescent beings. I have long forgotten the verses, but it would be difficult for me to forget her—her dark eyes—her long eyelashes—her completely Greek cast of face and figure! I was then about twelve—she rather older, perhaps a year. She died about a year or two afterwards, in consequence of a fall, which injured her spine, and induced consumption Her sister Augusta (by some thought still more beautiful) died of the same malady; and it was, indeed, in attending her, that Margaret met with the accident which occasioned her own death. My sister told me, that when she went to see her, shortly before her death, upon accidentally mentioning my name, Margaret coloured through the paleness of mortality to the eyes, to the great astonishment of my sister, who (residing with her grandmother, Lady Holderness, and seeing but little of me, for family reasons) knew nothing of our attachment, nor could conceive why my name should affect her at such a time. I knew nothing of her illness, being at Harrow and in the country, till she was gone. Some years after, I made an attempt at an elegy—a very dull one*

" I do not recollect scarcely any thing equal to the *transparent* beauty of my cousin, or to the sweetness of her temper, during the short period of our intimacy. She looked as if she had been made out of a rainbow—all beauty and peace.

" My passion had its usual effects upon me—I could not sleep—I could not eat—I could not rest; and although I had reason to know that

> Then he himself sunk down all dumb and shivering,
> And gave no sign of life, save his limbs quivering."
>
> DON JUAN, CANTO II.

In the collection of " Shipwrecks and Disasters at Sea," to which Lord Byron so skilfully had recourse for the technical knowledge and facts out of which he has composed his own powerful description, the reader will find the Account of the loss of the Juno here referred to.

This elegy is in his first (unpublished) volume.

she loved me, it was the texture of my life to think of the time which must elapse before we could meet again—being usually about twelve hours of separation! But I was a fool then, and am not much wise now."

He had been nearly two years under the tuition of Doctor Glennie when his mother, discontented at the slowness of his progress—though being, herself, as we have seen, the principal cause of it—entreated so urgently of Lord Carlisle to have him removed to a public school, that her wish was at length acceded to; and "accordingly," says Doctor Glennie, "to Harrow he went, as little prepared as it is natural to suppose from two years of elementary instruction, thwarted by every art that could estrange the mind of youth from preceptor, from school, and from all serious study."

This gentleman saw but little of Lord Byron after he left his care; but, from the manner in which both he and Mrs. Glennie spoke of their early charge, it was evident that his subsequent career had been watched by them with interest; that they had seen even his errors through the softening medium of their first feeling towards him, and had never, in his most irregular aberrations, lost the traces of those fine qualities which they had loved and admired in him when a child. Of the constancy, too, of this feeling, Doctor Glennie had to stand no ordinary trial, having visited Geneva in 1817, soon after Lord Byron had left it, when the private character of the poet was in the very crisis of its unpopularity, and when, among those friends who knew that Doctor Glennie had once been his tutor, it was made a frequent subject of banter with this gentleman that he had not more strictly disciplined his pupil, or, to use their own words, "made a better boy of him."

About the time when young Byron was removed, for his education, to London, his nurse May Gray left the service of Mrs. Byron, and returned to her native country, where she died about three years since. She had married respectably, and, in one of her last illnesses, was attended professionally by Doctor Ewing of Aberdeen, who, having been always an enthusiastic admirer of Lord Byron, was no less surprised than delighted to find that the person under his care had for so many years been an attendant on his favourite poet. With avidity, as may be supposed, he noted down from the lips of his patient all the particulars she could remember of his lordship's early days; and it is to the communications with which this gentleman has favoured me, that I am indebted for many of the anecdotes of that period which I have related.

As a mark of gratitude for her attention to him, I *ron had, in parting with May Gray, presented her with his watch,—the hrst of which he had ever been possessor. This watch the faithful nurse preserved fondly through life, and, when she died, it was given by her husband to Doctor Ewing, by whom, as a relic of genius, it is equally valued. The affectionate boy had also presented her with a full-length miniature of himself, which was painted by Kay of Edinburgh, in the year 1795, and which represents him standing with a bow and arrows in his hand, and a profusion of hair falling over his shoulders. This curious little drawing has likewise passed into the possession of Dr. Ewing.

The same thoughtful gratitude was evinced by Byron towards the sister of this woman, his first nurse, to whom he wrote some years after he left Scotland, in the most cordial terms, making inquiries of her welfare, and informing her, with much joy, that he had at last got his foot so far restored as to be able to put on a common boot,—" an event, for which he had long anxiously wished, and which he was sure would give her great pleasure."

In the summer of the year 1801 he accompanied his mother to Cheltenham, and the account which he himself gives of his sensations at that period* shows at what an early age those feelings that lead to poetry had unfolded themselves in his heart. A boy, gazing with emotion on the hills at sunset, because they remind him of the mountains among which he passed his childhood, is already, in heart and imagination, a poet. It was during their stay at Cheltenham that a fortune-teller, whom his mother consulted, pronounced a prediction concerning him which, for some time, left a strong impression on his mind. Mrs. Byron had, it seems, in her first visit to this person (who, if I mistake not, was the celebrated fortune-teller, Mrs. Williams) endeavoured to pass herself off as a maiden lady   The Sibyl, however, was not so easily deceived;—she

See page 17.

pronounced her wise consulter to be not only a married woman, but the mother of a son who was lame, and to whom, among other events which she read in the stars, it was predestined that his life should be in danger from poison before he was of age, and that he should be twice married,—the second time, to a foreign lady. About two years afterwards he himself mentioned these particulars to the person from whom I heard the story, and said that the thought of the first part of the prophecy very often occurred to him. The latter part, however, seems to have been the *nearer* guess of the two.

To a shy disposition, such as Byron's was in his youth—and such as, to a certain degree, it continued all his life—the transition from a quiet establishment, like that of Dulwich Grove, to the bustle of a great public school was sufficiently trying. Accordingly, we find from his own account, that, for the first year and a half, he "hated Harrow." The activity, however, and sociableness of his nature soon conquered this repugnance; and, from being, as he himself says, "a most unpopular boy," he rose at length to be a leader in all the sports, schemes, and mischief of the school.

For a general notion of his disposition and capacities at this period, we could not have recourse to a more trustworthy or valuable authority than that of the Rev. Dr. Drury, who was at this time head master of the school, and to whom Lord Byron has left on record a tribute of affection and respect, which, like the reverential regard of Dryden for Dr. Busby, will long associate together honourably the names of the poet and the master. From this venerable scholar I have received the following brief, but important, statement of the impressions which his early intercourse with the young noble left upon him:—

" Mr. Hanson, Lord Byron's solicitor, consigned him to my care at the age of 13½, with remarks, that his education had been neglected; that he was ill prepared for a public school, but that he thought there was a *cleverness* about him. After his departure I took my young disciple into my study, and endeavoured to bring him forward by inquiries as to his former amusements, employments, and associates, but with little or no effect;—and I soon found that a wild mountain colt had been submitted to my management. But there was mind in his eye. In the first place, it was necessary to attach him to an elder boy, in order to familiarize him with the objects before him, and with some parts of the system in which he was to move. But the information he received from his conductor gave him no pleasure, when he heard of the advances of some in the school, much younger than himself, and conceived by his own deficiency that he should be degraded, and humbled, by being placed below them. This I discovered, and having committed him to the care of one of the masters, as his tutor, I assured him he should not be placed till, by diligence, he might rank with those of his own age. He was pleased with this assurance, and felt himself on easier terms with his associates;—for a degree of shyness hung about him for some time. His manner and temper soon convinced me, that he might be led by a silken string to a point, rather than by a cable;—on that principle I acted. After some continuance at Harrow, and when the powers of his mind had begun to expand, the late Lord Carlisle, his relation, desired to see me in town;— I waited on his lordship. His object was to inform me of Lord Byron's expectations of property when he came of age, which he represented as contracted, and to inquire respecting his abilities. On the former circumstance I made no remark; as to the latter, I replied, ‘He has talents, my lord, which will *add lustre to his rank.*’ ‘Indeed!!!’ said his lordship, with a degree of surprise, that, according to my feeling, did not express in it all the satisfaction I expected.

“ The circumstance to which you allude, as to his declamatory powers, was as follows. The upper part of the school composed declamations, which, after a revisal by the tutors, were submitted to the master: to him the authors repeated them, that they might be improved in manner and action, before their public delivery. I certainly was much pleased with Lord Byron's attitude, gesture, and delivery, as well as with his composition. All who spoke on that day adhered, as usual, to the letter of their composition, as, in the earlier part of his delivery, did Lord Byron. But to my surprise he suddenly diverged from the written composition, with a boldness and rapidity sufficient to alarm me, lest he should fail in memory as to the conclusion. There was no failure;—he came round to the close of his composition without discovering any impediment and irregularity on the whole. I questioned him, why he had altered

his declamation? He declared he had made no alteration, and did n
know, in speaking, that he had deviated from it one letter. I believe
him, and from a knowledge of his temperament am convinced, that full
impressed with the sense and substance of the subject, he was hurrie
on to expressions and colourings more striking than what his pen ha
expressed."

In communicating to me these recollections of his illustrious pupi
Dr. Drury has added a circumstance which shows how strongly, even i
all the pride of his fame, that awe with which he had once regarded th
opinions of his old master still hung around the poet's sensitive mind :-

" After my retreat from Harrow, I received from him two ver
affectionate letters. In my occasional visits subsequently to Londor
when he had fascinated the public with his productions, I demanded o
him, why, as in *duty bound,* he had sent none to me? ' Because,' said he
' you are the only man I never wish to read them :'—but, in a few mo
ments, he added—' What do you think of the Corsair?' "

I shall now lay before the reader such notices of his school life as
find scattered through the various note-books he has left behind. Coming
as they do, from his own pen, it is needless to add, that they afford th
liveliest and best records of this period that can be furnished.

" Till I was eighteen years old (odd as it may seem) I had never rea
a Review. But while at Harrow, my general information was so great
on modern topics as to induce a suspicion that I could only collect sc
much information from *Reviews,* because I was never *seen* reading, but
always idle, and in mischief, or at play. The truth is, that I read eating
read in bed, read when no one else read, and had read all sorts of reading
since I was five years old, and yet never *met* with a Review, which is the
only reason I know of why I should not have read them. But it is true;
for I remember when Hunter and Curzon, in 1804, told me this opinion
at Harrow, I made them laugh by my ludicrous astonishment in asking
them ' *What is* a Review?' To be sure, they were then less common. In
three years more, I was better acquainted with that same; but the first I
ever read was in 1806-7.

" At school I was (as I have said) remarked for the extent and readiness of my *general* information; but in all other respects idle, capable of

great sudden exertions (such as thirty or forty Greek hexameters, of course with such prosody as it pleased God), but of few continuous drudgeries. My qualities were much more oratorical and martial than poetical, and Dr. Drury, my grand patron (our head master), had a great notion that I should turn out an orator, from my fluency, my turbulence, my voice, my copiousness of declamation, and my action*. I remember that my first declamation astonished him into some unwonted (for he was economical of such) and sudden compliments, before the declaimers at our first rehearsal. My first Harrow verses (that is, English, as exercises), a translation of a chorus from the Prometheus of Æschylus, were received by him but coolly. No one had the least notion that I should subside into poesy.

" Peel, the orator and statesman (' that was, or is, or is to be '), was my form-fellow, and we were both at the top of our remove (a public-school phrase). We were on good terms, but his brother was my intimate friend. There were always great hopes of Peel, amongst us all, masters and scholars—and he has not disappointed them. As a scholar he was greatly my superior; as a declaimer and actor, I was reckoned at least his equal; as a schoolboy, *out* of school, I was always *in* scrapes, and *he never;* and *in school,* he *always* knew his lesson, and I rarely,—but when I knew it, I knew it nearly as well. In general information, history, &c. &c. I think I was *his* superior, as well as of most boys of my standing.

" The prodigy of our school-days was George Sinclair (son of Sir John); he made exercises for half the school *(literally),* verses at will, and themes without it. * * * He was a friend of mine, and in the same remove, and used at times to beg me to let him do my exercise,—a request always most readily accorded upon a pinch, or when I wanted to do something else, which was usually once an hour. On the other hand, he was pacific and I savage; so I fought for him, or thrashed others for

---

* For the display of his declamatory powers, on the speech-days, he selected always the most vehement passages,—such as the speech of Zanga over the body of Alonzo, and Lear's address to the storm. On one of these public occasions, when it was arranged that he should take the part of Drances, and young Peel that of Turnus, Lord Byron suddenly changed his mind, and preferred the speech of Latinus,—fearing, it was supposed, some ridicule from the inappropriate taunt of Turnus, " Ventosa in linguâ, *pedibusque fugacibus istis.*"

him, or thrashed himself to make him thrash others, when it was neces sary, as a point of honour and stature, that he should so chastise;—o we talked politics, for he was a great politician, and were very goo friends. I have some of his letters, written to me from school, still *.

" Clayton was another school-monster of learning, and talent, an hope; but what has become of him I do not know. He was certainly geuius.

" My school-friendships were with *me passions* † (for I was alway violent), but I do not know that there is one which has endured (to b sure some have been cut short by death) till now. That with Lord Clar begun one of the earliest and lasted longest—being only interrupted by distance—that I know of. I never hear the word ' *Clare*' without beating of the heart even *now*, and I write it with the feelings of 1803-4- ad infinitum."

The following extract is from another of his manuscript journals.

" At Harrow I fought my way very fairly ‡. I think I lost but one

---

* His letters to Mr. Sinclair, in return, are unluckily lost,—one of them, as this gentleman tells me, having been highly characteristic of the jealous sensitiveness of his noble schoolfellow being written under the impression of some ideal slight, and beginning, angrily, " Sir."

† On a leaf of one of his note-books, dated 1808, I find the following passage from Marmontel, which no doubt struck him as applicable to the enthusiasm of his own youthful friendships :—" L'amitié, qui dans le monde est à peine un sentiment, est une passion dans les Cloîtres."—*Contes Moraux.*

‡ Mr. D'Israeli, in his ingenious work " on the Literary Character," has given it as his opinion, that a disinclination to athletic sports and exercises will be, in general, found among the peculiarities which mark a youth of genius. In support of this notion he quotes Beattie, who thus describes his ideal minstrel :—

> " Concourse, and noise, and toil, he ever fled,
>   Nor cared to mingle in the clamorous fray
>   Of squabbling imps, but to the forest sped."

His highest authority, however, is Milton, who says of himself,

> " When I was yet a child, no childish play
>   To me was pleasing."

Such general rules, however, are as little applicable to the dispositions of men of genius as to their powers. If, in the instances which Mr. D'Israeli adduces, an indisposition to bodily exertion was manifested, as many others may be cited in which the directly opposite propensity was remarkable. In war, the most turbulent of exercises, Æschylus, Dante, Camoens, and

battle out of seven; and that was to H——;—and the rascal did not win it, but by the unfair treatment of his own boarding-house, where we boxed—I had not even a second. I never forgave him, and I should be sorry to meet him now, as I am sure we should quarrel. My most memorable combats were with Morgan, Rice, Rainsford, and Lord Jocelyn,—but we were always friendly afterwards. I was a most unpopular boy, but *led* latterly, and have retained many of my school friendships, and all my dislikes—except to Doctor Butler, whom I treated rebelliously, and have been sorry ever since. Doctor Drury, whom I plagued sufficiently too, was the best, the kindest (and yet strict, too) friend I ever had—and I look upon him still as a father.

"P. Hunter, Curzon, Long, and Tatersall, were my principal friends. Clare, Dorset, C. Gordon, De Bath, Claridge, and J^{no}. Wingfield, were my juniors and favourites, whom I spoilt by indulgence. Of all human beings, I was, perhaps, at one time, the most attached to poor Wingfield, who died at Coimbra, 1811, before I returned to England."

One of the most striking results of the English system of education is, that while in no country are there so many instances of manly friendships early formed and steadily maintained, so in no other country, perhaps, are the feelings towards the parental home so early estranged, or, at the best, feebly cherished. Transplanted as boys are from the domestic circle, at a time of life when the affections are most disposed to cling, it is but natural that they should seek a substitute for the ties of home* in those boyish friendships which they form at school, and which, connected as they are with the scenes and events over which youth threw its charm,

---

long list of other poets distinguished themselves; and, though it may be granted that Horace was a bad rider, and Virgil no tennis-player, yet, on the other hand, Dante was, we know, a falconer as well as swordsman; Tasso, expert both as swordsman and dancer; Alfieri, a great rider; Klopstock, a skaiter; Cowper, famous, in his youth, at cricket and foot-ball; and Lord Byron pre-eminent in all sorts of exercises.

* "At eight or nine years of age the boy goes to school. From that moment he becomes a stranger in his father's house. The course of parental kindness is interrupted. The smiles of his mother, those tender admonitions, and the solicitous care of both his parents, are no longer before his eyes—year after year he feels himself more detached from them, till at last he is so effectually weaned from the connexion, as to find himself happier any where than in their company."—*Cowper, Letters.*

retain ever after the strongest hold upon their hearts. In Ireland and,
believe, also in France, where the system of education is more domesti
a different result is accordingly observable :—the paternal home comes i
for its due and natural share of affection, and the growth of friendship
out of this domestic circle, is proportionably diminished.

To a youth like Byron, abounding with the most passionate feeling
and finding sympathy with only the ruder parts of his nature at home
the little world of school afforded a vent for his affections, which was sur
to call them forth in their most ardent form. Accordingly, the friend
ships which he contracted both at school and college were little less tha
what he himself describes them, " passions." The want he felt at hom
of those kindred dispositions, which greeted him among " Ida's socia
band," is thus strongly described in one of his early poems*:—

> " Is there no cause beyond the common claim,
>   Endear'd to all in childhood's very name?
>   Ah! sure some stronger impulse vibrates here,
>   Which whispers, friendship will be doubly dear
>   To one who thus for kindred hearts must roam,
>   And seek abroad the love denied at home:
>   Those hearts, dear Ida, have I found in thee,
>   A home, a world, a paradise to me."

* Even previously to any of these school friendships, he had formed the same sort of ro
mantic attachment to a boy of his own age, the son of one of his tenants at Newstead; and there
are two or three of his most juvenile poems, in which he dwells no less upon the inequality than
the warmth of this friendship. Thus:—

> " Let Folly smile, to view the names
>   Of thee and me in friendship twined;
>   Yet Virtue will have greater claims
>   To love, than rank with Vice combined.
>
> " And though unequal is thy fate,
>   Since title deck'd my higher birth,
>   Yet envy not this gaudy state,
>   Thine is the pride of modest worth.
>
> " Our souls at least congenial meet,
>   Nor can thy lot my rank disgrace;
>   Our intercourse is not less sweet
>   Since worth of rank supplies the place.
>
>   November, 1820."

This early volume, indeed, abounds with the most affectionate tributes to his school-fellows. Even his expostulations to one of them, who had given him some cause for complaint, are thus tenderly conveyed:—

> " You knew that my soul, that my heart, my existence,
>   If danger demanded, were wholly your own ;
> You knew me unalter'd by years or by distance,
>   Devoted to love and to friendship alone.
>
> " You knew—but away with the vain retrospection,
>   The bond of affection no longer endures.
> Too late you may droop o'er the fond recollection,
>   And sigh for the friend who was formerly yours."

The following description of what he felt after leaving Harrow, when he encountered in the world any of his old schoolfellows, falls far short of the scene which actually occurred but a few years before his death, in Italy,—when, on meeting with his friend, Lord Clare, after a long separation, he was affected almost to tears by the recollections which rushed on him.

> ——" If chance some well remember'd face,
> Some old companion of my early race,
> Advance to claim his friend with honest joy,
> My eyes, my heart proclaim'd me still a boy;
> The glittering scene, the fluttering groups around,
> Were all forgotten when my friend was found."

It will be seen, by the extracts from his memorandum-book which I have given, that Mr. Peel was one of his contemporaries at Harrow; and the following interesting anecdote of an occurrence in which both were concerned, has been related to me by a friend of the latter gentleman, in whose words I shall endeavour as nearly as possible to give it.

While Lord Byron and Mr. Peel were at Harrow together, a tyrant some few years older, whose name was * * * * * *, claimed a right to fag little Peel, which claim (whether rightly or wrongly, I know not) Peel resisted. His resistance, however, was in vain:—* * * * * * not only subdued him, but determined also to punish the refractory slave; and proceeded forthwith to put this determination in practice, by inflicting a

kind of bastinado on the inner fleshy side of the boy's arm, which, durin
the operation, was twisted round with some degree of technical skill, t
render the pain more acute. While the stripes were succeeding eac
other, and poor Peel writhing under them, Byron saw and felt for th
misery of his friend; and, although he knew that he was not stron
enough to fight * * * * * * with any hope of success, and that it was dan
gerous even to approach him, he advanced to the scene of action, an
with a blush of rage, tears in his eyes, and a voice trembling betwee
terror and indignation, asked very humbly if * * * * * * would be please
to tell him, "how many stripes he meant to inflict?"—"Why," returne
the executioner, "you little rascal, what is that to you?"—"Because, i
you please," said Byron, holding out his arm, "I would take half!"

There is a mixture of simplicity and magnanimity in this little trai
which is truly heroic; and, however we may smile at the friendships o
boys, it is but rarely that the friendship of manhood is capable of any
thing half so generous.

Among his school favourites a great number, it may be observed
were nobles or of noble family—Lords Clare and Delaware, the Duke
of Dorset and young Wingfield—and that their rank may have had
some share in first attracting his regard to them, might appear from a
circumstance mentioned to me by one of his schoolfellows, who, being
monitor one day, had put Lord Delaware on his list for punishment.
Byron, hearing of this, came up to him, and said, "Wildman, I find
you've got Delaware on your list—pray don't lick him."—"Why not?"
—"Why, I don't know—except that he is a brother peer. But pray
don't." It is almost needless to add, that his interference, on such
grounds, was any thing but successful. One of the few merits, indeed,
of public schools is, that they level, in some degree, these artificial
distinctions, and that, however the peer may have his revenge, in the
world, afterwards, the young plebeian is, for once, at least, on something
like an equality with him.

It is true that Lord Byron's high notions of rank were, in his boyish
days, so little disguised or softened down, as to draw upon him, at times,
the ridicule of his companions; and it was at Dulwich, I think, that
from his frequent boast of the superiority of an old English barony over

all the later creations of the peerage, he got the nickname, among the
boys, of " the Old English Baron."　But it is a mistake to suppose that,
either at school or afterwards, he was at all guided in the selection of his
friends by aristocratic sympathies.　On the contrary, like most very proud
persons, he chose his intimates in general from a rank beneath his own,
and those boys whom he ranked as *friends* at school were mostly of this
description; while the chief charm that recommended to him his younger
favourites was their inferiority to himself in age and strength, which
enabled him to indulge his generous pride by taking upon himself, when
necessary, the office of their protector.

Among those whom he attached to himself by this latter tie, one of
the earliest (though he has omitted to mention his name) was William
Harness, who at the time of his entering Harrow was ten years of age,
while Byron was fourteen.　Young Harness, still lame from an accident
of his childhood, and but just recovered from a severe illness, was ill fitted
to struggle with the difficulties of a public school; and Byron, one day,
seeing him bullied by a boy much older and stronger than himself, interfered and took his part.　The next day, as the little fellow was standing
alone, Byron came to him and said, " Harness, if any one bullies you, tell
me, and I 'll thrash him, if I can."　The young champion kept his word,
and they were from this time, notwithstanding the difference of their
ages, inseparable friends.　A coolness, however, subsequently arose between them, to which and to the juvenile friendship it interrupted, Lord
Byron, in a letter addressed to Harness six years afterwards, alludes
with so much kindly feeling, so much delicacy and frankness, that I am
tempted to anticipate the date of the letter and give an extract from it
here.

" We both seem perfectly to recollect, with a mixture of pleasure
and regret, the hours we once passed together, and I assure you most
sincerely they are numbered among the happiest of my brief chronicle
of enjoyment.　I am now *getting into years*, that is to say, I was *twenty*
a month ago, and another year will send me into the world to run my
career of folly with the rest.　I was then just fourteen,—you were almost
the first of my Harrow friends, certainly the *first* in my esteem, if not in
date; but an absence from Harrow for some time, shortly after, and new

connexions on your side, and the difference in our conduct (an advantag
decidedly in your favour) from that turbulent and riotous disposition o
mine, which impelled me into every species of mischief,—all these ci
cumstances combined to destroy an intimacy, which Affection urged m
to continue, and Memory compels me to regret.   But there is not a ci
cumstance attending that period, hardly a sentence we exchanged, whic
is not impressed on my mind at this moment.   I need not say more,—
this assurance alone must convince you, had I considered them as trivia
they would have been less indelible.   How well I recollect the perusa
of your 'first flights!'   There is another circumstance you do not know
—the *first lines* I ever attempted at Harrow were addressed to *you*.   Yo
were to have seen them; but Sinclair had the copy in his possession
when we went home;—and, on our return, we were *strangers*.   They
were destroyed, and certainly no great loss; but you will perceive from
this circumstance my opinions at an age when we cannot be hypocrites.

   " I have dwelt longer on this theme than I intended, and I shall
now conclude with what I ought to have begun.   We were once friends
—nay, we have always been so, for our separation was the effect of
chance, not of dissension.   I do not know how far our destinations in
life may throw us together, but if opportunity and inclination allow you
to waste a thought on such a hare-brained being as myself, you will find
me at least sincere, and not so bigoted to my faults as to involve others
in the consequences.   Will you sometimes write to me?   I do not ask
it often, and, if we meet, let us be what we *should* be and what we *were*."

   Of the tenaciousness with which, as we see in this letter, he clung
to all the impressions of his youth there can be no stronger proof than
the very interesting fact, that, while so little of his own boyish correspondence has been preserved, there were found among his papers almost
all the notes and letters which his principal school favourites, even the
youngest, had ever addressed to him; and, in some cases, where the
youthful writers had omitted to date their scrawls, his faithful memory
had, at an interval of years after, supplied the deficiency.   Among these
memorials, so fondly treasured by him, there is one which it would be
unjust not to cite, as well on account of the manly spirit that dawns
through its own childish language, as for the sake of the tender and

amiable feeling which, it will be seen, the re-perusal of it, in other days, awakened in Byron :—

" TO THE LORD BYRON, &c. &c.

" Harrow on the Hill, July 28th, 1805.

" Since you have been so unusually unkind to me, in calling me names whenever you meet me, of late, I must beg an explanation, wishing to know whether you choose to be as good friends with me as ever. I must own that, for this last month, you have entirely cut me,—for, I suppose, your new cronies. But think not that I will (because you choose to take into your head some whim or other) be always going up to you, nor do, as I observe certain other fellows doing, to regain your friendship; nor think that I am your friend either through interest, or because you are bigger and older than I am. No,—it never was so, nor ever shall be so. I was only your friend, and am so still,—unless you go on in this way, calling me names whenever you see me. I am sure you may easily perceive I do not like it; therefore, why should you do it, unless you wish that I should no longer be your friend? And why should I be so, if you treat me unkindly? I have no interest in being so. Though you do not let the boys bully me, yet if *you* treat me unkindly, that is to me a great deal worse.

" I am no hypocrite, Byron, nor will I, for your pleasure, ever suffer you to call me names, if you wish me to be your friend. If not, I cannot help it. I am sure no one can say that I will cringe to regain a friendship that you have rejected. Why should I do so? Am I not your equal? Therefore, what interest can I have in doing so? When we meet again in the world (that is, if you choose it), *you* cannot advance or promote *me*, nor I you. Therefore I beg and entreat of you, if you value my friend-ship,—which, by your conduct, I am sure I cannot think you do,—not to call me the names you do, nor abuse me. Till that time, it will be out of my power to call you friend. I shall be obliged for an answer as soon as it is convenient; till then

" I remain yours,

* *

" I cannot say your friend."

VOL. I.   H

Endorsed on this letter, in the handwriting of Lord Byron, is the following:

"This and another letter were written, at Harrow, by my *then* and, hope, *ever* beloved friend, Lord * *, when we were both schoolboys, and sent to my study in consequence of some childish misunderstanding,—the only one which ever arose between us. It was of short duration, and I retain this note solely for the purpose of submitting it to his perusal, that we may smile over the recollection of the insignificance of our first and last quarrel.   " BYRON."

In a letter, dated two years afterwards, from the same boy *, there occurs the following characteristic trait:—" I think by your last letter that you are very much piqued with most of your friends; and, if I am not much mistaken, you are a little piqued with me. In one part you say, 'There is little or no doubt a few years, or months, will render us as politely indifferent to each other as if we had never passed a portion of our time together.' Indeed, Byron, you wrong me, and I have no doubt—at least, I hope—you wrong yourself."

As that propensity to self-delineation which so strongly pervades his maturer works is, to the full, as predominant in his early productions,

---

* There are, in other letters of the same writer, some curious proofs of the passionate and jealous sensibility of Byron. From one of them, for instance, we collect that he had taken offence at his young friend's addressing him " my dear Byron," instead of " my dearest;" and, from another, that his jealousy had been awakened by some expressions of regret which his correspondent had expressed at the departure of Lord John Russell for Spain:—

" You tell me," says the young letter-writer, " that you never knew me in such an agitation as I was when I wrote my last letter; and do you not think I had reason to be so? I received a letter from you on Saturday, telling me you were going abroad for six years in March, and on Sunday John Russell set off for Spain. Was not that sufficient to make me rather melancholy? But how can you possibly imagine that I was more agitated on John Russell's account, who is gone for a few months, and from whom I shall hear constantly, than at your going for six years to travel over most part of the world, when I shall hardly ever hear from you, and perhaps may never see you again?

" It has very much hurt me your telling me that you might be excused if you felt rather jealous at my expressing more sorrow for the departure of the friend who was with me than of that one who was absent. It is quite impossible you can think I am more sorry for John's absence than I shall be for yours;—I shall therefore finish the subject."

there needs no better record of his mode of life, as a schoolboy, than what these fondly circumstantial effusions supply. Thus the sports he delighted and excelled in are enumerated :—

> " Yet when confinement's lingering hour was done,
> Our sports, our studies, and our souls were one:
> Together we impell'd the flying ball,
>
> . . . .
>
> Together join'd in cricket's manly toil,
> Or shared the produce of the river's spoil;
> Or, plunging from the green, declining shore,
> Our pliant limbs the buoyant waters bore;
> In every element, unchanged, the same,
> All, all that brothers should be, but the name."

The danger which he incurred in a fight with some of the neighbouring farmers—an event well remembered by some of his schoolfellows—is thus commemorated :—

> " Still I remember, in the factious strife,
> The rustic's musket aim'd against my life;
> High poised in air the massy weapon hung,
> A cry of horror burst from every tongue :
> Whilst I, in combat with another foe,
> Fought on, unconscious of the impending blow,
> Your arm, brave boy, arrested his career—
> Forward you sprung, insensible to fear;
> Disarm'd and baffled by your conquering hand,
> The grovelling savage roll'd upon the sand."

Some feud, it appears, had arisen on the subject of the cricket-ground, between these " clods " (as in school-language they are called) and the boys, and one or two skirmishes had previously taken place. But the engagement here recorded was accidentally brought on by the breaking up of school and the dismissal of the volunteers from drill, both happening, on that occasion, at the same hour. This circumstance accounts for the use of the musket, the but-end of which was aimed at Byron's head, and would have felled him to the ground but for the interposition of his friend Tatersall, a lively, high-spirited boy, whom he addresses here under the name of Davus.

Notwithstanding these general habits of play and idleness, whi
might seem to indicate a certain absence of reflection and feeling, the
were moments when the youthful poet would retire thoughtfully with
himself, and give way to moods of musing uncongenial with the usu
cheerfulness of his age. They show a tomb in the churchyard at Harro
commanding a view over Windsor, which was so well known to be l
favourite resting-place, that the boys called it "Byron's tomb*;" and he
they say, he used to sit for hours, wrapt up in thought,—brooding loneli
over the first stirrings of passion and genius in his soul, and occasiona]
perhaps indulging in those bright forethoughts of fame, under t
influence of which, when little more than fifteen years of age, he wro
these remarkable lines :—

> " My epitaph shall be my name alone;
> If that with honour fail to crown my clay,
> Oh may no other fame my deeds repay;
> That, only that, shall single out the spot,
> By that remember'd, or with that forgot."

In the autumn of 1802 he passed a short time with his mother a
Bath, and entered, rather prematurely, into some of the gaieties of th
place. At a masquerade given by Lady Riddel, he appeared in th
character of a Turkish boy,—a sort of anticipation, both in beauty an
costume, of his own young Selim in "the Bride." On his entering int
the house, some person in the crowd attempted to snatch the diamon
crescent from his turban, but was prevented by the prompt interpositio
of one of the party. The lady who mentioned to me this circumstanc
and who was well acquainted with Mrs. Byron at that period, adds th
following remark in the communication with which she has favoure
me:—"At Bath I saw a good deal of Lord Byron,—his mother fre
quently sent for me to take tea with her. He was always very pleasan
and droll, and, when conversing about absent friends, showed a sligh
turn for satire, which after-years, as is well known, gave a finer edge to.

---

* To this tomb he thus refers in the "Childish Recollections," as printed in his first un
published volume :

> " Oft when, oppress'd with sad, foreboding gloom,
> I sat reclined upon our favourite tomb."

We come now to an event in his life which, according to his own deliberate persuasion, exercised a lasting and paramount influence over the whole of his subsequent character and career.

It was in the year 1803 that his heart, already twice, as we have seen, possessed with the childish notion that it loved, conceived an attachment which—young as he was, even then, for such a feeling—sunk so deep into his mind as to give a colour to all his future life.   That unsuccessful loves are generally the most lasting is a truth, however sad, which unluckily did not require this instance to confirm it.   To the same cause, I fear, must be traced the perfect innocence and romance, which distinguish this very early attachment to Miss Chaworth from the many others that succeeded, without effacing, it in his heart;—making it the only one whose details can be entered into with safety, or whose results, however darkening their influence on himself, can be dwelt upon with a pleasurable interest by others.

On leaving Bath, Mrs. Byron took up her abode, in lodgings, at Nottingham,—Newstead Abbey being at that time let to Lord Grey de Ruthen,—and during the Harrow vacations of this year she was joined there by her son.   So attached was he to Newstead that even to be in its neighbourhood was a delight to him; and before he became acquainted with Lord Grey, he used sometimes to sleep, for a night, at the small house near the gate which is still known by the name of "the Hut*."   An intimacy, however, soon sprung up between him and his noble tenant, and an apartment in the abbey was from thenceforth always at his service.   To the family of Miss Chaworth, who resided at Annesley, in the immediate neighbourhood of Newstead, he had been made known, some time before, in London, and now renewed his acquaintance with them. The young heiress herself combined with the many worldly advantages that encircled her, much personal beauty, and a disposition the most amiable and attaching.   Though already fully alive to her charms, it was at the period of which we are speaking that the young poet, who was then in his sixteenth year, while the object of his adoration was about two years older, seems to have drunk deepest of that fascination whose

---

* I find this circumstance, of his having occasionally slept at the Hut, though asserted by one of the old servants, much doubted by others.

effects were to be so lasting;—six short summer weeks which he no
passed in her company being sufficient to lay the foundation of a feelin
for all life.

He used, at first, though offered a bed at Annesley, to return ever
night to Newstead, to sleep; alleging as a reason that he was afraid
the family pictures of the Chaworths,—that he fancied " they had take
a grudge to him on account of the duel, and would come down from
their frames at night to haunt him*." At length, one evening, he sai
gravely to Miss Chaworth and her cousin, " In going home last night
saw a *bogle;*"—which Scotch term being wholly unintelligible to th
young ladies, he explained that he had seen a *ghost*, and would not there
fore return to Newstead that evening. From this time, he always slep
at Annesley during the remainder of his visit, which was interrupted onl
by a short excursion to Matlock and Castleton, in which he had the hap
piness of accompanying Miss Chaworth and her party, and of which th
following interesting notice appears in one of his memorandum-books :—

" When I was fifteen years of age, it happened that, in a cavern in
Derbyshire, I had to cross in a boat (in which two people only could li
down), a stream which flows under a rock, with the rock so close upon
the water as to admit the boat only to be pushed on by a ferryman (
sort of Charon) who wades at the stern, stooping all the time. The com
panion of my transit was M. A. C., with whom I had been long in love
and never told it, though *she* had discovered it without. I recollect my
sensations, but cannot describe them, and it is as well. We were a party
a Mr. W., two Miss W.s, Mr. and Mrs. Cl—ke, Miss R., and *my* M. A. C
Alas! why do I say MY? Our union would have healed feuds in which
blood had been shed by our fathers, it would have joined lands broad and
rich, it would have joined at least *one* heart, and two persons not ill

---

* It may possibly have been the recollection of these pictures that suggested to him the
following lines in the Siege of Corinth :—

> " Like the figures on arras that gloomily glare,
> Stirr'd by the breath of the wintry air,
> So seen by the dying lamp's fitful light,
> Lifeless, but life-like and awful to sight;
> As they seem, through the dimness, about to come down
> From the shadowy wall where their images frown."

matched in years (she is two years my elder), and—and—and—*what* has been the result?"

In the dances of the evening at Matlock, Miss Chaworth, of course, joined, while her lover sate looking on, solitary and mortified. It is not impossible, indeed, that the dislike which he always expressed for this amusement may have originated in some bitter pang, felt in his youth, on seeing " the lady of his love" led out by others to the gay dance from which he was himself excluded. On the present occasion, the young heiress of Annesley having had for her partner (as often happens at Matlock) some person with whom she was wholly unacquainted, on her resuming her seat, Byron said to her, pettishly, " I hope you like your friend." The words were scarce out of his lips when he was accosted by an ungainly-looking Scotch lady, who rather boisterously claimed him as " cousin," and was putting his pride to the torture with her vulgarity, when he heard the voice of his fair companion retorting archly in his ear, " I hope *you* like your friend."

His time at Annesley was mostly passed in riding with Miss Chaworth and her cousin,—sitting in idle reverie, as was his custom, pulling at his handkerchief, or in firing at a door which opens upon the terrace, and which still, I believe, bears the marks of his shots. But his chief delight was in sitting to hear Miss Chaworth play; and the pretty Welsh air, " Mary Anne," was (partly, of course, on account of the name) his especial favourite. During all this time he had the pain of knowing that the heart of her he loved was occupied by another;—that, as he himself expresses it,

> " Her sighs were not for him; to her he was
> Even as a brother—but no more."

Neither is it, indeed, probable, had even her affections been disengaged, that Lord Byron would, at this time, have been selected as the object of them. A seniority of two years gives to a girl, " on the eve of womanhood," an advance into life, with which the boy keeps no proportionate pace. Miss Chaworth looked upon Byron as a mere schoolboy. He was in his manners, too, at that period, rough and odd, and (as I have heard from more than one quarter) by no means popular among girls of his own age. If, at any moment, however, he had flattered himself with the hope of being loved by her, a circumstance mentioned in his " Me-

moranda," as one of the most painful of those humiliations to whic
the defect in his foot had exposed him, must have let the truth in, wit
dreadful certainty, upon his heart. He either was told of, or overhear
Miss Chaworth saying to her maid, " Do you think I could care any thir
for that lame boy?" This speech, as he himself described it, was like
shot through his heart. Though late at night when he heard it, I
instantly darted out of the house, and scarcely knowing whither he ra
never stopped till he found himself at Newstead.

The picture which he has drawn of this youthful love, in one of th
most interesting of his poems, " The Dream," shows how genius and fee
ing can elevate the realities of this life, and give to the commonest even
and objects an undying lustre. The old hall at Annesley, under th
name of " the antique oratory," will long call up to fancy the " maide
and the youth" who once stood in it; while the image of the " lover'
steed," though suggested by the unromantic race-ground of Nottinghan
will not the less conduce to the general charm of the scene, and share
portion of that light which only Genius could shed over it.

He appears already, at this boyish age, to have been so far a pro
ficient in gallantry as to know the use that may be made of the trophie
of former triumphs in achieving new ones; for he used to boast, witl
much pride, to Miss Chaworth, of a locket which some fair favourite ha
given him, and which probably may have been a present from that pretty
cousin, of whom he speaks with such warmth in one of the notice
already quoted. He was also, it appears, not a little aware of his owr
beauty, which, notwithstanding the tendency to corpulence derived from
his mother, gave promise, at this time, of that peculiar expression int
which his features refined and kindled afterwards.

With the summer holidays ended this dream of his youth. He saw
Miss Chaworth once more in the succeeding year, and took his last farewell of her (as he himself used to relate) on that hill near Annesley*

---

* Among the unpublished verses of his in my possession I find the following fragment
written not long after this period:

    " Hills of Annesley, bleak and barren,
      Where my thoughtless childhood stray'd,
     How the northern tempests, warring,
      Howl above thy tufted shade!

which, in his poem of " the Dream," he describes so happily as " crowned with a peculiar diadem." No one, he declared, could have told how *much* he felt—for his countenance was calm and his feelings restrained. " The next time I see you," said he, in parting with her, " I suppose you will be Mrs. Chaworth*,"—and her answer was, " I hope so." It was before this interview that he wrote, with a pencil, in a volume of Madame de Maintenon's letters belonging to her, the following verses, which have never, I believe, before been published:

> " Oh Memory, torture me no more,
>   The present's all o'ercast;
> My hopes of future bliss are o'er,
>   In mercy veil the past.
> Why bring those images to view
>   I henceforth must resign?
> Ah! why those happy hours renew,
>   That never can be mine?
> Past pleasure doubles present pain,
>   To sorrow adds regret,
> Regret and hope are both in vain,
>   I ask but to—forget."

In the following year, 1805, Miss Chaworth was married to his successful rival, Mr. John Musters; and a person who was present when the first intelligence of the event was communicated to him, thus describes the manner in which he received it.—" I was present when he first heard of the marriage. His mother said, ' Byron, I have some news for you.'—' Well, what is it?'—' Take out your handkerchief first, for you will want it.'—' Nonsense!'—' Take out your handkerchief, I say.' He did so, to humour her. ' Miss Chaworth is married.' An expression, very peculiar, impossible to describe, passed over his pale face, and he hurried his handkerchief into his pocket, saying, with an affected air of coldness and nonchalance, ' Is that all?'—' Why, I expected you would

> " Now no more, the hours beguiling,
>   Former favourite haunts I see;
> Now no more my Mary smiling
>   Makes ye seem a Heaven to me."

* The lady's husband, for some time, took her family name.

have been plunged in grief!'—He made no reply, and soon began to ta
about something else."

His pursuits at Harrow continued to be of the same truant descri
tion during the whole of his stay there;—" always," as he says himsel
" cricketing, rebelling*, *rowing*, and in all manner of mischiefs." Th
" rebelling," of which he here speaks (though it never, I believe, pro
ceeded to any act of violence), took place on the retirement of Dr. Drur
from his situation as head master, when three candidates for the vacan
chair presented themselves, Mark Drury, Evans, and Butler. On th
first movement to which this contest gave rise in the school, youn
Wildman was at the head of the party for Mark Drury, while Byron a
first held himself aloof from any. Anxious, however, to have him as an ally
one of the Drury faction said to Wildman—" Byron, I know, will no
join, because he does n't choose to act second to any one, but, by giving
up the leadership to him, you may at once secure him." This Wildman
accordingly did, and Byron took the command of the party.

The violence with which he opposed the election of Doctor Butle
on this occasion (chiefly from the warm affection which he had fel
towards the last master) continued to embitter his relations with tha
gentleman during the remainder of his stay at Harrow. Unluckily thei
opportunities of collision were the more frequent from Byron being a
resident in Dr. Butler's house. One day the young rebel, in a fit o
defiance, tore down all the gratings from the window in the hall; an
when called upon by his host to say why he had committed this violence
answered, with stern coolness, " because they darkened the hall." O
another occasion he explicitly, and so far manfully, avowed to thi
gentleman's face the pique he entertained against him. It has long been
customary, at the end of a term, for the master to invite the upper boy
to dine with him; and these invitations are generally considered as, like
royal ones, a sort of command. Lord Byron, however, when asked, sen
back a refusal, which rather surprising Doctor Butler, he, on the firs

---

* Gibbon, in speaking of public schools, says—" the mimic scene of a rebellion has dis
played, in their true colours, the ministers and patriots of the rising generation." Such pro
gnostics, however, are not always to be relied upon;—the mild, peaceful Addison was, when a
school, the successful leader of a *barring-out*.

opportunity that occurred, inquired of him, in the presence of the other boys, his motive for this step:—" Have you any other engagement?"——" No, sir."—" But you must have *some* reason, Lord Byron."—" I have."—" What is it?"—" Why, Dr. Butler," replied the young peer, with proud composure, " if you should happen to come into my neighbourhood when I was staying at Newstead, I certainly should not ask you to dine with me, and therefore feel that *I* ought not to dine with *you.*"

The general character which he bore among the masters at Harrow was that of an idle boy, who would never learn any thing; and, as far as regarded his tasks in school, this reputation was, by his own avowal, not ill founded. It is impossible, indeed, to look through the books which he had then in use, and which are scribbled over with clumsily interlined translations, without being struck with the narrow extent of his classical attainments. The most ordinary Greek words have their English signification scrawled under them,—showing too plainly that he was not sufficiently familiarized with their meaning to trust himself without this aid. Thus, in his Xenophon we find νεοι, *young*—σομασιν, *bodies*—ανθρωποις τοις αγαθοις, *good men*, &c. &c.—and even in the volumes of Greek Plays, which he presented to the library on his departure, we observe, among other instances, the common word χρυσος provided with its English representative in the margin.

But, notwithstanding his backwardness in the mere verbal scholarship, on which so large and precious a portion of life is wasted*, in all that general and miscellaneous knowledge, which is alone useful in the world, he was making rapid and even wonderful progress. With a mind too inquisitive and excursive to be imprisoned within statutable limits, he flew to subjects that interested his already manly tastes, with a zest which it is in vain to expect that the mere pedantries of school could

---

* " It is deplorable to consider the loss which children make of their time at most schools, employing, or rather casting away, six or seven years in the learning of words only, and that very imperfectly."—Cowley, *Essays.*

" Would not a Chinese, who took notice of our way of breeding, be apt to imagine that all our young gentlemen were designed to be teachers and professors of the dead languages of foreign countries, and not to be men of business in their own?"—Locke *on Education.*

inspire; and the irregular, but ardent, snatches of study which he caugh in this way gave to a mind like his an impulse forwards, which left mo disciplined and plodding competitors far behind. The list, indeed, whic he has left on record of the works, in all departments of literature, whic he thus hastily and greedily devoured before he was fifteen years of ag is such as almost to startle belief,—comprising, as it does, a range an variety of study, which might make much older "helluones librorun hide their heads.

Not to argue, however, from the powers and movements of a min like Byron's, which might well be allowed to take a privileged directio of its own, there is little doubt, that to *any* youth of talent and ambitio the plan of instruction pursued in the great schools and universities o England, wholly inadequate as it is to the intellectual wants of the age * presents an alternative of evils not a little embarrassing. Difficult, na utterly impossible, as he will find it, to combine a competent acquisitio of useful knowledge with that round of antiquated studies which a pu suit of scholastic honours requires, he must either, by devoting the whol of his attention and ambition to the latter object, remain ignorant on mos of those subjects upon which mind grapples with mind in life, or b adopting, as Lord Byron and other distinguished persons have done, th contrary system, consent to pass for a dunce or idler in the schools, i order to afford himself even a chance of attaining eminence in the world

From the memorandums scribbled by the young poet in his schoo books we might almost fancy that, even at so early an age, he had a sor of vague presentiment that every thing relating to him would one day be an object of curiosity and interest. The date of his entrance a Harrow†, the names of the boys who were, at that time, monitors, th list of his fellow-pupils under Doctor Drury‡,—all are noted down with

* "A finished scholar may emerge from the head of Westminster or Eton in tota ignorance of the business and conversation of English gentlemen in the latter end of th eighteenth century."—GIBBON.

† "Byron, Harrow on the Hill, Middlesex, Alumnus Scholæ Lyonensis primus in ann Domini 1801, Ellison Duce."

"Monitors, 1801.—Ellison, Royston, Hunxman, Rashleigh, Rokeby, Leigh."

‡ "Drury's Pupils, 1804.—Byron, Drury, Sinclair, Hoare, Bolder, Annesley, Calvert Strong, Acland, Gordon, Drummond."

a fond minuteness, as if to form points of retrospect in his after-life ; and that he sometimes referred to them with this feeling will appear from one touching instance. On the first leaf of his " Scriptores Græci" we find, in his schoolboy hand, the following memorial :—" George Gordon Byron, Wednesday, June 26th, A. D. 1805, 3 quarters of an hour past 3 o'clock in the afternoon, 3d school,—Calvert, monitor, Tom Wildman on my left hand, and Long on my right. Harrow on the Hill." On the same leaf, written five years after, appears this comment :

> " Eheu fugaces, Posthume ! Posthume !
> Labuntur anni.

" B. January 9th, 1809.—Of the four persons whose names are here mentioned, one is dead, another in a distant climate, *all* separated, and not five years have elapsed since they sat together in school, and none are yet twenty-one years of age."

The vacation of 1804 * he passed with his mother at Southwell, to which place she had removed from Nottingham, in the summer of this year, having taken the house on the Green, called Burgage Manor. There is a Southwell play-bill extant, dated August 8th, 1804, in which the play is announced as bespoke " by Mrs. and Lord Byron." The gentleman, from whom the house where they resided was rented, possesses a library of some extent, which the young poet, he says, ransacked with much eagerness on his first coming to Southwell; and one of the books that most particularly engaged and interested him was, as may be easily believed, the life of Lord Herbert of Cherbury.

In the month of October, 1805, he was removed to Trinity College, Cambridge, and his feelings on the change from his beloved Ida to this new scene of life are thus described by himself :—

" When I first went up to college, it was a new and a heavy-hearted scene for me: firstly, I so much disliked leaving Harrow, that though it was time (I being seventeen), it broke my very rest for the last quarter

---

* During one of the Harrow vacations he passed some time in the house of the Abbé de Rouffigny, in Took's-court, for the purpose of studying the French language ; but he was, according to the Abbé's account, very little given to study, and spent most of his time in boxing, fencing, &c., to the no small disturbance of the reverend teacher and his establishment.

with counting the days that remained. I always *hated* Harrow till th
last year and half, but then I liked it. Secondly, I wished to go t
Oxford, and not to Cambridge. Thirdly, I was so completely alone i
this new world, that it half broke my spirits. My companions were no
unsocial, but the contrary—lively, hospitable, of rank and fortune, an
gay far beyond my gaiety. I mingled with, and dined and supped, &
with them; but, I know not how, it was one of the deadliest and heavies
feelings of my life to feel that I was no longer a boy."

But though, for a time, he may have felt this sort of estrangemen
at Cambridge, to remain long without attaching himself was not in hi
nature; and the friendship which he now formed with a youth name
Eddleston, who was two years younger than himself, even exceeded i
warmth and romance all his schoolboy attachments. This boy, whos
musical talents first drew them together, was, at the commencement o
their acquaintance, one of the choir at Cambridge, though he afterwards
it appears, entered into a mercantile line of life; and this disparity in
their stations was by no means without its charm for Byron, as gratifyin
at once both his pride and good-nature, and founding the tie betwee
them on the mutually dependent relations of protection on the one side
and gratitude and devotion on the other;—the only relations *, according
to Lord Bacon, in which the little friendship that still remains in the
world is to be found. It was upon a gift presented to him by Eddleston
that he wrote those verses entitled " The Cornelian," which were printed
in his first, unpublished volume, and of which the following is a stanza:—

> " Some, who can sneer at friendship's ties,
>   Have for my weakness oft reproved me;
> Yet still the simple gift I prize,
>   For I am sure the giver loved me."

Another friendship, of a less unequal kind, which had been begun
at Harrow, and which he continued to cultivate during his first year at
Cambridge, is thus interestingly dwelt upon in one of his journals:—

---

* Between superior and inferior, " whose fortunes (as he expresses it) comprehend the one
the other."

" How strange are my thoughts!—The reading of the song of Milton, ' Sabrina fair,' has brought back upon me—I know not how or why—the happiest, perhaps, days of my life (always excepting, here and there, a Harrow holiday in the two latter summers of my stay there) when living at Cambridge with Edward Noel Long, afterwards of the Guards,—who, after having served honourably in the expedition to Copenhagen (of which two or three thousand scoundrels yet survive in plight and pay) was drowned early in 1809, on his passage to Lisbon with his regiment in the St. George transport, which was run foul of, in the night, by another transport. We were rival swimmers—fond of riding—reading—and of conviviality. We had been at Harrow together; but—*there*, at least—his was a less boisterous spirit than mine. I was always cricketing—rebelling—fighting—*row*ing (from *row*, not *boat*-rowing, a different practice), and in all manner of mischiefs; while he was more sedate and polished. At Cambridge—both of Trinity—my spirit rather softened, or his roughened, for we became very great friends. The description of Sabrina's seat reminds me of our rival feats in *diving*. Though Cam's is not a very ' translucent wave,' it was fourteen feet deep, where we used to dive for, and pick up—having thrown them in on purpose—plates, eggs, and even shillings. I remember, in particular, there was the stump of a tree (at least ten or twelve feet deep) in the bed of the river, in a spot where we bathed most commonly, round which I used to cling, and ' wonder how the devil I came there.'

" Our evenings we passed in music (he was musical, and played on more than one instrument, flute and violoncello), in which I was audience; and I think that our chief beverage was soda-water. In the day we rode, bathed, and lounged, reading occasionally. I remember our buying, with vast alacrity, Moore's new quarto (in 1806), and reading it together in the evenings.

" We only passed the summer together;—Long had gone into the Guards during the year I passed in Notts, away from college. *His* friendship and a violent, though *pure*, love and passion—which held me at the same period—were the then romance of the. most romantic period of my life.

*   *   *   *   *   *   *

" I remember that, in the spring of 1809, H * * laughed at m
being distressed at Long's death, and amused himself with makin
epigrams upon his name, which was susceptible of a pun—*Long, shor*
&c. But three years after he had ample leisure to repent it, when ou
mutual friend, and his, H * *'s, particular friend, Charles Matthews
was drowned also, and he, himself, was as much affected by a simila
calamity. But *I* did not pay him back in puns and epigrams, for
valued Matthews too much, myself, to do so;—and, even if I had not,
should have respected his griefs.

" Long's father wrote to me to write his son's epitaph. I promised
—but I had not the heart to complete it. He was such a good, amiable
being as rarely remains long in this world; with talent and accomplish
ments, too, to make him the more regretted. Yet, although a cheerfu
companion, he had strange melancholy thoughts sometimes. I remember
once that we were going to his uncle's, I think,—I went to accompany
him to the door merely, in some Upper or Lower Grosvenor or Brook-
street, I forget which, but it was in a street leading out of some square
—he told me that, the night before, he 'had taken up a pistol—not
knowing or examining whether it was loaded or no—and had snapped
it at his head, leaving it to chance whether it might, or might not, be
charged.' The letter, too, which he wrote me, on leaving college to join
the Guards, was as melancholy in its tenour as it could well be on such an
occasion. But he showed nothing of this in his deportment, being mild
and gentle;—and yet with much turn for the ludicrous in his disposition.
We were both much attached to Harrow, and sometimes made excursions
there together from London, to revive our schoolboy recollections."

These affecting remembrances are contained in a Journal, which he
kept during his residence at Ravenna, in 1821, and they are rendered
still more touching and remarkable by the circumstances under which
they were noted down. Domesticated in a foreign land, and even
connected with foreign conspirators, whose arms, at the moment he was
writing, were in his house, he could yet thus wholly disengage himself
from the scene around him, and, borne away by the current of memory
into other times, live over the lost friendships of his boyhood again.
An English gentleman (Mr. Wathen) who called upon him, at one of

his residences in Italy, having happened to mention in conversation that he had been acquainted with Long, the noble poet, from that moment, treated him with the most marked kindness, and talked with him of Long and of his amiable qualities, till (as this gentleman says) the tears could not be concealed in his eyes.

In the summer of this year (1806) he, as usual, joined his mother at Southwell,—among the small, but select, society of which place he had, during his visits, formed some intimacies and friendships, the memory of which is still cherished there fondly and proudly. With the exception, indeed, of the brief and bewildering interval which he passed, as we have seen, in the company of Miss Chaworth, it was at Southwell alone that an opportunity was ever afforded him of profiting by the bland influence of female society, or of seeing what woman is in the true sphere of her virtues, home. The amiable and intelligent family of the Pigots received him within their circle, as one of themselves; and in the Rev. John Becher* the youthful poet found not only an acute and judicious critic, but a sincere friend. There were also one or two other families—as the Leacrofts, the Housons—among whom his talents and vivacity made him always welcome; and the proud shyness with which, through the whole of his minority, he kept aloof from all intercourse with the neighbouring gentlemen seems to have been entirely familiarized away by the small, cheerful society of Southwell. One of the most intimate and valued of his friends, at this period, has given me the following account of her first acquaintance with him:—" The first time I was introduced to him was at a party at his mother's, when he was so shy that she was forced to send for him three times before she could persuade him to come into the drawing-room, to play with the young people at a round game. He was then a fat bashful boy, with his hair combed straight over his forehead, and extremely like a miniature picture that his mother had painted by M. de Chambruland. The next morning Mrs. Byron brought him to call at our house, when he still continued shy and formal in his manner. The conversation turned upon Chelten-

---

* A gentleman, who has since honourably distinguished himself by his philanthropic plans and suggestions for that most important object, the amelioration of the condition of the Poor.

ham, where we had been staying, the amusements there, the plays, &c.
and I mentioned that I had seen the character of Gabriel Lackbrain ver
well performed. His mother getting up to go, he accompanied he
making a formal bow, and I, in allusion to the play, said 'Good b
Gaby.' His countenance lighted up, his handsome mouth displayed
broad grin, all his shyness vanished, never to return, and, upon hi
mother's saying 'Come, Byron, are you ready?'—no, she might go b
herself, he would stay and talk a little longer; and, from that momen
he used to come in and go out at all hours, as it pleased him, and in ou
house considered himself perfectly at home."

To this lady was addressed the earliest letter from his pen that ha
fallen into my hands. He corresponded with many of his Harro
friends,—with Lord Clare, Lord Powerscourt, Mr. William Peel, M
William Bankes, and others. But it was then little foreseen what genera
interest would one day attach to these schoolboy letters, and accordingly
as I have already had occasion to lament, there are but few of them no
in existence. The letter, of which I have spoken, to his Southwell friend
though containing nothing remarkable, is perhaps for that very reaso
worth insertion, as serving to show, on comparing it with most of it
successors, how rapidly his mind acquired confidence in its powers
There is, indeed, one charm for the eye of curiosity in his juvenil
manuscripts which they necessarily want in their printed form; and tha
is, the strong evidence of an irregular education which they exhibit,—
the unformed and childish handwriting and, now and then, even
defective spelling of him who, in a very few years after, was to start u
one of the giants of English literature.

LETTER I.

TO MISS ——.

"Burgage Manor, August 29th, 1804.

"I received the arms, my dear Miss ——, and am very much
obliged to you for the trouble you have taken. It is impossible I should
have any fault to find with them. The sight of the drawings gives me
great pleasure for a double reason,—in the first place, they will ornamen

my books, in the next, they convince me that *you* have not entirely *forgot* me. I am, however, sorry you do not return sooner,—you have already been gone an *age*. I perhaps may have taken my departure for London before you come back; but, however, I will hope not. Do not overlook my watch-ribbon and purse, as I wish to carry them with me. Your note was given me by Harry, at the play, whither I attended Miss L—— and Doctor S——; and now I have set down to answer it before I go to bed. If I am at Southwell when you return,—and I sincerely hope you will soon, for I very much regret your absence,—I shall be happy to hear you sing my favourite, 'The Maid of Lodi.' My mother, together with myself, desires to be affectionately remembered to Mrs. Pigot, and believe me, my dear Miss ———, I remain your affectionate friend,   " BYRON.

" P.S. If you think proper to send me any answer to this, I shall be extremely happy to receive it. Adieu.

"P.S. 2d. As you say you are a novice in the art of knitting, I hope it do n't give you too much trouble. Go on *slowly*, but surely. Once more, adieu."

We shall often have occasion to remark the fidelity to early habits and tastes by which Lord Byron, though in other respects so versatile, was distinguished. In the juvenile letter, just cited, there are two characteristics of this kind which he preserved unaltered during the remainder of his life;—namely, his punctuality in immediately answering letters, and his love of the simplest ballad music. Among the chief favourites to which this latter taste led him at this time were the songs of the Duenna, which he had the good taste to delight in; and some of his Harrow contemporaries still remember the joyousness with which, when dining with his friends at the memorable mother Barnard's, he used to roar out, " This bottle 's the sun of our table."

His visit to Southwell this summer was interrupted, about the beginning of August, by one of those explosions of temper on the part of Mrs. Byron, to which, from his earliest childhood, he had been but too well accustomed, and in producing which his own rebel spirit was not always, it may be supposed, entirely blameless. In all his portraits of himself, so dark is the pencil which he employs, that the following account of his own temper, from one of his journals, must be taken with a due portion of that allowance for exaggeration, which his style of self portraiture, "overshadowing even the shade," requires.

"In all other respects" (he says, after mentioning his infant passion for Mary Duff,) "I differed not at all from other children, being neither tall nor short, dull nor witty, of my age, but rather lively—except in my sullen moods, and then I was always a Devil. They once (in one of my silent rages) wrenched a knife from me, which I had snatched from table at Mrs. B.'s dinner (I always dined earlier), and applied to my breast;—but this was three or four years after, just before the late Lord B.'s decease.

"My *ostensible* temper has certainly improved in later years; but I shudder, and must, to my latest hour, regret the consequence of it and my passions combined. One event—but no matter—there are others not much better to think of also—and to them I give the preference.....

"But I hate dwelling upon incidents. My temper is now under management—rarely *loud*, and, *when* loud, never deadly. It is when silent, and I feel my forehead and my cheek *paling*, that I cannot control it; and then..... but unless there is a woman (and not any or every woman) in the way, I have sunk into tolerable apathy."

Between a temper, at all resembling this, and the loud hurricane bursts of Mrs. Byron, the collision, it may be supposed, was not a little formidable; and the age at which the young poet was now arrived, when,—as most parents feel,—the impatience of youth begins to champ the bit, would but render the occasions for such shocks more frequent. It is told, as a curious proof of their opinion of each other's violence, that, after parting one evening in a tempest of this kind, they were known each to go privately that night to the apothecary's, inquiring anxiously whether the other had been to purchase poison, and cautioning the vender of drugs not to attend to such an application, if made.

It was but rarely, however, that the young lord allowed himself to be provoked into more than a passive share in these scenes. To the boisterousness of his mother he would oppose a civil and, no doubt, provoking silence,—bowing to her but the more profoundly the higher her voice rose in the scale. In general, however, when he perceived that a storm was at hand, in flight lay his only safe resource. To this summary expedient he was driven, at the period of which we are speaking; but not till after a scene had taken place between him and Mrs. Byron, in which the violence of her temper had proceeded to lengths, that, however outrageous they may be deemed, were not, it appears, unusual with her. The poet, Young, in describing a temper of this sort, says—

> " The cups and saucers, in a whirlwind sent,
>   Just intimate the lady's discontent."

But poker and tongs were, it seems, the missiles which Mrs. Byron preferred, and which she, more than once, sent resounding after her fugitive son. In the present instance, he was but just in time to avoid a blow aimed at him with the former of these weapons, and to make a hasty escape to the house of a friend in the neighbourhood; where, concerting the best means of baffling pursuit, he decided upon an instant flight to London. The letters, which I am about to give, were written, immediately on his arrival in town, to some friends at Southwell, from whose kind interference in his behalf it may fairly be concluded that the blame of the quarrel, whatever it may have been, did not rest with him. The first is to Mr. Pigot, a young gentleman about the same age as himself, who had just returned, for the vacation, from Edinburgh, where he was, at that time, pursuing his medical studies.

LETTER II.

TO MR. PIGOT.

" 16, Piccadilly, August 9th, 1806.

" MY DEAR PIGOT,

" Many thanks for your amusing narrative of the last proceedings of my *amiable Alecto*, who now begins to feel the effects of her folly. I have just received a penitential epistle, to which, apprehensive of pursuit, I have despatched a moderate answer, with a *kind* of promise to return in a fortnight;—this, however *(entre nous)*, I never mean to fulfil.

Her *soft warblings* must have delighted her auditors, her *higher* note being particularly *musical,* and on a calm moonlight evening would be heard to great advantage. Had I been present as a spectator, nothing would have pleased me more; but to have come forward as one of the ' dramatis personæ,'—St. Dominic defend me from such a scene Seriously, your mother has laid me under great obligations, and you with the rest of your family, merit my warmest thanks for your kind connivance at my escape from ' Mrs. Byron *furiosa.*'

"Oh! for the pen of Ariosto to rehearse, in *epic,* the *scolding* of that *momentous eve,*—or rather, let me invoke the shade of Danté to inspire me, for none but the author of the ' *Inferno*' could properly preside over such an attempt. But, perhaps, where the pen might fail the pencil would succeed. What a group!—Mrs. B. the principal figure you cramming your ears with *cotton,* as the only antidote to total deafness; Mrs. ——— in vain endeavouring to mitigate the wrath of the *lioness* robbed of her whelp; and last, though not least, Elizabeth and *Wousky,*—*wonderful to relate!*—both deprived of their parts of speech, and bringing up the rear in *mute* astonishment. How did S. B. receive the intelligence? How many *puns* did he utter on so *facetious* an event? In your next inform me on this point, and what excuse you made to A. You are probably by this time tired of deciphering this hieroglyphical letter;—like Tony Lumpkin, you will pronounce mine to be a d——d up and down hand. All Southwell, without doubt, is involved in amazement. Apropos, how does my blue-eyed nun, the fair * *? is she ' *robed in sable garb of woe ?*'

"Here I remain at least a week or ten days; previous to my departure you shall receive my address, but what it will be I have not determined. My lodgings must be kept secret from Mrs. B.; you may present my compliments to her, and say any attempt to pursue me will fail, as I have taken measures to retreat immediately to Portsmouth, on the first intimation of her removal from Southwell. You may add, I have now proceeded to a friend's house in the country, there to remain a fortnight.

"I have now *blotted* (I must not say written) a complete double letter, and in return shall expect a *monstrous budget.* Without doubt, the dames of Southwell reprobate the pernicious example I have shown, and tremble lest their *babes* should disobey their mandates, and quit in dudgeon their mammas on any grievance. Adieu. When you begin your next drop the 'lordship,' and put 'Byron' in its place. Believe me yours, &c.   " BYRON."

From the succeeding letters, it will be seen that the " lioness" was not behindhand, in energy and decision, with her offspring, but, immediately on discovering his flight, set off after him.

LETTER III.

TO MISS ———.

" London, August 10th, 1806.

" MY DEAR BRIDGET,

" As I have already troubled your brother with more than he will find pleasure in deciphering, you are the next to whom I shall assign the difficult employment of perusing this 2nd epistle. You will perceive from my 1st, that no idea of Mrs. B.'s arrival had disturbed me at the time it was written ; *not* so the present, since the appearance of a note from the *illustrious cause* of my *sudden decampment* has driven the 'natural ruby from my cheeks,' and completely blanched my woe-begone countenance. This gunpowder intimation of her arrival (confound her activity !) breathes less of terror and dismay than you will probably imagine from the *volcanic* temperament of her *ladyship*, and concludes with the comfortable assurance of all *present motion* being prevented by the fatigue of her journey, for which my *blessings* are due to the rough roads and restive quadrupeds of his majesty's highways. As I have not the smallest inclination to be chased round the country, I shall e'en make a merit of necessity, and since, like Macbeth, ' They 've tied me to the stake, I cannot fly,' I shall imitate that valorous tyrant, and ' bear-like fight the course,' all escape being precluded. I can now engage with less disadvantage, having drawn the enemy from her intrenchments, though, like the *prototype* to whom I have compared myself, with an excellent

chance of being knocked on the head. However, 'lay on, Macduff, an
d——d be he who first cries, hold, enough.'

"I shall remain in town for, at least, a week, and expect to hea
from *you* before its expiration. I presume the printer has brought yo
the offspring of my *poetic mania*. Remember, in the first line, to read
'*loud* the winds whistle,' instead of 'round,' which that blockhead Ridg
has inserted by mistake, and makes nonsense of the whole stanza. Addio
—Now to encounter my *Hydra*. Yours ever."

LETTER IV.

TO MR. PIGOT.

"London, Sunday, midnight, August 10th, 1806.

"DEAR PIGOT,

"This *astonishing* packet will, doubtless, amaze you, but having an
idle hour this evening, I wrote the enclosed stanzas, which I request you
to deliver to Ridge, to be printed *separate* from my other compositions,
as you will perceive them to be improper for the perusal of ladies; of
course, none of the females of your family must see them. I offer 1000
apologies for the trouble I have given you in this and other instances.
Yours truly."

LETTER V.

TO MR. PIGOT.

"Piccadilly, August 16th, 1806.

"I cannot exactly say with Cæsar, 'Veni, vidi, vici:' however, the
most important part of his laconic account of success applies to my present situation; for, though Mrs. Byron took the *trouble* of '*coming*' and
'*seeing*,' yet your humble servant proved the *victor*. After an obstinate
engagement of some hours, in which we suffered considerable damage,
from the quickness of the enemy's fire, they at length retired in confusion, leaving behind the artillery, field equipage, and some prisoners :

their defeat is decisive of the present campaign.   To speak more intelligibly, Mrs. B. returns immediately, but I proceed, with all my laurels, to Worthing, on the Sussex coast; to which place you will address (to be left at the post-office) your next epistle.   By the enclosure of a 2d *gingle* of *rhyme*, you will probably conceive my muse to be *vastly prolific;* her inserted production was brought forth a few years ago, and found by accident on Thursday among some old papers.   I have recopied it, and, adding the proper date, request it may be printed with the rest of the family.   I thought your sentiments on the last bantling would coincide with mine, but it was impossible to give it any other garb, being founded on *facts*.   My stay at Worthing will not exceed 3 weeks, and you may *possibly* behold me again at Southwell the middle of September.

*   *   *   *

" Will you desire Ridge to suspend the printing of my poems till he hears further from me, as I have determined to give them a new form entirely.   This prohibition does not extend to the two last pieces I have sent with my letters to you.   You will excuse the *dull vanity* of this epistle, as my brain is a *chaos* of absurd images, and full of business, preparations, and projects.

" I shall expect an answer with impatience;—believe me, there is nothing at this moment could give me greater delight than your letter."

LETTER VI.

TO MR. PIGOT.

" London, August 18th, 1806.

" I am just on the point of setting off for Worthing, and write merely to request you will send that *idle scoundrel Charles* with my horses immediately; tell him I am excessively provoked he has not made his appearance before, or written to inform me of the cause of his delay, particularly as I supplied him with money for his journey.   On *no* pretext is he to postpone his *march* one day longer, and if, in obedience to the *caprices* of Mrs. B. (who, I presume, is again spreading desolation through her little monarchy), he thinks proper to disregard my positive orders, I shall not, in future, consider him as my servant.   He must bring the surgeon's bill with him, which I will discharge immediately on receiving it. Nor can I conceive the reason of his not acquainting Frank with the state of my unfortunate quadrupeds. Dear Pigot, forgive this *petulant* effusion, and attribute it to the idle conduct of that *precious rascal*, who, instead of obeying my injunctions, is sauntering through the streets of that *political Pandemonium*, Nottingham. Present my remembrances to your family and the Leacrofts, and believe me, &c.

" P. S. I delegate to *you* the unpleasant task of despatching him on his journey—Mrs. B.'s orders to the contrary are not to be attended to: he is to proceed first to London, and then to Worthing, without delay. Every thing I have *left* must be sent to London. My *Poetics you will pack up* for the same place, and not even reserve a copy for yourself and sister, as I am about to give them an *entire new form:* when they are complete, you shall have the 1*st fruits*. Mrs. B. on no account is to *see or* touch them. Adieu."

LETTER VII.

TO MR. PIGOT.

" Little Hampton, August 26th, 1806.

" I this morning received your epistle, which I was obliged to send for to Worthing, whence I have removed to this place, on the same coast, about 8 miles distant from the former. You will probably not be displeased with this letter, when it informs you that I am £30,000 richer than I was at our parting, having just received intelligence from my lawyer that a cause has been gained at Lancaster assizes*, which will be worth that sum by the time I come of age. Mrs. B. is doubtless acquainted of this acquisition, though not apprized of its exact *value*, of which she had better be ignorant; for her behaviour on any sudden piece of favourable intelligence is, if possible, more ridiculous than her detestable conduct on the most trifling circumstance of an unpleasant nature. You may give my compliments to her, and say that her detaining my servant's

* In a suit undertaken for the recovery of the Rochdale property.

things shall only lengthen my absence; for unless they are immediately despatched to 16, Piccadilly, together with those which have been so long delayed belonging to myself, she shall never again behold my *radiant countenance* illuminating her gloomy mansion. If they are sent, I may probably appear in less than 2 years from the date of my present epistle.

" Metrical compliment is an ample reward for my strains; you are one of the few votaries of Apollo who unite the sciences over which that deity presides. I wish you to send my poems to my lodgings in London immediately, as I have several alterations and some additions to make; *every* copy must be sent, as I am about to *amend* them, and you shall soon behold them in all their glory. I hope you have kept them from that *Upas tree*, that *antidote* to the *arts*, Mrs. B. *Entre nous*,—you may expect to see me soon. Adieu. Yours ever."

From these letters it will be perceived that Lord Byron was already engaged in preparing a collection of his Poems for the press. The idea of printing them first occurred to him in the parlour of that cottage, which, during his visits to Southwell, had become his adopted home. Miss Pigot, who was not before aware of his turn for versifying, had been reading aloud the Poems of Burns, when young Byron said that " he, too, was a poet sometimes, and would write down for her some verses of his own which he remembered." He then, with a pencil, wrote those lines, beginning " In thee I fondly hoped to clasp*," which were printed in his first unpublished volume, but are not contained in the editions that followed. He also repeated to her the verses I have already referred to, " When in the hall my father's voice," so remarkable for the anticipations of his future fame that glimmer through them.

From this moment, the desire of appearing in print took entire possession of him;—though, for the present, his ambition did not extend its views beyond a small volume for private circulation. The person to whom fell the honour of receiving his first manuscripts was Ridge, the bookseller, at Newark; and, while the work was printing, the young author continued to pour fresh materials into his hands, with the same

---

* This precious pencilling is still, of course, preserved.

eagerness and rapidity that marked the progress of all his mature works.

His return to Southwell, which he announced in the last letter w have given, was but for a very short time. In a week or two after h again left that place, and, accompanied by his young friend Mr. Pigot set out for Harrowgate. The following extracts are from a letter written by the latter gentleman, at the time, to his sister.

" Harrowgate is still extremely full; Wednesday (to-day) is our ball night, and I meditate going into the room for an hour, although I am by no means fond of strange faces. Lord B., you know, is even more shy than myself; but for an hour this evening I will shake it off. * * * How do our theatricals proceed? Lord Byron can say *all* his part, and I *most* of mine. He certainly acts it inimitably. Lord B. is now *poetising* and, since he has been here, has written some very pretty verses*. He is very good in trying to amuse me as much as possible, but it is not in my nature to be happy without either female society or study. * * * There are many pleasant rides about here, which I have taken in company with Bo'swain, who, with Brighton†, is universally admired. *You* must read this to Mrs. B., as it is a little *Tony Lumpkinish.* Lord B. desires some space left: therefore, with respect to all the comedians *elect,* believe me to be, &c. &c."

To this letter the following note from Lord Byron was appended.

" MY DEAR BRIDGET,

" I have only just dismounted from my *Pegasus,* which has prevented me from descending to *plain* prose in an epistle of greater length to your *fair* self. You regretted in a former letter, that my poems were not more extensive; I now for your satisfaction announce that I have nearly doubled them, partly by the discovery of some I conceived to be lost, and partly by some new productions. We shall meet on Wednesday next; till then believe me yours affectionately,

" BYRON.

---

* The verses " To a beautiful Quaker," in his first volume, were written at Harrowgate.

† A horse of Lord Byron's:—the other horse that he had with him at this time was called Sultan.

" P. S. Your brother John is seized with a poetic mania, and is now rhyming away at the rate of three lines *per hour*—so much for *inspiration!* Adieu!"

By the gentleman, who was thus early the companion and intimate of Lord Byron, and who is now pursuing his profession with the success which his eminent talents deserve, I have been favoured with some further recollections of their visit together to Harrowgate, which I shall take the liberty of giving in his own words:—

" You ask me to recall some anecdotes of the time we spent together at Harrowgate in the summer of 1806, on our return from college, he from Cambridge, and I from Edinburgh; but so many years have elapsed since then that I really feel myself as if recalling a distant dream. We, I remember, went in Lord Byron's own carriage, with post-horses; and he sent his groom with two saddle-horses, and a beautifully formed, very ferocious, bull-mastiff, called Nelson, to meet us there. Boatswain* went, by the side of his valet Frank, on the box, with us.

" The bull-dog, Nelson, always wore a muzzle, and was occasionally sent for into our private room, when the muzzle was taken off, much to my annoyance, and he and his master amused themselves with throwing the room into disorder. There was always a jealous feud between this Nelson and Boatswain; and whenever the latter came into the room while the former was there, they instantly seized each other; and then, Byron, myself, Frank, and all the waiters that could be found, were vigorously engaged in parting them,—which was in general only effected by thrusting poker and tongs into the mouths of each. But, one day, Nelson unfortunately escaped out of the room without his muzzle, and going into the stable-yard fastened upon the throat of a horse, from which he could not be disengaged. The stable-boys ran in alarm to find Frank, who, taking one of his lord's Wogdon's pistols, always kept loaded in his room, shot poor Nelson through the head, to the great regret of Byron.

* The favourite dog, on which Lord Byron afterwards wrote the well-known epitaph.

" We were at the Crown Inn at Low Harrowgate. We always
dined in the public room, but retired very soon after dinner to our
private one; for Byron was no more a friend to drinking than myself.
We lived retired, and made few acquaintance; for he was naturally shy,
very shy, which people who did not know him mistook for pride. While
at Harrowgate he accidentally met with Professor Hailstone from Cambridge, and appeared much delighted to see him. The professor was at
Upper Harrowgate; we called upon him one evening to take him to the
theatre, I think,—and Lord Byron sent his carriage for him, another
time, to a ball at the Granby. This desire to show attention to one
of the professors of his college is a proof that, though he might choose
to satirize the mode of education in the university, and to abuse the
antiquated regulations and restrictions to which under-graduates are subjected, he had yet a due discrimination in his respect for the individuals
who belonged to it. I have always indeed heard him speak in high
terms of praise of Hailstone, as well as of his master, Bishop Mansel, of
Trinity College, and of others whose names I have now forgotten.

" Few people understood Byron, but *I* know that he had naturally
a kind and feeling heart, and that there was not a single spark of malice
in his composition*."

The private theatricals alluded to in the letters from Harrowgate
were, both in prospect and performance, a source of infinite delight to
him, and took place soon after his return to Southwell. How anxiously
he was expected back by all parties may be judged from the following
fragment of a letter which was received by his companion during their
absence from home:—

" Tell Lord Byron that, if any accident should retard his return, his
mother desires he will write to her, as she shall be *miserable* if he does
not arrive the day he fixes. Mr. W. B. has written a card to Mrs. H. to
offer for the character of ' Henry Woodville,'—Mr. and Mrs. * * * not
approving of their son's taking a part in the play: but I believe he will
persist in it. Mr. G. W. says that, sooner than the party should be dis-

---

* Lord Byron and Dr. Pigot continued to be correspondents for some time, but, after their
parting this autumn, they never met again.

appointed, *he* will take any part,—sing—dance—in short, do any thing to oblige. Till Lord Byron returns, nothing can be done; and positively he must not be later than Tuesday or Wednesday."

We have already seen that, at Harrow, his talent for declamation was the only one by which Lord Byron was particularly distinguished, and in one of his note-books he adverts, with evident satisfaction, both to his school displays and to the share which he took in these representations at Southwell:—

" When I was a youth, I was reckoned a good actor. Besides ' Harrow Speeches' (in which I shone), I enacted Penruddock, in the ' Wheel of Fortune,' and Tristram Fickle in Allingham's farce of the ' Weathercock,' for three nights (the duration of our compact), in some private theatricals at Southwell, in 1806, with great applause. The occasional prologue for our volunteer play was also of my composition. The other performers were young ladies and gentlemen of the neighbourhood, and the whole went off with great effect upon our good-natured audience."

It may, perhaps, not be altogether trifling to observe, that, in thus personating with such success two heroes so different, the young poet displayed both that love and power of versatility by which he was afterwards impelled, on a grander scale, to present himself under such opposite aspects to the world;—the gloom of Penruddock, and the whim of Tristram, being types, as it were, of the two extremes, between which his own character, in after-life, so singularly vibrated.

These representations, which form a memorable era at Southwell, took place, about the latter end of September, in the house of Mr. Leacroft, whose drawing-room was converted into a neat theatre on the occasion, and whose family contributed some of the fair ornaments of its boards. The prologue, which Lord Byron furnished, and which may be seen in his " Hours of Idleness," was written by him, between stages, on his way from Harrowgate. On getting into the carriage at Chesterfield, he said to his companion, " Now, Pigot, I 'll spin a prologue for our play;" and before they reached Mansfield, he had completed his task,—interrupting, only once, his rhyming reverie, to ask the proper pronunciation of the French word "*début*," and, on being told it, exclaiming, in the true spirit of Byshe, "Ay, that will do for rhyme to '*new*.'"

The epilogue on the occasion was from the pen of Mr. Becher; and for the purpose of affording to Lord Byron, who was to speak it, an opportunity of displaying his powers of mimicry, consisted of good humoured portraits of all the persons concerned in the representation. Some intimation of this design having got among the actors, an alarm was felt instantly at the ridicule thus in store for them; and to quiet their apprehensions, the author was obliged to assure them that, if after having heard his epilogue at rehearsal, they did not, of themselves, pronounce it harmless, and even request that it should be preserved, he would most willingly withdraw it. In the mean time, it was concerted between this gentleman and Lord Byron that the latter should, on the morning of rehearsal, deliver the verses in a tone as innocent and as free from all point as possible,—reserving his mimicry, in which the whole sting of the pleasantry lay, for the evening of representation. The desired effect was produced;—all the personages of the green-room were satisfied, and even wondered how a suspicion of waggery could have attached itself to so well-bred a production. Their wonder, however, was of a different nature a night or two after, when, on hearing the audience convulsed with laughter at this same composition, they discovered, at last, the trick which the unsuspected mimic had played on them, and had no other resource than that of joining in the laugh which his playful imitation of the whole dramatis personæ excited.

The small volume of Poems, which he had now, for some time, been preparing, was, in the month of November, ready for delivery to the select few among whom it was intended to circulate; and to Mr. Becher the first copy of the work was presented *. The influence which this gentleman had, by his love of poetry, his sociability and good sense, acquired at this period over the mind of Lord Byron, was frequently employed by him in guiding the taste of his young friend, no less in matters of conduct than of literature; and the ductility with which this

---

* Of this edition, which was in quarto, and consisted but of a few sheets, there are but two, or, at the utmost, three copies in existence.

influence was yielded to, in an instance I shall have to mention, will show
how far from untractable was the natural disposition of Byron, had he
more frequently been lucky enough to fall into hands, that "knew the
stops" of the instrument, and could draw out its sweetness as well as its
strength.

In the wild range which his taste was now allowed to take through
the light and miscellaneous literature of the day, it was but natural that
he should settle with most pleasure on those works, from which the
feelings of his age and temperament could extract their most congenial
food; and, accordingly, Lord Strang ord's Camoëns and Little's Poems
are said to have been, at this period, his favourite study. To the indulgence
of such a taste his reverend friend very laudably opposed himself,—representing with truth (as far, at least, as the latter author is concerned),
how much more worthy models, both in style and thought, he might find
among the established names of English literature. Instead of wasting
his time on the ephemeral productions of his contemporaries, he should
devote himself, his adviser said, to the pages of Milton and of Shakspeare,
and, above all, seek to elevate his fancy and taste by the contemplation
of the sublimer beauties of the Bible. In the latter study, this gentleman
acknowledges that his advice had been, to a great extent, anticipated, and
that with the poetical parts of the Scripture he found Lord Byron deeply
conversant;—a circumstance which corroborates the account given by his
early master, Doctor Glennie, of his great proficiency in scriptural knowledge while, yet but a child, under his care.

To Mr. Becher, as I have said, the first copy of his little work was
presented; and this gentleman, in looking over its pages, among many
things to commend and admire, as well as some almost too boyish to
criticise, found one poem in which, as it appeared to him, the imagination
of the young bard had indulged itself in a luxuriousness of colouring
beyond what even youth could excuse. Immediately, as the most gentle
mode of conveying his opinion, he sat down and addressed to Lord Byron
some expostulatory verses on the subject, to which an answer, also in
verse, was returned by the noble poet as promptly,—with, at the same
time, a note, in plain prose, to say, that he felt fully the justice of his reverend friend's censure, and that, rather than allow the poem in question

to be circulated, he would instantly recall all the copies that had been sent out, and cancel the whole impression. On the very same evening this prompt sacrifice was carried into effect;—Mr. Becher saw every copy of the edition burned, with the exception of that which he retained in his own possession, and another which had been despatched to Edinburgh and could not be recalled.

This trait of the young poet speaks sufficiently for itself;—the sensibility, the temper, the ingenuous pliableness which it exhibits, show a disposition capable, by nature, of every thing we most respect and love.

Of a no less amiable character were the feelings that, about this time, dictated the following letter;—a letter which it is impossible to peruse without acknowledging the noble candour and conscientiousness of the writer:—

LETTER VIII.

TO THE EARL OF CLARE.

" Southwell, Notts, February 6th, 1807.

" MY DEAREST CLARE,

" Were I to make all the apologies necessary to atone for my late negligence, you would justly say you had received a petition instead of a letter, as it would be filled with prayers for forgiveness; but instead of this, I will acknowledge my *sins* at once, and I trust to your friendship and generosity rather than to my own excuses. Though my health is not perfectly re-established, I am out of all danger, and have recovered every thing but my spirits, which are subject to depression. You will be astonished to hear I have lately written to Delawarre, for the purpose of explaining (as far as possible without involving some *old friends* of mine in the business) the cause of my behaviour to him during my last residence at Harrow (nearly two years ago), which you will recollect was rather ' *en cavalier.*' Since that period I have discovered he was treated with injustice, both by those who misrepresented his conduct, and by me in consequence of their suggestions. I have therefore made all the reparation in my power, by apologizing for my mistake, though with very faint hopes of success; indeed I never expected any answer, but desired one for form's sake; *that* has not yet arrived, and most probably never will. However, I have *eased* my own *conscience* by the atonement, which is humiliating enough to one of my disposition; yet I could not have slept satisfied with the reflection of having, *even unintentionally*, injured any individual. I have done all that could be done to repair the injury, and there the affair must end. Whether we renew our intimacy or not is of very trivial consequence.

" My time has lately been much occupied with very different pursuits. I have been *transporting* a servant*, who cheated me,—rather a disagreeable event:—performing in private theatricals;—publishing a volume of poems (at the request of my friends, for their perusal);—making *love*,—and taking physic. The two last amusements have not had the best effect *in the world;* for my attentions have been divided amongst so many *fair damsels,* and the drugs I swallow are of such variety in their composition, that between Venus and Æsculapius I am harassed to death; However, I have still leisure to devote some hours to the recollections of past, regretted friendships, and in the interval to take the advantage of the moment, to assure you how much I am, and ever will be, my dearest Clare,

" Your truly attached and sincere

" Byron."

Considering himself bound to replace the copies of his work which he had withdrawn, as well as to rescue the general character of the volume from the stigma this one offender might bring upon it, he set instantly about preparing a second edition for the press, and, during the ensuing six weeks, continued busily occupied with his task. In the beginning of January we find him forwarding a copy to his friend, Dr. Pigot, in Edinburgh :—

LETTER IX.

TO MR. PIGOT.

" Southwell, Jan. 13, 1807.

" I ought to begin with *sundry* apologies, for my own negligence, but the variety of my avocations in *prose* and *verse* must plead my excuse.

---

* His valet, Frank.

M 2

With this epistle you will receive a volume of all my *Juvenilia* published since your departure: it is of considerably greater size than the *copy* in your possession, which I beg you will destroy, as the present is much more complete. That *unlucky* poem to my poor Mary* has been the cause of some animadversion from *ladies in years*. I have not printed it in this collection, in consequence of my being pronounced a most *profligate sinner*, in short, a '*young Moore*,' by ————, your * * * friend. I believe in general they have been favourably received, and surely the age of their author will preclude *severe* criticism. The adventures of my life from sixteen to nineteen, and the dissipation into which I have been thrown in London, have given a voluptuous tint to my ideas; but the occasions which called forth my muse could hardly admit any other colouring. This volume is *vastly* correct and miraculously chaste. Apropos, talking of love, * * * * * * *

" If you can find leisure to answer this farrago of unconnected nonsense, you need not doubt what gratification will accrue from your reply to yours ever, &c."

To his schoolfellow Mr. William Bankes, who had met casually with a copy of the work, and wrote him a letter, conveying his opinion of it, he returned the following answer:

LETTER X.

TO MR. WILLIAM BANKES.

" Southwell, March 6, 1807.

" DEAR BANKES,

" Your critique is valuable for many reasons: in the first place, it is the only one in which flattery has borne so slight a part; in the *next*, I am *cloyed* with insipid compliments. I have a better opinion of your

---

* Of this "Mary," who is not to be confounded either with the heiress of Annesley, or "Mary" of Aberdeen, all I can record is, that she was of an humble, if not equivocal, station in life,—that she had long, light golden hair, of which he used to show a lock, as well as her picture, among his friends; and that the verses in his "Hours of Idleness," entitled "To Mary, on receiving her Picture," were addressed to her.

judgment and ability than your *feelings*. Accept my most sincere thanks for your kind decision, not less welcome, because totally unexpected. With regard to a more exact estimate, I need not remind you how few of the *best poems*, in our language, will stand the test of *minute* or *verbal* criticism : it can therefore hardly be expected the effusions of a boy (and most of these pieces have been produced at an early period) can derive much merit either from the subject or composition. Many of them were written under great depression of spirits, and during severe indisposition; —hence the gloomy turn of the ideas. We coincide in opinion that the ' *poesies érotiques*' are the most exceptionable; they were, however, grateful to the *deities*, on whose altars they were offered—more I seek not.

" The portrait of Pomposus was drawn at Harrow, after a *long sitting*; this accounts for the resemblance, or rather the *caricatura*. He is *your* friend, he *never was mine*—for both our sakes I shall be silent on this head. The *collegiate* rhymes are not personal—one of the notes may appear so, but could not be omitted. I have little doubt they will be deservedly abused—a just punishment for my unfilial treatment of so excellent an Alma Mater. I sent you no copy, lest *we* should be placed in the situation of *Gil Blas* and the *Archbishop* of Grenada: though running some hazard from the experiment, I wished your *verdict* to be unbiassed. Had my ' *Libellus*' been presented previous to your letter, it would have appeared a species of bribe to purchase compliment. I feel no hesitation in saying, I was more anxious to hear your critique however severe, than the praises of the *million*. On the same day I was honoured with the encomiums of *Mackenzie*, the celebrated author of the ' Man of Feeling.' Whether *his* approbation or *yours* elated me most, I cannot decide.

" You will receive my *Juvenilia*,—at least all yet published. I have a large volume in manuscript, which may in part appear hereafter; at present I have neither time nor inclination to prepare it for the press. In the spring I shall return to Trinity, to dismantle my rooms, and bid you a final adieu. The *Cam* will not be much increased by my *tears* on the occasion. Your further remarks, however *caustic* or bitter to a palate vitiated with the *sweets* of *adulation,* will be of service. Johnson has shown us that *no poetry* is perfect; but to correct mine would be an Herculean labour. In fact I never looked beyond the moment of composition, and published merely at the request of my friends. Notwithstanding so much has been said concerning the 'Genus irritabile vatum,' we shall never quarrel on the subject—poetic fame is by no means the 'acme' of my wishes. Adieu.

" Yours ever,

" BYRON."

This letter was followed by another, on the same subject, to Mr. Bankes, of which, unluckily, only the annexed fragment remains:

* * * * *

" For my own part, I have suffered severely in the decease of my two greatest friends, the only beings I ever loved (females excepted); I am therefore a solitary animal, miserable enough, and so perfectly a citizen of the world, that whether I pass my days in Great Britain or Kamschatka, is to me a matter of perfect indifference. I cannot evince greater respect for your alteration than by immediately adopting it— this shall be done in the next edition. I am sorry your remarks are not more frequent, as I am certain they would be equally beneficial. Since my last, I have received two critical opinions from Edinburgh, both too flattering for me to detail. One is from Lord Woodhouslee, at the head of the Scotch literati, and a most *voluminous* writer (his last work is a life of Lord Kaimes); the other from Mackenzie, who sent his decision a second time, more at length. I am not personally acquainted with either of these gentlemen, nor ever requested their sentiments on the subject: their praise is voluntary, and transmitted through the medium of a friend, at whose house they read the productions.

" Contrary to my former intention, I am now preparing a volume for the public at large: my amatory pieces will be exchanged, and others substituted in their place. The whole will be considerably enlarged, and appear the latter end of May. This is a hazardous experiment; but want of better employment, the encouragement I have met with, and my own vanity, induce me to stand the test, though not without *sundry palpitations*. The book will circulate fast enough in this country, from mere curiosity, what I prin——*"

*　　　*　　　*　　　*　　　*

The following modest letter accompanied a copy which he presented to Mr. Falkner, his mother's landlord:—

LETTER XI.

TO MR. FALKNER.

" SIR,

" The volume of little pieces which accompanies this, would have been presented before, had I not been apprehensive that Miss Falkner's indisposition might render such trifles unwelcome. There are some errors of the printer which I have not had time to correct in the collection: you have it thus, with ' all its imperfections on its head,' a heavy weight, when joined with the faults of its author. Such ' Juvenilia,' as they can claim no great degree of approbation, I may venture to hope, will also escape the severity of uncalled for, though perhaps *not* undeserved, criticism.

" They were written on many and various occasions, and are now published merely for the perusal of a friendly circle. Believe me, sir, if they afford the slightest amusement to yourself and the rest of my *social* readers, I shall have gathered all the *bays* I ever wish to adorn the head of

" yours, very truly,

" BYRON.

" P. S.—I hope Miss F. is in a state of recovery."

Notwithstanding this unambitious declaration of the young author, he had that within which would not suffer him to rest so easily; and the fame he had now reaped within a limited circle made him but more eager to try his chance on a wider field. The hundred copies of which this edition consisted were hardly out of his hands, when with fresh

* Here the imperfect sheet ends.

activity he went to press again,—and his first published volume, " The Hours of Idleness," made its appearance. Some new pieces which he had written in the interim were added, and no less than twenty of those contained in the former volume omitted ;—for what reason does not very clearly appear, as they are, most of them, equal, if not superior, to those retained.

In one of the pieces, reprinted in the " Hours of Idleness," there are some alterations and additions, which, as far as they may be supposed to spring from the known feelings of the poet respecting birth, are curious. This poem, which is entitled " Epitaph on a Friend," appears, from the lines I am about to give, to have been, in its original state, intended to commemorate the death of the same lowly-born youth, to whom some affectionate verses, cited in a preceding page, were addressed :—

> " Though low thy lot, since in a cottage born,
>   No titles did thy humble name adorn;
>   To me, far dearer was thy artless love
>   Than all the joys wealth, fame, and friends could prove."

But, in the altered form of the epitaph, not only this passage, but every other containing an allusion to the low rank of his young companion, is omitted; while, in the added parts, the introduction of such language as

> " What, though thy sire lament his failing line,"

seems calculated to give an idea of the youth's station in life, wholly different from that which the whole tenor of the original epitaph warrants. The other poem, too, which I have mentioned, addressed evidently to the same boy, and speaking in similar terms, of the " lowness" of his " lot," is, in the " Hours of Idleness," altogether omitted. That he grew more conscious of his high station, as he approached to manhood, is not improbable, and this wish to sink his early friendship with the young cottager may have been a result of that feeling.

As his visits to Southwell were, after this period, but few and transient, I shall take the present opportunity of mentioning such miscellaneous particulars respecting his habits and mode of life, while there, as I have been able to collect.

Though so remarkably shy, when he first went to Southwell, this reserve, as he grew more acquainted with the young people of the place, wore off; till, at length, he became a frequenter of their assemblies and dinner-parties, and even felt mortified if he heard of a rout to which he was not invited. His horror, however, at new faces still continued; and if, while at Mrs. Pigot's, he saw strangers approaching the house, he would instantly jump out of the window to avoid them. This natural shyness concurred with no small degree of pride to keep him aloof from the acquaintance of the gentlemen in the neighbourhood, whose visits, in more than one instance, he left unreturned;—some, under the plea that their ladies had not visited his mother, others, because they had neglected to pay him this compliment sooner. The true reason, however, of the haughty distance, at which, both now and afterwards, he stood apart from his more opulent neighbours, is to be found in his mortifying consciousness of the inadequacy of his own means to his rank, and the proud dread of being made to feel this inferiority by persons to whom, in every other respect, he knew himself superior. His friend Mr. Becher frequently expostulated with him on this unsociableness; and to his remonstrances, on one occasion, Lord Byron returned a poetical answer, so remarkably prefiguring the splendid burst, with which his own volcanic genius opened upon the world, that, as the volume containing the verses is in very few hands, I cannot resist the temptation of giving a few extracts here:—

> " Dear Becher, you tell me to mix with mankind,—
>   I cannot deny such a precept is wise;
> But retirement accords with the tone of my mind,
>   And I will not descend to a world I despise.

> " Did the Senate or Camp my exertions require,
>   Ambition might prompt me at once to go forth;
> And, when infancy's years of probation expire,
>   Perchance, I may strive to distinguish my birth.

> " *The fire, in the cavern of Ætna concealed,*
>   *Still mantles unseen, in its secret recess;—*
> *At length, in a volume terrific revealed,*
>   *No torrent can quench it, no bounds can repress.*

> " *Oh thus, the desire in my bosom for fame*
>   *Bids me live but to hope for Posterity's praise;*
>   *Could I soar, with the Phœnix, on pinions of flame,*
>   *With him I would wish to expire in the blaze.*

> " For the life of a Fox, of a Chatham the death,
>   What censure, what danger, what woe would I brave?
>   Their lives did not end when they yielded their breath,—
>   Their glory illumines the gloom of the grave!"

In his hours of rising and retiring to rest he was, like his mother, always very late; and this habit he never altered during the remainder of his life. The night, too, was at this period, as it continued afterwards, his favourite time for composition; and his first visit in the morning was generally paid to the fair friend who acted as his amanuensis, and to whom he then gave whatever new products of his brain the preceding night might have inspired. His next visit was usually to his friend Mr. Becher's, and from thence to one or two other houses on the Green, after which the rest of the day was devoted to his favourite exercises. The evenings he usually passed with the same family among whom he began his morning, either in conversation, or in hearing Miss Pigot play upon the piano-forte, and singing over with her a certain set of songs which he admired *,—among which the " Maid of Lodi " (with the words, " My heart with love is beating"), and " When Time who steals our years away," were, it seems, his particular favourites. He appears, indeed, to have, even thus early, shown a decided taste for that sort of regular routine of life,—bringing round the same occupations at the same stated periods,— which formed so much the system of his existence during the greater part of his residence abroad.

Those exercises, to which he flew for distraction in less happy days, formed his enjoyment now; and between swimming, sparring, firing at a mark, and riding†, the greater part of his time was passed. In the last

---

* Though always fond of music, he had very little skill in the performance of it. " It is very odd," he said, one day, to this lady,—" I sing much better to your playing than to any one else's."—" That is," she answered, " because I play to your singing."—In which few words, by the way, the whole secret of a skilful accompanier lies.

† Cricketing, too, was one of his most favourite sports, and it was wonderful, considering

of these accomplishments he was by no means very expert. As an instance of his little knowledge of horses, it is told, that, seeing a pair one day pass his window, he exclaimed, "What beautiful horses! I should like to buy them."—"Why, they are your own, my lord," said his servant. Those who knew him, indeed, at that period, were rather surprised, in after-life, to hear so much of his riding;—and the truth is, I am inclined to think, that he was at no time a very adroit horseman.

In swimming and diving, we have already seen by his own accounts, he excelled; and a lady in Southwell, among other precious relics of him, possesses a thimble which he borrowed of her one morning, when on his way to bathe in the Greet, and which, as was testified by her brother who accompanied him, he brought up three times successively from the bottom of the river. His practice of firing at a mark was the occasion, once, of some alarm to a very beautiful young person, Miss H.,—one of that numerous list of fair ones, by whom his imagination was dazzled while at Southwell. A poem relating to this occurrence, which may be found in his unpublished volume, is thus introduced:—
" As the author was discharging his pistols in a garden, two ladies, passing near the spot, were alarmed by the sound of a bullet hissing near them, to one of whom the following stanzas were addressed the next morning."

Such a passion, indeed, had he for arms of every description, that there generally lay a small sword by the side of his bed, with which he used to amuse himself, as he lay awake in the morning, by thrusting it through his bed-hangings. The person who purchased this bed at the sale of Mrs. Byron's furniture, on her removal to Newstead, gave out—with the view of attaching a stronger interest to the holes in the curtains—that they were pierced by the same sword with which the old lord had killed Mr. Chaworth, and which his descendant always kept as a memorial by his bedside. Such is the ready process by which fiction is often engrafted upon fact;—the sword in question being a most innocent and bloodless

---

his lameness, with what speed he could run. " Lord Byron (says Miss ———, in a letter, to her brother, from Southwell) is just gone past the window with his bat on his shoulder to cricket, which he is as fond of as ever."

weapon, which Lord Byron, during his visits at Southwell, used to borrow
of one of his neighbours.

His fondness for dogs—another fancy which accompanied him
through life—may be judged from the anecdotes already given, in th
account of his expedition to Harrowgate. Of his favourite dog, Boat
swain, whom he has immortalized in verse, and by whose side it wa
once his solemn purpose to be buried, some traits are told indicative, no
only of intelligence, but of a generosity of spirit, which might well win
for him the affections of such a master as Byron. One of these I shall
endeavour to relate as nearly as possible as it was told to me. Mrs
Byron had a fox-terrier, called Gilpin, with whom her son's dog, Boatswain, was perpetually at war*, taking every opportunity of attacking
and worrying him so violently, that it was very much apprehended he
would kill the animal. Mrs. Byron, therefore, sent off her terrier to a
tenant at Newstead, and on the departure of Lord Byron for Cambridge,
his "friend," Boatswain, with two other dogs, was intrusted to the care
of a servant till his return. One morning the servant was much alarmed
by the disappearance of Boatswain, and throughout the whole of the day
he could hear no tidings of him. At last, towards evening, the stray dog
arrived, accompanied by Gilpin, whom he led immediately to the kitchen
fire, licking him and lavishing upon him every possible demonstration of
joy. The fact was, he had been all the way to Newstead to fetch him,
and having now established his former foe under the roof once more,
agreed so perfectly well with him ever after, that he even protected him
against the insults of other dogs (a task which the quarrelsomeness of the
little terrier rendered no sinecure), and, if he but heard Gilpin's voice in
distress, would fly instantly to his rescue.

In addition to the natural tendency to superstition, which is usually
found connected with the poetical temperament, Lord Byron had also
the example and influence of his mother, acting upon him from infancy,

---

* In one of Miss ——'s letters, the following notice of these canine feuds occurs:—
"Boatswain has had another battle with Tippoo at the House of Correction, and came off conqueror. Lord B. brought Bo'sen to our window this morning, when Gilpin, who is almost
always here, got into an amazing fury with him."

to give his mind this tinge. Her implicit belief in the wonders of second sight, and the strange tales she told of this mysterious faculty, used to astonish not a little her sober English friends; and it will be seen, that, at so late a period as the death of his friend Shelley, the idea of fetches and forewarnings, impressed upon him by his mother, had not wholly lost possession of the poet's mind. As an instance of a more playful sort of superstition, I may be allowed to mention a slight circumstance told me of him by one of his Southwell friends. This lady had a large agate bead, with a wire through it, which had been taken out of a barrow, and lay always in her work-box. Lord Byron asking, one day, what it was, she told him that it had been given her as an amulet, and the charm was, that, as long as she had this bead in her possession, she should never be in love. "Then give it to me," he cried, eagerly, "for that's just the thing I want." The young lady refused;—but it was not long before the bead disappeared. She taxed him with the theft, and he owned it; but said, she never should see her amulet again.

Of his charity and kind-heartedness he left behind him at Southwell —as, indeed, at every place, throughout life, where he resided any time —the most cordial recollections. "He never," says a person, who knew him intimately at this period, "met with objects of distress, without affording them succour." Among many little traits of this nature which his friends delight to tell, I select the following,—less as a proof of his generosity, than from the interest which the simple incident itself, as connected with the name of Byron, presents. While yet a schoolboy he happened to be in a bookseller's shop at Southwell, when a poor woman came in to purchase a Bible. The price, she was told, by the shopman, was eight shillings. "Ah, dear sir," she exclaimed, "I cannot pay such a price;—I did not think it would cost half the money." The woman was then, with a look of disappointment, going away,—when young Byron called her back and made her a present of the Bible.

In his attention to his person and dress, to the becoming arrangement of his hair, and to whatever might best show off the beauty with which nature had gifted him, he manifested, even thus early, his anxiety to make himself pleasing to that sex, who were, from first to last, the ruling stars of his destiny. The fear of becoming, what he was naturally inclined to be, enormously fat, had induced him, from his first entrance a Cambridge, to adopt, for the purpose of reducing himself, a system o violent exercise and abstinence, together with the frequent use of warm baths. But the embittering circumstance of his life,—that, which haunted him, like a curse, amidst the buoyancy of youth, and the anticipations o fame and pleasure, was, strange to say, the trifling deformity of his foot By that one slight blemish (as in his moments of melancholy he persuaded himself) all the blessings that nature had showered upon him were counterbalanced. His reverend friend, Mr. Becher, finding him one day unusually dejected, endeavoured to cheer and rouse him by representing, in their brightest colours, all the various advantages with which Providence had endowed him,—and, among the greatest, that o " a mind which placed him above the rest of mankind." " Ah, my dear friend," said Byron, mournfully,—" if *this* (laying his hand on his forehead) places me above the rest of mankind, *that* (pointing to his foot) places me far, far below them."

It sometimes, indeed, seemed as if his sensitiveness on this point led him to fancy that he was the only person in the world afflicted with such an infirmity. When that accomplished scholar and traveller, Mr. D. Bailey, who was at the same school with him at Aberdeen, met him afterwards at Cambridge, the young peer had then grown so fat that, though accosted by him familiarly as his schoolfellow, it was not till he mentioned his name that Mr. Bailey could recognize him. " It is odd enough, too, that you shouldn't know me," said Byron—" I thought nature had set such a mark upon me, that I could never be forgot."

But, while this defect was such a source of mortification to his spirit, it was also, and in an equal degree, perhaps, a stimulus:—and more especially in whatever depended upon personal prowess or attractiveness, he seemed to feel himself piqued by this stigma, which nature, as he thought, had set upon him, to distinguish himself above those whom she had endowed with her more " fair proportion." In pursuits of gallantry he was, I have no doubt, a good deal actuated by this incentive; and the hope of astonishing the world, at some future period, as a chieftain and hero, mingled little less with his young dreams than the prospect of a poet's glory. " I will, some day or other," he used to say, when a boy,

" raise a troop,—the men of which shall be dressed in black, and ride on black horses.   They shall be called ' Byron's Blacks,' and you will hear of their performing prodigies of valour."

I have already adverted to the exceeding eagerness with which, while at Harrow, he devoured all sorts of learning,—excepting only that which, by the regimen of the school, was prescribed for him.   The same rapid and multifarious course of study he pursued during the holidays; and, in order to deduct as little as possible from his hours of exercise, he had given himself the habit, while at home, of reading all dinner-time*. In a mind so versatile as his, every novelty, whether serious or light, whether lofty or ludicrous, found a welcome and an echo; and I can easily conceive the glee—as a friend of his once described it to me—with which he brought to her, one evening, a copy of Mother Goose's Tales, which he had bought from a hawker that morning and read, for the first time, while he dined.

I shall now give, from a memorandum-book begun by him this year, the account, as I find it hastily and promiscuously scribbled out, of all the books in various departments of knowledge, which he had already perused at a period of life, when few of his schoolfellows had yet travelled beyond their *longs* and *shorts*.   The list is, unquestionably, a remarkable one;—and when we recollect that the reader of all these volumes was, at the same time, the possessor of a most retentive memory, it may be doubted whether, among what are called the regularly educated, the contenders for scholastic honours and prizes, there could be found a single one who, at the same age, has possessed any thing like the same stock of useful knowledge.

" LIST OF HISTORICAL WRITERS WHOSE WORKS I HAVE PERUSED IN DIFFERENT LANGUAGES.

" *History of England.*—Hume, Rapin, Henry, Smollet, Tindal, Belsham, Bisset, Adolphus, Holinshed, Froissart's Chronicles (belonging properly to France).

" *Scotland.*—Buchanan, Hector Boethius, both in the Latin.

---

* " It was the custom of Burns," says Mr. Lockhart, in his Life of that poet, " to read at table."

" *Ireland.*—Gordon.

" *Rome.*—Hooke, Decline and Fall by Gibbon, Ancient History b Rollin (including an account of the Carthaginians, &c.), besides Livy Tacitus, Eutropius, Cornelius Nepos, Julius Cæsar, Arrian, Sallust.

" *Greece.*—Mitford's Greece, Leland's Philip, Plutarch, Potter' Antiquities, Xenophon, Thucydides, Herodotus.

" *France.*—Mezeray, Voltaire.

" *Spain.*—I chiefly derived my knowledge of old Spanish History from a book, called the Atlas, now obsolete. The modern history, from the intrigues of Alberoni down to the Prince of Peace, I learned from its connexion with European politics.

" *Portugal.*—From Vertot; as also his account of the Siege of Rhodes,—though the last is his own invention, the real facts being totally different.—So much for his Knights of Malta.

" *Turkey.*—I have read Knolles, Sir Paul Rycaut, and Prince Cantemir, besides a more modern history, anonymous. Of the Ottoman History I know every event, from Tangralopi, and afterwards Othman I. to the peace of Passarowitz, in 1718,—the battle of Cutzka, in 1739, and the treaty between Russia and Turkey in 1790.

" *Russia.*—Tooke's Life of Catherine II., Voltaire's Czar Peter.

" *Sweden.*—Voltaire's Charles XII., also Norberg's Charles XII.— in my opinion the best of the two.—A translation of Schiller's Thirty Years' War, which contains the exploits of Gustavus Adolphus, besides Harte's Life of the same Prince. I have somewhere, too, read an account of Gustavus Vasa, the deliverer of Sweden, but do not remember the author's name.

" *Prussia.*—I have seen, at least, twenty Lives of Frederick II., the only prince worth recording in Prussian annals. Gillies, His own Works, and Thiebault,—none very amusing. The last is paltry, but circumstantial.

" *Denmark* I know little of. Of Norway I understand the natural history, but not the chronological.

" *Germany.*—I have read long histories of the house of Suabia, Wenceslaus, and, at length, Rodolph of Hapsburgh and his *thick-lipped* Austrian descendants.

" *Switzerland.*—Ah! William Tell, and the battle of Morgarten, where Burgundy was slain.

" *Italy.*—Davila, Guicciardini, the Guelphs and Ghibellines, the battle of Pavia, Massaniello, the revolutions of Naples, &c. &c.

" *Hindostan.*—Orme and Cambridge.

" *America.*—Robertson, Andrews' American War.

" *Africa.*—Merely from travels, as Mungo Park, Bruce.

" BIOGRAPHY.

" Robertson's Charles V.—Cæsar, Sallust (Catiline and Jugurtha), Lives of Marlborough and Eugene, Tekeli, Bonnard, Buonaparte, all the British Poets, both by Johnson and Anderson, Rousseau's Confessions, Life of Cromwell, British Plutarch, British Nepos, Campbell's Lives of the Admirals, Charles XII., Czar Peter, Catherine II., Henry Lord Kaimes, Marmontel, Teignmouth's Sir William Jones, Life of Newton, Belisaire, with thousands not to be detailed.

" LAW.

" Blackstone, Montesquieu.

" PHILOSOPHY.

" Paley, Locke, Bacon, Hume, Berkeley, Drummond, Beattie, and Bolingbroke. Hobbes I detest.

" GEOGRAPHY.

" Strabo, Cellarius, Adams, Pinkerton, and Guthrie.

" POETRY.

" All the British Classics, as before detailed, with most of the living poets, Scott, Southey, &c.—Some French, in the original, of which the Cid is my favourite.—Little Italian.—Greek and Latin without number; —these last I shall give up in future.—I have translated a good deal from both languages, verse as well as prose.

" ELOQUENCE.

" Demosthenes, Cicero, Quintilian, Sheridan, Austin's Chironomia, and Parliamentary Debates, from the Revolution to the year 1742.

" DIVINITY.

" Blair, Porteus, Tillotson, Hooker,—all very tiresome. I abhor books of religion, though I reverence and love my God, without the blasphemous notions of sectaries, or belief in their absurd and damnable heresies, mysteries, and Thirty-nine Articles.

" MISCELLANIES.

" Spectator, Rambler, World, &c. &c.—Novels by the thousand.

" All the books here enumerated I have taken down from memory. I recollect reading them, and can quote passages from any mentioned. I have, of course, omitted several in my catalogue; but the greater part of the above I perused before the age of fifteen. Since I left Harrow I have become idle and conceited, from scribbling rhyme and making love to women. " B.—Nov. 30, 1807.

" I have also read (to my regret at present) above four thousand novels, including the works of Cervantes, Fielding, Smollet, Richardson, Mackenzie, Sterne, Rabelais, and Rousseau, &c. &c. The book, in my opinion, most useful to a man who wishes to acquire the reputation of being well read, with the least trouble, is 'Burton's Anatomy of Melancholy,' the most amusing and instructive medley of quotations and classical anecdotes I ever perused. But a superficial reader must take care, or his intricacies will bewilder him. If, however, he has patience to go through his volumes, he will be more improved for literary conversation than by the perusal of any twenty other works with which I am acquainted,—at least, in the English language."

To this early and extensive study of English writers may be attributed that mastery over the resources of his own language, with which Lord Byron came furnished into the field of literature, and which enabled him, as fast as his youthful fancies sprung up, to clothe them with a diction worthy of their beauty. In general, the difficulty of young writers, at their commencement, lies far less in any lack of thoughts or images, than in that want of a fitting organ to give these conceptions vent, to which their unacquaintance with the great instrument of the man of genius, his native language, dooms them. It will be found, indeed, that the three most remarkable examples of early authorship, which, in their respective lines, the history of literature affords—Pope, Congreve, and Chatterton—were all of them persons self-educated *, according to their own intellectual wants and tastes, and left, undistracted by the worse than useless pedantries of the schools, to seek, in the pure " well of English undefiled," those treasures of which they accordingly so very early and intimately possessed themselves†. To these three instances may now be added, virtually, that of Lord Byron, who, though a disciple of the schools, was, intellectually speaking, *in* them, not *of* them, and who, while his comrades were prying curiously into the graves of dead languages, betook himself to the fresh, living sources of his own‡, and from thence drew those rich, varied stores of diction, which have placed his works, from the age of two-and-twenty upwards, among the most precious depositories of the strength and sweetness of the English language that our whole literature supplies.

In the same book that contains the above record of his studies, he has written out, also from memory, a " List of the different poets, dramatic or otherwise, who have distinguished their respective languages by their productions." After enumerating the various poets, both ancient

---

* " I took to reading by myself," says Pope, " for which I had a very great eagerness and enthusiasm ; . . . . . I followed every where, as my fancy led me, and was like a boy gathering flowers in the fields and woods, just as they fell in his way. These five or six years I still look upon as the happiest part of my life." It appears, too, that he was himself aware of the advantages which this free course of study brought with it :—" Mr. Pope," says Spence, " thought himself the better, in some respects, for not having had a regular education. He (as he observed in particular) read originally for the sense, whereas we are taught, for so many years, to read only for words."

† Before Chatterton was twelve years old, he wrote a catalogue, in the same manner as Lord Byron, of the books he had already read, to the number of seventy. Of these the chief subjects were history and divinity.

‡ The perfect purity with which the Greeks wrote their own language was, with justice perhaps, attributed by themselves to their entire abstinence from the study of any other. " If they became learned," says Ferguson, " it was only by studying what they themselves had produced."

and modern, of Europe, he thus proceeds with his catalogue throug
other quarters of the world :—

" *Arabia.*—Mahomet, whose Koran contains most sublime poetica
passages, far surpassing European poetry.

" *Persia.*—Ferdousi, author of the Shah Nameh, the Persian Iliad
—Sadi, and Hafiz, the immortal Hafiz, the oriental Anacreon. The las
is reverenced beyond any bard of ancient or modern times by the Per
sians, who resort to his tomb near Shiraz, to celebrate his memory. A
splendid copy of his works is chained to his monument.

" *America.*—An epic poet has already appeared in that hemisphere
Barlow, author of the Columbiad,—not to be compared with the work
of more polished nations.

" *Iceland, Denmark, Norway,* were famous for their Skalds. Among
these Lodburg was one of the most distinguished. His Death-Song
breathes ferocious sentiments, but a glorious and impassioned strain o
poetry.

" *Hindostan* is undistinguished by any great bard,—at least, the
Sanscrit is so imperfectly known to Europeans, we know not what poeti
cal relics may exist.

" *The Birman Empire.*—Here the natives are passionately fond of
poetry, but their bards are unknown.

" *China.*—I never heard of any Chinese poet but the Emperor Kien
Long, and his ode to *Tea.* What a pity their philosopher Confucius did
not write poetry, with his precepts of morality !

" *Africa.*—In Africa some of the native melodies are plaintive, and
the words simple and affecting ; but whether their rude strains of nature
can be classed with poetry, as the songs of the bards, the Skalds of
Europe, &c. &c. I know not.

" This brief list of poets I have written down from memory, without
any book of reference ; consequently some errors may occur, but I think,
if any, very trivial. The works of the European, and some of the Asiatic,
I have perused, either in the original or translations. In my list of En-

glish, I have merely mentioned the greatest;—to enumerate the minor poets would be useless, as well as tedious. Perhaps Gray, Goldsmith, and Collins, might have been added, as worthy of mention, in a *cosmopolite* account. But as for the others, from Chaucer down to Churchill, they are ' voces et præterea nihil;'—sometimes spoken of, rarely read, and never with advantage. Chaucer, notwithstanding the praises bestowed on him, I think obscene and contemptible:—he owes his celebrity merely to his antiquity, which he does not deserve so well as Pierce Plowman, or Thomas of Ercildoune. English living poets I have avoided mentioning;—we have none who will not survive their productions. Taste is over with us; and another century will sweep our empire, our literature, and our name, from all but a place in the annals of mankind.

" November 30, 1807. " BYRON."

Among the papers of his in my possession are several detached Poems (in all nearly six hundred lines), which he wrote about this period, but never printed—having produced most of them after the publication of his " Hours of Idleness." The greater number of these have little, besides his name, to recommend them; but there are a few that, from the feelings and circumstances that gave rise to them, will, I have no doubt, be interesting to the reader.

When he first went to Newstead, on his arrival from Aberdeen, he planted, it seems, a young oak in some part of the grounds, and had an idea that as *it* flourished so should *he*. Some six or seven years after, on revisiting the spot, he found his oak choked up by weeds, and almost destroyed. In this circumstance, which happened soon after Lord Grey de Ruthen left Newstead, originated one of these poems, which consists of five stanzas, but of which the few opening lines will be a sufficient specimen :—

> " Young Oak, when I planted thee deep in the ground,
> I hoped that thy days would be longer than mine;
> That thy dark-waving branches would flourish around,
> And ivy thy trunk with its mantle entwine.

> " Such, such was my hope, when, in infancy's years,
> On the land of my fathers I rear'd thee with pride;

They are past, and I water thy stem with my tears,——
　　Thy decay not the weeds, that surround thee, can hide.

" I left thee, my Oak, and, since that fatal hour,
　　A stranger has dwelt in the Hall of my Sire," &c. &c.

　　The subject of the verses that follow is sufficiently explained by the
notice which he has prefixed to them; and, as illustrative of the romantic
and almost love-like feeling which he threw into his school friendships,
they appeared to me, though rather quaint and elaborate, to be worth
preserving.

　　" Some years ago, when at H———, a friend of the author engraved
on a particular spot the names of both, with a few additional words as a
memorial. Afterwards, on receiving some real or imagined injury, the
author destroyed the frail record, before he left H——— On revisiting
the place in 1807, he wrote under it the following stanzas:—

1.

" Here once engaged the stranger's view
　　Young Friendship's record simply traced;
Few were her words,—but yet though few,
　　Resentment's hand the line defaced.

2.

" Deeply she cut—but, not erased,
　　The characters were still so plain,
That Friendship once return'd, and gazed,—
　　Till Memory hail'd the words again.

3.

" Repentance placed them as before;
　　Forgiveness join'd her gentle name;
So fair the inscription seem'd once more,
　　That Friendship thought it still the same.

4.

" Thus might the Record now have been;
　　But, ah, in spite of Hope's endeavour,
Or Friendship's tears, Pride rush'd between,
　　And blotted out the line for ever!"

The same romantic feeling of friendship breathes throughout another of these poems, in which he has taken for his subject the ingenious thought " l'Amitié est l'Amour sans ailes," and concludes every stanza with the words " Friendship is Love without his wings." Of the nine stanzas of which this poem consists, the three following appear the most worthy of selection:—

> " Why should my anxious breast repine,
>   Because my youth is fled?
> Days of delight may still be mine,
>   Affection is *not* dead.
> In tracing back the years of youth,
> One firm record, one lasting truth
>   Celestial consolation brings;
> Bear it, ye breezes, to the seat,
> Where first my heart responsive beat,—
>   ' Friendship is Love without his wings!'

*   *   *   *   *   *

> " Seat of my youth! thy distant spire
>   Recalls each scene of joy;
> My bosom glows with former fire,—
>   In mind again a boy.
> Thy grove of elms, thy verdant hill,
> Thy every path delights me still,
>   Each flower a double fragrance flings;
> Again, as once, in converse gay,
> Each dear associate seems to say
>   ' Friendship is Love without his wings !'

> " My Lycus! wherefore dost thou weep?
>   Thy falling tears restrain;
> Affection for a time may sleep,
>   But, oh, 'twill wake again.
> Think, think, my friend, when next we meet,
> Our long-wish'd intercourse, how sweet!
>   From this my hope of rapture springs,
> While youthful hearts thus fondly swell,
> Absence, my friend, can only tell,
>   ' Friendship is Love without his wings !' "

Whether the verses I am now about to give are, in any degree founded on fact, I have no accurate means of determining. Fond as h was of recording every particular of his youth, such an event, or rathe era, as is here commemorated, would have been, of all others, the leas likely to pass unmentioned by him;—and yet neither in conversatio nor in any of his writings do I remember even an allusion to it* O the other hand, so entirely was all that he wrote,—making allowanc for the embellishments of fancy,—the transcript of his actual life an feelings, that it is not easy to suppose a poem, so full of natural tender ness, to have been indebted for its origin to imagination alone.

" TO MY SON!

1.

" Those flaxen locks, those eyes of blue,
Bright as thy mother's in their hue;
Those rosy lips, whose dimples play
And smile to steal the heart away,
Recall a scene of former joy,
And touch thy father's heart, my Boy!

2.

" And thou canst lisp a father's name—
Ah, William, were thine own the same,
No self-reproach—but, let me cease—
My care for thee shall purchase peace;

---

* The only circumstance I know, that bears even remotely on the subject of this poem, i the following. About a year or two before the date affixed to it, he wrote to his mother, from Harrow (as I have been told by a person, to whom Mrs. Byron herself communicated th circumstance), to say, that he had lately had a good deal of uneasiness on account of a youn woman, whom he knew to have been a favourite of his late friend, Curzon, and who, findin herself after his death in a state of progress towards maternity, had declared Lord Byron wa the father of her child. This, he positively assured his mother, was not the case; but, believing as he did firmly, that the child belonged to Curzon, it was his wish that it should be brought u with all possible care, and he therefore entreated that his mother would have the kindness t take charge of it. Though such a request might well (as my informant expresses it) hav discomposed a temper more mild than Mrs. Byron's, she notwithstanding answered her son i the kindest terms, saying that she would willingly receive the child as soon as it was born and bring it up in whatever manner he desired. Happily, however, the infant died almos immediately, and was thus spared the being a tax on the good-nature of any body.

Thy mother's shade shall smile in joy,
And pardon all the past, my Boy!

3.

" Her lowly grave the turf has prest,
And thou hast known a stranger's breast.
Derision sneers upon thy birth,
And yields thee scarce a name on earth;
Yet shall not these one hope destroy,—
A Father's heart is thine, my Boy!

4.

" Why, let the world unfeeling frown,
Must I fond Nature's claim disown?
Ah, no—though moralists reprove,
I hail thee, dearest child of love,
Fair cherub, pledge of youth and joy—
A Father guards thy birth, my Boy!

5.

" Oh, 'twill be sweet in thee to trace,
Ere age has wrinkled o'er my face,
Ere half my glass of life is run,
At once a brother and a son;
And all my wane of years employ
In justice done to thee, my Boy!

6.

" Although so young thy heedless sire,
Youth will not damp parental fire;
And, wert thou still less dear to me,
While Helen's form revives in thee,
The breast, which beat to former joy,
Will ne'er desert its pledge, my Boy!

" B——, 1807 *."

But the most remarkable of these poems is one of a date prior to any I have given, being written in December, 1806; when he was not yet nineteen years old. It contains, as will be seen, his religious creed at that

* In this practice of dating his juvenile poems he followed the example of Milton, who (says Johnson), " by affixing the dates to his first compositions, a boast of which the learned

period, and shows how early the struggle between natural piety and doubt began in his mind.

" THE PRAYER OF NATURE.

" Father of Light ! great God of Heaven !
  Hear'st thou the accents of despair ?
Can guilt like man's be e'er forgiven ?
  Can vice atone for crimes by prayer ?
Father of Light, on thee I call !
  Thou see'st my soul is dark within ;
Thou who canst mark the sparrow's fall,
  Avert from me the death of sin.
No shrine I seek, to sects unknown,
  Oh point to me the path of truth !
Thy dread omnipotence I own,
  Spare, yet amend, the faults of youth.
Let bigots rear a gloomy fane,
  Let superstition hail the pile,
Let priests, to spread their sable reign,
  With tales of mystic rites beguile.
Shall man confine his Maker s sway
  To Gothic domes of mouldering stone ?
Thy temple is the face of day ;
  Earth, ocean, heaven, thy boundless throne.
Shall man condemn his race to hell
  Unless they bend in pompous form ;
Tell us that all, for one who fell,
  Must perish in the mingling storm ?

Politian had given him an example, seems to commend the earliness of his own compositions to the notice of posterity."

The following trifle, written also by him in 1807, has never, as far as I know, appeared in print :—

" EPITAPH ON JOHN ADAMS, OF SOUTHWELL, A CARRIER, WHO DIED OF DRUNKENNESS.

" John Adams lies here, of the parish of Southwell,
A *Carrier*, who *carried* his can to his mouth well ;
He *carried* so much, and he *carried* so fast,
He could *carry* no more—so was *carried* at last ;
For, the liquor he drank, being too much for one,
He could not *carry* off,—so he 's now *carri-on.*

                                        " B——, Sept. 1807."

Shall each pretend to reach the skies,
　　Yet doom his brother to expire,
Whose soul a different hope supplies,
　　Or doctrines less severe inspire?
Shall these, by creeds they can't expound,
　　Prepare a fancied bliss or woe?
Shall reptiles, groveling on the ground,
　　Their great Creator's purpose know?
Shall those, who live for self alone,
　　Whose years float on in daily crime—
Shall they by Faith for guilt atone,
　　And live beyond the bounds of Time?
Father! no prophet's laws I seek,—
　　Thy laws in Nature's works appear;—
I own myself corrupt and weak,
　　Yet will I pray, for thou wilt hear!
Thou, who canst guide the wandering star
　　Through trackless realms of Æther's space;
Who calm'st the elemental war,
　　Whose hand from pole to pole I trace:—
Thou, who in wisdom placed me here,
　　Who, when thou wilt, can take me hence,
Ah! whilst I tread this earthly sphere,
　　Extend to me thy wide defence.
To Thee, my God, to Thee I call!
　　Whatever weal or woe betide,
By thy command I rise or fall,
　　In thy protection I confide.
If, when this dust to dust restored,
　　My soul shall float on airy wing,
How shall thy glorious name adored
　　Inspire her feeble voice to sing!
But, if this fleeting spirit share
　　With clay the grave's eternal bed,
While life yet throbs I raise my prayer,
　　Though doom'd no more to quit the dead.
To Thee I breathe my humble strain,
　　Grateful for all thy mercies past,
And hope, my God, to thee again
　　This erring life may fly at last.

"29th Dec. 1806.   "BYRON."

In another of these poems, which extends to about a hundred lines, and which he wrote under the melancholy impression that he should soon die, we find him concluding with a prayer in somewhat the same spirit.   After bidding adieu to all the favourite scenes of his youth*, he thus continues,—

> " Forget this world, my restless sprite,
>   Turn, turn thy thoughts to Heav'n:
> There must thou soon direct thy flight,
>   If errors are forgiven.
> To bigots and to sects unknown,
> Bow down beneath th' Almighty's Throne;—
>   To him address thy trembling prayer;
> He, who is merciful and just,
> Will not reject a child of dust,
>   Although his meanest care.
> Father of Light! to thee I call,
>   My soul is dark within;
> Thou, who canst mark the sparrow fall,
>   Avert the death of sin.
> Thou, who canst guide the wandering star,
> Who calm'st the elemental war,
>   Whose mantle is yon boundless sky,
> My thoughts, my words, my crimes forgive;
> And, since I soon must cease to live,
>   Instruct me how to die.   1807."

We have seen, by a former letter, that the law proceedings for the recovery of his Rochdale property had been attended with success in some trial of the case at Lancaster.   The following note to one of his Southwell friends, announcing a second triumph of the cause, shows how sanguinely and, as it turned out, erroneously, he calculated on the results.

---

* Annesley is, of course, not forgotten among the number:—

> " And shall I here forget the scene,
>   Still nearest to my breast?
> Rocks rise and rivers roll between
>   The rural spot which passion blest;
> Yet, Mary, all thy beauties seem
> Fresh as in Love's bewitching dream," &c. &c.

"Feb. 9th, 1807.

"DEAR ————,

"I have the pleasure to inform you we have gained the Rochdale cause a 2d time, by which I am £60,000 *plus*.

"Yours ever,

"BYRON."

In the month of April we find him still at Southwell, and addressing to his friend Dr. Pigot, who was at Edinburgh, the following note*:—

"Southwell, April, 1807.

"MY DEAR PIGOT,

"Allow me to congratulate you on the success of your first examination—' *Courage*, mon ami.' The title of Dr. will do wonders with the damsels. I shall most probably be in Essex or London when you arrive at this d—d place, where I am detained by the publication of my *rhymes*.　　　"Adieu.—Believe me yours very truly,

"BYRON.

"P.S. Since we met, I have reduced myself by violent exercise, *much* physic, and *hot* bathing, from 14 stone 6 lb. to 12 stone 7 lb. In all I have lost 27 pounds. Bravo!—what say you?"

His movements and occupations for the remainder of this year will be best collected from a series of his own letters, which I am enabled, by the kindness of the lady to whom they were addressed, to give. Though these letters are boyishly† written, and a good deal of their pleasantry is

---

* It appears from a passage in one of Miss ————'s letters to her brother, that Lord Byron sent, through this gentleman, a copy of his Poems to Mr. Mackenzie, the author of the Man of Feeling:—" I am glad you mentioned Mr. Mackenzie's having got a copy of Lord B 's Poems, and what he thought of them—Lord B. was so *much* pleased!"

In another letter, the fair writer says:—" Lord Byron desired me to tell you that the reason you did not hear from him was because his publication was not so forward as he had flattered himself it would have been. I told him, ' he was no more to be depended on than a woman,' which instantly brought the softness of that sex into his countenance, for he blushed exceedingly."

† He was, indeed, a thorough boy, at this period, in every respect :—" Next Monday" (says

of that conventional kind which depends more upon phrase than thought, they will yet, I think, be found curious and interesting, not only as enabling us to track him through this period of his life, but as throwing light upon various little traits of character, and laying open to us the first working of his hopes and fears while waiting, in suspense, the opinions that were to decide, as he thought, his future fame. The first of the series, which is without date, appears to have been written before he had left Southwell. The other letters, it will be seen, are dated from Cambridge and from London.

LETTER XII.

TO MISS ———

"June 11th, 1807."

" DEAR QUEEN BESS,

" *Savage* ought to be *immortal*:—though not a *thorough-bred bull-dog*, he is the finest puppy I ever *saw*, and will answer much better; in his great and manifold kindness he has already bitten my fingers, and disturbed the *gravity* of old Boatswain, who is *grievously discomposed*. I wish to be informed what he *costs*, his *expenses*, &c. &c., that I may indemnify Mr. G———. My thanks are *all* I can give for the trouble he has taken, make a *long speech*, and conclude it with 1 2 3 4 5 6 7*. I am out of practice, so *deputize* you as Legate,—*ambassador* would not do in a matter concerning the *Pope*, which I presume this must, as the *whole* turns upon a *Bull*.   " Yours,

           " BYRON.

" P.S. I write in bed."

Miss ———) " is our great fair. Lord Byron talks of it with as much pleasure as little Henry, and declares he will ride in the Round-about,—but I think he will change his mind."

    * He here alludes to an odd fancy or trick of his own;—whenever he was at a loss for something to say, he used always to gabble over " 1 2 3 4 5 6 7."

LETTER XIII.

TO MISS ———.

"Cambridge, June 30th, 1807.

"'Better late than never, Pal,' is a saying of which you know the origin, and as it is applicable on the present occasion, you will excuse its conspicuous place in the front of my epistle. I am almost superannuated here. My old friends (with the exception of a very few) all departed, and I am preparing to follow them, but remain till Monday to be present at 3 *Oratorios*, 2 *Concerts*, a *Fair*, and a Ball. I find I am not only *thinner* but *taller* by an inch since my last visit. I was obliged to tell every body my *name*, nobody having the least recollection of my *visage*, or person. Even the hero of *my Cornelian* (who is now sitting *vis-à-vis*, reading a volume of my *Poetics*) passed me in Trinity walks without recognising me in the least, and was thunderstruck at the alteration which had taken place in my countenance, &c. &c. Some say I look *better*, others *worse*, but all agree I am *thinner*—more I do not require. I have lost 2 lb. in my weight since I left your *cursed, detestable,* and *abhorred* abode of *scandal**, where, excepting yourself and John Becher, I care not if the whole race were consigned to the *Pit* of *Acheron*, which I would visit in person rather than contaminate my *sandals* with the polluted dust of Southwell. *Seriously*, unless obliged by the *emptiness* of my purse to revisit Mrs. B., you will see me no more.

"On Monday I depart for London. I quit Cambridge with little regret, because our *set* are *vanished*, and my *musical protegé* before mentioned has left the choir, and is stationed in a mercantile house of con-

---

* Notwithstanding the abuse which, evidently more in sport than seriousness, he lavishes, in the course of these letters, upon Southwell, he was, in after days, taught to feel that the hours which he had passed in this place were far more happy than any he had known afterwards. In a letter written not long since to his servant, Fletcher, by a lady who had been intimate with him, in his young days, at Southwell, there are the following words:—"Your poor, good master always called me 'Old Piety,' when I preached to him. When he paid me his last visit, he said, 'Well, good friend, I shall never be so happy again as I was in old Southwell.'" His real opinion of the advantages of this town, as a place of residence, will be seen in a subsequent letter, where he most strenuously recommends it, in that point of view, to Mr. Dallas.

siderable eminence in the metropolis. You may have heard me observ
he is exactly to an hour, 2 years younger than myself. I found him
grown considerably, and, as you will suppose, very glad to see his forme
Patron. He is nearly my height, very *thin*, very fair complexion, dark
eyes, and light locks. My opinion of his mind you already know ;—
hope I shall never have occasion to change it. Every body here conceive
me to be an *invalid.* The University at present is very gay, from the
fêtes of divers kinds. I supped out last night, but eat (or ate) nothing
sipped a bottle of claret, went to bed at 2 and rose at 8. I have com
menced early rising, and find it agrees with me. The Masters and the
Fellows all very *polite*, but look a little *askance*—don't much admire
lampoons—truth always disagreeable.

"Write, and tell me how the inhabitants of your *Menagerie* go on,
and if my publication goes *off* well: do the quadrupeds *growl*? Apropos
my bull-dog is deceased—' Flesh both of cur and man is grass.' Address
your answer to Cambridge. If I am gone, it will be forwarded. Sad
news just arrived—Russians beat—a bad set, eat nothing but *oil*, consequently must melt before a *hard fire*. I get awkward in my academic
habiliments for want of practice. Got up in a window to hear the oratorio
at St. Mary's, popped down in the middle of the *Messiah*, tore a *woeful*
rent in the back of my best black silk gown, and damaged an egregious
pair of breeches. Mem.—never tumble from a church window during
service. Adieu, dear * * * *! do not remember me to any body:—to
forget and be forgotten by the people of Southwell is all I aspire to."

LETTER XIV.

TO MISS ———.

" Trin Coll. Camb. July 5th, 1807.

" Since my last letter I have determined to reside *another year* at
Granta, as my rooms, &c. &c. are finished in great style, several old friends
come up again, and many new acquaintances made; consequently my
inclination leads me forward, and I shall return to college in October, if
still *alive.* My life here has been one continued routine of dissipation—
out at different places every day, engaged to more dinners, &c. &c. than

my *stay* would permit me to fulfil. At this moment I write with a bottle of claret in my *head* and *tears* in my *eyes;* for I have just parted with my ' *Cornelian,*' who spent the evening with me. As it was our last interview, I postponed my engagement to devote the hours of the *Sabbath* to friendship:—Edleston and I have separated for the present, and my mind is a chaos of hope and sorrow. To-morrow I set out for London: you will address your answer to ' Gordon's Hotel, Albemarle-street,' where I *sojourn* during my visit to the metropolis.

" I rejoice to hear you are interested in my *protegé:* he has been my *almost constant* associate since October, 1805, when I entered Trinity College. His *voice* first attracted my attention, his *countenance* fixed it, and his *manners* attached me to him for ever. He departs for a *mercantile house* in *town* in October, and we shall probably not meet till the expiration of my minority, when I shall leave to his decision either entering as a *partner* through my interest, or residing with me altogether. Of course he would in his present frame of mind prefer the *latter,* but he may alter his opinion previous to that period;—however, he shall have his choice. I certainly love him more than any human being, and neither time or distance have had the least effect on my (in general) changeable disposition. In short, we shall put *Lady E. Butler* and *Miss Ponsonby* to the blush, *Pylades* and *Orestes* out of countenance, and want nothing but a catastrophe like *Nisus* and *Euryalus,* to give *Jonathan* and *David* the ' go by.' He certainly is perhaps more attached to *me* than even I am in return. During the whole of my residence at Cambridge we met every day, summer and winter, without passing *one* tiresome moment, and separated each time with increasing reluctance. I hope you will one day see us together, he is the only being I esteem, though I *like* many*.

---

* It may be as well to mention here the sequel of this enthusiastic attachment. In the year 1811 young Edleston died of a consumption, and the following letter, addressed by Lord Byron to the mother of his fair Southwell correspondent, will show with what melancholy faithfulness, among the many his heart had then to mourn for, he still dwelt on the memory of his young college friend.

" Cambridge, Oct. 28th, 1811.

" DEAR MADAM,

" I am about to write to you on a silly subject, and yet I cannot well do otherwise. You may remember a *cornelian,* which some years ago I consigned to Miss * * * *, indeed *gave to*

" The Marquis of Tavistock was down the other day; I supped with him at his tutor's—entirely a whig party. The opposition muster strong here now, and Lord Huntingdon, the Duke of Leinster, &c. &c. are to join us in October, so every thing will be *splendid*. The *music* is all over at present. Met with another '*accidency*'—upset a butter-boat in the lap of a lady—look'd very *blue*—*spectators* grinned—' curse 'em!' Apropos sorry to say, been *drunk* every day, and not quite *sober* yet—however touch no meat, nothing but fish, soup, and vegetables, consequently it does me no harm—sad dogs all the *Cantabs*. Mem.—*we mean* to reform next January. This place is a *monotony of endless variety*—like it—hate Southwell. Has Ridge sold well? or do the ancients demur? What ladies have bought?　＊　　　＊　　　＊　　　＊　　　＊

" Saw a girl at St. Mary's the image of Anne ＊ ＊ ＊, thought it was her—all in the wrong—the lady stared, so did I—I *blushed*, so did *not* the lady—sad thing—wish women had *more modesty*. Talking of women puts me in mind of my terrier Fanny—how is she? Got a headache, must go to bed, up early in the morning to travel. My protegé breakfasts with me; parting spoils my appetite—excepting from Southwell. Mem. *I hate Southwell*. Yours, &c."

her, and now I am going to make the most selfish and rude of requests. The person who gave it to me, when I was very young, is *dead*, and though a long time has elapsed since we met, as it was the only memorial I possessed of that person (in whom I was very much interested), it has acquired a value by this event I could have wished it never to have borne in my eyes. If, therefore, Miss ＊ ＊ ＊ ＊ should have preserved it, I must, under these circumstances, beg her to excuse my requesting it to be transmitted to me at No. 8, St. James's-street, London, and I will replace it by something she may remember me by equally well. As she was always so kind as to feel interested in the fate of him that formed the subject of our conversation, you may tell her that the giver of that cornelian died in May last of a consumption, at the age of twenty-one, making the sixth, within four months, of friends and relatives that I have lost between May and the end of August.

" Believe me, dear madam, yours very sincerely,

" BYRON.

" P. S. I go to London to-morrow."

The cornelian heart was, of course, returned, and Lord Byron, at the same time, reminded that he had left it with Miss ＊ ＊ ＊ ＊ as a deposit, *not* a gift.

LETTER XV.

TO MISS ———.

" Gordon's Hotel, July 13th, 1807.

" You write most excellent epistles—a fig for other correspondents, with their nonsensical apologies for ' *knowing nought about it*,'—you send me a delightful budget. I am here in a perpetual vortex of dissipation (very pleasant for all that), and, strange to tell, I get thinner, being now below 11 stone considerably. Stay in town a *month*, perhaps 6 weeks, trip into Essex, and then, as a favour, *irradiate* Southwell for 3 days with the light of my countenance; but nothing shall ever make me *reside* there again. I positively return to Cambridge in October; we are to be uncommonly gay, or in truth I should *cut* the University. An extraordinary circumstance occurred to me at Cambridge, a girl so very like * * made her appearance, that nothing but the most *minute inspection* could have undeceived me. I wish I had asked if *she* had ever been at H * * *.

" What the devil would Ridge have? is not 50 in a fortnight, before the advertisements, a sufficient sale? I hear many of the London booksellers have them, and Crosby has sent copies to the principal watering-places. Are they liked or not in Southwell? * * * * * I wish Boatswain had *swallowed* Damon! How is Bran? by the immortal gods, Bran ought to be a *Count* of the *Holy Roman Empire*. * * *

" The intelligence of London cannot be interesting to you, who have rusticated all your life—the annals of routs, riots, balls and boxing-matches, cards and crim. cons, parliamentary discussion, political details, masquerades, mechanics, Argyle-street Institution and aquatic races, love and lotteries, Brooks's and Buonaparte, opera-singers and oratorios, wine, women, wax-work, and weathercocks, can't accord with your *insulated* ideas of decorum and other *silly expressions* not inserted in *our vocabulary*.

" Oh! Southwell, Southwell, how I rejoice to have left thee, and how I curse the heavy hours I dragged along, for so many months, amongst the Mohawks who inhabit your kraals!—However, one thing I do not regret, which is having *pared off* a sufficient quantity of flesh to enable me to slip into ' an eel skin,' and vie with the *slim* beaux o modern times; though, I am sorry to say, it seems to be the mode amongst *gentlemen* to grow *fat*, and I am told I am at least 14lb. below the fashion.　However, I *decrease* instead of enlarging, which is extra ordinary, as *violent* exercise in London is impracticable; but I attribute the *phenomenon* to our *evening squeezes* at public and private parties. heard from Ridge this morning (the 14th, my letter was begun yester day): he says the Poems go on as well as can be wished, the 75 sent to town are circulated, and a demand for 50 more complied with, the day he dated his epistle, though the advertisements are not yet half published Adieu.

"P. S. Lord Carlisle, on receiving my Poems, sent, before he opened the book, a tolerably handsome letter:—I have not heard from him since. His opinions I neither know nor care about; if he is the least insolent, I shall enroll him with *Butler** and the other worthies.　He is in York shire, poor man! and very ill!　He said he had not had time to read the contents, but thought it necessary to acknowledge the receipt of the volume immediately.　Perhaps the earl ' *bears no brother near the throne,*' —*if so*, I will make his *sceptre* totter *in his hands*.—Adieu!"

LETTER XVI.

TO MISS ———.

"August 2d, 1807.

"London begins to disgorge its contents—town is empty—conse quently I can scribble at leisure, as occupations are less numerous.　In a fortnight I shall depart to fulfil a country engagement; but expect 2 epistles from you previous to that period.　Ridge does not proceed rapidly in Notts—very possible.　In town things wear a more promising aspect, and a man whose works are praised by *reviewers*, admired by *duchesses*, and sold by every bookseller of the metropolis, does not dedicate much consideration to *rustic readers*.　I have now a review before me, entitled

* In the Collection of his Poems printed for private circulation, he had inserted some severe verses on Doctor Butler, which he omitted in the subsequent publication,—at the same time explaining why he did so in a note little less severe than the verses.

'Literary Recreations,' where my *bardship* is applauded far beyond my deserts. I know nothing of the critic, but think *him* a very discerning gentleman, and *myself* a devilish *clever* fellow. His critique pleases me particularly, because it is of great length, and a proper quantum of censure is administered, just to give an agreeable *relish* to the praise. You know I hate insipid, unqualified, common-place compliment. If you would wish to see it, order the 13th Number of 'Literary Recreations' for the last month. I assure you I have not the most distant idea of the writer of the article—it is printed in a periodical publication—and though I have written a paper (a review of Wordsworth*), which appears in the same work, I am ignorant of every other person concerned in it—even the editor, whose name I have not heard. My cousin, Lord Alexander Gordon, who resided in the same hotel, told me his mother, her Grace of Gordon, requested he would introduce my *Poetical* Lordship to her *Highness*, as she had bought my volume, admired it exceedingly in common with the rest of the fashionable world, and wished to claim her relationship with the author. I was unluckily engaged on an excursion for some days afterwards, and as the duchess was on the eve of departing for Scotland, I have postponed my introduction till the winter, when I shall favour the lady, *whose taste I shall not dispute*, with my most sublime and edifying conversation. She is now in the Highlands, and Alexander took his departure a few days ago, for the same *blessed* seat of '*dark rolling winds.*'

" Crosby, my London publisher, has disposed of his second importation, and has sent to Ridge for a *third*—at least so he says. In every bookseller's window I see my *own name* and *say nothing*, but enjoy my

---

* This first attempt of Lord Byron at reviewing (for it will be seen that he, once or twice afterwards, tried his hand at this least poetical of employments) is remarkable only as showing how plausibly he could assume the established tone and phraseology of these minor judgment-seats of criticism. For instance :—" The volumes before us are by the Author of Lyrical Ballads, a collection which has not undeservedly met with a considerable share of public applause. The characteristics of Mr. Wordsworth's muse are simple and flowing, though occasionally inharmonious, verse,—strong and sometimes irresistible appeals to the feelings, with unexceptionable sentiments. Though the present work may not equal his former efforts, many of the poems possess a native elegance," &c. &c. &c. If Mr. Wordsworth ever chanced to cast his eye over this article, how little could he have suspected that under that dull prosaic mask lurked one who, in five short years from thence, would rival even *him* in poetry.

fame in secret.   My last reviewer kindly requests me to alter my deter
mination of writing no more, and ' a Friend to the Cause of Literature
begs I will *gratify* the *public* with some new work ' at no very distan
period.'   Who would not be a bard?—that is to say, if all critics would
be so polite.   However, the others will pay me off, I doubt not, for thi
gentle encouragement.   If so, have at 'em! By the by, I have written a
my intervals of leisure, after 2 in the morning, 380 lines in blank verse, o
Bosworth Field.   I have luckily got Hutton's account.   I shall extend
the Poem to 8 or 10 books, and shall have finished it in a year.   Whethe
it will be published or not must depend on circumstances.   So much fo
egotism! My *laurels* have turned my brain, but the *cooling acids* of forth
coming criticisms will probably restore me to *modesty.*

    " Southwell is a damned place—I have done with it—at least in al
probability: excepting yourself, I esteem no one within its precincts
You were my only *rational* companion; and in plain truth, I had more
respect for you than the whole *bevy*, with whose foibles I amused mysel
in compliance with their prevailing propensities.   You gave yoursel
more trouble with me and my manuscripts than a thousand *dolls* would
have done.   Believe me, I have not forgotten your good-nature in *thi
circle* of *sin*, and one day I trust I shall be able to evince my gratitude
Adieu, yours, &c.

    " P. S. Remember me to Dr. P."

LETTER XVII.

TO MISS ———.

                   " London, August 11th, 1807.

    " On Sunday next I set off for the Highlands *.   A friend of mine
accompanies me in my carriage to Edinburgh.   There we shall leave it,
and proceed in a *tandem* (a species of open carriage) through the

---

    * This plan (which he never put in practice) had been talked of by him before he left
Southwell, and is thus noticed in a letter of his fair correspondent to her brother:—" How can
you ask if Lord B. is going to visit the Highlands in the summer? Why, don't *you* know that
he never knows his own mind for ten minutes together? I tell him he is as fickle as the winds,
and as uncertain as the waves."

western passes to Inverary, where we shall purchase *shelties*, to enable us to view places inaccessible to *vehicular conveyances*. On the coast we shall hire a vessel and visit the most remarkable of the Hebrides, and, if we have time and favourable weather, mean to sail as far as Iceland, only 300 miles from the northern extremity of Caledonia, to peep at *Hecla*. This last intention you will keep a secret, as my nice *mamma* would imagine I was on a Voyage of *Discovery*, and raise the accustomed *maternal warwhoop*.

"Last week I swam in the Thames from Lambeth through the 2 bridges, Westminster and Blackfriars, a distance, including the different turns and tacks made on the way, of 3 miles! You see I am in excellent training in case of a *squall* at sea. I mean to collect all the Erse traditions, poems, &c. &c., and translate, or expand the subject to fill a volume, which may appear next spring under the denomination of ' *The Highland Harp*,' or some title equally *picturesque*. Of Bosworth Field, one book is finished, another just began. It will be a work of 3 or 4 years, and most probably never *conclude*. What would you say to some stanzas on Mount Hecla? they would be written at least with *fire*. How is the immortal Bran? and the Phœnix of canine quadrupeds, Boatswain? I have lately purchased a thorough-bred bull-dog, worthy to be the coadjutor of the aforesaid celestials—his name is *Smut!*—' bear it, ye breezes, on your *balmy* wings.'

"Write to me before I set off, I conjure you by the 5th rib of your grandfather. Ridge goes on well with the books—I thought that worthy had not done much in the country. In town they have been very successful; Carpenter (Moore's publisher) told me a few days ago they sold all theirs immediately, and had several inquiries made since, which, from the books being gone, they could not supply. The Duke of York, the Marchioness of Headfort, the Duchess of Gordon, &c. &c. were among the purchasers, and Crosby says the circulation will be still more extensive in the winter; the summer season being very bad for a sale, as most people are absent from London. However, they have gone off extremely well altogether. I shall pass very near you on my journey through Newark, but cannot approach. Don't tell this to Mrs. B., who supposes I travel a different road. If you have a letter, order it to be left at Ridge's shop, where I shall call, or the post-office, Newark, abou 6 or 8 in the evening. If your brother would ride over, I should b devilish glad to see him—he can return the same night, or sup with u and go home the next morning—the Kingston Arms is my inn.

" Adieu, yours ever,

" BYRON."

LETTER XVIII.

TO MISS ———.

" Trinity College, Cambridge, October 26th, 1807.

" MY DEAR ELIZABETH,

" Fatigued with sitting up till four in the morning for the last two days at hazard*, I take up my pen to inquire how your highness and the rest of my female acquaintance at the seat of archiepiscopal grandeur go on. I know I deserve a scolding for my negligence in not writing more frequently ; but racing up and down the country for these last three months, how was it possible to fulfil the duties of a correspondent? Fixed at last for six weeks, I write, as *thin* as ever (not having gained an ounce since my reduction), and rather in better humour ;—but, after all, Southwell was a detestable residence. Thank St. Dominica, I have done with it: I have been twice within eight miles of it, but could not prevail on myself to *suffocate* in its heavy atmosphere. This place is wretched enough—a villanous chaos of din and drunkenness, nothing but hazard and burgundy, hunting, mathematics and Newmarket, riot and racing. Yet it is a paradise compared with the eternal dullness of Southwell. Oh! the misery of doing nothing but make *love, enemies,* and *verses.*

" Next January (but this is *entre nous only*, and pray let it be so, or

---

* We observe here, as in other parts of his early letters, that sort of display and boast of rakishness which is but too common a folly at this period of life, when the young aspirant to manhood persuades himself that to be profligate is to be manly. Unluckily, this boyish desire of being thought worse than he really was remained with Lord Byron, as did some other feelings and foibles of his boyhood, long after the period when, with others, they are past and forgotten ; and his mind, indeed, was but beginning to outgrow them, when he was snatched away.

my maternal persecutor will be throwing her tomahawk at any of my curious projects) I am going to *sea*, for four or five months, with my cousin Capt. Bettesworth, who commands the Tartar, the finest frigate in the navy. I have seen most scenes, and wish to look at a naval life. We are going probably to the Mediterranean, or to the West Indies, or—to the d——l; and if there is a possibility of taking me to the latter, Bettesworth will do it; for he has received four and twenty wounds in different places, and at this moment possesses a letter from the late Lord Nelson, stating Bettesworth as the only officer in the navy who had more wounds than himself.

"I have got a new friend, the finest in the world, a *tame bear*. When I brought him here, they asked me what I meant to do with him, and my reply was, ' he should *sit for a fellowship*.' Sherard will explain the meaning of the sentence, if it is ambiguous. This answer delighted them not. We have several parties here, and this evening a large assortment of jockies, gamblers, boxers, authors, parsons, and poets, sup with me,—a precious mixture, but they go on well together; and for me, I am a *spice* of every thing, except a jockey; by the by, I was dismounted again the other day.

"Thank your brother in my name for his treatise. I have written 214 pages of a novel,—one poem of 380 lines*, to be published (without my name) in a few weeks, with notes,—560 lines of Bosworth Field, and 250 lines of another poem in rhyme, besides half a dozen smaller pieces. The poem to be published is a Satire. *Apropos*, I have been praised to the skies in the Critical Review†, and abused greatly in another publication‡. So much the better, they tell me, for the sale of the book; it

---

* The Poem afterwards enlarged and published under the title of "English Bards and Scotch Reviewers." It appears from this that the ground-work of that satire had been laid some time before the appearance of the article in the Edinburgh Review.

† Sept. 1807. This Review, in pronouncing upon the young author's future career, showed itself somewhat more "prophet-like" than the great oracle of the north. In noticing the Elegy on Newstead Abbey, the writer says, "We could not but hail with something of prophetic rapture, the hope conveyed in the closing stanza:

"Haply thy sun, emerging, yet may shine,
    Thee to irradiate with meridian ray," &c. &c.

‡ The first number of a monthly publication called " the Satirist," in which there appeared afterwards some low and personal attacks upon him.

keeps up controversy, and prevents it being forgotten. Besides, the first men of all ages have had their share, nor do the humblest escape;—so I bear it like a philosopher. It is odd two opposite critiques came out on the same day, and out of five pages of abuse my censor only quotes *two lines* from different poems, in support of his opinion. Now the proper way to *cut up* is to quote long passages, and make.them appear absurd, because simple allegation is no proof. On the other hand, there are seven pages of praise, and more than *my modesty* will allow said on the subject. Adieu.

"P.S. Write, write, write!!!"

It was at the beginning of the following year that an acquaintance commenced between Lord Byron and a gentleman, related to his family by marriage, Mr. Dallas,—the author of some novels, popular, I believe, in their day, and also of a sort of Memoir of the noble Poet published soon after his death, which, from being founded chiefly on original correspondence, is the most authentic and trust-worthy of any that have yet appeared. In the letters addressed by Lord Byron to this gentleman, among many details, curious in a literary point of view, we find, what is much more important for our present purpose, some particulars illustrative of the opinions which he had formed, at this time of his life, on the two subjects most connected with the early formation of character—morals and religion.

It is but rarely that infidelity or scepticism finds an entrance into youthful minds. That readiness to take the future upon trust, which is the charm of this period of life, would naturally, indeed, make it the season of belief as well as of hope. There are also then, still fresh in the mind, the impressions of early religious culture, which, even in those who begin soonest to question their faith, give way but slowly to the encroachments of doubt, and, in the mean time, extend the benefit of their moral restraint over a portion of life when it is acknowledged such restraints are most necessary. If exemption from the checks of religion be, as infidels themselves allow*, a state of freedom from responsibility dangerous

---

* " Look out for a people entirely destitute of religion : if you find them at all, be assured that they are but few degrees removed from brutes."—HUME.

The reader will find this avowal of Hume turned eloquently to the advantage of religion

at all times, it must be peculiarly so in that season of temptation, youth, when the passions are sufficiently disposed to usurp a latitude for themselves, without taking a licence also from infidelity to enlarge their range. It is, therefore, fortunate that, for the causes just stated, the inroads of scepticism and disbelief should be seldom felt in the mind till a period of life, when the character, already formed, is out of the reach of their disturbing influence,—when, being the result, however erroneous, of thought and reasoning, they are likely to partake of the sobriety of the process by which they were acquired, and, being considered but as matters of pure speculation, to have as little share in determining the mind towards evil as, too often, the most orthodox creed has, at the same age, in influencing it towards good.

While, in this manner, the moral qualities of the unbeliever himself are guarded from some of the mischiefs that might, at an earlier age, attend such doctrines, the danger also of his communicating the infection to others is, for reasons of a similar nature, considerably diminished. The same vanity or daring which may have prompted the youthful sceptic's opinions, will lead him likewise, it is probable, rashly and irreverently to avow them, without regard either to the effect of his example on those around him, or to the odium which, by such an avowal, he entails irreparably on himself. But, at a riper age, these consequences are, in general, more cautiously weighed. The infidel, if at all considerate of the happiness of others, will naturally pause before he chases from their hearts a hope of which his own feels the want so desolately. If regardful only of himself, he will no less naturally shrink from the promulgation of opinions which, in no age, have men uttered with impunity. In either case there is a tolerably good security for his silence ;—for, should benevolence not restrain him from making converts of others, prudence may, at least, prevent him from making a martyr of himself.

Unfortunately, Lord Byron was an exception to the usual course of such lapses. With him, the canker showed itself " in the morn and dew of youth," when the effect of such " blastments" is, for every

in a Collection of Sermons, entitled, " The Connexion of Christianity with Human Happiness," written by one of Lord Byron's earliest and most valued friends, the Rev. William Harness.

reason, most fatal,—and, in addition to the real misfortune of being an unbeliever at any age, he exhibited the rare and melancholy spectacle of an unbelieving schoolboy. The same prematurity of developement which brought his passions and genius so early into action, enabled him also to anticipate this worst, dreariest result of reason; and at the very time of life when a spirit and temperament like his most required control, those checks, which religious prepossessions best supply, were almost wholly wanting.

We have seen, in those two Addresses to the Deity which I have selected from among his unpublished Poems, and still more strongly in a passage of the Catalogue of his studies, at what a boyish age the authority of all systems and sects was avowedly shaken off by his inquiring spirit. Yet, even in these, there is a fervour of adoration mingled with his defiance of creeds, through which the piety implanted in his nature (as it is deeply in all poetic natures) unequivocally shows itself; and had he then fallen within the reach of such guidance and example as would have seconded and fostered these natural dispositions, the licence of opinion, into which he afterwards broke loose, might have been averted. His scepticism, if not wholly removed, might have been softened down into that humble doubt, which, so far from being inconsistent with a religious spirit, is, perhaps, its best guard against presumption and uncharitableness; and, at all events, even if his own views of religion had not been brightened or elevated, he would have learned not wantonly to cloud or disturb those of others. But there was no such monitor near him. After his departure from Southwell, he had not a single friend or relative to whom he could look up with respect; but was thrown alone on the world, with his passions and his pride, to revel in the fatal discovery which he imagined himself to have made of the nothingness of the future, and the all-paramount claims of the present. By singular ill-fortune, too, the individual who, among all his college friends, had taken the strongest hold on his admiration and affection, and whose loss he afterwards lamented with brotherly tenderness, was to the same extent as himself, if not more strongly, a sceptic. Of this remarkable young man, Matthews, who was so early snatched away, and whose career in after-life, had it been at all answerable to the extraordinary promise of his youth, must have placed him upon a level with the first men of his day, a Memoir was, at one time, intended to be published by his relatives; and to Lord Byron, among others of his college friends, application, for assistance in the task, was addressed. The letter which this circumstance drew forth from the noble poet, besides containing many amusing traits of his friend, affords such an insight into his own habits of life at this period, that, though infringing upon the chronological order of his correspondence, I shall insert it here.

LETTER XIX.

TO MR. MURRAY.

" Ravenna, 9bre 12, 1820.

" What you said of the late Charles Skinner Matthews has set me to my recollections; but I have not been able to turn up any thing which would do for the purposed Memoir of his brother,—even if he had previously done enough during his life to sanction the introduction of anecdotes so merely personal. He was, however, a very extraordinary man, and would have been a great one. No one ever succeeded in a more surpassing degree than he did, as far as he went. He was indolent too; but whenever he stripped, he overthrew all antagonists. His conquests will be found registered at Cambridge, particularly his *Downing* one, which was hotly and highly contested and yet easily *won*. Hobhouse was his most intimate friend, and can tell you more of him than any man. William Bankes also a great deal. I myself recollect more of his oddities than of his academical qualities, for we lived most together at a very idle period of *my* life. When I went up to Trinity in 1805, at the age of seventeen and a half, I was miserable and untoward to a degree. I was wretched at leaving Harrow, to which I had become attached during the two last years of my stay there; wretched at going to Cambridge instead of Oxford (there were no rooms vacant at Christ-church), wretched from some private domestic circumstances of different kinds, and consequently about as unsocial as a wolf taken from the troop. So that, although I knew Matthews, and met him often *then* at Bankes's (who was my collegiate pastor, and master, and patron), and at Rhode's,

Milnes's, Price's, Dick's, Macnamara's, Farrell's, Galley Knight's, and others of that *set* of cotemporaries, yet I was neither intimate with him nor with any one else, except my old schoolfellow Edward Long (with whom I used to pass the day in riding and swimming), and William Bankes, who was good-naturedly tolerant of my ferocities.

" It was not till 1807, after I had been upwards of a year away from Cambridge, to which I had returned again to *reside* for my degree, that I became one of Matthews's familiars, by means of H**, who, after hating me for two years, because I ' wore a *white hat* and a *gray* coat and rode a *gray* horse' (as he says himself), took me into his good graces because I had written some poetry. I had always lived a good deal, and got drunk occasionally, in their company—but now we became really friends in a morning. Matthews, however, was not at this period resident in College. I met *him* chiefly in London, and at uncertain periods at Cambridge. H**, in the mean time, did great things: he founded the Cambridge ' Whig Club' (which he seems to have forgotten), and the ' Amicable Society,' which was dissolved in consequence of the members constantly quarrelling, and made himself very popular with ' us youth,' and no less formidable to all tutors, professors, and heads of Colleges. William B** was gone; while he staid, he ruled the roast— or rather the *roasting*—and was father of all mischiefs.

" Matthews and I, meeting in London, and elsewhere, became great cronies. He was not good-tempered—nor am I—but with a little tact his temper was manageable, and I thought him so superior a man, that I was willing to sacrifice something to his humours, which were often, at the same time, amusing and provoking. What became of his *papers* (and he certainly had many), at the time of his death, was never known. I mention this by the way, fearing to skip it over, and *as* he *wrote* remarkably well, both in Latin and English. We went down to Newstead together, where I had got a famous cellar, and *Monks'* dresses from a masquerade warehouse. We were a company of some seven or eight, with an occasional neighbour or so for visitors, and used to sit up late in our Friars' dresses, drinking burgundy, claret, champagne, and what not, out of the *skull-cup*, and all sorts of glasses, and buffooning all round the house, in our conventual garments. Matthews always denominated me 'the Abbot,' and never called me by any other name in his good humours, to the day of his death. The harmony of these our symposia was somewhat interrupted, a few days after our assembling, by Matthews's threatening to throw '*bold* W**' (as he was called, from winning a foot-match, and a horse-match, the first from Ipswich to London, and the second from Brighthelmstone) by threatening to throw 'bold W**' out of a *window*, in consequence of I know not what commerce of jokes ending in this epigram. W** came to me and said, that ' his respect and regard for me as host would not permit him to call out any of my guests, and that he should go to town next morning.' He did. It was in vain that I represented to him that the window was not high, and that the turf under it was particularly soft. Away he went.

" Matthews and myself had travelled down from London together, talking all the way incessantly upon one single topic. When we got to Loughborough, I know not what chasm had made us diverge for a moment to some other subject, at which he was indignant. ' Come,' said he, ' don't let us break through—let us go on as we began, to our journey's end;' and so he continued, and was entertaining as ever to the very end. He had previously occupied, during my year's absence from Cambridge, my rooms in Trinity, with the furniture; and Jones the tutor, in his odd way, had said on putting him in, ' Mr. Matthews, I recommend to your attention not to damage any of the moveables, for Lord Byron, sir, is a young man *of tumultuous passions.*' Matthews was delighted with this; and whenever any body came to visit him, begged them to handle the very door with caution; and used to repeat Jones's admonition, in his tone and manner. There was a large mirror in the room, on which he remarked, ' that he thought his friends were grown uncommonly assiduous in coming to *see him*, but he soon discovered that they only came to *see themselves*.' Jones's phrase of ' *tumultuous passions*,' and the whole scene, had put him into such good humour, that I verily believe, that I owed to it a portion of his good graces.

" When at Newstead, somebody by accident rubbed against one of his white silk stockings, one day before dinner; of course the gentleman apologized. ' Sir,' answered Matthews, ' it may be all very well for you, who have a great many silk stockings, to dirty other people's; but to me,

who have only this *one pair*, which I have put on in honour of the Abbo
here, no apology can compensate for such carelessness; besides the expens
of washing.' He had the same sort of droll sardonic way about ever
thing. A wild Irishman, named F * *, one evening beginning to sa
something at a large supper at Cambridge, Matthews roared out ' Silence
and then, pointing to F * *, cried out, in the words of the oracle, ' *Orso*
is endowed with *reason*.' You may easily suppose that Orson lost wha
reason he had acquired, on hearing this compliment. When H * *
published his volume of Poems, the Miscellany (which Matthews *woul*
call the ' *Miss-sell-any*'), all that could be drawn from him was, that th
preface was ' extremely like *Walsh*.' H * * thought this at first a com
pliment; but we never could make out what it was, for all we know o
Walsh is his Ode to King William, and Pope's epithet of ' *knowing*
Walsh.' When the Newstead party broke up for London, H * * and
Matthews, who were the greatest friends possible, agreed, for a whim, to
walk together to town. They quarrelled by the way, and actually walked
the latter half of their journey, occasionally passing and repassing, without
speaking. When Matthews had got to Highgate, he had spent all his
money but threepence halfpenny, and determined to spend that also in
a pint of beer, which I believe he was drinking before a public-house, as
H * * passed him (still without speaking) for the last time on their route.
They were reconciled in London again.

" One of Matthews's passions was ' the Fancy ;' and he sparred
uncommonly well. But he always got beaten in rows, or combats with
the bare fist. In swimming too, he swam well; but with *effort* and *labour*,
and *too high* out of the water; so that Scrope Davies and myself, of
whom he was therein somewhat emulous, always told him that he would
be drowned if ever he came to a difficult pass in the water. He was so;
but surely Scrope and myself would have been most heartily glad that

> ' the Dean had lived,
> And our prediction proved a lie.'

" His head was uncommonly handsome, very like what *Pope*'s was
in his youth.

" His voice, and laugh, and features, are strongly resembled by his brother Henry's, if Henry be *he* of *King's College.* His passion for boxing was so great, that he actually wanted me to match him with Dogherty (whom I had backed and made the match for against Tom Belcher), and I saw them spar together at my own lodgings with the gloves on. As he was bent upon it, I would have backed Dogherty to please him, but the match went off. It was of course to have been a private fight in a private room.

"On one occasion, being too late to go home and dress, he was equipped by a friend (Mr. Bailey, I believe), in a magnificently fashionable and somewhat exaggerated shirt and neckcloth. He proceeded to the Opera, and took his station in Fop's Alley. During the interval between the opera and the ballet, an acquaintance took his station by him, and saluted him : ' Come round,' said Matthews, ' come round.' ' Why should I come round ?' said the other; ' you have only to turn your head—I am close by you.' ' That is exactly what I cannot do,' answered Matthews : ' don't you see the state I am in ?' pointing to his buckram shirt collar, and inflexible cravat,—and there he stood with his head always in the same perpendicular position during the whole spectacle.

"One evening, after dining together, as we were going to the Opera, I happened to have a spare Opera ticket (as subscriber to a box), and presented it to Matthews. ' Now, sir, said he to Hobhouse afterwards, ' this I call *courteous* in the Abbot—another man would never have thought that I might do better with half a guinea than throw it to a door-keeper ;—but here is a man not only asks me to dinner, but gives me a ticket for the theatre.' These were only his oddities, for no man was more liberal, or more honourable in all his doings and dealings than Matthews. He gave Hobhouse and me, before we set out for Constantinople, a most splendid entertainment, to which we did ample justice. One of his fancies was dining at all sorts of out of the way places. Somebody popped upon him, in I know not what coffee-house in the Strand—and what do you think was the attraction ? Why, that he paid a shilling (I think) to *dine with his hat on.* This he called his ' *hat* house,' and used to boast of the comfort of being covered at meal-times.

"When Sir Henry Smith was expelled from Cambridge for a row

with a tradesman named 'Hiron,' Matthews solaced himself with shouting under Hiron's windows every evening,

' Ah me ! What perils do environ
The man who meddles with *hot Hiron.*'

"He was also of that band of profane scoffers, who, under the auspices of ** **, used to rouse Lort Mansel (late Bishop of Bristol) from his slumbers in the lodge of Trinity, and when he appeared at the window foaming with wrath, and crying out ' I know you, gentlemen, I know you!' were wont to reply, 'We beseech thee to hear us, good *Lort*—Good *Lort*, deliver us!' (Lort was his christian name.) As he was very free in his speculations upon all kinds of subjects, although by no means either dissolute or intemperate in his conduct, and as I was no less independent, our conversation and correspondence used to alarm our friend Hobhouse to a considerable degree.

*   *   *   *

"You must be almost tired of my packets, which will have cost a mint of postage.

"Salute Gifford and all my friends.

"Yours, &c."

As already, before his acquaintance with Mr. Matthews commenced, Lord Byron had begun to bewilder himself in the mazes of scepticism, it would be unjust to impute to this gentleman any further share in the formation of his noble friend's opinions than what arose from the natural influence of example and sympathy;—an influence which, as it was felt perhaps equally on both sides, rendered the contagion of their doctrines, in a great measure, reciprocal. In addition, too, to this community of sentiment on such subjects, they were both, in no ordinary degree, possessed by that dangerous spirit of ridicule, whose impulses even the pious cannot always restrain, and which draws the mind on, by a sort of irresistible fascination, to disport itself most wantonly on the brink of all that is most solemn and awful. It is not wonderful, therefore, that, in such society, the opinions of the noble poet should have been, at least, accelerated in that direction to which their bias already leaned; and though he cannot be said to have become thus confirmed in these doctrines—as neither now, nor at any time of his life, was he a confirmed unbeliever,—he had undoubtedly learned to feel less uneasy under his scepticism, and even to mingle somewhat of boast and of levity with his expression of it. At the very first onset of his correspondence with Mr. Dallas, we find him proclaiming his sentiments on all such subjects with a flippancy and confidence, far different from the tone in which he had first ventured on his doubts,—from that fervid sadness, as of a heart loth to part with its illusions, which breathes through every line of those prayers, that, but a year before, his pen had traced.

Here again, however, we should recollect, there must be a considerable share of allowance for his usual tendency to make the most and the worst of his own obliquities. There occurs, indeed, in his first letter to Mr. Dallas an instance of this strange ambition,—the very reverse, it must be allowed, of hypocrisy,—which led him to court, rather than avoid, the reputation of profligacy, and to put, at all times, the worst face on his own character and conduct. His new correspondent having, in introducing himself to his acquaintance, passed some compliments on the tone of moral and charitable feeling which breathed through one of his poems, had added, that "it brought to his mind another noble author, who was not only a fine poet, orator, and historian, but one of the closest reasoners we have on the truth of that religion of which forgiveness is a prominent principle,—the great and the good Lord Lyttleton, whose fame will never die. His son," adds Mr. Dallas, "to whom he had transmitted genius, but not virtue, sparkled for a moment and went out like a star,—and with him the title became extinct." To this Lord Byron answers in the following letter.

LETTER XX.

TO MR. DALLAS.

" Dorant's Hotel, Albemarle-street, Jan. 20th, 1808.

" SIR,

" Your letter was not received till this morning, I presume from being addressed to me in Notts., where I have not resided since last June, and as the date is the 6th, you will excuse the delay of my answer.

" If the little volume you mention has given pleasure to the author of *Percival* and *Aubrey*, I am sufficiently repaid by his praise. Though our periodical censors have been uncommonly lenient, I confess a tribute from a man of acknowledged genius is still more flattering. But I am afraid I should forfeit all claim to candour, if I did not decline such praise as I do not deserve; and this is, I am sorry to say, the case in the present instance.

" My compositions speak for themselves, and must stand or fall by their own worth or demerit: *thus far* I feel highly gratified by your favourable opinion. But my pretensions to virtue are unluckily so few, that though I should be happy to merit, I cannot accept, your applause in that respect. One passage in your letter struck me forcibly: you mention the two Lords Lyttleton in a manner they respectively deserve, and will be surprised to hear the person who is now addressing you has been frequently compared to the *latter*. I know I am injuring myself in your esteem by this avowal, but the circumstance was so remarkable from your observation, that I cannot help relating the fact. The events of my short life have been of so singular a nature, that, though the pride commonly called honour has, and I trust ever will, prevent me from disgracing my name by a mean or cowardly action, I have been already held up as the votary of licentiousness, and the disciple of infidelity. How far justice may have dictated this accusation I cannot pretend to say, but, like the *gentleman* to whom my religious friends, in the warmth of their charity, have already devoted me, I am made worse than I really am. However, to quit myself (the worst theme I could pitch upon) and

return to my Poems, I cannot sufficiently express my thanks, and I hope
I shall some day have an opportunity of rendering them in person.
A second edition is now in the press, with some additions and considerable omissions; you will allow me to present you with a copy.
The Critical, Monthly, and Anti-Jacobin Reviews have been very
indulgent; but the Eclectic has pronounced a furious Philippic, not
against the *book* but the *author*, where you will find all I have mentioned
asserted by a reverend divine who wrote the critique.

　"Your name and connexion with our family have been long known
to me, and I hope your person will be not less so; you will find me an
excellent compound of a 'Brainless' and a 'Stanhope *.' I am afraid
you will hardly be able to read this, for my hand is almost as bad as my
character, but you will find me, as legibly as possible,

"Your obliged and obedient servant,

" BYRON."

　There is here, evidently, a degree of pride in being thought to
resemble the wicked Lord Lyttleton; and, lest his known irregularities
should not bear him out in the pretension, he refers mysteriously, as was
his habit, to certain untold events of his life, to warrant the parallel †.
Mr. Dallas, who seems to have been but little prepared for such a
reception of his compliments, escapes out of the difficulty by transferring
to the young lord's "candour" the praise he had so thanklessly bestowed
on his morals in general; adding, that from the design Lord Byron had
expressed in his preface of resigning the service of the Muses for a
different vocation, he had "conceived him bent on pursuits which lead
to the character of a legislator and statesman;—had imagined him at one
of the universities, training himself to habits of reasoning and eloquence,
and storing up a large fund of history and law." It is in reply to this
letter that the exposition of the noble poet's opinions to which I have
above alluded is contained.

---

　* Characters in the novel called *Percival.*
　† This appeal to the imagination of his correspondent was not altogether without effect.—
" I considered," says Mr. Dallas, " these letters, *though evidently grounded on some occurrences
in the still earlier part of his life,* rather as *jeux d'esprit* than as a true portrait."

LETTER XXI.

TO MR. DALLAS.

"Dorant's, January 21st, 1808.

"SIR,

"Whenever leisure and inclination permit me the pleasure of a visit, I shall feel truly gratified in a personal acquaintance with one whose mind has been long known to me in his writings.

"You are so far correct in your conjecture, that I am a member of the University of Cambridge, where I shall take my degree of A. M. this term; but were reasoning, eloquence, or virtue, the objects of my search, Granta is not their metropolis, nor is the place of her situation an 'El Dorado,' far less an Utopia. The intellects of her children are as stagnant as her Cam, and their pursuits limited to the church—not of Christ, but of the nearest benefice.

"As to my reading, I believe I may aver, without hyperbole, it has been tolerably extensive in the historical; so that few nations exist, or have existed, with whose records I am not in some degree acquainted, from Herodotus down to Gibbon. Of the classics, I know about as much as most schoolboys after a discipline of thirteen years; of the law of the land as much as enables me to keep 'within the statute'—to use the poacher's vocabulary. I did study the 'Spirit of Laws' and the Law of Nations; but when I saw the latter violated every month, I gave up my attempts at so useless an accomplishment;—of geography, I have seen more land on maps than I should wish to traverse on foot;—of mathematics, enough to give me the headache without clearing the part affected;—of philosophy, astronomy, and metaphysics, more than I can comprehend*; and of common sense so little, that I mean to leave a Byronian prize at each of our 'Almæ Matres' for the first discovery,—though I rather fear that of the Longitude will precede it.

"I once thought myself a philosopher, and talked nonsense with

---

* He appears to have had in his memory Voltaire's lively account of Zadig's learning:— "Il savait de la métaphysique ce qu'on en a su dans tous les âges,—c'est à dire, fort peu de chose," &c.

reat decorum : I defied pain, and preached up equanimity. For some ime this did very well, for no one 'was in *pain* for me but my friends, nd none lost their patience but my hearers. At last, a fall from my .orse convinced me bodily suffering was an evil; and the worst of an rgument overset my maxims and my temper at the same moment, so I [uitted Zeno for Aristippus, and conceive that pleasure constitutes the *ο καλον*. In morality, I prefer Confucius to the Ten Commandments, nd Socrates to St. Paul, though the two latter agree in their opinion of narriage. In religion, I favour the Catholic emancipation, but do not .cknowledge the Pope; and I have refused to take the Sacrament,)ecause I do not think eating bread or drinking wine from the hand of .n earthly vicar will make me an inheritor of heaven. I hold virtue in general, or the virtues severally, to be only in the disposition, each a *eeling*, not a principle*. I believe truth the prime attribute of the Deity; and death an eternal sleep, at least of the body. You have here . brief compendium of the sentiments of the *wicked* George Lord Byron; .nd, till I get a new suit, you will perceive I am badly clothed. I 'emain," &c.

Though such was, doubtless, the general cast of his opinions at this :ime, it must be recollected, before we attach any particular importance :o the details of his creed, that, in addition to the temptation, never easily resisted by him, of displaying his wit at the expense of his character, he was here addressing a person who, though, no doubt, well-meaning, was evidently one of those officious, self-satisfied advisers, whom it was the delight of Lord Byron at all times to astonish and *mystify*. The tricks which, when a boy, he played upon the Nottingham quack, Lavender, were but the first of a long series with which, through life, he amused himself, at the expense of all the numerous quacks, whom his celebrity and sociability drew around him.

The terms in which he speaks of the university in this letter agree in spirit with many passages both in the "Hours of Idleness," and his early Satire, and prove that, while Harrow was remembered by him with

---

* The doctrine of Hume, who resolves all virtue into sentiment.—See his "Enquiry concerning the Principles of Morals."

more affection, perhaps, than respect, Cambridge had not been able
inspire him with either. This feeling of distaste to his "nursir
mother" he entertained in common with some of the most illustrio
names of English literature. So great was Milton's hatred to Cambridg
that he had even conceived, says Warton, a dislike to the face of tl
country,—to the fields in its neighbourhood. The poet Gray thus speal
of the same university :—"Surely, it was of this place, now Cambridg
but formerly known by the name of Babylon, that the prophet spol
when he said, ' the wild beasts of the desert shall dwell there, and the
houses shall be full of doleful creatures, and owls shall build there, ar
satyrs shall dance there,'" &c. &c. The bitter recollections which Gibbc
retained of Oxford, his own pen has recorded; and the cool contempt b
which Locke avenged himself on the bigotry of the same seat of learnin
is even still more memorable*.

In poets, such distasteful recollections of their collegiate life ma
well be thought to have their origin in that antipathy to the tramme
of discipline, which is not unusually observable among the chara
teristics of genius, and which might be regarded, indeed, as a sort (
instinct, implanted in it for its own preservation, if there be any trut
in the opinion that a course of learned education is hurtful to th
freshness and elasticity of the imaginative faculty. A right reveren
writer† but little to be suspected of any desire to depreciate academic;
studies, not only puts the question, "whether the usual forms of learnin
be not rather injurious to the true poet, than really assisting to him?
but appears strongly disposed to answer it in the affirmative,—giving, ;
an instance, in favour of this conclusion, the classic Addison, who, ";
appears," he says, " from some original efforts in the sublime, allegoric;
way, had no want of natural talents for the greater poetry,—which ye
were so restrained and disabled by his constant and superstitious stud
of the old classics, that he was, in fact, but a very ordinary poet."

It was, no doubt, under some such impression of the malign influ

---

* See his Letter to Anthony Collins, 1703-4, where he speaks of "those sharp head
which were for damning his book, because of its discouraging the staple commodity of the plac
which in his time was called *hogs' shearing.*"

† Hurd, " Discourses on Poetical Imitation."

ence of a collegiate atmosphere upon genius that Milton, in speaking of Cambridge, gave vent to the exclamation, that it was "a place quite incompatible with the votaries of Phœbus," and that Lord Byron, versifying a thought of his own, in the letter to Mr. Dallas just given, declares,

> " Her Helicon is duller than her Cam."

The poet Dryden, too, who, like Milton, had incurred some mark of disgrace at Cambridge, seems to have entertained but little more veneration for his Alma Mater; and the verses in which he has praised Oxford at the expense of his own university* were, it is probable, dictated much less by admiration of the one than by a desire to spite and depreciate the other.

Nor is it Genius only that thus rebels against the discipline of the schools. Even the tamer quality of Taste, which it is the professed object of classical studies to cultivate, is sometimes found to turn restive under the pedantic *manège* to which it is subjected. It was not till released from the duty of reading Virgil as a task, that Gray could feel himself capable of enjoying the beauties of that poet; and Lord Byron was, to the last, unable to vanquish a similar prepossession, with which the same sort of school association had inoculated him, against Horace.

> ——" Though Time hath taught
> My mind to meditate what then it learn'd,
> Yet such the fix'd inveteracy wrought
> By the impatience of my early thought,
> That, with the freshness wearing out before
> My mind could relish what it might have sought,
> If free to choose, I cannot now restore
> Its health; but what it then detested, still abhor.
>
> Then farewell, Horace; whom I hated so,
> Not for thy faults, but mine; it is a curse
> To understand, not feel thy lyric flow,
> To comprehend, but never love thy verse."
>
> CHILDE HAROLD, CANTO IV.

---

* Prologue to the University of Oxford.

To the list of eminent poets, who have thus left on record the dislike and disapproval of the English system of education, are to l added, the distinguished names of Cowley, Addison, and Cowper; whil among the cases which, like those of Milton and Dryden, practicall demonstrate the sort of inverse ratio that may exist between colleg honours and genius, must not be forgotten those of Swift, Goldsmitl and Churchill, to every one of whom some mark of incompetency wa affixed by the respective universities, whose annals they adorn. Wher in addition, too, to this rather ample catalogue of poets, whom th universities have sent forth either disloyal or dishonoured, we come t number over such names as those of Shakspeare and of Pope, followe by Gay, Thomson, Burns, Chatterton, &c., all of whom have attaine their respective stations of eminence, without instruction or sanctio from any college whatever, it forms altogether, it must be owned, a larg portion of the poetical world, that must be subducted from the sphere c that nursing influence which the universities are supposed to exercis over the genius of the country.

The following letters, written at this time, contain some particular which will not be found uninteresting.

LETTER XXII.

TO MR. HENRY DRURY.

" Dorant's Hotel, January 13th, 1808.

" MY DEAR SIR,

" Though the stupidity of my servants, or the porter of the house in not showing you up stairs (where I should have joined you directly prevented me the pleasure of seeing you yesterday, I hoped to meet yo at some public place in the evening. However, my stars decreed otherwise as they generally do, when I have any favour to request of them. I thin! you would have been surprised at my figure, for, since our last meeting I am reduced four stone in weight. I then weighed fourteen stone seve pound, and now only *ten stone and a half.* I have disposed of m *superfluities* by means of hard exercise and abstinence. * * *

" Should your Harrow engagements allow you to visit town betwee his and February, I shall be most happy to see you in Albemarle-street. If I am not so fortunate, I shall endeavour to join you for an afternoon at Harrow, though, I fear, your cellar will by no means contribute to my cure. As for my worthy preceptor, Dr. B., our encounter would by no means prevent the *mutual endearments* he and I were wont to lavish on each other. We have only spoken once since my departure from Harrow in 1805, and then he politely told Tatersall I was not a proper associate for his pupils. This was long before my strictures in verse: but, in plain *prose*, had I been some years older, I should have held my tongue on his perfections. But, being laid on my back, when that schoolboy thing was written—or rather dictated—expecting to rise no more, my physician having taken his sixteenth fee, and I his prescription, I could not quit this earth without leaving a memento of my constant attachment to Butler in gratitude for his manifold good offices.

" I meant to have been down in July; but thinking my appearance, immediately after the publication, would be construed into an insult, I directed my steps elsewhere. Besides, I heard that some of the boys had got hold of my Libellus, contrary to my wishes certainly, for I never transmitted a single copy till October, when I gave one to a boy, since gone, after repeated importunities. You will, I trust, pardon this egotism. As you had touched on the subject, I thought some explanation necessary. Defence I shall not attempt, ' Hic murus aheneus esto, nil conscire sibi'— and ' so on' (as Lord Baltimore said on his trial for a rape)—I have been so long at Trinity as to forget the conclusion of the line; but, though I cannot finish my quotation, I will my letter, and entreat you to believe me, gratefully and affectionately, &c.

" P.S. I will not lay a tax on your time by requiring an answer, lest you say, as Butler said to Tatersall (when I had written his reverence an impudent epistle on the expression before mentioned), viz.—' that I wanted to draw him into a correspondence.' "

LETTER XXIII.

TO MR. HARNESS.

" Dorant's Hotel, Albemarle-street, Feb. 11th, 1808.

" MY DEAR HARNESS,

" As I had no opportunity of returning my verbal thanks, I trus
you will accept my written acknowledgments for the compliment yo
were pleased to pay some production of my unlucky muse last Novembe
—I am induced to do this not less from the pleasure I feel in the prais
of an old schoolfellow, than from justice to you, for I had heard th
story with some slight variations. Indeed, when we met this morning
Wingfield had not undeceived me, but he will tell you that I displaye
no resentment in mentioning what I had heard, though I was not sorr
to discover the truth. Perhaps you hardly recollect some years ago
short, though, for the time, a warm friendship between us? Why it wa
not of longer duration, I know not. I have still a gift of yours in m
possession, that must always prevent me from forgetting it. I als
remember being favoured with the perusal of many of your compositio
and several other circumstances very pleasant in their day, which I wil
not force upon your memory, but entreat you to believe me, with mucl
regret at their short continuance, and a hope they are not irrevocable
yours very sincerely, &c. " BYRON."

I have already mentioned the early friendship that subsisted betweer
this gentleman and Lord Byron, as well as the coolness that succeeded it
The following extract from a letter with which Mr. Harness favoure
me, in placing at my disposal those of his noble correspondent, wil
explain the circumstances that led, at this time, to their reconcilement
and the candid tribute, in the concluding sentences, to Lord Byron
will be found not less honourable to the reverend writer himself thar
to his friend.

" A coolness afterwards arose which Byron alludes to in the first o
the accompanying letters, and we never spoke during the last year of hi
remaining at school, nor till after the publication of his ' Hours o

dleness.' Lord Byron was then at Cambridge; I, in one of the upper orms at Harrow. In an English theme I happened to quote from the volume, and mention it with praise. It was reported to Byron that I had, on the contrary, spoken slightingly of his work and of himself, for the purpose of conciliating the favour of Dr. Butler, the master, who had been severely satirized in one of the poems. Wingfield, who was afterwards Lord Powerscourt, a mutual friend of Byron and myself, disabused him of the error into which he had been led, and this was the occasion of the first letter of the collection. Our conversation was renewed and continued from that time till his going abroad. Whatever faults Lord Byron might have had towards others, to myself he was always uniformly affectionate. I have many slights and neglects towards him to reproach myself with; but I cannot call to mind a single instance of caprice or unkindness, in the whole course of our intimacy, to allege against him."

In the spring of this year (1808) appeared the memorable critique upon the " Hours of Idleness" in the Edinburgh Review. That he had some notice of what was to be expected from that quarter appears by the following letter to his friend, Mr. Becher.

LETTER XXIV

TO MR. BECHER.

" Dorant's Hotel, Feb. 26, 1808.

" MY DEAR BECHER,

" *   *   *   *   * Now for Apollo. I am happy that you still retain your predilection, and that the public allow me some share of praise. I am of so much importance that a most violent attack is preparing for me in the next number of the Edinburgh Review. This I had from the authority of a friend who has seen the proof and manuscript of the critique. You know the system of the Edinburgh gentlemen is universal attack. They praise none; and neither the public nor the author expects praise from them. It is, however, something to be noticed, as they profess to pass judgment only on works requiring the public attention. You will see this, when it comes out;—it is, I understand, of

the most unmerciful description; but I am aware of it, and hope *you* w:
not be hurt by its severity.

" Tell Mrs. Byron not to be out of humour with them, and
prepare her mind for the greatest hostility on their part. It will do
injury whatever, and I trust her mind will not be ruffled. They defe
their object by indiscriminate abuse, and they never praise except th
partizans of Lord Holland and Co. It is nothing to be abused whe
Southey, Moore, Lauderdale, Strangford, and Payne Knight, share th
same fate.

" I am sorry—but ' Childish Recollections' must be suppressed durin
this edition. I have altered, at your suggestion, the *obnoxious allusior*
in the sixth stanza of my last ode.

" And now, my dear Becher, I must return my best acknowledg
ments for the interest you have taken in me and my poetical bantling;
and I shall ever be proud to show how much I esteem the *advice* an
the *adviser*. Believe me most truly," &c.

Soon after this letter appeared the dreaded article,—an article which
if not " witty in itself," deserves eminently the credit of causing " wit in
others." Seldom, indeed, has it fallen to the lot of the justest criticism
to attain celebrity such as injustice has procured for this; nor as long a
the short, but glorious race of Byron's genius is remembered, can the
critic, whoever he may be, that so unintentionally ministered to its firs
start, be forgotten.

It is but justice, however, to remark,—without at the same time
intending any excuse for the contemptuous tone of criticism assumed by
the reviewer,—that the early verses of Lord Byron, however distinguished
by tenderness and grace, give but little promise of those dazzling miracle
of poesy, with which he afterwards astonished and enchanted the world
and that, if his youthful verses now have a peculiar charm in our eyes
it is because we read them, as it were, by the light of his subsequent
glory.

There is, indeed, one point of view, in which these productions are
deeply and intrinsically interesting. As faithful reflections of his character
at that period of life, they enable us to judge of what he was in his yet

unadulterated state,—before disappointment had begun to embitter his ardent spirit, or the stirring up of the energies of his nature had brought into activity also its defects. Tracing him thus through these natural effusions of his young genius, we find him pictured exactly such, in all the features of his character, as every anecdote of his boyish days proves him really to have been,—proud, daring, and passionate,—resentful of slight or injustice, but still more so in the cause of others than in his own; and yet, with all this vehemence, docile and placable, at the least touch of a hand authorized by love to guide him. The affectionateness, indeed, of his disposition, traceable as it is through every page of this volume, is yet but faintly done justice to, even by himself;—his whole youth being, from earliest childhood, a series of the most passionate attachments,—of those overflowings of the soul, both in friendship and love, which are still more rarely responded to than felt, and which, when checked or sent back upon the heart, are sure to turn into bitterness.

We have seen also, in some of his early unpublished poems, how apparent, even through the doubts that already clouded them, are those feelings of piety which a soul like his could not but possess, and which, when afterwards diverted out of their legitimate channel, found a vent in the poetical worship of nature, and in that shadowy substitute for religion which superstition offers. When, in addition, too, to these traits of early character, we find scattered through his youthful poems such anticipations of the glory that awaited him—such, alternately, proud and saddened glimpses into the future, as if he already felt the elements of something great within him, but doubted whether his destiny would allow him to bring it forth,—it is not wonderful that, with the whole of his career present to our imaginations, we should see a lustre round these first puerile attempts, not really their own, but shed back upon them from the bright eminence which he afterwards attained; and that, in our indignation against the fastidious blindness of the critic, we should forget that he had not then the aid of this reflected charm, with which the subsequent achievements of the poet now irradiate all that bears his name.

The effect this criticism produced upon him can only be conceived by those, who, besides having an adequate notion of what most

poets would feel under such an attack, can understand all that there w
in the temper and disposition of Lord Byron to make him feel it wi
tenfold more acuteness than others.   We have seen with what feveri
anxiety he awaited the verdicts of all the minor Reviews, and, from h
sensibility to the praise of the meanest of these censors, may guess ho
painfully he must have writhed under the sneers of the highest.   .
friend, who found him in the first moments of excitement after readin
the article, inquired anxiously, whether he had just received a challeng
—not knowing how else to account for the fierce defiance of his look
It would, indeed, be difficult for sculptor or painter to imagine a subje
of more fearful beauty, than the fine countenance of the young po
must have exhibited in the collected energy of that crisis. His pride ha
been wounded to the quick, and his ambition humbled:—but this feelin
of humiliation lasted but for a moment.   The very reaction of his spiri
against aggression roused him to a full consciousness of his own powers*
and the pain and the shame of the injury were forgotten in the prou
certainty of revenge.

Among the less sentimental effects of this Review upon his mind
he used to mention that, on the day he read it, he drank three bottles o
claret, to his own share, after dinner;—that nothing, however, relieve
him, till he had given vent to his indignation in rhyme, and that " afte
the first twenty lines, he felt himself considerably better."   His chie
care, indeed, afterwards, was amiably devoted,—as we have seen it was
in like manner, *before* the criticism,—to allaying, as far as he could, th
sensitiveness of his mother; who, not having the same motive or powe
to summon up a spirit of resistance, was, of course, more helplessly aliv
to this attack upon his fame, and felt it far more than, after the firs
burst of indignation, he did himself.   But the state of his mind upor
the subject will be best understood from the following letter.

---

* " 'Tis a quality very observable in human nature, that any opposition which does no
entirely discourage and intimidate us has rather a contrary effect, and inspires us with a mor
than ordinary grandeur and magnanimity.   In collecting our force to overcome the opposition
we invigorate the soul, and give it an elevation with which otherwise it would never have bee
acquainted."—HUME, *Treatise of Human Nature.*

LETTER XXV.

TO MR. BECHER.

" Dorant's, March 28th, 1808.

" I have lately received a copy of the new edition from Ridge, and it is high time for me to return my best thanks to you for the trouble you have taken in the superintendence. This I do most sincerely, and only regret that Ridge has not seconded you as I could wish,—at least, in the bindings, paper, &c. of the copy he sent to me. Perhaps those for the public may be more respectable in such articles.

" You have seen the Edinburgh Review, of course. I regret that Mrs. Byron is so much annoyed. For my own part, these ' paper bullets of the brain' have only taught me to stand fire; and, as I have been lucky enough upon the whole, my repose and appetite are not discomposed. Pratt, the gleaner, author, poet, &c. &c. addressed a long rhyming epistle to me on the subject, by way of consolation; but it was not well done, so I do not send it, though the name of the man might make it go down. The E. R's. have not performed their task well;—at least, the literati tell me this, and I think *I* could write a more sarcastic critique on *myself* than any yet published. For instance, instead of the remark,—ill-natured enough, but not keen,—about Macpherson, I (quoad reviewers) could have said, ' Alas, this imitation only proves the assertion of Doctor Johnson, that many men, women, and *children*, could write such poetry as Ossian's.'

" I am *thin* and in exercise. During the spring or summer I trust we shall meet. I hear Lord Ruthyn leaves Newstead in April. * * * As soon as he quits it for ever, I wish much you would take a ride over, survey the mansion, and give me your candid opinion on the most advisable mode of proceeding with regard to the *house*. *Entre nous*, I am cursedly dipped; my debts, *every* thing inclusive, will be nine or ten thousand before I am twenty-one. But I have reason to think my property will turn out better than general expectation may conceive. Of Newstead I have little hope or care; but Hanson, my agent, intimated

my Lancashire property was worth three Newsteads. I believe w
have it hollow; though the defendants are protracting the surrender,
possible, till after my majority, for the purpose of forming some arrang
ment with me, thinking I shall probably prefer a sum in hand to
reversion. Newstead I may *sell*;—perhaps I will not,—though of th
more anon. I will come down in May or June. * * * *

"Yours most truly, &c."

The sort of life which he led at this period, between the dissipation
of London and of Cambridge, without a home to welcome, or even th
roof of a single relative to receive him, was but little calculated to rende
him satisfied either with himself or the world. Unrestricted as he wa
by deference to any will but his own*, even the pleasures to which h
was naturally most inclined prematurely palled upon him, for want o
those best zests of all enjoyment, rarity and restraint. I have alread
quoted, from one of his note-books, a passage descriptive of his feeling
on first going to Cambridge, in which he says that "one of the deadlies
and heaviest feelings of his life was to feel that he was no longer a boy.
—" From that moment (he adds) I began to grow old in my own esteem
and in my esteem age is not estimable. I took my gradations in th
vices with great promptitude, but they were not to my taste; for m
early passions, though violent in the extreme, were concentrated, an
hated division or spreading abroad. I could have left or lost the whol
world with, or for, that which I loved; but, though my temperamen
was naturally burning, I could not share in the common-place libertinism
of the place and time without disgust. And yet this very disgust, an
my heart thrown back upon itself, threw me into excesses perhaps mor
fatal than those from which I shrunk, as fixing upon one (at a time) th
passions which spread amongst many would have hurt only myself."

Though, from the causes here alleged, the irregularities he, at thi
period, gave way to, were of a nature far less gross and miscellaneou
than those, perhaps, of any of his associates, yet, partly from the vehe-

---

* " The colour of our whole life is generally such as the three or four first years in which
we are our own masters make it."—Cowper.

nence which this concentration caused, and, still more, from that strange pride in his own errors, which led him always to bring them forth in he most conspicuous light, it so happened that one single indiscretion, n his hands, was made to go *farther*, if I may so express it, than a thousand in those of others. An instance of this, that occurred about the time of which we are speaking, was, I am inclined to think, the sole foundation of the mysterious allusions just cited. An amour (if it may be dignified with such a name) of that sort of casual description which less attachable natures would have forgotten, and more prudent ones at least concealed, was by him converted, at this period, and with circumstances of most unnecessary display, into a connexion of some continuance,—the object of it not only becoming domesticated with him in lodgings at Brompton, but accompanying him afterwards, disguised in boy's clothes, to Brighton. He introduced this young person, who used to ride about with him in her male attire, as his younger brother; and the late Lady P**, who was at Brighton at the time, and had some suspicion of the real nature of the relationship, said one day to the poet's companion, " What a pretty horse that is you are riding!"— " Yes," answered the pretended cavalier, " it was *gave* me by my brother!"

Beattie tells us, of his ideal poet,—

> " The exploits of strength, dexterity, or speed,
>   To him nor vanity nor joy could bring."

But far different were the tastes of the real poet, Byron;—and, among the least romantic, perhaps, of the exercises in which he took delight was that of boxing, or sparring. This taste it was that, at a very early period, brought him acquainted with the distinguished professor of that art, Mr. Jackson, for whom he continued through life to entertain the sincerest regard,—one of his latest works containing a most cordial tribute not only to the professional, but social qualities of this sole prop and ornament of pugilism*. During his stay at Brighton this year,

* " I refer to my old friend and corporeal pastor and master, John Jackson, Esq. Professor of Pugilism, who I trust still retains the strength and symmetry of his model of a form, together with his good-humour and athletic, as well as mental, accomplishments."—*Note on Don Juan, Canto II.*

Jackson was one of his most constant visitors,—the expense of t
professor's chaise thither and back being always defrayed by his nol
patron. He also honoured with his notice, at this time, D'Egville, t
ballet-master, and Grimaldi, to the latter of whom he sent, as I understar
on one of his benefit-nights, a present of five guineas.

Having been favoured by Mr. Jackson with copies of the few not
and letters, which he has preserved out of the many addressed to him l
Lord Byron, I shall here lay before the reader one or two, which be
the date of the present year, and which, though referring to matters.
no interest in themselves, give, perhaps, a better notion of the actual li
and habits of the young poet, at this time, than could be afforded by tl
most elaborate and, in other respects, important correspondence. The
will show, at least, how very little akin to romance were the early pu
suits and associates of the author of Childe Harold, and, combined wit
what we know of the still less romantic youth of Shakspeare, prove ho
unhurt the vital principle of genius can preserve itself even in atmospher(
apparently the most ungenial and noxious to it.

LETTER XXVI.

TO MR. JACKSON.

"N. A. Notts.   September 18, 1808.

" DEAR JACK,

" I wish you would inform me what has been done by Jekyll, a
No. 40, Sloane-square, concerning the pony I returned as unsound.

" I have also to request you will call on Louch at Brompton, an
inquire what the devil he meant by sending such an insolent letter to m
at Brighton; and at the same time tell him I by no means can compl
with the charge he has made for things pretended to be damaged.

" Ambrose behaved most scandalously about the pony. You ma
tell Jekyll if he does not refund the money, I shall put the affair int
my lawyer's hands. Five and twenty guineas is a sound price for a pony
and by ——, if it costs me five hundred pounds, I will make an exampl(
of Mr. Jekyll, and that immediately, unless the cash is returned.

" Believe me, dear Jack, &c."

LETTER XXVII.

TO MR. JACKSON.

"N. A. Notts. October 4, 1808.

"You will make as good a bargain as possible with this Master Jekyll, if he is not a gentleman. If he is a *gentleman*, inform me, for I shall take very different steps. If he is not, you must get what you can of the money, for I have too much business on hand at present to commence an action. Besides, Ambrose is the man who ought to refund,— but I have done with him. You can settle with L. out of the balance, and dispose of the bidets, &c. as you best can.

"I should be very glad to see you here; but the house is filled with workmen and undergoing a thorough repair. I hope, however, to be more fortunate before many months have elapsed.

"If you see Bold Webster, remember me to him, and tell him I have to regret Sydney, who has perished, I fear, in my rabbit warren, for we have seen nothing of him for the last fortnight.

"Adieu.—Believe me, &c."

LETTER XXVIII.

TO MR. JACKSON.

"N. A. Notts. December 12, 1808.

"MY DEAR JACK,

"You will get the greyhound from the owner at any price, and as many more of the same breed (male or female) as you can collect.

"Tell D'Egville his dress shall be returned—I am obliged to him for the pattern. I am sorry you should have so much trouble, but I was not aware of the difficulty of procuring the animals in question. I shall have finished part of my mansion in a few weeks, and, if you can pay me a visit at Christmas, I shall be very glad to see you.

"Believe me, &c."

The dress alluded to here was, no doubt, wanted for a private play,

which he, at this time, got up at Newstead, and of which there are som
further particulars in the annexed letter to Mr. Becher.

LETTER XXIX.

TO MR. BECHER.

"Newstead Abbey, Notts, Sept. 14th, 1808.

"MY DEAR BECHER,

"I am much obliged to you for your inquiries, and shall profit by
them accordingly. I am going to get up a play here: the hall will con
stitute a most admirable theatre. I have settled the dram. pers., and can
do without ladies, as I have some young friends who will make tolerabl
substitutes for females, and we only want three male characters, besid
Mr. Hobhouse and myself, for the play we have fixed on, which will b
the Revenge. Pray direct Nicholson the carpenter to come over to me
immediately, and inform me what day you will dine and pass the nigh
here. "Believe me, &c."

It was in the autumn of this year, as the letters I have just giver
indicate, that he, for the first time, took up his residence at Newstead
Abbey. Having received the place in a most ruinous condition from
the hands of its last occupant, Lord Grey de Ruthyn, he proceeded
immediately to repair and fit up some of the apartments, so as to render
them—more with a view to his mother's accommodation than his own—
comfortably habitable. In one of his letters to Mrs. Byron, published
by Mr. Dallas, he thus explains his views and intentions on this subject.

LETTER XXX.

TO THE HONOURABLE* MRS. BYRON.

"Newstead Abbey, Notts, October 7th, 1808.

"DEAR MADAM,

"I have no beds for the H**s, or any body else at present. The
H**s sleep at Mansfield. I do not know that I resemble Jean Jacques

* Thus addressed always by Lord Byron, but without any right to the distinction.

Rousseau. I have no ambition to be like so illustrious a madman—but this I know, that I shall live in my own manner, and as much alone as possible. When my rooms are ready I shall be glad to see you; at present it would be improper, and uncomfortable to both parties. You can hardly object to my rendering my mansion habitable, notwithstanding my departure for Persia in March (or May at farthest), since *you* will be *tenant* till my return; and in case of any accident (for I have already arranged my will to be drawn up the moment I am twenty-one), I have taken care you shall have the house and manor for *life*, besides a sufficient income. So you see my improvements are not entirely selfish. As I have a friend here, we will go to the Infirmary Ball on the 12th; we will drink tea with Mrs. Byron at eight o'clock, and expect to see you at the ball. If that lady will allow us a couple of rooms to dress in, we shall be highly obliged:—if we are at the ball by ten or eleven it will be time enough, and we shall return to Newstead about three or four.

" Adieu. Believe me,

" Yours very truly,

" BYRON."

The idea, entertained by Mrs. Byron, of a resemblance between her son and Rousseau was founded chiefly, we may suppose, on those habits of solitariness, in which he had even already shown a disposition to follow that self-contemplative philosopher, and which, manifesting themselves thus early, gained strength as he advanced in life. In one of his Journals, to which I frequently have occasion to refer[*], he thus, in questioning the justice of this comparison between himself and Rousseau, gives,—as usual, vividly,—some touches of his own disposition and habitudes:—

" My mother, before I was twenty, would have it that I was like Rousseau, and Madame de Staël used to say so too in 1813, and the Edinburgh Review has something of the sort in its critique on the fourth Canto of Childe Harold. I can't see any point of resemblance:—

---

* The Journal, entitled by himself, " Detached Thoughts."

he wrote prose; I verse: he was of the people; I of the aristocracy
he was a philosopher; I am none: he published his first work at forty
I mine at eighteen: his first essay brought him universal applause
mine the contrary: he married his housekeeper; I could not keep house
with my wife: he thought all the world in a plot against him; my little
world seems to think me in a plot against it, if I may judge by their abuse
in print and coterie: he liked botany; I like flowers, herbs, and trees
but know nothing of their pedigrees: he wrote music; I limit my
knowledge of it to what I catch by *ear*—I never could learn any thing
by *study*, not even a *language*—it was all by rote, and ear, and memory
he had a *bad* memory; I *had*, at least, an excellent one (ask Hodgson
the poet—a good judge, for he has an astonishing one): he wrote with
hesitation and care; I with rapidity, and rarely with pains: *he* could
never ride, nor swim, nor 'was cunning of fence;' *I* am an excellent
swimmer, a decent, though not at all a dashing rider (having staved in
a rib at eighteen in the course of scampering), and was sufficient of
fence, particularly of the Highland broadsword,—not a bad boxer, when
I could keep my temper, which was difficult, but which I strove to do
ever since I knocked down Mr. Purling, and put his knee-pan out (with
the gloves on), in Angelo's and Jackson's rooms, in 1806, during the
sparring,—and I was besides a very fair cricketer—one of the Harrow
eleven, when we played against Eton in 1805.   Besides, Rousseau's way
of life, his country, his manners, his whole character, were so very
different, that I am at a loss to conceive how such a comparison could
have arisen, as it has done three several times, and all in rather a
remarkable manner.   I forgot to say that *he* was also short-sighted, and
that hitherto my eyes have been the contrary, to such a degree that in
the largest theatre of Bologna I distinguished and read some busts and
inscriptions painted near the stage from a box so distant and so *darkly*
lighted, that none of the company (composed of young and very bright-
eyed people, some of them in the same box) could make out a letter,

---

* Few philosophers, however, have been so indulgent to the pride of birth as Rousseau
—" S'il est un orgueil pardonnable (he says) après celui qui se tire du mérite personnel, c'est
celui qui se tire de la naissance."—*Confess.*

nd thought it was a trick, though I had never been in that theatre before.

" Altogether, I think myself justified in thinking the comparison not well founded. I don't say this out of pique, for Rousseau was a great man, and the thing, if true, were flattering enough;—but I have no idea of being pleased with the chimera."

In another letter to his mother, dated some weeks after the preceding one, he explains further his plans both with respect to Newstead and his projected travels:—

LETTER XXXI.

TO MRS. BYRON.

" Newstead Abbey, November 2d, 1808.

" DEAR MOTHER,

" If you please, we will forget the things you mention. I have no desire to remember them. When my rooms are finished, I shall be happy to see you; as I tell but the truth, you will not suspect me of evasion. I am furnishing the house more for you than myself, and I shall establish you in it before I sail for India, which I expect to do in March, if nothing particularly obstructive occurs. I am now fitting up the *green* drawing-room; the red for a bed-room, and the rooms over as sleeping-rooms. They will be soon completed;—at least, I hope so.

" I wish you would inquire of Major Watson (who is an old Indian) what things will be necessary to provide for my voyage. I have already procured a friend to write to the Arabic Professor at Cambridge for some information I am anxious to procure. I can easily get letters from government to the ambassadors, consuls, &c., and also to the governors at Calcutta and Madras. I shall place my property and my will in the hands of trustees till my return, and I mean to appoint you one. From H ** I have heard nothing—when I do, you shall have the particulars.

" After all, you must own my project is not a bad one. If I do not travel now, I never shall, and all men should one day or other. I have at present no connexions to keep me at home; no wife, or unprovided sisters, brothers, &c. I shall take care of you, and when I return I may

possibly become a politician.   A few years' knowledge of other countri
than our own will not incapacitate me for that part.   If we see no natio
but our own, we do not give mankind a fair chance—it is from *experienc*
not books, we ought to judge of them.   There is nothing like inspectio
and trusting to our own senses.   Yours, &c."

In the November of this year he lost his favourite dog, Boatswai
—the poor animal having been seized with a fit of madness, at th
commencement of which so little aware was Lord Byron of the natur
of the malady, that he, more than once, with his bare hand, wiped awa
the slaver from the dog's lips during the paroxysms.   In a letter to hi
friend, Mr. Hodgson *, he thus announces this event: "Boatswain i
dead!—he expired in a state of madness on the 18th, after sufferin
much, yet retaining all the gentleness of his nature to the last, neve
attempting to do the least injury to any one near him.   I have now los
every thing except old Murray."

The monument raised by him to this dog,—the most memorabl
tribute of the kind, since the Dog's Grave, of old, at Salamis,—is still
conspicuous ornament of the gardens of Newstead.   The misanthropi
verses engraved upon it may be found among his poems, and th
following is the inscription by which they are introduced:—

> " Near this spot
> Are deposited the Remains of one
> Who possessed Beauty without Vanity,
> Strength without Insolence,
> Courage without Ferocity,
> And all the Virtues of Man without his Vices.
> This Praise, which would be unmeaning Flattery
> If inscribed over human ashes,
> Is but a just tribute to the Memory of
> BOATSWAIN, a Dog,
> Who was born at Newfoundland, May, 1803,
> And died at Newstead Abbey, Nov. 18, 1808."

---

* The Reverend Francis Hodgson, author of a spirited translation of Juvenal, and c
other works of distinguished merit.   To this gentleman, who was long in correspondence wit

The poet, Pope, when about the same age as the writer of this inscription, passed a similar eulogy on his dog* at the expense of human nature, adding, that " Histories are more full of examples of the fidelity of dogs than of friends." In a still sadder and bitterer spirit, Lord Byron writes of his favourite,

> " To mark a friend's remains these stones arise;
> I never knew but *one*, and *here* he lies †."

Melancholy, indeed, seems to have been gaining fast upon his mind at this period. In another letter to Mr. Hodgson he says,—" You know laughing is the sign of a rational animal—so says Dr. Smollet. I think so too, but unluckily my spirits don't always keep pace with my opinions."

Old Murray, the servant, whom he mentions in a preceding extract, as the only faithful follower now remaining to him, had long been in the service of the former lord, and was regarded by the young poet with a fondness of affection which it has seldom been the lot of age and

---

Lord Byron, I am indebted for some interesting letters of his noble friend, which shall be given in the course of the following pages.

* He had also, at one time, as appears from an anecdote preserved by Spence, some thoughts of burying this dog in his garden, and placing a monument over him, with the inscription, " Oh rare Bounce !"

In speaking of the members of Rousseau's domestic establishment, Hume says, " She (Thérése) governs him as absolutely as a nurse does a child. In her absence, his dog has acquired that ascendant. His affection for that creature is beyond all expression or conception." —*Private Correspondence.* See an instance which he gives of this dog's influence over the philosopher, p. 143.

In Burns's elegy on the death of his favourite Mailie, we find the friendship even of a sheep set on a level with that of man :—

> " Wi' kindly bleat, when she did spy him,
> She ran wi' speed :
> A friend mair faithful ne'er came nigh him,
> Than Mailie dead."

In speaking of the favourite dogs of great poets, we must not forget Cowper's little spaniel ' Beau ;" nor will posterity fail to add to the list the name of Sir Walter Scott's " Maida."

† In the epitaph, as first printed in his friend's Miscellany, this line runs thus :—

> " I knew but one unchanged—and here he lies."

dependence to inspire. " I have more than once," says a gentleman wh was, at this time, a constant visitor at Newstead, " seen Lord Byron the dinner-table fill out a tumbler of madeira, and hand it over h shoulder to Joe Murray, who stood behind his chair, saying, with cordiality that brightened his whole countenance, 'Here, my old fellow.'

The unconcern with which he could sometimes allude to the defec in his foot is manifest from another passage in one of these letters t Mr. Hodgson. That gentleman having said jestingly that some of th verses in the " Hours of Idleness" were calculated to make schoolboy rebellious, Lord Byron answers—" If my songs have produced th glorious effects you mention, I shall be a complete Tyrtæus;—though am sorry to say I resemble that interesting harper more in his persor than in his poesy." Sometimes, too, even an allusion to this infirmity by others, when he could perceive that it was not offensively intended was borne by him with the most perfect good-humour. " I was onc present," says the friend I have just mentioned, " in a large and mixed company, when a vulgar person asked him aloud—' Pray, my lord, how is that foot of yours?'—' Thank you, sir,' answered Lord Byron, with the utmost mildness—' much the same as usual.' "

The following extract, relating to a reverend friend of his lordship is from another of his letters to Mr. Hodgson, this year:—

" A few weeks ago I wrote to * * *, to request he would receive the son of a citizen of London, well known to me, as a pupil; the family having been particularly polite during the short time I was with them induced me to this application. Now, mark what follows,—as somebody sublimely saith. On this day arrives an epistle signed * * *, containing, not the smallest reference to tuition, or intuition, but a petition for Robert Gregson, of pugilistic notoriety, now in bondage for certain paltry pounds sterling, and liable to take up his everlasting abode in Banco Regis. Had the letter been from any of my lay acquaintance, or, in short, from any person but the gentleman whose signature it bears, I should have marvelled not. If * * * is serious, I congratulate pugilism on the acquisition of such a patron, and shall be most happy to advance any sum necessary for the liberation of the captive Gregson. But I certainly hope to be certified from you, or some respectable housekeeper of the fact, before I write to * * * on the subject. When I say the *fact*, I mean of the letter being written by * * *, not having any doubt as to the authenticity of the statement. The letter is now before me, and I keep it for your perusal."

His time at Newstead during this autumn was principally occupied in enlarging and preparing his Satire for the press; and with the view, perhaps, of mellowing his own judgment of its merits, by keeping it some time before his eyes in a printed form*, he had proofs taken off from the manuscript by his former publisher at Newark. It is somewhat remarkable, that, excited as he was by the attack of the Reviewers, and possessing, at all times, such rapid powers of composition, he should have allowed so long an interval to elapse between the aggression and the revenge. But the importance of his next move in literature seems to have been fully appreciated by him. He saw that his chances of future eminence now depended upon the effort he was about to make, and therefore deliberately collected all his energies for the spring. Among the preparatives by which he disciplined his talent to the task was a deep study of the writings of Pope; and I have no doubt that from this period may be dated the enthusiastic admiration which he ever after cherished for this great poet,—an admiration which at last extinguished in him, after one or two trials, all hope of pre-eminence in the same track, and drove him thenceforth to seek renown in fields more open to competition.

The misanthropic mood of mind into which he had fallen at this time, from disappointed affections and thwarted hopes, made the office of satirist but too congenial and welcome to his spirit. Yet it is evident that this bitterness existed far more in his fancy than his heart; and that the sort of relief he now found in making war upon the world arose much less from the indiscriminate wounds he dealt around, than from the new sense of power he became conscious of in dealing them, and by which he more than recovered his former station in his own esteem.

* We are told that Wieland used to have his works printed thus for the purpose of correction, and said that he found great advantage in it. The practice is, it appears, not unusual in Germany.

In truth, the versatility and ease with which, as shall presently be shown he could, on the briefest consideration, shift from praise to censure, and sometimes, almost as rapidly, from censure to praise, shows how fanciful and transient were the impressions under which he, in many instances pronounced his judgments; and, though it may in some degree deduct from the weight of his eulogy, absolves him also from any great depth of malice in his satire.

His coming of age in 1809 was celebrated at Newstead by such festivities as his narrow means and society could furnish. Besides the ritual roasting of an ox, there was a ball, it seems, given on the occasion —of which the only particular I could collect, from the old domestic who mentioned it, was that Mr. Hanson, the agent of her lord, was among the dancers. Of Lord Byron's own method of commemorating the day, I find the following curious record in a letter written from Genoa in 1822 :—" Did I ever tell you that the day I came of age I dined on eggs and bacon and a bottle of ale ?—For once in a way they are my favourite dish and drinkable; but, as neither of them agree with me, I never use them but on great jubilees,—once in four or five years or so." The pecuniary supplies necessary towards his outset, at this epoch, were procured from money-lenders at an enormously usurious interest, the payment of which for a long time continued to be a burden to him.

It was not till the beginning of this year that he took his Satire,— in a state ready, as he thought, for publication,—to London. Before, however, he had put the work to press, new food was unluckily furnished to his spleen by the neglect with which he conceived himself to have been treated by his guardian, Lord Carlisle. The relations between this nobleman and his ward had, at no time, been of such a nature as to afford opportunities for the cultivation of much friendliness on either side; and to the temper and influence of Mrs. Byron must mainly be attributed the blame of widening, if not of producing, this estrangement between them. The coldness with which Lord Carlisle had received the dedication of the young poet's first volume was, as we have seen from one of the letters of the latter, felt by him most deeply. He, however, allowed himself to be so far governed by prudential considerations as not only to stifle this displeasure, but even to introduce into his Satire, as originally intended for the press, the following compliment to his guardian :—

> " On one alone Apollo deigns to smile,
>   And crowns a new Roscommon in Carlisle."

The crown, however, thus generously awarded, did not long remain where it had been placed. In the interval between the inditing of this couplet and the delivery of the manuscript to the press, Lord Byron, with the natural hope that his guardian would, of himself, make an offer to introduce him to the House of Lords on his first taking his seat, wrote to remind his lordship that he should be of age at the commencement of the session. Instead, however, of the courtesy which he had thus, not unreasonably, counted upon, a mere formal reply, acquainting him with the technical mode of proceeding on such occasions, was all that, it appears, in return to this application, he received. It is not wonderful therefore that, disposed as he had been, by preceding circumstances, to suspect his noble guardian of no very friendly inclinations towards him, such backwardness, at a moment when the countenance of so near a connexion might have been of service to him, should have roused in his sensitive mind a strong feeling of resentment. The indignation, thus excited, found a vent, but too temptingly, at hand ;—the laudatory couplet I have just cited was instantly expunged, and his Satire went forth charged with those vituperative verses against Lord Carlisle, of which, gratifying as they must have been to his revenge at the moment, he, not long after, with the placability so inherent in his generous nature, repented*.

During the progress of his Poem through the press, he increased its length by more than a hundred lines ; and made several alterations, one or two of which may be mentioned, as illustrative of that prompt

---

* See his lines on Major Howard, the son of Lord Carlisle, who was killed at Waterloo :—
> " Their praise is hymn'd by loftier harps than mine ;
>   Yet one I would select from that proud throng,
>   Partly because they blend me with his line,
>   And *partly that I did his sire some wrong*."
>   CHILDE HAROLD, CANTO III.

susceptibility of new impressions and influences which rendered both hi
judgment and feelings so variable. In the Satire, as it originally stoo
was the following couplet:—

> " Though printers condescend the press to soil
>   With odes by Smythe and epic songs by Hoyle."

Of the injustice of these lines (unjust, it is but fair to say, to both th
writers mentioned) he, on the brink of publication, repented; and,—a
far, at least, as regarded one of the intended victims,—adopted a ton
directly opposite in his printed Satire, where the name of Professor
Smythe is mentioned honourably, as it deserved, in conjunction with
that of Mr. Hodgson, one of the poet's most valued friends:—

> " Oh dark asylum of a vandal race !
>   At once the boast of learning and disgrace;
>   So sunk in dulness and so lost in shame,
>   That Smythe and Hodgson scarce redeem thy fame."

In another instance we find him " changing his hand" with equal
facility and suddenness. The original manuscript of the Satire contained
this line,—

> " I leave topography to coxcomb Gell;"

but having, while the work was printing, become acquainted with Sir
William Gell, he, without difficulty, by the change of a single epithet,
converted satire into eulogy, and the line now descends to posterity
thus:—

> " I leave topography to *classic* Gell*."

---

* In the fifth edition of the Satire (suppressed by him in 1812), he again changed his
mind respecting this gentleman, and altered the line to

> " I leave topography to *rapid* Gell,"

explaining his reasons for the change in the following note:—"' Rapid,' indeed;—he topogra-
phized and typographized King Priam's dominions in three days. I called him ' classic' before
I saw the Troad, but, since, have learned better than to tack to his name what don't belong
to it."

He is not, however, the only satirist who has been thus capricious and changeable in his

Among the passages added to the Poem during its progress through
the press were those lines, denouncing the licentiousness of the Opera,
" Then let Ausonia, &c." which the young satirist wrote one night, after
returning, brimful of morality, from the Opera, and sent them early next
morning to Mr. Dallas for insertion.   The just and animated tribute to
Mr. Crabbe was also among the after-thoughts with which his Poem was
adorned; nor can we doubt that both this, and the equally merited eulogy
on Mr. Rogers, were the disinterested and deliberate result of the young
poet's judgment, as he had never at that period seen either of these
distinguished persons, and the opinion he then expressed of their genius
remained unchanged through life.   With the author of the Pleasures of
Memory he afterwards became intimate, but with him, whom he has so
well designated as " Nature's sternest painter, yet the best," he was never
lucky enough to form any acquaintance;—though, as my venerated friend
and neighbour, Mr. Crabbe himself, tells me, they were once, without
being aware of it, in the same inn together for a day or two, and must
have frequently met, as they went in and out of the house, during the
time.

Almost every second day, while the Satire was printing, Mr. Dallas,
who had undertaken to superintend it through the press, received fresh
matter, for the enrichment of its pages, from the author, whose mind,
once excited on any subject, knew no end to the outpourings of its
wealth.   In one of his short notes to Mr. Dallas, he says, " Print soon,
or I shall overflow with rhyme;" and it was, in the same manner, in all
his subsequent publications,—as long, at least, as he remained within
reach of the printer,—that he continued thus to feed the press, to the
very last moment, with new and " thick-coming fancies," which the
re-perusal of what he had already written suggested to him.   It would
almost seem, indeed, from the extreme facility and rapidity with which
he produced some of his brightest passages during the progress of his
works through the press, that there was in the very act of printing an

judgments.   The variations of this nature in Pope's Dunciad are well known; and the Abbé
Cotin, it is said, owed the " painful pre-eminence" of his station in Boileau's Satires to the
unlucky convenience of his name as a rhyme.   Of the generous change from censure to praise,
the poet Dante had already set an example, having, in his " Convito," lauded some of those
persons whom in his Commedia he had most severely lashed.

excitement to his fancy, and that the rush of his thoughts towards th
outlet gave increased life and freshness to their flow.

Among the passing events from which he now caught illustratio
for his Poem was the melancholy death of Lord Falkland,—a gallar
but dissipated naval officer, with whom the habits of his town life h
brought him acquainted, and who, about the beginning of March, w
killed in a duel by Mr. Powell.   That this event affected Lord Byr
very deeply, the few touching sentences devoted to it in his Satire prov
" On Sunday night (he says) I beheld Lord Falkland presiding at h
own table in all the honest pride of hospitality; on Wednesday mornin
at three o'clock I saw stretched before me all that remained of courag
feeling, and a host of passions."   But it was not by words only that h
gave proof of sympathy on this occasion.   The family of the unfortunat
nobleman were left behind in circumstances, which needed somethin
more than the mere expression of compassion to alleviate them; an
Lord Byron, notwithstanding the pressure of his own difficulties at th
time, found means, seasonably and delicately, to assist the widow an
children of his friend.   In the following letter to Mrs. Byron, he men
tions this, among other matters of interest,—and in a tone of unosten
tatious sensibility, highly honourable to him :—

LETTER XXXII.

TO MRS. BYRON.

" 8, St. James's-street, March 6th, 1809.

" DEAR MOTHER,

" My last letter was written under great depression of spirits from
poor Falkland's death, who has left without a shilling four children an
his wife.   I have been endeavouring to assist them, which, God know
I cannot do as I could wish, from my own embarrassments and the man
claims upon me from other quarters.

" What you say is all very true: come what may, *Newstead* an
I *stand* or fall together.   I have now lived on the spot, I have fixe
my heart upon it, and no pressure, present or future, shall induce me t
barter the last vestige of our inheritance.   I have that pride within m

which will enable me to support difficulties. I can endure privations; but could I obtain in exchange for Newstead Abbey the first fortune in the country, I would reject the proposition. Set your mind at ease on that score; Mr. H** talks like a man of business on the subject, I feel like a man of honour, and I will not sell Newstead.

" I shall get my seat on the return of the affidavits from Carhais, in Cornwall, and will do something in the House soon: I must dash, or it is all over. My Satire must be kept secret for a month; after that you may say what you please on the subject. Lord C. has used me infamously, and refused to state any particulars of my family to the Chancellor. I have *lashed* him in my rhymes, and perhaps his lordship may regret not being more conciliatory. They tell me it will have a sale; I hope so, for the bookseller has behaved well, as far as publishing well goes.

" Believe me, &c.

" P. S. You shall have a mortgage on one of the farms."

The affidavits which he here mentions, as expected from Cornwall, were those required in proof of the marriage of Admiral Byron with Miss Trevanion, the solemnization of which having taken place, as it appears, in a private chapel at Carhais, no regular certificate of the ceremony could be produced. The delay in procuring other evidence, coupled with the rather ungracious refusal of Lord Carlisle to afford any explanations respecting his family, interposed those difficulties which he alludes to in the way of his taking his seat. At length, all the necessary proofs having been obtained, he, on the 13th of March, presented himself in the House of Lords, in a state more lone and unfriended, perhaps, than any youth of his high station had ever before been reduced to on such an occasion,— not having a single individual of his own class either to introduce him as friend or receive him as acquaintance. To chance alone was he even indebted for being accompanied as far as the bar of the House by a very distant relative, who had been, little more than a year before, an utter stranger to him. This relative was Mr. Dallas, and the account which he has given of the whole scene is too striking, in all its details, to be related in any other words than his own :—

" The Satire was published about the middle of March, previous to

Y 2

which he took his seat in the House of Lords, on the 13th of the sam month. On that day, passing down St. James's-street, but with a intention of calling, I saw his chariot at his door, and went in. H countenance, paler than usual, showed that his mind was agitated, an that he was thinking of the nobleman to whom he had once looked f a hand and countenance in his introduction to the House. He said me—'1 am glad you happened to come in; I am going to take my sea perhaps you will go with me.' I expressed my readiness to attend him while, at the same time, I concealed the shock I felt on thinking tha this young man, who, by birth, fortune, and talent, stood high in lif should have lived so unconnected and neglected by persons of his ow rank, that there was not a single member of the senate to which h belonged, to whom he could or would apply to introduce him in a manne becoming his birth. I saw that he felt the situation, and I fully partoo his indignation. * * *

" After some talk about the Satire, the last sheets of which were i the press, I accompanied Lord Byron to the House. He was received i one of the antechambers by some of the officers in attendance, with whom he settled respecting the fees he had to pay. One of them went t apprize the Lord Chancellor of his being there, and soon returned fo him. There were very few persons in the House. Lord Eldon wa going through some ordinary business. When Lord Byron entered, thought he looked still paler than before; and he certainly wore countenance in which mortification was mingled with, but subduec by, indignation. He passed the woolsack without looking round, an advanced to the table where the proper officer was attending to administe the oaths. When he had gone through them, the Chancellor quitted hi seat, and went towards him with a smile, putting out his hand warml to welcome him; and, though I did not catch his words, I saw that h paid him some compliment. This was all thrown away upon Lord Byron who made a stiff bow, and put the tips of his fingers into the Chancellor' hand. * * * * The Chancellor did not press a welcome so received but resumed his seat; while Lord Byron carelessly seated himself for few minutes on one of the empty benches to the left of the throne, usuall occupied by the lords in opposition. When, on his joining me, I expresse what I had felt, he said: 'If I had shaken hands heartily, he would have set me down for one of his party—but I will have nothing to do with any of them, on either side; I have taken my seat, and now I will go abroad.' We returned to St. James's-street, but he did not recover his spirits."

To this account of a ceremonial so trying to the proud spirit engaged in it, and so little likely to abate the bitter feeling of misanthropy now growing upon him, I am enabled to add, from his own report in one of his note-books, the particulars of the short conversation which he held with the Lord Chancellor on the occasion:—

" When I came of age, some delays, on account of some birth and marriage certificates from Cornwall, occasioned me not to take my seat for several weeks. When these were over and I had taken the oaths, the Chancellor apologized to me for the delay, observing ' that these forms were a part of his *duty*.' I begged him to make no apology, and added (as he certainly had shown no violent hurry), ' Your lordship was exactly like Tom Thumb' (which was then being acted)—' you did your *duty*, and you did *no more*.' "

In a few days after, the Satire made its appearance, and one of the first copies was sent, with the following letter, to his friend Mr. Harness.

LETTER XXXIII.

TO MR. HARNESS.

" 8, St. James's-street, March 18th, 1809

" There was no necessity for your excuses: if you have time and inclination to write, ' for what we receive, the Lord make us thankful,'— if I do not hear from you, I console myself with the idea that you are much more agreeably employed.

" I send down to you by this post a certain Satire lately published, and in return for the three and sixpence expenditure upon it, only beg that if you should guess the author, you will keep his name secret; at least for the present. London is full of the Duke's business. The Commons have been at it these last three nights, and are not yet come to a decision. I do not know if the affair will be brought before our

House, unless in the shape of an impeachment. If it makes its appearanc in a debatable form, I believe I shall be tempted to say something o the subject.—I am glad to hear you like Cambridge: firstly, because, t know that you are happy is pleasant to one who wishes you all possibl sublunary enjoyment; and, secondly, I admire the morality of th sentiment. *Alma Mater* was to me *injusta noverca:* and the old Belda only gave me my M.A. degree because she could not avoid it*.—Yo know what a farce a noble Cantab. must perform.

" I am going abroad, if possible, in the spring, and before I depar I am collecting the pictures of my most intimate schoolfellows; I hav already a few, and shall want yours, or my cabinet will be incomplete. have employed one of the first miniature-painters of the day to take them of course at my own expense, as I never allow my acquaintance to incu the least expenditure to gratify a whim of mine. To mention this may seem indelicate; but when I tell you a friend of ours first refused to sit under the idea that he was to disburse on the occasion, you will see that i is necessary to state these preliminaries to prevent the recurrence of any similar mistake. I shall see you in time, and will carry you to the *limner* It will be a tax on your patience for a week, but pray excuse it, as it i, possible the resemblance may be the sole trace I shall be able to preserv of our past friendship and present acquaintance. Just now it seem foolish enough, but in a few years, when some of us are dead, and other are separated by inevitable circumstances, it will be a kind of satisfactior to retain in these images of the living the idea of our former selves and to contemplate in the resemblances of the dead, all that remains o judgment, feeling, and a host of passions. But all this will be dull enough for you, and so good night, and to end my chapter, or rather my homily believe me, my dear H., yours most affectionately."

In this romantic design of collecting together the portraits of hi school friends, we see the natural working of an ardent and disappointed

---

* In another letter to Mr. Harness, dated February, 1809, he says, " I do not know how you and Alma Mater agree. I was but an untoward child myself, and I believe the good lad and her brat were equally rejoiced when I was weaned; and, if I obtained her benediction a parting, it was, at best, equivocal."

heart, which, as the future began to darken upon it, clung with fondness to the recollections of the past, and in despair of finding new and true friends saw no happiness but in preserving all it could of the old. But even here, his sensibility had to encounter one of those freezing checks, to which feelings, so much above the ordinary temperature of the world, are but too constantly exposed;—it being from one of the very friends thus fondly valued by him, that he experienced, on leaving England, that mark of neglect of which he so indignantly complains in a note on the second Canto of Childe Harold,—contrasting with this conduct the fidelity and devotedness he had just found in his Turkish servant, Dervish. Mr. Dallas, who witnessed the immediate effect of this slight upon him, thus describes his emotion:—

" I found him bursting with indignation. ' Will you believe it?' said he, ' I have just met * * *, and asked him to come and sit an hour with me: he excused himself; and what do you think was his excuse? He was engaged with his mother and some ladies to go shopping! And he knows I set out to-morrow, to' be absent for years, perhaps never to return!—Friendship! I do not believe I shall leave behind me, yourself and family excepted, and perhaps my mother, a single being who will care what becomes of me.' "

From his expressions in a letter to Mrs. Byron, already cited, that he must " do something in the House soon," as well as from a more definite intimation of the same intention to Mr. Harness, it would appear that he had, at this time, serious thoughts of at once entering on the high pohtical path, which his station as an hereditary legislator opened to him. But, whatever may have been the first movements of his ambition in this direction, they were soon relinquished. Had he been connected with any distinguished political families, his love of eminence, seconded by such example and sympathy, would have impelled him, no doubt, to seek renown in the fields of party warfare, where it might have been his fate to afford a signal instance of that transmuting process by which, as Pope says, the corruption of a poet sometimes leads to the generation of a statesman. Luckily, however, for the world (though, whether luckily for himself may be questioned), the brighter empire of poesy was destined to claim him all its own. The loneliness, indeed, of

his position in society at this period, left destitute, as he was, of all thos
sanctions and sympathies, by which youth, at its first start, is usual
surrounded, was, of itself, enough to discourage him from embarking
a pursuit, where it is chiefly on such extrinsic advantages that any chan
of success must depend. So far from taking an active part in th
proceedings of his noble brethren, he appears to have regarded even th
ceremony of his attendance among them as irksome and mortifying
and, in a few days after his admission to his seat, he withdrew himse
in disgust to the seclusion of his own Abbey, there to brood over th
bitterness of premature experience, or meditate, in the scenes an
adventures of other lands, a freer outlet for his impatient spirit than i
could command at home.

It was not long, however, before he was summoned back to tow
by the success of his Satire,—the quick sale of which already rendere
the preparation of a new edition necessary. His zealous agent, M
Dallas, had taken care to transmit to him, in his retirement, all th
favourable opinions of the work he could collect; and it is not una
musing, as showing the sort of steps by which Fame at first mounts, t
find the approbation of such authorities as Pratt and the magazine-writer
put forward among the first rewards and encouragements of a Byron.

"You are already (he says) pretty generally known to be the author
So Cawthorn tells me, and a proof occurred to myself at Hatchard's, th
Queen's bookseller. On inquiring for the Satire, he told me that he hac
sold a great many, and had none left, and was going to send for more
which I afterwards found he did. I asked who was the author? He
said it was believed to be Lord Byron's. Did *he* believe it? Yes, he
did. On asking the ground of his belief, he told me that a lady o
distinction had, without hesitation, asked for it as Lord Byron's Satire
He likewise informed me that he had inquired of Mr. Gifford, who
frequents his shop, if it was yours. Mr. Gifford denied any knowledge
of the author, but spoke very highly of it, and said a copy had been sen
to him. Hatchard assured me that all who came to his reading-room
admired it. Cawthorn tells me it is universally well spoken of, not only
among his own customers, but generally at all the booksellers'. I hear
it highly praised at my own publisher's, where I have lately called severa

times.　At Phillip's it was read aloud by Pratt to a circle of literary guests, who were unanimous in their applause:—The *Antijacobin*, as well as the *Gentleman's Magazine*, has already blown the trump of fame for you.　We shall see it in the other Reviews next month, and probably in some severely handled, according to the connexion of the proprietors and editors with those whom it lashes."

On his arrival in London, towards the end of April, he found the first edition of his Poem nearly exhausted; and set immediately about preparing another, to which he determined to prefix his name.　The additions he now made to the work were considerable,—near a hundred new lines being introduced at the very opening *,—and it was not till about the middle of the ensuing month that the new edition was ready to go to press.　He had, during his absence from town, fixed definitively with his friend Mr. Hobhouse that they should leave England together early in the following June, and it was his wish to see the last proofs of the volume corrected before his departure.

Among the new features of this edition was a Postscript to the Satire, in prose, which Mr. Dallas, much to the credit of his discretion and taste, most earnestly entreated the poet to suppress.　It is to be regretted that the adviser did not succeed in his efforts, as there runs a tone of bravado through this ill-judged effusion, which it is, at all times, painful to see a really brave man assume.　For instance:—" It may be said," he observes, " that I quit England because I have censured these ' persons of honour and wit about town;' but I am coming back again, and their vengeance will keep hot till my return.　Those who know me can testify that my motives for leaving England are very different from fears, literary or personal; those, who do not, may one day be convinced.　Since the publication of this thing, my name has not been concealed; I have been mostly in London, ready to answer for my transgressions, and in daily expectation of sundry cartels; but, alas, ' the age of chivalry is over,' or, in the vulgar tongue, there is no spirit now-a-days."

But, whatever may have been the faults or indiscretions of this

---

* The Poem, in the first edition, began at the line,

　　" Time was ere yet, in these degenerate days."

Satire, there are few who would now sit in judgment upon it so severel
as did the author himself, on reading it over nine years after, when h
had quitted England, never to return. The copy which he then peruse
is now in the possession of Mr. Murray, and the remarks which he ha
left scribbled over its pages are well worth transcribing. On the firs
leaf we find—

"The binding of this volume is considerably too valuable for it
contents.

"Nothing but the consideration of its being the property of anothe
prevents me from consigning this miserable record of misplaced ange
and indiscriminate acrimony to the flames.   "B."

Opposite the passage,

> "to be misled
> By Jeffrey's heart, or Lamb's Bœotian head,"

is written, "This was not just. Neither the heart nor the head of these
gentlemen are, at all, what they are here represented." Along the whole
of the severe verses against Mr. Wordsworth he has scrawled, "Unjust,"
—and the same verdict is affixed to those against Mr. Coleridge. On his
unmeasured attack upon Mr. Bowles, the comment is,—"Too savage all
this on Bowles;" and down the margin of the page containing the lines,
"Health to immortal Jeffrey," &c. he writes,—"Too ferocious—this is
mere insanity,"—adding, on the verses that follow ("Can none remember
that eventful day?" &c.) "All this is bad, because personal."

Sometimes, however, he shows a disposition to stand by his original
decisions. Thus, on the passage relating to a writer of certain obscure
Epics (v. 379), he says,—"All right;" adding, of the same person, "I
saw some letters of this fellow to an unfortunate poetess, whose productions (which the poor woman by no means thought vainly of) he
attacked so roughly and bitterly, that I could hardly regret assailing
him;—even were it unjust, which it is not; for, verily, he *is* an ass."
On the strong lines, too (v. 953), upon Clarke (a writer in a magazine
called the Satirist), he remarks,—"Right enough,—this was well deserved,
and well laid on."

To the whole paragraph, beginning "Illustrious Holland," are affixed
the words "Bad enough;—and on mistaken grounds, besides." The

bitter verses against Lord Carlisle he pronounces " Wrong also—the provocation was not sufficient to justify such acerbity;"—and of a subsequent note respecting the same nobleman he says, " Much too savage, whatever the foundation may be." Of Rosa Matilda (v. 738) he tells us, " She has since married the Morning Post,—an exceeding good match." To the verses " When some brisk youth, the tenant of a stall," &c. he has appended the following interesting note :—" This was meant at poor Blackett, who was then patronized by A. I. B.*—but *that* I did not know, or this would not have been written; at least, I think not."

Farther on, where Mr. Campbell and other poets are mentioned, the following gingle on the names of their respective poems is scribbled :—

> " Pretty Miss Jacqueline
> Had a nose aquiline;
> And would assert rude
> Things of Miss Gertrude;
> While Mr. Marmion
> Led a great army on,
> Making Kehama look
> Like a fierce Mamaluke."

Opposite the paragraph in praise of Mr. Crabbe he has written, " I consider Crabbe and Coleridge as the first of these times in point of power and genius." On his own line, in a subsequent paragraph, " And glory, like the Phœnix mid her fires," he says, comically, " The Devil take that Phœnix—how came it there?" and his concluding remark on the whole Poem is as follows :—

" The greater part of this Satire, I most sincerely wish had never been written; not only on account of the injustice of much of the critical and some of the personal part of it, but the tone and temper are such as I cannot approve.   " BYRON."

" Diodati, Geneva, July 14, 1816.

While engaged in preparing his new edition for the press, he was also gaily dispensing the hospitalities of Newstead to a party of young college

* Lady Byron, then Miss Milbank.

friends, whom, with the prospect of so long an absence from Englan
he had assembled round him at the Abbey, for a sort of festive farewe
The following letter from one of the party, Charles Skinner Matthew
though containing much less of the noble host himself than we cou
have wished, yet, as a picture, taken freshly and at the moment, of
scene so pregnant with character, will, I have little doubt, be highl
acceptable to the reader.

LETTER FROM CHARLES SKINNER MATTHEWS, ESQ. TO MISS I. M.

" London, 22 May, 1809.

" MY DEAR ————,

      *   *   *   *   *

" I must begin with giving you a few particulars of the singula
place which I have lately quitted.

" Newstead Abbey is situate 136 miles from London,—4 on thi
side Mansfield. It is so fine a piece of antiquity that I should thin
there must be a description and, perhaps, a picture of it in Grose. Th
ancestors of its present owner came into possession of it at the time o
the dissolution of the monasteries,—but the building itself is of a muc
earlier date. Though sadly fallen to decay, it is still completely a
Abbey, and most part of it is still standing in the same state as when i
was first built. There are two tiers of cloisters, with a variety of cell
and rooms about them, which, though not inhabited, nor in an inhabitabl
state, might easily be made so; and many of the original rooms, amongs
which is a fine stone hall, are still in use. Of the Abbey Church onl
one end remains; and the old kitchen, with a long range of apartment
is reduced to a heap of rubbish. Leading from the Abbey to the moder
part of the habitation is a noble room, seventy feet in length and twenty
three in breadth: but every part of the house displays neglect and decay
save those which the present Lord has lately fitted up.

" The house and gardens are entirely surrounded by a wall witl
battlements. In front is a large lake, bordered here and there witl
castellated buildings, the chief of which stands on an eminence at th
further extremity of it. Fancy all this surrounded with bleak an

barren hills, with scarce a tree to be seen for miles, except a solitary
clump or two, and you will have some idea of Newstead. For the late
Lord being at enmity with his son, to whom the estate was secured by
entail, resolved, out of spite to the same, that the estate should descend
to him in as miserable a plight as he could possibly reduce it to; for
which cause, he took no care of the mansion, and fell to lopping of every
tree he could lay his hands on so furiously, that he reduced immense
tracts of woodland country to the desolate state I have just described.
However, his son died before him, so that all his rage was thrown away.

" So much for the place, concerning which I have thrown together
these few particulars, meaning my account to be, like the place itself,
without any order or connexion. But if the place itself appear rather
strange to you, the ways of the inhabitants will not appear much less so.
Ascend, then, with me the hall steps, that I may introduce you to my
Lord and his visitants. But have a care how you proceed; be mindful
to go there in broad daylight, and with your eyes about you. For,
should you make any blunder,—should you go to the right of the hall
steps, you are laid hold of by a bear; and, should you go to the left,
your case is still worse, for you run full against a wolf!—Nor, when you
have attained the door, is your danger over; for the hall being decayed,
and therefore standing in need of repair, a bevy of inmates are very
probably banging at one end of it with their pistols; so that if you enter
without giving loud notice of your approach, you have only escaped the
wolf and the bear to expire by the pistol-shots of the merry Monks of
Newstead.

" Our party consisted of Lord Byron and four others; and was,
now and then, increased by the presence of a neighbouring parson. As
for our way of living, the order of the day was generally this:—For
breakfast we had no set hour, but each suited his own convenience,—
every thing remaining on the table till the whole party had done;
though had one wished to breakfast at the early hour of ten, one would
have been rather lucky to find any of the servants up. Our average hour
of rising was one. I, who generally got up between eleven and twelve,
was always,—even when an invalid,—the first of the party, and was
esteemed a prodigy of early rising. It was frequently past two before

the breakfast party broke up. Then, for the amusements of the mornin
there was reading, fencing, single-stick, or shuttle-cock, in the great roon
practising with pistols in the hall; walking—riding—cricket—sailing o
the lake, playing with the bear, or teazing the wolf. Between seven ar
eight we dined, and our evening lasted from that time till one, two, o
three in the morning. The evening diversions may be easily conceive

" I must not omit the custom of handing round, after dinner, c
the removal of the cloth, a human skull filled with burgundy. Aft
revelling on choice viands, and the finest wines of France, we adjourne
to tea, where we amused ourselves with reading, or improving convers:
tion,—each, according to his fancy,—and, after sandwiches, &c. retire
to rest. A set of monkish dresses, which had been provided, with a
the proper apparatus of crosses, beads, tonsures, &c. often gave a variet
to our appearance, and to our pursuits.

" You may easily imagine how chagrined I was at being ill nearl
the first half of the time I was there. But I was led into a very differen
reflection from that of Dr. Swift, who left Pope's house without cere
mony, and afterwards informed him, by letter, that it was impossible fo
two sick friends to live together; for I found my shivering and invali
frame so perpetually annoyed by the thoughtless and tumultuous healtl
of every one about me, that I heartily wished every soul in the house to
be as ill as myself.

" The journey back I performed on foot, together with another o
the guests. We walked about 25 miles a day; but were a week on th
road, from being detained by the rain.

*   *   *   *   *   *

" So here I close my account of an expedition which has somewha
extended my knowledge of this country. And where do you think]
am going next? To Constantinople!—at least, such an excursion ha
been proposed to me. Lord B. and another friend of mine are going
thither next month, and have asked me to join the party; but it seem:
to be but a wild scheme, and requires twice thinking upon. * * *

" Addio, my dear I., yours very affectionately,

" C. S. MATTHEWS."

Having put the finishing hand to his new edition, he, without waiting for the fresh honours that were in store for him, took leave of London (whither he had returned) on the 11th of June, and, in about a fortnight after, sailed for Lisbon.

Great as was the advance which his powers had made, under the influence of that resentment from which he now drew his inspiration, they were yet, even in his Satire, at an immeasurable distance from the point to which they afterwards so triumphantly rose. It is, indeed, remarkable that, essentially as his genius seemed connected with, and, as it were, springing out of his character, the developement of the one should so long have preceded the full maturity of the resources of the other. By her very early and rapid expansion of his sensibilities, Nature had given him notice of what she destined him for, long before he understood the call; and those materials of poetry with which his own fervid temperament abounded were but by slow degrees, and after much self-meditation, revealed to him. In his Satire, though vigorous, there is but little foretaste of the wonders that followed it. His spirit was stirred, but he had not yet looked down into its depths, nor does even his bitterness taste of the bottom of the heart, like those sarcasms which he afterwards flung in the face of mankind. Still less had the other countless feelings and passions, with which his soul had been long labouring, found an organ worthy of them;—the gloom, the grandeur, the tenderness of his nature, all were left without a voice, till his mighty genius, at last, awakened in its strength.

In stooping, as he did, to write after established models, as well in the Satire as in his still earlier poems, he showed how little he had yet explored his own original resources, or found out those distinctive marks by which he was to be known through all time. But, bold and energetic as was his general character, he was, in a remarkable degree, diffident in his intellectual powers. The consciousness of what he could achieve was but by degrees forced upon him, and the discovery of so rich a mine of genius in his soul came with no less surprise on himself than on the world. It was from the same slowness of self-appreciation that, afterwards, in the full flow of his fame, he long doubted, as we shall see, his own aptitude for works of wit and humour,—till the happy

experiment of " Beppo" at once dissipated this distrust, and opened
new region of triumph to his versatile and boundless powers.

But, however far short of himself his first writings must be cons
dered, there is in his Satire a liveliness of thought, and, still more,
vigour and courage, which, concurring with the justice of his cause an
the sympathies of the public on his side, could not fail to attach instan
celebrity to his name. Notwithstanding, too, the general boldness an
recklessness of his tone, there were occasionally mingled with this defianc
some allusions to his own fate and character, whose affecting earnestnes
seemed to answer for their truth, and which were of a nature strongly t
awaken curiosity as well as interest. One or two of these passages, a
illustrative of the state of his mind at this period, I shall here extract
The loose and unfenced state in which his youth was left to grow wil
upon the world is thus touchingly alluded to:—

> " Ev'n I—least thinking of a thoughtless throng,
> Just skill'd to know the right and choose the wrong,
> Freed at that age when Reason's shield is lost
> To fight my course through Passion's countless host,
> Whom every path of Pleasure's flowery way
> Has lured in turn, and all have led astray—*
> Ev'n I must raise my voice, ev'n 1 must feel
> Such scenes, such men destroy the public weal:
> Although some kind, censorious friend will say,
> ' What art thou better, meddling fool †, than they ?'
> And every brother Rake will smile to see
> That miracle, a Moralist, in me."

But the passage in which, hastily thrown off as it is, we find the
strongest trace of that wounded feeling, which bleeds, as it were, through
all his subsequent writings, is the following :—

> " The time hath been, when no harsh sound would fall
> From lips that now may seem imbued with gall,

---

* In the MS. remarks on his Satire, to which I have already referred, he says, on thi
passage—" Yea, and a pretty dance they have led me."
† " Fool then, and but little wiser now."—*MS. ibid.*

Nor fools nor follies tempt me to despise
The meanest thing that crawl'd beneath my eyes.
But now so callous grown, so changed from youth," &c.

Some of the causes that worked this change in his character have been intimated in the course of the preceding pages. That there was no tinge of bitterness in his natural disposition we have abundant testimony, besides his own, to prove. Though, as a child, occasionally passionate and headstrong, his docility and kindness, towards those who were, themselves, kind, is acknowledged by all; and "playful" and "affectionate" are invariably the epithets by which those who knew him in his childhood convey their impression of his character.

Of all the qualities, indeed, of his nature, affectionateness seems to have been the most ardent and most deep. A disposition, on his own side, to form strong attachments, and a yearning desire after affection in return, were the feeling and the want that formed the dream and torment of his existence. We have seen with what passionate enthusiasm he threw himself into his boyish friendships. The all-absorbing and unsuccessful love that followed was, if I may so say, the agony, without being the death, of this unsated desire, which lived on through his life, filled his poetry with the very soul of tenderness, lent the colouring of its light to even those unworthy ties which vanity or passion led him afterwards to form, and was the last aspiration of his fervid spirit in those stanzas written but a few months before his death :—

" 'Tis time this heart should be unmoved,
    Since others it has ceased to move;
Yet, though I cannot be beloved,
    Still let me love !"

It is much, I own, to be questioned, whether, even under the most favourable circumstances, a disposition such as I have here described could have escaped ultimate disappointment, or found anywhere a resting-place for its imaginings and desires. But, in the case of Lord Byron, disappointment met him on the very threshold of life. His mother, to whom his affections first, naturally and with ardour, turned, either repelled them rudely or capriciously trifled with them. In speaking of

his early days to a friend at Genoa, a short time before his departure f
Greece, he traced the first feelings of pain and humiliation he had ev
known to the coldness with which his mother had received his caress
in infancy, and the frequent taunts on his personal deformity with whi
she had wounded him.

The sympathy of a sister's love, of all influences on the mind of
youth the most softening, was also, in his early days, denied to him,—
his sister Augusta and he having seen but little of each other whi
young. A vent through the calm channel of domestic affections mig
have brought down the high current of his feelings to a level nearer th
of the world he had to traverse, and thus saved them from the tumu
tuous rapids and falls to which this early elevation, in their after-cours
exposed them. In the dearth of all home endearments, his heart had n
other resource but in those boyish friendships which he formed at school
and when these were interrupted by his removal to Cambridge, he wa
again thrown back, isolated, on his own restless desires. Then followe
his ill-fated attachment to Miss Chaworth, to which, more than to an
other cause, he himself attributed the desolating change then wrought i
his disposition.

"I doubt sometimes" (he says, in his "Detached Thoughts"
"whether, after all, a quiet and unagitated life would have suited me; ye
I sometimes long for it. My earliest dreams (as most boys' dreams are
were martial; but a little later they were all for *love* and retirement, til
the hopeless attachment to M*** C*** began and continued (thoug
sedulously concealed) *very* early in my teens; and so upwards for a time
This threw me out again 'alone on a wide, wide sea.' In the year 180
I recollect meeting my sister at General Harcourt's in Portland Place.
was then *one thing*, and *as* she had always till then found me. When w
met again in 1805 (she told me since) that my temper and dispositio
were so completely altered that I was hardly to be recognized. I wa
not then sensible of the change; but I can believe it, and accoun
for it."

I have already described his parting with Miss Chaworth previously
to her marriage. Once again, after that event, he saw her, and for the
last time,—being invited by Mr. Chaworth to dine at Annesley not long

before his departure from England. The few years that had elapsed since their last meeting had made a considerable change in the appearance and manners of the young poet. The fat, unformed schoolboy was now a slender and graceful young man. Those emotions and passions, which, at first, heighten, and then destroy, beauty, had, as yet, produced only their favourable effects on his features; and, though with but little aid from the example of refined society, his manners had subsided into that tone of gentleness and self-possession which more than any thing marks the well-bred gentleman. Once only was the latter of these qualities put to the trial, when the little daughter of his fair hostess was brought into the room. At the sight of the child, he started involuntarily, —it was with the utmost difficulty he could conceal his emotion; and to the sensations of that moment we are indebted for those touching stanzas, "Well—thou art happy," &c.* which appeared afterwards in a Miscellany published by one of his friends, and are now to be found in the general collection of his works. Under the influence of the same despondent passion he wrote two other poems at this period, from which, as they exist only in the Miscellany I have just alluded to, and that collection has for some time been out of print, a few stanzas may, not improperly, be extracted here.

" THE FAREWELL—TO A LADY†.

" When man, expell'd from Eden's bowers,
 A moment linger'd near the gate,
Each scene recall'd the vanish'd hours,
 And bade him curse his future fate.

" But, wandering on through distant climes,
 He learnt to bear his load of grief;
Just gave a sigh to other times,
 And found in busier scenes relief.

---

* Dated, in his original copy, Nov. 2, 1808.

 † Entitled, in his original manuscript, "To Mrs. * * *, on being asked my reason for quitting England in the spring." The date subjoined is Dec. 2, 1808.

" Thus, lady*, must it be with me,
 And I must view thy charms no more;
For, whilst I linger near to thee,
 I sigh for all I knew before." &c. &c.

The other poem is, throughout, full of tenderness; but I shall give only what appear to me the most striking stanzas.

" STANZAS TO * * * ON LEAVING ENGLAND.

" 'Tis done—and shivering in the gale
 The bark unfurls her snowy sail;
And whistling o'er the bending mast,
 Loud sings on high the fresh'ning blast;
And I must from this land be gone,
 Because I cannot love but one.
 * * * *

" As some lone bird, without a mate,
 My weary heart is desolate;
I look around, and cannot trace
 One friendly smile or welcome face,
And ev'n in crowds am still alone,
 Because I cannot love but one.

" And I will cross the whitening foam,
 And I will seek a foreign home;
Till I forget a false fair face,
 I ne'er shall find a resting-place;
My own dark thoughts I cannot shun,
 But ever love, and love but one.
 * * * *

" I go—but wheresoe'er I flee
 There's not an eye will weep for me;
There's not a kind congenial heart,
 Where I can claim the meanest part;
Nor thou, who hast my hopes undone,
 Wilt sigh, although I love but one.

---

* In his first copy, " Thus, Mary."

" To think of every early scene,
　　Of what we are, and what we 've been,
　　Would whelm some softer hearts with woe—
　　But mine, alas! has stood the blow;
　　Yet still beats on as it begun,
　　And never truly loves but one.

" And who that dear loved one may be
　　Is not for vulgar eyes to see,
　　And why that early love was crost,
　　Thou know'st the best, I feel the most;
　　But few that dwell beneath the sun
　　Have loved so long, and loved but one.

" I 've tried another's fetters too,
　　With charms, perchance, as fair to view;
　　And I would fain have loved as well,
　　But some unconquerable spell
　　Forbade my bleeding breast to own
　　A kindred care for aught but one.

" 'Twould soothe to take one lingering view,
　　And bless thee in my last adieu;
　　Yet wish I not those eyes to weep
　　For him that wanders o'er the deep;
　　His home, his hope, his youth are gone,
　　Yet still he loves, and loves but one *."

While thus, in all the relations of the heart, his thirst after affection was thwarted, in another instinct of his nature, not less strong—the desire of eminence and distinction—he was, in an equal degree, checked in his aspirings, and mortified. The inadequacy of his means to his station was early a source of embarrassment and humiliation to him; and those high, patrician notions of birth in which he indulged but made the disparity between his fortune and his rank the more galling. Ambition, however, soon whispered to him that there were other and nobler ways

* Thus corrected by himself in a copy of the Miscellany now in my possession;—the two last lines being, originally, as follows:—

　　" Though wheresoe'er my bark may run,
　　　I love but thee, I love but one."

to distinction. The eminence which talent builds for itself might, on day, he proudly felt, be his own; nor was it too sanguine to hope tha under the favour accorded usually to youth, he might with impunit venture on his first steps to fame. But here, as in every other object of his heart, disappointment and mortification awaited him. Instead of experiencing the ordinary forbearance, if not indulgence, with whic young aspirants for fame are received by their critics, he found himsel instantly the victim of such unmeasured severity as is not often deal out even to veteran offenders in literature; and, with a heart fresh from the trials of disappointed love, saw those resources and consolation which he had sought in the exercise of his intellectual strength also invaded.

While thus prematurely broken into the pains of life, a no les darkening effect was produced upon him by too early an initiation into its pleasures. That charm with which the fancy of youth invests an untried world was, in his case, soon dissipated. His passions had, at the very onset of their career, forestalled the future; and the blank void tha followed was by himself considered as one of the causes of that melan choly, which now settled so deeply into his character.

" My passions" (he says, in his " Detached Thoughts,") " were developed very early—so early that few would believe me if I were to state the period and the facts which accompanied it. Perhaps this was one of the reasons which caused the anticipated melancholy of my thoughts,—having anticipated life. My earlier poems are the thoughts of one at least ten years older than the age at which they were written,— I don't mean for their solidity, but their experience. The two first Cantos of Childe Harold were completed at twenty-two; and they are written as if by a man older than I shall probably ever be."

Though the allusions in the first sentence of this extract have reference to a much earlier period, they afford an opportunity of remark- ing, that however dissipated may have been the life which he led during the two or three years previous to his departure on his travels, yet the notion caught up by many, from his own allusions, in Childe Harold, to irregularities and orgies of which Newstead had been the scene, is, like most other imputations against him founded on his own testimony, greatly exaggerated. He describes, it is well known, the home of his poetical representative as a "monastic dome, condemned to uses vile," and then adds,—

> " Where Superstition once had made her den,
>   Now Paphian girls were known to sing and smile."

Mr. Dallas, too, giving in to the same strain of exaggeration, says, in speaking of the poet's preparations for his departure, " already satiated with pleasure, and disgusted with those companions who have no other resource, he had resolved on mastering his appetites ;—he broke up his harams." The truth, however, is that the narrowness of Lord Byron's means would alone have prevented such oriental luxuries. The mode of his life at Newstead was simple and unexpensive. His companions, though not averse to convivial indulgences, were of habits and tastes too intellectual for mere vulgar debauchery; and, with respect to the alleged " Harams," it appears certain that one or two suspected " *Subintroductæ*" (as the ancient monks of the Abbey would have styled them), and those, too, among the ordinary menials of the establishment, were all that even scandal itself could ever fix upon to warrant such an assumption.

That gaming was among his follies at this period, he himself tells us in the Journal I have just cited :—

" I have a notion (he says) that gamblers are as happy as many people, being always *excited*. Women, wine, fame, the table,—even ambition, *sate* now and then ; but every turn of the card and cast of the dice keeps the gamester alive : besides, one can game ten times longer than one can do any thing else. I was very fond of it when young, that is to say, of hazard, for I hate all *card* games,—even faro. When macco (or whatever they spell it) was introduced, I gave up the whole thing, for I loved and missed the *rattle* and *dash* of the box and dice, and the glorious uncertainty, not only of good luck or bad luck, but of *any luck at all*, as one had sometimes to throw *often* to decide at all. I have thrown as many as fourteen mains running, and carried off all the cash upon the table occasionally ; but I had no coolness, or judgment, or calculation. It was the delight of the thing that pleased me. Upon the whole, I left off in time, without being much a winner or loser. Since one-and-twenty

years of age I played but little, and then never above a hundred, or tw
or three."

To this, and other follies of the same period, he alludes in th
following note :—

TO MR. WILLIAM BANKES.

"Twelve o'clock, Friday night.

"MY DEAR BANKES,

"I have just received your note; believe me I regret most sincerely
that I was not fortunate enough to see it before, as I need not repeat to
you, that your conversation for half an hour would have been much
more agreeable to me than gambling or drinking, or any other fashionabl
mode of passing an evening abroad or at home.—I really am very sorry
that I went out previous to the arrival of your despatch: in future pray
let me hear from you before six, and whatever my engagements may be
I will always postpone them.—Believe me, with that deference which I
have always from my childhood paid to your *talents*, and with somewha
a better opinion of your heart than I have hitherto entertained,

"Yours ever, &c."

Among the causes—if not rather among the results—of that disposition to melancholy, which, after all, perhaps, naturally belonged to
his temperament, must not be forgotten those sceptical views of religion,
which clouded, as has been shown, his boyish thoughts, and, at the time
of which I am speaking, gathered still more darkly over his mind. In
general, we find the young too ardently occupied with the enjoyments
which this life gives or promises to afford either leisure or inclination for
much inquiry into the mysteries of the next. But with him it was
unluckily otherwise; and to have, at once, anticipated the worst experience both of the voluptuary and the reasoner,—to have reached, as he
supposed, the boundary of this world's pleasures, and see nothing but
"clouds and darkness" beyond, was the doom, the anomalous doom,
which a nature, premature in all its passions and powers, inflicted on
Lord Byron.

When Pope, at the age of five-and-twenty, complained of being weary of the world, he was told by Swift that he " had not yet acted or suffered enough in the world to have become weary of it*." But far different was the youth of Pope and of Byron;—what the former but anticipated in thought, the latter had drunk deep of in reality;—at an age when the one was but looking forth on the sea of life, the other had plunged in, and tried its depths. Swift himself, in whom early disappointments and wrongs had opened a vein of bitterness that never again closed, affords a far closer parallel to the fate of our noble poet†, as well in the untimeliness of the trials he had been doomed to encounter, as in the traces of their havoc which they left in his character.

That the romantic fancy of youth, which courts melancholy as an indulgence, and loves to assume a sadness it has not had time to earn, may have had some share in, at least, fostering the gloom by which the mind of the young poet was overcast, I am not disposed to deny. The circumstance, indeed, of his having, at this time, among the ornaments of his study, a number of skulls highly polished, and placed on light stands round the room, would seem to indicate that he rather courted than shunned such gloomy associations‡. Being a sort of boyish mimickry, too, of the use to which the poet Young is said to have applied a skull, such a display might well induce some suspicion of the sincerity of his gloom, did we not, through the whole course of his subsequent life and writings, track visibly the deep vein of melancholy which nature had imbedded in his character.

Such was the state of mind and heart,—as, from his own testimony and that of others, I have collected it,—in which Lord Byron now set

* I give the words as Johnson has reported them ;—in Swift's own letter they are, if I recollect right, rather different.

† There is, at least, one striking point of similarity between their characters in the disposition which Johnson has thus attributed to Swift :—" The suspicions of Swift's irreligion," he says, " proceeded, in a great measure, from his dread of hypocrisy ; *instead of wishing to seem better, he delighted in seeming worse than he was.*"

‡ Another use to which he appropriated one of the skulls found in digging at Newstead was the having it mounted in silver, and converted into a drinking-cup. This whim has been commemorated in some well-known verses of his own ; and the cup itself, which, apart from any revolting ideas it may excite, forms by no means an inelegant object to the eye, is, with many other interesting relics of Lord Byron, in the possession of the present proprietor of Newstead Abbey, Colonel Wildman.

out on his indefinite pilgrimage; and never was there a change wrough
in disposition and character to which Shakspeare's fancy of " sweet bel
jangled out of tune" more truly applied. The unwillingness of Lor
Carlisle to countenance him, and his humiliating position in consequenc
completed the full measure of that mortification towards which so man
other causes had concurred. Baffled, as he had been, in his own arden
pursuit of affection and friendship, his sole revenge and consolatio
lay in doubting that any such feelings really existed. The variou
crosses he had met with, in themselves sufficiently irritating and wound
ing,—were rendered still more so by the high, impatient temper wit
which he encountered them. What others would have bowed to, a
misfortunes, his proud spirit rose against, as wrongs; and the vehemenc
of this reaction produced, at once, a revolution throughout his whol
character*, in which, as in revolutions of the political world, all that wa
bad and irregular in his nature burst forth with all that was mos
energetic and grand. The very virtues and excellencies of his dispositior
ministered to the violence of this change. The same ardour that hac
burned through his friendships and loves now fed the fierce explosion
of his indignation and scorn. His natural vivacity and humour but lent
a fresher flow to his bitterness†, till he, at last, revelled in it as an
indulgence; and that hatred of hypocrisy, which had hitherto only
shown itself in a too shadowy colouring of his own youthful frailties
now hurried him, from his horror of all false pretensions to virtue, into
the still more dangerous boast and ostentation of vice.

The following letter to his mother, written a few days before he
sailed, gives some particulars respecting the persons who composed his
suite. Robert Rushton, whom he mentions so feelingly in the Postscript,
was the boy introduced, as his Page, in the First Canto of Childe Harold.

* Rousseau appears to have been conscious of a similar sort of change in his own nature:—
" They have laboured without intermission," he says, in a letter to Madame de Boufflers, " to
give to my heart, and, perhaps, at the same time to my genius, a spring and stimulus of action,
which they have not inherited from nature. I was born weak,—ill-treatment has made me
strong."—HUME's *Private Correspondence.*

† " It was bitterness that they mistook for frolic."—Johnson's account of himself at the
university, in Boswell.

LETTER XXXIV.

TO MRS. BYRON.

"Falmouth, June 22d, 1809.

" DEAR MOTHER,

" I am about to sail in a few days; probably before this reaches you. Fletcher begged so hard, that I have continued him in my service. If he does not behave well abroad, I will send him back in a *transport*. I have a German servant (who has been with Mr. Wilbraham in Persia before, and was strongly recommended to me by Dr. Butler of Harrow), Robert and William; they constitute my whole suite. I have letters in plenty—you shall hear from me at the different ports I touch upon; but you must not be alarmed if my letters miscarry. The continent is in a fine state—an insurrection has broken out at Paris, and the Austrians are beating Buonaparte—the Tyrolese have risen.

" There is a picture of me in oil, to be sent down to Newstead soon. —I wish the Miss P**s had something better to do than carry my miniatures to Nottingham to copy. Now they have done it, you may ask them to copy the others, which are greater favourites than my own. As to money matters, I am ruined—at least till Rochdale is sold; and if that does not turn out well, I shall enter into the Austrian or Russian service—perhaps the Turkish, if I like their manners. The world is all before me, and I leave England without regret, and without a wish to revisit any thing it contains, except *yourself*, and your present residence.

" P.S.—Pray tell Mr. Rushton his son is well, and doing well; so is Murray, indeed better than I ever saw him; he will be back in about a month. I ought to add, the leaving Murray to my few regrets, as his age perhaps will prevent my seeing him again. Robert I take with me; I like him, because, like myself, he seems a friendless animal."

To those who have in their remembrance his poetical description of the state of mind in which he now took leave of England, the gaiety and levity of the letters I am about to give will appear, it is not improbable, strange and startling. But, in a temperament like that of Lord

Byron, such bursts of vivacity on the surface are by no means incompatibl
with a wounded spirit underneath*; and the light, laughing tone tha
pervades these letters, but makes the feeling of solitariness that break
out in them the more striking and affecting.

LETTER XXXV.

TO MR. HENRY DRURY.

"Falmouth, June 25th, 1809.

" MY DEAR DRURY,

" We sail to-morrow in the Lisbon packet, having been detained till
now by the lack of wind, and other necessaries. These being at last
procured, by this time to-morrow evening we shall be embarked on the
*v*ide *v*orld of *v*aters, *v*or all the *v*orld like Robinson Crusoe. The Malta
vessel not sailing for some weeks, we have determined to go by way
of Lisbon, and, as my servants term it, to see ' that there Portingale;'—
thence to Cadiz and Gibraltar, and so on our old route to Malta and
Constantinople, if so be that Captain Kidd, our gallant commander,
understands plain sailing and Mercator, and takes us on our voyage all
according to the chart.

" Will you tell Dr. Butler† that I have taken the treasure of a

---

* The poet Cowper, it is well known, produced that master-piece of humour, John Gilpin,
during one of his fits of morbid dejection, and he himself says, " Strange as it may seem, the
most ludicrous lines I ever wrote have been written in the saddest mood, and but for that
saddest mood, perhaps, had never been written at all."

† The reconciliation which took place between him and Dr. Butler, before his departure,
is one of those instances of placability and pliableness with which his life abounded. We have
seen, too, from the manner in which he mentions the circumstance in one of his note-books, that
the reconcilement was of that generously retrospective kind, in which not only the feeling of
hostility is renounced in future, but a strong regret expressed that it had been ever entertained.
Not content with this private atonement to Dr. Butler, it was his intention, had he
published another edition of the Hours of Idleness, to substitute for the offensive verses against
that gentleman, a frank avowal of the wrong he had been guilty of in giving vent to them.
This fact, so creditable to the candour of his nature, I learn from a loose sheet in his handwriting, containing the following corrections. In place of the passage beginning " Or if my
Muse a pedant's portrait drew," he meant to insert—

" If once my Muse a harsher portrait drew,
    Warm with her wrongs, and deem'd the likeness true,

servant, Friese, the native of Prussia Proper, into my service from his recommendation. He has been all among the Worshippers of Fire in Persia, and has seen Persepolis and all that.

" H ＊＊ has made woundy preparations for a book on his return;— 100 pens, two gallons of japan ink, and several volumes of best blank, is no bad provision for a discerning public. I have laid down my pen, but have promised to contribute a chapter on the state of morals, &c. &c.

> ' The cock is crowing,
> I must be going,
> And can no more.'—GHOST OF GAFFER THUMB.

> " Adieu.—Believe me, &c. &c."

LETTER XXXVI.

TO MR. HODGSON.

> " Falmouth, June 25th, 1809.

" MY DEAR HODGSON,

" Before this reaches you, Hobhouse, two officers' wives, three children, two waiting-maids, ditto subalterns for the troops, three Portuguese esquires and domestics, in all nineteen souls, will have sailed in the Lisbon packet, with the noble Captain Kidd, a gallant commander as ever smuggled an anker of right Nantz.

" We are going to Lisbon first, because the Malta packet has sailed, d'ye see?—from Lisbon to Gibraltar, Malta, Constantinople, and ' all that,' as Orator Henley said, when he put the Church, and ' all that,' in danger.

> By cooler judgment taught, her fault she owns,—
> With noble minds a fault, confess'd, atones."

And to the passage immediately succeeding his warm praise of Dr. Drury,—" Pomposus fills his magisterial chair," it was his intention to give the following turn :—

> " Another fills his magisterial chair ;
> Reluctant Ida owns a stranger's care ;
> Oh may like honours crown his future name,—
> If such his virtues, such shall be his fame."

" This town of Falmouth, as you will partly conjecture, is no grea
ways from the sea. It is defended on the sea-side by tway castles, S†
Maws and Pendennis, extremely well calculated for annoying every bod†
except an enemy. St. Maws is garrisoned by an able-bodied person o†
fourscore, a widower. He has the whole command and sole managemen†
of six most unmanageable pieces of ordnance, admirably adapted for th†
destruction of Pendennis, a like tower of strength on the opposite side
of the Channel. We have seen St. Maws, but Pendennis they will no†
let us behold, save at a distance, because Hobhouse and I are suspected
of having already taken St. Maws by a coup de main.

" The town contains many quakers and salt-fish—the oysters have a
taste of copper, owing to the soil of a mining country—the women
(blessed be the Corporation therefor!) are flogged at the cart's tail when
they pick and steal, as happened to one of the fair sex yesterday noon.
She was pertinacious in her behaviour, and damned the mayor.　　*　　*

" Hodgson! remember me to the Drury, and remember me to—
yourself, when drunk:—I am not worth a sober thought. Look to my
Satire at Cawthorne's, Cockspur-street.　　*　　*　　*

" I don't know when I can write again, because it depends on that
experienced navigator, Captain Kidd, and the ' stormy winds that (don't)
blow' at this season. I leave England without regret—I shall return to
it without pleasure. I am like Adam, the first convict, sentenced to
transportation, but I have no Eve, and have eaten no apple but what was
sour as a crab;—and thus ends my first chapter. Adieu. Yours, &c."

In this letter the following lively verses were enclosed:—

" Falmouth Roads, June 30th, 1809.

1.

" Huzza! Hodgson, we are going,
　　Our embargo's off at last;
Favourable breezes blowing
　　Bend the canvas o'er the mast.
From aloft the signal's streaming,
　　Hark! the farewell gun is fired,

Women screeching, tars blaspheming,
   Tell us that our time's expired.
      Here's a rascal
      Come to task all,
   Prying from the Custom-house;
      Trunks unpacking,
      Cases cracking,
   Not a corner for a mouse
Scapes unsearch'd amid the racket,
Ere we sail on board the Packet.

2

" Now our boatmen quit their mooring,
   And all hands must ply the oar;
Baggage from the quay is lowering,
   We're impatient—push from shore.
' Have a care! that case holds liquor—
   ' Stop the boat—I'm sick—oh Lord!'
' Sick, ma'am, damme, you'll be sicker
   ' Ere you've been an hour on board.'
      Thus are screaming
      Men and women,
   Gemmen, ladies, servants, Jacks;
      Here entangling,
      All are wrangling,
Stuck together close as wax.—
Such the general noise and racket,
Ere we reach the Lisbon Packet.

3.

" Now we've reach'd her, lo! the captain,
   Gallant Kidd, commands the crew;
Passengers their births are clapt in,
   Some to grumble, some to spew.
' Hey day! call you that a cabin?
   Why 'tis hardly three feet square;
Not enough to stow Queen Mab in—
   Who the deuce can harbour there?'
      ' Who, sir? plenty—
      Nobles twenty
Did at once my vessel fill'—

'Did they? Jesus,
How you squeeze us!
Would to God they did so still:
Then I'd scape the heat and racket
Of the good ship, Lisbon Packet.'

4.

" Fletcher! Murray! Bob! where are you?
Stretch'd along the deck like logs—
Bear a hand, you jolly tar, you!
Here's a rope's end for the dogs.
H * * muttering fearful curses,.
As the hatchway down he rolls;
Now his breakfast, now his verses,
Vomits forth—and damns our souls.
' Here's a stanza
On Braganza—
Help!'—'A couplet?'—'No, a cup
Of warm water—'
' What's the matter?'
' Zounds! my liver's coming up;
I shall not survive the racket
Of this brutal Lisbon Packet.'

5.

" Now at length we're off for Turkey,
Lord knows when we shall come back!
Breezes foul and tempests murky
May unship us in a crack.
But, since life at most a jest is,
As philosophers allow,
Still to laugh by far the best is,
Then laugh on—as I do now.
Laugh at all things,
Great and small things,
Sick or well, at sea or shore;
While we're quaffing,
Let's have laughing—
Who the devil cares for more?—
Some good wine! and who would lack it,
Ev'n on board the Lisbon Packet?

" BYRON."

On the 2d of July the packet sailed from Falmouth, and, after a favourable passage of four days and a half, the voyagers reached Lisbon, and took up their abode in that city*.

The following letters, from Lord Byron to his friend Mr. Hodgson, though written in his most light and schoolboy strain, will give some idea of the first impressions that his residence in Lisbon made upon him. Such letters, too, contrasted with the noble stanzas on Portugal in " Childe Harold," will show how various were the moods of his versatile mind, and what different aspects it could take when in repose or on the wing.

LETTER XXXVII.

TO MR. HODGSON.

"Lisbon, July 16th, 1809.

" Thus far have we pursued our route, and seen all sorts of marvellous sights, palaces, convents, &c.—which, being to be heard in my friend Hobhouse's forthcoming Book of Travels, I shall not anticipate by smuggling any account whatsoever to you in a private and clandestine manner. I must just observe that the village of Cintra in Estremadura is the most beautiful, perhaps, in the world.　*　*　*

" I am very happy here, because I loves oranges, and talk bad Latin to the monks, who understand it, as it is like their own,—and I goes

---

* Lord Byron used sometimes to mention a strange story, which the commander of the packet, Captain Kidd, related to him on the passage. This officer stated that, being asleep, one night, in his birth, he was awakened by the pressure of something heavy on his limbs, and, there being a faint light in the room, could see, as he thought, distinctly, the figure of his brother, who was, at that time, in the naval service in the East Indies, dressed in his uniform and stretched across the bed. Concluding it to be an illusion of the senses, he shut his eyes and made an effort to sleep. But still the same pressure continued, and still, as often as he ventured to take another look, he saw the figure lying across him in the same position. To add to the wonder, on putting his hand forth to touch this form, he found the uniform, in which it appeared to be dressed, dripping wet. On the entrance of one of his brother officers, to whom he called out in alarm, the apparition vanished; but in a few months after, he received the startling intelligence that on that night his brother had been drowned in the Indian seas. Of the supernatural character of this appearance, Captain Kidd himself did not appear to have the slightest doubt.

into society (with my pocket-pistols), and I swims in the Tagus all across at once, and I rides on an ass or a mule, and swears Portuguese, and have got a diarrhœa and bites from the mosquitoes. But what of that? Comfort must not be expected by folks that go a pleasuring.   *   *   *

"When the Portuguese are pertinacious, I say, 'Carracho!'—the great oath of the grandees, that very well supplies the place of 'Damme,' —and, when dissatisfied with my neighbour, I pronounce him 'Ambra di merdo.' With these two phrases, and a third, 'Avra Bouro,' which signifieth 'Get an ass,' I am universally understood to be a person of degree and a master of languages. How merrily we lives that travellers be!—if we had food and raiment. But, in sober sadness, any thing is better than England, and I am infinitely amused with my pilgrimage as far as it has gone.

"To-morrow we start to ride post near 400 miles as far as Gibraltar, where we embark for Melita and Byzantium. A letter to Malta will find me, or to be forwarded, if I am absent. Pray embrace the Drury and Dwyer and all the Ephesians you encounter. I am writing with Butler's donative pencil, which makes my bad hand worse. Excuse illegibility.   *   *   *

"Hodgson! send me the news, and the deaths and defeats and capital crimes and the misfortunes of one's friends; and let us hear of literary matters, and the controversies and the criticisms. All this will be pleasant—'Suave mari magno,' &c. Talking of that, I have been seasick, and sick of the sea. Adieu. Yours faithfully, &c."

LETTER XXXVIII.

TO MR. HODGSON.

"Gibraltar, August 6, 1809.

"I have just arrived at this place after a journey through Portugal, and a part of Spain, of nearly 500 miles. We left Lisbon and travelled on horseback * to Seville and Cadiz, and thence in the Hyperion frigate to Gibraltar. The horses are excellent—we rode seventy miles a day.

---

* The baggage and part of the servants were sent by sea to Gibraltar.

Eggs and wine and hard beds are all the accommodation we found, and, in such torrid weather, quite enough. My health is better than in England. * * *

" Seville is a fine town, and the Sierra Morena, part of which we crossed, a very sufficient mountain,—but damn description, it is always disgusting. Cadiz, sweet Cadiz!—it is the first spot in the creation. * * * The beauty of its streets and mansions is only excelled by the loveliness of its inhabitants. For, with all national prejudice, I must confess the women of Cadiz are as far superior to the English women in beauty as the Spaniards are inferior to the English in every quality that dignifies the name of man. * * * Just as I began to know the principal persons of the city, I was obliged to sail.

" You will not expect a long letter after my riding so far ' on hollow pampered jades of Asia.' Talking of Asia puts me in mind of Africa, which is within five miles of my present residence. I am going over before I go on to Constantinople.

" * * * Cadiz is a complete Cythera. Many of the grandees who have left Madrid during the troubles reside there, and I do believe it is the prettiest and cleanest town in Europe. London is filthy in the comparison. * * * The Spanish women are all alike, their education the same. The wife of a duke is, in information, as the wife of a peasant,—the wife of a peasant, in manner, equal to a duchess. Certainly, they are fascinating; but their minds have only one idea, and the business of their lives is intrigue. * * *

" I have seen Sir John Carr at Seville and Cadiz, and, like Swift's barber, have been down on my knees to beg he would not put me into black and white. Pray remember me to the Drurys and the Davies, and all of that stamp who are yet extant*. Send me a letter and news to Malta. My next epistle shall be from Mount Caucasus or Mount

---

* " This sort of passage," says Mr. Hodgson, in a note on his copy of this letter, " constantly occurs in his correspondence. Nor was his interest confined to mere remembrances and inquiries after health. Were it possible to state all he has done for numerous friends, he would appear amiable indeed. For myself, I am bound to acknowledge, in the fullest and warmest manner, his most generous and well-timed aid; and, were my poor friend Bland alive, he would as gladly bear the like testimony;—though I have most reason, of all men, to do so."

Sion. I shall return to Spain before I see England, for I am enamoured of the country. Adieu, and believe me, &c."

In a letter to Mrs. Byron, dated a few days later, from Gibraltar, he recapitulates the same account of his progress, only dwelling rather more diffusely on some of the details. Thus, of Cintra and Mafra,—" To make amends for this *, the village of Cintra, about fifteen miles from the capital, is, perhaps in every respect, the most delightful in Europe; it contains beauties of every description, natural and artificial. Palaces and gardens rising in the midst of rocks, cataracts, and precipices; convents on stupendous heights—a distant view of the sea and the Tagus; and, besides (though that is a secondary consideration), is remarkable as the scene of Sir H. D.'s Convention †. It unites in itself all the wildness of the western highlands, with the verdure of the south of France. Near this place, about ten miles to the right, is the palace of Mafra, the boast of Portugal, as it might be of any country, in point of magnificence without elegance. There is a convent annexed; the monks, who possess large revenues, are courteous enough, and understand Latin, so that we had a long conversation: they have a large library, and asked me if the *English* had *any books* in their country."

An adventure which he met with at Seville, characteristic both of the country and of himself, is thus described in the same letter to Mrs. Byron:—

" We lodged in the house of two Spanish unmarried ladies, who possess *six* houses in Seville, and gave me a curious specimen of Spanish manners. They are women of character, and the eldest a fine woman, the youngest pretty, but not so good a figure as Donna Josepha. The freedom of manner, which is general here, astonished me not a little; and in the course of further observation I find that reserve is not the characteristic of the Spanish belles, who are, in general, very handsome,

---

* The filthiness of Lisbon and its inhabitants.

† Colonel Napier, in a note in his able History of the Peninsular War, notices the mistake into which Lord Byron and others were led on this subject;—the signature of the Convention, as well as all the other proceedings connected with it, having taken place at a distance of thirty miles from Cintra.

with large black eyes, and very fine forms. The eldest honoured your *unworthy* son with very particular attention, embracing him with great tenderness at parting (I was there but three days), after cutting off a lock of his hair, and presenting him with one of her own, about three feet in length, which I send, and beg you will retain till my return Her last words were, ' Adios, tu hermoso! me gusto mucho.'—' Adieu, you pretty fellow, you please me much.' She offered a share of her apartment, which my *virtue* induced me to decline; she laughed, and said I had some English ' amante' (lover), and added that she was going to be married to an officer in the Spanish army."

Among the beauties of Cadiz, his imagination, dazzled by the attractions of the many, was on the point, it would appear from the following, of being fixed by *one*:—

" Cadiz, sweet Cadiz, is the most delightful town I ever beheld, very different from our English cities in every respect, except cleanliness (and it is as clean as London), but still beautiful and full of the finest women in Spain, the Cadiz belles being the Lancashire witches of their land. Just as I was introduced and began to like the grandees, I was forced to leave it for this cursed place; but before I return to England I will visit it again.

" The night before I left it, I sat in the box at the Opera with Admiral ***'s family, an aged wife and a fine daughter, Sennorita *** The girl is very pretty, in the Spanish style; in my opinion, by no means inferior to the English in charms, and certainly superior in fascination. Long, black hair, dark languishing eyes, clear olive complexions, and forms more graceful in motion than can be conceived by an Englishman used to the drowsy, listless air of his countrywomen, added to the most becoming dress, and, at the same time, the most decent in the world, render a Spanish beauty irresistible.

" Miss *** and her little brother understood a little French, and, after regretting my ignorance of the Spanish, she proposed to become my preceptress in that language. I could only reply by a low bow, and express my regret that I quitted Cadiz too soon to permit me to make the progress which would doubtless attend my studies under so charming a directress. I was standing at the back of the box, which resembles our Opera boxes (the theatre is large, and finely decorated, the music admirable), in the manner in which Englishmen generally adopt, for fear of incommoding the ladies in front, when this fair Spaniard dispossessed an old woman (an aunt or a duenna) of her chair, and commanded me to be seated next herself, at a tolerable distance from her mamma. At the close of the performance I withdrew, and was lounging with a party of men in the passage, when, *en passant*, the lady turned round and called me, and I had the honour of attending her to the admiral's mansion. I have an invitation on my return to Cadiz, which I shall accept, if I re-pass through the country on my return from Asia."

To these adventures, or rather glimpses of adventures, which he met with in his hasty passage through Spain, he adverted, I recollect, briefly, in the early part of his " Memoranda;" and it was the younger, I think, of his fair hostesses at Seville, whom he there described himself as having made earnest love to, with the help of a dictionary. " For some time," he said, " I went on prosperously both as a linguist and a lover*, till, at length, the lady took a fancy to a ring which I wore, and set her heart on my giving it to her, as a pledge of my sincerity. This, however, could not be;—any thing but the ring, I declared, was at her service, and much more than its value,—but the ring itself I had made a vow never to give away." The young Spaniard grew angry as the contention went on, and it was not long before the lover became angry also; till, at length, the affair ended by their separating unsuccessful on both sides. " Soon after this," said he, " I sailed for Malta, and there parted with both my heart and ring."

In the letter from Gibraltar, just cited, he adds—" I am going over to Africa to-morrow; it is only six miles from this fortress. My next stage is Cagliari in Sardinia, where I shall be presented to his majesty. I have a most superb uniform as a court-dress, indispensable in tra-velling." His plan of visiting Africa was, however, relinquished. After a short stay at Gibraltar, during which he dined one day with Lady Westmoreland, and another with General Castanos, he, on the 19th of

---

* We find an allusion to this incident in Don Juan :—

> " 'Tis pleasing to be school'd in a strange tongue
> By female lips and eyes—that is, I mean,
> When both the teacher and the taught are young,
> As was the case, at least, where I have been," &c. &c.

August, took his departure for Malta in the packet, having first sent Joe Murray and young Rushton back to England,—the latter being unable, from ill health, to accompany him any further. "Pray," he says to his mother, "show the lad every kindness, as he is my great favourite *."

He also wrote a letter to the father of the boy, which gives so favourable an impression of his thoughtfulness and kindliness that I have much pleasure in being enabled to introduce it here.

LETTER XXXIX.

TO MR. RUSHTON.

"Gibraltar, August 15th, 1809.

"MR. RUSHTON,

"I have sent Robert home with Mr. Murray, because the country which I am about to travel through is in a state which renders it unsafe, particularly for one so young. I allow you to deduct five-and-twenty pounds a year for his education for three years, provided I do not return before that time, and I desire he may be considered as in my service. Let every care be taken of him, and let him be sent to school. In case of my death I have provided enough in my will to render him independent. He has behaved extremely well, and has travelled a great deal for the time of his absence. Deduct the expense of his education from your rent.

"BYRON."

It was the fate of Lord Byron, throughout life, to meet, wherever he went, with persons who, by some tinge of the extraordinary in their own fates or characters, were prepared to enter, at once, into full sympathy with his; and to this attraction, by which he drew towards him all strange and eccentric spirits, he owed some of the most agreeable connexions of his life, as well as some of the most troublesome. Of the

* The postscript to this letter is as follows:—

"P. S. So Lord G. is married to a rustic! Well done! If I wed, I will bring you home a Sultana, with half a dozen cities for a dowry, and reconcile you to an Ottoman daughter-in-law with a bushel of pearls, not larger than ostrich eggs, or smaller than walnuts."

former description was an intimacy which he now cultivated during his short sojourn at Malta. The lady with whom he formed this acquaintance was the same addressed by him under the name of "Florence" in Childe Harold, and in a letter to his mother from Malta, he thus describes her in prose:—"This letter is committed to the charge of a very extraordinary woman, whom you have doubtless heard of, Mrs. S* S*, of whose escape the Marquis de Salvo published a narrative a few years ago. She has since been shipwrecked, and her life has been from its commencement so fertile in remarkable incidents, that in a romance they would appear improbable. She was born at Constantinople, where her father, Baron H*, was Austrian ambassador; married unhappily, yet has never been impeached in point of character; excited the vengeance of Buonaparte by a part in some conspiracy; several times risked her life; and is not yet twenty-five. She is here on her way to England, to join her husband, being obliged to leave Trieste, where she was paying a visit to her mother, by the approach of the French, and embarks soon in a ship of war. Since my arrival here, I have had scarcely any other companion. I have found her very pretty, very accomplished, and extremely eccentric. Buonaparte is even now so incensed against her, that her life would be in some danger if she were taken prisoner a second time."

The tone in which he addresses this fair heroine in Childe Harold is (consistently with the above dispassionate account of her) that of the purest admiration and interest, unwarmed by any more ardent sentiment:—

> " Sweet Florence ! could another ever share
>   This wayward, loveless heart, it would be thine:
>   But, check'd by every tie, I may not dare
>   To cast a worthless offering at thy shrine,
> Nor ask so dear a breast to feel one pang for mine.
>
> " Thus Harold deem'd, as on that lady's eye
>   He look'd, and met its beam without a thought,
>   Save admiration, glancing harmless by," &c. &c.

In one so imaginative as Lord Byron, who, while he infused so much of his life into his poetry, mingled also not a little of poetry with his life, it is difficult, in unravelling the texture of his feelings, to distinguish at all times between the fanciful and the real. His description here, for instance, of the unmoved and "loveless heart," with which he contemplated even the charms of this attractive person, is wholly at variance, not only with the anecdote from his " Memoranda" which I have recalled, but with the statements in many of his subsequent letters, and, above all, with one of the most graceful of his lesser poems, purporting to be addressed to this same lady during a thunder-storm on his road to Zitza*.

Notwithstanding, however, these counter evidences, I am much disposed to believe that the representation of the state of his heart in the foregoing extract from Childe Harold may be regarded as the true one; and that the notion of his being in love was but a dream that sprung up afterwards, when the image of the fair Florence had become idealized in his fancy, and every remembrance of their pleasant hours among " Calypso's isles" came invested by his imagination with the warm aspect of love. It will be recollected that to the chilled and sated feelings which early indulgence, and almost as early disenchantment, had left behind, he attributes in these verses the calm and passionless regard, with which even attractions like those of Florence were viewed by him. That such was actually his distaste, at this period, to all real objects of love or passion (however his fancy could call up creatures of its own to worship)

* The following stanzas from this little poem have a music in them, which, independently of all meaning, is enchanting:—

> " And since I now remember thee
> In darkness and in dread,
> As in those hours of revelry,
> Which mirth and music sped;
>
> " Do thou, amidst the fair white walls,
> If Cadiz yet be free,
> At times, from out her latticed halls,
> Look o'er the dark blue sea;
>
> " Then think upon Calypso's isles,
> Endear'd by days gone by;
> To others give a thousand smiles,
> To me a single sigh," &c. &c.

there is every reason to believe; and the same morbid indifference to those pleasures he had once so ardently pursued still continued to be professed by him on his return to England. No anchoret, indeed, could claim for himself much more apathy towards all such allurements than he did at that period. But to be *thus* saved from temptation was a dear-bought safety, and, at the age of three-and-twenty, satiety and disgust are but melancholy substitutes for virtue.

While at Malta, in consequence of some trifling misunderstanding, he was on the point of fighting a duel with an officer of the Staff of General Oakes. To this circumstance we shall find him, in some of his subsequent letters, alluding; and I have more than once heard the gentleman who acted as his adviser on the occasion, speak of the cool and manly courage with which he conducted himself through the whole affair. The meeting being appointed for a very early hour in the morning, his companion had to awake him from a sound sleep; but, on their arrival at the place of rendezvous on the sea-shore, the adverse party, from some mistake in the arrangements, was not forthcoming. Though their baggage was already on board the brig that was to convey them to Albania, Lord Byron determined to give his antagonist the chances of, at least, another hour, and for nearly that space of time his friend and he sauntered about the shore. At length an officer, deputed by his expected adversary, arrived, and not only accounted satisfactorily for the delay that had taken place, but made every other explanation, with respect to the supposed offence, that the two friends could require.

The brig of war, in which they sailed, having been ordered to convoy a fleet of small merchant-men to Patras and Prevesa, they remained, for two or three days, at anchor off the former place. From thence, proceeding to their ultimate destination, and catching a sunset view of Missolonghi in their way, they landed on the 29th of September, at Prevesa.

The route which Lord Byron now took through Albania, as well as those subsequent journeys through other parts of Turkey, which he performed in company with his friend Mr. Hobhouse, may be traced, by such as are desirous of details on the subject, in the account which the latter gentleman has given of his travels;—an account which, interesting from its own excellence in every merit that should adorn such a work, becomes still more so from the feeling that Lord Byron is, as it were, present through its pages, and that we there follow his first youthful footsteps into the land, with whose name he has intertwined his own for ever. As I am enabled, however, by the letters of the noble poet to his mother, as well as by others, still more curious, which are now for the first time published, to give his own rapid and lively sketches of his wanderings, I shall content myself, after this general reference to the volume of Mr. Hobhouse, with such occasional extracts from its pages as may throw light upon the letters of his friend.

LETTER XL.

TO MRS. BYRON.

" Prevesa, November 12, 1809.

" MY DEAR MOTHER,

" I have now been some time in Turkey: this place is on the coast, but I have traversed the interior of the province of Albania on a visit to the Pacha. I left Malta in the Spider, a brig of war, on the 21st of September, and arrived in eight days at Prevesa. I thence have been about 150 miles, as far as Tepaleen, his highness's country palace, where I stayed three days. The name of the Pacha is *Ali*, and he is considered a man of the first abilities: he governs the whole of Albania (the ancient Illyricum), Epirus, and part of Macedonia. His son, Vely Pacha, to whom he has given me letters, governs the Morea, and has great influence in Egypt; in short, he is one of the most powerful men in the Ottoman empire. When I reached Yanina, the capital, after a journey of three days over the mountains, through a country of the most picturesque beauty, I found that Ali Pacha was with his army in Illyricum, besieging Ibrahim Pacha in the castle of Berat. He had heard that an Englishman of rank was in his dominions, and had left orders in Yanina with the commandant to provide a house, and supply me with every kind of necessary *gratis;* and, though I have been allowed to make presents to the slaves, &c., I have not been permitted to pay for a single article of household consumption.

" I rode out on the vizier's horses, and saw the palaces of himself

and grandsons: they are splendid, but too much ornamented with sill
and gold. I then went over the mountains through *Zitza*, a village with
a Greek monastery (where I slept on my return), in the most beautiful
situation (always excepting Cintra, in Portugal) I ever beheld. In nine
days I reached Tepaleen. Our journey was much prolonged by the
torrents that had fallen from the mountains, and intersected the roads.
I shall never forget the singular scene* on entering Tepaleen at five in

* The following is Mr. Hobhouse's less embellished description of this scene:—" The
court at Tepellene, which was enclosed on two sides by the palace, and on the other two sides
by a high wall, presented us, at our first entrance, with a sight something like what we might
have, perhaps, beheld some hundred years ago in the castle-yard of a great feudal lord.
Soldiers, with their arms piled against the wall near them, were assembled in different parts of
the square: some of them pacing slowly backwards and forwards, and others sitting on the
ground in groups. Several horses, completely caparisoned, were leading about, whilst others
were neighing under the hands of the grooms. In the part farthest from the dwelling, preparations were making for the feast of the night; and several kids and sheep were being
dressed by cooks who were themselves half armed. Every thing wore a most martial look,
though not exactly in the style of the head-quarters of a christian general; for many of the
soldiers were in the most common dress, without shoes, and having more wildness in their air
and manner than the Albanians we had before seen."

On comparing this description, which is itself sufficiently striking, with those which Lord
Byron has given of the same scene, both in the letter to his mother, and in the Second Canto
of Childe Harold, we gain some insight into the process by which imagination elevates, without
falsifying, reality, and facts become brightened and refined into poetry. Ascending from the
representation drawn faithfully on the spot by the traveller, to the more fanciful arrangement
of the same materials in the letter of the poet, we at length, by one step more, arrive at that
consummate, idealized picture, the result of both memory and invention combined, which in
the following splendid stanzas is presented to us:

> " Amidst no common pomp the despot sate,
> 　While busy preparation shook the court,
> 　Slaves, eunuchs, soldiers, guests, and santons wait;
> 　Within, a palace, and without, a fort:
> Here men of every clime appear to make resort.

> " Richly caparison'd, a ready row
> 　Of armed horse, and many a warlike store,
> 　Circled the wide extending court below;
> 　Above, strange groups adorn'd the corridore;
> 　And oft-times through the area's echoing door
> 　Some high-capp'd Tartar spurr'd his steed away:
> 　The Turk, the Greek, the Albanian, and the Moor,
> 　Here mingled in their many-hued array,
> While the deep war-drum's sound announced the close of day.

the afternoon, as the sun was going down. It brought to my mind (with some change of *dress*, however) Scott's description of Branksome Castle in his *Lay*, and the feudal system. The Albanians, in their dresses (the most magnificent in the world, consisting of a long *white kilt*, gold-worked cloak, crimson velvet gold-laced jacket and waistcoat, silver-mounted pistols and daggers), the Tartars with their high caps, the Turks in their vast pelisses and turbans, the soldiers and black slaves with the horses, the former in groups in an immense large open gallery in front of the palace, the latter placed in a kind of cloister below it, two hundred steeds ready caparisoned to move in a moment, couriers entering or passing out with despatches, the kettle-drums beating, boys calling the hour from the minaret of the mosque, altogether, with the singular appearance of the building itself, formed a new and delightful spectacle to a stranger. I was conducted to a very handsome apartment, and my health inquired after by the vizier's secretary, ' à-la-mode Turque!'

" The next day I was introduced to Ali Pacha. I was dressed in a full suit of staff uniform, with a very magnificent sabre, &c. The vizier received me in a large room paved with marble; a fountain was playing in the centre; the apartment was surrounded by scarlet ottomans. He received me standing, a wonderful compliment from a Mussulman, and

" The wild Albanian kirtled to his knee,
　　With shawl-girt head and ornamented gun,
　　And gold-embroider'd garments, fair to see;
　　·The crimson-scarfed men of Macedon;
　　The Delhi with his cap of terror on,
　　And crooked glaive; the lively, supple Greek;
　　And swarthy Nubia's mutilated son;
　　The bearded Turk that rarely deigns to speak,
Master of all around, too potent to be meek,

" Are mix'd conspicuous: some recline in groups,
　　Scanning the motley scene that varies round;
　　There some grave Moslem to devotion stoops,
　　And some that smoke, and some that play, are found;
　　Here the Albanian proudly treads the ground;
　　Half whispering there the Greek is heard to prate;
　　Hark! from the mosque the nightly solemn sound,
　　The Muezzin's call doth shake the minaret,
' There is no god but God!—to prayer—lo! God is great!' "
CHILDE HAROLD, CANTO II.

made me sit down on his right hand. I have a Greek interpreter for general use, but a physician of Ali's, named Femlario, who understands Latin, acted for me on this occasion. His first question was, why, at so early an age, I left my country?—(the Turks have no idea of travelling for amusement). He then said, the English minister, Captain Leake, had told him I was of a great family, and desired his respects to my mother; which I now, in the name of Ali Pacha, present to you. He said he was certain I was a man of birth, because I had small ears, curling hair, and little white hands*, and expressed himself pleased with my appearance and garb. He told me to consider him as a father whilst I was in Turkey, and said he looked on me as his son. Indeed, he treated me like a child, sending me almonds and sugared sherbet, fruit and sweetmeats, twenty times a day. He begged me to visit him often, and at night, when he was at leisure. I then, after coffee and pipes, retired for the first time. I saw him thrice afterwards. It is singular, that the Turks, who have no hereditary dignities, and few great families, except the Sultans, pay so much respect to birth; for I found my pedigree more regarded than my title†.

* * * *

"To-day I saw the remains of the town of Actium, near which Antony lost the world, in a small bay, where two frigates could hardly manœuvre: a broken wall is the sole remnant. On another part of the gulf stand the ruins of Nicopolis, built by Augustus in honour of his victory. Last night I was at a Greek marriage; but this and a thousand things more I have neither time nor space to describe.

"I am going to-morrow, with a guard of fifty men, to Patras in the Morea, and thence to Athens, where I shall winter. Two days ago I was

---

* In the shape of the hands, as a mark of high birth, Lord Byron himself had as implicit faith as the Pacha: see his note on the line, "Though on more *thorough-bred* or fairer fingers," in Don Juan.

† A few sentences are here and elsewhere omitted, as having no reference to Lord Byron himself, but merely containing some particulars relating to Ali and his grandsons, which may be found in various books of travels.

Ali had not forgotten his noble guest when Dr. Holland, a few years after, visited Albania: —" I mentioned to him, generally (says this intelligent traveller), Lord Byron's poetical description of Albania, the interest it had excited in England, and Mr. Hobhouse's intended publication of his travels in the same country. He seemed pleased with these circumstances, and stated his recollections of Lord Byron."

nearly lost in a Turkish ship of war, owing to the ignorance of the captain and crew, though the storm was not violent. Fletcher yelled after his wife, the Greeks called on all the saints, the Mussulmans on Alla; the captain burst into tears and ran below deck, telling us to call on God; the sails were split, the main-yard shivered, the wind blowing fresh, the night setting in, and all our chance was to make Corfu, which is in possession of the French, or (as Fletcher pathetically termed it) 'a watery grave.' I did what I could to console Fletcher, but finding him incorrigible, wrapped myself up in my Albanian capote (an immense cloak), and lay down on deck to wait the worst*. I have learnt to philosophize in my travels, and if I had not, complaint was useless. Luckily the wind abated, and only drove us on the coast of Suli, on the main land, where we landed, and proceeded, by the help of the natives, to Prevesa again; but I shall not trust Turkish sailors in future, though the Pacha had ordered one of his own galliots to take me to Patras. I am therefore going as far as Missolonghi by land, and there have only to cross a small gulf to get to Patras.

" Fletcher's next epistle will be full of marvels: we were one night lost for nine hours in the mountains in a thunder-storm †, and since nearly wrecked. In both cases, Fletcher was sorely bewildered, from appre-

---

* I have heard the poet's fellow-traveller describe this remarkable instance of his coolness and courage even still more strikingly than it is here stated by himself. Finding that, from his lameness, he was unable to be of any service in the exertions which their very serious danger called for, after a laugh or two at the panic of his valet, he not only wrapped himself up and lay down, in the manner here mentioned, but, when their difficulties were surmounted, was found fast asleep.

† In the route from Ioannina to Zitza, Mr. Hobhouse and the Secretary of Ali, accompanied by one of the servants, had rode on before the rest of the party, and arrived at the village just as the evening set in. After describing the sort of hovel in which they were to take up their quarters for the night, Mr. Hobhouse thus continues:—" Vasilly was despatched into the village to procure eggs and fowls, that would be ready, as we thought, by the arrival of the second party. But an hour passed away and no one appeared. It was seven o'clock, and the storm had increased to a fury I had never before, and, indeed, have never since, seen equalled. The roof of our hovel shook under the clattering torrents and gusts of wind. The thunder roared, as it seemed, without any intermission; for the echoes of one peal had not ceased to roll in the mountains, before another tremendous crash burst over our heads; whilst the plains and the distant hills (visible through the cracks of the cabin) appeared in a perpetual blaze. The tempest was altogether terrific and worthy of the Grecian Jove; and the peasants, no less

hensions of famine and banditti in the first, and drowning in the second instance.   His eyes were a little hurt by the lightning, or crying (I don' know which), but are now recovered.   When you write, address to me at Mr. Strané's, English consul, Patras, Morea.

" I could tell you I know not how many incidents that I think would amuse you, but they crowd on my mind as much as they would swell my paper, and I can neither arrange them in the one, nor put them down on the other, except in the greatest confusion.   I like the Albanians much; they are not all Turks; some tribes are Christians.   But their religion makes little difference in their manner or conduct.   They are esteemed the best troops in the Turkish service.   I lived on my route

religious than their ancestors, confessed their alarm. The women wept, and the men, calling on the name of God, crossed themselves at every repeated peal.

" We were very uneasy that the party did not arrive; but the Secretary assured me that the guides knew every part of the country, as did also his own servant, who was with them, and that they had certainly taken shelter in a village at an hour's distance. Not being satisfied with the conjecture, I ordered fires to be lighted on the hill above the village, and some musquets to be discharged: this was at eleven o'clock, and the storm had not abated. I lay down in my great coat; but all sleeping was out of the question, as any pauses in the tempest were filled up by the barking of the dogs, and the shouting of the shepherds in the neighbouring mountains.

" A little after midnight, a man, panting and pale, and drenched with rain, rushed into the room, and, between crying and roaring, with a profusion of action, communicated something to the Secretary, of which I understood only—that they had all fallen down. I learnt, however, that no accident had happened, except the falling of the luggage horses, and losing their way, and that they were now waiting for fresh horses and guides. Ten were immediately sent to them, together with several men with pine torches; but it was not till two o'clock in the morning that we heard they were approaching, and my Friend, with the priest and the servants, did not enter our hut before three.

" I now learnt from him that they had lost their way from the commencement of the storm, when not above three miles from the village; and that, after wandering up and down in total ignorance of their position, they had, at last, stopped near some Turkish tombstones and a torrent which they saw by the flashes of lightning. They had been thus exposed for nine hours; and the guides, so far from assisting them, only augmented the confusion, by running away, after being threatened with death by George the Dragoman, who, in an agony of rage and fear, and without giving any warning, fired off both his pistols, and drew from the English servant an involuntary scream of horror; for he fancied they were beset by robbers.

" I had not, as you have seen, witnessed the distressing part of this adventure myself; but from the lively picture drawn of it by my Friend, and from the exaggerated descriptions of George, I fancied myself a good judge of the whole situation, and should consider this to have been one of the most considerable of the few adventures that befel either of us during our tour in Turkey.   It was long before we ceased to talk of the thunder-storm in the plain of Zitza."

two days at once, and three days again, in a barrack at Salora, and never found soldiers so tolerable, though I have been in the garrisons of Gibraltar and Malta, and seen Spanish, French, Sicilian, and British troops in abundance. I have had nothing stolen, and was always welcome to their provision and milk. Not a week ago an Albanian chief (every village has its chief, who is called Primate), after helping us out of the Turkish galley in her distress, feeding us, and lodging my suite, consisting of Fletcher, a Greek, two Athenians, a Greek priest, and my companion, Mr. Hobhouse, refused any compensation but a written paper stating that I was well received; and when I pressed him to accept a few sequins, ' No,' he replied; ' I wish you to love me, not to pay me.' These are his words.

" It is astonishing how far money goes in this country. While I was in the capital, I had nothing to pay, by the vizier's order; but since, though I have generally had sixteen horses, and generally six or seven men, the expense has not been *half* as much as staying only three weeks in Malta, though Sir A. Ball, the governor, gave me a house for nothing, and I had only *one servant.* By the by, I expect H * * to remit regularly; for I am not about to stay in this province for ever. Let him write to me at Mr. Strané's, English consul, Patras. The fact is, the fertility of the plains is wonderful, and specie is scarce, which makes this remarkable cheapness. I am going to Athens to study modern Greek, which differs much from the ancient, though radically similar. I have no desire to return to England, nor shall I, unless compelled by absolute want, and H * *'s neglect; but I shall not enter into Asia for a year or two, as I have much to see in Greece, and I may perhaps cross into Africa, at least the Egyptian part. Fletcher, like all Englishmen, is very much dissatisfied, though a little reconciled to the Turks by a present of eighty piastres from the vizier, which, if you consider every thing, and the value of specie here, is nearly worth ten guineas English. He has suffered nothing but from cold, heat, and vermin, which those who lie in cottages and cross mountains in a cold country must undergo, and of which I have equally partaken with himself; but he is not valiant, and is afraid of robbers and tempests. I have no one to be remembered

to in England, and wish to hear nothing from it, but that you are well
and a letter or two on business from H**, whom you may tell to write
I will write when I can, and beg you to believe me

"Your affectionate son,

"BYRON."

About the middle of November, the young traveller took his
departure from Prevesa (the place where the foregoing letter was
written), and proceeded, attended by his guard of fifty Albanians*,
through Acarnania and Ætolia, towards the Morea.

> "And therefore did he take a trusty band
> To traverse Acarnania's forest wide,
> In war well season'd, and with labours tann'd,
> Till he did greet white Achelous' tide,
> And from his further bank Ætolia's wolds espied."

CHILDE HAROLD, CANTO II.

His description of the night-scene at Utraikey (a small place situated
in one of the bays of the Gulf of Arta) is, no doubt, vividly in the
recollection of every reader of these pages; nor will it diminish their
enjoyment of the wild beauties of that picture to be made acquainted
with the real circumstances on which it was founded, in the following
animated details of the same scene by his fellow-traveller :—

"In the evening the gates were secured, and preparations were
made for feeding our Albanians. A goat was killed and roasted whole,
and four fires were kindled in the yard, round which the soldiers seated
themselves in parties. After eating and drinking, the greater part of
them assembled round the largest of the fires, and whilst ourselves and
the elders of the party were seated on the ground, danced round the
blaze to their own songs, in the manner before described, but with an
astonishing energy. All their songs were relations of some robbing
exploits. One of them, which detained them more than an hour, began

---

* Mr. Hobhouse, I think, makes the number of this guard but thirty-seven, and Lord
Byron, in a subsequent letter, rates them at forty.

thus—' When we set out from Parga there were sixty of us:—then came the burden of the verse,

> ' Robbers all at Parga!
> Robbers all at Parga!'
>
> ' Κλεφτεις ποτε Παργα!
> Κλεφτεις ποτε Παργα!'

And as they roared out this stave they whirled round the fire, dropped and rebounded from their knees, and again whirled round as the chorus was again repeated.   The rippling of the waves upon the pebbly margin where we were seated filled up the pauses of the song with a milder and not more monotonous music.   The night was very dark, but by the flashes of the fires we caught a glimpse of the woods, the rocks, and the lake, which, together with the wild appearance of the dancers, presented us with a scene that would have made a fine picture in the hands of such an artist as the author of the Mysteries of Udolpho."

Having traversed Acarnania, the travellers passed to the Ætolian side of the Achelous, and on the 21st of November reached Missolonghi. And here,—it is impossible not to pause, and send a mournful thought forward to the visit which, fifteen years after, he paid to this same spot, —when, in the full meridian both of his age and fame, he came to lay down his life as the champion of that land, through which he now wandered a stripling and a stranger.   Could some Spirit have here revealed to him the events of that interval,—have shown him, on the one side, the triumphs that awaited him, the power his varied genius would acquire over all hearts, alike to elevate or depress, to darken or illuminate them,—and then place, on the other side, all the penalties of this gift, the waste and wear of the heart through the imagination, the havoc of that perpetual fire within, which, while it dazzles others, consumes the possessor,—the invidiousness of such an elevation in the eyes of mankind, and the revenge they take on him who compels them to look up to it,—*would* he, it may be asked, have welcomed glory on such conditions? would he not rather have felt that the purchase was too costly, and that such warfare with an ungrateful world, while living, would be ill recompensed even by the immortality it might award him afterwards?

At Missolonghi he dismissed his whole band of Albanians, with the exception of one, named Dervish, whom he took into his service, and who, with Basilius, the attendant allotted him by Ali Pacha, continued with him during the remainder of his stay in the East. After a residence of near a fortnight at Patras, he next directed his course to Vostizza,— on approaching which town the snowy peak of Parnassus, towering on the other side of the Gulf, first broke on his eyes; and, in two days after, among the sacred hollows of Delphi, the stanzas, with which that vision had inspired him, were written*.

It was at this time that, in riding along the sides of Parnassus, he saw an unusually large flight of eagles in the air,—a phenomenon which seems to have affected his imagination with a sort of poetical superstition, as he, more than once, recurs to the circumstance in his journals. Thus, "Going to the fountain of Delphi (Castri) in 1809, I saw a flight of twelve eagles (H. says they were vultures—at least, in conversation), and I seized the omen. On the day before, I composed the lines to Parnassus (in Childe Harold), and, on beholding the birds, had a hope that Apollo had accepted my homage. I have at least had the name and fame of a poet during the poetical part of life (from twenty to thirty); —whether it will *last* is another matter."

He has also, in reference to this journey from Patras, related a little anecdote of his own sportsmanship, which, by all *but* sportsmen, will be thought creditable to his humanity. "The last bird I ever fired at was an eaglet, on the shore of the Gulf of Lepanto, near Vostizza. It was only wounded, and I tried to save it,—the eye was so bright. But it pined, and died in a few days; and I never did since, and never will, attempt the death of another bird."

* " Oh, thou Parnassus! whom I now survey,
　　Not in the phrensy of a dreamer's eye,
　　Not in the fabled landscape of a lay,
　　But soaring snow-clad through thy native sky,
　　In the wild pomp of mountain majesty!"

CHILDE HAROLD, CANTO I.

To a traveller in Greece, there are few things more remarkable than the diminutive extent of those countries, which have filled such a wide space in fame. "A man might very easily," says Mr. Hobhouse, "at a moderate pace, ride from Livadia to Thebes and back again between breakfast and dinner; and the tour of all Bœotia might certainly be made in two days without baggage." Having visited, within a very short space of time, the fountains of Memory and Oblivion at Livadia, and the haunts of the Ismenian Apollo at Thebes, the travellers at length turned towards Athens, the city of their dreams, and, after crossing Mount Cithæron, arrived in sight of the ruins of Phyle, on the evening of Christmas-day, 1809.

Though the poet has left, in his own verses, an ever-during testimony of the enthusiasm with which he now contemplated the scenes around him, it is not difficult to conceive that, to superficial observers, Lord Byron at Athens might have appeared an untouched spectator of much that throws ordinary travellers into, at least, verbal raptures. For pretenders of every sort, whether in taste or morals, he entertained, at all times, the most profound contempt; and if, frequently, his real feelings of admiration disguised themselves under an affected tone of indifference and mockery, it was out of pure hostility to the cant of those, who, he well knew, praised without any feeling at all. It must be owned, too, that while he thus justly despised the raptures of the common herd of travellers, there were some pursuits, even of the intelligent and tasteful, in which he took but very little interest. With the antiquarian and connoisseur his sympathies were few and feeble;—"I am not a collector," he says, in one of his notes on Childe Harold, "nor an admirer of collections." For antiquities, indeed, unassociated with high names and deeds, he had no value whatever; and of works of art he was content to admire the general effect, without professing, or aiming at, any knowledge of the details. It was to nature, in her lonely scenes of grandeur and beauty, or, as at Athens, shining, unchanged, among the ruins of glory and of art, that the true, fervid homage of his whole soul was paid. In the few notices of his travels, appended to Childe Harold, we find the sites and scenery of the different places he visited far more fondly dwelt upon than their classic or historical associations. To the valley of Zitza

he reverts, both in prose and verse, with a much warmer recollection tha
to Delphi or the Troad; and the plain of Athens itself is chiefly praise
by him as "a more glorious prospect than even Cintra or Istambol.
Where, indeed, could Nature assert such claims to his worship as i
scenes like these, where he beheld her blooming, in indestructible beauty
amid the wreck of all that Man deems most worthy of duration. "Humar
institutions," says Harris, "perish, but Nature is permanent:"—or, a
Lord Byron has amplified this thought* in one of his most splendid
passages :—

> " Yet are thy skies as blue, thy crags as wild;
> Sweet are thy groves, and verdant are thy fields,
> Thine olive ripe as when Minerva smiled,
> And still his honied wealth Hymettus yields;
> There the blithe bee his fragrant fortress builds,
> The free-born wanderer of thy mountain-air;
> Apollo still thy long, long summer gilds,
> Still in his beam Mendeli's marbles glare;
> Art, Glory, Freedom fail, but Nature still is fair."
>
> CHILDE HAROLD, CANTO II.

At Athens, on this his first visit, he made a stay of between two and
three months, not a day of which he let pass without employing some
of its hours in visiting the grand monuments of ancient genius around
him, and calling up the spirit of other times among their ruins. He made
frequently, too, excursions to different parts of Attica, and it was in one
of his visits to Cape Colonna, at this time, that he was near being seized
by a party of Mainotes, who were lying hid in the caves under the cliff
of Minerva Sunias. These pirates, it appears, were only deterred from
attacking him (as a Greek, who was then their prisoner, informed him
afterwards) by a supposition that the two Albanians, whom they saw
attending him, were but part of a complete guard he had at hand.

In addition to all the magic of its names and scenes, the city of

---

* The passage of Harris, indeed, contains the pith of the whole stanza:—" Notwithstanding the various fortune of Athens, as a city, Attica is still famous for olives, and Mount
Hymettus for honey. Human institutions perish, but Nature is permanent."—*Philolog.
Inquiries*. I recollect having once pointed out this coincidence to Lord Byron, but he assured
me that he had never read this work of Harris.

Minerva possessed another sort of attraction for the poet, to which, wherever he went, his heart, or rather imagination, was but too sensible. His pretty song, " Maid of Athens, ere we part," is said to have been addressed to the eldest daughter of the Greek lady at whose house he lodged; and that the fair Athenian, when he composed these verses, may have been the tenant, for the time being, of his fancy, is highly possible.   Theodora Macri, his hostess, was the widow of the late English vice-consul, and derived a livelihood from letting, chiefly to English travellers, the apartments which Lord Byron and his friend now occupied, and of which the latter gentleman gives us the following description: —" Our lodgings consisted of a sitting-room and two bed-rooms, opening into a court-yard where there were five or six lemon-trees, from which, during our residence in the place, was plucked the fruit that seasoned the pilaf, and other national dishes served up at our frugal table."

The fame of an illustrious poet is not confined to his own person and writings, but imparts a share of its splendour to whatever has been, even remotely, connected with him; and not only ennobles the objects of his friendships, his loves, and even his likings, but on every spot where he has sojourned, through life, leaves traces of its light that do not easily pass away.   Little did the Maid of Athens, while listening innocently to the compliments of the young Englishman, foresee that a day would come, when he should make her name and home so celebrated, that travellers, on their return from Greece, would find few things more interesting to their hearers, than such details of herself and her family as the following :—

" Our servant, who had gone before to procure accommodation, met us at the gate and conducted us to Theodora Macri, the Consulina's, where we at present live.   This lady is the widow of the consul, and has three lovely daughters; the eldest, celebrated for her beauty, and said to be the subject of those stanzas by Lord Byron,

' Maid of Athens, ere we part,
    Give, oh, give me back my heart!' &c.

" At Orchomenus, where stood the Temple of the Graces, I was tempted to exclaim, ' Whither have the Graces fled ?'—Little did I

expect to find them here. Yet here comes one of them with golden cup
and coffee, and another with a book. The book is a register of names
some of which are far sounded by the voice of fame. Among them is
Lord Byron's, connected with some lines which I shall send you:

> ‘ Fair Albion smiling sees her son depart,
> To trace the birth and nursery of art;
> Noble his object, glorious is his aim,
> He comes to Athens, and he—writes his name.’

" The counterpoise by Lord Byron:

> ‘ This modest bard, like many a bard unknown,
> Rhymes on our names, but wisely hides his own,
> But yet, whoe'er he be, to say no worse,
> His name would bring more credit than his verse.’

" The mention of the three Athenian Graces will, I can foresee,
rouse your curiosity, and fire your imagination; and I may despair of
your farther attention till I attempt to give you some description of
them. Their apartment is immediately opposite to ours, and, if you
could see them, as we do now, through the gently waving aromatic plants
before our window, you would leave your heart in Athens.

" Theresa, the Maid of Athens, Catinco, and Mariana, are of middle
stature. On the crown of the head of each is a red Albanian skull-cap,
with a blue tassel spread out and fastened down like a star. Near the
edge or bottom of the skull-cap is a handkerchief of various colours
bound round their temples. The youngest wears her hair loose, falling
on her shoulders,—the hair behind descending down the back nearly to
the waist, and, as usual, mixed with silk. The two eldest generally
have their hair bound, and fastened under the handkerchief. Their
upper robe is a pelisse edged with fur, hanging loose down to the ancles;
below is a handkerchief of muslin covering the bosom, and terminating
at the waist, which is short; under that, a gown of striped silk or muslin,
with a gore round the swell of the loins, falling in front in graceful
negligence;—white stockings and yellow slippers complete their attire.
The two eldest have black, or dark, hair and eyes; their visage oval, and
complexion somewhat pale, with teeth of dazzling whiteness. Their

cheeks are rounded, and noses straight, rather inclined to aquiline. The youngest, Mariana, is very fair, her face not so finely rounded, but has a gayer expression than her sisters', whose countenances, except when the conversation has something of mirth in it, may be said to be rather pensive. Their persons are elegant, and their manners pleasing and ladylike, such as would be fascinating in any country. They possess very considerable powers of conversation, and their minds seem to be more instructed than those of the Greek women in general. With such attractions it would, indeed, be remarkable, if they did not meet with great attentions from the travellers who occasionally are resident in Athens. They sit in the eastern style, a little reclined, with their limbs gathered under them on the divan, and without shoes. Their employments are the needle, tambouring, and reading.

" I have said that I saw these Grecian beauties through the waving aromatic plants before their window. This, perhaps, has raised your imagination somewhat too high, in regard to their condition. You may have supposed their dwelling to have every attribute of eastern luxury. The golden cups, too, may have thrown a little witchery over your excited fancy. Confess, do you not imagine that the doors

> ' Self-open'd into halls, where, who can tell
> What elegance and grandeur wide expand,
> The pride of Turkey and of Persia's land;
> Soft quilts on quilts, on carpets carpets spread,
> And couches stretch'd around in seemly band,
> And endless pillows rise to prop the head,
> So that each spacious room was one full swelling bed.'

" You will shortly perceive the propriety of my delaying, till now, to inform you that the aromatic plants which I have mentioned are neither more nor less than a few geraniums and Grecian balms, and that the room in which the ladies sit is quite unfurnished, the walls neither painted nor decorated by ' cunning hand.' Then, what would have become of the Graces had I told you sooner that a single room is all they have, save a little closet and a kitchen? You see how careful I have been to make the first impression good; not that they do not merit every praise, but that it is in man's august and elevated nature to think a little slightingly of merit, and even of beauty, if not supported by some worldly show.   Now, I shall communicate to you a secret, but in the lowest whisper.

" These ladies, since the death of the consul their father, depend on strangers living in their spare room and closet,—which we now occupy. But, though so poor, their virtue shines as conspicuously as their beauty.

" Not all the wealth of the East, or the complimentary lays even of the first of England's poets, could render them so truly worthy of love and admiration *."

Ten weeks had flown rapidly away, when the unexpected offer of a passage in an English sloop of war to Smyrna induced the travellers to make immediate preparations for departure, and, on the 5th of March, they reluctantly took leave of Athens.   " Passing," says Mr. Hobhouse, " through the gate leading to the Piræus, we struck into the olive-wood on the road going to Salamis, galloping at a quick pace, in order to rid ourselves, by hurry, of the pain of parting."   He adds, " we could not refrain from looking back, as we passed rapidly to the shore, and we continued to direct our eyes towards the spot, where we had caught the last glimpse of the Theséum and the ruins of the Parthenon through the vistas in the woods, for many minutes after the city and the Acropolis had been totally hidden from our view."

At Smyrna Lord Byron took up his residence in the house of the consul-general, and remained there, with the exception of two or three days employed in a visit to the ruins of Ephesus, till the 11th of April. It was during this time, as appears from a memorandum of his own, that the two first Cantos of Childe Harold, which he had begun five months before at Ioannina, were completed.   The memorandum alluded to, which I find prefixed to his original manuscript of the Poem, is as follows.

" Byron, Ioannina in Albania.
Begun October 31st, 1809 ;
Concluded Canto 2d, Smyrna,
March 28th, 1810.

BYRON."

* Travels in Italy, Greece, &c. by H. W. Williams, Esq.

From Smyrna the only letter, at all interesting, which I am enabled to present to the reader, is the following.

LETTER XLI.

TO MRS. BYRON.

"Smyrna, March 19, 1810.

"DEAR MOTHER,

"I cannot write you a long letter, but as I know you will not be sorry to receive any intelligence of my movements, pray accept what I can give. I have traversed the greatest part of Greece, besides Epirus, &c. &c., resided ten weeks at Athens, and am now on the Asiatic side on my way to Constantinople. I have just returned from viewing the ruins of Ephesus, a day's journey from Smyrna. I presume you have received a long letter I wrote from Albania, with an account of my reception by the Pacha of the province.

"When I arrive at Constantinople, I shall determine whether to proceed into Persia or return, which latter I do not wish, if I can avoid it. But I have no intelligence from Mr. H**, and but one letter from yourself. I shall stand in need of remittances whether I proceed or return. I have written to him repeatedly, that he may not plead ignorance of my situation for neglect. I can give you no account of any thing, for I have not time or opportunity, the frigate sailing immediately. Indeed the further I go the more my laziness increases, and my aversion to letter-writing becomes more confirmed. I have written to no one but yourself and Mr. H**, and these are communications of business and duty rather than of inclination.

"F** is very much disgusted with his fatigues, though he has undergone nothing that I have not shared. He is a poor creature; indeed English servants are detestable travellers. I have, besides him, two Albanian soldiers and a Greek interpreter; all excellent in their way. Greece, particularly in the vicinity of Athens, is delightful,—cloudless skies and lovely landscapes. But I must reserve all account of my adventures till we meet. I keep no journal, but my friend H. writes incessantly. Pray take care of Murray and Robert, and tell the boy it

F F 2

is the most fortunate thing for him that he did not accompany me to Turkey. Consider this as merely a notice of my safety, and believe me

" Yours, &c. &c.

" BYRON."

On the 11th of April he left Smyrna in the Salsette frigate, which had been ordered to Constantinople for the purpose of conveying the ambassador, Mr. Adair, to England, and, after an exploratory visit to the ruins of Troas, arrived, at the beginning of the following month, in the Dardanelles.—While the frigate was at anchor in these straits, the following letters to his friends Mr. Drury and Mr. Hodgson were written.

LETTER XLII.

TO MR. HENRY DRURY.

" Salsette Frigate, May 3d, 1810.

" MY DEAR DRURY,

" When I left England, nearly a year ago, you requested me to write to you—I will do so. I have crossed Portugal, traversed the south of Spain, visited Sardinia, Sicily, Malta, and thence passed into Turkey, where I am still wandering. I first landed in Albania, the ancient Epirus, where we penetrated as far as Mount Tomarit—excellently treated by the chief Ali Pacha,—and, after journeying through Illyria, Chaonia, &c., crossed the Gulf of Actium, with a guard of 50 Albanians, and passed the Achelous in our route through Acarnania and Ætolia. We stopped a short time in the Morea, crossed the Gulf of Lepanto, and landed at the foot of Parnassus ;—saw all that Delphi retains, and so on to Thebes and Athens, at which last we remained ten weeks.

" His majesty's ship, Pylades, brought us to Smyrna; but not before we had topographised Attica, including, of course, Marathon and the Sunian promontory. From Smyrna to the Troad (which we visited when at anchor, for a fortnight, off the tomb of Antilochus) was our next stage; and now we are in the Dardanelles, waiting for a wind to proceed to Constantinople.

" This morning I *swam* from *Sestos* to *Abydos*. The immediate distance is not above a mile, but the current renders it hazardous;—so much so that I doubt whether Leander's conjugal affection must not have been a little chilled in his passage to Paradise. I attempted it a week ago, and failed,—owing to the north wind, and the wonderful rapidity of the tide,—though I have been from my childhood a strong swimmer. But, this morning being calmer, I succeeded, and crossed the ' broad Hellespont' in an hour and ten minutes.

" Well, my dear sir, I have left my home, and seen part of Africa and Asia, and a tolerable portion of Europe. I have been with generals and admirals, princes and pashas, governors and ungovernables,—but I have not time or paper to expatiate. I wish to let you know that I live with a friendly remembrance of you, and a hope to meet you again; and, if I do this as shortly as possible, attribute it to any thing but forgetfulness.

" Greece, ancient and modern, you know too well to require description. Albania, indeed, I have seen more of than any Englishman (except a Mr. Leake), for it is a country rarely visited, from the savage character of the natives, though abounding in more natural beauties than the classical regions of Greece,—which, however, are still eminently beautiful, particularly Delphi and Cape Colonna in Attica. Yet these are nothing to parts of Illyria and Epirus, where places without a name, and rivers not laid down in maps, may, one day, when more known, be justly esteemed superior subjects, for the pencil and the pen, to the dry ditch of the Ilissus and the bogs of Bœotia.

" The Troad is a fine field for conjecture and snipe-shooting, and a good sportsman and an ingenious scholar may exercise their feet and faculties to great advantage upon the spot;—or, if they prefer riding, lose their way (as I did) in a cursed quagmire of the Scamander, who wriggles about as if the Dardan virgins still offered their wonted tribute. The only vestige of Troy, or her destroyers, are the barrows supposed to contain the carcasses of Achilles, Antilochus, Ajax, &c.—but Mount Ida is still in high feather, though the shepherds are now-a-days not much like Ganymede. But why should I say more of these things? are they not written in the *Boke* of *Gell?* and has not H. got a journal? I keep none, as I have renounced scribbling.

"I see not much difference between ourselves and the Turks, save that we have * *, and they have none—that they have long dresses, and we short, and that we talk much, and they little. * * * * * They are sensible people. Ali Pacha told me he was sure I was a man of rank, because I had *small ears* and *hands*, and *curling hair*. By the by, I speak the Romaic, or modern Greek, tolerably. It does not differ from the ancient dialects so much as you would conceive; but the pronunciation is diametrically opposite. Of verse, except in rhyme, they have no idea.

"I like the Greeks, who are plausible rascals,—with all the Turkish vices, without their courage. However, some are brave, and all are beautiful, very much resembling the busts of Alcibiades:—the women not quite so handsome. I can swear in Turkish; but, except one horrible oath, and 'pimp,' and 'bread,' and 'water,' I have got no great vocabulary in that language. They are extremely polite to strangers of any rank, properly protected; and as I have two servants and two soldiers, we get on with great éclat. We have been occasionally in danger of thieves, and once of shipwreck,—but always escaped.

"At Malta I fell in love with a married woman, and challenged an aide-de-camp of General * * (a rude fellow, who grinned at something,—I never rightly knew what)—but he explained and apologized, and the lady embarked for Cadiz, and so I escaped murder and crim. con. Of Spain I sent some account to our Hodgson, but have subsequently written to no one, save notes to relations and lawyers, to keep them out of my premises. I mean to give up all connexion, on my return, with many of my best friends—as I supposed them—and to snarl all my life. But I hope to have one good-humoured laugh with you, and to embrace Dwyer, and pledge Hodgson, before I commence cynicism.

"Tell Doctor Butler I am now writing with the gold pen he gave me before I left England, which is the reason my scrawl is more unintelligible than usual. I have been at Athens and seen plenty of these reeds for scribbling, some of which he refused to bestow upon me, because topographic Gell had brought them from Attica. But I will not describe,—no—you must be satisfied with simple detail till my return; and then we will unfold the flood-gates of colloquy. I am in a 36-gun frigate, going up to fetch Bob Adair from Constantinople, who will have the honour to carry this letter.

"And so H.'s *boke* is out*, with some sentimental sing-song of my own to fill up,—and how does it take, eh? and where the devil is the 2nd edition of my Satire, with additions? and my name on the title-page? and more lines tagged to the end, with a new exordium and what not, hot from my anvil before I cleared the Channel? The Mediterranean and the Atlantic roll between me and criticism; and the thunders of the Hyperborean Review are deafened by the roar of the Hellespont.

"Remember me to Claridge, if not translated to college, and present to Hodgson assurances of my high consideration. Now, you will ask, what shall I do next? and I answer, I do not know. I may return in a few months, but I have intents and projects after visiting Constantinople. —Hobhouse, however, will probably be back in September.

"On the 2d of July we have left Albion one year—'oblitus meorum obliviscendus et illis.' I was sick of my own country, and not much prepossessed in favour of any other; but I 'drag on' 'my chain' without 'lengthening it at each remove.' I am like the Jolly Miller, caring for nobody, and not cared for. All countries are much the same in my eyes. I smoke, and stare at mountains, and twirl my mustachios very independently. I miss no comforts, and the mosquitoes that rack the morbid frame of H. have, luckily for me, little effect on mine, because I live more temperately.

"I omitted Ephesus in my catalogue, which I visited during my sojourn at Smyrna; but the Temple has almost perished, and St. Paul need not trouble himself to epistolize the present brood of Ephesians, who have converted a large church built entirely of marble into a mosque, and I don't know that the edifice looks the worse for it.

"My paper is full, and my ink ebbing—good afternoon! If you address to me at Malta, the letter will be forwarded wherever I may be.

---

* The Miscellany, to which I have more than once referred.

H. greets you; he pines for his poetry,—at least, some tidings of it.
almost forgot to tell you that I am dying for love of three Greek girl
at Athens, sisters. I lived in the same house. Teresa, Mariana, and
Katinka*, are the names of these divinities,—all of them under 15.

Your ταπεινοτατος δϩλος,

" BYRON."

LETTER XLIII.

TO MR. HODGSON.

" Salsette Frigate, in the Dardanelles, off Abydos, May 5th, 1810.

" I am on my way to Constantinople, after a tour through Greece,
Epirus, &c. and part of Asia Minor, some particulars of which I have
just communicated to our friend and host, H. Drury With these, then,
I shall not trouble you; but, as you will perhaps be pleased to hear that
I am well, &c., I take the opportunity of our ambassador's return to
forward the few lines I have time to despatch. We have undergone
some inconveniences, and incurred partial perils, but no events worthy of
communication, unless you will deem it one that two days ago I swam
from Sestos to Abydos. This,—with a few alarms from robbers, and
some danger of shipwreck in a Turkish galliot six months ago, a visit to
a Pacha, a passion for a married woman at Malta, a challenge to an
officer, an attachment to three Greek girls at Athens, with a great deal
of buffoonery and fine prospects,—form all that has distinguished my
progress since my departure from Spain.

" H. rhymes and journalizes; I stare and do nothing—unless smoking
can be deemed an active amusement. The Turks take too much care of
their women to permit them to be scrutinized; but I have lived a good
deal with the Greeks, whose modern dialect I can converse in enough
for my purposes. With the Turks I have also some male acquaintances

---

* He has adopted this name in his description of the Seraglio in Don Juan, Canto VI.
It was, if I recollect right, in making love to one of these girls that he had recourse to an act of
courtship often practised in that country,—namely, giving himself a wound across the breast
with his dagger. The young Athenian, by his own account, looked on very coolly during the
operation, considering it a fit tribute to her beauty, but in no degree moved to gratitude.

—female society is out of the question. I have been very well treated by the Pachas and Governors, and have no complaint to make of any kind. Hobhouse will one day inform you of all our adventures,—were I to attempt the recital, neither *my* paper nor *your* patience would hold out during the operation.

"Nobody, save yourself, has written to me since I left England; but indeed I did not request it. I except my relations, who write quite as often as I wish. Of Hobhouse's volume I know nothing, except that it is out; and of my 2d edition I do not even know *that*, and certainly do not, at this distance, interest myself in the matter. * * * * I hope you and Bland roll down the stream of sale with rapidity.

"Of my return I cannot positively speak, but think it probable Hobhouse will precede me in that respect. We have been very nearly one year abroad. I should wish to gaze away another, at least, in these ever-green climates; but I fear business, law business, the worst of employments, will recall me previous to that period, if not very quickly. If so, you shall have due notice.

"I hope you will find me an altered personage,—I do not mean in body, but in manner, for I begin to find out that nothing but virtue will do in this d—d world. I am tolerably sick of vice, which I have tried in its agreeable varieties, and mean, on my return, to cut all my dissolute acquaintance, leave off wine and carnal company, and betake myself to politics and decorum. I am very serious and cynical, and a good deal disposed to moralize; but, fortunately for you, the coming homily is cut off by default of pen and defection of paper.

"Good morrow! If you write, address to me at Malta, whence your letters will be forwarded. You need not remember me to any body, but believe me yours with all faith,

"BYRON."

From Constantinople, where he arrived on the 14th of May, he addressed four or five letters to Mrs. Byron, in almost every one of which his achievement in swimming across the Hellespont is commemorated. The exceeding pride, indeed, which he took in this classic feat (the particulars of which he has himself abundantly detailed) may be cited among the instances of that boyishness of character, which he carried with him so remarkably into his maturer years, and which, while it puzzled distant observers of his conduct, was not among the least amusing or attaching of his peculiarities to those who knew him intimately. So late as eleven years from this period, when some sceptical traveller ventured to question, after all, the practicability of Leander's exploit, Lord Byron, with that jealousy on the subject of his own personal prowess which he retained from boyhood, entered again, with fresh zeal, into the discussion, and brought forward two or three other instances of his own feats in swimming*, to corroborate the statement originally made by him.

In one of these letters to his mother from Constantinople, dated May 24th, after referring, as usual, to his notable exploit, " in humble imitation of Leander, of amorous memory, though," he adds, " I had no Hero to receive me on the other side of the Hellespont," he continues thus :—

" When our ambassador takes his leave, I shall accompany him to see the sultan, and afterwards probably return to Greece. I have heard nothing of Mr. Hanson, but one remittance, without any letter from that legal gentleman. If you have occasion for any pecuniary supply, pray use my funds as far as they *go* without reserve ; and, lest this should not be enough, in my next to Mr. Hanson I will direct him to advance any sum you may want, leaving it to your discretion how much, in the present state of my affairs, you may think proper to require. I have already seen the most interesting parts of Turkey in Europe and Asia Minor, but shall not proceed further till I hear from England: in the

---

* Among others, he mentions his passage of the Tagus in 1809, which is thus described by Mr. Hobhouse :—" My companion had before made a more perilous, but less celebrated, passage ; for I recollect that, when we were in Portugal, he swam from old Lisbon to Belem Castle, and having to contend with a tide and counter current, the wind blowing freshly, was but little less than two hours in crossing the river." In swimming from Sestos to Abydos, he was one hour and ten minutes in the water.

In the year 1808, he had been nearly drowned, while swimming at Brighton with Mr. L. Stanhope. His friend, Mr. Hobhouse, and other bystanders, sent in some boatmen, with ropes tied round them, who at last succeeded in dragging Lord Byron and Mr. Stanhope from the surf, and thus saved their lives.

mean time I shall expect occasional supplies, according to circumstances; and shall pass my summer amongst my friends, the Greeks of the Morea."

He then adds, with his usual kind solicitude about his favourite servants:—

" Pray take care of my boy Robert, and the old man Murray. It is fortunate they returned; neither the youth of the one, nor the age of the other, would have suited the changes of climate and fatigue of travelling."

LETTER XLIV.

TO MR. HENRY DRURY.

" Constantinople, June 17th, 1810.

" Though I wrote to you so recently, I break in upon you again to congratulate you on a child being born, as a letter from Hodgson apprizes me of that event, in which I rejoice.

" I am just come from an expedition through the Bosphorus to the Black Sea and the Cyanean Symplegades, up which last I scrambled at as great a risk as ever the Argonauts escaped in their hoy. You remember the beginning of the nurse's dole in the Medea, of which I beg you to take the following translation, done on the summit.

> " Oh how I wish that an embargo
> Had kept in port the good ship Argo!
> Who, still unlaunch'd from Grecian docks,
> Had never pass'd the Azure rocks;
> But now I fear her trip will be a
> Damn'd business for my Miss Medea, &c. &c.

as it very nearly was to me;—for, had not this sublime passage been in my head, I should never have dreamed of ascending the said rocks, and bruising my carcass in honour of the ancients.

" I have now sat on the Cyaneans, swam from Sestos to Abydos (as I trumpeted in my last), and, after passing through the Morea again, shall set sail for Santa Maura, and toss myself from the Leucadian promontory;—surviving which operation, I shall probably rejoin you in England. H., who will deliver this, is bound straight for these parts;

and, as he is bursting with his travels, I shall not anticipate his narrative but merely beg you not to believe one word he says, but reserve your ear for me, if you have any desire to be acquainted with the truth. * *

"I am bound for Athens once more, and thence to the Morea; but my stay depends so much on my caprice, that I can say nothing of its probable duration. I have been out a year already, and may stay another; but I am quicksilver, and say nothing positively. We are all very much occupied doing nothing, at present. We have seen every thing but the mosques, which we are to view with a firman on Tuesday next. But of these and other sundries let H. relate, with this proviso that *I* am to be referred to for authenticity; and I beg leave to contradict all those things whereon he lays particular stress. But, if he soars at any time, into wit, I give you leave to applaud, because that is necessarily stolen from his fellow-pilgrim. Tell Davies that H. has made excellent use of his best jokes in many of his majesty's ships of war; but add, also, that I always took care to restore them to the right owner; in consequence of which he (Davies) is no less famous by water than by land, and reigns unrivalled in the cabin, as in the 'Cocoa Tree.'

"And Hodgson has been publishing more poesy—I wish he would send me his 'Sir Edgar,' and 'Bland's Anthology' to Malta, where they will be forwarded. In my last, which I hope you received, I gave an outline of the ground we have covered. If you have not been overtaken by this despatch, H.'s tongue is at your service. Remember me to Dwyer, who owes me eleven guineas. Tell him to put them in my banker's hands at Gibraltar or Constantinople. I believe he paid them once, but that goes for nothing, as it was an annuity.

"I wish you would write. I have heard from Hodgson frequently. Malta is my post-office. I mean to be with you by next Montem. You remember the last,—I hope for such another; but, after having swam across the 'broad Hellespont,' I disdain Datchett*. Good afternoon! I am yours, very sincerely,   " BYRON."

---

* Alluding to his having swum across the Thames with Mr. H. Drury, after the Montem, to see how many times they could perform the passage backwards and forwards without touching land In this trial (which took place at night, after supper, when both were heated with drinking), Lord Byron was the conqueror.

About ten days after the date of this letter we find another, addressed to Mrs. Byron, which—with much that is merely a repetition of what he had detailed in former communications—contains also a good deal worthy of being extracted.

LETTER XLV.

TO MRS. BYRON.

" DEAR MOTHER,

" Mr. Hobhouse, who will forward or deliver this, and is on his return to England, can inform you of our different movements, but I am very uncertain as to my own return. He will probably be down in Notts. some time or other; but Fletcher, whom I send back as an incumbrance (English servants are sad travellers), will supply his place in the interim, and describe our travels, which have been tolerably extensive.

      *   *   *   *   *

" I remember Mahmout Pacha, the grandson of Ali Pacha, at Yanina (a little fellow of ten years of age, with large black eyes, which our ladies would purchase at any price, and those regular features which distinguish the Turks), asked me how I came to travel so young, without any body to take care of me. This question was put by the little man with all the gravity of threescore. I cannot now write copiously; I have only time to tell you that I have passed many a fatiguing, but never a tedious moment; and that all I am afraid of is, that I shall contract a gipsy-like wandering disposition, which will make home tiresome to me: this, I am told, is very common with men in the habit of peregrination, and, indeed, I feel it so. On the third of May, I swam from *Sestos* to *Abydos*. You know the story of Leander, but I had no *Hero* to receive me at landing.

      *   *   *   *   *

" I have been in all the principal mosques by the virtue of a firman; this is a favour rarely permitted to infidels, but the ambassador's departure obtained it for us. I have been up the Bosphorus into the Black Sea, round the walls of the city, and, indeed, I know more of it by sight

than I do of London. I hope to amuse you some winter's evening with
the details, but at present you must excuse me ;—I am not able to write
long letters in June. I return to spend my summer in Greece.

*   *   *   *   *

"F. is a poor creature, and requires comforts that I can dispense
with. He is very sick of his travels, but you must not believe his account of the country. He sighs for ale, and idleness, and a wife, and the
devil knows what besides. I have not been disappointed or disgusted.
I have lived with the highest and the lowest. I have been for days in
a Pacha's palace, and have passed many a night in a cowhouse, and I find
the people inoffensive and kind. I have also passed some time with the
principal Greeks in the Morea and Livadia, and, though inferior to the
Turks, they are better than the Spaniards, who, in their turn, excel the
Portuguese. Of Constantinople you will find many descriptions in different travels; but Lady Wortley errs strangely when she says ' St.
Paul's would cut a strange figure by St. Sophia's.' I have been in both,
surveyed them inside and out attentively. St. Sophia's is undoubtedly
the most interesting from its immense antiquity, and the circumstance
of all the Greek emperors, from Justinian, having been crowned there,
and several murdered at the altar, besides the Turkish sultans who attend
it regularly. But it is inferior in beauty and size to some of the
mosques, particularly ' Soleyman,' &c., and not to be mentioned in the
same page with St. Paul's (I speak like a *Cockney*). However, I prefer
the Gothic cathedral of Seville to St. Paul's, St. Sophia's, and any religious building I have ever seen.

"The walls of the Seraglio are like the walls of Newstead gardens,
only higher, and much in the same order; but the ride by the walls of
the city, on the land side, is beautiful. Imagine four miles of immense
triple battlements, covered with ivy, surmounted with 218 towers, and,
on the other side of the road, Turkish burying-grounds (the loveliest
spots on earth), full of enormous cypresses. I have seen the ruins of
Athens, of Ephesus, and Delphi. I have traversed great part of Turkey,
and many other parts of Europe, and some of Asia; but I never beheld
a work of nature or art which yielded an impression like the prospect
on each side from the Seven Towers to the end of the Golden Horn.

" Now for England.   I am glad to hear of the progress of ' English Bards,' &c.—of course, you observed I have made great additions to the new edition.   Have you received my picture from Sanders, Vigo-lane, London?   It was finished and paid for long before I left England: pray, send for it.   You seem to be a mighty reader of magazines: where do you pick up all this intelligence, quotations, &c. &c.?   Though I was happy to obtain my seat without the assistance of Lord Carlisle, I had no measures to keep with a man who declined interfering as my relation on that occasion, and I have done with him, though I regret distressing Mrs. Leigh, poor thing !—I hope she is happy.

" It is my opinion that Mr. B** ought to marry Miss R**.   Our first duty is not to do evil; but, alas! that is impossible: our next is to repair it, if in our power.   The girl is his equal: if she were his inferior, a sum of money and provision for the child would be some, though a poor compensation: as it is, he should marry her.   I will have no gay deceivers on my estate, and I shall not allow my tenants a privilege I do not permit myself, *that* of debauching each other's daughters.   God knows, I have been guilty of many excesses; but, as I have laid down a resolution to reform, and lately kept it, I expect this Lothario to follow the example, and begin by restoring this girl to society, or, by the beard of my father! he shall hear of it.   Pray take some notice of Robert, who will miss his master: poor boy, he was very unwilling to return.   I trust you are well and happy.   It will be a pleasure to hear from you.

" Believe me yours very sincerely,

" BYRON.

" P. S.—How is Joe Murray ?

" P. S.—I open my letter again to tell you that Fletcher having petitioned to accompany me into the Morea, I have taken him with me, contrary to the intention expressed in my letter."

The reader has not, I trust, passed carelessly over the latter part of this letter.   There is a healthfulness in the moral feeling so unaffectedly expressed in it, which seems to answer for a heart sound at the core,

however passion might have scorched it. Some years after, when he ha
become more confirmed in that artificial tone of banter, in which it wa
unluckily, his habit to speak of his own good feelings, as well as o
those of others, however capable he might still have been of the sam
amiable sentiments, I question much whether the perverse fear of being
thought desirous to pass for moral would not have prevented him from
thus naturally and honestly avowing them.

The following extract from a communication addressed to a distinguished monthly work, by a traveller who, at this period, happened to
meet with Lord Byron at Constantinople, bears sufficiently the features
of authenticity to be presented, without hesitation, to my readers.

" We were interrupted in our debate by the entrance of a stranger,
whom, on the first glance, I guessed to be an Englishman but lately
arrived at Constantinople. He wore a scarlet coat, richly embroidered
with gold, in the style of an English aide-de-camp's dress-uniform, with
two heavy epaulettes. His countenance announced him to be about the
age of two-and-twenty. His features were remarkably delicate, and
would have given him a feminine appearance, but for the manly expression of his fine blue eyes. On entering the inner shop, he took off his
feathered cocked-hat, and showed a head of curly auburn hair, which
improved in no small degree the uncommon beauty of his face. The
impression which his whole appearance made on my mind was such, that
it has ever since remained deeply engraven on it; and although fifteen
years have since gone by, the lapse of time has not in the slightest degree
impaired the freshness of the recollection. He was attended by a Janis-
sary attached to the English embassy, and by a person who professionally
acted as a Cicerone to strangers. These circumstances, together with a
very visible lameness in one of his legs, convinced me at once he was
Lord Byron. I had already heard of his lordship, and of his late arrival
in the Salsette frigate, which had come up from the Smyrna station, to
fetch away Mr. Adair, our ambassador to the Porte. Lord Byron had
been previously travelling in Epirus and Asia Minor, with his friend
Mr. Hobhouse, and had become a great amateur of smoking; he was
conducted to this shop for the purpose of purchasing a few pipes. The

indifferent Italian, in which language he spoke to his Cicerone, and the latter's still more imperfect Turkish, made it difficult for the shopkeeper to understand their wishes, and as this seemed to vex the stranger, I addressed him in English, offering to interpret for him. When his lordship thus discovered me to be an Englishman, he shook me cordially by the hand, and assured me, with some warmth in his manner, that he always felt great pleasure when he met with a countryman abroad. His purchase and my bargain being completed, we walked out together, and rambled about the streets, in several of which I had the pleasure of directing his attention to some of the most remarkable curiosities in Constantinople. The peculiar circumstances under which our acquaintance took place established between us, in one day, a certain degree of intimacy, which two or three years frequenting each other's company in England would most likely not have accomplished. I frequently addressed him by his name, but he did not think of inquiring how I came to learn it, nor of asking mine. His lordship had not yet laid the foundation of that literary renown which he afterwards acquired; on the contrary, he was only known as the author of his Hours of Idleness; and the severity with which the Edinburgh Reviewers had criticised that production was still fresh in every English reader's recollection. I could not, therefore, be supposed to seek his acquaintance from any of those motives of vanity which have actuated so many others since: but it was natural that, after our accidental rencontre, and all that passed between us on that occasion, I should, on meeting him in the course of the same week at dinner at the English ambassador's, have requested one of the secretaries, who was intimately acquainted with him, to introduce me to him in regular form. His lordship testified his perfect recollection of me, but in the coldest manner, and immediately after turned his back on me. This unceremonious proceeding, forming a striking contrast with previous occurrences, had something so strange in it, that I was at a loss how to account for it, and felt at the same time much disposed to entertain a less favourable opinion of his lordship than his apparent frankness had inspired me with at our first meeting. It was not, therefore, without surprise, that, some days after, I saw him in the streets, coming up to me with a smile of good-nature in his countenance. He accosted me in a familiar manner, and offering me his hand, said,—' I am an enemy to English etiquette, especially out of England; and I always make my own acquaintance without waiting for the formality of an introduction. If you have nothing to do, and are disposed for another ramble, I shall be glad of your company.' There was that irresistible attraction in his manner, of which those who have had the good fortune to be admitted into his intimacy can alone have felt the power in his moments of good-humour; and I readily accepted his proposal. We visited again more of the most remarkable curiosities of the capital, a description of which would here be but a repetition of what a hundred travellers have already detailed with the utmost minuteness and accuracy; but his lordship expressed much disappointment at their want of interest. He praised the picturesque beauties of the town itself, and its surrounding scenery; and seemed of opinion that nothing else was worth looking at. He spoke of the Turks in a manner which might have given reason to suppose that he had made a long residence among them, and closed his observations with these words:—' The Greeks will, sooner or later, rise against them; but if they do not make haste, I hope Buonaparte will come and drive the useless rascals away *.' "

During his stay at Constantinople, the English minister, Mr. Adair, being indisposed the greater part of the time, had but few opportunities of seeing him. He, however, pressed him, with much hospitality, to accept a lodging at the English palace, which Lord Byron, preferring the freedom of his homely inn, declined. At the audience granted to the ambassador, on his taking leave, by the Sultan, the noble poet attended, in the train of Mr. Adair,—having shown an anxiety as to the place he was to hold in the procession, not a little characteristic of his jealous pride of rank. In vain had the minister assured him that no particular station could be allotted to him;—that the Turks, in their arrangements for the ceremonial, considered only the persons connected with the embassy, and neither attended to, or acknowledged, the precedence which our forms assign to nobility. Seeing the young peer still unconvinced

* New Monthly Magazine.

by these representations, Mr. Adair was, at length, obliged to refer him to an authority, considered infallible on such points of etiquette, the old Austrian Internuncio,—on consulting whom, and finding his opinions agree fully with those of the English minister, Lord Byron declared himself perfectly satisfied.

On the 14th of July his fellow-traveller and himself took their departure from Constantinople on board the Salsette frigate,—Mr. Hobhouse with the intention of accompanying the ambassador to England, and Lord Byron with the resolution of visiting his beloved Greece again. To Mr. Adair he appeared, at this time (and I find that Mr. Bruce, who met him afterwards at Athens, conceived the same impression of him), to be labouring under great dejection of spirits. One circumstance related to me, as having occurred in the course of the passage, is not a little striking. Perceiving, as he walked the deck, a small yataghan, or Turkish dagger, on one of the benches, he took it up, unsheathed it, and, having stood for a few moments contemplating the blade, was heard to say, in an under voice, " I should like to know how a person feels, after committing a murder!" In this startling speech we may detect, I think, the germ of his future Giaours and Laras. This intense *wish* to explore the dark workings of the passions was what, with the aid of imagination, at length generated the *power;* and that faculty which entitled him afterwards to be so truly styled " the searcher of dark bosoms," may be traced to, perhaps, its earliest stirrings in the sort of feeling that produced these words.

On their approaching the island of Zea, he expressed a wish to be put on shore. Accordingly, having taken leave of his companion, he was landed upon this small island, with his two Albanians, a Tartar, and one English servant; and in one of his manuscripts, he has, himself, described the proud, solitary feeling with which he stood to see the ship sail swiftly away—leaving him there, in a land of strangers, alone.

A few days after, he addressed the following letter to Mrs. Byron from Athens.

LETTER XLVI.

TO MRS. BYRON.

"Athens, July 25, 1810.

"DEAR MOTHER,

"I have arrived here in four days from Constantinople, which is considered as singularly quick, particularly for the season of the year. You northern gentry can have no conception of a Greek summer; which, however, is a perfect frost compared with Malta and Gibraltar, where I reposed myself in the shade last year, after a gentle gallop of four hundred miles, without intermission, through Portugal and Spain. You see, by my date, that I am at Athens again, a place which I think I prefer, upon the whole, to any I have seen. * * *

"My next movement is to-morrow into the Morea, where I shall probably remain a month or two, and then return to winter here, if I do not change my plans, which, however, are very variable, as you may suppose; but none of them verge to England.

"The Marquis of Sligo, my old fellow collegian, is here, and wishes to accompany me into the Morea. We shall go together for that purpose. Lord S. will afterwards pursue his way to the capital; and Lord B. having seen all the wonders in that quarter, will let you know what he does next, of which at present he is not quite certain. Malta is my perpetual post-office, from which my letters are forwarded to all parts of the habitable globe:—by the by, I have now been in Asia, Africa, and the east of Europe, and, indeed, made the most of my time, without hurrying over the most interesting scenes of the ancient world. F**, after having been toasted, and roasted, and baked, and grilled, and eaten by all sorts of creeping things, begins to philosophize, is grown a refined as well as resigned character, and promises at his return to become an ornament to his own parish, and a very prominent person in the future family pedigree of the F**s, who I take to be Goths by their accomplishments, Greeks by their acuteness, and ancient Saxons by their appetite. He (F**) begs leave to send half a dozen sighs to Sally his spouse, and wonders (though I do not) that his ill written and worse spelt letters have never come to hand; as for that matter, there is no great loss in either of our letters, saving and except that I wish you to know we are well, and warm enough at this present writing, God knows. You must not expect long letters at present, for they are written with the sweat of my brow, I assure you. It is rather singular that Mr. H * * has not written a syllable since my departure. Your letters I have mostly received, as well as others; from which I conjecture that the man of law is either angry or busy.

" I trust you like Newstead, and agree with your neighbours; but you know *you* are a *vixen*—is not that a dutiful appellation? Pray, take care of my books, and several boxes of papers in the hands of Joseph; and pray leave me a few bottles of champagne to drink, for I am very thirsty;—but I do not insist on the last article, without you like it. I suppose you have your house full of silly women, prating scandalous things. Have you ever received my picture in oil from Sanders, London? It has been paid for these sixteen months: why do you not get it? My suite, consisting of two Turks, two Greeks, a Lutheran, and the nondescript, Fletcher, are making so much noise that I am glad to sign myself

" Yours, &c. &c.

" BYRON."

A day or two after the date of this letter, he left Athens in company with the Marquis of Sligo. Having travelled together as far as Corinth, they from thence branched off in different directions,—Lord Sligo to pay a visit to the capital of the Morea, and Lord Byron to proceed to Patras, where he had some business, as will be seen by the following letter, with the English consul, Mr. Strané.

LETTER XLVII.

TO MRS. BYRON.

" Patras, July 30, 1810.

" DEAR MADAM,

" In four days from Constantinople, with a favourable wind, I arrived in the frigate at the island of Ceos, from whence I took a boat to Athens, where I met my friend the Marquis of Sligo, who expressed a wish to proceed with me as far as Corinth.   At Corinth we separated he for Tripolitza, I for Patras, where I had some business with the consul, Mr. Strané, in whose house I now write.   He has rendered me every service in his power since I quitted Malta on my way to Constantinople, whence I have written to you twice or thrice.   In a few days I visit the Pacha at Tripolitza, make the tour of the Morea, and return again to Athens, which at present is my head-quarters.   The heat is at present intense.   In England, if it reaches 98°, you are all on fire: the other day, in travelling between Athens and Megara, the thermometer was at 125°!!   Yet I feel no inconvenience; of course I am much bronzed, but I live temperately, and never enjoyed better health.

" Before I left Constantinople, I saw the Sultan (with Mr. Adair), and the interior of the mosques, things which rarely happen to travellers. Mr. Hobhouse is gone to England: I am in no hurry to return, but have no particular communications for your country, except my surprise at Mr. H * *'s silence, and my desire that he will remit regularly.   I suppose some arrangement has been made with regard to Wymondham and Rochdale.   Malta is my post-office, or to Mr. Strané, consul-general, Patras, Morea.   You complain of my silence—I have written twenty or thirty times within the last year: never less than twice a month, and often more.   If my letters do not arrive, you must not conclude that we are eaten, or that there is a war, or a pestilence, or famine : neither must you credit silly reports, which I dare say you have in Notts., as usual.   I am very well, and neither more or less happy than I usually am; except that I am very glad to be once more alone, for I was sick of my companion,—not that he was a bad one, but because my nature leads me to solitude, and that every day adds to this disposition.   If I chose, here are many men who would wish to join me—one wants me to go to Egypt, another to Asia, of which I have seen enough.   The greater part of Greece is already my own, so that I shall only go over my old ground, and look upon my old seas and mountains, the only acquaintances I ever found improve upon me.

" I have a tolerable suite, a Tartar, two Albanians, an interpreter, besides Fletcher; but in this country these are easily maintained.   Adair received me wonderfully well, and indeed I have no complaints against any one. Hospitality here is necessary, for inns are not. I have lived in the houses of Greeks, Turks, Italians, and English—to-day in a palace, to-morrow in a cowhouse; this day with the Pacha, the next with a shepherd. I shall continue to write briefly, but frequently, and am glad to hear from you; but you fill your letters with things from the papers, as if English papers were not found all over the world. I have at this moment a dozen before me. Pray take care of my books, and believe me, my dear mother, yours, &c."

The greater part of the two following months he appears to have occupied in making a tour of the Morea*; and the very distinguished reception he met with from Vely Pacha, the son of Ali, is mentioned with much pride, in more than one of his letters.

On his return from this tour to Patras, he was seized with a fit of illness, the particulars of which are mentioned in the following letter to Mr. Hodgson; and they are, in many respects, so similar to those of the last fatal malady, with which, fourteen years afterwards, he was attacked, in nearly the same spot, that, livelily as the account is written, it is difficult to read it without melancholy.

LETTER XLVIII.

TO MR. HODGSON.

" Patras, Morea, October 3d, 1810.

" As I have just escaped from a physician and a fever, which confined me five days to bed, you won't expect much ' allegrezza' in the ensuing letter. In this place there is an indigenous distemper, which, when the wind blows from the Gulf of Corinth (as it does five months

---

* In a note upon the Advertisement prefixed to his Siege of Corinth, he says—"I visited all three (Tripolitza, Napoli, and Argos) in 1810-11, and in the course of journeying through the country, from my first arrival in 1809, crossed the Isthmus eight times in my way from Attica to the Morea, over the mountains, or in the other direction, when passing from the Gulf of Athens to that of Lepanto."

out of six) attacks great and small, and makes woeful work with visitors
Here be also two physicians, one of whom trusts to his genius (never
having studied)—the other to a campaign of eighteen months against the
sick of Otranto, which he made in his youth with great effect.

" When I was seized with my disorder, I protested against both
these assassins;—but what can a helpless, feverish, toasted-and-watered
poor wretch do? In spite of my teeth and tongue, the English consul,
my Tartar, Albanians, dragoman, forced a physician upon me, and in
three days vomited and glystered me to the last gasp. In this state I
made my epitaph—take it.

> " Youth, Nature, and relenting Jove,
>   To keep my lamp *in* strongly strove;
>   But Romanelli was so stout
>   He beat all three—and *blew* it *out*.

But Nature and Jove, being piqued at my doubts, did, in fact, at last, beat
Romanelli, and here I am, well but weakly, at your service.

" Since I left Constantinople, I have made a tour of the Morea, and
visited Vely Pacha, who paid me great honours and gave me a pretty
stallion. H. is doubtless in England before even the date of this letter—
he bears a despatch from me to your bardship. He writes to me from
Malta, and requests my journal, if I keep one. I have none, or he should
have it; but I have replied, in a consolatory and exhortatory epistle,
praying him to abate three and sixpence in the price of his next Boke,
seeing that half-a-guinea is a price not to be given for any thing save an
opera-ticket.

" As for England, it is long since I have heard from it. Every one
at all connected with my concerns is asleep, and you are my only correspondent, agents excepted. I have really no friends in the world;
though all my old school-companions are gone forth into that world, and
walk about there in monstrous disguises, in the garb of guardsmen,
lawyers, parsons, fine gentlemen, and such other masquerade dresses.
So, I here shake hands and cut with all these busy people, none of whom
write to me Indeed, I asked it not;—and here I am, a poor traveller

and heathenish philosopher, who hath perambulated the greatest part of the Levant, and seen a great quantity of very improvable land and sea, and, after all, am no better than when I set out—Lord help me!

"I have been out fifteen months this very day, and I believe my concerns will draw me to England soon; but of this I will apprize you regularly from Malta. On all points, Hobhouse will inform you, if you are curious as to our adventures. I have seen some old English papers up to the 15th of May. I see the 'Lady of the Lake' advertised. Of course it is in his old ballad style, and pretty. After all, Scott is the best of them. The end of all scribblement is to amuse, and he certainly succeeds there. I long to read his new romance.

"And how does 'Sir Edgar?' and your friend, Bland? I suppose you are involved in some literary squabble. The only way is to despise all brothers of the quill. I suppose you won't allow me to be an author, but I contemn you all, you dogs!—I do.

"You don't know D——s, do you? He had a farce ready for the stage before I left England, and asked me for a prologue, which I promised, but sailed in such a hurry, I never penned a couplet. I am afraid to ask after his drama, for fear it should be damned—Lord forgive me for using such a word!—but the pit, sir, you know, the pit—they will do those things, in spite of merit. I remember this farce from a curious circumstance. When Drury-lane was burnt to the ground, by which accident Sheridan and his son lost the few remaining shillings they were worth, what doth my friend D—— do? Why, before the fire was out, he writes a note to Tom Sheridan, the manager of this combustible concern, to inquire whether this farce was not converted into fuel, with about two thousand other unactable manuscripts, which of course were in great peril, if not actually consumed. Now, was not this characteristic?—the ruling passions of Pope are nothing to it. Whilst the poor distracted manager was bewailing the loss of a building only worth £300,000, together with some twenty thousand pounds of rags and tinsel in the tiring rooms, Blue-beard's elephants, and all that—in comes a note from a scorching author, requiring at his hands two acts and odd scenes of a farce!!

"Dear H., remind Drury that I am his well-wisher, and let Scrope

Davies be well affected towards me. I look forward to meeting you at Newstead and renewing our old champagne evenings with all the glee of anticipation. I have written by every opportunity, and expect responses as regular as those of the liturgy, and somewhat longer. As it is impossible for a man in his senses to hope for happy days, let us at least look forward to merry ones, which come nearest to the other in appearance, if not in reality; and in such expectations I remain, &c."

He was a good deal weakened and thinned by his illness at Patras, and, on his return to Athens, standing, one day, before a looking-glass, he said to Lord Sligo—"How pale I look!—I should like, I think, to die of a consumption."—"Why of a consumption?" asked his friend. "Because then (he answered) the women would all say, 'See that poor Byron—how interesting he looks in dying!'" In this anecdote,—which, slight as it is, the relater remembered, as a proof of the poet's consciousness of his own beauty,—may be traced also the habitual reference of his imagination to that sex, which, however he affected to despise it, influenced, more or less, the flow and colour of all his thoughts.

He spoke often of his mother to Lord Sligo, and with a feeling that seemed little short of aversion. "Some time or other," he said, "I will tell you *why* I feel thus towards her."—A few days after, when they were bathing together in the Gulf of Lepanto, he referred to this promise, and, pointing to his naked leg and foot, exclaimed—"Look there! —it is to her false delicacy at my birth I owe that deformity; and yet, as long as I can remember, she has never ceased to taunt and reproach me with it. Even a few days before we parted, for the last time, on my leaving England, she, in one of her fits of passion, uttered an imprecation upon me, praying that I might prove as ill-formed in mind as I am in body!" His look and manner, in relating this frightful circumstance, can be conceived only by those who have ever seen him in a similar state of excitement.

The little value he had for those relics of ancient art, in pursuit of which he saw all his classic fellow-travellers so ardent, was, like every thing he ever thought or felt, unreservedly avowed by him. Lord Sligo having it in contemplation to expend some money in digging for antiquities, Lord Byron, in offering to act as his agent, and to see the money, at least, honestly applied, said—"You may safely trust *me*—I am no Dilettante. Your connoisseurs are all thieves;—but I care too little for these things ever to steal them."

The system of thinning himself, which he had begun before he left England, was continued, still more rigidly, abroad. While at Athens, he took the hot bath, for this purpose, three times a week,—his usual drink being vinegar and water, and his food seldom more than a little rice.

Among the persons, besides Lord Sligo, whom he saw most of at this time, were Lady Hester Stanhope and Mr. Bruce. One of the first objects, indeed, that met the eyes of these two distinguished travellers, on their approaching the coast of Attica, was Lord Byron, disporting in his favourite element, under the rocks of Cape Colonna. They were afterwards made acquainted with each other by Lord Sligo, and it was in the course, I believe, of their first interview, at his table, that Lady Hester, with that lively eloquence for which she is so remarkable, took the poet briskly to task for the depreciating opinion, which, as she understood, he entertained of all female intellect. Being but little inclined, were he even able, to sustain such a heresy, against one who was, in her own person, such an irresistible refutation of it, Lord Byron had no other refuge from the fair orator's arguments than in assent and silence; and this well-bred deference being, in a sensible woman's eyes, equivalent to concession, they became, from thenceforward, most cordial friends. In recalling some recollections of this period in his "Memoranda," after relating the circumstance of his being caught bathing by an English party at Sunium, he added, "This was the beginning of the most delightful acquaintance which I formed in Greece." He then went on to assure Mr. Bruce, if ever those pages should meet his eyes, that the days they had passed together at Athens were remembered by him with pleasure.

During this period of his stay in Greece, we find him forming one of those extraordinary friendships,—if attachment to persons so inferior to himself can be called by that name,—of which I have already mentioned two or three instances in his younger days, and in which the pride of being a protector, and the pleasure of exciting gratitude, seem to have constituted to his mind the chief, pervading charm. The person, whom he now adopted in this manner, and from similar feelings to those which had inspired his early attachments to the cottage-boy near Newstead and the young chorister at Cambridge, was a Greek youth, named Nicolo Giraud, the son, I believe, of a widow lady, in whose house the artist Lusieri, lodged. In this young man he appears to have taken the most lively, and even brotherly, interest;—so much so, as not only to have presented to him, on their parting, at Malta, a considerable sum of money, but to have subsequently designed for him, as the reader will learn, a still more munificent, as well as permanent, provision.

Though he occasionally made excursions through Attica and the Morea, his head-quarters were fixed at Athens, where he had taken lodgings in a Franciscan convent, and, in the intervals of his tours, employed himself in collecting materials for those notices on the state of modern Greece which he has appended to the second Canto of Childe Harold. In this retreat also, as if in utter defiance of the "genius loci," he wrote his "Hints from Horace,"—a satire which, impregnated as it is with London life from beginning to end, bears the date, "Athens, Capuchin Convent, March 12, 1811."

From the few remaining letters addressed to his mother, I shall content myself with selecting the two following.

LETTER XLIX.

TO MRS. BYRON.

"Athens, January 14, 1811.

"MY DEAR MADAM,

"I seize an occasion to write as usual, shortly, but frequently, as the arrival of letters, where there exists no regular communication, is, of course, very precarious. * * * I have lately made several small tours of some hundred or two miles about the Morea, Attica, &c., as I have finished my grand giro by the Troad, Constantinople, &c. and am returned down again to Athens. I believe I have mentioned to you more than once, that I swam (in imitation of Leander, though without his lady) across the Hellespont, from Sestos to Abydos. Of this, and all other particulars, F., whom I have sent home with papers, &c. will apprize you. I cannot find that he is any loss; being tolerably master of the Italian and modern Greek languages, which last I am also studying with a master, I can order and discourse more than enough for a reasonable man. Besides, the perpetual lamentations after beef and beer, the stupid bigoted contempt for every thing foreign, and insurmountable incapacity of acquiring even a few words of any language, rendered him, like all other English servants, an incumbrance. I do assure you, the plague of speaking for him, the comforts he required (more than myself by far), the pilaws (a Turkish dish of rice and meat), which he could not eat, the wines which he could not drink, the beds where he could not sleep, and the long list of calamities, such as stumbling horses, want of *tea!!!* &c., which assailed him, would have made a lasting source of laughter to a spectator, and inconvenience to a master. After all, the man is honest enough, and, in Christendom, capable enough; but in Turkey, Lord forgive me! my Albanian soldiers, my Tartars and Janizary, worked for him and us too, as my friend Hobhouse can testify.

"It is probable I may steer homewards in spring; but, to enable me to do that, I must have remittances. My own funds would have lasted me very well; but I was obliged to assist a friend, who, I know, will pay me; but, in the mean time, I am out of pocket. At present, I do not care to venture a winter's voyage, even if I were otherwise tired of travelling; but I am so convinced of the advantages of looking at mankind instead of reading about them, and the bitter effects of staying at home with all the narrow prejudices of an islander, that I think there should be a law amongst us, to set our young men abroad, for a term, among the few allies our wars have left us.

"Here I see and have conversed with French, Italians, Germans, Danes, Greeks, Turks, Americans, &c. &c. &c.; and, without losing sight of my own, I can judge of the countries and manners of others. Where I see the superiority of England (which, by the by, we are a good deal mistaken about in many things), I am pleased, and where I find her inferior, I am at least enlightened. Now, I might have staid, smoked in your towns, or fogged in your country, a century, without being sure of this, and without acquiring any thing more useful or amusing at home. I keep no journal, nor have I any intention of scribbling my travels. I have done with authorship; and if, in my last production, I have convinced the critics or the world I was something more than they took me for, I am satisfied; nor will I hazard *that reputation* by a future effort. It is true I have some others in manuscript, but I leave them for those who come after me; and, if deemed worth publishing, they may serve to prolong my memory when I myself shall cease to remember. I have a famous Bavarian artist taking some views of Athens, &c. &c. for me. This will be better than scribbling, a disease I hope myself cured of. I hope, on my return, to lead a quiet, recluse life, but God knows and does best for us all; at least, so they say, and I have nothing to object, as, on the whole, I have no reason to complain of my lot. I am convinced, however, that men do more harm to themselves than ever the devil could do to them. I trust this will find you well, and as happy as we can be; you will, at least, be pleased to hear I am so, and yours ever."

LETTER L.

TO MRS. BYRON.

"Athens, February 28, 1811.

" DEAR MADAM,

"As I have received a firman for Egypt, &c. I shall proceed to that quarter in the spring, and I beg you will state to Mr. H. that it is necessary to further remittances. On the subject of Newstead, I answer, as before, *no*. If it is necessary to sell, sell Rochdale. Fletcher will have arrived by this time with my letters to that purport. I will tell you fairly, I have, in the first place, no opinion of funded property; if, by any particular circumstances, I shall be led to adopt such a determination, I will, at all events, pass my life abroad, as my only tie to England is Newstead, and, that once gone, neither interest nor inclination lead me northward. Competence in your country is ample wealth in the east, such is the difference in the value of money and the abundance of the necessaries of life; and I feel myself so much a citizen of the world, that the spot where I can enjoy a delicious climate, and every luxury, at a less expense than a common college life in England, will always be a country to me; and such are in fact the shores of the Archipelago. This then is the alternative—if I preserve Newstead, I return; if I sell it, I stay away. I have had no letters since yours of June, but I have written several times, and shall continue, as usual, on the same plan.

" Believe me, yours ever,

" BYRON.

" P.S.—I shall most likely see you in the course of the summer, but, of course, at such a distance, I cannot specify any particular month."

The voyage to Egypt, which he appears from this letter to have contemplated, was, probably for want of the expected remittances, relinquished; and, on the 3d of June, he set sail from Malta, in the Volage frigate, for England, having, during his short stay at Malta, suffered a severe attack of the tertian fever. The feelings with which he returned home may be collected from the following melancholy letters.

LETTER LI.

TO MR. HODGSON.

" Volage frigate, at sea, June 29th, 1811.

" In a week, with a fair wind, we shall be at Portsmouth, and on the 2d of July, I shall have completed (to a day) two years of peregrination, from which I am returning with as little emotion as I set out. I think, upon the whole, I was more grieved at leaving Greece than England, which I am impatient to see simply because I am tired of a long voyage.

" Indeed, my prospects are not very pleasant. Embarrassed in my private affairs, indifferent to public, solitary without the wish to be social, with a body a little enfeebled by a succession of fevers, but a spirit, I trust, yet unbroken, I am returning *home* without a hope, and almost without a desire. The first thing I shall have to encounter will be a lawyer, the next a creditor, then colliers, farmers, surveyors, and all the agreeable attachments to estates out of repair and contested coal-pits.

In short, I am sick and sorry, and when I have a little repaired my irreparable affairs, away I shall march, either to campaign in Spain, or back again to the East, where I can at least have cloudless skies and a cessation from impertinence.

"I trust to meet, or see you, in town or at Newstead, whenever you can make it convenient—I suppose you are in love and in poetry, as usual. That husband, H. Drury, has never written to me, albeit I have sent him more than one letter;—but I dare say the poor man has a family, and of course all his cares are confined to his circle.

> ' For children fresh expenses get,
>   And Dicky now for school is fit.'
>
> WARTON.

If you see him, tell him I have a letter for him from Tucker, a regimental chirurgeon and friend of his, who prescribed for me,   *   *   * and is a very worthy man, but too fond of hard words. I should be too late for a speech-day, or I should probably go down to Harrow.

 * * * * * * *

I regretted very much in Greece having omitted to carry the Anthology with me—I mean Bland and Merivale's.

 * * * * * * *

What has Sir Edgar done? And the Imitations and Translations—where are they? I suppose you don't mean to let the public off so easily, but charge them home with a quarto. For me, I am 'sick of fops and poesy and prate,' and shall leave the 'whole Castalian state' to Bufo, or any body else. But you are a sentimental and sensibilitous person, and will rhyme to the end of the chapter. Howbeit, I have written some 4000 lines, of one kind or another, on my travels.

"I need not repeat that I shall be happy to see you. I shall be in town about the 8th, at Dorant's Hotel, in Albemarle-street, and proceed in a few days to Notts., and thence to Rochdale on business.

"I am, here and there, yours, &c."

LETTER LII.

TO MRS. BYRON.

"Volage frigate, at sea, June 25th, 1811.

"DEAR MOTHER,

"This letter, which will be forwarded on our arrival at Portsmouth, probably about the fourth of July, is begun about twenty-three days after our departure from Malta. I have just been two years (to a day, on the 2d of July) absent from England, and I return to it with much the same feelings which prevailed on my departure, viz. indifference; but within that apathy I certainly do not comprise yourself, as I will prove by every means in my power. You will be good enough to get my apartments ready at Newstead, but don't disturb yourself on any account, particularly mine, nor consider me in any other light than as a visitor. I must only inform you that for a long time I have been restricted to an entire vegetable diet, neither fish nor flesh coming within my regimen; so I expect a powerful stock of potatoes, greens, and biscuit: I drink no wine. I have two servants, middle-aged men, and both Greeks. It is my intention to proceed first to town, to see Mr. H**, and thence to Newstead, on my way to Rochdale. I have only to beg you will not forget my diet, which it is very necessary for me to observe. I am well in health, as I have generally been, with the exception of two agues, both of which I quickly got over.

"My plans will so much depend on circumstances, that I shall not venture to lay down an opinion on the subject. My prospects are not very promising, but I suppose we shall wrestle through life like our neighbours; indeed, by H.'s last advices, I have some apprehensions of finding Newstead dismantled by Messrs. Brothers, &c., and he seems determined to force me into selling it, but he will be baffled. I don't suppose I shall be much pestered with visitors; but if I am, you must receive them, for I am determined to have nobody breaking in upon my retirement: you know that I never was fond of society, and I am less so than before. I have brought you a shawl, and a quantity of attar of roses, but these I must smuggle, if possible. I trust to find my library in tolerable order.

" Fletcher is no doubt arrived. I shall separate the mill from Mr B**'s farm, for his son is too gay a deceiver to inherit both, and place Fletcher in it, who has served me faithfully, and whose wife is a good woman; besides, it is necessary to sober young Mr. B**, or he will people the parish with bastards. In a word, if he had seduced a dairy-maid, he might have found something like an apology; but the girl is his equal, and in high life or low life reparation is made in such circum-stances. But I shall not interfere further than (like Buonaparte) by dis-membering Mr. B.'s *kingdom*, and erecting part of it into a principality for field-marshal Fletcher! I hope you govern my little *empire* and its sad load of national debt with a wary hand. To drop my metaphor, I beg leave to subscribe myself, yours, &c.

" P.S.—This letter was written to be sent from Portsmouth, but, on arriving there, the squadron was ordered to the Nore, from whence I shall forward it. This I have not done before, supposing you might be alarmed by the interval mentioned in the letter being longer than expected between our arrival in port and my appearance at Newstead."

LETTER LIII.

TO MR. HENRY DRURY.

" Volage frigate, off Ushant, July 17th, 1811.

" MY DEAR DRURY,

" After two years' absence (on the 2d) and some odd days, I am approaching your country. The day of our arrival you will see by the outside date of my letter. At present, we are becalmed comfortably, close to Brest Harbour;—I have never been so near it since I left Duck Puddle. * * * * * * * *
We left Malta thirty-four days ago, and have had a tedious passage of it. You will either see or hear from or of me, soon after the receipt of this, as I pass through town to repair my irreparable affairs; and thence I want to go to Notts. and raise rents, and to Lancs. and sell collieries,

and back to London and pay debts,—for it seems I shall neither have coals or comfort till I go down to Rochdale in person.

" I have brought home some marbles for Hobhouse;—for myself, four ancient Athenian skulls*, dug out of Sarcophagi—a phial of attic hemlock†—four live tortoises—a greyhound (died on the passage)—two live Greek servants, one an Athenian, t' other a Yaniote, who can speak nothing but Romaic and Italian—and *myself*, as Moses in the Vicar of Wakefield says, slily, and I may say it too, for I have as little cause to boast of my expedition as he had of his to the fair.

" I wrote to you from the Cyanean Rocks, to tell you I had swam from Sestos to Abydos—have you received my letter?   *   *   *
Hodgson, I suppose, is four deep by this time. What would he have given to have seen, like me, the *real Parnassus*, where I robbed the Bishop of Chrissæ of a book of geography;—but this I only call plagiarism, as it was done within an hour's ride of Delphi."

Having landed the young pilgrim once more in England, it may be worth while, before we accompany him into the scenes that awaited him at home, to consider how far the general character of his mind and disposition may have been affected by the course of travel and adventure, in which he had been, for the last two years, engaged. A life less savouring of poetry and romance than that which he had pursued previously to his departure on his travels, it would be difficult to imagine. In his childhood, it is true, he had been a dweller and wanderer among scenes well calculated, according to the ordinary notion, to implant the first rudiments of poetic feeling. But, though the poet may afterwards feed on the recollection of such scenes, it is more than questionable, as has been already observed, whether he ever has been formed by them. If a childhood, indeed, passed among mountainous scenery were so favourable to the awakening of the imaginative power, both the Welsh, among ourselves, and the Swiss, abroad, ought to rank much higher on the scale of poetic excellence than they do at present. But, even allowing the picturesqueness of his early haunts to have had some share in giving a

---

* Given afterwards to Sir Walter Scott.

† At present in the possession of Mr. Murray.

direction to the fancy of Byron, the actual operation of this influence whatever it may have been, ceased with his childhood; and the life which he led afterwards, during his school-days at Harrow, was,—as, naturally the life of so idle and daring a schoolboy must be,—the very reverse of poetical. For a soldier or an adventurer, the course of training through which he then passed would have been perfect;—his athletic sports, his battles, his love of dangerous enterprise, gave every promise of a spirit fit for the most stormy career. But to the meditative pursuits of poesy, these dispositions seemed, of all others, the least friendly; and, however they might promise to render him, at some future time, a subject for bards, gave, assuredly, but little hope of his shining first among bards himself.

The habits of his life at the university were even still less intellectual and literary. While a schoolboy, he had read abundantly and eagerly, though desultorily; but even this discipline of his mind, irregular and undirected as it was, he had, in a great measure, given up, after leaving Harrow; and among the pursuits that occupied his academic hours, those of playing at hazard, sparring, and keeping a bear and bull-dogs, were, if not the most favourite, at least, perhaps, the most innocent. His time in London passed equally unmarked either by mental cultivation or refined amusement. Having no resources in private society, from his total want of friends and connexions, he was left to live loosely about town among the loungers in coffee-houses; and to those who remember what his two favourite haunts, Limmer's and Stevens's, were at that period, it is needless to say that, whatever else may have been the merits of these establishments, they were any thing but fit schools for the formation of poetic character.

But however incompatible such a life must have been with those habits of contemplation, by which, and which only, the faculties he had already displayed could be ripened, or those that were still latent could be unfolded, yet, in another point of view, the time, now apparently squandered by him, was, in after-days, turned most invaluably to account. By thus initiating him into a knowledge of the varieties of human character,—by giving him an insight into the details of society, in their least artificial form,—in short, by mixing him up, thus early, with the world, its businesses and its pleasures, his London life but contributed its share in forming that wonderful combination, which his mind afterwards exhibited, of the imaginative and the practical—the heroic and the humorous—of the keenest and most dissecting views of real life, with the grandest and most spiritualized conceptions of ideal grandeur.

To the same period, perhaps, another predominant characteristic of his maturer mind and writings may be traced. In this anticipated experience of the world which his early mixture with its crowd gave him, it is but little probable that many of the more favourable specimens of human kind should have fallen under his notice. On the contrary, it is but too likely that some of the lightest and least estimable of both sexes may have been among the models, on which, at an age when impressions sink deepest, his earliest judgments of human nature were formed. Hence, probably, those contemptuous and debasing views of humanity, with which he was so often led to alloy his noblest tributes to the loveliness and majesty of general nature. Hence the contrast that appeared between the fruits of his imagination and of his experience,— between those dreams, full of beauty and kindliness, with which the one teemed at his bidding, and the dark, desolating bitterness that overflowed when he drew from the other.

Unpromising, however, as was his youth of the high destiny that awaited him, there was one unfailing characteristic of the imaginative order of minds—his love of solitude—which very early gave signs of those habits of self-study and introspection, by which alone the "diamond quarries" of genius are worked and brought to light. When but a boy, at Harrow, he had shown this disposition strongly,—being often known, as I have already mentioned, to withdraw himself from his playmates, and sitting alone upon a tomb in the churchyard, give himself up, for hours, to thought. As his mind began to disclose its resources, this feeling grew upon him; and, had his foreign travel done no more than, by detaching him from the distractions of society, to enable him, solitarily and freely, to commune with his own spirit, it would have been an all-important step gained towards the full expansion of his faculties. It was only then, indeed, that he began to feel himself capable of the abstraction which self-study requires, or to enjoy that freedom from the intrusion of others' thoughts, which alone leaves the contemplative mind master of its

own. In the solitude of his nights at sea, in his lone wanderings throug
Greece, he had sufficient leisure and seclusion to look within himself, an
there catch the first "glimpses of his glorious mind." One of his chie
delights, as he mentioned in his "Memoranda," was, when bathing i
some retired spot, to seat himself on a high rock above the sea, and ther
remain for hours, gazing upon the sky and the waters*, and lost in that
sort of vague reverie, which, however formless and indistinct at th
moment, settled afterwards, on his pages, into those clear, bright pictures
which will endure for ever.

Were it not for the doubt and diffidence that hang round the firs
steps of genius, this growing consciousness of his own power, these
openings into a new domain of intellect where he was to reign supreme,
must have made the solitary hours of the young traveller one dream of
happiness. But it will be seen that, even yet, he distrusted his own
strength, nor was at all aware of the height to which the spirit he was
now calling up would grow So enamoured, nevertheless, had he become
of these lonely musings, that even the society of his fellow-traveller,
though with pursuits so congenial to his own, grew at last to be a chain
and a burthen on him; and it was not till he stood, companionless, on
the shore of the little island in the Ægean that he found his spirit breathe
freely. If any stronger proof were wanting of his deep passion for
solitude, we shall find it, not many years after, in his own written avowal,
that even, when in the company of the woman he most loved, he not
unfrequently found himself sighing to be alone.

It was not only, however, by affording him the concentration
necessary for this silent drawing out of his feelings and powers, that

---

* To this he alludes in those beautiful stanzas,

"To sit on rocks, to muse o'er flood and fell," &c.

Alfieri, before his dramatic genius had yet unfolded itself, used to pass hours, as he tells us,
in this sort of dreaming state, gazing upon the ocean:—"Après le spectacle un de mes amuse-
mens, à Marseille, était de me baigner presque tous les soirs dans la mer. J'avais trouvé un petit
endroit fort agréable, sur une langue de terre placée à droite hors du port, où, en m'asseyant sur
le sable, le dos appuyé contre un petit rocher qui empêchait qu'on ne pût me voir du coté de la
terre, je n'avais plus devant moi que le ciel et la mer. Entre ces deux immensités qu'embel-
lissaient les rayons d'un soleil couchant, je passai en rêvant des heures delicieuses ; et là, je serais
devenu poëte, si j'avais su écrire dans une langue quelconque."

travel conduced so essentially to the formation of his poetical character. To the East he had looked, with the eyes of romance, from his very childhood. Before he was ten years of age, the perusal of Rycaut's History of the Turks had taken a strong hold of his imagination, and he read eagerly, in consequence, every book concerning the East he could find *. In visiting, therefore, those countries, he was but realizing the dreams of his childhood; and this return of his thoughts to that innocent time gave a freshness and purity to their current which they had long wanted. Under the spell of such recollections, the attraction of novelty was among the least that the scenes, through which he wandered, presented, Fond traces of the past—and few have ever retained them so vividly—mingled themselves with the impressions of the objects before him; and as, among the Highlands, he had often traversed, in fancy, the land of the Moslem, so memory, from the wild hills of Albania, now "carried him back to Morven."

While such sources of poetic feeling were stirred at every step, there was also in his quick change of place and scene—in the diversity of men and manners surveyed by him—in the perpetual hope of adventure and thirst of enterprise, such a succession and variety of ever fresh excitement as not only brought into play, but invigorated, all the energies of his character: as he, himself, describes his mode of living, it was "To-day in a palace, to-morrow in a cow-house—this day with the Pacha, the next with a shepherd." Thus were his powers of observation

---

* But a few months before he died, in a conversation with Maurocordato at Missolonghi, Lord Byron said—"The Turkish History was one of the first books that gave me pleasure when a child; and I believe it had much influence on my subsequent wishes to visit the Levant, and gave perhaps the oriental colouring which is observed in my poetry."—COUNT GAMBA'S Narrative.

In the last edition of Mr. D'Israeli's work on "the Literary Character," that gentleman has given some curious marginal notes, which he found written by Lord Byron in a copy of this work that belonged to him. Among them is the following enumeration of the writers that, besides Rycaut, had drawn his attention so early to the East:—

"Knolles, Cantemir, De Tott, Lady M. W. Montague, Hawkins's Translation from Mignot's History of the Turks, the Arabian Nights, all travels, or histories, or books upon the East I could meet with, I had read, as well as Rycaut, before I was *ten years' old*. I think, the Arabian Nights first. After these, I preferred the history of naval actions, Don Quixote and Smollet's novels, particularly Roderick Random, and I was passionate for the Roman History. When a boy, I could never bear to read any Poetry whatever without disgust and reluctance."

quickened, and the impressions on his imagination multiplied. Thus schooled, too, in some of the roughnesses and privations of life, and, so far, made acquainted with the flavour of adversity, he learned to enlarge more than is common in his high station, the circle of his sympathies and became inured to that manly and vigorous cast of thought which is so impressed on all his writings. Nor must we forget, among these strengthening and animating effects of travel, the ennobling excitement of danger, which he more than once experienced,—having been placed in situations, both on land and sea, well calculated to call forth that pleasurable sense of energy, which perils, calmly confronted, never fail to inspire.

The strong interest which—in spite of his assumed philosophy on this subject, in Childe Harold—he took in every thing connected with a life of warfare, found frequent opportunities of gratification, not only on board the English ships of war in which he sailed, but in his occasional intercourse with the soldiers of the country. At Salora, a solitary place on the Gulf of Arta, he once passed two or three days, lodged in a small miserable barrack. Here, he lived the whole time, familiarly, among the soldiers; and a picture of the singular scene which their evenings presented—of those wild, half-bandit warriors, seated round the young poet, and examining, with savage admiration, his fine Manton gun* and English sword—might be contrasted, but too touchingly, with another and a later picture of the same poet dying, as a chieftain, on the same land, with Suliotes for his guards and all Greece for his mourners.

It is true, amid all this stimulating variety of objects, the melancholy which he had brought from home still lingered around his mind. To Mr. Adair and Mr. Bruce, as I have before mentioned, he gave the idea of a person labouring under deep dejection; and Colonel Leake, who was, at that time, resident at Ioannina, conceived very much the same impression of the state of his mind†. But, assuredly, even this

---

* " It rained hard the next day, and we spent another evening with our soldiers. The captain, Elmas, tried a fine Manton gun belonging to my Friend, and hitting his mark every time was highly delighted."—HOBHOUSE's *Journey, &c.*

† It must be recollected that by two of these gentlemen he was seen chiefly under the restraints of presentation and etiquette, when whatever gloom there was on his spirits would, in a shy nature like his, most show itself. The account which his fellow-traveller gives of him is

melancholy, habitually as it still clung to him, must, under the stirring
and healthful influences of his roving life, have become a far more
elevated and abstract feeling than it ever could have expanded to within
reach of those annoyances, whose tendency was to keep it wholly concentrated round self. Had he remained idly at home, he would have
sunk, perhaps, into a querulous satirist. But, as his views opened on a
freer and wider horizon, every feeling of his nature kept pace with their
enlargement; and this inborn sadness, mingling itself with the effusions
of his genius, became one of the chief constituent charms not only of
their pathos, but their grandeur. For, when did ever a sublime thought
spring up in the soul, that melancholy was not to be found, however
latent, in its neighbourhood?

We have seen, from the letters written by him on his passage homeward, how far from cheerful or happy was the state of mind in which he
returned. In truth, even for a disposition of the most sanguine cast,
there was quite enough in the discomforts that now awaited him in
England, to sadden its hopes and check its buoyancy. "To be happy at
home," says Johnson, "is the ultimate result of all ambition, the end to
which every enterprise and labour tends." But Lord Byron had no
home,—at least none that deserved this endearing name. A fond, family
circle, to accompany him with its prayers, while away, and draw round
him, with listening eagerness, on his return, was what, unluckily, he
never knew, though with a heart, as we have seen, by nature formed for

altogether different. In introducing the narration of a short tour to Negroponte, in which his
noble friend was unable to accompany him, Mr. Hobhouse expresses strongly the deficiency of
which he is sensible, from the absence, on this occasion, of "a companion, who, to quickness of
observation and ingenuity of remark, united that gay good-humour which keeps alive the
attention under the pressure of fatigue and softens the aspect of every difficulty and danger."
In some lines, too, of the "Hints from Horace," addressed evidently to Mr. Hobhouse, Lord
Byron not only renders the same justice to his own social cheerfulness, but gives a somewhat
more distinct idea of the frame of mind out of which it rose:—

> " Moschus! with whom I hope once more to sit,
> And smile at folly, if we can't at wit;
> Yes, friend, for thee I'll quit my Cynic cell,
> And bear Swift's motto, ' Vive la bagatelle!'
> Which charm'd our days in each Ægean clime,
> And oft at home with revelry and rhyme."

it. In the absence, too, of all that might cheer and sustain, he had every
thing to encounter that could distress and humiliate. To the dreariness
of a home without affection was added the burden of an establishment
without means, and he had thus all the embarrassments of domestic life
without its charms. His affairs had, during his absence, been suffered to
fall into confusion, even greater than their inherent tendency to such a
state warranted. There had been, the preceding year, an execution on
Newstead, for a debt of £1500 owing to the Messrs. Brothers, uphol-
sterers; and a circumstance, told of the veteran, Joe Murray, on this
occasion, well deserves to be mentioned. To this faithful old servant,
jealous of the ancient honour of the Byrons, the sight of the notice of
sale, pasted up on the abbey-door, could not be otherwise than an
unsightly and intolerable nuisance. Having enough, however, of the
fear of the law before his eyes, not to tear the writing down, he was at
last forced, as his only consolatory expedient, to paste a large piece of
brown paper over it.

Notwithstanding the resolution, so recently expressed by Lord
Byron, to abandon for ever the vocation of authorship, and leave " the
whole Castalian state" to others, he was hardly landed in England when
we find him busily engaged in preparations for the publication of some
of the Poems which he had produced abroad. So eager was he, indeed,
to print, that he had already, in a letter written at sea, announced himself
to Mr. Dallas, as ready for the press. Of this letter, which, from its
date, ought to have preceded some of the others that have been given, I
shall here lay before the reader the most material parts.

LETTER LIV.

TO MR. DALLAS.

" Volage Frigate, at sea, June 28th, 1811.

" After two years' absence (to a day, on the 2d of July, before which
we shall not arrive at Portsmouth), I am retracing my way to England.

*   *   *   *   *   *   *

" I am coming back with little prospect of pleasure at home, and with
a body a little shaken by one or two smart fevers, but a spirit I hope yet

unbroken. My affairs, it seems, are considerably involved, and much business must be done with lawyers, colliers, farmers, and creditors. Now this, to a man who hates bustle as he hates a bishop, is a serious concern. But enough of my home department.

*   *   *   *   *   *   *

" My Satire, it seems, is in a fourth edition, a success rather above the middling run, but not much for a production which, from its topics, must be temporary, and of course be successful at first, or not at all. At this period, when I can think and act more coolly, I regret that I have written it, though I shall probably find it forgotten by all except those whom it has offended.

" Yours and Pratt's *protégé*, Blackett, the cobbler, is dead, in spite of his rhymes, and is probably one of the instances where death has saved a man from damnation. You were the ruin of that poor fellow amongst you: had it not been for his patrons, he might now have been in very good plight, shoe- (not verse-) making: but you have made him immortal with a vengeance. I write this, supposing poetry, patronage, and strong waters to have been the death of him. If you are in town in or about the beginning of July, you will find me at Dorant's, in Albemarle-street, glad to see you. I have an imitation of Horace's Art of Poetry ready for Cawthorn, but don't let that deter you, for I sha'n't inflict it upon you. You know I never read my rhymes to visitors. I shall quit town in a few days for Notts., and thence to Rochdale. Yours, &c."

Immediately, on Lord Byron's arrival in London, Mr. Dallas called upon him. " On the 15th of July," says this gentleman, " I had the pleasure of shaking hands with him at Reddish's Hotel in St. James's-street. I thought his looks belied the report he had given me of his bodily health, and his countenance did not betoken melancholy, or displeasure at his return. He was very animated in the account of his travels, but assured me he had never had the least idea of writing them. He said he believed satire to be his *forte*, and to that he had adhered, having written, during his stay at different places abroad, a Paraphrase of Horace's Art of Poetry, which would be a good finish to English Bards and Scotch Reviewers. He seemed to promise himself additional fame

from it, and I undertook to superintend its publication, as I had don
that of the Satire. I had chosen the time ill for my visit, and we ha
hardly any time to converse uninterruptedly, he therefore engaged m
to breakfast with him next morning."

In the interval Mr. Dallas looked over this Paraphrase, which h
had been permitted by Lord Byron to take home with him for the pur
pose, and his disappointment was, as he himself describes it, "grievous,'
on finding, that a pilgrimage of two years to the inspiring lands of th
East had been attended with no richer poetical result. On their meeting
again next morning, though unwilling to speak disparagingly of the work,
he could not refrain, as he informs us, from expressing some surprise that
his noble friend should have produced nothing else during his absence.
" Upon this," he continues, " Lord Byron told me that he had occasionally
written short poems, besides a great many stanzas in Spenser's measure,
relative to the countries he had visited. ' They are not worth troubling
you with, but you shall have them all with you, if you like.' So came I
by Childe Harold's Pilgrimage. He took it from a small trunk, with a
number of verses. He said they had been read but by one person, who
had found very little to commend and much to condemn: that he himself was of that opinion, and he was sure I should be so too. Such as it
was, however, it was at my service: but he was urgent that ' The Hints
from Horace' should be immediately put in train, which I promised to
have done."

The value of the treasure thus presented to him, Mr. Dallas was not
slow in discovering. That very evening he despatched a letter to his
noble friend, saying—" You have written one of the most delightful
poems I ever read. If I wrote this in flattery, I should deserve your
contempt rather than your friendship. I have been so fascinated with
Childe Harold that I have not been able to lay it down. I would almost
pledge my life on its advancing the reputation of your poetical powers,
and on its gaining you great honour and regard, if you will do me
the credit and favour of attending to my suggestions respecting," &c.
&c. &c.

Notwithstanding this just praise, and the secret echo it must have
found in a heart so awake to the slightest whisper of fame, it was some

time before Lord Byron's obstinate repugnance to the idea of publishing Childe Harold could be removed.

" Attentive," says Mr. Dallas, " as he had hitherto been to my opinions and suggestions, and natural as it was that he should be swayed by such decided praise, I was surprised to find that I could not at first obtain credit with him for my judgment on Childe Harold's Pilgrimage. ' It was any thing but poetry—it had been condemned by a good critic— had I not myself seen the sentences on the margins of the manuscript?' He dwelt upon the Paraphrase of the Art of Poetry with pleasure, and the manuscript of that was given to Cawthorn, the publisher of the Satire, to be brought forth without delay. I did not, however, leave him so: before I quitted him I returned to the charge, and told him that I was so convinced of the merit of Childe Harold's Pilgrimage, that, as he had given it to me, I should certainly publish it, if he would have the kindness to attend to some corrections and alterations."

Among the many instances, recorded in literary history, of the false judgments of authors respecting their own productions, this preference given by Lord Byron to a work so little worthy of his genius, over a poem of such rare and original beauty as the first Cantos of Childe Harold, may be accounted, perhaps, one of the most extraordinary and inexplicable*. " It is in men as in soils," says Swift, " where sometimes there is a vein of gold which the owner knows not of." But Lord Byron had made the discovery of the vein, without, as it would seem, being aware of its value. I have already had occasion to observe that, even while occupied with the composition of Childe Harold, it is questionable whether he himself was yet fully conscious of the new powers, both of thought and feeling, that had been awakened in him ; and the strange estimate we now find him forming of his own production appears to warrant the remark. It would seem, indeed, as if, while the imaginative powers of his mind had received such an impulse forward, the faculty of

---

* It is, however, less wonderful that authors should thus misjudge their productions, when whole generations have sometimes fallen into the same sort of error. The Sonnets of Petrarch were, by the learned of his day, considered only worthy of the ballad-singers by whom they were chanted about the streets ; while his Epic Poem, " Africa," of which few now even know the existence, was sought for on all sides, and the smallest fragment of it begged from the author, for the libraries of the learned.

judgment, slower in its developement, was still immature, and that of *self*-judgment, the most difficult of all, still unattained.

On the other hand, from the deference which, particularly at this period of his life, he was inclined to pay to the opinions of those with whom he associated, it would be fairer, perhaps, to conclude that this erroneous valuation arose rather from a diffidence in his own judgment than from any deficiency of it. To his college companions, almost all of whom were his superiors in scholarship, and some of them even, at this time, his competitors in poetry, he looked up with a degree of fond and admiring deference, for which his ignorance of his own intellectual strength alone could account; and the example, as well as tastes, of these young writers being mostly on the side of established models, their authority, as long as it influenced him, would, to a certain degree, interfere with his striking confidently into any new or original path. That some remains of this bias, with a little leaning, perhaps, towards school-recollections*, may have had a share in prompting his preference of the Horatian Paraphrase, is by no means improbable;—at least, that it was enough to lead him, untried as he had yet been in the new path, to content himself, for the present, with following up his success in the old. We have seen, indeed, that the manuscript of the two Cantos of Childe Harold had, previously to its being placed in the hands of Mr. Dallas, been submitted by the noble author to the perusal of some friend—the first and only one, it appears, who at that time had seen them. Who this fastidious critic was, Mr. Dallas has not mentioned; but the sweeping tone of censure in which he conveyed his remarks was such as, at any period of his career, would have disconcerted the judgment of one, who, years after, in all the plenitude of his fame, confessed, that " the depreciation of the lowest of mankind was more painful to him than the applause of the highest was pleasing†."

---

* Gray, under the influence of a similar predilection, preferred, for a long time, his Latin poems to those by which he has gained such a station in English literature. " Shall we attribute this," says Mason, " to his having been educated at Eton, or to what other cause? Certain it is, that when I first knew him, he seemed to set a greater value on his Latin poetry than on that which he had composed in his native language."

† One of the manuscript notes of Lord Byron on Mr. D'Israeli's work, already referred to. —Vol. i. p. 144.

Though on every thing that, after his arrival at the age of manhood, he produced, some mark or other of the master-hand may be traced, yet, to print the whole of his Paraphrase of Horace, which extends to nearly 800 lines, would be, at the best, but a questionable compliment to his memory. That the reader, however, may be enabled to form some opinion of a performance, which—by an error or caprice of judgment, unexampled, perhaps, in the annals of literature—its author, for a time, preferred to the sublime musings of Childe Harold, I shall here select a few such passages from the Paraphrase as may seem calculated to give an idea as well of its merits as its defects.

The opening of the poem is, with reference to the original, ingenious :—

> " Who would not laugh, if Lawrence, hired to grace
> His costly canvas with each flatter'd face,
> Abused his art, till Nature, with a blush,
> Saw cits grow centaurs underneath his brush ?
> Or should some limner join, for show or sale,
> A maid of honour to a mermaid's tail ?
> Or low Dubost (as once the world has seen)
> Degrade God's creatures in his graphic spleen ?
> Not all that forced politeness, which defends
> Fools in their faults, could gag his grinning friends.
> Believe me, Moschus, like that picture seems
> The book, which sillier than a sick man's dreams,
> Displays a crowd of figures incomplete,
> Poetic nightmares, without head or feet."

The following is pointed, and felicitously expressed :—

> " Then glide down Grub-street, fasting and forgot,
> Laugh'd into Lethe by some quaint Review,
> Whose wit is never troublesome till—true."

Of the graver parts, the annexed is a favourable specimen :—

> " New words find credit in these latter days,
> If neatly grafted on a Gallic phrase:
> What Chaucer, Spenser, did, we scarce refuse
> To Dryden's or to Pope's maturer muse.

If you can add a little, say, why not,
As well as William Pitt and Walter Scott,
Since they, by force of rhyme, and force of lungs,
Enrich'd our island's ill-united tongues?
'Tis then, and shall be, lawful to present
Reforms in writing as in parliament.

As forests shed their foliage by degrees,
So fade expressions which in season please;
And we and ours, alas! are due to fate,
And works and words but dwindle to a date.
Though, as a monarch nods and commerce calls,
Impetuous rivers stagnate in canals;
Though swamps subdued, and marshes drain'd, sustain
The heavy ploughshare and the yellow grain;
And rising ports along the busy shore
Protect the vessel from old Ocean's roar—
All, all must perish. But, surviving last,
The love of letters half preserves the past:
True,—some decay, yet not a few survive,
Though those shall sink which now appear to thrive,
As custom arbitrates, whose shifting sway
Our life and language must alike obey."

I quote what follows chiefly for the sake of the note attached to it :—

" Satiric rhyme first sprang from selfish spleen.
You doubt?—See Dryden, Pope, St. Patrick's Dean*.

Blank verse is now with one consent allied
To tragedy, and rarely quits her side ;—
Though mad Almanzor rhymed in Dryden's days,
No sing-song hero rants in modern plays ;—
While modest comedy her verse foregoes
For jest and pun in very middling prose.

---

* " MacFlecknoe, the Dunciad, and all Swift's lampooning ballads.—Whatever their other works may be, these originated in personal feelings and angry retort on unworthy rivals; and though the ability of these satires elevates the poetical, their poignancy detracts from the personal, character of the writers."

> Not that our Bens or Beaumonts show the worse,
> Or lose one point because they wrote in verse;
> But so Thalia pleases to appear,—
> Poor virgin!—damn'd some twenty times a year!"

There is more of poetry in the following verses upon Milton than in any other passage throughout the Paraphrase :—

> " ' Awake a louder and a loftier strain'—
> And, pray, what follows from his boiling brain?
> He sinks to S * *'s level in a trice,
> Whose epic mountains never fail in mice !
> Not so of yore awoke your mighty sire
> The temper'd warblings of his master lyre;
> Soft as the gentler breathing of the lute,
> ' Of man's first disobedience and the fruit'
> He speaks; but as his subject swells along,
> Earth, Heaven, and Hades, echo with the song."

The annexed sketch contains some lively touches :—

> " Behold him Freshman !—forced no more to groan
> O'er Virgil's devilish verses *, and—his own;
> Prayers are too tedious, lectures too abstruse,
> He flies from T⸺ll's frown to ' Fordham's Mews;'
> (Unlucky T⸺ll, doom'd to daily cares
> By pugilistic pupils and by bears!)
> Fines, tutors, tasks, conventions, threat in vain,
> Before hounds, hunters, and Newmarket plain :
> Rough with his elders; with his equals rash;
> Civil to sharpers; prodigal of cash.
> *   *   *   *   *

---

* " Harvey, the *circulator* of the *circulation* of the blood, used to fling away Virgil in his ecstasy of admiration, and say, ' the book had a devil.' Now, such a character as I am copying would probably fling it away also, but rather wish that the devil had the book; not from dislike to the poet, but a well-founded horror of hexameters. Indeed, the public-school penance of ' Long and Short' is enough to beget an antipathy to poetry for the residue of a man's life, and perhaps so far may be an advantage."

Fool'd, pillaged, dunn'd, he wastes his terms away;
And, unexpell'd perhaps, retires M. A. : —
Master of Arts!—as Hells and Clubs* proclaim,
Where scarce a blackleg bears a brighter name.

Launch'd into life, extinct his early fire,
He apes the selfish prudence of his sire;
Marries for money; chooses friends for rank;
Buys land, and shrewdly trusts not to the Bank;
Sits in the senate; gets a son and heir;
Sends him to Harrow—for himself was there;
Mute though he votes, unless when call'd to cheer,
His son's so sharp—he'll see the dog a peer!

Manhood declines; age palsies every limb;
He quits the scene, or else the scene quits him;
Scrapes wealth, o'er each departing penny grieves,
And Avarice seizes all Ambition leaves;
Counts cent. per cent. and smiles, or vainly frets
O'er hoards diminish'd by young Hopeful's debts;
Weighs well and wisely what to sell or buy,
Complete in all life's lessons—but to die;
Peevish and spiteful, doting, hard to please,
Commending every time save times like these;
Crazed, querulous, forsaken, half forgot,
Expires unwept, is buried—let him rot!"

In speaking of the opera, he says :—

" Hence the pert shopkeeper, whose throbbing ear
Aches with orchestras which he pays to hear,
Whom shame, not sympathy, forbids to snore,
His anguish doubled by his own ' encore !'
Squeezed in ' Fop's Alley,' jostled by the beaux,
Teazed with his hat, and trembling for his toes,
Scarce wrestles through the night, nor tastes of ease
Till the dropp'd curtain gives a glad release :
Why this and more he suffers, can ye guess?—
Because it costs him dear, and makes him dress!"

---

* " ' Hell,' a gaming-house so called, where you risk little and are cheated a good deal :
' Club,' a pleasant purgatory, where you lose more, and are not supposed to be cheated at all."

The concluding couplet of the following lines is amusingly characteristic of that mixture of fun and bitterness with which their author sometimes spoke in conversation;—so much so that those who knew him might almost fancy they hear him utter the words:—

> " But every thing has faults, nor is 't unknown
> That harps and fiddles often lose their tone,
> And wayward voices at their owner's call,
> With all his best endeavours, only squall;
> Dogs blink their covey, flints withhold the spark,
> And double barrels (damn them) miss their mark*!"

One more passage, with the humorous note appended to it, will complete the whole amount of my favourable specimens:—

> " And that 's enough—then write and print so fast,—
> If Satan take the hindmost, who 'd be last?
> They storm the types, they publish one and all,
> They leap the counter, and they leave the stall :—
> Provincial maidens, men of high command,
> Yea, baronets, have ink'd the bloody hand!
> Cash cannot quell them—Pollio play'd this prank :
> (Then Phœbus first found credit in a bank!)
> Not all the living only, but the dead
> Fool on, as fluent as an Orpheus' head!
> Damn'd all their days, they posthumously thrive,
> Dug up from dust, though buried when alive!
> Reviews record this epidemic crime,
> Those books of martyrs to the rage for rhyme :
> Alas! woe worth the scribbler, often seen
> In Morning Post or Monthly Magazine!
> There lurk his earlier lays, but soon, hot-press'd,
> Behold a quarto!—tarts must tell the rest!
> Then leave, ye wise, the lyre's precarious chords
> To muse-mad baronets or madder lords,

---

* " As Mr. Pope took the liberty of damning Homer, to whom he was under great obligations—' And Homer (damn him) calls'—it may be presumed that any body or any thing may be damned in verse by poetical licence ; and in case of accident, I beg leave to plead so illustrious a precedent."

Or country Crispins, now grown somewhat stale,
Twin Doric minstrels, drunk with Doric ale!
Hark to those notes, narcotically soft,
The cobbler-laureates sing to Capel Lofft*!"

From these select specimens, which comprise, altogether, little more
than an eighth of the whole Poem, the reader may be enabled to form
some notion of the remainder, which is, for the most part, of a very inferior
quality, and, in some parts, descending to the depths of doggerel. Who,
for instance, could trace the hand of Byron in such "prose, fringed with
rhyme," as the following?—

" Peace to Swift's faults ! his wit hath made them pass
Unmatch'd by all, save matchless Hudibras,
Whose author is perhaps the first we meet
Who from our couplet lopp'd two final feet;

---

* " This well-meaning gentleman has spoilt some excellent shoemakers, and been accessary
to the poetical undoing of many of the industrious poor. Nathaniel Bloomfield and his brother
Bobby have set all Somersetshire singing. Nor has the malady confined itself to one county.
Pratt, too (who once was wiser), has caught the contagion of patronage, and decoyed a poor
fellow, named Blackett, into poetry; but he died during the operation, leaving one child and
two volumes of 'Remains,' utterly destitute. The girl, if she don't take a poetical twist, and
come forth as a shoemaking Sappho, may do well, but the 'Tragedies' are as rickety as if they
had been the offspring of an Earl or a Seatonian prize-poet. The patrons of this poor lad are
certainly answerable for his end, and it ought to be an indictable offence. But this is the least
they have done; for, by a refinement of barbarity, they have made the (late) man posthumously
ridiculous, by printing what he would have had sense enough never to print himself. Certes,
these rakers of 'Remains' come under the statute against resurrection-men. What does it signify
whether a poor dear dead dunce is to be stuck up in Surgeons' or in Stationers' Hall? is it so bad
to unearth his bones as his blunders? is it not better to gibbet his body on a heath than his soul
in an octavo? 'We know what we are, but we know not what we may be,' and it is to be
hoped we never shall know, if a man who has passed through life with a sort of éclat is to find
himself a mountebank on the other side of Styx, and made, like poor Joe Blackett, the laughing-
stock of purgatory. The plea of publication is to provide for the child. Now, might not some
of this 'sutor ultra crepidam's' friends and seducers have done a decent action without inveigling
Pratt into biography? And then, his inscription split into so many modicums! 'To the Duchess
of So Much, the Right Honble. So-and-so, and Mrs and Miss Somebody, these volumes are,'
&c. &c. Why, this is doling out the 'soft milk of dedication' in gills; there is but a quart, and
he divides it among a dozen. Why, Pratt! hadst thou not a puff left? dost thou think six
families of distinction can share this in quiet? There is a child, a book, and a dedication: send
the girl to her grace, the volumes to the grocer, and the dedication to the d-v-l."

Nor less in merit than the longer line
This measure moves, a favourite of the Nine.
*   *   *   *   *   *

Though at first view, eight feet may seem in vain
Form'd, save in odes, to bear a serious strain,
Yet Scott has shown our wondering isle of late
This measure shrinks not from a theme of weight,
And varied skilfully, surpasses far
Heroic rhyme, but most in love or war,
Whose fluctuations, tender or sublime,
Are curb'd too much by long recurring rhyme.
*   *   *   *   *   *

In sooth, I do not know, or greatly care
To learn, who our first English strollers were,
Or if—till roofs received the vagrant art—
Our Muse—like that of Thespis—kept a cart.
But this is certain, since our Shakspeare's days,
There's pomp enough, if little else, in plays;
Nor will Melpomene ascend her throne
Without high heels, white plume, and Bristol stone.
*   *   *   *   *   *

Where is that living language which could claim
Poetic more, as philosophic fame,
If all our bards, more patient of delay,
Would stop like Pope to polish by the way?"

In tracing the fortunes of men, it is not a little curious to observe, how often the course of a whole life has depended on one single step. Had Lord Byron now persisted in his original purpose of giving this Poem to the press, instead of Childe Harold, it is more than probable that he would have been lost, as a great poet, to the world*. Inferior as the Paraphrase is, in every respect, to his former Satire, and, in some places, even descending below the level of under-graduate versifiers, its failure, there can be little doubt, would have been certain and signal;—his former assailants would have resumed their advantage over him, and

---

* That he himself attributed every thing to fortune, appears from the following passage in one of his journals: " Like Sylla, I have always believed that all things depend upon fortune, and nothing upon ourselves. I am not aware of any one thought or action worthy of being called good to myself or others, which is not to be attributed to the good goddess, FORTUNE!"

either, in the bitterness of his mortification, he would have flung Childe
Harold into the fire, or, had he summoned up sufficient confidence to
publish that Poem, its reception, even if sufficient to retrieve him in
the eyes of the public and his own, could never have, at all, resembled
that explosion of success,—that instantaneous and universal acclaim of
admiration into which, coming, as it were, fresh from the land of song,
he now surprised the world, and in the midst of which he was borne,
buoyant and self-assured, along, through a succession of new triumphs,
each more splendid than the last.

Happily, the better judgment of his friends averted such a risk;
and he, at length, consented to the immediate publication of Childe
Harold,—still, however, to the last, expressing his doubts of its merits,
and his alarm at the sort of reception it might meet with in the
world.

" I did all I could," says his adviser, " to raise his opinion of this
composition, and I succeeded; but he varied much in his feelings about
it, nor was he, as will appear, at his ease until the world decided on its
merit.   He said again and again that I was going to get him into a scrape
with his old enemies, and that none of them would rejoice more than the
Edinburgh Reviewers at an opportunity to humble him.   He said I
must not put his name to it.   I entreated him to leave it to me, and that
I would answer for this Poem silencing all his enemies."

The publication being now determined upon, there arose some
doubts and difficulty as to a publisher.   Though Lord Byron had
intrusted Cawthorn with what he considered to be his surer card, the
" Hints from Horace," he did not, it seems, think him of sufficient
station in the trade to give a sanction or fashion to his more hazardous
experiment,   The former refusal of the Messrs. Longman to publish his
" English Bards and Scotch Reviewers" was not forgotten; and he
expressly stipulated with Mr. Dallas that the manuscript should not be
offered to that house.   An application was, at first, made to Mr. Miller,
of Albemarle-street; but, in consequence of the severity with which
Lord Elgin was treated in the Poem, Mr. Miller (already the publisher
and bookseller of this latter nobleman) declined the work.   Even this
circumstance,—so apprehensive was the poet for his fame,—began to

re-awaken all the qualms and terrors he had, at first, felt; and, had any further difficulties or objections arisen, it is more than probable he might have relapsed into his original intention. It was not long, however, before a person was found willing and proud to undertake the publication. Mr. Murray, who, at this period, resided in Fleet-street, having, some time before, expressed a desire to be allowed to publish some work of Lord Byron, it was in his hands that Mr. Dallas now placed the manuscript of Childe Harold;—and thus was laid the first foundation of that connexion between this gentleman and the noble poet, which continued, with but a temporary interruption, throughout the lifetime of the one, and has proved an abundant source of honour, as well as emolument, to the other.

While thus busily engaged in his literary projects, and having, besides, some law affairs to transact with his agent, he was called suddenly away to Newstead by the intelligence of an event, which seems to have affected his mind far more deeply than, considering all the circumstances of the case, could have been expected. Mrs. Byron, whose excessive corpulence rendered her, at all times, rather a perilous subject for illness, had been of late indisposed, but not to any alarming degree ; nor does it appear that, when the following note was written, there existed any grounds for apprehension as to her state.

" Reddish's Hotel, St. James's-street, London, July 23d, 1811.

" MY DEAR MADAM,

" I am only detained by Mr. H ** to sign some copyhold papers, and will give you timely notice of my approach. It is with great reluctance I remain in town. I shall pay a short visit as we go on to Lancashire on Rochdale business. I shall attend to your directions of course, and am,

" With great respect, yours ever,

" BYRON.

" P. S. You will consider Newstead as your house, not mine ; and me only as a visitor."

On his going abroad, she had conceived a sort of superstitious fancy that she should never see him again; and when he returned, safe and well, and wrote to inform her that he should soon see her at Newstead, she said to her waiting-woman, "If I should be dead before Byron comes down, what a strange thing it would be!"—and so, in fact, it happened. At the end of July, her illness took a new and fatal turn; and, so sadly characteristic was the close of the poor lady's life, that a fit of rage, brought on, it is said, by reading over the upholsterer's bills, was the ultimate cause of her death. Lord Byron had, of course, prompt intelligence of the attack. But, though he started instantly from town, he was too late,—she had breathed her last.

The following letter, it will be perceived, was written on his way to Newstead.

LETTER LV.

TO DOCTOR PIGOT.

"Newport Pagnell, August 2, 1811.

"MY DEAR DOCTOR,

"My poor mother died yesterday! and I am on my way from town to attend her to the family vault. I heard *one* day of her illness, the *next* of her death.—Thank God her last moments were most tranquil. I am told she was in little pain, and not aware of her situation.—I now feel the truth of Mr. Gray's observation, 'That we can only have *one* mother.'—Peace be with her! I have to thank you for your expressions of regard, and as in six weeks I shall be in Lancashire on business, I may extend to Liverpool and Chester,—at least I shall endeavour.

"If it will be any satisfaction, I have to inform you that in November next the Editor of the Scourge will be tried for two different libels on the late Mrs. B. and myself (the decease of Mrs. B. makes no difference in the proceedings), and as he is guilty, by his very foolish and unfounded assertion, of a breach of privilege, he will be prosecuted with the utmost rigour.

"I inform you of this, as you seem interested in the affair, which is now in the hands of the attorney-general.

" I shall remain at Newstead the greater part of this month, where I shall be happy to hear from you, after my two years' absence in the East.

" I am, dear Pigot, yours very truly,

" BYRON."

It can hardly have escaped the observation of the reader, that the general tone of the noble poet's correspondence with his mother is that of a son, performing, strictly and conscientiously, what he deems to be his duty, without the intermixture of any sentiment of cordiality to sweeten the task. The very title of " Madam," by which he addresses her—and which he but seldom exchanges for the endearing name of " mother*"—is, of itself, a sufficient proof of the sentiments he entertained for her. That such should have been his dispositions towards such a parent can be matter neither of surprise or blame,—but that, notwithstanding this alienation, which her own unfortunate temper produced, he should have continued to consult her wishes, and minister to her comforts, with such unfailing thoughtfulness as is evinced not only in the frequency of his letters, but in the almost exclusive appropriation of Newstead to her use, redounds, assuredly, in no ordinary degree, to his honour; and was even the more strikingly meritorious from the absence of that affection, which renders kindnesses to a beloved object little more than an indulgence of self.

But, however estranged from her his feelings must be allowed to have been while she lived, her death seems to have restored them into their natural channel. Whether from a return of early fondness and the all-atoning power of the grave, or from the prospect of that void in his future life, which this loss of his only link with the past would leave, it is certain that he felt the death of his mother acutely, if not deeply. On the night after his arrival at Newstead, the waiting-woman of Mrs. Byron, in passing the door of the room where the deceased lady lay, heard a

---

* In many instances the mothers of illustrious poets have had reason to be proud no less of the affection than of the glory of their sons; and Tasso, Pope, Gray, and Cowper, are among these memorable examples of filial tenderness. In the lesser poems of Tasso there are few things so beautiful as his description, in the Canzone to the Metauro, of his first parting with his mother:—

" Me dal sen della madre empia fortuna
Pargoletto divelse," &c.

sound, as of some one sighing heavily from within; and, on entering the chamber, found, to her surprise, Lord Byron sitting, in the dark, beside the bed. On her representing to him the weakness of thus giving way to grief, he burst into tears and exclaimed, "Oh, Mrs. By, I had but one friend in the world, and she is gone!"

While his real thoughts were thus confided to silence and darkness, there was, in other parts of his conduct more open to observation, a degree of eccentricity and indecorum which, with superficial observers, might well bring the sensibility of his nature into question. On the morning of the funeral, having declined following the remains himself, he stood looking, from the abbey door, at the procession, till the whole had moved off;—then, turning to young Rushton, who was the only person left besides himself, he desired him to fetch the sparring-gloves, and proceeded to his usual exercise with the boy. He was silent and abstracted all the time, and, as if from an effort to get the better of his feelings, threw more violence, Rushton thought, into his blows than was his habit; but, at last,—the struggle seeming too much for him,—he flung away the gloves, and retired to his room.

Of Mrs. Byron, sufficient, perhaps, has been related in these pages to enable the reader to form fully his own opinion, as well with respect to the character of this lady herself, as to the degree of influence her temper and conduct may have exercised on those of her son. It was said by one of the most extraordinary of men *,—who was, himself, as he avowed, principally indebted to maternal culture for the unexampled elevation to which he subsequently rose,—that " the future good or bad conduct of a child depends entirely on the mother." How far the leaven that sometimes mixed itself with the better nature of Byron,—his uncertain and wayward impulses,—his defiance of restraint,—the occasional bitterness of his hate, and the precipitance of his resentments,—may have had their origin in his early collisions with maternal caprice and violence, is an inquiry for which sufficient materials have been, perhaps, furnished in these pages, but which every one will decide upon, according to the more or less weight he may attribute to the influence of such causes on the formation of character.

* Napoleon.

That, notwithstanding her injudicious and coarse treatment of him, Mrs. Byron loved her son, with that sort of fitful fondness of which alone such a nature is capable, there can be little doubt,—and still less, that she was ambitiously proud of him. Her anxiety for the success of his first literary essays may be collected from the pains which he so considerately took to tranquillize her on the appearance of the hostile article in the Review. As his fame began to brighten, that notion of his future greatness and glory, which, by a singular forecast of superstition, she had entertained from his very childhood, became proportionably confirmed. Every mention of him in print was watched by her with eagerness, and she had got bound together in a volume, which a friend of mine once saw, a collection of all the literary notices, that had then appeared, of his early Poems and Satire,—written over, on the margin, with observations of her own, which to my informant appeared indicative of much more sense and ability than, from her general character, we should be inclined to attribute to her.

Among those lesser traits of his conduct through which an observer can trace a filial wish to uphold, and throw respect round, the station of his mother, may be mentioned his insisting, while a boy, on being called " George Byron Gordon"—giving thereby precedence to the maternal name,—and his continuing, to the last, to address her as " the Honourable Mrs. Byron,"—a mark of rank, to which, he must have been aware, she had no claim whatever. Neither does it appear that, in his habitual manner towards her, there was any thing denoting a want of either affection or deference,—with the exception, perhaps, occasionally, of a somewhat greater degree of familiarity than comports with the ordinary notions of filial respect. Thus, the usual name he called her by, when they were on good-humoured terms together, was " Kitty Gordon ;" and I have heard an eye-witness of the scene describe the look of arch, dramatic humour, with which, one day, at Southwell, when they were in the height of their theatrical rage, he threw open the door of the drawing-room, to admit his mother, saying, at the same time, " Enter the Honourable Kitty."

The pride of birth was a feeling common alike to mother and son, and, at times, even became a point of rivalry between them, from their respective claims, English and Scotch, to high lineage. In a letter written by him from Italy, referring to some anecdote which his mother had told him, he says,—" My mother, who was as haughty as Lucifer with her descent from the Stuarts, and her right line from the *old Gordons* —*not* the *Seyton Gordons,* as she disdainfully termed the ducal branch,— told me the story, always reminding me how superior *her* Gordons were to the southern Byrons, notwithstanding our Norman, and always masculine descent, which has never lapsed into a female, as my mother's Gordons had done in her own person."

If, to be able to depict powerfully the painful emotions, it is necessary first to have experienced them, or, in other words, if, for the poet to be great, the man must suffer, Lord Byron, it must be owned, paid early this dear price of mastery. Few as were the ties by which his affections held, whether within, or without, the circle of relationship, he was now doomed, within a short space, to see the most of them swept away by death *. Besides the loss of his mother, he had to mourn over, in quick succession, the untimely fatalities that carried off, within a few weeks of each other, two or three of his most loved and valued friends. " In the short space of one month," he says, in a note on Childe Harold, " I have lost *her* who gave me being, and most of those who made that being tolerable†." Of these, young Wingfield, whom we have seen high on the list of his Harrow favourites, died of a fever at Coimbra; and Matthews, the idol of his admiration at college, was drowned while bathing in the waters of the Cam.

The following letter, written immediately after the latter event, bears the impress of strong and even agonized feeling, to such a degree as renders it almost painful to read it.

* In a letter, written between two and three months after his mother's death, he states no less a number than six persons, all friends or relatives, who had been snatched away from him by death between May and the end of August.

† In continuation of the note quoted in the text, he says of Matthews—" His powers of mind, shown in the attainment of greater honours, against the *ablest candidates,* than those of any graduate on record at Cambridge, have sufficiently established his fame on the spot where it was acquired." One of the candidates, thus described, was Mr. Thomas Barnes, a gentleman whose career since has kept fully the promise of his youth, though, from the nature of the channels through which his literary labours have been directed, his great talents are far more extensively known than his name.

LETTER LVI.

TO MR. SCROPE DAVIES.

" Newstead Abbey, August 7, 1811.

" MY DEAREST DAVIES,

" Some curse hangs over me and mine. My mother lies a corpse in this house: one of my best friends is drowned in a ditch. What can I say, or think, or do? I received a letter from him the day before yesterday. My dear Scrope, if you can spare a moment, do come down to me, I want a friend. Matthews's last letter was written on *Friday*,—on Saturday he was not. In ability, who was like Matthews? How did we all shrink before him? You do me but justice in saying, I would have risked my paltry existence to have preserved his. This very evening did I mean to write, inviting him, as I invite you, my very dear friend, to visit me. God forgive * * * for his apathy! What will our poor Hobhouse feel! His letters breathe but of Matthews. Come to me, Scrope, I am almost desolate—left almost alone in the world—I had but you, and H. and M. and let me enjoy the survivors whilst I can. Poor M. in his letter of Friday, speaks of his intended contest for Cambridge*, and a speedy journey to London. Write or come, but come if you can, or one or both. Yours ever."

Of this remarkable young man, Charles Skinner Matthews†, I have already had occasion to speak; but the high station which he held in Lord Byron's affection and admiration may justify a somewhat ampler tribute to his memory.

There have seldom, perhaps, started together in life so many youths

---

* It had been the intention of Mr. Matthews to offer himself, at the ensuing election, for the university. In reference to this purpose, a manuscript Memoir of him, now lying before me, says—" If acknowledged and successful talents—if principles of the strictest honour—if the devotion of many friends could have secured the success of an ' independent pauper' (as he jocularly called himself in a letter on the subject), the vision would have been realized."

† He was the third son of the late John Matthews, Esq. of Belmont, Herefordshire, representative of that county in the parliament of 1802-6. The author of " The Diary of an Invalid," also untimely snatched away, was another son of the same gentleman, as is likewise the

of high promise and hope as were to be found among the society of which Lord Byron formed a part at Cambridge. Of some of these, the names have since eminently distinguished themselves in the world, as the mere mention of Mr. Hobhouse and Mr. William Bankes is sufficient to testify; while in the instance of another of this lively circle, Mr. Scrope Davies*, the only regret of his friends is, that the social wit of which he is such a master should, in the memories of his hearers alone, be likely to leave any record of its brilliancy. Among all these young men of learning and talent (including Byron himself, whose genius was, however, as yet, " an undiscovered world"), the superiority, in almost every department of intellect, seems to have been, by the ready consent of all, awarded to Matthews;—a concurrence of homage which, considering the persons from whom it came, gives such a high notion of the powers of his mind at that period as renders the thought of what he might have been, if spared, a matter of interesting, though vain and mournful, speculation. To mere mental pre-eminence, unaccompanied by the kindlier qualities of the heart, such a tribute, however deserved, might not, perhaps, have been so uncontestedly paid. But young Matthews appears,—in spite of some little asperities of temper and manner, which he was already beginning to soften down when snatched away,—to have been one of those rare individuals who, while they command deference, can, at the same time, win regard, and who, as it were, relieve the intense feeling of admiration which they excite by blending it with love.

To his religious opinions, and their unfortunate coincidence with those of Lord Byron, I have before adverted. Like his noble friend, ardent in the pursuit of Truth, he, like him too, unluckily lost his way in

present Prebendary of Hereford, the Reverend Arthur Matthews, who, by his ability and attainments, sustains worthily the reputation of the name.

The father of this accomplished family was himself a man of considerable talent, and the author of several unavowed poetical pieces; one of which, a Parody of Pope's Eloisa, written in early youth, has been erroneously ascribed to the late Professor Porson, who was in the habit of reciting it, and even printed an edition of the verses.

* " One of the cleverest men I ever knew, in conversation, was Scrope Berdmore Davies. Hobhouse is also very good in that line, though it is of less consequence to a man who has other ways of showing his talents than in company. Scrope was always ready and often witty—Hobhouse as witty, but not always so ready, being more diffident."—MS. Journal of Lord Byron.

seeking her,—" the light that led astray" being by both friends mistaken for hers. That in his scepticism he proceeded any farther than Lord Byron, or ever suffered his doubting, but still ingenuous, mind to persuade itself into the " incredible creed" of atheism, is, I find, (notwithstanding an assertion in a letter of the noble poet to this effect) disproved by the testimony of those among his relations and friends, who are the most ready to admit and, of course, lament his other heresies;—nor should I have felt that I had any right to allude thus to the religious opinions of one who had never, by promulgating his heterodoxy, brought himself within the jurisdiction of the public, had not the wrong impression, as it appears, given of those opinions, on the authority of Lord Byron, rendered it an act of justice to both friends to remove the imputation.

In the letters to Mrs. Byron, written previously to the departure of her son on his travels, there occurs, it will be recollected, some mention of a Will, which it was his intention to leave behind him in the hands of his trustees. Whatever may have been the contents of this former instrument, we find that, in about a fortnight after his mother's death, he thought it right to have a new form of will drawn up, and the following letter, enclosing his instructions for that purpose, was addressed to the late Mr. Bolton, a solicitor of Nottingham. Of the existence, in any serious or formal shape, of the strange directions here given, respecting his own interment, I was, for some time, I confess, much inclined to doubt; but the curious documents here annexed put this remarkable instance of his eccentricity beyond all question.

TO ——— BOLTON, ESQ.

" Newstead Abbey, August 12th, 1811.

" SIR,

" I enclose a rough draft of my intended Will, which I beg to have drawn up as soon as possible in the firmest manner. The alterations are principally made in consequence of the death of Mrs. Byron. I have only to request that it may be got ready in a short time, and have the honour to be,

" Your most obedient, humble servant,

" BYRON."

"Newstead Abbey, August 12th, 1811.

"DIRECTIONS FOR THE CONTENTS OF A WILL TO BE DRAWN UP
IMMEDIATELY.

"The estate of Newstead to be entailed (subject to certain de
ductions) on George Anson Byron, heir at law, or whoever may be the
heir at law on the death of Lord B. The Rochdale property to be sold
in part or the whole, according to the debts and legacies of the present
Lord B.

"To Nicolo Giraud of Athens, subject of France, but born in
Greece, the sum of seven thousand pounds sterling, to be paid from the
sale of such parts of Rochdale, Newstead, or elsewhere, as may enable
the said Nicolo Giraud (resident at Athens and Malta in the year 1810)
to receive the above sum on his attaining the age of twenty-one years.

"To William Fletcher, Joseph Murray, and Demetrius Zograffo *
(native of Greece), servants, the sum of fifty pounds p^r. ann. each, for
their natural lives. To W^m. Fletcher the Mill at Newstead, on condition
that he payeth rent, but not subject to the caprice of the landlord. To
R^t. Rushton the sum of fifty pounds per ann. for life, and a further sum
of one thousand pounds on attaining the age of twenty-five years.

"To J^n. Hanson, Esq. the sum of two thousand pounds sterling.

"The claims of S. B. Davies, Esq. to be satisfied on proving the
amount of the same.

"The body of Lord B. to be buried in the vault of the garden of
Newstead, without any ceremony or burial-service whatever, or any
inscription, save his name and age. His dog not to be removed from the
said vault.

"My library and furniture of every description to my friends

---

* "If the papers lie not (which they generally do), Demetrius Zograffo of Athens is at the
head of the Athenian part of the Greek insurrection. He was my servant in 1809, 1810, 1811,
1812, at different intervals in those years (for I left him in Greece when I went to
Constantinople), and accompanied me to England in 1811; he returned to Greece, spring, 1812.
He was a clever, but not *apparently* an enterprising man; but circumstances make men. His
two sons (*then* infants) were named Miltiades and Alcibiades: may the omen be happy!"—*MS.
Journal.*

Jⁿ. Cam Hobhouse, Esq., and S. B. Davies, Esq., my executors. In case of their decease, the Rev. J. Becher, of Southwell, Notts., and R. C. Dallas, Esq., of Mortlake, Surrey, to be executors.

"The produce of the sale of Wymondham in Norfolk, and the late Mrs. B.'s Scotch property *, to be appropriated in aid of the payment of debts and legacies."

In sending a copy of the Will, framed on these instructions, to Lord Byron, the solicitor accompanied some of the clauses with marginal queries, calling the attention of his noble client to points which he considered inexpedient or questionable; and as the short, pithy answers to these suggestions are strongly characteristic of their writer, I shall here give one or two of the clauses in full, with the respective queries and answers annexed.

"This is the last will and testament of me the Rt. Honble. George Gordon Lord Byron, Baron Byron of Rochdale in the county of Lancaster.—I desire that my body may be buried in the vault of the garden of Newstead without any ceremony or burial-service whatever, and that no inscription, save my name and age, be written on the tomb or tablet; and it is my will that my faithful dog may not be removed from the said vault. To the performance of this my particular desire, I rely on the attention of my executors hereinafter named."

"*It is submitted to Lord Byron whether this clause relative to the funeral had not better be omitted. The substance of it can be given in a letter from his lordship to the executors, and accompany the will; and the will may state that the funeral shall be performed in such manner as his lordship may by letter direct, and, in default of any such letter, then at the discretion of his executors.*"

"It must stand. "B."

"I do hereby specifically order and direct that all the claims of the said S. B. Davies upon me shall be fully paid and satisfied as soon as

---

* On the death of his mother, a considerable sum of money, the remains of the price of the estate of Gight, was paid into his hands by her trustee, Baron Clerk.

conveniently may be after my decease, on his proving [by vouchers, or otherwise, to the satisfaction of my executors hereinafter named] * the amount thereof and the correctness of the same."

"*If Mr. Davies has any unsettled claims upon Lord Byron, that circumstance is a reason for his not being appointed executor; each executor having an opportunity of paying himself his own debt without consulting his co-executors.*"

" So much the better—if possible, let him be an executor.

" B."

The two following letters contain further instructions on the same subject.

LETTER LVII.

TO MR. BOLTON.

" Newstead Abbey, August 16th, 1811.

" SIR,

" I have answered the queries on the margin †. I wish Mr. Davies's claims to be most fully allowed, and, further, that he be one of my executors. I wish the will to be made in a manner to prevent all discussion, if possible, after my decease; and this I leave to you, as a professional gentleman.

" With regard to the few and simple directions for the disposal of my *carcass*, I must have them implicitly fulfilled, as they will, at least, prevent trouble and expense;—and (what would be of little consequence to me, but may quiet the conscience of the survivors) the garden is *consecrated* ground. These directions are copied verbatim from my former will; the alterations in other parts have arisen from the death of Mrs. B.

" I have the honour to be your most obedient, humble servant,

" BYRON."

* Over the words which I have here placed between brackets, Lord Byron drew his pen.

† In the clause enumerating the names and places of abode of the executors, the solicitor had left blanks for the christian names of these gentlemen, and Lord Byron, having filled up all but that of Dallas, writes in the margin—" I forget the christian name of Dallas—cut him out."

LETTER LVIII.

TO MR. BOLTON.

" Newstead Abbey, August 20, 1811.

" SIR,

" The witnesses shall be provided from amongst my tenants, and I shall be happy to see you on any day most convenient to yourself. I forgot to mention that it must be specified by codicil, or otherwise, that my body is on no account to be removed from the vault where I have directed it to be placed; and, in case any of my successors within the entail (from bigotry, or otherwise) might think proper to remove the carcass, such proceeding shall be attended by forfeiture of the estate, which, in such case, shall go to my sister, the Honble. Augusta Leigh and her heirs on similar conditions. I have the honour to be, sir,

" Your very obedient, humble servant,

" BYRON."

In consequence of this last letter, a proviso and declaration, in conformity with its instructions, were inserted in the will. He also executed, on the 28th of this month, a codicil, by which he revoked the bequest of his " household goods and furniture, library, pictures, sabres, watches, plate, linen, trinkets, and other personal estate (except money and securities) situate within the walls of the mansion-house and premises at his decease—and bequeathed the same (except his wine and spirituous liquors) to his friends, the said J. C. Hobhouse, J. B. Davies, and Francis Hodgson, their executors, &c. to be equally divided between them for their own use;—and he bequeathed his wine and spirituous liquors, which should be in the cellars and premises at Newstead, unto his friend the said J. Becher for his own use, and requested the said J. C. Hobhouse, J. B. Davies, F. Hodgson, and J. Becher, respectively, to accept the bequest therein contained, to them respectively, as a token of his friendship."

The following letters, written while his late losses were fresh in his mind, will be read with painful interest.

LETTER LIX.

TO MR. DALLAS.

"Newstead Abbey, Notts., August 12th, 1811.

"Peace be with the dead! Regret cannot wake them. With a sigh to the departed, let us resume the dull business of life, in the certainty that we also shall have our repose. Besides her who gave me being, I have lost more than one who made that being tolerable.—The best friend of my friend Hobhouse, Matthews, a man of the first talents, and also not the worst of my narrow circle, has perished miserably in the muddy waves of the Cam, always fatal to genius:—my poor school-fellow, Wingfield, at Coimbra—within a month; and whilst I had heard from *all three*, but not seen *one*. Matthews wrote to me the very day before his death; and though I feel for his fate, I am still more anxious for Hobhouse, who, I very much fear, will hardly retain his senses; his letters to me since the event have been most incoherent. But let this pass—we shall all one day pass along with the rest—the world is too full of such things, and our very sorrow is selfish.

"I received a letter from you, which my late occupations prevented me from duly noticing,—I hope your friends and family will long hold together. I shall be glad to hear from you, on business, on common-place, or any thing, or nothing—but death—I am already too familiar with the dead. It is strange that I look on the skulls which stand beside me (I have always had *four* in my study) without emotion, but I cannot strip the features of those I have known of their fleshy covering, even in idea, without a hideous sensation; but the worms are less ceremonious. —Surely, the Romans did well when they burned the dead.—I shall be happy to hear from you, and am, yours, &c."

LETTER LX.

TO MR. HODGSON.

"Newstead Abbey, August 22d, 1811.

"You may have heard of the sudden death of my mother, and poor Matthews, which, with that of Wingfield (of which I was not fully aware till just before I left town, and indeed hardly believed it), has made a sad chasm in my connexions. Indeed the blows followed each other so rapidly that I am yet stupid from the shock, and though I do eat and drink and talk, and even laugh, at times, yet I can hardly persuade myself that I am awake, did not every morning convince me mournfully to the contrary.—I shall now wave the subject,—the dead are at rest, and none but the dead can be so.

" You will feel for poor Hobhouse,—Matthews was the ' god of his idolatry;' and if intellect could exalt a man above his fellows, no one could refuse him pre-eminence. I knew him most intimately, and valued him proportionably, but I am recurring—so let us talk of life and the living.

" If you should feel a disposition to come here, you will find ' beef and a sea-coal fire,' and not ungenerous wine. Whether Otway's two other requisites for an Englishman or not, I cannot tell, but probably one of them.—Let me know when I may expect you, that I may tell you when I go and when return.—I have not yet been to Lancs. *

* * * * * * * * *

Davies has been here, and has invited me to Cambridge for a week in October, so that, peradventure, we may encounter glass to glass. His gaiety (death cannot mar it) has done me service; but, after all, ours was a hollow laughter.

" You will write to me? I am solitary, and I never felt solitude irksome before. Your anxiety about the critique on * *'s book is amusing; as it was anonymous, certes it was of little consequence: I wish it had produced a little more confusion, being a lover of literary malice. Are you doing nothing? writing nothing? printing nothing? why not your Satire on Methodism? the subject (supposing the public to be blind to merit) would do wonders. Besides, it would be as well for a destined deacon to prove his orthodoxy.—It really would give me pleasure to see you properly appreciated. I say *really*, as, being an author, my humanity might be suspected. Believe me, dear H., yours always."

LETTER LXI.

TO MR. DALLAS.

" Newstead, August 21, 1811.

" Your letter gives me credit for more acute feelings than I possess; for though I feel tolerably miserable, yet I am at the same time subject to a kind of hysterical merriment, or rather laughter without merriment, which I can neither account for nor conquer, and yet I do not feel relieved by it; but an indifferent person would think me in excellent spirits. 'We must forget these things,' and have recourse to our old selfish comforts, or rather comfortable selfishness. I do not think I shall return to London immediately, and shall therefore accept freely what is offered courteously—your mediation between me and Murray. I don't think my name will answer the purpose, and you must be aware that my plaguy Satire will bring the north and south Grub-streets down upon the ' Pilgrimage ;'—but, nevertheless, if Murray makes a point of it, and you coincide with him, I will do it daringly; so let it be entitled, ' By the Author of English Bards and Scotch Reviewers.' My remarks on the Romaic, &c. once intended to accompany the ' Hints from Horace,' shall go along with the other, as being indeed more appropriate; also the smaller poems now in my possession, with a few selected from those published in **'s Miscellany. I have found amongst my poor mother's papers all my letters from the East, and one in particular of some length from Albania. From this, if necessary, I can work up a note or two on that subject. As I kept no journal, the letters written on the spot are the best. But of this anon, when we have definitively arranged.

" Has Murray shown the work to any one? He may—but I will have no traps for applause. Of course there are little things I would wish to alter, and perhaps the two stanzas of a buffooning cast on London's Sunday are as well left out. I much wish to avoid identifying Childe Harold's character with mine, and that, in sooth, is my second objection to my name appearing in the title-page. When you have made arrangements as to time, size, type, &c., favour me with a reply. I am giving you an universe of trouble, which thanks cannot atone for. I made a kind of prose apology for my scepticism at the head of the MS., which, on recollection, is so much more like an attack than a defence, that, haply, it might better be omitted:—perpend, pronounce. After all, I fear Murray will be in a scrape with the orthodox; but I cannot help it, though I wish him well through it. As for me, ' I have supped full of criticism,' and I don't think that the ' most dismal treatise' will stir and rouse my ' fell of hair' till ' Birnam wood do come to Dunsinane.'

" I shall continue to write at intervals, and hope you will pay me in kind. How does Pratt get on, or rather get off Joe Blackett's posthumous stock? You killed that poor man amongst you, in spite of your Ionian friend and myself, who would have saved him from Pratt, poetry, present poverty, and posthumous oblivion. Cruel patronage! to ruin a man at his calling; but then he is a divine subject for subscription and biography; and Pratt, who makes the most of his dedications, has inscribed the volume to no less than five families of distinction.

" I am sorry you don't like Harry White; with a great deal of cant, which in him was sincere (indeed it killed him as you killed Joe Blackett), certes there is poesy and genius. I don't say this on account of my simile and rhymes; but surely he was beyond all the Bloomfields and Blacketts, and their collateral cobblers, whom Lofft and Pratt have or may kidnap from their calling into the service of the trade. You must excuse my flippancy, for I am writing I know not what, to escape from myself. Hobhouse is gone to Ireland. Mr. Davies has been here on his way to Harrowgate.

" You did not know M.; he was a man of the most astonishing powers, as he sufficiently proved at Cambridge, by carrying off more prizes and fellowships, against the ablest candidates, than any other graduate on record; but a most decided atheist, indeed noxiously so, for he proclaimed his principles in all societies. I knew him well, and feel a loss not easily to be supplied to myself—to Hobhouse never. Let me hear from you, and believe me, &c."

The progress towards publication of his two forthcoming works will be best traced in his letters to Mr. Murray and Mr. Dallas.

LETTER LXII.

TO MR. MURRAY.

"Newstead Abbey, Notts., August 23, 1811.

"SIR,

"A domestic calamity in the death of a near relation has hitherto prevented my addressing you on the subject of this letter.—My friend Mr. Dallas has placed in your hands a manuscript poem written by me in Greece, which he tells me you do not object to publishing. But he also informed me in London that you wished to send the MS. to Mr. Gifford. Now, though no one would feel more gratified by the chance of obtaining his observations on a work than myself, there is in such a proceeding a kind of petition for praise, that neither my pride—or whatever you please to call it—will admit. Mr. G. is not only the first satirist of the day, but editor of one of the principal Reviews. As such, he is the last man whose censure (however eager to avoid it) I would deprecate by clandestine means. You will therefore retain the MS. in your own care, or, if it must needs be shown, send it to another. Though not very patient of censure, I would fain obtain fairly any little praise my rhymes might deserve, at all events not by extortion and the humble solicitations of a bandied about MS. I am sure a little consideration will convince you it would be wrong.

"If you determine on publication, I have some smaller poems (never published), a few notes, and a short dissertation on the literature of the modern Greeks (written at Athens), which will come in at the end of the volume.—And if the present poem should succeed, it is my intention, at some subsequent period, to publish some selections from my first work,—my Satire,—another nearly the same length, and a few other things, with the MS. now in your hands, in two volumes.—But of these hereafter. You will apprize me of your determination. I am, sir, your very obedient, &c."

LETTER LXIII.

TO MR. DALLAS.

"Newstead Abbey, August 25, 1811.

"Being fortunately enabled to frank, I do not spare scribbling, having sent you packets within the last ten days. I am passing solitary, and do not expect my agent to accompany me to Rochdale before the second week in September, a delay which perplexes me, as I wish the business over, and should at present welcome employment. I sent you exordiums, annotations, &c. for the forthcoming quarto, if quarto it is to be; and I also have written to Mr. Murray my objection to sending the MS. to Juvenal, but allowing him to show it to any others of the calling. Hobhouse is amongst the types already; so, between his prose and my verse, the world will be decently drawn upon for its paper-money and patience. Besides all this, my 'Imitation of Horace' is gasping for the press at Cawthorn's, but I am hesitating as to the *how* and the *when*, the single or the double, the present or the future. You must excuse all this, for I have nothing to say in this lone mansion but of myself, and yet I would willingly talk or think of aught else.

"What are you about to do? Do you think of perching in Cumberland, as you opined when I was in the metropolis? If you mean to retire, why not occupy Miss ***'s 'Cottage of Friendship,' late the seat of Cobbler Joe, for whose death you and others are answerable? His 'Orphan Daughter' (pathetic Pratt!) will, certes, turn out a shoemaking Sappho. Have you no remorse? I think that elegant address to Miss Dallas should be inscribed on the cenotaph which Miss *** means to stitch to his memory.

"The newspapers seem much disappointed at his majesty's not dying, or doing something better. I presume it is almost over. If parliament meets in October, I shall be in town to attend. I am also invited to Cambridge for the beginning of that month, but am first to jaunt to Rochdale. Now Matthews is gone, and Hobhouse in Ireland, I have hardly one left there to bid me welcome, except my inviter. At

three-and-twenty I am left alone, and what more can we be at seventy ?
It is true, I am young enough to begin again, but with whom can I
retrace the laughing part of life? It is odd how few of my friends have
died a quiet death,—I mean, in their beds. But a quiet life is of more
consequence. Yet one loves squabbling and jostling better than yawning. This *last word* admonishes me to relieve you from yours very
truly, &c."

LETTER LXIV.

TO MR. DALLAS.

"Newstead Abbey, August 27th, 1811.

"I was so sincere in my note on the late Charles Matthews, and do
feel myself so totally unable to do justice to his talents, that the passage
must stand for the very reason you bring against it. To him all the men
I ever knew were pigmies. He was an intellectual giant. It is true I
loved W. better; he was the earliest and the dearest, and one of the few
one could never repent of having loved: but in ability—ah! you did
not know Matthews!

"'Childe Harold' may wait and welcome—books are never the worse
for delay in the publication. So you have got our heir, George Anson
Byron, and his sister, with you.

*   *   *   *   *

*   *   *   *   *

"You may say what you please, but you are one of the *murderers*
of Blackett, and yet you won't allow Harry White's genius. Setting
aside his bigotry, he surely ranks next Chatterton. It is astonishing how
little he was known; and at Cambridge no one thought or heard of such
a man, till his death rendered all notice useless. For my own part, I
should have been most proud of such an acquaintance: his very prejudices were respectable. There is a sucking epic poet at Granta, a Mr.
Townsend, *protégé* of the late Cumberland. Did you ever hear of him
and his 'Armageddon?' I think his plan (the man I don't know)
borders on the sublime; though, perhaps, the anticipation of the 'Last

Day' (according to you Nazarenes), is a little too daring: at least, it looks like telling the Lord what he is to do, and might remind an ill-natured person of the line—

> ' And fools rush in where angels fear to tread.'

"But I don't mean to cavil, only other folks will, and he may bring all the lambs of Jacob Behmen about his ears.   However, I hope he will bring it to a conclusion, though Milton is in his way.

"Write to me—I dote on gossip—and make a bow to Ju—, and shake George by the hand for me; but, take care, for he has a sad sea paw.

"P.S. I would ask George here, but I don't know how to amuse him —all my horses were sold when I left England, and I have not had time to replace them.   Nevertheless, if he will come down and shoot in September, he will be very welcome; but he must bring a gun, for I gave away all mine to Ali Pacha, and other Turks.   Dogs, a keeper, and plenty of game, with a very large manor, I have—a lake, a boat, house-room, and *neat wines*."

LETTER LXV.

TO MR. MURRAY.

" Newstead Abbey, Notts., Sept. 5th, 1811.

" SIR,

"The time seems to be past when (as Dr. Johnson said) a man was certain to 'hear the truth from his bookseller,' for you have paid me so many compliments, that, if I was not the veriest scribbler on earth, I should feel affronted.   As I accept your compliments, it is but fair I should give equal or greater credit to your objections, the more so, as I believe them to be well founded.   With regard to the political and metaphysical parts, I am afraid I can alter nothing; but I have high authority for my errors in that point, for even the *Æneid* was a *political* poem, and written for a *political* purpose; and as to my unlucky opinions on subjects of more importance, I am too sincere in them for recantation. On Spanish affairs I have said what I saw, and every day confirms me in that notion of the result formed on the spot; and I rather think honest John Bull is beginning to come round again to that sobriety which Massena's retreat had begun to reel from its centre—the usual consequence of *un*usual success. So you perceive I cannot alter the sentiments; but if there are any alterations in the structure of the versification you would wish to be made, I will tag rhymes and turn stanzas as much as you please. As for the '*orthodox*,' let us hope they will buy, on purpose to abuse—you will forgive the one, if they will do the other. You are aware that any thing from my pen must expect no quarter, on many accounts; and as the present publication is of a nature very different from the former, we must not be sanguine.

"You have given me no answer to my question—tell me fairly, did you show the MS. to some of your corps?—I sent an introductory stanza to Mr. Dallas, to be forwarded to you; the poem else will open too abruptly. The stanzas had better be numbered in Roman characters. There is a disquisition on the literature of the modern Greeks and some smaller poems to come in at the close. These are now at Newstead, but will be sent in time. If Mr. D. has lost the stanza and note annexed to it, write, and I will send it myself.—You tell me to add two Cantos, but I am about to visit my *collieries* in Lancashire on the 15th inst. which is so unpoetical an employment that I need say no more. I am, sir, your most obedient, &c."

The manuscripts of both his Poems having been shown, much against his own will, to Mr. Gifford, the opinion of that gentleman was thus reported to him by Mr. Dallas:—"Of your Satire he spoke highly; but this Poem (Childe Harold) he pronounces not only the best you have written, but equal to any of the present age."

LETTER LXVI.

TO MR. DALLAS.

"Newstead Abbey, September 7th, 1811.

"As Gifford has been ever my 'Magnus Apollo,' any approbation, such as you mention, would, of course, be more welcome than 'all Bokara's

vaunted gold, than all the gems of Samarkand.' But I am sorry the
MS. was shown to him in such a manner, and I had written to Murray to
say as much, before I was aware that it was too late.

" Your objection to the expression ' central line,' I can only meet by
saying that, before Childe Harold left England, it was his full intention
to traverse Persia, and return by India, which he could not have done
without passing the equinoctial.

" The other errors you mention, I must correct in the progress
through the press. I feel honoured by the wish of such men that the
poem should be continued, but to do that, I must return to Greece and
Asia; I must have a warm sun and a blue sky; I cannot describe scenes
so dear to me by a sea-coal fire. I had projected an additional Canto
when I was in the Troad and Constantinople, and if I saw them again, it
would go on; but under existing circumstances and *sensations*, I have
neither harp, ' heart, nor voice' to proceed. I feel that *you are all right*
as to the metaphysical part; but I also feel that I am sincere, and that if
I am only to write ' *ad captandum vulgus*,' I might as well edit a magazine at once, or spin canzonettas for Vauxhall.

    *   *   *   *   *

" My work must make its way as well as it can; I know I have
every thing against me, angry poets and prejudices; but if the poem is
a *poem*, it will surmount these obstacles, and if *not*, it deserves its fate.
Your friend's Ode I have read—it is no great compliment to pronounce
it far superior to S * *'s on the same subject, or to the merits of the new
Chancellor. It is evidently the production of a man of taste, and a poet,
though I should not be willing to say it was fully equal to what might
be expected from the author of ' *Horæ Ionicæ*.' I thank you for it, and
that is more than I would do for any other Ode of the present day.

" I am very sensible of your good wishes, and, indeed, I have need
of them. My whole life has been at variance with propriety, not to say
decency; my circumstances are become involved; my friends are dead
or estranged, and my existence a dreary void. In Matthews I have lost
my ' guide, philosopher, and friend;' in Wingfield a friend only, but one
whom I could have wished to have preceded in his long journey.

" Matthews was indeed an extraordinary man; it has not entered into the heart of a stranger to conceive such a man; there was the stamp of immortality in all he said or did; and now what is he? When we see such men pass away and be no more—men, who seem created to display what the Creator *could make* his creatures, gathered into corruption, before the maturity of minds that might have been the pride of posterity, what are we to conclude? For my own part, I am bewildered. To me he was much, to Hobhouse every thing.—My poor Hobhouse doted on Matthews. For me, I did not love quite so much as I honoured him; I was indeed so sensible of his infinite superiority, that though I did not envy, I stood in awe of it. He, Hobhouse, Davies, and myself, formed a coterie of our own at Cambridge and elsewhere. Davies is a wit and man of the world, and feels as much as such a character can do; but not as Hobhouse has been affected. Davies, who is not a scribbler, has always beaten us all in the war of words, and by his colloquial powers at once delighted and kept us in order. H. and myself always had the worst of it with the other two; and even M. yielded to the dashing vivacity of S. D. But I am talking to you of men, or boys, as if you cared about such beings.

" I expect mine agent down on the 14th to proceed to Lancashire, where, I hear from all quarters, that I have a very valuable property in coals, &c. I then intend to accept an invitation to Cambridge in October, and shall, perhaps, run up to town. I have four invitations—to Wales, Dorset, Cambridge, and Chester; but I must be a man of business. I am quite alone, as these long letters sadly testify. I perceive, by referring to your letter, that the Ode is from the author; make my thanks acceptable to him. His muse is worthy a nobler theme. You will write, as usual, I hope. I wish you a good evening, and am, &c."

LETTER LXVII.

TO MR. MURRAY.

" Newstead Abbey, Notts., Sept. 14, 1811.

" SIR,

" Since your former letter, Mr. Dallas informs me that the MS. has been submitted to the perusal of Mr. Gifford, most contrary to my wishes, as Mr. D. could have explained, and as my own letter to you did, in fact, explain, with my motives for objecting to such a proceeding. Some late domestic events, of which you are probably aware, prevented my letter from being sent before; indeed, I hardly conceived you would so hastily thrust my productions into the hands of a stranger, who could be as little pleased by receiving them, as their author is at their being offered in such a manner, and to such a man.

"My address, when I leave Newstead, will be to 'Rochdale, Lancashire;' but I have not yet fixed the day of departure, and I will apprize you when ready to set off.

"You have placed me in a very ridiculous situation, but it is past, and nothing more is to be said on the subject. You hinted to me that you wished some alterations to be made; if they have nothing to do with politics or religion, I will make them with great readiness. I am, sir, &c. &c."

TO MR. MURRAY.

"Newstead Abbey, Sept. 16, 1811 *.

"I return the proof, which I should wish to be shown to Mr. Dallas, who understands typographical arrangements much better than I can pretend to do. The printer may place the notes in his *own way*, or any *way*, so that they are out of *my way*; I care nothing about types or margins.

"If you have any communication to make, I shall be here at least a week or ten days longer.

"I am, sir, &c. &c."

* On a leaf of one of his paper-books I find an Epigram, written at this time, which, though not perhaps particularly good, I consider myself bound to insert :—

"ON MOORE'S LAST OPERATIC FARCE, OR FARCICAL OPERA.

"Good plays are scarce,
So Moore writes farce:
The poet's fame grows brittle—
We knew before
That *Little*'s Moore,
But now 'tis Moore that's *little*.

"Sept. 14, 1811."

LETTER LXVIII.

TO MR. DALLAS.

" Newstead Abbey, Sept. 17, 1811.

" I can easily excuse your not writing, as you have, I hope, something better to do, and you must pardon my frequent invasions on your attention, because I have at this moment nothing to interpose between you and my epistles.

" I cannot settle to any thing, and my days pass, with the exception of bodily exercise to some extent, with uniform indolence, and idle insipidity. I have been expecting, and still expect, my agent, when I shall have enough to occupy my reflections in business of no very pleasant aspect. Before my journey to Rochdale, you shall have due notice where to address me—I believe at the post-office of that township. From Murray I received a second proof of the same pages, which I requested him to show you, that any thing which may have escaped my observation may be detected before the printer lays the corner-stone of an *errata* column.

" I am now not quite alone, having an old acquaintance and school-fellow with me, so *old*, indeed, that we have nothing *new* to say on any subject, and yawn at each other in a sort of *quiet inquietude*. I hear nothing from Cawthorn, or Captain Hobhouse, and *their quarto*—Lord have mercy on mankind! We come on like Cerberus with our triple publications. As for *myself*, by *myself*, I must be satisfied with a comparison to *Janus*.

" I am not at all pleased with Murray for showing the MS.; and I am certain Gifford must see it in the same light that I do. His praise is nothing to the purpose: what could he say? He could not spit in the face of one who had praised him in every possible way. I must own that I wish to have the impression removed from his mind, that I had any concern in such a paltry transaction. The more I think, the more it disquiets me; so I will say no more about it. It is bad enough to be a scribbler, without having recourse to such shifts to extort praise, or deprecate censure. It is anticipating, it is begging, kneeling, adulating

—the devil! the devil! the devil! and all without my wish, and contrary to my express desire. I wish Murray had been tied to *Payne*'s neck when he jumped into the Paddington Canal*, and so tell him,—*that* is the proper receptacle for publishers. You have thoughts of settling in the country, why not try Notts.? I think there are places which would suit you in all points, and then you are nearer the metropolis. But of this anon.　　　　　　　　　　　　　" I am yours, &c."

LETTER LXIX.

TO MR. DALLAS.

" Newstead Abbey, Sept. 21, 1811.

" I have shown my respect for your suggestions by adopting them; but I have made many alterations in the first proof, over and above; as, for example:

" Oh Thou, in *Hellas* deem'd of heavenly birth,
&c. &c.

" Since *shamed full oft* by *later lyres* on earth,
Mine, &c.

" Yet there *I've wander'd* by the vaunted rill;

---

* In a note on his " Hints from Horace," he thus humorously applies this incident :—

" A literary friend of mine walking out one lovely evening last summer on the eleventh bridge of the Paddington Canal, was alarmed by the cry of ' one in jeopardy.' He rushed along, collected a body of Irish haymakers (supping on butter-milk in an adjoining paddock), procured three rakes, one eel-spear, and a landing-net, and at last (*horresco referens*) pulled out—his own publisher. The unfortunate man was gone for ever, and so was a large quarto wherewith he had taken the leap, which proved, on inquiry, to have been Mr. S——'s last work. Its ' alacrity of sinking' was so great, that it has never since been heard of, though some maintain that it is at this moment concealed at Alderman Birch's pastry-premises, Cornhill. Be this as it may, the coroner's inquest brought in a verdict of ' Felo de Bibliopolâ' against a ' quarto unknown,' and circumstantial evidence being since strong against the ' Curse of Kehama' (of which the above words are an exact description), it will be tried by its peers next session in Grub-street. Arthur, Alfred, Davideis, Richard Cœur de Lion, Exodus, Exodiad, Epigoniad, Calvary, Fall of Cambria, Siege of Acre, Don Roderick, and Tom Thumb the Great, are the names of the twelve jurors. The judges are Pye, * * *, and the bellman of St. Sepulchre's."

and so on. So I have got rid of Dr. Lowth and ' drunk' to boot, an very glad I am to say so. I have also sullenised the line as heretofore and in short have been quite conformable.

" Pray write; you shall hear when I remove to Lancs. I have brought you and my friend Juvenal Hodgson upon my back, on the score of revelation. You are fervent, but he is quite *glowing;* and if he take: half the pains to save his own soul, which he volunteers to redeem mine great will be his reward hereafter. I honour and thank you both, but am convinced by neither. Now for notes. Besides those I have sent, I shall send the observations on the Edinburgh Reviewer's remarks on the modern Greek, an Albanian song in the Albanian *(not Greek)* language, specimens of modern Greek from their New Testament, a comedy of Goldoni's translated, *one scene,* a prospectus of a friend's book, and perhaps a song or two, *all* in Romaic, besides their Pater Noster; so there will be enough, if not too much, with what I have already sent. Have you received the ' Noctes Atticæ?' I sent also an annotation on Portugal. Hobhouse is also forthcoming."

LETTER LXX.

TO MR. DALLAS.

" Newstead Abbey, Sept. 23, 1811.

" *Lisboa* is the Portuguese word, consequently the very best. Ulissipont is pedantic; and, as I have *Hellas* and *Eros* not long before, there would be something like an affectation of Greek terms, which I wish to avoid, since I shall have a perilous quantity of *modern* Greek in my notes, as specimens of the tongue; therefore Lisboa may keep its place. You are right about the ' Hints;' they must not precede the ' Romaunt;' but Cawthorn will be savage if they don't; however, keep *them* back, and *him* in *good humour,* if we can, but do not let him publish.

" I have adopted, I believe, most of your suggestions, but ' Lisboa' will be an exception, to prove the rule. I have sent a quantity of notes, and shall continue; but pray let them be copied; no devil can read my hand. By the by, I do not mean to exchange the ninth verse of the ' Good Night.' I have no reason to suppose my dog better than his

brother brutes, mankind; and *Argus* we know to be a fable. The
'Cosmopolite' was an acquisition abroad. I do not believe it is to be
found in England. It is an amusing little volume, and full of French
flippancy. I read, though I do not speak, the language.

"I *will* be angry with Murray. It was a bookselling, back-shop,
Paternoster-row, paltry proceeding, and if the experiment had turned
out as it deserved, I would have raised all Fleet-street, and borrowed the
giant's staff from St. Dunstan's church, to immolate the betrayer of trust.
I have written to him as he never was written to before by an author,
I'll be sworn, and I hope you will amplify my wrath, till it has an effect
upon him. You tell me always you have much to write about. Write
it, but let us drop metaphysics;—on that point we shall never agree. I
am dull and drowsy, as usual. I do nothing, and even that nothing
fatigues me. Adieu."

LETTER LXXI.

TO MR. DALLAS.

"Newstead Abbey, October 11, 1811.

"I have returned from Lancs., and ascertained that my property
there may be made very valuable, but various circumstances very much
circumscribe my exertions at present. I shall be in town on business in
the beginning of November, and perhaps at Cambridge before the end of
this month; but of my movements you shall be regularly apprized.
Your objections I have in part done away by alterations, which I hope
will suffice; and I have sent two or three additional stanzas for both
'Fyttes.' I have been again shocked with a *death*, and have lost one
very dear to me in happier times; but 'I have almost forgot the taste of
grief,' and 'supped full of horrors' till I have become callous, nor have I
a tear left for an event which five years ago would have bowed down my
head to the earth. It seems as though I were to experience in my youth
the greatest misery of age. My friends fall around me, and I shall be
left a lonely tree before I am withered. Other men can always take
refuge in their families; I have no resource but my own reflections, and

they present no prospect here or hereafter, except the selfish satisfactio
of surviving my betters. I am indeed very wretched, and you wil
excuse my saying so, as you know I am not apt to cant of sensibility.

" Instead of tiring yourself with *my* concerns, I should be glad to hea
your plans of retirement. I suppose you would not like to be wholl
shut out of society? Now I know a large village, or small town, abou
twelve miles off, where your family would have the advantage of ver
genteel society, without the hazard of being annoyed by mercantil
affluence; where *you* would meet with men of information and independence; and where I have friends to whom I should be proud to
introduce you. There are, besides, a coffee-room, assemblies, &c. &c.
which bring people together. My mother had a house there some years,
and I am well acquainted with the economy of Southwell, the name of
this little commonwealth. Lastly, you will not be very remote from me;
and though I am the very worst companion for young people in the
world, this objection would not apply to *you*, whom I could see frequently.
Your expenses too would be such as best suit your inclinations, more or
less, as you thought proper; but very little would be requisite to enable
you to enter into all the gaieties of a country life. You could be as quiet
or bustling as you liked, and certainly as well situated as on the lakes of
Cumberland, unless you have a particular wish to be *picturesque*.

" Pray, is your Ionian friend in town? You have promised me an
introduction.—You mention having consulted some friends on the MSS.
—Is not this contrary to our usual way? Instruct Mr. Murray not to
allow his shopman to call the work ' Child of Harrow's Pilgrimage !!!!!'
as he has done to some of my astonished friends, who wrote to inquire
after my *sanity* on the occasion, as well they might. I have heard nothing
of Murray, whom I scolded heartily.—Must I write more notes?—Are
there not enough?—Cawthorn must be kept back with the ' Hints.'—I
hope he is getting on with Hobhouse's quarto.

" Good evening. Yours ever, &c."

Of the same date with this melancholy letter are the following
verses, never before printed, which he wrote in answer to some lines

received from a friend, exhorting him to be cheerful, and to " banish care."
They will show with what gloomy fidelity, even while under the pressure of recent sorrow, he reverted to the disappointment of his early affection, as the chief source of all his sufferings and errors, present and to come.

" Newstead Abbey, October 11, 1811.

" ' Oh ! banish care'—such ever be
The motto of *thy* revelry !
Perchance of *mine*, when wassail nights
Renew those riotous delights,
Wherewith the children of Despair
Lull the lone heart, and ' banish care.'
But not in morn's reflecting hour,
When present, past, and future lower,
When all I loved is changed or gone,
Mock with such taunts the woes of one,
Whose every thought—but let them pass—
Thou know'st I am not what I was.
But, above all, if thou would'st hold
Place in a heart that ne'er was cold,
By all the powers that men revere,
By all unto thy bosom dear,
Thy joys below, thy hopes above,
Speak—speak of any thing but love.
  'Twere long to tell, and vain to hear,
The tale of one who scorns a tear;
And there is little in that tale
Which better bosoms would bewail.
But mine has suffer'd more than well
'T would suit Philosophy to tell.
I 've seen my bride another's bride,—
Have seen her seated by his side,—
Have seen the infant, which she bore,
Wear the sweet smile the mother wore,
When she and I in youth have smiled
As fond and faultless as her child ;—
Have seen her eyes, in cold disdain,
Ask if I felt no secret pain,

And *I* have acted well my part,
And made my cheek belie my heart,
Return'd the freezing glance she gave,
Yet felt the while *that* woman's slave;—
Have kiss'd, as if without design,
The babe which ought to have been mine,
And show'd, alas! in each caress
Time had not made me love the less.
　　But let this pass—I'll whine no more,
Nor seek again an eastern shore;
The world befits a busy brain,—
I'll hie me to its haunts again.
But if, in some succeeding year,
When Britain's ' May is in the Sere,'
Thou hear'st of one, whose deepening crimes
Suit with the sablest of the times,
Of one, whom Love nor Pity sways,
Nor hope of fame, nor good men's praise,
One, who in stern Ambition's pride,
Perchance not Blood shall turn aside,
One rank'd in some recording page
With the worst anarchs of the age,
Him wilt thou *know*—and, *knowing*, pause,
Nor with the *effect* forget the cause."

The anticipations of his own future career in these concluding lines are of a nature, it must be owned, to awaken more of horror than of interest, were we not prepared, by so many instances of his exaggeration in this respect, not to be startled at any lengths to which the spirit of self-libelling would carry him. It seemed as if, with the power of painting fierce and gloomy personages, he had also the ambition to be, himself, the dark "sublime he drew," and that, in his fondness for the delineation of heroic crime, he endeavoured to fancy, where he could not find, in his own character, fit subjects for his pencil.

It was about the time when he was thus bitterly feeling, and expressing, the blight which his heart had suffered from a *real* object of affection, that his poems on the death of an *imaginary* one, " Thyrza," were written;—nor is it any wonder, when we consider the peculiar circumstances under which these beautiful effusions flowed from his fancy, that of all his strains of pathos, they should be the most touching and most pure. They were, indeed, the essence, the abstract spirit, as it were, of many griefs;—a confluence of sad thoughts from many sources of sorrow, refined and warmed in their passage through his fancy, and forming thus one deep reservoir of mournful feeling. In retracing the happy hours he had known with the friends now lost, all the ardent tenderness of his youth came back upon him. His school-sports with the favourites of his boyhood, Wingfield and Tattersall,—his summer days with Long*, and those evenings of music and romance, which he had dreamed away in the society of his adopted brother, Eddle-stone,—all these recollections of the young and dead now came to mingle themselves in his mind with the image of her, who, though living, was, for him, as much lost as they, and diffused that general feeling of sadness and fondness through his soul, which found a vent in these poems. No friendship, however warm, could have inspired sorrow so passionate; as no love, however pure, could have kept passion so chastened. It was the blending of the two affections, in his memory and imagination, that thus gave birth to an ideal object combining the best features of both, and drew from him these saddest and tenderest of love-poems, in which we find all the depth and intensity of real feeling touched over with such a light as no reality ever wore.

The following letter gives some further account of the course of his thoughts and pursuits at this period.

LETTER LXXII.

TO MR. HODGSON.

" Newstead Abbey, Oct. 13th, 1811.

" You will begin to deem me a most liberal correspondent; but as my letters are free, you will overlook their frequency. I have sent you answers in prose and verse† to all your late communications, and though

* See the extract from one of his journals, page 63.
† The verses in a preceding page, dated October 11th.

I am invading your ease again, I don't know why, or what to put down
that you are not acquainted with already. I am growing *nervous* (how
you will laugh!)—but it is true,—really, wretchedly, ridiculously, fine
ladically *nervous*. Your climate kills me; I can neither read, write, o
amuse myself, or any one else. My days are listless, and my nights rest
less; I have very seldom any society, and when I have, I run out of it
At ' this present writing' there are in the next room three *ladies*, and
have stolen away to write this grumbling letter.—I don't know that
sha'n't end with insanity, for I find a want of method in arranging my
thoughts that perplexes me strangely; but this looks more like silliness
than madness, as Scrope Davies would facetiously remark in his consoling
manner. I must try the hartshorn of your company; and a session of
Parliament would suit me well,—any thing to cure me of conjugating
the accursed verb ' *ennuyer.*'

"When shall you be at Cambridge? You have hinted, I think,
that your friend Bland is returned from Holland. I have always had a
great respect for his talents, and for all that I have heard of his character;
but of me, I believe, he knows nothing, except that he heard my 6th
form repetitions ten months together, at the average of two lines a
morning, and those never perfect. I remembered him and his ' Slaves'
as I passed between Capes Matapan, St. Angelo, and his Isle of Ceriga,
and I always bewailed the absence of the Anthology. I suppose he
will now translate Vondel, the Dutch Shakspeare, and ' Gysbert van
Amstel' will easily be accommodated to our stage in its present state;
and I presume he saw the Dutch poem, where the love of Pyramus and
Thisbe is compared to the *passion* of *Christ;* also the love of *Lucifer* for
Eve, and other varieties of Low Country literature. No doubt you will
think me crazed to talk of such things, but they are all in black and
white and good repute on the banks of every canal from Amsterdam to
Alkmaar.

"Yours ever,

"B.

" My Poesy is in the hands of its various publishers; but the
' Hints from Horace' (to which I have subjoined some savage lines on
Methodism, and ferocious notes on the vanity of the triple Editory of
the Edin. Annual Register), my ' *Hints,*' I say, stand still, and why?—I
have not a friend in the world (but you and Drury) who can construe
Horace's Latin, or my English, well enough to adjust them for the press,
or to correct the proofs in a grammatical way. So that, unless you have
bowels when you return to town (I am too far off to do it for myself),
this ineffable work will be lost to the world for—I don't know how many
weeks.

" ' Childe Harold's Pilgrimage' must wait till *Murray*'s is finished.
He is making a tour in Middlesex, and is to return soon, when high
matter may be expected. He wants to have it in quarto, which is a
cursed unsaleable size; but it is pestilent long, and one must obey one's
bookseller. I trust Murray will pass the Paddington Canal without
being seduced by Payne and Mackinlay's example,—I say Payne and
Mackinlay, supposing that the partnership held good. Drury, the villain,
has not written to me; ' I am never (as Mrs. Lumpkin says to Tony) to
be gratified with the monster's dear wild notes.'

" So you are going (going indeed!) into orders. You must make
your peace with the Eclectic Reviewers—they accuse you of impiety, I
fear, with injustice. Demetrius, the ' Sieger of Cities,' is here, with
' Gilpin Horner.' The painter* is not necessary, as the portraits he
already painted are (by anticipation) very like the new animals.—Write,
and send me your ' Love Song'—but I want ' paulo majora' from you.
Make a dash before you are a deacon, and try a *dry* publisher.

" Yours always,

" B."

It was at this period that I first had the happiness of seeing and
becoming acquainted with Lord Byron. The correspondence, in which
our acquaintance originated, is, in a high degree, illustrative of the frank
manliness of his character; and, as it was begun on my side, some egotism

---

* Barber, whom he had brought down to Newstead to paint his wolf and his bear.

must be tolerated in the detail which I have to give of the circumstance
that led to it. So far back as the year 1806, on the occasion of a meeting
which took place at Chalk Farm between Mr. Jeffrey and myself, a good
deal of ridicule and raillery, founded on a false representation of what
occurred before the magistrates at Bow-street, appeared in almost all the
public prints. In consequence of this, I was induced to address a letter
to the Editor of one of the Journals, contradicting the falsehood that
had been circulated, and stating briefly the real circumstances of the
case. For some time, my letter seemed to produce the intended effect
—but, unluckily, the original story was too tempting a theme for
humour and sarcasm to be so easily superseded by mere matter of
fact. Accordingly, after a little time, whenever the subject was
publicly alluded to,—more especially by those who were at all " willing
to wound,"—the old falsehood was, for the sake of its ready sting
revived.

In the year 1809, on the first appearance of " English Bards and
Scotch Reviewers," I found the author, who was then generally understood to be Lord Byron, not only jesting on this subject—and with
sufficiently provoking pleasantry and cleverness—in his verse, but giving
also, in the more responsible form of a note, an outline of the transaction
in accordance with the original misreport, and, therefore, in direct contradiction to my published statement. Still, as the Satire was anonymous
and unacknowledged, I did not feel that I was, in any way, called upon
to notice it, and therefore dismissed the matter entirely from my mind.
In the summer of the same year appeared the Second Edition of the
work, with Lord Byron's name prefixed to it. I was, at the time, in
Ireland, and but little in the way of literary society; and it so happened
that some months passed away before the appearance of this new edition
was known to me. Immediately on being apprized of it,—the offence
now assuming a different form,—I addressed the following letter to Lord
Byron, and, transmitting it to a friend in London, requested that he
would have it delivered into his lordship's hands*.

* This is the only entire letter of my own that, in the course of this work, I mean to
obtrude upon my readers. Being short, and in terms more explanatory of the feeling on which
I acted than any others that could be substituted, it might be suffered, I thought, to form the

" Dublin, January 1st, 1810.

" MY LORD,

" Having just seen the name of ' Lord Byron' prefixed to a work, entitled ' English Bards and Scotch Reviewers,' in which, as it appears to me, *the lie is given* to a public statement of mine, respecting an affair with Mr. Jeffrey some years since, I beg you will have the goodness to inform me whether I may consider your lordship as the author of this publication.

" I shall not, I fear, be able to return to London for a week or two; but, in the mean time, I trust your lordship will not deny me the satisfaction of knowing whether you avow the insult contained in the passages alluded to.

" It is needless to suggest to your lordship the propriety of keeping our correspondence secret.

" I have the honour to be

" Your lordship's very humble servant,

" THOMAS MOORE.

" 22, Molesworth-street."

In the course of a week, the friend to whom I intrusted this letter wrote to inform me that Lord Byron had, as he learned on inquiring of his publisher, gone abroad immediately on the publication of his Second Edition; but that my letter had been placed in the hands of a gentleman, named Hodgson, who had undertaken to forward it carefully to his lordship. Though the latter step was not exactly what I could have wished, I thought it as well, on the whole, to let my letter take its chance, and again postponed all consideration of the matter.

During the interval of a year and a half which elapsed before Lord Byron's return, I had taken upon myself obligations, both as husband and father, which make most men,—and especially those who have nothing to bequeath,—less willing to expose themselves unnecessarily to danger. On hearing, therefore, of the arrival of the noble traveller

single exception to my general rule. In all other cases, I shall merely give such extracts from my own letters, as may be necessary to elucidate those of my correspondent.

from Greece, though still thinking it due to myself to follow up my first request of an explanation, I resolved, in prosecuting that object, to adopt such a tone of conciliation as should not only prove my sincere desire of a pacific result, but show the entire freedom from any angry or resentful feeling with which I took the step. The death of Mrs. Byron, for some time, delayed my purpose. But as soon after that event as was consistent with decorum, I addressed a letter to Lord Byron, in which, referring to my former communication, and expressing some doubts as to its having ever reached him, I re-stated, in pretty nearly the same words, the nature of the insult, which, as it appeared to me, the passage in his note was calculated to convey. " It is now useless," I continued, " to speak of the steps with which it was my intention to follow up that letter. The time which has elapsed since then, though it has done away neither the injury nor the feeling of it, has, in many respects, materially altered my situation; and the only object which I have now in writing to your lordship is to preserve some consistency with that former letter, and to prove to you that the injured feeling still exists, however circumstances may compel me to be deaf to its dictates, at present. When I say 'injured feeling,' let me assure your lordship that there is not a single vindictive sentiment in my mind towards you. I mean but to express that uneasiness, under (what I consider to be) a charge of falsehood, which must haunt a man of any feeling to his grave, unless the insult be retracted or atoned for; and which, if I did *not* feel, I should, indeed, deserve far worse than your lordship's satire could inflict upon me." In conclusion I added, that, so far from being influenced by any angry or resentful feeling towards him, it would give me sincere pleasure, if, by any satisfactory explanation, he would enable me to seek the honour of being henceforward ranked among his acquaintance*.

To this letter, Lord Byron returned the following answer.

---

* Finding two different draughts of this letter among my papers, I cannot be quite certain as to some of the terms employed; but have little doubt that they are here given correctly.

LETTER LXXIII.

TO MR. MOORE.

" Cambridge, October 27th, 1811.

" SIR,

" Your letter followed me from Notts. to this place, which will account for the delay of my reply. Your former letter I never had the honour to receive;—be assured, in whatever part of the world it had found me, I should have deemed it my duty to return and answer it in person.

" The advertisement you mention, I know nothing of.—At the time of your meeting with Mr. Jeffrey, I had recently entered College, and remember to have heard and read a number of squibs on the occasion, and from the recollection of these I derived all my knowledge on the subject, without the slightest idea of ' giving the lie' to an address which I never beheld. When I put my name to the production, which has occasioned this correspondence, I became responsible to all whom it might concern,—to explain where it requires explanation, and, where insufficiently or too sufficiently explicit, at all events to satisfy. My situation leaves me no choice; it rests with the injured and the angry to obtain reparation in their own way.

" With regard to the passage in question, *you* were certainly *not* the person towards whom I felt personally hostile. On the contrary, my whole thoughts were engrossed by one, whom I had reason to consider as my worst literary enemy, nor could I foresee that his former antagonist was about to become his champion. You do not specify what you would wish to have done: I can neither retract nor apologize for a charge of falsehood which I never advanced.

" In the beginning of the week, I shall be at No. 8, St. James's-street. —Neither the letter or the friend to whom you stated your intention ever made their appearance.

" Your friend, Mr. Rogers, or any other gentleman delegated by you, will find me most ready to adopt any conciliatory proposition

which shall not compromise my own honour,—or, failing in that, to make
the atonement you deem it necessary to require.

> " I have the honour to be, sir,
>
>   " your most obedient, humble servant,
>
>   " BYRON."

In my reply to this, I commenced by saying that his lordship's
letter was, upon the whole, as satisfactory as I could expect. It
contained all that, in the strict *diplomatique* of explanation, could be
required, namely,—that he had never seen the statement which I
supposed him wilfully to have contradicted,—that he had no intention
of bringing against me any charge of falsehood, and that the objectionable passage of his work was not levelled personally at *me*. This, I
added, was all the explanation that I had a right to expect, and I was, of
course, satisfied with it.

I then entered into some detail relative to the transmission of
my first letter from Dublin,—giving, as my reason for descending to
these minute particulars, that I did not, I must confess, feel quite easy
under the manner in which his lordship had noticed the miscarriage of
that first application to him.

My reply concluded thus :—" As your lordship does not show any
wish to proceed beyond the rigid formulary of explanation, it is not for
me to make any further advances. We, Irishmen, in businesses of this
kind, seldom know any medium between decided hostility and decided
friendship ;—but, as any approaches towards the latter alternative must
now depend entirely on your lordship, I have only to repeat that I am
satisfied with your letter, and that I have the honour to be," &c. &c.

On the following day, I received the annexed rejoinder from Lord
Byron.

LETTER LXXIV.

TO MR. MOORE.

"8, St. James's-street, October 29th, 1811.

"SIR,

"Soon after my return to England, my friend, Mr. Hodgson, apprized me that a letter for me was in his possession; but a domestic event hurrying me from London, immediately after, the letter (which may most probably be your own) is still *unopened in his keeping*. If, on examination of the address, the similarity of the handwriting should lead to such a conclusion, it shall be opened in your presence, for the satisfaction of all parties. Mr. H. is at present out of town;—on Friday I shall see him, and request him to forward it to my address.

"With regard to the latter part of both your letters, until the principal point was discussed between us, I felt myself at a loss in what manner to reply. Was I to anticipate friendship from one, who conceived me to have charged him with falsehood? Were not *advances*, under such circumstances, to be misconstrued,—not, perhaps, by the person to whom they were addressed, but by others? In *my* case, such a step was impracticable. If you, who conceived yourself to be the offended person, are satisfied that you had no cause for offence, it will not be difficult to convince me of it. My situation, as I have before stated, leaves me no choice. I should have felt proud of your acquaintance, had it commenced under other circumstances; but it must rest with you to determine how far it may proceed after so *auspicious* a beginning.

"I have the honour to be, &c."

Somewhat piqued, I own, at the manner in which my efforts towards a more friendly understanding,—ill-timed as I confess them to have been,—were received, I hastened to close our correspondence by a short note, saying, that his lordship had made me feel the imprudence I was guilty of, in wandering from the point immediately in discussion between us; and I should now, therefore, only add, that if, in my last letter, I had correctly stated the substance of his explanation, our correspondence might, from this moment, cease for ever, as with that explanation I declared myself satisfied.

This brief note drew immediately from Lord Byron the following frank and open-hearted reply.

LETTER LXXV.

TO MR. MOORE.

"8, St James's-street, October 30th, 1811.

" SIR,

" You must excuse my troubling you once more upon this very unpleasant subject. It would be a satisfaction to me, and I should think, to yourself, that the unopened letter in Mr. Hodgson's possession (supposing it to prove your own) should be returned 'in statu quo' to the writer; particularly as you expressed yourself 'not quite easy under the manner in which I had dwelt on its miscarriage.'

" A few words more, and I shall not trouble you further. I felt, and still feel, very much flattered by those parts of your correspondence, which held out the prospect of our becoming acquainted. If I did not meet them, in the first instance, as perhaps I ought, let the situation in which I was placed be my defence. You have *now* declared yourself *satisfied*, and on that point we are no longer at issue. If, therefore, you still retain any wish to do me the honour you hinted at, I shall be most happy to meet you, when, where, and how you please, and I presume you will not attribute my saying thus much to any unworthy motive.

" I have the honour to remain, &c."

On receiving this letter, I went instantly to my friend, Mr. Rogers, who was, at that time, on a visit at Holland House, and, for the first time, informed him of the correspondence in which I had been engaged. With his usual readiness to oblige and serve, he proposed that the meeting between Lord Byron and myself should take place at his table, and requested of me to convey to the noble lord his wish, that he would do him the honour of naming some day for that purpose. The following is Lord Byron's answer to the note which I then wrote.

LETTER LXXVI.

TO MR. MOORE.

"8, St. James's-street, November 1st, 1811.

" SIR,

" As I should be very sorry to interrupt your Sunday's engagement, if Monday, or any other day of the ensuing week, would be equally convenient to yourself and friend, I will then have the honour of accepting his invitation. Of the professions of esteem with which Mr. Rogers has honoured me, I cannot but feel proud, though undeserving. I should be wanting to myself, if insensible to the praise of such a man; and, should my approaching interview with him and his friend lead to any degree of intimacy with both or either, I shall regard our past correspondence as one of the happiest events of my life.

" I have the honour to be,
" Your very sincere and obedient servant,
" BYRON."

It can hardly, I think, be necessary to call the reader's attention to the good sense, self-possession, and frankness of these letters of Lord Byron. I had placed him,—by the somewhat national confusion which I had made of the boundaries of peace and war, of hostility and friendship,—in a position which, ignorant as he was of the character of the person who addressed him, it required all the watchfulness of his sense of honour to guard from surprise or snare. Hence, the judicious reserve with which he abstained from noticing my advances towards acquaintance, till he should have ascertained exactly whether the explanation which he was willing to give would be such as his correspondent would be satisfied to receive. The moment he was set at rest on this point, the frankness of his nature displayed itself; and th disregard of all further mediation or etiquette with which he at onc professed himself ready to meet me "when, where, and how" I pleased showed that he could be as pliant and confiding *after* such an under standing, as he had been judiciously reserved and punctilious *before* it.

Such did I find Lord Byron, on my first experience of him; ane such,—so open and manly-minded,—did I find him to the last.

It was, at first, intended by Mr. Rogers that his company at dinne should not extend beyond Lord Byron and myself; but Mr. Thoma Campbell, having called upon our host that morning, was invited to joi the party, and consented. Such a meeting could not be otherwise than interesting to us all. It was the first time that Lord Byron was eve seen by any of his three companions; while he, on his side, for the first time, found himself in the society of persons, whose names had been associated with his first literary dreams, and to *two** of whom he looked up with that tributary admiration, which youthful genius is ever ready to pay to its precursors.

Among the impressions which this meeting left upon me, what I chiefly remember to have remarked was the nobleness of his air, his beauty, the gentleness of his voice and manners, and—what was, naturally, not the least attraction—his marked kindness to myself. Being in mourn-ing for his mother, the colour, as well of his dress, as of his glossy, curling, and picturesque hair, gave more effect to the pure, spiritual paleness of his features, in the expression of which, when he spoke, there was a perpetual play of lively thought, though melancholy was their habitual character, when in repose.

As we had none of us been apprized of his peculiarities with respect to food, the embarrassment of our host was not a little, on discovering that there was nothing upon the table which his noble guest could eat or drink. Neither meat, fish, or wine would Lord Byron touch; and of biscuits and soda-water, which he asked for, there had been, unluckily, no

---

* In speaking thus, I beg to disclaim all affected modesty. Lord Byron had already made the same distinction himself in the opinions which he expressed of the living poets; and I cannot but be aware that, for the praises which he afterwards bestowed on my writings, I was, in a great degree, indebted to his partiality to myself.

provision. He professed, however, to be equally well pleased with potatoes and vinegar; and of these meagre materials contrived to make rather a hearty dinner.

I shall now resume the series of his correspondence with other friends.

LETTER LXXVII.

TO MR. HARNESS.

"8, St. James's-street, December 6th, 1811.

" MY DEAR HARNESS,

" I. write again, but don't suppose I mean to lay such a tax on your pen and patience as to expect regular replies. When you are inclined, write; when silent, I shall have the consolation of knowing that you are much better employed. Yesterday, Bland and I called on Mr. Miller, who, being then out, will call on Bland * to-day or to-morrow. I shall certainly endeavour to bring them together.—You are censorious, child; when you are a little older, you will learn to dislike every body, but abuse nobody.

" With regard to the person of whom you speak, your own good sense must direct you. I never pretend to advise, being an implicit believer in the old proverb. This present frost is detestable. It is the first I have felt these three years, though I longed for one in the oriental summer, when no such thing is to be had, unless I had gone to the top of Hymettus for it.

" I thank you most truly for the concluding part of your letter. I have been of late not much accustomed to kindness from any quarter, and I am not the less pleased to meet with it again from one, where I had known it earliest. I have not changed in all my ramblings,—Harrow and, of course, yourself never left me, and the

' Dulces reminiscitur Argos'

---

* The Rev. Robert Bland, one of the authors of " Collections from the Greek Anthology." Lord Byron was, at this time, endeavouring to secure for Mr. Bland the task of translating Lucien Buonaparte's Poem.

attended me to the very spot to which that sentence alludes in the min of the fallen Argive.—Our intimacy began before we began to date a all, and it rests with you to continue it till the hour which must numbe it and me with the things that *were*.

"Do read mathematics.—I should think *X plus Y* at least a amusing as the Curse of Kehama, and much more intelligible. Maste S.'s poems *are*, in fact, what parallel lines might be—viz., prolonged *a infinitum* without meeting any thing half so absurd as themselves.

> "What news, what news? Queen Oreaca,
>   What news of scribblers five?
> S———, W———, C———e, L—d and L—e?—
>   All damn'd, though yet alive.

C———e is lecturing. 'Many an old fool,' said Hannibal to some sucl lecturer, 'but such as this, never.'

"Ever yours, &c."

LETTER LXXVIII.

TO MR. HARNESS.

"8, St. James-street, Dec. 8th, 1811.

"Behold a most formidable sheet, without gilt or black edging and consequently very vulgar and indecorous, particularly to one of you precision; but this being Sunday, I can procure no better, and will atone for its length by not filling it. Bland I have not seen since my las letter; but on Tuesday he dines with me and will meet M * * e, the epitome of all that is exquisite in poetical or personal accomplishments How Bland has settled with Miller, I know not. I have very little interest with either, and they must arrange their concerns according to their own gusto. I have done my endeavours, *at your request*, to bring them together, and hope they may agree to their mutual advantage.

"Coleridge has been lecturing against Campbell. Rogers wa present, and from him I derive the information. We are going to make a party to hear this Manichean of poesy.—Pole is to marry Miss Long

and will be a very miserable dog for all that.   The present ministers are
to continue, and his majesty *does* continue in the same state.   So there's
folly and madness for you, both in a breath.

"I never heard but of one man truly fortunate, and he was
Beaumarchais, the author of Figaro, who buried two wives and gained
three lawsuits before he was thirty.

"And now, child, what art thou doing? *Reading, I trust.*   I want
to see you take a degree.   Remember this is the most important period
of your life; and don't disappoint your papa and your aunt, and all your
kin—besides myself.   Don't you know that all male children are begotten
for the express purpose of being graduates? and that even I am an A.M.,
though how I became so, the Public Orator only can resolve.   Besides,
you are to be a priest; and to confute Sir William Drummond's late
book about the Bible (printed, but not published), and all other infidels
whatever.   Now leave master H.'s gig, and master S.'s Sapphics, and
become as immortal as Cambridge can make you.

"You see, Mio Carissimo, what a pestilent correspondent I am
likely to become; but then you shall be as quiet at Newstead as you
please, and I won't disturb your studies, as I do now.   When do you fix
the day, that I may take you up according to contract?   Hodgson talks
of making a third in our journey: but we can't stow him, inside at least.
Positively you shall go with me as was agreed, and don't let me have
any of your *politesse* to H. on the occasion.   I shall manage to arrange
for both with a little contrivance.   I wish H. was not quite so fat, and
we should pack better.   Has he left off vinous liquors?   He is an
excellent soul; but I don't think water would improve him, at least
*in*ternally.   You will want to know what I am doing—chewing tobacco.

"You see nothing of my allies, Scrope Davies and Matthews *—
they don't suit you; and how does it happen that I—who am a pipkin
of the same pottery—continue in your good graces?   Good night,—I will
go on in the morning.

"Dec. 9th. In a morning I'm always sullen, and to-day is as sombre
as myself.   Rain and mist are worse than a sirocco, particularly in a

* The brother of his late friend, Charles Skinner Matthews.

beef-eating and beer-drinking country. My bookseller, Cawthorne, ha
just left me, and tells me, with a most important face, that he is i
treaty for a novel of Madame D'Arblay's, for which 1000 guineas ar
asked! He wants me to read the MS. (if he obtains it), which I shal
do with pleasure; but I should be very cautious in venturing an opinio
on her, whose Cecilia Dr. Johnson superintended. If he lends it to me
I shall put it into the hands of Rogers and M * * e, who are truly me
of taste. I have filled the sheet, and beg your pardon; I will not do i
again. I shall, perhaps, write again, but if not, believe, silent o
scribbling, that I am, my dearest William, ever, &c."

LETTER LXXIX.

TO MR. HODGSON.

" London, Dec. 8th, 1811.

" I sent you a sad Tale of Three Friars the other day, and now take
a dose in another style. I wrote it a day or two ago, on hearing a song
of former days.

" Away, away, ye notes of woe *, &c. &c.

" I have gotten a book by Sir W. Drummond (printed, but no
published), entitled Œdipus Judaicus, in which he attempts to prove the
greater part of the Old Testament an allegory, particularly Genesis and
Joshua. He professes himself a theist in the preface, and handles the
literal interpretation very roughly. I wish you could see it. Mr. W * *
has lent it me, and I confess, to me, it is worth fifty Watsons.

" You and Harness must fix on the time for your visit to Newstead;
I can command mine at your wish, unless any thing particular occurs in
the interim.   *   *   *   Bland dines with me on Tuesday to meet
Moore. Coleridge has attacked the ' Pleasures of Hope,' and all other
pleasures whatsoever. Mr. Rogers was present, and heard himself indirectly *rowed* by the lecturer. We are going in a party to hear the new
Art of Poetry by this reformed schismatic; and were I one of these

* This poem is now printed in Lord Byron's Works.

poetical luminaries, or of sufficient consequence to be noticed by the man of lectures, I should not hear him without an answer. For, you know, 'an' a man will be beaten with brains, he shall never keep a clean doublet.' C * * will be desperately annoyed. I never saw a man (and of him I have seen very little) so sensitive;—what a happy temperament! I am sorry for it; what can *he* fear from criticism? I don't know if Bland has seen Miller, who was to call on him yesterday.

"To-day is the Sabbath,—a day I never pass pleasantly, but at Cambridge; and, even there, the organ is a sad remembrancer. Things are stagnant enough in town,—as long as they don't retrograde, 'tis all very well. H * * writes and writes and writes, and is an author. I do nothing but eschew tobacco. I wish parliament were assembled, that I may hear, and perhaps some day be heard;—but on this point I am not very sanguine. I have many plans;—sometimes I think of the East again, and dearly beloved Greece. I am well, but weakly. Yesterday Kinnaird told me I looked very ill, and sent me home happy.

"You will never give up wine;—see what it is to be thirty; if you were six years younger, you might leave off any thing. You drink and repent, you repent and drink. Is Scrope still interesting and invalid? And how does Hinde with his cursed chemistry? To Harness I have written, and he has written, and we have all written, and have nothing now to do but write again, till death splits up the pen and the scribbler.

"The Alfred has 354 candidates for six vacancies. The cook has run away and left us liable, which makes our committee very plaintive. Master Brook, our head serving-man, has the gout, and our new cook is none of the best. I speak from report,—for what is cookery to a leguminous-eating ascetic? So now you know as much of the matter as I do. Books and quiet are still there, and they may dress their dishes in their own way for me. Let me know your determination as to Newstead, and believe me,

"Yours ever,

"Νωαιρῶν."

LETTER LXXX.

TO MR. HODGSON.

"8, St. James s-street, Dec. 12th, 1811.

" Why, Hodgson! I fear you have left off wine and me at the sam time,—I have written and written and written, and no answer! M· dear Sir Edgar, water disagrees with you,—drink sack and write. Blan did not come to his appointment, being unwell, but M * * e supplied al other vacancies most delectably. I have hopes of his joining us a Newstead. I am sure you would like him more and more as h developes,—at least I do.

" How Miller and Bland go on, I don't know. Cawthorne talks o being in treaty for a novel of M^e. D'Arblay's, and if he obtains it (a 1000 gs.!!) wishes me to see the MS. This I should read with pleasure,— not that I should ever dare to venture a criticism on her whose writing Dr. Johnson once revised, but for the pleasure of the thing. If my worthy publisher wanted a sound opinion, I should send the MS. t Rogers and M * * e, as men most alive to true taste. I have had frequen letters from Wm. Harness, and *you* are silent; certes, you are not schoolboy. However, I have the consolation of knowing that you ar better employed, viz. reviewing. You don't deserve that I should ad another syllable, and I won't. Yours, &c.

" P. S. I only wait for your answer to fix our meeting."

LETTER LXXXI.

TO MR. HARNESS.

"8, St. James's-street, December 15, 1811.

" I wrote you an answer to your last, which, on reflection, please me as little as it probably has pleased yourself. I will not wait for you rejoinder; but proceed to tell you, that I had just then been greete with an epistle of * *'s, full of his petty grievances, and this at th moment when (from circumstances it is not necessary to enter upon) was bearing up against recollections to which *his* imaginary suffering are as a scratch to a cancer. These things combined, put me out of humour with him and all mankind. The latter part of my life has been a perpetual struggle against affections which imbittered the earliest portion; and though I flatter myself I have in a great measure conquered them, yet there are moments (and this was one) when I am as foolish as formerly. I never said so much before, nor had I said this now, if I did not suspect myself of having been rather savage in my letter, and wish to inform you thus much of the cause. You know I am not one of your dolorous gentlemen: so now let us laugh again.

"Yesterday I went with Moore to Sydenham to visit Campbell *. He was not visible, so we jogged homeward, merrily enough. To-morrow I dine with Rogers, and am to hear Coleridge, who is a kind of rage at present. Last night I saw Kemble in Coriolanus;—he *was glorious*, and exerted himself wonderfully. By good luck, I got an excellent place in the best part of the house, which was more than overflowing. Clare and Delawarre, who were there on the same speculation, were less fortunate. I saw them by accident,—we were not together. I wished for you, to gratify your love of Shakspeare and of fine acting to its fullest extent. Last week I saw an exhibition of a different kind in a Mr. Coates, at the Haymarket, who performed Lothario in a *damned* and damnable manner.

"I told you of the fate of B. and H. in my last. So much for these sentimentalists, who console themselves in their stews for the loss—the never to be recovered loss—the despair of the refined attachment of a couple of drabs! You censure *my* life, Harness,—when I compare myself with these men, my elders and my betters, I really begin to conceive myself a monument of prudence—a walking statue—without feeling or failing; and yet the world in general hath given me a proud pre-eminence over them in profligacy. Yet I like the men, and, God

---

* On this occasion, another of the noble poet's peculiarities was, somewhat startlingly, introduced to my notice. When we were on the point of setting out from his lodgings in St. James's-street, it being then about mid-day, he said to the servant, who was shutting the door of the vis-à-vis, "Have you put in the pistols?" and was answered in the affirmative. It was difficult,—more especially, taking into account the circumstances under which we had just become acquainted,—to keep from smiling at this singular noon-day precaution.

knows, ought not to condemn their aberrations. But I own I feel pro
voked when they dignify all this by the name of *love*—romantic attach
ments for things marketable for a dollar!

"Dec. 16th.—I have just received your letter;—I feel your kindnes
very deeply. The foregoing part of my letter, written yesterday, will,
hope, account for the tone of the former, though it cannot excuse it
I do *like* to hear from you—more than *like*. Next to seeing you, I hav
no greater satisfaction. But you have other duties and greater pleasures
and I should regret to take a moment from either. H** was to cal
to-day, but I have not seen him. The circumstances you mention a
the close of your letter is another proof in favour of my opinion of man
kind. Such you will always find them—selfish and distrustful. I excep
none. The cause of this is the state of society. In the world, every one
is to stir for himself—it is useless, perhaps selfish, to expect any thing
from his neighbour. But I do not think we are born of this disposition
for you find *friendship*, as a schoolboy, and *love* enough before twenty

"I went to see **; he keeps me in town, where I don't wish to be at
present. He is a good man, but totally without conduct. And now,
my dearest William, I must wish you good morrow, and remain ever
most sincerely and affectionately yours, &c."

From the time of our first meeting, there seldom elapsed a day that
Lord Byron and I did not see each other; and our acquaintance ripened
into intimacy and friendship with a rapidity of which I have seldom
known an example. I was, indeed, lucky in all the circumstances that
attended my first introduction to him. In a generous nature like his,
the pleasure of repairing an injustice would naturally give a zest to
any partiality I might have inspired in his mind; while the manner in
which I had sought this reparation, free as it was from resentment or
defiance, left nothing painful to remember in the transaction between
us,—no compromise or concession that could wound self-love, or take
away from the grace of that frank friendship, to which he at once, so
cordially and so unhesitatingly, admitted me. I was also not a little
fortunate in forming my acquaintance with him, before his success had
yet reached its meridian burst,—before the triumphs that were in store

for him had brought the world all in homage at his feet, and, among the splendid crowds that courted his society, even claims less humble than mine had but a feeble chance of fixing his regard. As it was, the new scene of life that opened upon him with his success, instead of detaching us from each other, only multiplied our opportunities of meeting, and increased our intimacy. In that society where his birth entitled him to move, circumstances had already placed me, notwithstanding mine; and when, after the appearance of " Childe Harold," he began to mingle with the world, the same persons, who had long been *my* intimates and friends, became his; our visits were mostly to the same places, and, in the gay and giddy round of a London spring, we were generally (as in one of his own letters he expresses it) " embarked in the same Ship of Fools together."

But, at the time when we first met, his position in the world was most solitary. Even those coffee-house companions who, before his departure from England, had served him as a sort of substitute for more worthy society, were either relinquished or had dispersed; and, with the exception of three or four associates of his college days (to whom he appeared strongly attached), Mr. Dallas and his solicitor seemed to be the only persons whom, even in their very questionable degree, he could boast of as friends. Though too proud to complain of this loneliness, it was evident that he felt it; and that the state of cheerless isolation, " unguided and unfriended," to which, on entering into manhood, he had found himself abandoned, was one of the chief sources of that resentful disdain of mankind, which even their subsequent worship of him came too late to remove. The effect, indeed, which his short commerce with society afterwards had, for the period it lasted, in softening and exhilarating his temper, showed how fit a soil his heart would have been for the growth of all the kindlier feelings, had but a portion of this sunshine of the world's smiles shone on him earlier.

At the same time, in all such speculations and conjectures as to what *might* have been, under more favourable circumstances, his character, it is invariably to be borne in mind, that his very defects were among the elements of his greatness, and that it was out of the struggle between the good and evil principles of his nature that his mighty genius drew

its strength. A more genial and fostering introduction into life, whil
it would doubtless have softened and disciplined his mind, might hav
impaired its vigour; and the same influences that would have diffuse
smoothness and happiness over his life might have been fatal to its glory
In a short poem of his*, which appears to have been produced at Athen
(as I find it written on a leaf of the original MS. of Childe Harold, an
dated "Athens, 1811,") there are two lines which, though hardly intel
ligible as connected with the rest of the poem, may, taken separately, b
interpreted as implying a sort of prophetic consciousness that it was ou
of the wreck and ruin of all his hopes the immortality of his name wa
to arise.

> " Dear object of defeated care,
>   Though now of love and thee bereft,
> To reconcile me with despair,
>   Thine image and my tears are left.
> 'Tis said with sorrow Time can cope,
>   But this, I feel, can ne'er be true;
> For, *by the death-blow of my hope,*
>   *My Memory immortal grew!*"

We frequently, during the first months of our acquaintance, dined
together alone; and as we had no club, in common, to resort to,—the
Alfred being the only one to which he, at that period, belonged, and I
being then a member of none but Watier's,—our dinners used to be either
at the St. Alban's, or at his old haunt, Stevens's. Though at times he
would drink freely enough of claret, he still adhered to his system of
abstinence in food. He appeared, indeed, to have conceived a notion
that animal food has some peculiar influence on the character; and I
remember, one day, as I sat opposite to him, employed, I suppose, rather
earnestly over a beef-steak, after watching me for a few seconds, he said,
in a grave tone of inquiry—"Moore, don't you find eating beef-steak
makes you ferocious?"

Understanding me to have expressed a wish to become a member
of the Alfred, he very good-naturedly lost no time in proposing me a

---

* " Written beneath the picture of ———."

a candidate; but as the resolution which I had then nearly formed of betaking myself to a country life rendered an additional club in London superfluous, I wrote to beg that he would, for the present, at least, withdraw my name; and his answer, though containing little, being the first familiar note he ever honoured me with, I may be excused for feeling a peculiar pleasure in inserting it.

LETTER LXXXII.

TO MR. MOORE.

"December 11th, 1811.

"MY DEAR MOORE,

"If you please, we will drop our formal monosyllables, and adhere to the appellations sanctioned by our godfathers and godmothers. If you make it a point, I will withdraw your name; at the same time there is no occasion, as I have this day postponed your election ' sine die,' till it shall suit your wishes to be amongst us. I do not say this from any awkwardness the erasure of your proposal would occasion to *me*, but simply such is the state of the case; and, indeed, the longer your name is up, the stronger will become the probability of success, and your voters more numerous. Of course you will decide—your wish shall be my law. If my zeal has already outrun discretion, pardon me, and attribute my officiousness to an excusable motive.

"I wish you would go down with me to Newstead. Hodgson will be there, and a young friend, named Harness, the earliest and dearest I ever had from the third form at Harrow to this hour. I can promise you good wine, and, if you like shooting, a manor of 4000 acres, fires, books, your own free will, and my own very indifferent company. ' Balnea, vina * *' * * *

"Hodgson will plague you, I fear, with verse;—for my own part, I will conclude, with Martial, ' nil recitabo tibi;' and surely the last inducement is not the least. Ponder on my proposition, and believe me, my dear Moore,

"Yours ever,

"BYRON."

Among those acts of generosity and friendship by which every yea of Lord Byron's life was signalized, there is none, perhaps, that, for i own peculiar seasonableness and delicacy, as well as for the perfec worthiness of the person who was the object of it, deserves more honou able mention than that which I am now about to record, and which too place nearly at the period of which I am speaking. The friend, whos good fortune it was to inspire the feeling thus testified, was Mr. Hodgso the gentleman to whom so many of the preceding letters are addressec and as it would be unjust to rob him of the grace and honour of being himself, the testimony of obligations so signal, I shall here lay before m readers an extract from the letter with which, in reference to a passag in one of his noble friend's Journals, he has favoured me.

" I feel it incumbent upon me to explain the circumstances to whic this passage alludes, however private their nature. They are, indeec calculated to do honour to the memory of my lamented friend. Havin become involved, unfortunately, in difficulties and embarrassments, received from Lord Byron (besides former pecuniary obligations) assist ance, at the time in question, to the amount of a thousand pounds. Ai of such magnitude was equally unsolicited and unexpected on my part but it was the long-cherished, though secret, purpose of my friend t afford that aid; and he only waited for the period when he thought i would be of most service. His own words were, on the occasion of con ferring this overwhelming favour, '*I always intended to do it.*'"

During all this time, and through the months of January an February, his Poem of " Childe Harold" was in its progress through th press; and to the changes and additions which he made in the course o printing, some of the most beautiful passages of the work owe their existence. On comparing, indeed, his rough draft of the two Canto with the finished form in which they exist at present, we are mad sensible of the power which the man of genius possesses, not only o surpassing others, but of improving on himself. Originally, the " little Page" and " Yeoman" of the Childe were introduced to the reader' notice in the following tame stanzas, by expanding the substance of which into their present light, lyric shape, it is almost needless to remark how much the poet has gained in variety and dramatic effect:—

" And of his train there was a henchman page,
     A peasant boy, who served his master well;
     And often would his pranksome prate engage
     Childe Burun's * ear, when his proud heart did swell
     With sullen thoughts that he disdain'd to tell.
     Then would he smile on him, and Alwin† smiled,
     When aught that from his young lips archly fell
     The gloomy film from Harold's eye beguiled.

. . . .

" Him and one yeoman only did he take
     To travel eastward to a far countrie;
     And, though the boy was grieved to leave the lake,
     On whose fair banks he grew from infancy,
     Eftsoons his little heart beat merrily,
     With hope of foreign nations to behold,
     And many things right marvellous to see,
     Of which our vaunting travellers oft have told,
From Mandeville . . . .‡"

In place of that mournful song " to Ines," in the First Canto, which contains some of the dreariest touches of sadness that even his pen ever let fall, he had, in the original construction of the Poem, been so little fastidious as to content himself with such ordinary sing-song as the following :—

" Oh never tell again to me
     Of Northern climes and British ladies,
It has not been your lot to see,
     Like me, the lovely girl of Cadiz.
Although her eye be not of blue,
     Nor fair her locks, like English lasses," &c. &c.

There were also, originally, several stanzas full of direct personality, and some that degenerated into a style still more familiar and ludicrous than that of the description of a London Sunday, which still disfigures the

* If there could be any doubt as to his intention of delineating himself in his hero, this adoption of the old Norman name of his family, which he seems to have at first contemplated, would be sufficient to remove it.

† In the MS. the names " Robin" and " Rupert" had been successively inserted here and scratched out again.

‡ Here the manuscript is illegible.

Poem. In thus mixing up the light with the solemn, it was the intentio
of the poet to imitate Ariosto.' But it is far easier to rise, with grace, fro
the level of a strain generally familiar, into an occasional short burst ‹
pathos or splendour, than to interrupt thus a prolonged tone of solemnit
by any descent into the ludicrous or burlesque*. In the former cas‹
the transition may have the effect of softening or elevating, while, ͏
the latter, it almost invariably shocks;—for the same reason, perhap
that a trait of pathos or high feeling, in comedy, has a peculiar charm
while the intrusion of comic scenes into tragedy, however sanctione
among us by habit and authority, rarely fails to offend. The noble poe
was, himself, convinced of the failure of the experiment, and in none o
the succeeding Cantos of Childe Harold repeated it.

Of the satiric parts, some verses on the well-known traveller, S͏
John Carr, may supply us with, at least, a harmless specimen :—

> " Ye, who would more of Spain and Spaniards know,
> Sights, saints, antiques, arts, anecdotes, and war,
> Go, hie ye hence to Paternoster-row,—
> Are they not written in the boke of Carr?
> Green Erin's Knight, and Europe's wandering star !
> Then listen, readers, to the Man of Ink,
> Hear what he did, and sought, and wrote afar,
> All these are coop'd within one Quarto's brink,
> This borrow, steal (don't buy), and tell us what you think."

Among those passages which, in the course of revisal, he introduced
like pieces of " rich inlay," into the Poem, was that fine stanza—

> " Yet if, as holiest men have deem'd, there be
> A land of souls beyond that sable shore," &c.

through which lines though, it must be confessed, a tone of scepticism
breathes, (as well as in those tender verses,

> " Yes,—I will dream that we may meet again),"

it is a scepticism whose sadness calls far more for pity than blame; ther‹

---

* Among the acknowledged blemishes of Milton's great Poem is his abrupt transition, i͏
this manner, into an imitation of Ariosto's style, in the " Paradise of Fools."

being discoverable, even through its very doubts, an innate warmth of piety, which they had been able to obscure, but not to chill. To use the words of the poet himself, in a note which it was once his intention to affix to these stanzas, " Let it be remembered that the spirit they breathe is desponding, not sneering, scepticism,"—a distinction never to be lost sight of; as, however hopeless may be the conversion of the scoffing infidel, he who feels pain in doubting has still alive within him the seeds of belief.

At the same time with Childe Harold, he had three other works in the press,—his " Hints from Horace," " The Curse of Minerva," and a fifth edition of " English Bards and Scotch Reviewers." The note upon the latter Poem, which had been the lucky origin of our acquaintance, was withdrawn in this edition, and a few words of explanation, which he had the kindness to submit to my perusal, substituted in its place.

In the month of January, the whole of the Two Cantos being printed off, some of the poet's friends, and, among others, Mr. Rogers and myself, were so far favoured as to be indulged with a perusal of the sheets. In adverting to this period in his " Memoranda," Lord Byron, I remember, mentioned,—as one of the ill omens which preceded the publication of the Poem,—that some of the literary friends to whom it was shown expressed doubts of its success, and that one among them had told him " it was too good for the age." Whoever may have pronounced this opinion,—and I have some suspicion that I am, myself, the guilty person,—the age has, it must be owned, most triumphantly refuted the calumny upon its taste which the remark implied.

It was in the hands of Mr. Rogers I first saw the sheets of the Poem, and glanced hastily over a few of the stanzas which he pointed out to me as beautiful. Having occasion, the same morning, to write a note to Lord Byron, I expressed strongly the admiration which this foretaste of his work had excited in me; and the following is,—as far as relates to literary matters,—the answer I received from him.

LETTER LXXXIII.

TO MR. MOORE.

"January 29th, 1812.

"MY DEAR MOORE,

"I wish very much I could have seen you; I am in a state o
ludicrous tribulation.

    *   *   *   *   *   *

"Why do you say that I dislike your poesy?   I have expressed n
such opinion, either in *print* or elsewhere.   In scribbling, myself, it wa
necessary for me to find fault, and I fixed upon the trite charge o
immorality, because I could discover no other, and was so perfectl
qualified, in the innocence of my heart, to 'pluck that mote from m
neighbour's eye.'

"I feel very, very much obliged by your approbation; but, at *thi
moment*, praise, even *your* praise, passes by me like 'the idle wind.'
meant and mean to send you a copy the moment of publication; bu
now, I can think of nothing but damned, deceitful,—delightful woman
as Mr. Liston says in the Knight of Snowdon.

"Believe me, my dear Moore,

"ever yours, most affectionately,

"BYRON."

The passages, here omitted, contain rather *too* amusing an accoun
of a disturbance that had just occurred in the establishment at Newstead
in consequence of the detected misconduct of one of the maid-servants
who had been supposed to stand rather too high in the favour of he
master, and, by the airs of authority which she thereupon assumed, hac
disposed all the rest of the household to regard her with no very
charitable eyes.   The chief actors in the strife were this Sultana and
young Rushton; and the first point in dispute that came to Lord Byron'
knowledge (though circumstances, far from creditable to the damsel
afterwards transpired) was, whether Rushton was bound to carry letter:
to "the Hut" at the bidding of this female.   To an episode of such a

nature I should not have thought of alluding, were it not for the two rather curious letters that follow, which show how gravely and coolly the young lord could arbitrate on such an occasion, and with what considerate leaning towards the servant whose fidelity he had proved, in preference to any new liking or fancy, by which it might be suspected he was actuated towards the other.

LETTER LXXXIV.

TO ROBERT RUSHTON.

" 8, St James's-street, Jan. 21st, 1812.

" Though I have no objection to your refusal to carry *letters* to Mealey's, you will take care that the letters are taken by *Spero* at the proper time. I have also to observe, that Susan is to be treated with civility, and not *insulted* by any person over whom I have the smallest control, or, indeed, by any one whatever, while I have the power to protect her. I am truly sorry to have any subject of complaint against *you;* I have too good an opinion of you to think I shall have occasion to repeat it, after the care I have taken of you, and my favourable intentions in your behalf. I see no occasion for any communication whatever between *you* and the *women*, and wish you to occupy yourself in preparing for the situation in which you will be placed. If a common sense of decency cannot prevent you from conducting yourself towards them with rudeness, I should at least hope that your *own interest*, and regard for a master who has *never* treated you with unkindness, will have some weight.

" Yours, &c.

" BYRON.

" P.S.—I wish you to attend to your arithmetic, to occupy yourself in surveying, measuring, and making yourself acquainted with every particular relative to the *land* of Newstead, and you will *write* to me *one letter every week*, that I may know how you go on."

LETTER LXXXV.

TO ROBERT RUSHTON.

"8, St. James's-street, January 25th, 1812.

"Your refusal to carry the letter was not a subject of remonstranc it was not a part of your business; but the language you used to th girl was (as *she* stated it) highly improper.

"You say that you also have something to complain of; then stat it to me immediately; it would be very unfair, and very contrary to m disposition, not to hear both sides of the question.

"If any thing has passed between you *before* or since my last vis to Newstead, do not be afraid to mention it. I am sure *you* would nd deceive me, though *she* would Whatever it is, *you* shall be forgive I have not been without some suspicions on the subject, and am certai that, at your time of life, the blame could not attach to you. You wi not *consult* any one as to your answer, but write to me immediately. shall be more ready to hear what you have to advance, as I do nd remember ever to have heard a word from you before *against* any huma being, which convinces me you would not maliciously assert an untrutl There is not any one who can do the least injury to you while yor conduct yourself properly. I shall expect your answer immediately.

"Yours, &c.

"BYRON."

It was after writing these letters that he came to the knowledge o some improper levities on the part of the girl, in consequence of whicl he dismissed her and another female servant from Newstead; and how strongly he allowed this discovery to affect his mind, will be seen in a subsequent letter to Mr. Hodgson.

LETTER LXXXVI.

TO MR. HODGSON.

" 8, St. James's-street, February 16th, 1812.

" DEAR HODGSON,

" I send you a proof. Last week I was very ill and confined to bed with stone in the kidney, but I am now quite recovered. If the stone had got into my heart instead of my kidneys, it would have been all the better. The women are gone to their relatives, after many attempts to explain what was already too clear. However, I have quite recovered *that* also, and only wonder at my folly in excepting my own strumpets from the general corruption,—albeit a two months' weakness is better than ten years. I have one request to make, which is, never mention a woman again in any letter to me, or even allude to the existence of the sex. I won't even read a word of the feminine gender;—it must all be ' propria quæ maribus.'

" In the spring of 1813 I shall leave England for ever. Every thing in my affairs tends to this, and my inclinations and health do not discourage it. Neither my habits nor constitution are improved by your customs or your climate. I shall find employment in making myself a good oriental scholar. I shall retain a mansion in one of the fairest islands, and retrace, at intervals, the most interesting portions of the East. In the mean time, I am adjusting my concerns, which will (when arranged) leave me with wealth sufficient even for home, but enough for a principality in Turkey. At present they are involved, but I hope, by taking some necessary but unpleasant steps, to clear every thing. Hobhouse is expected daily in London; we shall be very glad to see him; and, perhaps, you will come up and ' drink deep ere he depart,' if not, ' Mahomet must go to the mountain;'—but Cambridge will bring sad recollections to him, and worse to me, though for very different reasons. I believe the only human being that ever loved me in truth and entirely was of, or belonging to, Cambridge, and, in that, no change can now take place. There is one consolation in death—where he sets his

seal, the impression can neither be melted or broken, but endureth fo
ever.

> " Yours always,
>
> " B."

Among those lesser memorials of his good-nature and mindfulnes
which, while they are precious to those who possess them, are not un
worthy of admiration from others, may be reckoned such letters as th
following, to a youth at Eton, recommending another, who was about t
be entered at that school, to his care.

LETTER LXXXVII.

TO MASTER JOHN COWELL.

> "8, St. James's-street, February 12th, 1812.

" MY DEAR JOHN,

" You have probably long ago forgotten the writer of these lines
who would, perhaps, be unable to recognise *yourself*, from the differenc
which must naturally have taken place in your stature and appearance
since he saw you last. I have been rambling through Portugal, Spain
Greece, &c. &c. for some years, and have found so many changes on my
return, that it would be very unfair not to expect that you should have
had your share of alteration and improvement with the rest. I write to
request a favour of you: a little boy of eleven years, the son of Mr. * *
my particular friend, is about to become an Etonian, and I should esteem
any act of protection or kindness to him as an obligation to myself; let
me beg of you then to take some little notice of him at first, till he is able
to shift for himself.

" I was happy to hear a very favourable account of you from a
schoolfellow a few weeks ago, and should be glad to learn that you
family are as well as I wish them to be. I presume you are in the uppe
school;—as an *Etonian*, you will look down upon a *Harrow* man; but I
never, even in my boyish days, disputed your superiority, which I once

experienced in a cricket match, where I had the honour of making one of eleven, who were beaten to their hearts' content by your college in *one innings*.

"Believe me to be, with great truth, &c. &c."

On the 27th of February, a day or two before the appearance of Childe Harold, he made the first trial of his eloquence in the House of Lords; and it was on this occasion he had the good fortune to become acquainted with Lord Holland,—an acquaintance no less honourable than gratifying to both, as having originated in feelings the most generous, perhaps, of our nature, a ready forgiveness of injuries, on the one side, and a frank and unqualified atonement for them, on the other. The subject of debate was the Nottingham Frame-breaking Bill, and, Lord Byron having mentioned to Mr. Rogers his intention to take a part in the discussion, a communication was, by the intervention of that gentleman, opened between the noble poet and Lord Holland, who, with his usual courtesy, professed himself ready to afford all the information and advice in his power. The following letters, however, will best explain their first advances towards acquaintance.

LETTER LXXXVIII.

TO MR. ROGERS.

"February 4th, 1812.

"MY DEAR SIR,

"With my best acknowledgments to Lord Holland, I have to offer my perfect concurrence in the propriety of the question previously to be put to ministers. If their answer is in the negative, I shall, with his lordship's approbation, give notice of a motion for a Committee of Inquiry. I would also gladly avail myself of his most able advice, and any information or documents with which he might be pleased to intrust me, to bear me out in the statement of facts it may be necessary to submit to the House.

" From all that fell under my own observation during my Christma visit to Newstead, I feel convinced that, if *conciliatory* measures are no very soon adopted, the most unhappy consequences may be apprehende Nightly outrage and daily depredation are already at their height, an not only the masters of frames, who are obnoxious on account of the occupation, but persons in no degree connected with the malcontents their oppressors, are liable to insult and pillage.

" I am very much obliged to you for the trouble you have take on my account, and beg you to believe me ever your obliged an sincere, &c."

LETTER LXXXIX.

"8, St. James's-street, February 25th, 1812.

" MY LORD,

" With my best thanks, I have the honour to return the Nott letter to your lordship. I have read it with attention, but do not thin I shall venture to avail myself of its contents, as my view of the questio differs in some measure from Mr. Coldham's. I hope I do not wron him, but *his* objections to the bill appear to me to be founded on certai apprehensions that he and his coadjutors might be mistaken for th ' *original advisers*' (to quote him) of the measure. For my own part, consider the manufacturers as a much injured body of men, sacrificed t the views of certain individuals who have enriched themselves by thos practices which have deprived the frame-workers of employment. Fo instance ;—by the adoption of a certain kind of frame, one man perform the work of seven—six are thus thrown out of business. But it is to b observed that the work thus done is far inferior in quality, hardl marketable at home, and hurried over with a view to exportation Surely, my lord, however we may rejoice in any improvement in th arts which may be beneficial to mankind, we must not allow mankind t be sacrificed to improvements in mechanism. The maintenance an well-doing of the industrious poor is an object of greater consequence t the community than the enrichment of a few monopolists by any im provement in the implements of trade, which deprives the workman of his bread, and renders the labourer 'unworthy of his hire.' My own motive for opposing the bill is founded on its palpable injustice, and its certain inefficacy. I have seen the state of these miserable men, and it is a disgrace to a civilized country. Their excesses may be condemned, but cannot be subject of wonder. The effect of the present bill would be to drive them into actual rebellion. The few words I shall venture to offer on Thursday will be founded upon these opinions formed from my own observations on the spot. By previous inquiry, I am convinced these men would have been restored to employment and the county to tranquillity. It is, perhaps, not yet too late, and is surely worth the trial. It can never be too late to employ force in such circumstances. I believe your lordship does not coincide with me entirely on this subject, and most cheerfully and sincerely shall I submit to your superior judgment and experience, and take some other line of argument against the bill, or be silent altogether, should you deem it more advisable. Condemning, as every one must condemn, the conduct of these wretches, I believe in the existence of grievances which call rather for pity than punishment. I have the honour to be, with great respect, my lord,

" Your lordship's

" most obedient and obliged servant,

" BYRON.

" P.S. I am a little apprehensive that your lordship will think me too lenient towards these men, and half a *framebreaker myself.*"

It would have been, no doubt, the ambition of Lord Byron to acquire distinction as well in oratory as in poesy; but Nature seems to set herself against pluralities in fame. He had prepared himself for this debate,—as most of the best orators have done, in their first essays,—not only by composing, but writing down, the whole of his speech beforehand. The reception he met with was flattering; some of the noble speakers on his own side complimented him very warmly; and that he was himself highly pleased with his success appears from the annexed account of Mr. Dallas, which gives a lively notion of his boyish elation on the occasion.

"When he left the great chamber, I went and met him in the passage; he was glowing with success, and much agitated. I had an umbrella in my right hand, not expecting that he would put out his hand to me;—in my haste to take it when offered, I had advanced my left hand—'What,' said he, 'give your friend your left hand upon such an occasion?' I showed the cause, and immediately changing the umbrella to the other hand, I gave him my right hand, which he shook and pressed warmly. He was greatly elated, and repeated some of the compliments which had been paid him, and mentioned one or two of the peers who had desired to be introduced to him. He concluded with saying, that he had, by his speech, given me the best advertisement for Childe Harold's Pilgrimage."

The speech itself, as given by Mr. Dallas from the noble speaker's own manuscript, is pointed and vigorous; and the same sort of interest that is felt in reading the poetry of a Burke, may be gratified, perhaps, by a few specimens of the oratory of a Byron. In the very opening of his speech he thus introduces himself by the melancholy avowal, that in that assembly of his brother nobles he stood almost a stranger.

"As a person in some degree connected with the suffering county, though a stranger not only to this House in general, but to almost every individual whose attention I presume to solicit, I must claim some portion of your lordships' indulgence."

The following extracts comprise, I think, the passages of most spirit.

"When we are told that these men are leagued together, not only for the destruction of their own comfort, but of their very means of subsistence, can we forget that it is the bitter policy, the destructive warfare, of the last eighteen years which has destroyed their comfort, your comfort, all men's comfort;—that policy which, originating with 'great statesmen now no more,' has survived the dead to become a curse on the living, unto the third and fourth generation! These men never destroyed their looms till they were become useless, worse than useless; till they were become actual impediments to their exertions in obtaining their daily bread. Can you then wonder that, in times like these, when bankruptcy, convicted fraud, and imputed felony, are found in a station not far beneath that of your lordships, the lowest, though once most useful portion of the people, should forget their duty in their distresses, and become only less guilty than one of their representatives? But while the exalted offender can find means to baffle the law, new capital punishments must be devised, new snares of death must be spread for the wretched mechanic who is famished into guilt. These men were willing to dig, but the spade was in other hands: they were not ashamed to beg, but there was none to relieve them. Their own means of subsistence were cut off; all other employments pre-occupied; and their excesses, however to be deplored and condemned, can hardly be the subject of surprise.

*　　*　　*　　*　　*　　*

" I have traversed the seat of war in the peninsula; I have been in some of the most oppressed provinces of Turkey; but never, under the most despotic of infidel governments, did I behold such squalid wretchedness as I have seen since my return, in the very heart of a Christian country. And what are your remedies? After months of inaction, and months of action worse than inactivity, at length comes forth the grand specific, the never-failing nostrum of all state-physicians, from the days of Draco to the present time. After feeling the pulse and shaking the head over the patient, prescribing the usual course of warm water and bleeding—the warm water of your mawkish police, and the lancets of your military—these convulsions must terminate in death, the sure consummation of the prescriptions of all political Sangrados. Setting aside the palpable injustice and the certain inefficiency of the bill, are there not capital punishments sufficient on your statutes? Is there not blood enough upon your penal code, that more must be poured forth to ascend to heaven and testify against you? How will you carry this bill into effect? Can you commit a whole county to their own prisons? Will you erect a gibbet in every field, and hang up men like scarecrows? or will you proceed (as you must, to bring this measure into effect,) by decimation; place the country under martial law; depopulate and lay waste all around you, and restore Sherwood Forest as an acceptable gift to the crown in its former condition of a royal chase and an asylum for outlaws? Are these the remedies for a starving and desperate populace? Will the famished wretch who has braved your bayonets be appalled by

x x 2

your gibbets? When death is a relief, and the only relief it appear
that you will afford him, will he be dragooned into tranquillity? Wi
that which could not be effected by your grenadiers be accomplished b
your executioners? If you proceed by the forms of law, where is you
evidence? Those who refused to impeach their accomplices, when trans
portation only was the punishment, will hardly be tempted to witnes
against them when death is the penalty. With all due deference to th
noble lords opposite, I think a little investigation, some previous inquiry
would induce even them to change their purpose. That most favourit
state measure, so marvellously efficacious in many and recent instances
temporizing, would not be without its advantage in this. When a pro
posal is made to emancipate or relieve, you hesitate, you deliberate fo
years, you temporize and tamper with the minds of men; but a death
bill must be passed off hand, without a thought of the consequences."

In reference to his own parliamentary displays, and to this maider
speech in particular, I find the following remarks in one of his Journals.

"Sheridan's liking for me (whether he was not mystifying me, I d
not know, but Lady Caroline Lamb and others told me that he said the
same both before and after he knew me) was founded upon 'English
Bards and Scotch Reviewers.' He told me that he did not care about
poetry (or about mine—at least, any but *that* poem of mine), but he was
sure, from *that* and other symptoms, I should make an orator, if I would
but take to speaking and grow a parliament man. He never ceased
harping upon this to me to the last; and I remember my old tutor, Dr.
Drury, had the same notion when I was a *boy;* but it never was my turn
of inclination to try. I spoke once or twice, as all young peers do, as a
kind of introduction into public life; but dissipation, shyness, haughty
and reserved opinions, together with the short time I lived in England
after my majority (only about five years in all), prevented me from
resuming the experiment. As far as it went, it was not discouraging,
particularly my *first* speech (I spoke three or four times in all), but just
after it, my poem of Childe Harold was published, and nobody ever
thought about my *prose* afterwards, nor indeed did I; it became to me a
secondary and neglected object, though I sometimes wonder to myself if
I should have succeeded."

His immediate impressions with respect to the success of his first speech may be collected from a letter addressed soon after to Mr. Hodgson.

LETTER XC.

TO MR. HODGSON.

"8, St. James's-street, March 5th, 1812.

" MY DEAR HODGSON,

" *We* are not answerable for reports of speeches in the papers, they are always given incorrectly, and on this occasion more so than usual, from the debate in the Commons on the same night. The Morning Post should have said *eighteen years*. However, you will find the speech, as spoken, in the Parliamentary Register, when it comes out. Lords Holland and Grenville, particularly the latter, paid me some high compliments in the course of their speeches, as you may have seen in the papers, and Lords Eldon and Harrowby answered me. I have had many marvellous eulogies repeated to me since, in person and by proxy, from divers persons *ministerial*—yea, *ministerial!*—as well as oppositionists; of them I shall only mention Sir F. Burdett. *He* says it is the best speech by a *lord* since the 'Lord knows when,' probably from a fellow-feeling in the sentiments. Lord H. tells me I shall beat them all if I persevere, and Lord G. remarked that the construction of some of my periods are very like *Burke*'s!! And so much for vanity. I spoke very violent sentences with a sort of modest impudence, abused every thing and every body, and put the Lord Chancellor very much out of humour; and if I may believe what I hear, have not lost any character by the experiment. As to my delivery, loud and fluent enough, perhaps a little theatrical. I could not recognise myself or any one else in the newspapers. * * *

" My poesy comes out on Saturday. Hobhouse is here; I shall tell him to write. My stone is gone for the present, but I fear is part of my habit. We *all* talk of a visit to Cambridge.

" Yours ever,

" B."

Of the same date as the above is the following letter to Lord Holland, accompanying a copy of his new publication, and written in a tone that cannot fail to give a high idea of his good feeling and candour.

LETTER XCI.

"St. James's-street, March 5th, 1812.

"MY LORD,

"May I request your lordship to accept a copy of the thing which accompanies this note? You have already so fully proved the truth of the first line of Pope's couplet,

'Forgiveness to the injured doth belong,'

that I long for an opportunity to give the lie to the verse that follows. If I were not perfectly convinced that any thing I may have formerly uttered in the boyish rashness of my misplaced resentment had made as little impression as it deserved to make, I should hardly have the confidence—perhaps your lordship may give it a stronger and more appropriate appellation—to send you a quarto of the same scribbler. But your lordship, I am sorry to observe to-day, is troubled with the gout: if my book can produce a *laugh* against itself or the author, it will be of some service. If it can set you to *sleep*, the benefit will be yet greater; and as some facetious personage observed half a century ago, that 'poetry is a mere drug,' I offer you mine as a humble assistant to the 'eau médecinale.' I trust you will forgive this and all my other buffooneries, and believe me to be, with great respect,

"Your lordship's
"obliged and sincere servant,
"BYRON."

It was within two days after his speech in the House of Lords, that Childe Harold appeared*;—and the impression which it produced upon the public was as instantaneous as it has proved deep and lasting. The permanence of such success genius alone could secure, but to its instant and enthusiastic burst, other causes, besides the merit of the work, concurred.

There are those who trace in the peculiar character of Lord Byron's genius strong features of relationship to the times in which he lived; who think that the great events which marked the close of the last century, by giving a new impulse to men's minds, by habituating them to the daring and the free, and allowing full vent to " the flash and outbreak of fiery spirits," had led naturally to the production of such a poet as Byron; and that he was, in short, as much the child and representative of the Revolution, in poesy, as another great man of the age, Napoleon, was in statesmanship and warfare. Without going the full length of this notion, it will, at least, be conceded, that the free loose which had been given to all the passions and energies of the human mind, in the great struggle of that period, together with the constant spectacle of such astounding vicissitudes as were passing, almost daily, on the theatre of the world, had created, in all minds, and in every walk of intellect, a taste for strong excitement, which the stimulants supplied from ordinary sources were insufficient to gratify;—that a tame deference to established authorities had fallen into disrepute, no less in literature than in politics, and that the poet who should breathe into his songs the fierce and passionate spirit of the age, and assert, untrammeled and unawed, the high dominion of genius, would be the most sure of an audience toned in sympathy with his strains.

It is true that, to the licence on religious subjects, which revelled through the first acts of that tremendous drama, a disposition of an

---

* To his sister, Mrs. Leigh, one of the first presentation copies was sent, with the following inscription in it:—

" To Augusta, my dearest sister, and my best friend, who has ever loved me much better than I deserved, this volume is presented by her *father's* son, and most affectionate brother,

" B."

opposite tendency had, for some time, succeeded. Against the wit o
the scoffer not only piety, but a better taste, revolted; and had Lor
Byron, in touching on such themes in Childe Harold, adopted a tone o
levity or derision (such as, unluckily, he sometimes afterwards descende
to), not all the originality and beauty of his work would have secure
for it a prompt or uncontested triumph. As it was, however, the few
dashes of scepticism with which he darkened his strain, far from checkin
his popularity, were among those attractions which, as I have said, inde
pendent of all the charms of the poetry, accelerated and heightened it
success. The religious feeling that has sprung up through Europe sinc
the French revolution—like the political principles that have emerge
out of the same event—in rejecting all the licentiousness of that period
have preserved much of its spirit of freedom and inquiry; and, amon
the best fruits of this enlarged and enlightened piety is the liberty whic
it disposes men to accord to the opinions, and even heresies, of others
To persons thus sincerely, and, at the same time, tolerantly, devout, th
spectacle of a great mind, like that of Byron, labouring in the eclipse o
scepticism, could not be otherwise than an object of deep and solem
interest. If they had already known what it was to doubt, themselves
they would enter into his fate with mournful sympathy; while, if saf
in the tranquil haven of faith, they would look with pity on one wh
was still a wanderer. Besides, erring and dark as might be his views a
that moment, there were circumstances in his character and fate tha
gave a hope of better thoughts yet dawning upon him. From his tem
perament and youth, there could be little fear that he was yet hardene
in his heresies, and as, for a heart wounded like his, there was, the
knew, but one true source of consolation, so it was hoped that the lov
of truth, so apparent in all he wrote, would, one day, enable him to find it

Another, and not the least of those causes which concurred with th
intrinsic claims of his genius to give an impulse to the tide of succes
that now flowed upon him, was, unquestionably, the peculiarity of hi
personal history and character. There had been, in his very first in
troduction of himself to the public, a sufficient portion of singularit
to excite strong attention and interest. While all other youths o

talent, in his high station, are heralded into life by the applauses and anticipations of a host of friends, young Byron stood forth alone, unannounced by either praise or promise,—the representative of an ancient house, whose name, long lost in the gloomy solitudes of Newstead, seemed to have just awakened from the sleep of half a century in his person. The circumstances that, in succession, followed,—the prompt vigour of his reprisals upon the assailants of his fame,—his disappearance, after this achievement, from the scene of his triumph, without deigning even to wait for the laurels which he had earned, and his departure on a far pilgrimage, whose limits he left to chance and fancy,—all these successive incidents had thrown an air of adventure round the character of the young poet, which prepared his readers to meet half-way the impressions of his genius. Instead of finding him, on a nearer view, fall short of their imaginations, the new features of his disposition now disclosed to them far outwent, in peculiarity and interest, whatever they might have preconceived; while the curiosity and sympathy awakened by what he suffered to transpire of his history were still more heightened by the mystery of his allusions to much that yet remained untold. The late losses, by death, which he had sustained, and mourned, it was manifest, so deeply, gave a reality to the notion formed of him by his admirers which seemed to authorise them in imagining still more; and what has been said of the poet Young, that he found out the art of " making the public a party to his private sorrows," may be, with infinitely more force and truth, applied to Lord Byron.

On that circle of society with whom he came immediately in contact, these personal influences acted with increased force, from being assisted by others, which, to female imaginations especially, would have presented a sufficiency of attraction, even without the great qualities joined with them. His youth,—the noble beauty of his countenance, and its constant play of lights and shadows,—the gentleness of his voice and manner to women, and his occasional haughtiness to men,—the alleged singularities of his mode of life, which kept curiosity alive and inquisitive,—all these lesser traits and habitudes concurred towards the quick spread of his fame; nor can it be denied that, among many purer sources of interest in his Poem, the allusions which he makes to instance of "*successful* passion" in his career* were not without their influence on the fancies of that sex, whose weakness it is to be most easily won by those who come recommended by the greatest number of triumphs over others.

That his rank was also to be numbered among these extrinsic advantages appears to have been,—partly, perhaps, from a feeling of modesty at the time,—his own persuasion. " I may place a great deal of it," said he to Mr. Dallas, " to my being a lord." It might be supposed that it is only on a rank inferior to his own such a charm could operate; but this very speech is, in itself, a proof, that in no class whatever is the advantage of being noble more felt and appreciated than among nobles themselves. It was, also, natural that, in that circle, the admiration of the new poet should be, at least, quickened by the consideration that he had sprung up among themselves, and that their order had, at length, produced a man of genius, by whom the arrears of contribution, long due from them to the treasury of English literature, would be at once fully and splendidly discharged.

Altogether, taking into consideration the various points I have here enumerated, it may be asserted, that never did there exist before, and, it is most probable, never will exist again, a combination of such vast mental power and surpassing genius, with so many other of those advantages and attractions, by which the world is, in general, dazzled and captivated. The effect was, accordingly, electric;—his fame had not to wait for any of the ordinary gradations, but seemed to spring up, like the palace of a fairy tale, in a night. As he himself briefly described it in

* " Little knew she, that seeming marble heart,
　　Now mask'd in silence, or withheld by pride,
　　Was not unskilful in the spoiler's art,
　　And spread its snares licentious far and wide."
　　　　　　　　　　　　　CHILDE HAROLD, CANTO II.

We have here another instance of his propensity to self-misrepresentation. However great might have been the irregularities of his college life, such phrases as the " art of the spoiler" and " spreading snares" were in nowise applicable to them.

his Memoranda,—" I awoke one morning and found myself famous." The first edition of his work was disposed of instantly; and, as the echoes of its reputation multiplied on all sides, " Childe Harold" and " Lord Byron" became the theme of every tongue. At his door, most of the leading names of the day presented themselves,—some of them persons whom he had much wronged in his Satire, but who now forgot their resentment in generous admiration. From morning till night the most flattering testimonies of his success crowded his table,—from the grave tributes of the statesman and the philosopher down to (what flattered him still more) the romantic billet of some *incognita,* or the pressing note of invitation from some fair leader of fashion; and, in place of the desert which London had been to him but a few weeks before, he now not only saw the whole splendid interior of High Life thrown open to receive him, but found himself, among its illustrious crowds, the most distinguished object.

The copyright of the Poem, which was purchased by Mr. Murray for 600*l.*, he presented, in the most delicate and unostentatious manner, to Mr. Dallas *, saying, at the same time, that he " never would receive money for his writings;"—a resolution, the mixed result of generosity and pride, which he afterwards wisely abandoned, though borne out by the example of Swift † and Voltaire, the latter of whom gave away most of his copyrights to Prault and other booksellers, and received books, not money, for those he disposed of otherwise. To his young friend, Mr. Harness, it had been his intention, at first, to dedicate the work, but, on further consideration, he relinquished his design; and in a letter to that gentleman (which, with some others, is unfortunately lost) alleged, as his reason for this change, the prejudice which, he foresaw, some parts of the poem would raise against himself, and his fear lest, by any pos-

---

* " After speaking to him of the sale, and settling the new edition, I said, ' How can I possibly think of this rapid sale, and the profits likely to ensue, without recollecting—' ' What?' —' Think what sum your work may produce.' ' I shall be rejoiced, and wish it doubled and trebled; but do not talk to me of money. I never will receive money for my writings.' "— DALLAS's *Recollections.*

† In a letter to Pulteney, 12th May, 1735, Swift says " I never got a farthing for any thing I writ, except once."

sibility, a share of the odium might so far extend itself to his friend, as to injure him in the profession to which he was about to devote himself.

Not long after the publication of Childe Harold, the noble author paid me a visit, one morning, and, putting a letter into my hand, which he had just received, requested that I would undertake to manage for him whatever proceedings it might render necessary. This letter, I found, had been delivered to him by Mr. Leckie (a gentleman well known by a work on Sicilian affairs), and came from a once active and popular member of the fashionable world, Colonel Greville,—it purport being to require of his lordship, as author of " English Bards &c." such reparation as it was in his power to make for the injury which, as Colonel Greville conceived, certain passages in that satire, reflecting upon his conduct, as manager of the Argyle Institution, were calculated to inflict upon his character. In the appeal of the gallant colonel, there were some expressions of rather an angry cast, which Lord Byron, though fully conscious of the length to which he himself had gone, was but little inclined to brook, and, on my returning the letter into his hands, he said, " To such a letter as that there can be but one sort of answer." He agreed, however, to trust the matter entirely to my discretion, and I had, shortly after, an interview with the friend of Colonel Greville. By this gentleman, who was then an utter stranger to me, I was received with much courtesy, and with every disposition to bring the affair intrusted to us to an amicable issue. On my premising that the tone of his friend's letter stood in the way of negotiation, and that some obnoxious expressions which it contained must be removed before I could proceed a single step towards explanation, he most readily consented to remove this obstacle. At his request I drew a pen across the parts I considered objectionable, and he undertook to send me the letter, re-written, next morning. In the mean time I received from Lord Byron the following paper for my guidance.

" With regard to the passage on Mr. Way's loss, no unfair play was hinted at, as may be seen by referring to the book; and it is expressly added that the *managers were ignorant* of that transaction. As to the prevalence of play at the Argyle, it cannot be denied that there were *billiards* and *dice* ;—Lord B. has been a witness to the use of both at the Argyle Rooms. These, it is presumed, come under the denomination of play. If play be allowed, the President of the Institution can hardly complain of being termed the ' Arbiter of Play,'— or what becomes of his authority ?

" Lord B. has no personal animosity to Colonel Greville. A public institution, to which he, himself, was a subscriber, he considered himself to have a right to notice *publicly*. Of that institution, Colonel Greville was the avowed director ;—it is too late to enter into the discussion of its merits or demerits.

" Lord B. must leave the discussion of the reparation, for the real or supposed injury, to Colonel G.'s friend and Mr. Moore, the friend of Lord B.—begging them to recollect that, while they consider Colonel G.'s honour, Lord B. must also maintain his own. If the business can be settled amicably, Lord B. will do as much as can and ought to be done by a man of honour towards conciliation ;—if not, he must satisfy Colonel G. in the manner most conducive to his further wishes."

In the morning I received the letter, in its new form, from Mr. Leckie, with the annexed note.

" MY DEAR SIR,

" I found my friend very ill in bed; he has, however, managed to copy the inclosed, with the alterations proposed. Perhaps you may wish to see me in the morning ; I shall therefore be glad to see you any time till twelve o'clock. If you rather wish me to call on you, tell me, and I shall obey your summons.

" Yours, very truly,

" G. T. LECKIE."

With such facilities towards pacification, it is almost needless to add that there was but little delay in settling the matter amicably.

While upon this subject, I shall avail myself of the opportunity which it affords of extracting an amusing account given by Lord Byron himself of some affairs of this description, in which he was, at differer times, employed as mediator.

"I have been called in as mediator, or second, at least twenty time in violent quarrels, and have always contrived to settle the busine without compromising the honour of the parties, or leading them t mortal consequences, and this too sometimes in very difficult and delicat circumstances, and having to deal with very hot and haughty spirits,– Irishmen, gamesters, guardsmen, captains, and cornets of horse, and th like. This was, of course, in my youth, when I lived in hot-heade company. I have had to carry challenges from gentlemen to noblemer from captains to captains, from lawyers to counsellors, and once from clergyman to an officer in the life-guards; but I found the latter by fa the most difficult,

> ' to compose
> The bloody duel without blows,'

the business being about a woman: I must add too, that I never saw . *woman* behave so ill, like a cold-blooded, heartless b— as she was,– but very handsome, for all that. A certain Susan C** was she called I never saw her but once; and that was to induce her but to say tw words (which in no degree compromised herself), and which would hav had the effect of saving a priest or a lieutenant of cavalry. She woul *not* say them, and neither N** or myself (the son of Sir E. N**, and friend to one of the parties) could prevail upon her to say them, thoug both of us used to deal in some sort with womankind. At last I manage to quiet the combatants without her talisman, and, I believe, to her grea disappointment: she was the damnedest b— that I ever saw, and I hav seen a great many. Though my clergyman was sure to lose either hi life or his living, he was as warlike as the Bishop of Beauvais, and woul hardly be pacified; but then he was in love, and that is a martial passion.'

However disagreeable it was to find the consequences of his Satir thus rising up against him in a hostile shape, he was far more embarrasse in those cases where the retribution took a friendly form. Being now daily in the habit of meeting and receiving kindnesses from persons who

either in themselves, or through their relatives, had been wounded by
his pen, he felt every fresh instance of courtesy from such quarters to be
(as he sometimes, in the strong language of scripture, expressed it) like
" heaping coals of fire upon his head." He was, indeed, in a remarkable
degree, sensitivè to the kindness or displeasure of those he lived with;
and had he passed a life subject to the immediate influence of society,
it may be doubted whether he ever would have ventured upon those
unbridled bursts of energy, in which he, at once, demonstrated and
abused his power. At the period when he ran riot in his Satire, society
had not yet caught him within its pale; and in the time of his Cains
and Don Juans, he had again broken loose from it. Hence, his instinct
towards a life of solitude and independence, as the true element of his
strength. In his own domain of imagination he could defy the whole
world; while, in real life, a frown or smile could rule him. The facility
with which he sacrificed his first volume, at the mere suggestion of his
friend, Mr. Becher, is a strong proof of this pliableness; and in the
instance of Childe Harold, such influence had the opinions of Mr. Gifford
and Mr. Dallas on his mind, that he not only shrunk from his original
design of identifying himself with his hero, but surrendered to them
one of his most favourite stanzas, whose heterodoxy they had objected
to; nor is it too much, perhaps, to conclude, that had a more extended force of such influence then acted upon him, he would have
consented to omit the sceptical parts of his poem altogether. Certain
it is that, during the remainder of his stay in England, no such doctrines
were ever again obtruded on his readers; and in all those beautiful
creations of his fancy, with which he brightened that whole period,
keeping the public eye in one prolonged gaze of admiration, both the
bitterness and the licence of his impetuous spirit were kept effectually
under control. The world, indeed, had yet to witness what he was
capable of, when emancipated from this restraint. For, graceful and
powerful as were his flights while society had still a hold of him, it was
not till let loose from the leash that he rose into the true region of his
strength; and though almost in proportion to that strength was, too
frequently, his abuse of it, yet so magnificent are the very excesses of
such energy, that it is impossible, even while we condemn, not to admire.

The occasion by which I have been led into these remarks,—namely his sensitiveness on the subject of his Satire,—is one of those instances that show how easily his gigantic spirit could be, if not held down, at least entangled, by the small ties of society. The aggression of which he had been guilty was not only past, but, by many of those most injured, forgiven; and yet,—highly, it must be allowed, to the credit of his social feelings,—the idea of living familiarly and friendly with persons respecting whose character or talents there were such opinions of his on record, became, at length, insupportable to him; and, though far advanced in a fifth edition of " English Bards, &c." he came to the resolution of suppressing the Satire altogether; and orders were sent to Cawthorn, the publisher, to commit the whole impression to the flames. At the same time, and from similar motives,—aided, I rather think, by friendly remonstrance from Lord Elgin, or some of his connexions,—the " Curse of Minerva," a poem levelled against that nobleman, and already in progress towards publication, was also sacrificed; while the " Hint from Horace," though containing far less personal satire than either of the others, shared their fate.

To exemplify what I have said of his extreme sensibility to the passing sunshine or clouds of the society in which he lived, I need but cite the following notes, addressed by him to his friend Mr. William Bankes, under the apprehension that this gentleman was, for some reason or other, displeased with him.

LETTER XCII.

TO MR. WILLIAM BANKES.

" April 20th, 1812.

" MY DEAR BANKES,

" I feel rather hurt (not savagely) at the speech you made to me last night, and my hope is, that it was only one of your *profane* jests. I should be very sorry that any part of my behaviour should give you cause to suppose that I think higher of myself, or otherwise of you, than I have always done. I can assure you that I am as much the humblest of your servants as at Trin. Coll.; and if I have not been at home when you favoured me with a call, the loss was more mine than yours. In the bustle of buzzing parties, there is, there can be, no rational conversation; but when I can enjoy it, there is nobody's I can prefer to your own.

"Believe me ever faithfully

"and most affectionately yours,

"BYRON."

LETTER XCIII.

TO MR. WILLIAM BANKES.

"MY DEAR BANKES,

"My eagerness to come to an explanation has, I trust, convinced you that whatever my unlucky manner might inadvertently be, the change was as unintentional as (if intended) it would have been ungrateful. I really was not aware that, while we were together, I had evinced such caprices; that we were not so much in each other's company as I could have wished, I well know, but I think so *acute* an *observer* as yourself must have perceived enough to *explain this*, without supposing any slight to one in whose society I have pride and pleasure. Recollect that I do not allude here to ' extended' or ' extending' acquaintances, but to circumstances you will understand, I think, on a little reflection.

" And now, my dear Bankes, do not distress me by supposing that I can think of you, or you of me, otherwise than I trust we have long thought. You told me not long ago that my temper was improved, and I should be sorry that opinion should be revoked. Believe me, your friendship is of more account to me than all those absurd vanities in which, I fear, you conceive me to take too much interest. I have never disputed your superiority, or doubted (seriously) your good will, and no one shall ever ' make mischief between us' without the sincere regret on the part of your ever affectionate, &c.

" P.S. I shall see you, I hope, at Lady Jersey's. Hobhouse goes also."

In the month of April he was again tempted to try his success in the House of Lords, and, on the motion of Lord Donoughmore for taking into consideration the claims of the Irish catholics, delivered his sentiments strongly in favour of the proposition. His display, on this occasion, seems to have been less promising than in his first essay. His delivery was thought mouthing and theatrical, being infected, I take for granted (having never heard him speak in Parliament), with the same chanting tone that disfigured his recitation of poetry,—a tone contracted at most of the public schools, but more particularly, perhaps, at Harrow, and encroaching just enough on the boundaries of song to offend those ears most by which song is best enjoyed and understood.

On the subject of the negotiations for a change of ministry which took place during this session, I find the following anecdotes recorded in his note-book.

" At the opposition meeting of the Peers, in 1812, at Lord Grenville's, when Lord Grey and he read to us the correspondence upon Moira's negotiation, I sate next to the present Duke of Grafton, and said, ' What is to be done next?'—' Wake the Duke of Norfolk' (who was snoring away near us), replied he: ' I don't think the negotiators have left any thing else for us to do this turn.'

" In the debate, or rather discussion, afterwards in the House of Lords upon that very question, I sate immediately behind Lord Moira, who was extremely annoyed at Grey's speech upon the subject; and, while Grey was speaking, turned round to me repeatedly, and asked me whether I agreed with him. It was an awkward question to me, who had not heard both sides. Moira kept repeating to me, ' It was *not so, it was so and so,*' &c. I did not know very well what to think, but I sympathised with the acuteness of his feelings upon the subject."

The subject of the catholic claims was, it is well known, brought forward a second time this session by Lord Wellesley, whose motion for a future consideration of the question was carried by a majority of one. In reference to this division, another rather amusing anecdote is thus related.

" Lord * * affects an imitation of two very different Chancellors, Thurlow and Loughborough, and can indulge in an oath now and then. On one of the debates on the catholic question, when we were either equal or within one (I forget which), I had been sent for in great haste to a ball, which I quitted, I confess, somewhat reluctantly, to emancipate five millions of people.   I came in late, and did not go immediately into the body of the House, but stood just behind the woolsack.   * * turned round, and, catching my eye, immediately said to a peer (who had come to him for a few minutes on the woolsack, as is the custom of his friends), ' Damn them! they 'll have it now,—by G-d! the vote that is just come in will give it them.' "

During all this time, the impression which he had produced in society, both as a poet and a man, went on daily increasing; and the facility with which he gave himself up to the current of fashionable life, and mingled in all the gay scenes through which it led, showed that the novelty, at least, of this mode of existence had charms for him, however he might estimate its pleasures.   That sort of vanity which is almost inseparable from genius, and which consists in an extreme sensitiveness on the subject of self, Lord Byron, I need not say, possessed in no ordinary degree; and never was there a career in which this sensibility to the opinions of others was exposed to more constant and various excitement than that on which he was now entered.   I find in a note of my own to him, written at this period, some jesting allusions to the " circle of star-gazers" whom I had left around him at some party on the preceding night;—and such, in fact, was the flattering ordeal he had to undergo wherever he went.   On these occasions,—particularly before the range of his acquaintance had become sufficiently extended to set him wholly at his ease,—his air and port were those of one whose better thoughts were elsewhere, and who looked with melancholy abstraction on the gay crowd around him.   This deportment, so rare in such scenes, and so accordant with the romantic notions entertained of him, was the result partly of shyness, and partly, perhaps, of that love of effect and impression to which the poetical character of his mind naturally led.   Nothing, indeed, could be more amusing and delightful than the contrast which his manner afterwards, when we were alone, presented to his proud reserve in the brilliant circle we had just left.   It was like the bursting gaiety of a boy let loose from school, and seemed as if there was no extent of fun or tricks of which he was not capable.   Finding him invariably thus lively when we were together, I often rallied him on the gloomy tone of his poetry, as assumed; but his constant answer was (and I soon ceased to doubt of its truth), that, though thus merry and full of laughter with those he liked, he was, at heart, one of the most melancholy wretches in existence.

Among the numerous notes which I received from him at this time —some of them relating to our joint engagements in society, and others to matters now better forgotten,—I shall select a few that (as showing his haunts and habits) may not, perhaps, be uninteresting.

" March 25th, 1812.

" Know all men by these presents, that you, Thomas Moore, stand indicted—no—invited, by special and particular solicitation, to Lady C. L**'s to-morrow even, at half-past nine o'clock, where you will meet with a civil reception and decent entertainment. Pray, come—I was so examined after you this morning, that I entreat you to answer in person.

" Believe me, &c."

" Friday, noon.

" I should have answered your note yesterday, but I hoped to have seen you this morning. I must consult with you about the day we dine with Sir Francis. I suppose we shall meet at Lady Spencer's to-night. I did not know that you were at Miss Berry's the other night, or I should have certainly gone there.

" As usual, I am in all sorts of scrapes, though none, at present, of a martial description. Believe me, &c."

" May 8th, 1812.

" I am too proud of being your friend to care with whom I am linked in your estimation, and, God knows, I want friends more at this time than at any other. I am ' taking care of myself' to no great purpose. If you knew my situation in every point of view, you would excuse apparent and unintentional neglect. * * * * * * * I shall leave town, I think; but do not you leave it without seeing me.

I wish you, from my soul, every happiness you can wish yourself; and I think you have taken the road to secure it. Peace be with you! I fear she has abandoned me. Ever, &c."

" May 20th, 1812.

" On Monday, after sitting up all night, I saw Bellingham launched into eternity*, and at three the same day I saw *** launched into the country.　　*　　*　　*　　*

" I believe, in the beginning of June, I shall be down for a few days in Notts. If so, I shall beat you up ' en passant' with Hobhouse, who is endeavouring, like you and every body else, to keep me out of scrapes.

" I meant to have written you a long letter, but I find I cannot. If any thing remarkable occurs, you will hear it from me—if good; if *bad*, there are plenty to tell it. In the mean time, do you be happy.

" Ever yours, &c.

" P.S. My best wishes and respects to Mrs. **;—she is beautiful. I may say so even to you, for I never was more struck with a countenance."

Among the tributes to his fame, this spring, it should have been mentioned that, at some evening party, he had the honour of being

---

* He had taken a window opposite for the purpose, and was accompanied on the occasion by his old schoolfellows, Mr. Bailey and Mr. John Madocks. They went together from some assembly, and, on their arriving at the spot, about three o'clock in the morning, not finding the house that was to receive them open, Mr. Madocks undertook to rouse the inmates, while Lord Byron and Mr. Bailey sauntered, arm and arm, up the street. During this interval, rather a painful scene occurred. Seeing an unfortunate woman lying on the steps of a door, Lord Byron, with some expression of compassion, offered her a few shillings; but, instead of accepting them, she violently pushed away his hand, and, starting up with a yell of laughter, began to mimic the lameness of his gait. He did not utter a word, but " I could feel," said Mr. Bailey, " his arm trembling within mine, as we left her."

I may take this opportunity of mentioning another anecdote connected with his lameness. In coming out, one night, from a ball, with Mr. Rogers, as they were on their way to their carriage, one of the link-boys ran on before Lord Byron, crying " This way, my lord." " He seems to know you," said Mr. Rogers. " Know me!" answered Lord Byron, with some degree of bitterness in his tone—" every one knows me,—I am deformed."

presented, at that royal personage's own desire, to the Prince Regent "The Regent," says Mr. Dallas, "expressed his admiration of Childe Harold's Pilgrimage, and continued a conversation, which so fascinated the poet, that, had it not been for an accidental deferring of the next levee, he bade fair to become a visitor at Carlton House, if not a complete courtier."

After this wise prognostic, the writer adds,—" I called on him on the morning for which the levee had been appointed, and found him in a full-dress court suit of clothes, with his fine black hair in powder which by no means suited his countenance. I was surprised, as he had not told me that he should go to court; and it seemed to me as if he thought it necessary to apologize for his intention, by his observing that he could not in decency but do it, as the Regent had done him the honour to say that he hoped to see him soon at Carlton House."

In the two letters that follow we find his own account of the introduction.

LETTER XCIV.

TO LORD HOLLAND.

"June 25th, 1812.

" MY DEAR LORD,

" I must appear very ungrateful, and have, indeed, been very negligent, but till last night I was not apprized of Lady Holland's restoration, and I shall call to-morrow to have the satisfaction, I trust, of hearing that she is well.—I hope that neither politics nor gout have assailed your lordship since I last saw you, and that you also are 'as well as could be expected.'

" The other night, at a ball, I was presented by order to our gracious Regent, who honoured me with some conversation, and professed a predilection for poetry.—I confess it was a most unexpected honour, and I thought of poor B——s's adventure, with some apprehensions of a similar blunder. I have now great hope, in the event of Mr. Pye's decease, of 'warbling truth at court,' like Mr. Mallet of indifferent memory.—Consider, 100 marks a year! besides the wine and the disgrace; but then 'emorse would make me drown myself in my own butt before the year's ·nd, or the finishing of my first dithyrambic.—So that, after all, I shall ·ot meditate our laureate's death by pen or poison.

"Will you present my best respects to Lady Holland, and believe ·ne hers and yours very sincerely."

The second letter, entering much more fully into the particulars of this interview with Royalty, was in answer, it will be perceived, to some inquiries which Sir Walter Scott (then Mr. Scott) had addressed to him on the subject; and the whole account reflects even still more honour on the Sovereign himself than on the two poets.

LETTER XCV.

TO SIR WALTER SCOTT, BART.

"St. James's-street, July 6th, 1812.

"SIR,

"I have just been honoured with your letter.—I feel sorry that you should have thought it worth while to notice the 'evil works of my non-age,' as the thing is suppressed *voluntarily*, and your explanation is too kind not to give me pain. The Satire was written when I was very young and very angry, and fully bent on displaying my wrath and my wit, and now I am haunted by the ghosts of my wholesale assertions. I cannot sufficiently thank you for your praise; and now, waving myself, let me talk to you of the Prince Regent. He ordered me to be presented to him at a ball; and after some sayings peculiarly pleasing from royal lips, as to my own attempts, he talked to me of you and your immortalities: he preferred you to every bard past and present, and asked which of your works pleased me most. It was a difficult question. I answered, I thought the 'Lay.' He said his own opinion was nearly similar. In speaking of the others, I told him that I thought you more particularly the poet of *Princes*, as *they* never appeared more fascinating than in 'Marmion' and the 'Lady of the Lake. He was pleased to coincide, and to dwell on the description of your Jameses as no less royal than poetical. He spoke alternately of Homer and yourself, and seemed

well acquainted with both; so that (with the exception of the Turks ar
your humble servant) you were in very good company. I défy Murr;
to have exaggerated his royal highness's opinion of your powers, nor c;
I pretend to enumerate all he said on the subject; but it may give yc
pleasure to hear that it was conveyed in language which would onl
suffer by my attempting to transcribe it, and with a tone and taste whic
gave me a very high idea of his abilities and accomplishments, which
had hitherto considered as confined to *manners*, certainly superior t
those of any living *gentleman*.

"This interview was accidental. I never went to the levee; fc
having seen the courts of Mussulman and Catholic sovereigns, my curic
sity was sufficiently allayed; and my politics being as perverse as m
rhymes, I had, in fact, 'no business there.' To be thus praised by you
Sovereign must be gratifying to you; and if that gratification is nc
alloyed by the communication being made through me, the bearer of i
will consider himself very fortunately and sincerely

"Your obliged and obedient servant,

"Byron.

"P.S. Excuse this scrawl, scratched in a great hurry and just afte
a journey."

During the summer of this year he paid visits to some of his nobl·
friends, and, among others, to the Earl of Jersey and the Marquis o
Lansdowne. "In 1812," he says, "at Middleton (Lord Jersey's), amongs
a goodly company of lords, ladies, and wits, &c., there was * * *†

"Erskine, too! Erskine was there; good, but intolerable. H·
jested, he talked, he did every thing admirably, but then he *would* b·
applauded for the same thing twice over. He would read his owr
verses, his own paragraph, and tell his own story, again and again; ano
then 'the Trial by Jury!!!' I almost wished it abolished, for I sate nex
him at dinner. As I had read his published speeches, there was nc
occasion to repeat them to me.

"C * * (the fox-hunter), nicknamed '*Cheek* C * *', and I, sweatec
the claret, being the only two who did so. C * *, who loves his bottle

† A review, somewhat too critical, of some of the guests is here omitted.

and had no notion of meeting with a 'bon-vivant' in a scribbler*, in making my eulogy to somebody one evening, summed it up in—' By G—d, he drinks like a man !'

"Nobody drank, however, but C * * and I. To be sure, there was little occasion, for we swept off what was on the table (a most splendid board, as may be supposed, at Jersey's) very sufficiently. However, we carried our liquor discreetly, like the Baron of Bradwardine."

In the month of August this year, on the completion of the new Theatre Royal, Drury-lane, the Committee of Management, desirous of procuring an Address for the opening of the theatre, took the rather novel mode of inviting, by an advertisement in the newspapers, the competition of all the poets of the day towards this object. Though the contributions that ensued were sufficiently numerous, it did not appear to the Committee that there was any one among the number worthy of selection. In this difficulty, it occurred to Lord Holland that they could not do better than have recourse to Lord Byron, whose popularity would give additional vogue to the solemnity of their opening, and to whose transcendant claims, as a poet, it was taken for granted (though without sufficient allowance, as it proved, for the irritability of the brotherhood), even the rejected candidates themselves would bow without a murmur. The first result of this application to the noble poet will be learned from what follows.

LETTER XCVI.

TO LORD HOLLAND.

"Cheltenham, September 10th, 1812.

" MY DEAR LORD,

" The lines which I sketched off on your hint are still, or rather *were*, in an unfinished state, for I have just committed them to a flame more decisive than that of Drury. Under all the circumstances, I should

---

* For the first day or two, at Middleton, he did not join his noble host's party till after dinner, but took his scanty repast of biscuits and soda water in his own room. Being told by somebody that the gentleman above-mentioned had pronounced such habits to be " effeminate,"

hardly wish a contest with Philo-drama—Philo-Drury—Asbestos, H * * and all the anonymes and synonymes of the Committee candidate Seriously, I think you have a chance of something much better; fc prologuizing is not my forte, and, at all events, either my pride or m modesty won't let me incur the hazard of having my rhymes buried i next month's Magazine, under 'Essays on the Murder of Mr. Perceval and 'Cures for the Bite of a Mad Dog,' as poor Goldsmith complaine of the fate of far superior performances.

"I am still sufficiently interested to wish to know the successfu candidate; and, amongst so many, I have no doubt some will be ex cellent, particularly in an age when writing verse is the easiest of al attainments.

"I cannot answer your intelligence with the 'like comfort,' unless as you are deeply theatrical, you may wish to hear of Mr. * *, whose acting is, I fear, utterly inadequate to the London engagement into which the managers of Covent-garden have lately entered. His figure is fat, his features flat, his voice unmanageable, his action ungraceful and, as Diggory says, 'I defy him to extort that d—d muffin face of hi into madness.' I was very sorry to see him in the character of the 'Elephant on the slack rope;' for, when I last saw him, I was in rapture with his performance. But then I was sixteen,—an age to which al London then condescended to subside. After all, much better judge have admired, and may again; but I venture to 'prognosticate a prophecy (see the Courier) that he will not succeed.

"So, poor dear Rogers has stuck fast on 'the brow of the mighty Helvellyn'—I hope not for ever. My best respects to Lady H.—her departure, with that of my other friends, was a sad event for me, now reduced to a state of the most cynical solitude. 'By the waters of Cheltenham I sat down and *drank*, when I remembered thee, oh Georgiana Cottage! As for our *harps*, we hanged them up upon the willows that grew thereby. Then they said, Sing us a song of Drury-lane,' &c.—but I am dumb and dreary as the Israelites. The waters

he resolved to show the "fox-hunter" that he could be, on occasion, as good a *bon-vivant* as him-self, and, by his prowess at the claret next day, after dinner, drew forth from Mr. C * * the eulogium here recorded.

have disordered me to my heart's content,—you were *right*, as you always are.

> " Believe me ever your obliged
> " and affectionate servant,
> " BYRON."

The request of the Committee for his aid having been, still more urgently, repeated, he, at length, notwithstanding the difficulty and invidiousness of the task, from his strong wish to oblige Lord Holland, consented to undertake it ; and the following series of quick succeeding notes and letters, which he addressed, during the completion of the Address, to his noble friend, will, by the literary reader, at least, be thought well worth perusal,—as affording a proof (in conjunction with others, of still more interest, yet to be cited) of the pains he, at this time, took in improving and polishing his first conceptions, and the importance he wisely attached to a judicious choice of epithets as a means of enriching both the music and meaning of his verse.   They also show,—what, as an illustration of his character, is even still more valuable,—the exceeding pliancy and good humour with which he could yield to friendly suggestions and criticisms ; nor can it be questioned, I think, but that the docility thus invariably exhibited by him, on points where most poets are found to be tenacious and irritable, was a quality natural to his disposition, and which might have been turned to account in far more important matters, had he been fortunate enough to meet with persons capable of understanding and guiding him.

TO LORD HOLLAND.

" September 22d, 1812.

" MY DEAR LORD,

" In a day or two I will send you something which you will still have the liberty to reject if you dislike it.   I should like to have had more time, but will do my best,—but too happy if I can oblige *you*, though I may offend 100 scribblers and the discerning public.

" Ever yours.

" Keep *my name* a *secret;* or I shall be beset by all the rejected, an
perhaps, damned by a party."

LETTER XCVII.

TO LORD HOLLAND.

" Cheltenham, September 23d, 1812.

" Ecco!—I have marked some passages with *double* readings—choos
between them—*cut*—*add*—*reject*—or *destroy*—do with them as you will—
I leave it to you and the Committee—you cannot say so called ' a no
committendo.' What will *they* do (and I do) with the hundred and on
rejected Troubadours? ' With trumpets, yea, and with shawms,' wi
you be assailed in the most diabolical doggerel. I wish my name not t
transpire till the day is decided. I shall not be in town, so it won'
much matter; but let us have a good *deliverer.* I think Elliston shoul
be the man, or Pope; *not* Raymond, I implore you, by the love o
Rhythmus!

" The passages marked thus = =, above and below, are for you t
choose between epithets, and such like poetical furniture. Pray, writ
me a line, and believe me ever, &c.

" My best remembrances to Lady H. Will you be good enough t
decide between the various readings marked, and erase the other; or ou
deliverer may be as puzzled as a commentator, and belike repeat both
If these *versicles* won't do, I will hammer out some more endecasyllables

" P. S. Tell Lady H. I have had sad work to keep out the Phœni
—I mean the Fire-Office of that name. It has insured the theatre, an
why not the Address?"

TO LORD HOLLAND.

" September 24th.

" I send a recast of the four first lines of the concluding paragraph.

" This greeting o'er, the ancient rule obey'd,
The drama's homage by her Herald paid,
Receive *our welcome too*, whose every tone
Springs from our hearts, and fain would win your own.
The curtain rises, &c. &c.

And do forgive all this trouble.   See what it is to have to do even with the *genteelest* of us.   Ever, &c."

LETTER XCVIII.

TO LORD HOLLAND.

"Cheltenham, Sept. 25th, 1812.

"Still 'more matter for a May morning.' Having patched the middle and end of the Address, I send one more couplet for a part of the beginning, which, if not too turgid, you will have the goodness to add. After that flagrant image of the *Thames* (I hope no unlucky wag will say I have set it on fire, though Dryden, in his 'Annus Mirabilis,' and Churchill, in his 'Times,' did it before me), I mean to insert this:

> "As flashing far the new Volcano shone
> And swept the skies with { *meteors* / lightnings } not their own,
> While thousands throng'd around the burning dome, &c. &c.

I think 'thousands' less flat than 'crowds collected'—but don't let me plunge into the bathos, or rise into Nat. Lee's *Bedlam* metaphors. By the by, the best view of the said fire (which I myself saw from a house-top in Covent-garden) was at Westminster Bridge, from the reflection on the Thames.

"Perhaps the present couplet had better come in after 'trembled for their homes,' the two lines after;—as otherwise the image certainly sinks, and it will run just as well.

"The lines themselves, perhaps, may be better thus—('choose,' or 'refuse'—but please *yourself,* and don't mind 'Sir Fretful')—

> "As flash'd the volumed blaze, and { *sadly* / ghastly } shone
> The skies with lightnings awful as their own.

The last *runs* smoothest and, I think, best; but you know *better* than *best*. 'Lurid' is also a less indistinct epithet than 'livid wave,' and, if you think so, a dash of the pen will do.

"I expected one line this morning; in the mean time, I shall remode
and condense, and, if I do not hear from you, shall send another copy.

"I am ever, &c."

LETTER XCIX.

TO LORD HOLLAND.

"September 26th, 1812.

"You will think there is no end to my villanous emendations. The
fifth and sixth lines I think to alter thus:

> "Ye who beheld—oh sight admired and mourn'd,
> Whose radiance mock'd the ruin it adorn'd;

because 'night' is repeated the next line but one; and, as it now stands
the conclusion of the paragraph, 'worthy him (Shakspeare) and *you*,
appears to apply the '*you*' to those only who were out of bed and in
Covent-garden market on the night of conflagration, instead of the audi
ence or the discerning public at large, all of whom are intended to be
comprised in that comprehensive and, I hope, comprehensible pronoun.

"By the by, one of my corrections in the fair copy sent yesterday
has dived into the bathos some sixty fathom—

> "When Garrick died, and Brinsley ceased to write.

Ceasing to *live* is a much more serious concern, and ought not to be first
therefore I will let the old couplet stand, with its half rhymes 'sought
and 'wrote*.' Second thoughts in every thing are best, but, in rhyme
third and fourth don't come amiss. I am very anxious on this business
and I do hope that the very trouble I occasion you will plead its own

* "Such are the names that here your plaudits sought,
> When Garrick acted, and when Brinsley wrote."

At present, the couplet stands thus:—

> "Dear are the days that made our annals bright,
> Ere Garrick fled, or Brinsley ceased to write."

excuse, and that it will tend to show my endeavour to make the most of the time allotted. I wish I had known it months ago, for in that case I had not left one line standing on another. I always scrawl in this way, and smooth as much as I can, but never sufficiently; and, latterly, I can weave a nine-line stanza faster than a couplet, for which measure I have not the cunning. When I began ' Childe Harold,' I had never tried Spenser's measure, and now I cannot scribble in any other.

" After all, my dear lord, if you can get a decent Address elsewhere, don't hesitate to put this aside. Why did you not trust your own Muse? I am very sure she would have been triumphant, and saved the Committee their trouble—' 'tis a joyful one' to me, but I fear I shall not satisfy even myself. After the account you sent me, 'tis no compliment to say, you would have beaten your candidates; but I mean that, in *that* case, there would have been no occasion for their being beaten at all.

" There are but two decent prologues in our tongue—Pope's to Cato—Johnson's to Drury-lane. These, with the epilogue to the ' Distrest Mother,' and, I think, one of Goldsmith's, and a prologue of old Coleman's to Beaumont and Fletcher's Philaster, are the best things of the kind we have.

" P. S. I am diluted to the throat with medicine for the stone; and Boisragon wants me to try a warm climate for the winter—but I won't."

LETTER C.

TO LORD HOLLAND.

" September 27th, 1812.

" I have just received your very kind letter, and hope you have met with a second copy corrected and addressed to Holland house, with some omissions and this new couplet,

" As glared each rising flash *, and ghastly shone
The skies with lightnings awful as their own.

---

* At present, " As glared the volumed blaze."

As to remarks, I can only say I will alter and acquiesce in any thing
With regard to the part which Whitbread wishes to omit, I believe th
Address will go off *quicker* without it, though, like the agility of th
Hottentot, at the expense of its vigour. I leave to your choice entirel
the different specimens of stucco-work; and a *brick* of your own will als
much improve my Babylonish turret. I should like Elliston to have it
with your leave. ' Adorn' and ' mourn' are lawful rhymes in Pope'
Death of the unfortunate Lady—Gray has ' forlorn' and ' mourn'—an
' torn' and ' mourn' are in Smollet's famous Tears of Scotland.

" As there will probably be an outcry amongst the rejected, I hop
the Committee will testify (if it be needful) that I sent in nothing to th
congress whatever, with or without a name, as your lordship well knows
All I have to do with it is with and through you; and though I, o
course, wish to satisfy the audience, I do assure you my first object is t
comply with your request, and in so doing to show the sense I have o
the many obligations you have conferred upon me.

" Yours ever,

" B."

TO LORD HOLLAND.

" September 27th, 1812.

" I believe this is the third scrawl since yesterday—all about epithets
I think the epithet ' intellectual' won't convey the meaning I intend
and, though I hate compounds, for the present I will try (col' permesso
the word ' *genius-gifted* patriarchs of our line*' instead. Johnson ha
' many-coloured life,' a compound—but they are always best avoided
However, it is the only one in ninety lines, but will be happy to giv
way to a better. I am ashamed to intrude any more remembrances or
Lady H., or letters upon you; but you are, fortunately for me, gifted
with patience already too often tried by

" Your, &c. &c."

This, as finally altered, is

" Immortal names, emblazon'd on our line."

LETTER CI.

TO LORD HOLLAND.

"September 28th, 1812.

"Will this do better? the metaphor is more complete.

"Till slowly ebb'd the { *lava of the* / spent volcanic } wave,
  And blackening ashes mark'd the Muse's grave.

If not, we will say 'burning' wave, and instead of 'burning clime,' in the line some couplets back, have 'glowing.'

"Is Whitbread determined to castrate all my *cavalry* lines*? I don't see why t'other house should be spared; besides, it is the public, who ought to know better; and you recollect Johnson's was against similar buffooneries of Rich's—but, certes, I am not Johnson.

"Instead of 'effects,' say 'labours'—'degenerate' will do, will it? Mr. Betty is no longer a babe, therefore the line cannot be personal.

---

* The lines he here alludes to, and which, in spite of all his efforts to retain them, were omitted by the Committee, ran thus:

"*Nay, lower still, the Drama yet deplores*
That late she deign'd to crawl upon all-fours.
When Richard roars in Bosworth for a horse,
If you command, the steed must come in course.
If you decree, the Stage must condescend
To soothe the sickly taste we dare not mend.
Blame not our judgment should we acquiesce,
And gratify you more by showing less.
Oh, since your Fiat stamps the Drama's laws,
Forbear to mock us with misplaced applause;
That public praise be ne'er again disgraced,
From { brutes to man recall / babes and brutes redeem } a nation's taste;
Then pride shall doubly nerve the actors' powers,
When Reason's voice is echoed back by ours."

The last couplet but one was again altered in a subsequent copy thus:—

"*The past reproach let present scenes refute,*
Nor shift from man to babe, from babe to brute."

" Will this do?

$$\text{" Till ebb'd the lava of } \left\{ \begin{array}{c} \textit{the burning} \\ \text{that molten} \end{array} \right\} \text{ wave *,}$$

with 'glowing dome,' in case you prefer 'burning' added to this 'wave
metaphorical. The word 'fiery pillar' was suggested by the 'pillar o
fire' in the book of Exodus, which went before the Israelites through th
Red Sea. I once thought of saying 'like Israel's pillar,' and making i
a simile, but I did not know,—the great temptation was leaving th
epithet 'fiery' for the supplementary wave. I want to work up tha
passage, as it is the only new ground us prologuizers can go upon—

> " This is the place where, if a poet
> Shined in description, he might show it."

If I part with the possibility of a future conflagration, we lessen the
compliment to Shakspeare. However, we will e'en mend it thus:

> " Yes, it shall be—the magic of that name,
> That scorns the scythe of Time, the torch of Flame,
> On the same spot, &c. &c.

There—the deuce is in it, if that is not an improvement to Whitbread'
content. Recollect, it is the 'name,' and not the 'magic,' that has a
noble contempt for those same weapons. If it were the 'magic,' my
metaphor would be somewhat of the maddest—so the 'name' is the
antecedent. But, my dear lord, your patience is not quite so immortal
—therefore, with many and sincere thanks, I am

" Yours ever most affectionately.

" P. S. I foresee there will be charges of partiality in the papers
but you know I sent in no Address; and glad both you and I must be
that I did not, for, in that case, their plea had been plausible. I doubt
the Pit will be testy; but conscious innocence (a novel and pleasing
sensation) makes me bold."

---

* The form of this couplet, as printed, is as follows:—

> " Till blackening ashes and the lonely wall
> Usurp'd the Muse's realm, and mark'd her fall."

LETTER CII.

TO LORD HOLLAND.

"Sept. 28.

" I have altered the *middle* couplet, so as I hope partly to do away with W.'s objection. I do think, in the present state of the stage, it had been unpardonable to pass over the horses and Miss Mudie, &c. As Betty is no longer a boy, how can this be applied to him ? He is now to be judged as a man. If he acts still like a boy, the public will but be more ashamed of their blunder. I have, you see, *now* taken it for granted that these things are reformed. I confess, I wish that part of the Address to stand; but if W. is inexorable, e'en let it go. I have also new cast the lines, and softened the hint of future combustion *, and sent them off this morning. Will you have the goodness to add, or insert, the *approved* alterations as they arrive? They ' come like shadows, so depart;' occupy me, and, I fear, disturb you.

" Do not let Mr. W. put his Address into Elliston's hands till you have settled on these alterations. E. will think it too long :—much depends on the speaking. I fear it will not bear much curtailing, without *chasms* in the sense.

" It is certainly too long in the reading; but if Elliston exerts himself, such a favourite with the public will not be thought tedious. *I* should think it so, if *he* were not to speak it.

" Yours ever, &c.

" P.S. On looking again, I doubt my idea of having obviated W.'s objection. To the other House, allusion is a ' non sequitur'—but I wish to plead for this part, because the thing really is not to be passed over. Many after-pieces at the Lyceum by the *same company* have already attacked this ' Augean *Stable*'—and Johnson, in his prologue against ' Lunn' (the harlequin manager, Rich),—' Hunt,'—' Mahomet,' &c. is surely a fair precedent."

---

* It had been, originally,

" *Though other piles may sink in future flame,*
  On the same spot," &c. &c.

LETTER CIII.

TO LORD HOLLAND.

" September 29th, 1812.

" Shakspeare certainly ceased to reign in *one* of his kingdoms, as George III. did in America and George IV. may in Ireland*. Now, we have nothing to do out of our own realms, and when the monarchy was gone, his majesty had but a barren sceptre. I have *cut away*, you will see, and altered, but make it what you please; only I do implore, for my *own* gratification, one lash on those accursed quadrupeds—' a long shot, Sir Lucius, if you love me.' I have altered ' wave,' &c. and the ' fire,' and so forth, for the timid.

" Let me hear from you when convenient, and believe me, &c.

" P.S. Do let *that* stand, and cut out elsewhere. I shall choke, if we must overlook their d—-d menagerie."

LETTER CIV.

TO LORD HOLLAND.

" September 30th, 1812.

" I send you the most I can make of it; for I am not so well as I was, and find I ' pall in resolution.'

" I wish much to see you, and will be at Tetbury by twelve on Saturday; and from thence I go on to Lord Jersey's. It is impossible not to allude to the degraded state of the Stage, but I have lightened *it*, and endeavoured to obviate your *other* objections. There is a new couplet for Sheridan, allusive to his Monody. All the alterations I have marked thus |,— as you will see by comparison with the other copy. I have cudgelled my brains with the greatest willingness, and only wish I had more time to have done better.

" You will find a sort of clap-trap laudatory couplet inserted for the quiet of the Committee, and I have added, towards the end, the couplet you were pleased to *like*. The whole Address is seventy-three lines, still

---

* Some objection, it appears from this, had been made to the passage, " and Shakspeare *ceased to reign.*"

perhaps too long; and, if shortened, you will save time, but, I fear, a little of what I meant for sense also.

> "With myriads of thanks, I am ever, &c.

"My sixteenth edition of respects to Lady H.—How she must laugh at all this!

"I wish Murray, my publisher, to print off some copies as soon as your lordship returns to town—it will ensure correctness in the papers afterwards."

LETTER CV.

TO LORD HOLLAND.

> "Far be from him that hour which asks in vain
> Tears such as flow for Garrick in his strain;
>
> *or,*
>
> Far be that hour that vainly asks in turn
> $\left\{\begin{array}{c}\textit{crown'd his}\\ \textit{wept o'er}\end{array}\right\}$
> Such verse for him as Garrick's urn.

> "Sept. 30, 1812.

"Will you choose between these added to the lines on Sheridan*? I think they will wind up the panegyric, and agree with the train of thought preceding them.

"Now, one word as to the Committee—how could they resolve on a rough copy of an Address never sent in, unless you had been good enough to retain in memory, or on paper, the thing they have been good enough to adopt? By the by, the circumstances of the case should make the Committee less 'avidus gloriæ,' for all praise of them would look plaguy suspicious. If necessary to be stated at all, the simple facts bear them out. They surely had a right to act as they pleased. My sole object is one which, I trust, my whole conduct has shown; viz. that I did nothing insidious—sent in no Address *whatever*—but, when applied to, did my best for them and myself; but above all, that there was no undue partiality, which will be what the rejected will endeavour to make out.

* These added lines, as may be seen by reference to the printed Address, were not retained.

Fortunately—most fortunately—I sent in no lines on the occasion. Fo[r] I am sure that had they, in that case, been preferred, it would have bee[n] asserted that *I* was known, and owed the preference to private friendship This is what we shall probably have to encounter, but, if once spoke[n] and approved, we sha'n't be much embarrassed by their brilliant conjec tures, and, as to criticism, an *old* author, like an old bull, grows coole[r] (or ought) at every baiting.

" The only thing would be to avoid a party on the night of delivery —afterwards, the more the better, and the whole transaction inevitably tends to a good deal of discussion. Murray tells me there are myriads of ironical Addresses ready—*some*, in imitation of what is called *my style.* If they are as good as the Probationary Odes, or Hawkins's Pipe of Tobacco, it will not be bad fun for the imitated. " Ever, &c."

LETTER CVI.

TO LORD HOLLAND.

" October 2, 1812.

" A copy of this *still altered* is sent by the post, but this will arrive first. It must be ' humbler'—'*yet aspiring*' does away the modesty, and, after all, *truth is truth.* Besides, there is a puff direct altered, to please your *plaguy renters.*

" I shall be at Tetbury by 12 or 1—but send this for you to ponder over. There are several little things marked thus altered for your perusal. I have dismounted the cavalry, and, I hope, arranged to your *general* satisfaction. " Ever, &c.

" At Tetbury by noon.—I hope, after it is sent, there will be no more elisions. It is not now so long—73 lines—two less than allotted. I will alter all Committee objections, but I hope you won't permit *Elliston* to have any *voice* whatever,—except in speaking it."

The time comprised in this series of letters to Lord Holland,— which, as being exclusively on one subject, I have thought it right to give without interruption,—Lord Byron passed, for the most part, at Cheltenham ; and during the same period, the following letters to other correspondents were written.

LETTER CVII.

TO MR. MURRAY.

" High-street, Cheltenham, Sept. 5th, 1812.

" Pray have the goodness to send those despatches, and a No. of the Edinburgh Review with the rest. I hope you have written to Mr. Thompson, thanked him in my name for his present, and told him that I shall be truly happy to comply with his request.—How do you go on? and when is the graven image, ' with *bays and wicked rhyme upon' t*,' to grace, or disgrace, some of our tardy editions?

" Send me ' *Rokeby.*' Who the devil is he?—no matter, he has good connexions, and will be well introduced. I thank you for your inquiries: I am so, so, but my thermometer is sadly below the poetical point. What will you give *me* or *mine* for a poem of six Cantos (*when complete —no* rhyme, *no* recompense), as like the last two as I can make them? I have some ideas that one day may be imbodied, and till winter I shall have much leisure.

" P.S. My last question is in the true style of Grub-street; but, like Jeremy Diddler, I only ' ask for information.'—Send me Adair on Diet and Regimen, just republished by Ridgway."

LETTER CVIII.

TO MR. MURRAY.

" Cheltenham, Sept. 14, 1812.

" The parcels contained some letters and verses, all (but one) anonymous and complimentary, and very anxious for my conversion from certain infidelities into which my good-natured correspondents conceive me to have fallen. The books were presents of a *convertible* kind. Also, ' Christian Knowledge' and the ' Bioscope,' a religious Dial of Life explained;—and to the author of the former (Cadell, publisher), I beg you will forward my best thanks for his letter, his present, and, above all, his good intentions. The ' Bioscope' contained a MS. copy of very excellent verses, from whom I know not, but evidently the composition of some one in the habit of writing, and of writing well. I do not know

if he be the author of the 'Bioscope' which accompanied them; bu
whoever he is, if you can discover him, thank him from me most heartily
The other letters were from ladies, who are welcome to convert m
when they please; and if I can discover them, and they be young, a
they say they are, I could convince them perhaps of my devotion.   I had
also a letter from Mr. Walpole on matters of this world, which I have
answered.

   " So you are Lucien's publisher? I am promised an interview with
him, and think I shall ask *you* for a letter of introduction, as ' the gods
have made him poetical.'   From whom could it come with a better grace
than from *his* publisher and mine?   Is it not somewhat treasonable in
you to have to do with a relative of the ' direful foe,' as the Morning
Post calls his brother?

   " But my book on ' Diet and Regimen,' where is it?   I thirst for
Scott's Rokeby; let me have your first-begotten copy.   The Anti-jacobin
Review is all very well, and not a bit worse than the Quarterly, and at
least less harmless.   By the by, have you secured my books?   I want
all the Reviews, at least the critiques, quarterly, monthly, &c. Portuguese
and English, extracted, and bound up in one volume for my *old age ;*
and pray, sort my Romaic books, and get the volumes lent to Mr.
Hobhouse—he has had them now a long time.   If any thing occurs,
you will favour me with a line, and in winter we shall be nearer
neighbours.

   " P.S. I was applied to, to write the Address for Drury-lane, but the
moment I heard of the contest, I gave up the idea of contending against
all Grub-street, and threw a few thoughts on the subject into the fire.
I did this out of respect to you, being sure you would have turned off
any of your authors who had entered the lists with such scurvy competitors.   To triumph would have been no glory ; and to have been
defeated—'sdeath !—I would have choked myself, like Otway, with a
quartern loaf; so, remember I had, and have, nothing to do with it,
upon *my honour !*"

LETTER CIX.

TO MR. WILLIAM BANKES.

" Cheltenham, September 28th, 1812.

" MY DEAR BANKES,

" When you point out to one how people can be intimate at the distance of some seventy leagues, I will plead guilty to your charge, and accept your farewell, but not *wittingly*, till you give me some better reason than my silence, which merely proceeded from a notion founded on your own declaration of *old*, that you hated writing and receiving letters. Besides, how was I to find out a man of many residences? If I had addressed you *now*, it had been to your borough, where I must have conjectured you were amongst your constituents. So now, in despite of Mr. N. and Lady W., you shall be as 'much better' as the Hexham post-office will allow me to make you. I do assure you I am much indebted to you for thinking of me at all, and can't spare you even from amongst the superabundance of friends with whom you suppose me surrounded.

" You heard that Newstead * is sold—the sum £140,000; sixty to remain in mortgage on the estate for three years, paying interest, of course. Rochdale is also likely to do well—so my worldly matters are mending. I have been here some time drinking the waters, simply because there are waters to drink, and they are very medicinal, and sufficiently disgusting. In a few days I set out for Lord Jersey's, but return here, where I am quite alone, go out very little, and enjoy in its fullest extent the ' dolce far niente.' What you are about, I cannot guess, even from your date;—not dauncing to the sound of the gitourney in the Halls of the Lowthers? one of whom is here, ill, poor thing, with a

---

* " Early in the autumn of 1812," says Mr. Dallas, " he told me that he was urged by his man of business, and that Newstead *must* be sold." It was accordingly brought to the hammer at Garraway's, but not, at that time, sold, only £90,000 being offered for it. The private sale to which he alludes in this letter took place soon after,—Mr. Claughton, the agent for Mr. Leigh, being the purchaser. It was never, however, for reasons which we shall see, completed.

phthisic. I heard that you passed through here (at the sordid inn where
I first alighted), the very day before I arrived in these parts. We had
a very pleasant set here; at first the Jerseys, Melbournes, Cowpers, and
Hollands, but all gone; and the only persons I know are the Rawdons
and Oxfords, with some later acquaintances of less brilliant descent.

"But I do not trouble them much; and as for your rooms and your
assemblies, 'they are not dreamed of in our philosophy!!'—Did you read
of a sad accident in the Wye t' other day? a dozen drowned, and Mr
Rossoe, a corpulent gentleman, preserved by a boat-hook or an eel-spear
begged, when he heard his wife was saved—no—*lost*—to be thrown in
again!!—as if he could not have thrown himself in, had he wished it;
but this passes for a trait of sensibility. What strange beings men are,
in and out of the Wye!

"I have to ask you a thousand pardons for not fulfilling some orders
before I left town; but if you knew all the cursed entanglements I *had*
to wade through, it would be unnecessary to beg your forgiveness.—
When will Parliament (the new one) meet?—in sixty days, on account of
Ireland, I presume: the Irish election will demand a longer period for
completion than the constitutional allotment. Yours, of course, is safe,
and all your side of the question. Salamanca is the ministerial watch-
word, and all will go well with you. I hope you will speak more
frequently, I am sure at least you *ought*, and it will be expected. I see
Portman means to stand again. Good night.

"Ever yours most affectionately,

" Νωαίρων*."

LETTER CX.

TO MR. MURRAY.

"Cheltenham, Sept. 27, 1812.

"I sent in no Address whatever to the Committee; but out of
nearly one hundred (this is *confidential*), none have been deemed worth
acceptance; and in consequence of their *subsequent* application to *me*, I

---

* A mode of signature he frequently adopted at this time.

have written a prologue, which *has* been received, and will be spoken. The MS. is now in the hands of Lord Holland.

" I write this merely to say, that (however it is received by the audience) you will publish it in the next edition of Childe Harold; and I only beg you at present to keep my name secret till you hear further from me, and as soon as possible I wish you to have a correct copy, to do with as you think proper.

" P.S. I should wish a few copies printed off *before*, that the newspaper copies may be correct *after* the *delivery*."

LETTER CXI.

TO MR MURRAY.

" Cheltenham, Oct. 12, 1812.

" I have a very *strong objection* to the engraving of the portrait*, and request that it may, on no account, be prefixed; but let *all* the proofs be burnt, and the plate broken. I will be at the expense which has been incurred; it is but fair that *I* should, since I cannot permit the publication. I beg, as a particular favour, that you will lose no time in having this done, for which I have reasons that I will state when I see you. Forgive all the trouble I have occasioned you.

" I have received no account of the reception of the Address, but see it is vituperated in the papers, which does not much embarrass an *old author*. I leave it to your own judgment to add it, or not, to your next edition when required. Pray comply *strictly* with my wishes as to the engraving, and believe me, &c.

" P.S. Favour me with an answer, as I shall not be easy till I hear that the proofs, &c. are destroyed. I hear that the *Satirist* has reviewed Childe Harold, in what manner I need not ask; but I wish to know if the old personalities are revived? I have a better reason for

---

* A miniature by Sanders. Besides this miniature, Sanders had also painted a full length of his lordship, from which the portrait prefixed to this work is engraved. In reference to the latter picture, Lord Byron says, in a note to Mr. Rogers, " If you think the picture you saw at Murray's worth your acceptance, it is yours; and you may put a *glove* or masque on it, if you like."

asking this than any that merely concerns myself; but in publications o
that kind, others, particularly female names, are sometimes introduced."

LETTER CXII.

TO LORD HOLLAND.

"Cheltenham, Oct. 14, 1812.

" MY DEAR LORD,

" I perceive that the papers, yea, even Perry's, are somewhat ruffled
at the injudicious preference of the Committee. My friend Perry has,
indeed, ' et tu Brute'-d me rather scurvily, for which I will send him, for
the M.C., the next epigram I scribble, as a token of my full forgiveness.

" Do the Committee mean to enter into no explanation of their proceedings? You must see there is a leaning towards a charge of partiality.
You will, at least, acquit me of any great anxiety to push myself before
so many elder and better anonymous, to whom the 20 guineas (which I
take to be about two thousand pounds *Bank* currency) and the honour
would have been equally welcome. ' Honour,' I see, ' hath no skill in
paragraph-writing.'

" I wish to know how it went off at the second reading, and whether
any one has had the grace to give it a glance of approbation. I have
seen no paper but Perry's, and two Sunday ones. Perry is severe, and
the others silent. If, however, you and your Committee are not now
dissatisfied with your own judgments, I shall not much embarrass myself
about the brilliant remarks of the journals. My own opinion upon it is
what it always was, perhaps pretty near that of the public.

" Believe me, my dear lord, &c. &c.

" P.S. My best respects to Lady H., whose smiles will be very
consolatory, even at this distance."

LETTER CXIII.

TO MR. MURRAY.

"Cheltenham, Oct. 18th, 1812

"Will you have the goodness to get this Parody of a peculiar kind * (for all the first lines are *Busby*'s entire) inserted in several of the papers (*correctly*—and copied *correctly; my hand* is difficult)—particularly the Morning Chronicle? Tell Mr. Perry I forgive him all he has said, and may say against *my address*, but he will allow me to deal with the doctor—*(audi alteram partem)*—and not *betray* me. I cannot think what has befallen Mr. Perry, for of yore we were very good friends;—but no matter, only get this inserted.

"I have a poem on Waltzing for *you*, of which I make *you* a present; but it must be anonymous. It is in the old style of English Bards and Scotch Reviewers.

"P.S. With the next edition of Childe Harold you may print the first fifty or a hundred opening lines of the 'Curse of Minerva' down to the couplet beginning

"Mortal ('twas thus she spake, &c.

Of course, the moment the *Satire* begins, there you will stop, and the opening is the best part."

---

* Among the Addresses sent in to the Drury-lane Committee was one by Dr. Busby, entitled a Monologue, of which the Parody was enclosed in this letter. A short specimen of this trifle will be sufficient. The four first lines of the Doctor's Address are as follows:—

"When energizing objects men pursue,
What are the prodigies they cannot do?
A magic Edifice you here survey,
Shot from the ruins of the other day!"

Which verses are thus ridiculed, unnecessarily, in the Parody:—

"'When energizing objects men pursue,
The Lord knows what is writ by Lord knows who.
'A modest Monologue you here survey,'
Hiss'd from the theatre the 'other day.'"

LETTER CXIV.

TO MR MURRAY.

"Oct. 19, 1812.

"Many thanks, but I *must* pay the *damage*, and will thank you to tell me the amount for the engraving. I think the 'Rejected Addresses' by far the best thing of the kind since the Rolliad, and wish *you* had published them. Tell the author 'I forgive him, were he twenty times over a satirist;' and think his imitations not at all inferior to the famous ones of Hawkins Browne. He must be a man of very lively wit, and less scurrilous than wits often are: altogether, I very much admire the performance, and wish it all success. The *Satirist* has taken a new tone, as you will see: we have now, I think, finished with Childe Harold's critics. I have in *hand* a *Satire* on *Waltzing*, which you must publish anonymously; it is not long, not quite two hundred lines, but will make a very small boarded pamphlet. In a few days you shall have it.

"P.S. The editor of the *Satirist* ought to be thanked for his revocation; it is done handsomely, after five years' warfare."

LETTER CXV.

TO MR. MURRAY.

"Oct 23, 1812.

"Thanks, as usual. You go on boldly; but have a care of *glutting* the public, who have by this time had enough of Childe Harold. 'Waltzing' shall be prepared. It is rather above two hundred lines, with an introductory Letter to the Publisher. I think of publishing, with Childe Harold, the opening lines of the Curse of Minerva, as far as the first speech of Pallas,—because some of the readers like that part better than any I have ever written, and as it contains nothing to affect the subject of the subsequent portion, it will find a place as a *Descriptive Fragment*.

"The *plate* is *broken?* between ourselves, it was unlike the picture;

and besides, upon the whole, the frontispiece of an author's visage is but a paltry exhibition. At all events, *this* would have been no recommendation to the book. I am sure Sanders would not have *survived* the engraving. By the by, the *picture* may remain with *you* or *him* (which you please), till my return. The *one* of two remaining copies is at your service till I can give you a *better;* the other must be *burned peremptorily.* Again, do not forget that I have an account with you, and *that* this is *included.* I give you too much *trouble* to allow you to incur *expense* also.

" You best know how far this ' Address riot' will affect the future sale of Childe Harold. I like the volume of ' Rejected Addresses' better and better. The other parody which Perry has received is mine also (I believe). It is Dr. Busby's speech versified. You are removing to Albemarle-street, I find, and I rejoice that we shall be nearer neighbours. I am going to Lord Oxford's, but letters here will be forwarded. When at leisure, all communications from you will be willingly received by the humblest of your scribes. Did Mr. Ward write the review of Horne Tooke's Life in the Quarterly? it is excellent."

LETTER CXVI.

TO MR. MURRAY.

" Cheltenham, November 22, 1812.

" On my return here from Lord Oxford's, I found your obliging note, and will thank you to retain the letters, and any other subsequent ones to the same address, till I arrive in town to claim them, which will probably be in a few days. I have in charge a curious and very long MS. poem, written by Lord Brooke (the *friend* of Sir *Philip Sidney*), which I wish to submit to the inspection of Mr. Gifford, with the following queries:—first, whether it has ever been published, and, secondly (if not), whether it is worth publication? It is from Lord Oxford's library, and must have escaped or been overlooked amongst the MSS. of the Harleian Miscellany. The writing is Lord Brooke's, except a different hand towards the close. It is very long, and in the six-line stanza. It is not for me to hazard an opinion upon its merits; but I would take the liberty, if not too troublesome, to submit it to Mr.

Gifford's judgment, which, from his excellent edition of Massinger, I
should conceive to be as decisive on the writings of that age as on those
of our own.

"Now for a less agreeable and important topic.—How came Mr
Mac-Somebody, without consulting you or me, to prefix the Address to
his volume* of ' *Dejected* Addresses?' Is not this somewhat larcenous?
I think the ceremony of leave might have been asked, though I have no
objection to the thing itself; and leave the ' hundred and eleven' to tire
themselves with ' base comparisons.' I should think the ingenuous
public tolerably sick of the subject, and, except the Parodies, I have not
interfered, nor shall; indeed I did not know that Dr. Busby had published his Apologetical Letter and Postscript, or I should have recalled
them. But I confess I looked upon his conduct in a different light
before its appearance. I see some mountebank has taken Alderman
Birch's name to vituperate Dr. Busby; he had much better have pilfered
his pastry, which I should imagine the more valuable ingredient—at
least for a puff.—Pray secure me a copy of Woodfall's new Junius, and
believe me, &c."

LETTER CXVII.

TO MR. WILLIAM BANKES.

"December 26.

"The multitude of your recommendations has already superseded
my humble endeavours to be of use to you, and, indeed, most of my
principal friends are returned. Leake from Joannina, Canning and Adair
from the city of the Faithful, and at Smyrna no letter is necessary, as the
consuls are always willing to do every thing for personages of respecta-
bility. I have sent you *three*, one to Gibraltar, which, though of no
great necessity, will, perhaps, put you on a more intimate footing with
a very pleasant family there. You will very soon find out that a man of

---

* "The Genuine Rejected Addresses, presented to the Committee of Management for
Drury-lane Theatre; preceded by that written by Lord Byron and adopted by the Committee:"
—published by B. M'Millan.

any consequence has very little occasion for any letters but to ministers and bankers, and of them you have already plenty, I will be sworn.

"It is by no means improbable that I shall go in the spring, and if you will fix any place of rendezvous about August, I will *write* or *join* you.—When in Albania, I wish you would inquire after Dervise Tahiri and Vascillie (or Basil), and make my respects to the viziers, both there and in the Morea. If you mention my name to Suleyman of Thebes, I think it will not hurt you; if I had my dragoman, or wrote Turkish, I could have given you letters of *real service;* but to the English they are hardly requisite, and the Greeks themselves can be of little advantage. Liston you know already, and I do not, as he was not then minister. Mind you visit Ephesus and the Troad, and let me hear from you when you please. I believe G. Forresti is now at Yanina, but if not, whoever is there will be too happy to assist you. Be particular about *firmauns;* never allow yourself to be bullied, for you are better protected in Turkey than any where; trust not the Greeks; and take some *knick-nackeries* for presents—*watches, pistols,* &c. &c. to the Beys and Pachas. If you find one Demetrius, at Athens or elsewhere, I can recommend him as a good dragoman. I hope to join you, however; but you will find swarms of English now in the Levant.

"Believe me, &c."

LETTER CXVIII.

TO MR. MURRAY.

"February 20th, 1813.

"In 'Horace in London,' I perceive some stanzas on Lord Elgin, in which (waving the kind compliment to myself*) I heartily concur. I

---

* In the Ode entitled "The Parthenon," Minerva thus speaks:—

> "All who behold my mutilated pile
> Shall brand its ravager with classic rage;
> And soon a titled bard from Britain's isle
> Thy country's praise and suffrage shall engage,
> And fire with Athens' wrongs an angry age!"

HORACE IN LONDON.

wish I had the pleasure of Mr. Smith's acquaintance, as I could communicate the curious anecdote you read in Mr. T.'s letter. If he would like it, he can have the *substance* for his second edition; if not, I shall add it to our next, though I think we already have enough of Lord Elgin.

"What I have read of this work seems admirably done. My praise, however, is not much worth the author's having; but you may thank him in my name for *his*. The idea is new—we have excellent imitations of the Satires, &c. by Pope; but I remember but one imitative Ode in his works, and *none* any where else. I can hardly suppose that *they* have lost any fame by the fate of the *farce;* but even should this be the case, the present publication will again place them on their pinnacle.

"Yours, &c."

It has already been stated that the pecuniary supplies, which he found it necessary to raise on arriving at majority, were procured for him on ruinously usurious terms*. To some transactions connected with this subject, the following characteristic letter refers.

LETTER CXIX.

TO MR. ROGERS.

"March 25th, 1813.

"I enclose you a draft for the usurious interest due to Lord * *'s *protégé;*—I also could wish you would state thus much for me to his lordship   Though the transaction speaks plainly in itself for the borrower's folly and the lender's usury, it never was my intention to *quash*

---

* " 'Tis said that persons living on annuities
    Are longer lived than others,—God knows why,
Unless to plague the grantors,—yet so true it is,
    That some, I really think, *do* never die.
Of any creditors, the worst a Jew it is;
    And *that*'s their mode of furnishing supply:
In my young days they lent me cash that way,
Which I found very troublesome to pay."

DON JUAN, CANTO II.

the demand, as I *legally* might, nor to withhold payment of principal, or, perhaps, even *unlawful* interest. You know what my situation has been, and what it is. I have parted with an estate (which has been in my family for nearly three hundred years, and was never disgraced by being in possession of a *lawyer*, a *churchman*, or a *woman*, during that period), to liquidate this and similar demands; and the payment of the purchase is still withheld, and may be, perhaps, for years. If, therefore, I am under the necessity of making those persons *wait* for their money (which, considering the terms, they can afford to suffer), it is my misfortune.

"When I arrived at majority in 1809, I offered my own security on *legal* interest, and it was refused. *Now*, I will not accede to this. This man I may have seen, but I have no recollection of the names of any parties but the *agents* and the securities. The moment I can, it is assuredly my intention to pay my debts. This person's case may be a hard one; but, under all circumstances, what is mine? I could not foresee that the purchaser of my estate was to demur in paying for it.

"I am glad it happens to be in my power so far to accommodate my Israelite, and only wish I could do as much for the rest of the Twelve Tribes.

"Ever yours, dear R.

"BN."

At the beginning of this year, Mr. Murray having it in contemplation to publish an edition of the two Cantos of Childe Harold with engravings, the noble author entered with much zeal into his plan; and, in a note on the subject to Mr. Murray, says:—"Westall has, I believe, agreed to illustrate your book, and I fancy one of the engravings will be from the pretty little girl you saw the other day *, though without her name, and merely as a model for some sketch connected with the subject. I would also have the portrait (which you saw to-day) of the friend who is mentioned in the text at the close of Canto 1st, and in the notes,—which are subjects sufficient to authorize that addition."

* Lady Charlotte Harley, to whom, under the name of Ianthe, the introductory lines to Childe Harold were afterwards addressed.

Early in the spring he brought out, anonymously, his poem on Waltzing, which, though full of very lively satire, fell so far short of what was now expected from him by the public, that the disavowal of it, which, as we see by the following letter, he thought right to put forth, found ready credence.

LETTER CXX.

TO MR. MURRAY.

" April 21st, 1813.

" I shall be in town by Sunday next, and will call and have some conversation on the subject of Westall's designs. I am to sit to him for a picture at the request of a friend of mine, and as Sanders's is not a good one, you will probably prefer the other. I wish you to have Sanders's taken down and sent to my lodgings immediately—before my arrival. I hear that a certain malicious publication on Waltzing is attributed to me. This report, I suppose, you will take care to contradict, as the author, I am sure, will not like that I should wear his cap and bells. Mr. Hobhouse's quarto will be out immediately; pray send to the author for an early copy, which I wish to take abroad with me.

" P.S. I see the Examiner threatens some observations upon you next week. What can you have done to share the wrath which has heretofore been principally expended upon the Prince? I presume all your Scribleri will be drawn up in battle array in defence of the modern Tonson—Mr. Bucke, for instance.

" Send in my account to Bennet-street, as I wish to settle it before sailing."

In the month of May appeared his wild and beautiful " Fragment," *The Giaour;*—and though, in its first flight from his hands, some of the fairest feathers of its wing were yet wanting, the public hailed this new offspring of his genius with wonder and delight. The idea of writing a Poem in fragments had been suggested to him by the *Columbus* of Mr. Rogers; and, whatever objections may lie against such a plan in general, it must be allowed to have been well suited to the impatient temperament of Byron, as enabling him to overleap those mechanical difficulties, which, in a regular narrative, embarrass, if not chill, the poet, —leaving it to the imagination of his readers to fill up the intervals between those abrupt bursts of passion in which his chief power lay. The story, too, of the Poem possessed that stimulating charm for him, almost indispensable to his fancy, of being in some degree connected with himself,—an event in which he had been personally concerned, while on his travels, having supplied the groundwork on which the fiction was founded. After the appearance of the Giaour, some incorrect statement of this romantic incident having got into circulation, the noble author requested of his friend, the Marquis of Sligo, who had visited Athens soon after it happened, to furnish him with his recollections on the subject; and the following is the answer which Lord Sligo returned.

" Albany, Monday, August 31st, 1813.

" MY DEAR BYRON,

" You have requested me to tell you all that I heard at Athens about the affair of that girl who was so near being put an end to while you were there; you have asked me to mention every circumstance, in the remotest degree relating to it, which I heard. In compliance with your wishes, I write to you all I heard, and I cannot imagine it to be very far from the fact, as the circumstance happened only a day or two before I arrived at Athens, and consequently was a matter of common conversation at the time.

" The new governor, unaccustomed to have the same intercourse with the Christians as his predecessor, had of course the barbarous Turkish ideas with regard to women. In consequence, and in compliance with the strict letter of the Mahommedan law, he ordered this girl to be sewed up in a sack, and thrown into the sea,—as is, indeed, quite customary at Constantinople. As you were returning from bathing in the Piræus, you met the procession going down to execute the sentence of the Waywode on this unfortunate girl. Report continues to say, that on finding out what the object of their journey was, and who was the miserable sufferer, you immediately interfered; and on some delay in obeying your orders, you were obliged to inform the leader of the escort, that force should make him comply;—that, on farther hesitation, you drew a pistol, and told him, that if he did not immediately obey your orders, and come back with you to the Aga's house, you would shoot him dead. On this, the man turned about and went with you to the governor's house; here you succeeded, partly by personal threats, and partly by bribery and entreaty, to procure her pardon on condition of her leaving Athens. I was told that you then conveyed her in safety to the convent, and despatched her off at night to Thebes, where she found a safe asylum. Such is the story I heard, as nearly as I can recollect it at present. Should you wish to ask me any further questions about it, I shall be very ready and willing to answer them.

> "I remain, my dear Byron,
>> "yours, very sincerely,
>>> "SLIGO.

"I am afraid you will hardly be able to read this scrawl; but I am so hurried with the preparations for my journey, that you must excuse it."

Of the prodigal flow of his fancy, when its sources were once opened on any subject, the *Giaour* affords one of the most remarkable instances, —this Poem having accumulated under his hand, both in printing and through successive editions, till from four hundred lines, of which it consisted in his first copy, it at present amounts to nearly fourteen hundred. The plan, indeed, which he had adopted, of a series of fragments, —a set of "orient pearls at random strung,"—left him free to introduce, without reference to more than the general complexion of his story, whatever sentiments or images his fancy, in its excursions, could collect; and how little fettered he was by any regard to connexion in these additions appears from a note which accompanied his own copy of the paragraph, commencing "Fair clime, where every season smiles,"—in which he says, "I have not yet fixed the place of insertion for the following lines, but will, when I see you—as I have no copy."

Even into this new passage, rich as it was at first, his fancy afterwards poured a fresh infusion,—the whole of its most picturesque portion, from the line "For there, the Rose o'er crag or vale," down to "And turn to groans his roundelay," having been suggested to him during revision. In order to show, however, that though so rapid in the first heat of composition, he formed no exception to that law which imposes labour as the price of perfection, I shall here extract a few verses from his original draft of this paragraph, by comparing which with the form they wear at present* we may learn to appreciate the value of these after-touches of the master.

> " Fair clime ! where *ceaseless summer* smiles
> Benignant o'er those blessed isles,
> Which, seen from far Colonna's height,
> Make glad the heart that hails the sight,
> And *give* to loneliness delight.
> There *shine the bright abodes ye seek,*
> *Like dimples upon Ocean's cheek,*—
> *So smiling round the waters lave*
> These Edens of the eastern wave.
> Or if, at times, the transient breeze
> Break the *smooth* crystal of the seas,
> Or *brush* one blossom from the trees,
> How *grateful* is the gentle air
> That wakes and wafts the *fragrance* there."

---

* The following are the lines in their present shape, and it will be seen that there is not a single alteration in which the music of the verse has not been improved as well as the thought.

> " Fair clime ! where every season smiles
> Benignant o'er those blessed isles,
> Which, seen from far Colonna's height,
> Make glad the heart that hails the sight,
> And lend to loneliness delight.
> There, mildly dimpling, Ocean's cheek
> Reflects the tints of many a peak
> Caught by the laughing tides that lave
> These Edens of the eastern wave :
> And if at times a transient breeze
> Break the blue crystal of the seas,
> Or sweep one blossom from the trees,
> How welcome is each gentle air
> That wakes and wafts the odours there !"

Among the other passages added to this edition (which was eithe[
the third or fourth, and between which and the first there intervened bu[
about six weeks) was that most beautiful and melancholy illustration o[
the lifeless aspect of Greece, beginning " He who hath bent him o'er th[
dead,"—of which the most gifted critic of our day* has justly pro[
nounced, that "it contains an image more true, more mournful, and
more exquisitely finished, than any we can recollect in the whole com[
pass of poetry†." To the same edition also were added, among othe[
accessions of wealth‡, those lines, " The cygnet proudly walks the water,'
and the impassioned verses, " My memory now is but the tomb."

On my rejoining him in town this spring, I found the enthusiasm
about his writings and himself, which I had left so prevalent, both in
the world of literature and in society, grown, if any thing, still more
general and intense. In the immediate circle, perhaps, around him,
familiarity of intercourse might have begun to produce its usual disen-
chanting effects. His own liveliness and unreserve, on a more intimate
acquaintance, would not be long in dispelling that charm of poetic sadness, which to the eyes of distant observers hung about him; while the
romantic notions, connected by some of his fair readers with those past and
nameless loves alluded to in his poems, ran some risk of abatement from too
near an acquaintance with the supposed objects of his fancy and fondness
at present. A poet's mistress should remain, if posssible, as imaginary
a being to others, as, in most of the attributes he clothes her with, she
has been to himself;—the reality, however fair, being always sure to fall
short of the picture which a too lavish fancy has drawn of it. Could we
call up in array before us all the beauties whom the love of poets has
immortalized, from the high-born dame to the plebeian damsel,—from

* Mr. Jeffrey.

† In Dallaway's Constantinople, a book which Lord Byron is not unlikely to have consulted, I find a passage quoted from Gillies's History of Greece, which contains, perhaps, the
first seed of the thought thus expanded into full perfection by genius:—"The present state of
Greece compared to the ancient is the silent obscurity of the grave contrasted with the vivid
lustre of active life."

‡ Among the recorded instances of such happy after-thoughts in poetry may be mentioned,
as one of the most memorable, Denham's four lines, "Oh could I flow like thee," &c., which
were added in the second edition of his Poem.

the Lauras and Sacharissas down to the Cloes and Jeannies,—we should, it is to be feared, sadly unpeople our imaginations of many a bright tenant that poesy has lodged there, and find, in more than one instance, our admiration of the faith and fancy of the worshipper increased by our discovery of the worthlessness of the idol.

But, whatever of its first romantic impression the personal character of the poet may, from such causes, have lost in the circle he most frequented, this disappointment of the imagination was far more than compensated by the frank, social, and engaging qualities, both of disposition and manner, which, on a nearer intercourse, he disclosed, as well as by that entire absence of any literary assumption or pedantry, which entitled him fully to the praise bestowed by Sprat upon Cowley, that few could " ever discover he was a great poet by his discourse." While thus, by his intimates, and those who had got, as it were, behind the scenes of his fame, he was seen in his true colours, as well of weakness as of amiableness, on strangers and such as were out of this immediate circle, the spell of his poetical character still continued to operate; and the fierce gloom and sternness of his imaginary personages were, by the greater number of them, supposed to belong, not only as regarded mind, but manners, to himself. So prevalent and persevering has been this notion, that, in some disquisitions on his character published since his death, and containing otherwise many just and striking views, we find, in the professed portrait drawn of him, such features as the following :—" Lord Byron had a stern, direct, severe mind: a sarcastic, disdainful, gloomy temper. He had no light sympathy with heartless cheerfulness ;—upon the surface was sourness, discontent, displeasure, ill-will. Beneath all this weight of clouds and darkness*," &c. &c.

Of the sort of double aspect which he thus presented, as viewed by the world and by his friends, he was himself fully aware; and it not only amused him, but, as a proof of the versatility of his powers, flattered his pride. He was, indeed, as I have already remarked, by no means insensible or inattentive to the effect he produced personally on society; and though the brilliant station he had attained, since the commencement of

---

* Letters on the Character and Poetical Genius of Lord Byron, by Sir Egerton Brydges, Bart.

my acquaintance with him, made not the slightest alteration in the unaf
fectedness of his private intercourse, I could perceive, I thought, with
reference to the external world, some slight changes in his conduct which
seemed indicative of the effects of his celebrity upon him.　Among other
circumstances, I observed that, whether from shyness of the general gaze
or from a notion, like Livy's, that men of eminence should not too much
familiarize the public to their persons*, he avoided showing himself in
the mornings, and in crowded places, much more than was his custom
when we first became acquainted.　The preceding year, before his name
had grown " so rife and celebrated," we had gone together to the
exhibition at Somerset-house, and other such places†; and the true reason,
no doubt, of his present reserve, in abstaining from all such miscellaneous
haunts, was the sensitiveness, so often referred to, on the subject of his
lameness,—a feeling which the curiosity of the public eye, now attracted
to this infirmity by his fame, could not fail, he knew, to put rather painfully to the proof.

Among the many gay hours we passed together this spring, I remember particularly the wild flow of his spirits one evening, when we
had accompanied Mr. Rogers home from some early assembly, and when
Lord Byron, who, according to his frequent custom, had not dined for
the last two days, found his hunger no longer governable, and called
aloud for " something to eat."　Our repast,—of his own choosing,—was
simple bread and cheese; and seldom have I partaken of so joyous a
supper.　It happened that our host had just received a presentation copy
of a volume of Poems, written professedly in imitation of the old English
writers, and containing, like many of these models, a good deal that was
striking and beautiful, mixed up with much that was trifling, fantastic,
and absurd.　In our mood, at the moment, it was only with these latter
qualities that either Lord Byron or I felt disposed to indulge ourselves;

---

* " Continuus aspectus minus verendos magnos homines facit."

† The only peculiarity that struck me on those occasions was the uneasy restlessness which
he seemed to feel in wearing a hat,—an article of dress which, from his constant use of a
carriage while in England, he was almost wholly unaccustomed to, and which, after that year, I
do not remember to have ever seen upon him again.　Abroad, he always wore a kind of
foraging cap.

and, in turning over the pages, we found, it must be owned, abundant matter for mirth. In vain did Mr. Rogers, in justice to the author, endeavour to direct our attention to some of the beauties of the work;— it suited better our purpose (as is too often the case with more deliberate critics) to pounce only on such passages as ministered to the laughing humour that possessed us. In this sort of hunt through the volume, we, at length, lighted on the discovery that our host, in addition to his sincere approbation of some of its contents, had also the motive of gratitude for standing by its author, as one of the poems was a warm and, I need not add, well-deserved panegyric on himself. We were, however, too far gone in nonsense for even this eulogy, in which we both so heartily agreed, to stop us. The opening line of the poem was, as well as I can recollect, " When Rogers o'er this labour bent;" and Lord Byron undertook to read it aloud;—but he found it impossible to get beyond the first two words. Our laughter had now increased to such a pitch that nothing could restrain it. Two or three times he began; but no sooner had the words " When Rogers" passed his lips, than our fit burst forth afresh,—till even Mr. Rogers himself, with all his feeling of our injustice, found it impossible not to join us; and we were, at last, all three, in such a state of inextinguishable laughter that, had the author himself been of the party, I question whether he could have resisted the infection.

A day or two after, Lord Byron sent me the following.

" MY DEAR MOORE,

" ' When Rogers' must not see the enclosed, which I send for your perusal. I am ready to fix any day you like for our visit. Was not Sheridan good upon the whole? The ' Poulterer' was the first and best *.

" Ever yours, &c."

* He here alludes to a dinner at Mr. Rogers's, of which I have elsewhere given the following account.

" The company consisted but of Mr. Rogers himself, Lord Byron, Mr. Sheridan, and the writer of this Memoir. Sheridan knew the admiration his audience felt for him; the presence of the young poet, in particular, seemed to bring back his own youth and wit; and the details

1.

" When T * * this damn'd nonsense sent,
  (I hope I am not violent)
  Nor men nor gods knew what he meant.

2.

" And since not ev'n our Rogers' praise
  To common sense his thoughts could raise—
  Why *would* they let him print his lays?

3.

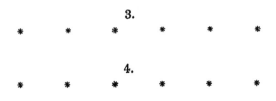

4.

*   *   *   *   *   *

5.

" To me, divine Apollo, grant—O!
  Hermilda's first and second canto,
  I'm fitting up a new portmanteau;

6.

" And thus to furnish decent lining,
  My own and others' bays I'm twining—
  So, gentle T * *, throw me thine in."

On the same day I received from him the following additional scraps. The lines in Italics are from the eulogy that provoked his waggish comments.

he gave of his early life were not less interesting and animating to himself than delightful to us. It was in the course of this evening that, describing to us the poem which Mr. Whitbread had written, and sent in, among the other addresses for the opening of Drury-lane theatre, and which, like the rest, turned chiefly on allusions to the Phœnix, he said—' But Whitbread made more of this bird than any of them :—he entered into particulars, and described its wings, beak, tail, &c.—in short, it was a *Poulterer's* description of a Phœnix.' "—*Life of Sheridan.*

TO ———

1.

" I lay my branch of laurel down."

———

" *Thou* ' lay thy branch of *laurel* down !'
    Why, what thou'st stole is not enow;
And, were it lawfully thine own,
    Does Rogers want it most, or thou?
Keep to thyself thy wither'd bough,
    Or send it back to Doctor Donne—
Were justice done to both, I trow,
    He'd have but little, and thou—none.

2.

" Then thus to form Apollo's crown."

———

" A crown ! why, twist it how you will,
    Thy chaplet must be foolscap still.
When next you visit Delphi's town,
    Inquire amongst your fellow-lodgers,
They'll tell you Phœbus gave his crown,
    Some years before your birth, to Rogers.

3.

" Let every other bring his own."

———

" When coals to Newcastle are carried,
    And owls sent to Athens, as wonders,
From his spouse when the * *'s unmarried,
    Or Liverpool weeps o'er his blunders;
When Tories and Whigs cease to quarrel,
    When C * *'s wife has an heir,
Then Rogers shall ask us for laurel,
    And thou shalt have plenty to spare."

The mention which he makes of Sheridan in the note just cited affords a fit opportunity of producing, from one of his Journals, some

particulars which he has noted down respecting this extraordinary man
for whose talents he entertained the most unbounded admiration,—
rating him, in natural powers, far above all his great political contemporaries.

    *   *   *   *   *   *   *

    " In society I have met Sheridan frequently : he was superb ! He
had a sort of liking for me, and never attacked me, at least to my face,
and he did every body else—high names, and wits, and orators, some of
them poets also. I have seen him cut up Whitbread, quiz Madame de
Staël, annihilate Colman, and do little less by some others (whose names,
as friends, I set not down) of good fame and ability.

    " The last time I met him was, I think, at Sir Gilbert Elliot's,
where he was as quick as ever—no, it was not the last time ; the last
time was at Douglas Kinnaird's.

    " I have met him in all places and parties—at Whitehall with the
Melbournes, at the Marquis of Tavistock's, at Robins's the auctioneer's,
at Sir Humphrey Davy's, at Sam Rogers's,—in short, in most kinds of
company, and always found him very convivial and delightful.

    " I have seen Sheridan weep two or three times. It may be that he
was maudlin ; but this only renders it more impressive, for who would
see

> ' From Marlborough's eyes the tears of dotage flow,
>   And Swift expire a driveller and a show ?'

Once I saw him cry at Robins's the auctioneer's, after a splendid dinner,
full of great names and high spirits. I had the honour of sitting next
to Sheridan. The occasion of his tears was some observation or other
upon the subject of the sturdiness of the Whigs in resisting office and
keeping to their principles : Sheridan turned round :—' Sir, it is easy
for my Lord G. or Earl G. or Marquis B. or Lord H., with thousands
upon thousands a year, some of it either *presently* derived, or *inherited*
in sinecure or acquisitions from the public money, to boast of their
patriotism and keep aloof from temptation ; but they do not know from
what temptation those have kept aloof who had equal pride, at least

equal talents, and not unequal passions, and nevertheless knew not in the course of their lives what it was to have a shilling of their own.' And in saying this he wept.

"I have more than once heard him say, ' that he never had a shilling of his own.' To be sure, he contrived to extract a good many of other people's.

"In 1815, I had occasion to visit my lawyer in Chancery-lane: he was with Sheridan. After mutual greetings, &c., Sheridan retired first. Before recurring to my own business, I could not help inquiring *that* of Sheridan. ' Oh,' replied the attorney, ' the usual thing! to stave off an action from his wine-merchant, my client.'—' Well,' said I, ' and what do you mean to do?'—' Nothing at all for the present,' said he: ' would you have us proceed against old Sherry? what would be the use of it?' and here he began laughing, and going over Sheridan's good gifts of conversation.

"Now, from personal experience, I can vouch that my attorney is by no means the tenderest of men, or particularly accessible to any kind of impression out of the statute or record; and yet Sheridan, in half an hour, had found the way to soften and seduce him in such a manner, that I almost think he would have thrown his client (an honest man, with all the laws, and some justice, on his side) out of the window, had he come in at the moment.

"Such was Sheridan! he could soften an attorney! There has been nothing like it since the days of Orpheus.

"One day I saw him take up his own ' Monody on Garrick.' He lighted upon the Dedication to the Dowager Lady * *. On seeing it, he flew into a rage, and exclaimed, ' that it must be a forgery, that he had never dedicated any thing of his to such a d—d canting,' &c. &c. &c. —and so went on for half an hour abusing his own dedication, or at least the object of it. If all writers were equally sincere, it would be ludicrous.

"He told me that, on the night of the grand success of his School for Scandal, he was knocked down and put into the watch-house for making a row in the street, and being found intoxicated by the watchmen.

" When dying, he was requested to undergo ' an operation.' He replied, that he had already submitted to *two*, which were enough for one man's lifetime. Being asked what they were, he answered, ' having his hair cut, and sitting for his picture.'

" I have met George Colman occasionally, and thought him extremely pleasant and convivial. Sheridan's humour, or rather wit, was always saturnine, and sometimes savage; he never laughed (at least that *I* saw, and I watched him), but Colman did. If I had to *choose*, and could not have both at a time, I should say, ' Let me begin the evening with Sheridan, and finish it with Colman.' Sheridan for dinner, Colman for supper; Sheridan for claret or port, but Colman for every thing, from the madeira and champagne at dinner, the claret with a *layer* of *port* between the glasses, up to the punch of the night, and down to the grog, or gin and water, of daybreak;—all these I have threaded with both the same. Sheridan was a grenadier company of life-guards, but Colman a whole regiment—of *light infantry*, to be sure, but still a regiment."

It was at this time that Lord Byron became acquainted (and, I regret to have to add, partly through my means) with Mr. Leigh Hunt, the editor of a well-known weekly journal, the Examiner. This gentleman I had myself formed an acquaintance with in the year 1811, and, in common with a large portion of the public, entertained a sincere admiration of his talents and courage as a journalist. The interest I took in him personally had been recently much increased by the manly spirit which he had displayed throughout a prosecution instituted against himself and his brother, for a libel that had appeared in their paper on the Prince Regent, and in consequence of which they were both sentenced to imprisonment for two years. It will be recollected that there existed among the Whig party, at this period, a strong feeling of indignation at the late defection from themselves and their principles of the illustrious personage who had been so long looked up to as the friend and patron of both. Being myself, at the time, warmly—perhaps, intemperately—under the influence of this feeling, I regarded the fate of Mr. Hunt with more than common interest, and, immediately on my arrival in town, paid him a visit in his prison. On mentioning the circumstance, soon after, to Lord Byron, and describing my surprise at the sort of luxurious comforts with which I had found the "wit in the dungeon" surrounded,—his trellised flower-garden without, and his books, busts, pictures, and piano-forte within,—the noble poet, whose political view of the case coincided entirely with my own, expressed a strong wish to pay a similar tribute of respect to Mr. Hunt, and accordingly, a day or two after, we proceeded for that purpose to the prison. The introduction which then took place was soon followed by a request from Mr. Hunt that we would dine with him, and the noble poet having good-naturedly accepted the invitation, the Cold Bath Fields prison had, in the month of June, 1813, the honour of receiving Lord Byron, as a guest, within its walls.

On the morning of our first visit to the journalist, I received from Lord Byron the following lines, written, it will be perceived, the night before.

"May 19th, 1813.

> " Oh you, who in all names can tickle the town,
>   Anacreon, Tom Little, Tom Moore, or Tom Brown,—
>   For hang me if I know of which you may most brag,
>   Your Quarto two-pounds, or your Twopenny Post Bag;
>   *　　　*　　　*　　　*　　　*　　　*
>   But now to my letter—to *yours* 'tis an answer—
>   To-morrow be with me, as soon as you can, sir,
>   All ready and dress'd for proceeding to spunge on
>   (According to compact) the wit in the dungeon—
>   Pray Phœbus at length our political malice.
>   May not get us lodgings within the same palace!
>   I suppose that to-night you 're engaged with some codgers,
>   And for Sotheby's Blues have deserted Sam Rogers;
>   And I, though with cold I have nearly my death got,
>   Must put on my breeches, and wait on the Heathcote.
>   But to-morrow, at four, we will both play the *Scurra*,
>   And you 'll be Catullus, the R—t Mamurra.

" Dear M.—having got thus far, I am interrupted by　*　*　*　* 10 o'clock.

" Half-past 11. *　*　*　* is gone. I must dress for Lady Heathcote's.—Addio."

Our day in the prison was, if not agreeable, at least novel and odd
I had, for Lord Byron's sake, stipulated with our host beforehand, tha
the party should be, as much as possible, confined to ourselves; and, a
far as regarded dinner, my wishes had been attended to;—there being
present, besides a member or two of Mr. Hunt's own family, no othe
stranger, that I can recollect, but Mr. Mitchell, the ingenious translato
of Aristophanes.   Soon after dinner, however, there dropped in some o
our host's literary friends, who, being utter strangers to Lord Byron and
myself, rather disturbed the ease into which we were all settling. Among
these, I remember, was Mr. John Scott,—the writer, afterwards, of
some severe attacks on Lord Byron; and it is painful to think that
among the persons then assembled round the poet, there should have been
one so soon to step forth the assailant of his living fame, while *another*
less manful, would reserve the cool venom for his grave.

On the 2d of June, in presenting a petition to the House of Lords,
he made his third, and last, appearance, as an orator, in that assembly.
In his way home from the House that day, he called, I remember, at my
lodgings, and found me dressing in a very great hurry for dinner. He was,
I recollect, in a state of most humorous exaltation after his display, and,
while I hastily went on with my task in the dressing-room, continued to
walk up and down the adjoining chamber, spouting forth for me, in a
sort of mock-heroic voice, detached sentences of the speech he had just
been delivering. " I told them," he said, " that it was a most flagrant
violation of the Constitution—that, if such things were permitted, there
was an end of English freedom, and that——"   " But what was this
dreadful grievance?" I asked, interrupting him in his eloquence.—" The
grievance?" he repeated, pausing as if to consider—" Oh, *that* I forget *."
It is impossible, of course, to convey an idea of the dramatic humour
with which he gave effect to these words; but his look and manner on
such occasions were irresistibly comic, and it was, indeed, rather in such
turns of fun and oddity than in any more elaborate exhibition of wit
that the pleasantry of his conversation consisted.

* His speech was on presenting a Petition from Major Cartwright.

Though it is evident that, after the brilliant success of Childe Harold, he had ceased to think of Parliament as an arena of ambition, yet, as a field for observation, we may take for granted it was not unstudied by him.   To a mind of such quick and various views, every place and pursuit presented some aspect of interest; and whether in the ball-room, the boxing-school, or the senate, all must have been, by genius like his, turned to profit.   The following are a few of the recollections and impressions which I find recorded by himself of his short parliamentary career.

" I have never heard any one who fulfilled my ideal of an orator. Grattan would have been near it, but for his harlequin delivery.   Pitt I never heard.   Fox but once, and then he struck me as a debater, which to me seems as different from an orator as an improvisatore, or a versifier, from a poet.   Grey is great, but it is not oratory.   Canning is sometimes very like one.   Windham I did not admire, though all the world did ; it seemed sad sophistry.   Whitbread was the Demosthenes of bad taste and vulgar vehemence, but strong, and English.   Holland is impressive from sense and sincerity.   Lord Lansdowne good, but still a debater only. Grenville I like vastly, if he would prune his speeches down to an hour's delivery.   Burdett is sweet and silvery as Belial himself, and I think the greatest favourite in Pandemonium, at least I always heard the country gentlemen and the ministerial devilry praise his speeches *up* stairs, and run down from Bellamy's when he was upon his legs.   I heard Bob Milnes make his *second* speech ; it made no impression.   I like Ward—studied, but keen, and sometimes eloquent.   Peel, my school and form-fellow (we sate within two of each other), strange to say, I have never heard, though I often wished to do so ; but from what I remember of him at Harrow, he *is*, or *should* be, among the best of them.   Now, I do *not* admire Mr. Wilberforce's speaking ; it is nothing but a flow of words—' words, words alone.'

" I doubt greatly if the English *have* any eloquence, properly so called ; and am inclined to think that the Irish *had* a great deal, and that the French *will* have, and have had in Mirabeau.   Lord Chatham and Burke are the nearest approaches to orators in England.   I don't

know what Erskine may have been at the *bar*, but in the House, I wish
him at the bar once more. Lauderdale is shrill, and Scotch, and acute

*   *   *   *   *   *   *

"But amongst all these, good, bad, and indifferent, I never heard
the speech which was not too long for the auditors, and not very intelligible, except here and there. The whole thing is a grand deception,
and as tedious and tiresome as may be to those who must be often
present. I heard Sheridan only once, and that briefly, but I liked his
voice, his manner, and his wit; and he is the only one of them I ever
wished to hear at greater length.

"The impression of Parliament upon me was, that its members are
not formidable as *speakers*, but very much so as an *audience;* because in
so numerous a body there may be little eloquence (after all, there were
but *two* thorough orators in all antiquity, and I suspect still *fewer* in
modern times), but there must be a leaven of thought and good sense
sufficient to make them *know* what is right, though they can't express it
nobly.

"Horne Tooke and Roscoe both are said to have declared that they
left Parliament with a higher opinion of its aggregate integrity and
abilities than that with which they entered it. The general amount of
both in most Parliaments is probably about the same, as also the number
of *speakers* and their talent. I except *orators*, of course, because they are
things of ages, and not of septennial or triennial reunions. Neither
House ever struck me with more awe or respect than the same number
of Turks in a divan, or of Methodists in a barn, would have done.
Whatever diffidence or nervousness I felt (and I felt both, in a great
degree) arose from the number rather than the quality of the assemblage,
and the thought rather of the *public without* than the persons within,—
knowing (as all know) that Cicero himself, and probably the Messiah,
could never have altered the vote of a single lord of the bedchamber or
bishop. I thought *our* House dull, but the other animating enough
upon great days.

"I have heard that when Grattan made his first speech in the
English Commons, it was for some minutes doubtful whether to laugh

at or cheer him*. The *début* of his predecessor Flood had been a complete failure under nearly similar circumstances. But when the ministerial part of our senators had watched Pitt (their thermometer) for the cue, and saw him nod repeatedly his stately nod of approbation, they took the hint from their huntsman, and broke out into the most rapturous cheers. Grattan's speech, indeed, deserved them; it was a *chef-d'œuvre*. I did not hear *that* speech of his (being then at Harrow), but heard most of his others on the same question—also that on the war of 1815. I differed from his opinions on the latter question, but coincided in the general admiration of his eloquence.

"When I met old Courtenay, the orator, at Rogers the poet's, in 1811-12, I was much taken with the portly remains of his fine figure, and the still acute quickness of his conversation. It was *he* who silenced Flood in the English House by a crushing reply to a hasty *début* of the rival of Grattan in Ireland. I asked Courtenay (for I like to trace motives) if he had not some personal provocation; for the acrimony of his answer seemed to me, as I had read it, to involve it. Courtenay said ' he had; that, when in Ireland (being an Irishman), at the bar of the Irish House of Commons, Flood had made a personal and unfair attack upon *himself,* who, not being a member of that House, could not defend himself, and that some years afterwards, the opportunity of retort offering in the English Parliament, he could not resist it.' He certainly repaid Flood with interest, for Flood never made any figure, and only a speech or two afterwards, in the English House of Commons. I must except, however, his speech on Reform in 1790, which Fox called ' the best he ever heard upon that subject.'"

For some time he had entertained thoughts of going again abroad; and it appeared, indeed, to be a sort of relief to him, whenever he felt melancholy or harassed, to turn to the freedom and solitude of a life of travel, as his resource. During the depression of spirits which he laboured under, while printing Childe Harold, " he would frequently,"

---

* Of Grattan he says, in another place,—" I was much struck with the simplicity of Grattan's manners in private life ;—they were odd, but they were natural. Curran used to take him off, bowing to the very ground, and ' thanking God that he had no peculiarities of gesture or appearance,' in a way irresistibly ludicrous."

says Mr. Dallas, "talk of selling Newstead, and of going to reside at
Naxos, in the Grecian Archipelago,—to adopt the eastern costume and
customs, and to pass his time in studying the Oriental languages and
literature." The excitement of the triumph that soon after ensued, and
the success which, in other pursuits besides those of literature, attended
him, again diverted his thoughts from these migratory projects. But the
roving fit soon returned; and we have seen, from one of his letters to
Mr. William Bankes, that he looked forward to finding himself, in the
course of this spring, among the mountains of his beloved Greece once
more. For a time, this plan was exchanged for the more social project
of accompanying his friends, the family of Lord Oxford, to Sicily; and
it was while engaged in his preparatives for this expedition that the
annexed letters were written.

LETTER CXXI.

TO MR. MURRAY.

"Maidenhead, June 13th, 1813.

" * * * I have read the 'Strictures,' which are just enough, and
not grossly abusive, in very fair couplets. There is a note against
Massinger near the end, and one cannot quarrel with one's company, at
any rate. The author detects some incongruous figures in a passage of
English Bards, page 23, but which edition I do not know. In the *sole*
copy in your possession—I mean the *fifth* edition—you may make these
alterations, that I may profit (though a little too late) by his remarks :—
For ' *hellish* instinct,' substitute ' *brutal* instinct;' ' *harpies*' alter to ' *felons;*'
and for ' blood-hounds' write 'hell-hounds*.' These be ' very bitter words,
by my troth,' and the alterations not much sweeter; but as I shall not

---

* In an article on this Satire (written for Cumberland's Review, but never printed) by that
most amiable man and excellent poet, the late Rev. Wm. Crowe, the incongruity of these metaphors is thus noticed :—" Within the space of three or four couplets he transforms a man into
as many different animals. Allow him but the compass of three lines, and he will metamorphose
him from a wolf into a harpy, and in three more he will make him a blood-hound."

There are also in this MS. critique some curious instances of oversight or ignorance adduced
from the Satire ; such as " *Fish* from *Helicon*"—" *Attic* flowers *Aonian* odours breathe," &c. &c.

publish the thing, they can do no harm, but are a satisfaction to me in the way of amendment. The passage is only twelve lines.

"You do not answer me about H.'s book; I want to write to him, and not to say any thing unpleasing. If you direct to Post-office, Portsmouth, till *called* for, I will send and receive your letter. You never told me of the forthcoming critique on Columbus, which is not *too* fair; and I do not think justice quite done to the 'Pleasures,' which surely entitle the author to a higher rank than that assigned him in the Quarterly. But I must not cavil at the decisions of the *invisible infallibles;* and the article is very well written. The general horror of '*fragments*' makes me tremulous for the 'Giaour;' but you would publish it—I presume, by this time, to your repentance. But as I consented, whatever be its fate, I won't now quarrel with you, even though I detect it in my pastry; but I shall not open a pie without apprehension for some weeks.

"The books which may be marked G. O. I will carry out. Do you know Clarke's Naufragia? I am told that he asserts the *first* volume of Robinson Crusoe was written by the first Lord Oxford, when in the Tower, and given by him to Defoe; if true, it is a curious anecdote. Have you got back Lord Brooke's MS.? and what does Heber say of it? Write to me at Portsmouth.

"Ever yours, &c.
"N."

TO MR. MURRAY.

"June 18th, 1813.

"DEAR SIR,

"Will you forward the enclosed answer to the kindest letter I ever received in my life, my sense of which I can neither express to Mr. Gifford himself nor to any one else.

"Ever yours,
"N."

LETTER CXXII.

TO W. GIFFORD, ESQ.

"June 18th, 1813.

" MY DEAR SIR,

" I feel greatly at a loss how to write to you at all—still more to thank you as I ought. If you knew the veneration with which I have ever regarded you, long before I had the most distant prospect of becoming your acquaintance, literary or personal, my embarrassment would not surprise you.

" Any suggestion of yours, even were it conveyed in the less tender shape of the text of the Baviad, or a Monk Mason note in Massinger, would have been obeyed; I should have endeavoured to improve myself by your censure: judge then if I should be less willing to profit by your kindness. It is not for me to bandy compliments with my elders and my betters: I receive your approbation with gratitude, and will not return my brass for your gold, by expressing more fully those sentiments of admiration, which, however sincere, would, I know, be unwelcome.

" To your advice on religious topics, I shall equally attend. Perhaps the best way will be by avoiding them altogether. The already published objectionable passages have been much commented upon, but certainly have been rather strongly interpreted. I am no bigot to infidelity, and did not expect that, because I doubted the immortality of man, I should be charged with denying the existence of a God. It was the comparative insignificance of ourselves and *our world,* when placed in comparison with the mighty whole, of which it is an atom, that first led me to imagine that our pretensions to eternity might be overrated.

" This, and being early disgusted with a calvinistic Scotch school, where I was cudgelled to church for the first ten years of my life. afflicted me with this malady; for, after all, it is, I believe, a disease of the mind as much as other kinds of hypochondria*."

*　　　*　　　*　　　*　　　*

* The remainder of this letter, it appears, has been lost.

LETTER CXXIII.

TO MR. MOORE.

"June 22d, 1813.

*　　*　　*　　*　　*　　*　　*

"Yesterday I dined in company with '* *, the Epicene,' whose politics are sadly changed. She is for the Lord of Israel and the Lord of Liverpool—a vile antithesis of a Methodist and a Tory—talks of nothing but devotion and the ministry, and, I presume, expects that God and the government will help her to a pension.

*　　*　　*　　*　　*　　*　　*

"Murray, the $αναξ$ of publishers, the Anac of stationers, has a design upon you in the paper line. He wants you to become the staple and stipendiary Editor of a periodical work. What say you? Will you be bound, like 'Kit Smart, to write for ninety-nine years in the Universal Visitor?' Seriously, he talks of hundreds a year, and—though I hate prating of the beggarly elements—his proposal may be to your honour and profit, and, I am very sure, will be to our pleasure.

"I don't know what to say about 'friendship.' I never was in friendship but once, in my nineteenth year, and then it gave me as much trouble as love. I am afraid, as Whitbread's sire said to the king, when he wanted to knight him, that I am 'too old:' but, nevertheless, no one wishes you more friends, fame, and felicity than

"Yours, &c."

Having relinquished his design of accompanying the Oxfords to Sicily, he again thought of the East, as will be seen by the following letters, and proceeded so far in his preparations for the voyage as to purchase of Love, the jeweller, of Old Bond-street, about a dozen snuffboxes, as presents for some of his old Turkish acquaintances.

LETTER CXXIV.

TO MR. MOORE.

" 4, Benedictine-street, St. James's, July 8th, 1813.

" I presume by your silence that I have blundered into something noxious in my reply to your letter, for the which I beg leave to send, beforehand, a sweeping apology, which you may apply to any, or all, parts of that unfortunate epistle. If I err in my conjecture, I expect the like from you, in putting our correspondence so long in quarantine. God he knows what I have said; but he also knows (if he is not as indifferent to mortals as the *nonchalant* deities of Lucretius), that you are the last person I want to offend. So, if I have,—why the devil don't you say it at once, and expectorate your spleen?

" Rogers is out of town with Madame de Staël, who hath published an Essay against Suicide, which, I presume, will make somebody shoot himself;—as a sermon by Blinkensop, in *proof* of Christianity, sent a hitherto most orthodox acquaintance of mine out of a chapel of ease a perfect atheist. Have you found or founded a residence yet? and have you begun or finished a Poem? If you won't tell me what *I* have done, pray say what you have done, or left undone, yourself. I am still in equipment for voyaging, and anxious to hear from, or of, you *before* I go, which anxiety you should remove more readily, as you think I sha'n't cogitate about you afterwards. I shall give the lie to that calumny by fifty foreign letters, particularly from any place where the plague is rife,—without a drop of vinegar or a whiff of sulphur to save you from infection. Pray write: I am sorry to say that * * * *.

" The Oxfords have sailed almost a fortnight, and my sister is in town, which is a great comfort—for, never having been much together, we are naturally more attached to each other. I presume the illuminations have conflagrated to Derby (or wherever you are) by this time. We are just recovering from tumult and train oil, and transparent fripperies, and all the noise and nonsense of victory. Drury-lane had a large *M. W.* which some thought was Marshal Wellington; others, that it might be translated into Manager Whitbread; while the ladies of the vicinity and the saloon conceived the last letter to be complimentary to themselves. I leave this to the commentators to illuminate. If you don't answer this, I sha'n't say what *you* deserve, but I think *I* deserve a reply. Do you conceive there is no Post-Bag but the Twopenny? Sunburn me, if you are not too bad."

LETTER CXXV.

TO MR. MOORE.

" July 13th, 1813.

*   *   *   *   *   *   *

" Your letter set me at ease; for I really thought (as I hear of your susceptibility) that I had said—I know not what—but something I should have been very sorry for, had it, or I, offended you;—though I don't see how a man with a beautiful wife—*his own* children—quiet—fame—competency and friends (I will vouch for a thousand, which is more than I will for a unit in my own behalf), can be offended with any thing.

" Do you know, Moore, I am amazingly inclined—remember I say but *inclined*—to be seriously enamoured with Lady A. F.—but this * * has ruined all my prospects. However, you know her;—is she *clever*, or sensible, or good-tempered? either *would* do—I scratch out the *will*. I don't ask as to her beauty—that I see; but my circumstances are mending, and were not my other prospects blackening, I would take a wife, and that should be the woman, had I a chance. I do not yet know her much, but better than I did.   *   *   *   *

" I want to get away, but find difficulty in compassing a passage in a ship of war. They had better let me go; if I cannot, patriotism is the word—' nay, an' they 'll mouth, I 'll rant as well as they.' Now, what are you doing?—writing, we all hope, for our own sakes. Remember you must edite my posthumous works, with a Life of the Author, for which I will send you Confessions, dated ' Lazaretto,' Smyrna, Malta, or Palermo—one can die any where.

" There is to be a thing on Tuesday ycleped a national fete. The

Regent and * * * are to be there, and every body else, who has shillings enough for what was once a guinea. Vauxhall is the scene— there are six tickets issued for the modest women, and it is supposed there will be three to spare. The passports for the lax are beyond my arithmetic.

"P.S. The Staël last night attacked me most furiously—said that I had 'no right to make love—that I had used * * barbarously—that I had no feeling, and was totally *insensible* to *la belle passion*, and *had* been all my life.' I am very glad to hear it, but did not know it before. Let me hear from you anon."

LETTER CXXVI.

TO MR. MOORE.

"July 25th, 1813.

" I am not well versed enough in the ways of single woman to make much matrimonial progress. * * * * * * *

" I have been dining like the dragon of Wantley for this last week. My head aches with the vintage of various cellars, and my brains are muddled as their dregs. I met your friends, the D * *s:—she sung one of your best songs so well, that, but for the appearance of affectation, I could have cried; he reminds me of Hunt, but handsomer, and more musical in soul, perhaps. I wish to God he may conquer his horrible anomalous complaint. The upper part of her face is beautiful, and she seems much attached to her husband. He is right, nevertheless, in leaving this nauseous town. The first winter would infallibly destroy her complexion,—and the second, very probably, every thing else.

" I must tell you a story. M * * (of indifferent memory) was dining out the other day, and complaining of the P—e's coldness to his old wassailers. D' * * (a learned Jew) bored him with questions—why this? and why that? 'Why did the P—e act thus?'—'Why, sir, on account of Lord * *, who ought to be ashamed of himself.' 'And why ought Lord * * to be ashamed of himself?'—'Because the P—e, sir, * * * * * * * *.' 'And why, sir, did the P—e cut *you?*'—'Because, G—d d—mme, sir, I stuck to my principles.' 'And *why* did you stick to your principles?'

" Is not this last question the best that ever was put, when you consider to whom? It nearly killed M * *. Perhaps you may think it stupid, but, as Goldsmith said about the peas, it was a very good joke when I heard it—as I did from an ear-witness—and is only spoilt in my narration.

" The season has closed with a Dandy Ball;—but I have dinners with the Harrowbys, Rogers, and Frere and Mackintosh, where I shall drink your health in a silent bumper, and regret your absence till ' too much canaries' wash away my memory, or render it superfluous by a vision of you at the opposite side of the table. Canning has disbanded his party by a speech from his * * * *—the true throne of a Tory. Conceive his turning them off in a formal harangue, and bidding them think for themselves. ' I have led my ragamuffins where they are well peppered. There are but three of the 150 left alive, and they are for the *Town's-end* (*query*, might not Falstaff mean the Bow-street officer? I dare say Malone's posthumous edition will have it so) for life.'

" Since I wrote last, I have been into the country. I journeyed by night—no incident or accident, but an alarm on the part of my valet on the outside, who, in crossing Epping Forest, actually, I believe, flung down his purse before a mile-stone, with a glow-worm in the second figure of number XIX—mistaking it for a footpad and dark lantern. I can only attribute his fears to a pair of new pistols, wherewith I had armed him; and he thought it necessary to display his vigilance by calling out to me whenever we passed any thing—no matter whether moving or stationary. Conceive ten miles, with a tremor every furlong. I have scribbled you a fearfully long letter. This sheet must be blank, and is merely a wrapper, to preclude the tabellarians of the post from peeping. You once complained of my *not* writing;—I will heap ' coals of fire upon your head' by *not* complaining of your *not* reading. Ever. my dear Moore, your'n (isn't that the Staffordshire termination?)

"BYRON."

LETTER CXXVII.

TO MR. MOORE.

"July 27th, 1813.

" When you next imitate the style of 'Tacitus,' pray add, 'de moribus Germanorum;'—this last was a piece of barbarous silence, and could only be taken from the *Woods*, and, as such, I attribute it entirely to your sylvan sequestration at Mayfield Cottage. You will find, on casting up accounts, that you are my debtor by several sheets and one epistle. I shall bring my action;—if you don't discharge, expect to hear from my attorney. I have forwarded your letter to Ruggiero; but don't make a postman of me again, for fear I should be tempted to violate your sanctity of wax or wafer.

" Believe me ever yours *indignantly*,

" Bn."

LETTER CXXVIII.

TO MR. MOORE.

"July 28th, 1813.

" Can't you be satisfied with the pangs of my jealousy of Rogers, without actually making me the pander of your epistolary intrigue? This is the second letter you have enclosed to my address, notwithstanding a miraculous long answer, and a subsequent short one or two of your own. If you do so again, I can't tell to what pitch my fury may soar. I shall send you verse or arsenic, as likely as any thing,— four thousand couplets on sheets beyond the privilege of franking; that privilege, sir, of which you take an undue advantage over a too susceptible senator, by forwarding your lucubrations to every one but himself. I won't frank *from* you, or *for* you, or *to* you—may I be curst if I do, unless you mend your manners. I disown you—I disclaim you—and by all the powers of Eulogy, I will write a panegyric upon you—or dedicate a quarto—if you don't make me ample amends.

"P.S. I am in training to dine with Sheridan and Rogers this evening. I have a little spite against R. and will shed his 'Clary wines pottle-deep.' This is nearly my ultimate or penultimate letter; for I am quite equipped, and only wait a passage. Perhaps I may wait a few weeks for Sligo; but not if I can help it."

He had, with the intention of going to Greece, applied to Mr. Croker, the Secretary of the Admiralty, to procure him a passage on board a king's ship to the Mediterranean; and, at the request of this gentleman, Captain Barlton, of the Boyne, who was just then ordered to reinforce Sir Edward Pellew, consented to receive Lord Byron into his cabin for the voyage. To the letter announcing this offer, the following is the reply.

LETTER CXXIX.

TO MR. CROKER.

"Bt. Str. August 2d, 1813.

"DEAR SIR,

"I was honoured with your unexpected* and very obliging letter when on the point of leaving London, which prevented me from acknowledging my obligation as quickly as I felt it sincerely. I am endeavouring all in my power to be ready before Saturday—and even if I should not succeed, I can only blame my own tardiness, which will not the less enhance the benefit I have lost. I have only to add my hope of forgiveness for all my trespasses on your time and patience, and with my best wishes for your public and private welfare, I have the honour to be, most truly,

"Your obliged and most obedient servant,

"BYRON."

* He calls the letter of Mr. Croker "unexpected," because, in their previous correspondence and interviews on the subject, that gentleman had not been able to hold out so early a prospect of a passage, nor one which was likely to be so agreeable in point of society.

So early as the autumn of this year, a fifth edition of the Giaour was required; and again his fancy teemed with fresh materials for its pages. The verses commencing " The browsing camels' bells are tinkling," and the four pages that follow the line, " Yes, love indeed is light from heaven," were all added at this time.   Nor had the overflowings of his mind even yet ceased, as I find in the Poem, as it exists at present, still further additions,—and, among them, those four brilliant lines,—

> " She was a form of life and light,
> That, seen, became a part of sight,
> And rose, where'er I turn'd mine eye,
> The Morning-star of memory !"

The following notes and letters to Mr. Murray, during these out-pourings, will show how irresistible was the impulse under which he vented his thoughts.

" If you send more proofs, I shall never finish this infernal story— ' Ecce signum'—thirty-three more lines enclosed! to the utter discomfiture of the printer, and, I fear, not to your advantage.

" B."

" Half past two in the morning, August 10th, 1813.

" DEAR SIR,

" Pray suspend the *proofs*, for I am *bitten* again, and have *quantities* for other parts of the bravura.   Yours ever,

" B.

" P.S. You shall have them in the course of the day."

LETTER CXXX.

TO MR. MURRAY.

" August 26th, 1813.

" I have looked over and corrected one proof, but not so carefully (God knows if you can read it through, but I can't) as to preclude your eye from discovering some *o*mission of mine or *com*mission of your printer. If you have patience, look it over. Do you know any body who can stop—I mean *point*—commas, and so forth? for I am, I hear, a sad hand at your punctuation. I have, but with some difficulty, *not* added any more to this snake of a Poem, which has been lengthening its rattles every month. It is now fearfully long, being more than a Canto and a half of Childe Harold, which contains but 882 lines per book, with all late additions inclusive.

" The last lines Hodgson likes. It is not often he does, and when he don't, he tells me with great energy, and I fret and alter. I have thrown them in to soften the ferocity of our Infidel, and, for a dying man, have given him a good deal to say for himself. * * * *

" I was quite sorry to hear you say you staid in town on my account, and I hope sincerely you did not mean so superfluous a piece of politeness.

" Our *six* critiques!—they would have made half a Quarterly by themselves; but this is the age of criticism."

The following refer apparently to a still later edition.

LETTER CXXXI.

TO MR. MURRAY.

" Stilton, Oct. 3d, 1813.

" I have just recollected an alteration you may make in the proof to be sent to Aston.—Among the lines on Hassan's Serai, not far from the beginning, is this—

" Unmeet for Solitude to share.

Now to share implies more than *one*, and Solitude is a single gentleman; it must be thus—

" For many a gilded chamber's there,
Which Solitude might well forbear;

and so on.—My address is Aston-Hall, Rotherham.

" Will you adopt this correction? and pray accept a Stilton cheese from me for your trouble.   Ever yours,   " B."

" If * the old line stands, let the other run thus—

> " Nor there will weary traveller halt,
> To bless the sacred bread aud salt.

" *Note.*—To partake of food—to break bread and taste salt with your host, ensures the safety of the guest; even though an enemy, his person from that moment becomes sacred.

" There is another additional note sent yesterday—on the Priest in the Confessional.

" P.S. I leave this to your discretion; if any body thinks the old line a good one, or the cheese a bad one, don't accept either.   But, in that case, the word *share* is repeated soon after in the line—

> " To share the master's bread and salt;

and must be altered to—

> " To break the master's bread and salt.

This is not so well, though—confound it!"

LETTER CXXXII.

TO MR. MURRAY.

" Oct. 12th, 1813.

" You must look the Giaour again over carefully; there are a few lapses, particularly in the last page.—' I *know* 'twas false; she could not die;' it was, and ought to be—' I *knew.*'   Pray observe this and similar mistakes.

" I have received and read the British Review.   I really think the writer in most points very right.   The only mortifying thing is the

---

* This is written on a separate slip of paper enclosed.

accusation of imitation. *Crabbe's* passage I never saw*; and Scott I no further meant to follow than in his *lyric* measure, which is Gray's, Milton's, and any one's who likes it. The Giaour is certainly a bad character, but not dangerous; and I think his fate and his feelings will meet with few proselytes. I shall be very glad to hear from or of you, when you please; but don't put yourself out of your way on my account."

LETTER CXXXIII.

TO MR. MOORE.

"Bennet-street, August 22d, 1813.

*　　　*　　　*　　　*　　　*

"As our late—I might say, deceased—correspondence had too much of the town-life leaven in it, we will now, ' paulo majora,' prattle a little of literature in all its branches; and first of the first—criticism. The Prince is at Brighton, and Jackson, the boxer, gone to Margate, having, I believe, decoyed Yarmouth to see a milling in that polite neighbourhood. Mad^e de Staël Holstein has lost one of her young barons, who has been carbonadoed by a vile Teutonic adjutant,—kilt and killed in a coffee-house at Scrawsenhawsen. Corinne is, of course, what all mothers must be,—but will, I venture to prophesy, do what few mothers could—write an Essay upon it. She cannot exist without a grievance—and somebody to see, or read, how much grief becomes her. I have not seen her since the event; but merely judge (not very charitably) from prior observation.

---

* The passage referred to by the Reviewers is in the Poem entitled " Resentment;" and the following is, I take for granted, the part which Lord Byron is accused by them of having imitated.

"Those are like wax—apply them to the fire,
　Melting, they take th' impressions you desire;
　Easy to mould, and fashion as you please,
　And again moulded with an equal ease:
　Like smelted iron these the forms retain,
　But, once impress'd, will never melt again."

3 H 2

" In a 'mail-coach copy' of the Edinburgh, I perceive the Giaour is 2d article. The numbers are still in the Leith smack—*pray, which way is the wind?* The said article is so very mild and sentimental, that it must be written by Jeffrey *in love;*—you know he is gone to America to marry some fair one, of whom he has been, for several *quarters, éperdument amoureux.* Seriously—as Winifred Jenkins says of Lismahago—Mr. Jeffrey (or his deputy) ' has done the handsome thing by me,' and I say *nothing.* But this I will say,—if you and I had knocked one another on the head in his quarrel, how he would have laughed, and what a mighty bad figure we should have cut in our posthumous works. By the by, I was called *in* the other day to mediate between two gentlemen bent upon carnage, and,—after a long struggle between the natural desire of destroying one's fellow-creatures, and the dislike of seeing men play the fool for nothing,—I got one to make an apology, and the other to take it, and left them to live happy ever after. One was a peer, the other a friend untitled, and both fond of high play;—and one, I can swear for, though very mild, ' not fearful,' and so dead a shot, that, though the other is the thinnest of men, he would have split him like a cane. They both conducted themselves very well, and I put them out of *pain* as soon as I could.

*　　*　　*　　*　　*　　*　　*

" There is an American Life of G. F. Cooke, *Scurra* deceased, lately published. Such a book!—I believe, since Drunken Barnaby's Journal, nothing like it has drenched the press. All green-room and tap-room—drams and the drama—brandy, whisky-punch, and, *latterly,* toddy, overflow every page. Two things are rather marvellous—first, that a man should live so long drunk, and, next, that he should have found a sober biographer. There are some very laughable things in it, nevertheless;—but the pints he swallowed and the parts he performed are too regularly registered.

" All this time you wonder I am not gone: so do I; but the accounts of the plague are very perplexing—not so much for the thing itself as the quarantine established in all ports, and from all places, even from England. It is true the forty or sixty days would, in all probability, be as foolishly spent on shore as in the ship; but one likes to have one's choice, nevertheless. Town is awfully empty; but not the worse for that. I am really puzzled with my perfect ignorance of what I mean to do;—not stay, if I can help it, but where to go*? Sligo is for the North,—a pleasant place, Petersburgh, in September, with one's ears and nose in a muff, or else tumbling into one's neckcloth or pocket-hand-kerchief! If the winter treated Buonaparte with so little ceremony, what would it inflict upon your solitary traveller?—Give me a *sun*, I care not how hot, and sherbet, I care not how cool, and *my* Heaven is as easily made as your Persian's†. The Giaour is now 1000 and odd lines. 'Lord Fanny spins a thousand such a day,' eh, Moore?—thou wilt needs be a wag, but I forgive it.   " Yours ever,

" BN.

" P.S. I perceive I have written a flippant and rather cold hearted letter; let it go, however. I have said nothing, either, of the brilliant sex; but the fact is, I am, at this moment, in a far more serious, and entirely new, scrape than any of the last twelvemonths,—and that is saying a good deal. * * * It is unlucky we can neither live with nor without these women.

" I am now thinking and regretting that, just as I have left New-stead, you reside near it. Did you ever see it? do—but don't tell me that you like it. If I had known of such intellectual neighbourhood, I don't think I should have quitted it. You could have come over so

---

* One of his travelling projects appears to have been a visit to Abyssinia:—at least, I have found, among his papers, a letter founded on that supposition, in which the writer entreats of him to procure information concerning " a kingdom of Jews mentioned by Bruce as residing on the mountain of Samen in that country. I have had the honour," he adds, " of some corre-spondence with the Rev. Dr. Buchanan and the reverend and learned G. S. Faber, on the subject of the existence of this kingdom of Jews, which, if it prove to be a fact, will more clearly elucidate many of the scripture prophecies; . . . . and, if Providence favours your lordship's mission to Abyssinia, an intercourse might be established between England and that country, and the English ships, according to the Rev. Mr. Faber, might be the principal means of transporting the kingdom of Jews, now in Abyssinia, to Egypt, in their way to their own country, Palestine."

† " A Persian's Heav'n is easily made—
'Tis but black eyes and lemonade."

often, as a bachelor,—for it was a thorough bachelor's mansion—plenty of wine and such sordid sensualities—with books enough, room enough, and an air of antiquity about all (except the lasses) that would have suited you, when pensive, and served you to laugh at when in glee. I had built myself a bath and a *vault*—and now I sha'n't even be buried in it. It is odd that we can't even be certain of a *grave*, at least a particular one. I remember, when about fifteen, reading your poems there,—which I can repeat almost now,—and asking all kinds of questions about the author, when I heard that he was not dead according to the preface; wondering if I should ever see him—and though, at that time, without the smallest poetical propensity myself, very much taken, as you may imagine, with that volume. Adieu—I commit you to the care of the gods—Hindoo, Scandinavian, and Hellenic!

"P.S. 2d. There is an excellent review of Grimm's Correspondence and Mad². de Staël in this N°. of the E. R. * * * * * Jeffrey, himself, was my critic last year; but this is, I believe, by another hand. I hope you are going on with your *grand coup*—pray do—or that damned Lucien Buonaparte will.beat us all. I have seen much of his poem in MS., and he really surpasses every thing beneath Tasso. Hodgson is translating him *against* another bard. You and (I believe, Rogers) Scott, Gifford and myself, are to be referred to as judges between the twain,—that is, if you accept the office. Conceive our different opinions! I think we, most of us (I am talking very impudently, you will think—*us*, indeed!) have a way of our own,—at least, you and Scott certainly have."

LETTER CXXXIV.

TO MR. MOORE.

"August 28th, 1813.

"Ay, my dear Moore, 'there *was* a time'—I have heard of your tricks, when 'you was campaigning at the King of Bohemy.' I am much mistaken if, some fine London spring, about the year 1815, that time does not come again. After all, we must end in marriage; and I can conceive nothing more delightful than such a state in the country, reading the county newspaper, &c. and kissing one's wife's maid. Seriously, I would incorporate with any woman of decent demeanour to-morrow—that is, I would a month ago, but, at present,   *   *   *   *   *.

" Why don't you ' parody that Ode * ?'—Do you think I should be *tetchy*? or have you done it, and won't tell me?—You are quite right about Giamschid, and I have reduced it to a dissyllable within this half-hour †. I am glad to hear you talk of Richardson, because it tells me what you won't—that you are going to beat Lucien. At least, tell me how far you have proceeded. Do you think me less interested about your works, or less sincere than our friend Ruggiero? I am not—and never was. In that thing of mine, the ' English Bards,' at the time when I was angry with all the world, I never ' disparaged your parts,' although I did not know you personally;—and have always regretted that you don't give us an *entire* work, and not sprinkle yourself in detached pieces —beautiful, I allow, and quite *alone* in our language ‡, but still giving us a right to expect a *Shah Nameh* (is that the name?) as well as Gazels.

---

* The Ode of Horace,

              " Natis in usum lætitiæ," &c.

some passages of which I told him might be parodied, in allusion to some of his late adventures:

          " Quanta laboras in Charybdi!
            Digne puer meliore flammâ !"

   † In his first edition of the Giaour he had used this word as a trisyllable,—" Bright as the gem of Giamschid,"—but on my remarking to him, upon the authority of Richardson's Persian Dictionary, that this was incorrect, he altered it to " Bright as the ruby of Giamschid." On seeing this, however, I wrote to him " that, as the comparison of his heroine's eye to a ' ruby' might unluckily call up the idea of its being bloodshot, he had better change the line to ' Bright as the jewel of Giamschid;' "—which he accordingly did in the following edition.

   ‡ Having already endeavoured to obviate the charge of vanity to which I am aware I expose myself by being thus accessory to the publication of eulogies, so warm and so little merited, on myself, I shall here only add, that it will abundantly console me under such a charge, if, in whatever degree the judgment of my noble friend may be called in question for these praises, he shall, in the same proportion, receive credit for the good-nature and warm-heartedness by which they were dictated.

Stick to the East;—the oracle, Staël, told me it was the only poetical policy. The North, South, and West, have all been exhausted; but from the East, we have nothing but S**'s unsaleables,—and these he has contrived to spoil, by adopting only their most outrageous fictions. His personages don't interest us, and yours will. You will have no competitor; and, if you had, you ought to be glad of it. The little I have done in that way is merely a ' voice in the wilderness' for you; and, if it has had any success, that also will prove that the public are orientalizing, and pave the path for you.

" I have been thinking of a story, grafted on the amours of a Peri and a mortal—something like, only more *philanthropical* than, Cazotte's Diable Amoureux. It would require a good deal of poesy, and tenderness is not my forte. For that, and other reasons, I have given up the idea, and merely suggest it to you, because, in intervals of your greater work, I think it a subject you might make much of*. If you want any more books, there is ' Castellan's Mœurs des Ottomans,' the best compendium of the kind I ever met with, in six small tomes. I am really taking a liberty by talking in this style to my ' elders and my betters;'—pardon it, and don't *Rochefoucault* my motives."

LETTER CXXXV.

TO MR. MOORE.

" August—September, I mean—1st, 1813.

" I send you, begging your acceptance, Castellan, and three vols. on Turkish Literature, not yet looked into. The *last* I will thank you to

---

* I had already, singularly enough, anticipated this suggestion, by making the daughter of a Peri the heroine of one of my stories, and detailing the love-adventures of her aërial parent in an episode. In acquainting Lord Byron with this circumstance, in my answer to the above letter, I added, " All I ask of your friendship is—not that you will abstain from Peris on my account, for that is too much to ask of human (or, at least, author's) nature—but that, whenever you mean to pay your addresses to any of these aërial ladies, you will, at once, tell me so, frankly and instantly, and let me, at least, have my choice whether I shall be desperate enough to go on, with such a rival, or at once surrender the whole race into your hands, and take, for the future, to Antediluvians with Mr. Montgomery."

read, extract what you want, and return in a week, as they are lent to me by that brightest of Northern constellations, Mackintosh,—amongst many other kind things into which India has warmed him, for I am sure your *home* Scotsman is of a less genial description.

"Your Peri, my dear M., is sacred and inviolable; I have no idea of touching the hem of her petticoat. Your affectation of a dislike to encounter me is so flattering, that I begin to think myself a very fine fellow. But you are laughing at me—' stap my vitals, Tam! thou art a very impudent person;' and, if you are not laughing at me, you deserve to be laughed at. Seriously, what on earth can you, or have you, to dread from any poetical flesh breathing? It really puts me out of humour to hear you talk thus.

*　　*　　*　　*　　*　　*

"The 'Giaour' I have added to a good deal; but still in foolish fragments. It contains about 1200 lines, or rather more—now printing. You will allow me to send you a copy. You delight me much by telling me that I am in your good graces, and more particularly as to temper; for, unluckily, I have the reputation of a very bad one. But they say the devil is amusing when pleased, and I must have been more venomous than the old serpent, to have hissed or stung in your company. It may be, and would appear to a third person, an incredible thing, but I know *you* will believe me when I say that I am as anxious for your success as one human being can be for another's,—as much as if I had never scribbled a line. Surely the field of fame is wide enough for all; and if it were not, I would not willingly rob my neighbour of a rood of it. Now you have a pretty property of some thousand acres there, and when you have passed your present Inclosure Bill, your income will be doubled (there's a metaphor, worthy of a Templar, namely, pert and low), while my wild common is too remote to incommode you, and quite incapable of such fertility. I send you (which return per post, as the printer would say) a curious letter from a friend of mine*, which will let you into the origin of 'the Giaour.' Write soon.

"Ever, dear Moore, yours most entirely, &c.

"P.S. This letter was written to me on account of a *different story*

---

* The letter of Lord Sligo, already given.

circulated by some gentlewomen of our acquaintance, a little too close to
the text. The part erased contained merely some Turkish names, and
circumstantial evidence of the girl's detection, not very important or
decorous."

LETTER CXXXVI.

TO MR. MOORE.

"Sept. 5, 1813.

" You need not tie yourself down to a day with Toderini, but send
him at your leisure, having anatomized him into such annotations as you
want; I do not believe that he has ever undergone that process before,
which is the best reason for not sparing him now.

" * * has returned to town, but not yet recovered of the Quarterly.
What fellows these reviewers are! 'these bugs do fear us all.' They
made you fight, and me (the milkiest of men) a satirist, and will end by
making * * madder than Ajax. I have been reading Memory again,
the other day, and Hope together, and retain all my preference of the
former. His elegance is really wonderful—there is no such thing as a
vulgar line in his book. *   *   *   *   *   *   *   *   *

" What say you to Buonaparte? Remember, I back him against the
field, barring Catalepsy and the Elements. Nay, I almost wish him success
against all countries but this,—were it only to choke the Morning Post,
and his undutiful father-in-law, with that rebellious bastard of Scandinavian adoption, Bernadotte. Rogers wants me to go with him on a
crusade to the Lakes, and to besiege you on our way. This last is a
great temptation, but I fear it will not be in my power, unless you
would go on with one of us somewhere—no matter where. It is too late
for Matlock, but we might hit upon some scheme, high life or low,—the
last would be much the best for amusement. I am so sick of the other,
that I quite sigh for a cider-cellar, or a cruise in a smuggler's sloop.

" You cannot wish more than I do that the Fates were a little more
accommodating to our parallel lines, which prolong ad infinitum without
coming a jot the nearer. I almost wish I were married, too—which is
saying much. All my friends, seniors and juniors, are in for it, and ask

me to be godfather,—the only species of parentage which, I believe, will ever come to my share in a lawful way; and, in an unlawful one, by the blessing of Lucina, we can never be certain,—though the parish may. I suppose I shall hear from you to-morrow. If not, this goes as it is; but I leave room for a P.S., in case any thing requires an answer. Ever, &c.

" No letter—*n'importe*. R. thinks the Quarterly will be at *me* this time: if so, it shall be a war of extermination—no *quarter*. From the youngest devil down to the oldest woman of that Review, all shall perish by one fatal lampoon. The ties of nature shall be torn asunder, for I will not even spare my bookseller; nay, if one were to include readers also, all the better."

LETTER CXXXVII.

TO MR. MOORE.

" Sept. 8, 1813.

" I am sorry to see Tod. again so soon, for fear your scrupulous conscience should have prevented you from fully availing yourself of his spoils. By this coach I send you a copy of that awful pamphlet ' the Giaour,' which has never procured me half so high a compliment as your modest alarm. You will (if inclined in an evening) perceive that I have added much in quantity,—a circumstance which may truly diminish your modesty upon the subject.

" You stand certainly in great need of a ' lift' with Mackintosh. My dear Moore, you strangely underrate yourself. I should conceive it an affectation in any other; but I think I know you well enough to believe that you don't know your own value. However, 'tis a fault that generally mends; and, in your case, it really ought. I have heard him speak of you as highly as your wife could wish; and enough to give all your friends the jaundice.

" Yesterday I had a letter from *Ali Pacha!* brought by Doctor Holland, who is just returned from Albania. It is in Latin, and begins ' Excellentissime, *nec non* Carissime,' and ends about a gun he wants made for him;—it is signed ' Ali Vizir.' What do you think he has

been about?　H. tells me that, last spring, he took a hostile town
where, forty-two years ago, his mother and sisters were treated as Miss
Cunigunde was by the Bulgarian cavalry.　He takes the town, selects all
the survivors of this exploit—children, grand-children, &c. to the tune
of six hundred, and has them shot before his face.　Recollect, he spared
the rest of the city, and confined himself to the Tarquin pedigree,—
which is more than I would.　So much for 'dearest friend.'"

LETTER CXXXVIII.

TO MR. MOORE.

"Sept. 9, 1813.

"I write to you from Murray's, and I may say, from Murray, who,
if you are not predisposed in favour of any other publisher, would be
happy to treat with you, at a fitting time, for your work.　I can safely
recommend him, as fair, liberal, and attentive, and certainly, in point of
reputation, he stands among the first of 'the trade.'　I am sure he would
do you justice.　I have written to you so much lately, that you will be
glad to see so little now.　Ever, &c. &c."

LETTER CXXXIX.

TO MR. MOORE.

"September 27, 1813.

"THOMAS MOORE,

"(Thou wilt never be called 'true Thomas,' like He of Ercildoune),
why don't you write to me?—as you won't, I must.　I was near you at
Aston the other day, and hope I soon shall be again.　If so, you must
and shall meet me, and go to Matlock and elsewhere, and take what, in
flash dialect, is poetically termed 'a lark,' with Rogers and me for
accomplices.　Yesterday, at Holland-house, I was introduced to Southey
—the best looking bard I have seen for some time.　To have that poet's
head and shoulders, I would almost have written his Sapphics.　He is
certainly a prepossessing person to look on, and a man of talent, and all
that, and—*there* is his eulogy.

" * * read me *part* of a letter from you. By the foot of Pharaoh, I believe there was abuse, for he stopped short, so he did, after a fine saying about our correspondence, and *looked*—I wish I could revenge myself by attacking you, or by telling you that I have *had* to defend you—an agreeable way which one's friends have of recommending themselves by saying—' Ay, ay, *I* gave it Mr. Such-a-one for what he said about your being a plagiary and a rake, and so on.' But do you know that you are one of the very few whom I never have the satisfaction of hearing abused, but the reverse;—and do you suppose I will forgive *that?*

" I have been in the country, and ran away from the Doncaster races. It is odd,—I was a visitor in the same house which came to my sire as a residence with Lady Carmarthen (with whom he adulterated before his majority—by the by, remember, *she* was not my mamma)—and they thrust me into an old room, with a nauseous picture over the chimney, which I should suppose my papa regarded with due respect, and which, inheriting the family taste, I looked upon with great satisfaction. I staid a week with the family, and behaved very well—though the lady of the house is young and religious, and pretty, and the master is my particular friend. I felt no wish for any thing but a poodle dog, which they kindly gave me. Now, for a man of my courses, not even to have *coveted* is a sign of great amendment. Pray pardon all this nonsense, and don't ' snub me when I 'm in spirits.'

" Ever yours,
" BN.

" Here 's an impromptu for you by a ' person of quality,' written last week, on being reproached for low spirits.

> " When from the heart where Sorrow sits *,
>   Her dusky shadow mounts too high,
> And o'er the changing aspect flits,
>   And clouds the brow, or fills the eye:
> Heed not that gloom, which soon shall sink;
>   My Thoughts their dungeon know too well—
> Back to my breast the wanderers shrink,
>   And bleed within their silent cell."

---

* Now printed in his Works.

LETTER CXL.

TO MR. MOORE.

" October 2, 1813.

" You have not answered some six letters of mine. This, therefore, is my penultimate. I will write to you once more, but, after that—I swear by all the saints—I am silent and supercilious. I have met Curran at Holland-house—he beats every body;—his imagination is beyond human, and his humour (it is difficult to define what is wit) perfect. Then he has fifty faces, and twice as many voices, when he mimics;—I never met his equal. Now, were I a woman, and eke a virgin, that is the man I should make my Scamander. He is quite fascinating. Remember, I have met him but once; and you, who have known him long, may probably deduct from my panegyric. I almost fear to meet him again, lest the impression should be lowered. He talked a great deal about you—a theme never tiresome to me, nor any body else that I know. What a variety of expression he conjures into that naturally not very fine countenance of his! He absolutely changes it entirely. I have done—for I can't describe him, and you know him. On Sunday I return to * *, where I shall not be far from you. Perhaps I shall hear from you in the mean time. Good night.

" Saturday morn.—Your letter has cancelled all my anxieties. I did *not suspect* you in *earnest*. Modest again! Because I don't do a very shabby thing, it seems, I ' don't fear your competition.' If it were reduced to an alternative of preference, I *should* dread you, as much as Satan does Michael. But is there not room enough in our respective regions? Go on—it will soon be my turn to forgive. To-day I dine with Mackintosh and Mrs. *Stale*—as John Bull may be pleased to denominate Corinne—whom I saw last night, at Covent-garden, yawning over the humour of Falstaff.

" The reputation of ' gloom,' if one's friends are not included in the *reputants*, is of great service; as it saves one from a legion of impertinents, in the shape of common-place acquaintance. But thou know'st I can be a right merry and conceited fellow, and rarely ' larmoyant.'

Murray shall reinstate your line forthwith *.　I believe the blunder in the motto was mine;—and yet I have, in general, a memory for *you*, and am sure it was rightly printed at first.

"I do 'blush' very often, if I may believe Ladies H. and M.—but luckily, at present, no one sees me.　Adieu."

LETTER CXLI.

TO MR. MOORE.

"November 30th, 1813.

"Since I last wrote to you, much has occurred, good, bad, and indifferent,—not to make me forget you, but to prevent me from reminding you of one who, nevertheless, has often thought of you, and to whom *your* thoughts, in many a measure, have frequently been a consolation.　We were once very near neighbours this autumn; and a good and bad neighbourhood it has proved to me.　Suffice it to say, that your French quotation was confoundedly to the purpose,—though very *unexpectedly* pertinent, as you may imagine by what I *said* before, and my silence since.　*　*　*　*　*　*　*　*　*　* However, 'Richard's himself again,' and, except all night and some part of the morning, I don't think very much about the matter.

"All convulsions end with me in rhyme; and, to solace my midnights, I have scribbled another Turkish story †—not a Fragment— which you will receive soon after this.　It does not trench upon your kingdom in the least, and, if it did, you would soon reduce me to my proper boundaries.　You will think, and justly, that I run some risk of losing the little I have gained in fame, by this further experiment on public patience; but I have really ceased to care on that head.　I have written this, and published it, for the sake of the *employment*,—to wring my thoughts from reality, and take refuge in 'imaginings,' however

---

* The motto to the Giaour, which is taken from one of the Irish Melodies, had been quoted by him incorrectly in the first editions of the Poem.　He made afterwards a similar mistake in the lines from Burns prefixed to the Bride of Abydos.

† The Bride of Abydos.

'horrible;' and, as to success! those who succeed will console me for failure—excepting yourself and one or two more, whom luckily I lov? too well to wish one leaf of their laurels a tint yellower. This is th? work of a week, and will be the reading of an hour to you, or even less —and so, let it go * * * * *.

"P.S. Ward and I *talk* of going to Holland. I want to see how ? Dutch canal looks, after the Bosphorus. Pray respond."

LETTER CXLII.

TO MR. MOORE.

"December 8th, 1813.

"Your letter, like all the best, and even kindest, things in this world, is both painful and pleasing. But, first, to what sits nearest. Do you know I was actually about to dedicate to you,—not in a formal inscription, as to one's *elders*,—but through a short prefatory letter, in which I boasted myself your intimate, and held forth the prospect of *your* Poem; when, lo, the recollection of your strict injunctions of secrecy as to the said Poem, more than *once* repeated by word and letter, flashed upon me, and marred my intents. I could have no motive for repressing my own desire of alluding to you (and not a day passes that I do not think and talk of you), but an idea that you might, yourself, dislike it. You cannot doubt my sincere admiration, waving personal friendship for the present, which, by the by, is not less sincere and deep-rooted. I have you by rote and by heart; of which 'ecce signum!' When I was at ·* *, on my first visit, I have a habit, in passing my time a good deal alone, of—I won't call it singing, for that I never attempt except to myself—but of uttering, to what I think tunes, your 'Oh breathe not,' 'When the last glimpse,' and 'When he who adores thee,' with others of the same minstrel;—they are my matins and vespers. I assuredly did not intend them to be overheard, but, one morning, in comes, not La Donna, but Il Marito, with a very grave face, saying, 'Byron, I must request you won't sing any more, at least of *those* songs.' I stared, and said, 'Certainly, but why?'—'To tell you the truth,' quoth he, 'they make my wife *cry*, and so melancholy, that I wish her to hear no more of them.'

" Now, my dear M., the effect must have been from your words, and certainly not my music. I merely mention this foolish story, to show you how much I am indebted to you for even your pastimes. A man may praise and praise, but no one recollects but that which pleases —at least, in composition. Though I think no one equal to you in that department, or in satire,—and surely no one was ever so popular in both, —I certainly am of opinion that you have not yet done all *you* can do, though more than enough for any one else. I want, and the world expects, a longer work from you; and I see in you what I never saw in poet before, a strange diffidence of your own powers, which I cannot account for, and which must be unaccountable, when a *Cossac* like me can appal a *cuirassier*. Your story I did not, could not, know,—I thought only of a Peri. I wish you had confided in me, not for your sake, but mine, and to prevent the world from losing a much better poem than my own, but which, I yet hope, this *clashing* will not even now deprive them of*. Mine is the work of a week, written, *why* I have partly told you, and partly I cannot tell you by letter—some day I will.

*　　　*　　　*　　　*　　　*

"Go on—I shall really be very unhappy if I at all interfere with you. The success of mine is yet problematical; though the public will pro-

---

* Among the stories, intended to be introduced into Lalla Rookh, which I had begun, but, from various causes, never finished, there was one which I had made some progress in, at the time of the appearance of " the Bride," and which, on reading that Poem, I found to contain such singular coincidences with it, not only in locality and costume, but in plot and characters, that I immediately gave up my story altogether, and began another on an entirely new subject, the Fire-worshippers. To this circumstance, which I immediately communicated to him, Lord Byron alludes in this letter. In my hero (to whom I had even given the name of " Zelim," and who was a descendant of Ali, outlawed, with all his followers, by the reigning Caliph,) it was my intention to shadow out, as I did afterwards in another form, the national cause of Ireland. To quote the words of my letter to Lord Byron on the subject:—" I chose this story because one writes best about what one feels most, and I thought the parallel with Ireland would enable me to infuse some vigour into my hero's character. But to aim at vigour and strong feeling after *you*, is hopeless;—that region ' was made for Cæsar.'"

bably purchase a certain quantity, on the presumption of their own propensity for 'the Giaour' and such 'horrid mysteries.' The only advantage I have is being on the spot; and that merely amounts to saving me the trouble of turning over books, which I had better read again. If *your chamber* was furnished in the same way, you have no need to *go there* to describe—I mean only as to *accuracy*—because I drew it from recollection.

* * * * *

"This last thing of mine *may* have the same fate, and I assure you I have great doubts about it. But, even if not, its little day will be over before you are ready and willing. Come out—'screw your courage to the sticking-place.' Except the Post Bag (and surely you cannot complain of a want of success there), you have not been *regularly* out for some years. No man stands higher,—whatever you may think on a rainy day, in your provincial retreat. 'Aucun homme, dans aucune langue, n'a été, peut-être, plus complètement le poëte du cœur et le poëte des femmes. Les critiques lui reprochent de n'avoir representé le monde ni tel qu'il est, ni tel qu'il doit être; *mais les femmes répondent qu'il l'a representé tel qu'elles le désirent.*'—I should have thought Sismondi had written this for you instead of Metastasio.

"Write to me, and tell me of *yourself.* Do you remember what Rousseau said to some one—'Have we quarrelled? you have talked to me often, and never once mentioned yourself.'

"P.S. The last sentence is an indirect apology for my own egotism, —but I believe in letters it is allowed. I wish it was *mutual.* I have met with an odd reflection in Grimm; it shall not—at least, the bad part—be applied to you or me, though *one* of us has certainly an indifferent name—but this it is: 'Many people have the reputation of being wicked, with whom we should be too happy to pass our lives.' I need not add it is a woman's saying—a Mademoiselle de Sommery's."

* * * * *

At this time Lord Byron commenced a Journal, or Diary, from the pages of which I have already selected a few extracts, and of which I shall now lay as much more as is producible before the reader. Employed chiefly,—as such a record, from its nature, must be,—about persons still living and occurrences still recent, it would be impossible, of course, to submit it to the public eye, without the omission of some portion of its contents, and unluckily, too, of that very portion which, from its reference to the secret pursuits and feelings of the writer, would the most livelily pique and gratify the curiosity of the reader. Enough, however, will, I trust, still remain, even after all this necessary winnowing, to enlarge still further the view we have here opened into the interior of the poet's life and habits, and to indulge harmlessly that taste, as general as it is natural, which leads us to contemplate with pleasure a great mind in its undress, and to rejoice in the discovery, so consoling to human pride, that even the mightiest, in their moments of ease and weakness, resemble ourselves *.

" JOURNAL, BEGUN NOVEMBER 14, 1813.

" If this had been begun ten years ago, and faithfully kept!!!— heigho! there are too many things I wish never to have remembered, as it is. Well,—I have had my share of what are called the pleasures of this life, and have seen more of the European and Asiatic world than I have made a good use of. They say ' virtue is its own reward,'—it certainly should be paid well for its trouble. At five-and-twenty, when the better part of life is over, one should be *something;*—and what am I? nothing but five-and-twenty—and the odd months. What have I seen? the same man all over the world,—ay, and woman too. Give *me* a Mussulman who never asks questions, and a she of the same race who saves one the trouble of putting them. But for this same plague— yellow-fever—and Newstead delay, I should have been by this time a second time close to the Euxine. If I can overcome the last, I don't so much mind your pestilence; and, at any rate, the spring shall see me there,—provided I neither marry myself nor unmarry any one else in the

---

* " C'est surtout aux hommes qui sont hors de toute comparaison par le génie qu'on aime à ressembler au moins par les foiblesses."—GINGUENÉ.

interval. I wish one was—I don't know what I wish. It is odd I neve
set myself seriously to wishing without attaining it—and repenting.
begin to believe with the good old Magi, that one should only pray fo
the nation, and not for the individual;—but, on my principle, this woul
not be very patriotic.

    " No more reflections.—Let me see—last night I finished ' Zuleika
my second Turkish Tale. I believe the composition of it kept me aliv
—for it was written to drive my thoughts from the recollection of—

            ' Dear sacred name, rest ever unreveal'd.'

At least, even here, my hand would tremble to write it. This afternoor
I have burnt the scenes of my commenced comedy. I have some idea o
expectorating a romance; or rather a tale, in prose;—but what romance
could equal the events—

                ' quæque ipse . . . . . vidi,
            Et quorum pars magna fui.'

    " To-day Henry Byron called on me with my little cousin Eliza.
She will grow up a beauty and a plague; but, in the mean time, it is the
prettiest child! dark eyes and eyelashes, black and long as the wing of a
raven. I think she is prettier even than my niece, Georgina,—yet I
don't like to think so neither; and, though older, she is not so clever.

    " Dallas called before I was up, so we did not meet. Lewis, too—who
seems out of humour with every thing. What can be the matter? he is
not married—has he lost his own mistress, or any other person's wife?
Hodgson, too, came. He is going to be married, and he is the kind of
man who will be the happier. He has talent, cheerfulness, every thing
that can make him a pleasing companion; and his intended is handsome
and young, and all that. But I never see any one much improved by
matrimony. All my coupled contemporaries are bald and discontented.
W. and S. have both lost their hair and good-humour; and the last of
the two had a good deal to lose. But it don't much signify what falls *off*
a man's temples in that state.

" Mem. I must get a toy to-morrow for Eliza, and send the device for the seals of myself and * * * * * Mem. too, to call on the Staël and Lady Holland to-morrow, and on * *, who has advised me (without seeing it, by the by,) not to publish ' Zuleika;' I believe he is right, but experience might have taught him that not to print is *physically* impossible. No one has seen it but Hodgson and Mr. Gifford. I never in my life *read* a composition, save to Hodgson, as he pays me in kind. It is a horrible thing to do too frequently;—better print, and they who like may read, and, if they don't like, you have the satisfaction of knowing that they have, at least, *purchased* the right of saying so.

" I have declined presenting the Debtor's Petition, being sick of parliamentary mummeries. I have spoken thrice; but I doubt my ever becoming an orator. My first was liked; the second and third—I don't know whether they succeeded or not. I have never yet set to it *con amore*;—one must have some excuse to oneself for laziness, or inability, or both, and this is mine. ' Company, villanous company, hath been the spoil of me;'—and then, I have ' drunk medicines,' not to make me love others, but certainly enough to hate myself.

" Two nights ago, I saw the tigers sup at Exeter 'Change. Except Veli Pacha's lion in the Morea,—who followed the Arab keeper like a dog,—the fondness of the hyæna for her keeper amused me most. Such a conversazione!—There was a ' hippopotamus,' like Lord L——l in the face; and the ' Ursine Sloth' hath the very voice and manner of my valet—but the tiger talked too much. The elephant took and gave me my money again—took off my hat—opened a door—*trunked* a whip— and behaved so well, that I wish he was my butler. The handsomest animal on earth is one of the panthers; but the poor antelopes were dead. I should hate to see one *here*:—the sight of the *camel* made me pine again for Asia Minor. ' Oh quando te aspiciam ?'

     *   *   *   *   *   *

" Nov. 16th.

" Went last night with Lewis to see the first of Antony and Cleopatra. It was admirably got up and well acted—a salad of Shak-

speare and Dryden. Cleopatra strikes me as the epitome of her sex—
fond, lively, sad, tender, teasing, humble, haughty, beautiful, the devil
—coquettish to the last, as well with the 'asp' as with Antony. Afte
doing all she can to persuade him that—but why do they abuse him fo
cutting off that poltroon Cicero's head? Did not Tully tell Brutus i
was a pity to have spared Antony? and did he not speak the Philippics
and are not '*words things?*' and such '*words*' very pestilent '*things*' too
If he had had a hundred heads, they deserved (from Antony) a rostrur
(his was stuck up there) apiece—though, after all, he might as well have
pardoned him, for the credit of the thing. But to resume—Cleopatra
after securing him, says, 'yet go'—'it is your interest,' &c.—how like the
sex! and the questions about Octavia—it is woman all over.

"To-day received Lord Jersey's invitation to Middleton—to trave
sixty miles to meet Madame * *! I once travelled three thousand to get
among silent people; and this same lady writes octavos and *talks* folios
I have read her books—like most of them, and delight in the last; so]
won't hear it, as well as read. * * * * * *

"Read Burns to-day. What would he have been, if a patrician?
We should have had more polish—less force—just as much verse, but no
immortality—a divorce and a duel or two, the which had he survived, as
his potations must have been less spirituous, he might have lived as long
as Sheridan, and outlived as much as poor Brinsley. What a wreck is
that man! and all from bad pilotage; for no one had ever better gales,
though now and then a little too squally. Poor dear Sherry! I shall
never forget the day he and Rogers and Moore and I passed together;
when *he* talked, and *we* listened, without one yawn, from six till one in
the morning.

"Got my seals * * * * * *. Have again forgot a plaything
for *ma petite cousine* Eliza; but I must send for it to-morrow. I hope
Harry will bring her to me. I sent Lord Holland the proofs of the last
'Giaour,' and the 'Bride of Abydos.' He won't like the latter, and I
don't think that I shall long. It was written in four nights to distract
my dreams from * *. Were it not thus, it had never been composed;
and had I not done something at that time, I must have gone mad, by

eating my own heart—bitter diet!—Hodgson likes it better than the Giaour, but nobody else will,—and he never liked the Fragment. I am sure, had it not been for Murray, *that* would never have been published, though the circumstances which are the groundwork make it * * * heigh-ho!

"To-night I saw both the sisters of * *; my God! the youngest so like! I thought I should have sprung across the house, and am so glad no one was with me in Lady H.'s box. I hate those likenesses— the mock-bird, but not the nightingale—so like as to remind, so different as to be painful*. One quarrels equally with the points of resemblance and of distinction.

"Nov. 17th.

"No letter from * *;—but I must not complain. The respectable Job says, 'Why should a *living man* complain?' I really don't know, except it be that a *dead man* can't; and he, the said patriarch, *did* complain, nevertheless, till his friends were tired, and his wife recommended that pious prologue, 'Curse—and die;' the only time, I suppose, when but little relief is to be found in swearing. I have had a most kind letter from Lord Holland on 'The Bride of Abydos,' which he likes, and so does Lady H. This is very good-natured in both, from whom I don't deserve any quarter. Yet I *did* think, at the time, that my cause of enmity proceeded from Holland-house, and am glad I was wrong, and wish I had not been in such a hurry with that confounded satire, of which I would suppress even the memory;—but people, now they can't get it, make a fuss, I verily believe, out of contradiction.

"George Ellis and Murray have been talking something about Scott and me, George pro Scoto,—and very right too. If they want to depose him, I only wish they would not set me up as a competitor. Even if I

---

* " Earth holds no other like to thee,
      Or, if it doth, in vain for me:
      For worlds I dare not view the dame
      Resembling thee, yet not the same."

THE GIAOUR.

had my choice, I would rather be the Earl of Warwick than all the king he ever made! Jeffrey and Gifford I take to be the monarch-makers i poetry and prose. The British Critic, in their Rokeby Review, hav presupposed a comparison, which I am sure my friends never thought o and W. Scott's subjects are injudicious in descending to. I like th man—and admire his works to what Mr. Braham calls *Entusymusy* All such stuff can only vex him, and do me no good. Many hate hi politics—(I hate all politics); and, here, a man's politics are like th Greek *soul*—an εἰδωλον, besides God knows what *other soul;* but thei estimate of the two generally go together.

"Harry has not brought *ma petite cousine.* I want us to go t the play together;—she has been but once. Another short note from Jersey, inviting Rogers and me on the 23d. I must see my agen to-night. I wonder when that Newstead business will be finished. I cost me more than words to part with it—and to *have* parted with it! What matters it what I do? or what becomes of me?—bu let me remember Job's saying, and console myself with being 'a living man.'

"I wish I could settle to reading again,—my life is monotonous, and yet desultory. I take up books, and fling them down again. I began a comedy, and burnt it because the scene ran into *reality;*—a novel, for the same reason. In rhyme, I can keep more away from facts; but the thought always runs through, through . . . . yes, yes, through. I have had a letter from Lady Melbourne—the best friend I ever had in my life, and the cleverest of women. * * * · * *

"Not a word from * *. Have they set out from * *? or has my last precious epistle fallen into the Lion's jaws? If so—and this silence looks suspicious—I must clap on 'my musty morion' and 'hold out my iron.' I am out of practice,—but I won't begin again at Manton's now. Besides, I would not return his shot. I was once a famous wafer-splitter; but then the bullies of society made it necessary. Ever since I began to feel that I had a bad cause to support, I have left off the exercise.

"What strange tidings from that Anakim of anarchy—Buonaparte!

Ever since I defended my bust of him at Harrow against the rascally time-servers, when the war broke out in 1803, he has been a 'Héros de Roman' of mine—on the continent; I don't want him here. But I don't like those same flights,—leaving of armies, &c. &c. I am sure when I fought for his bust at school, I did not think he would run away from himself. But I should not wonder if he banged them yet. To be beat by men would be something; but by three stupid, legitimate-old-dynasty boobies of regular-bred sovereigns—O-hone-a-rie!—O-hone-a-rie! It must be, as Cobbett says, his marriage with the thick-lipped and thick-headed *Autrichienne* brood. He had better have kept to her who was kept by Barras. I never knew any good come of your young wife, and legal espousals, to any but your 'sober-blooded boy' who 'eats fish' and drinketh 'no sack.' Had he not the whole opera? all Paris? all France? But a mistress is just as perplexing—that is, *one*—two or more are manageable by division.

"I have begun, or had begun, a song, and flung it into the fire. It was in remembrance of Mary Duff, my first of flames, before most people begin to burn. I wonder what the devil is the matter with me! I can do nothing, and—fortunately there is nothing to do. It has lately been in my power to make two persons (and their connexions) comfortable, *pro tempore*, and one happy *ex tempore*,—I rejoice in the last particularly, as it is an excellent man *. I wish there had been more inconvenience and less gratification to my self-love in it, for then there had been more merit. We are all selfish—and I believe, ye gods of Epicurus! I believe in Rochefoucault about *men*, and in Lucretius (not Busby's translation) about yourselves. Your bard has made you very *nonchalant* and blest; but as he has excused *us* from damnation, I don't envy you your blessedness *much*—a little, to be sure. I remember, last year, * * said to me, at * *, 'Have we not passed our last month like the gods of Lucretius?' And so we had. She is an adept in the text of the original (which I like too); and when that booby Bus. sent his translating prospectus, she subscribed. But, the devil prompting him to add a specimen, she transmitted him a subsequent answer, saying, that, 'after perusing

---

* Evidently, Mr. Hodgson.

it, her conscience would not permit her to allow her name to remain o¿
the list of subscribblers.'   *   *   *   *   *   *   *   ¿

Last night, at Lord H.'s—Mackintosh, the Ossulstones, Puységur, &c¿
there—I was trying to recollect a quotation (as *I* think) of Staël's, from
some Teutonic sophist about architecture. 'Architecture,' says thi¿
Macoronico Tedescho, 'reminds me of frozen music.' It is somewhere—
but where?—the demon of perplexity must know and won't tell. ¿
asked M., and he said it was not in her; but P——r said it must be *hers,*
it was so *like.*   *   *   *   *   *   *   *   *   *   *

H. laughed, as he does at all 'De l'Allemagne,'—in which, however, I
think he goes a little too far. B., I hear, contemns it too. But there are
fine passages;—and, after all, what is a work—any—or every work—but
a desert with fountains, and, perhaps, a grove or two, every day's journey?
To be sure, in Madame, what we often mistake, and 'pant for,' as the
'cooling stream,' turns out to be the '*mirage*' (criticé, *verbiage*); but we
do, at last, get to something like the temple of Jove Ammon, and then
the waste we have passed is only remembered to gladden the contrast.
        *   *   *   *   *   *   *

"Called on C * *, to explain   *   *   *. She is very beautiful, to
my taste, at least; for on coming home from abroad, I recollect being
unable to look at any woman but her—they were so fair, and unmeaning,
and *blonde.* The darkness and regularity of her features reminded me
of my 'Jannat al Aden.' But this impression wore off; and now I can
look at a fair woman, without longing for a Houri. She was very good-
tempered, and every thing was explained.

"To-day, great news—'the Dutch have taken Holland,'—which, I
suppose, will be succeeded by the actual explosion of the Thames. Five
provinces have declared for young Stadt, and there will be inundation,
conflagration, constupration, consternation, and every sort of nation and
nations, fighting away, up to their knees, in the damnable quags of
this will-o'-the-wisp abode of Boors. It is said Bernadotte is amongst
them, too; and, as Orange will be there soon, they will have (Crown)
Prince Stork and King Log in their Loggery at the same time. Two
to one on the new dynasty!

"Mr. Murray has offered me one thousand guineas for the 'Giaour' and the 'Bride of Abydos.' I won't—it is too much, though I am strongly tempted, merely for the *say* of it. No bad price for a fortnight's (a week each) what?—the gods know—it was intended to be called Poetry.

" I have dined regularly to-day, for the first time since Sunday last —this being Sabbath, too. All the rest, tea and dry biscuits—six *per diem*. I wish to God I had not dined now!—It kills me with heaviness, stupor, and horrible dreams;—and yet it was but a pint of bucellas, and fish *. Meat I never touch,—nor much vegetable diet. I wish I were in the country, to take exercise,—instead of being obliged to *cool* by abstinence, in lieu of it. I should not so much mind a little accession of flesh,—my bones can well bear it. But the worst is, the devil always came with it,—till I starve him out,—and I will *not* be the slave of *any* appetite. If I do err, it shall be my heart, at least, that heralds the way. Oh my head—how it aches!—the horrors of digestion! I wonder how Buonaparte's dinner agrees with him?

" Mem. I must write to-morrow to 'Master Shallow, who owes me a thousand pounds,' and seems, in his letter, afraid I should ask him for it †;—as if I would!—I don't want it (just now, at least), to begin with; and though I have often wanted that sum, I never asked for the repayment of £10 in my life—from a friend. His bond is not due this year, and I told him, when it was, I should not enforce it. How often must he make me say the same thing?

" I am wrong—I did once ask * * * ‡ to repay me. But it was under circumstances that excused me *to him*, and would to any one. I took no interest, nor required security. He paid me soon,—at least, his *padre*. My head! I believe it was given me to ache with. Good even.

---

* He had this year so far departed from his strict plan of diet as to eat fish occasionally.

† We have here another instance, in addition to the munificent aid afforded to Mr. Hodgson, of the generous readiness of the poet, notwithstanding his own limited means, to make the resources he possessed available for the assistance of his friends.

‡ Left blank thus in the original.

"Nov. 22d, 1813.

"'Orange Boven!' So the bees have expelled the bear that broke open their hive. Well,—if we are to have new De Witts and De Ruyters, God speed the little republic! I should like to see the Hague and the village of Brock, where they have such primitive habits. Yet, I don't know,—their canals would cut a poor figure by the memory of the Bosphorus; and the Zuyder Zee look awkwardly after 'Ak Degnity.' No matter,—the bluff burghers, puffing freedom out of their short tobacco-pipes, might be worth seeing; though I prefer a cigar, or a hooka, with the rose-leaf mixed with the milder herb of the Levant. I don't know what liberty means,—never having seen it,—but wealth is power all over the world; and as a shilling performs the duty of a pound (besides sun and sky and beauty for nothing) in the East,— *that* is the country. How I envy Herodes Atticus!—more than Pomponius. And yet a little *tumult*, now and then, is an agreeable quickener of sensation;—such as a revolution, a battle, or an *aventure* of any lively description. I think I rather would have been Bonneval, Ripperda, Alberoni, Hayreddin, or Horuc Barbarossa, or even Wortley Montague, than Mahomet himself.

"Rogers will be in town soon?—the 23d is fixed for our Middleton visit. Shall I go? umph!—In this island, where one can't ride out without overtaking the sea, it don't much matter where one goes.

* * * * * *

"I remember the effect of the *first* Edinburgh Review on me. I heard of it six weeks before,—read it the day of its denunciation,— dined and drank three bottles of claret (with S. B. Davies, I think),— neither ate nor slept the less, but, nevertheless, was not easy till I had vented my wrath and my rhyme, in the same pages, against every thing and every body. Like George, in the Vicar of Wakefield, 'the fate of my paradoxes' would allow me to perceive no merit in another. I remembered only the maxim of my boxing-master, which, in my youth, was found useful in all general riots,—'Whoever is not for you is against you—*mill* away right and left,' and so I did;—like Ishmael, my hand was against all men, and all men's anent me. I did wonder, to be sure, at my own success—

> ' And marvels so much wit is all his own,'

as Hobhouse sarcastically says of somebody (not unlikely myself, as we are old friends);—but were it to come over again, I would *not*. I have since redde* the cause of my couplets, and it is not adequate to the effect. C** told me that it was believed I alluded to poor Lord Carlisle's nervous disorder in one of the lines. I thank Heaven I did not know it —and would not, could not, if I had. I must naturally be the last person to be pointed on defects or maladies.

" Rogers is silent,—and, it is said, severe. When he does talk, he talks well; and, on all subjects of taste, his delicacy of expression is pure as his poetry. If you enter his house—his drawing-room—his library— you of yourself say, this is not the dwelling of a common mind. There is not a gem, a coin, a book thrown aside on his chimney-piece, his sofa, his table, that does not bespeak an almost fastidious elegance in the possessor. But this very delicacy must be the misery of his existence. Oh the jarrings his disposition must have encountered through life!

" Southey, I have not seen much of. His appearance is *Epic*; and he is the only existing entire man of letters. All the others have some pursuit annexed to their authorship. His manners are mild, but not those of a man of the world, and his talents of the first order. His prose is perfect. Of his poetry there are various opinions: there is, perhaps, too much of it for the present generation;—posterity will probably select. He has *passages* equal to any thing. At present, he has *a party*, but no *public*— except for his prose writings. The life of Nelson is beautiful.

" * * is a *Littérateur*, the Oracle of the Coteries, of the * * s, L* W* (Sydney Smith's ' Tory Virgin,') Mrs. Wilmot (she, at least, is a swan, and might frequent a purer stream), Lady B * *, and all the Blues, with Lady C * * at their head—but I say nothing of *her*—' look in her face and you forget them all,' and every thing else. Oh that face!—by ' te,

---

* It was thus that he, in general, spelled this word.

Diva potens Cypri,' I would, to be beloved by that woman, build and burn another Troy.

" M * * e has a peculiarity of talent, or rather talents,—poetry, music, voice, all his own; and an expression in each, which never was, nor will be, possessed by another. But he is capable of still higher flights in poetry. By the by, what humour, what—every thing in the 'Post-Bag!' There is nothing M * * e may not do, if he will but seriously set about it. In society, he is gentlemanly, gentle, and altogether more pleasing than any individual with whom I am acquainted. For his honour, principle, and independence, his conduct to * * * * speaks 'trumpet-tongued.' He has but one fault—and that one I daily regret —he is not *here*.

" Nov. 23d.

" Ward—I like Ward *. By Mahomet! I begin to think I like every body;—a disposition, not to be encouraged;—a sort of social gluttony, that swallows every thing set before it. But I like Ward. He is *piquant*; and, in my opinion, will stand *very* high in the House and every where else—if he applies *regularly*. By the by, I dine with him to-morrow, which may have some influence on my opinion. It is as well not to trust one's gratitude *after* dinner. I have heard many a host libelled by his guests, with his burgundy yet reeking on their rascally lips.

* * * * * *

" I have taken Lord Salisbury's box at Covent-garden for the season;—and now I must go and prepare to join Lady Holland and party, in theirs, at Drury-lane, *questa sera*.

" Holland doesn't think the man *is Junius*; but that the yet unpublished journal throws great light on the obscurities of that part of George the Second's reign.—What is this to George the Third's? I don't know what to think. Why should Junius be yet dead? If suddenly apoplexed, would he rest in his grave without sending his εἰδωλον to shout in the ears of posterity, 'Junius was X. Y. Z. Esq.

---

* The present Lord Dudley.

buried in the parish of * * *   Repair his monument, ye church-wardens! Print a new Edition of his Letters, ye booksellers!' Impossible, —the man must be alive, and will never die without the disclosure.   I like him;—he was a good hater.

"Came home unwell and went to bed,—not so sleepy as might be desirable.

> "Tuesday morning.

"I awoke from a dream—well! and have not others dreamed?—Such a dream!—but she did not overtake me.   I wish the dead would rest, however.   Ugh! how my blood chilled—and I could not wake—and—and—heigho!

> 'Shadows to-night
> Have struck more terror to the soul of Richard,
> Than could the substance of ten thousand * * s,
> Arm'd all in proof, and led by shallow * *.'

I do not like this dream,—I hate its 'foregone conclusion.'   And am I to be shaken by shadows?   Ay, when they remind us of—no matter—but, if I dream thus again, I will try whether *all* sleep has the like visions.   Since I rose, I've been in considerable bodily pain also; but it is gone, and now, like Lord Ogleby, I am wound up for the day.

"A note from Mountnorris—I dine with Ward;—Canning is to be there, Frere, and Sharpe,—perhaps Gifford.   I am to be one of 'the five' (or rather six), as Lady * * said a little sneeringly yesterday.   They are all good to meet, particularly Canning, and—Ward, when he likes.   I wish I may be well enough to listen to these intellectuals.

"No letters to-day;—so much the better,—there are no answers. I must not dream again;—it spoils even reality.   I will go out of doors, and see what the fog will do for me.   Jackson has been here: the boxing world much as usual;—but the Club increases.   I shall dine at Crib's to-morrow:—I like energy—even animal energy—of all kinds; and I have need of both mental and corporeal.   I have not dined out, nor, indeed, *at all*, lately; have heard no music—have seen nobody.   Now for a *plunge*—high life and low life.   'Amant *alterna* Camœnæ!'

" I have burnt my *Roman*—as I did the first scenes and sketch o
my comedy—and, for aught I see, the pleasure of burning is quite a
great as that of printing. These two last would not have done. I ran
into *realities* more than ever; and some would have been recognised an
others guessed at.

" Redde the Ruminator—a collection of Essays, by a strange, but
able, old man (Sir E. B.) and a half-wild young one, author of a Poem
on the Highlands, called ' Childe Alarique.' The word ' sensibility
(always my aversion) occurs a thousand times in these Essays; and, it
seems, is to be an excuse for all kinds of discontent. This young man
can know nothing of life; and, if he cherishes the disposition which runs
through his papers, will become useless,—and, perhaps, not even a poet,
after all, which he seems determined to be. God help him! no one
should be a rhymer who could be any thing better. And this is what
annoys one, to see Scott and Moore, and Campbell and Rogers, who
might have all been agents and leaders, now mere spectators. For,
though they may have other ostensible avocations, these last are reduced
to a secondary consideration. * *, too, frittering away his time among
dowagers and unmarried girls. If it advanced any *serious* affair, it were
some excuse; but, with the unmarried, that is a hazardous speculation,
and tiresome enough, too; and, with the veterans, it is not much worth
trying,—unless, perhaps, one in a thousand.

" If I had any views in this country, they would probably be
parliamentary. But I have no ambition; at least, if any, it would be
' aut Cæsar aut nihil.' My hopes are limited to the arrangement of my
affairs, and settling either in Italy or the East (rather the last), and
drinking deep of the languages and literature of both. Past events have
unnerved me; and all I can now do is to make life an amusement, and
look on, while others play. After all—even the highest game of crowns
and sceptres, what is it? *Vide* Napoleon's last twelvemonth. It has completely upset my system of fatalism. I thought, if crushed, he would have
fallen, when ' fractus illabatur orbis,' and not have been pared away to
gradual insignificance;—that all this was not a mere *jeu* of the gods, but
a prelude to greater changes and mightier events. But Men never
advance beyond a certain point;—and here we are, retrograding to the

dull, stupid, old system,—balance of Europe—poising straws upon kings' noses, instead of wringing them off! Give me a republic, or a despotism of one, rather than the mixed government of one, two, three. A republic!—look in the history of the Earth—Rome, Greece, Venice, France, Holland, America, our short (eheu) Commonwealth, and compare it with what they did under masters. The Asiatics are not qualified to be republicans, but they have the liberty of demolishing despots,— which is the next thing to it. To be the first man—not the Dictator— not the Sylla, but the Washington or the Aristides—the leader in talent and truth—is next to the Divinity! Franklin, Penn, and, next to these, either Brutus or Cassius—even Mirabeau—or St. Just. I shall never be any thing, or rather always be nothing. The most I can hope is, that some will say, ' He might, perhaps, if he would.'

" 12, midnight.

" Here are two confounded proofs from the printer. I have looked at the one, but, for the soul of me, I can't look over that ' Giaour' again, —at least, just now, and at this hour—and yet there is no moon.

" Ward talks of going to Holland, and we have partly discussed an *ensemble* expedition. It must be in ten days, if at all—if we wish to be in at the Revolution. And why not? * * is distant, and will be at * *, still more distant, till spring. No one else, except Augusta, cares for me—no ties—no trammels—*andiamo dunque—se torniamo, bene—se non, ch' importa?* Old William of Orange talked of dying in ' the last ditch' of his dingy country. It is lucky I can swim, or I suppose I should not well weather the first. But let us see. I have heard hyænas and jackalls in the ruins of Asia; and bull-frogs in the marshes,—besides wolves and angry Mussulmans. Now, I should like to listen to the shout of a free Dutchman.

" Alla! Viva! For ever! Hourra! Huzza!—which is the most rational or musical of these cries? ' Orange Boven,' according to the Morning Post.

"Wednesday, 24th.

"No dreams last night of the dead nor the living—so—I am 'firm as the marble, founded as the rock'—till the next earthquake.

"Ward's dinner went off well. There was not a disagreeable person there—unless *I* offended any body, which I am sure I could not by contradiction, for I said little, and opposed nothing. Sharpe (a man of elegant mind, and who has lived much with the best—Fox, Horne Tooke, Windham, Fitzpatrick, and all the agitators of other times and tongues) told us the particulars of his last interview with Windham, a few days before the fatal operation, which sent 'that gallant spirit to aspire the skies.' Windham,—the first in one department of oratory and talent, whose only fault was his refinement beyond the intellect of half his hearers,—Windham, half his life an active participator in the events of the earth, and one of those who governed nations,—*he* regretted, and dwelt much on that regret, that 'he had not entirely devoted himself to literature and science!!!' His mind certainly would have carried him to eminence there, as elsewhere;—but I cannot comprehend what debility of that mind could suggest such a wish. I, who have heard him, cannot regret any thing but that I shall never hear him again. What! would he have been a plodder? a metaphysician?—perhaps a rhymer? a scribbler? Such an exchange must have been suggested by illness. But he is gone, and Time 'shall not look upon his like again.'

"I am tremendously in arrear with my letters,—except to * *, and to her my thoughts overpower me,—my words never compass them. To Lady Melbourne I write with most pleasure—and her answers, so sensible, so *tactique*—I never met with half her talent. If she had been a few years younger, what a fool she would have made of me, had she thought it worth her while,—and I should have lost a valuable and most agreeable *friend*. Mem.—a mistress never is nor can be a friend. While you agree, you are lovers; and, when it is over, any thing but friends.

"I have not answered W. Scott's last letter,—but I will. I regret to hear from others that he has lately been unfortunate in pecuniary involvements. He is undoubtedly the Monarch of Parnassus, and the most *English* of bards. I should place Rogers next in the living list—

(I value him more as the last of the *best* school)—Moore and Campbell both *third*—Southey and Wordsworth and Coleridge—the rest, οἱ πολλοί —thus:

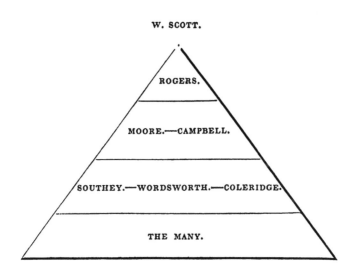

W. SCOTT.

ROGERS.

MOORE.——CAMPBELL.

SOUTHEY.—WORDSWORTH.—COLERIDGE.

THE MANY.

There is a triangular ' Gradus ad Parnassum!'—the names are too numerous for the base of the triangle. Poor Thurlow has gone wild about the poetry of Queen Bess's reign—*c'est dommage.* I have ranked the names upon my triangle more upon what I believe popular opinion than any decided opinion of my own. For, to me, some of M * * e's last *Erin* sparks—' As a beam o'er the face of the waters'—' When he who adores thee'—' Oh blame not'—and ' Oh breathe not his name'—are worth all the Epics that ever were composed.

" * * thinks the Quarterly will attack me next. Let them. I have been ' peppered so highly' in my time, *both* ways, that it must be cayenne or aloes to make me taste. I can sincerely say that I am not very much alive *now* to criticism. But—in tracing this—I rather believe, that it proceeds from my not attaching that importance to authorship which many do, and which, when young, I did also. ' One gets tired of every thing, my angel,' says Valmont. The ' angels' are the only things of which I am not a little sick—but I do think the preference of *writers* to *agents*—the mighty stir made about scribbling and scribes, by themselves and others—a sign of effeminacy, degeneracy, and weakness. Who would write, who had any thing better to do? ' Action'—' action'— ' action'—said Demosthenes: ' Action*s*—action*s*,' I say, and not writing —least of all, rhyme. Look at the querulous and monotonous lives of the ' genus;'—except Cervantes, Tasso, Dante, Ariosto, Kleist (who were brave and active citizens), Æschylus, Sophocles, and some other of the antiques also—what a worthless, idle brood it is!

" 12, Mezza notte.

" Just returned from dinner, with Jackson (the Emperor of Pugilism) and another of the select, at Crib's the champion's. I drank more than I like, and have brought away some three bottles of very fair claret—for I have no headache. We had Tom * * up after dinner ;—very facetious, though somewhat prolix. He don't like his situation—wants to fight again—pray Pollux (or Castor, if he was the *miller*) he may! Tom has been a sailor—a coal-heaver—and some other genteel profession, before he took to the cestus. Tom has been in action at sea, and is now only three-and-thirty. A great man! has a wife and a mistress, and conversations well—bating some sad omissions and misapplications of the aspirate. Tom is an old friend of mine; I have seen some of his best battles in my nonage. He is now a publican, and, I fear, a sinner;—for Mrs. * * is on alimony, and * *'s daughter lives with the champion. *This* * * told me,—Tom, having an opinion of my morals, passed her off as a legal spouse. Talking of her, he said ' she was the truest of women'— from which I immediately inferred she could *not* be his wife, and so it turned out.

" These panegyrics don't belong to matrimony ;—for, if ' true,' a man don't think it necessary to say so; and if not, the less he says the better. * * * * is the only man, except * * * *, I ever heard harangue upon his wife's virtue; and I listened to both with great credence and patience, and stuffed my handkerchief into my mouth, when I found yawning irresistible.—By the by, I am yawning now—so, good night to thee.—Νωαιρων.

"" Thursday, 26th November.

" Awoke a little feverish, but no headache—no dreams neither, thanks to stupor! Two letters, one from * * * *, the other from Lady Melbourne—both excellent in their respective styles. * * * *'s contained also a very pretty lyric on ' concealed griefs'—if not her own, yet very like her. Why did she not say that the stanzas were, or were not, of her composition?—I do not know whether to wish them *hers* or not. I have no great esteem for poetical persons, particularly women;—they have so much of the ' ideal' in *practics*, as well as *ethics*.

" I have been thinking lately a good deal of Mary Duff, &c. &c. &c. &c.*

" Lord Holland invited me to dinner to-day; but three days' dining would destroy me. So, without eating at all since yesterday, I went to my box at Covent-garden.

*   *   *   *   *   *

" Saw * * * * looking very pretty, though quite a different style of beauty from the other two. She has the finest eyes in the world, out of which she pretends *not* to see, and the longest eyelashes I ever saw, since Leila's and Phannio's Moslem curtains of the light. She has much beauty,—just enough,—but is, I think, *méchante*.

*   *   *   *   *   *

" I have been pondering on the miseries of separation, that—oh how seldom we see those we love! yet we live ages in moments, *when met.* The only thing that consoles me during absence is the reflection that no mental or personal estrangement, from ennui or disagreement, can take place;—and when people meet hereafter, even though many changes may have taken place in the mean time, still—unless they are *tired* of each other—they are ready to re-unite, and do not blame each other for the circumstances that severed them.   *   *   *   *

" Saturday, 27th (I believe—or rather am in *doubt,* which
is the ne plus ultra of mortal faith).

" I have missed a day; and, as the Irishman said, or Joe Miller says for him, ' have gained a loss,' or *by* the loss. Every thing is settled for

* This passage has been already extracted.

Holland, and nothing but a cough, or a caprice of my fellow-traveller's, can stop us. Carriage ordered—funds prepared—and, probably, a gale of wind into the bargain. *N'importe*—I believe, with Clym o' the Clow, or Robin Hood, ' By our Mary (dear name!) that art both Mother and May, I think it never was a man's lot to die before his day.' Heigh for Helvoetsluys, and so forth!

" To-night I went with young Henry Fox to see ' Nourjahad'—a drama, which the Morning Post hath laid to my charge, but of which I cannot even guess the author. I wonder what they will next inflict upon me. They cannot well sink below a Melodrama; but that is better than a Satire (at least, a personal one), with which I stand truly arraigned, and in atonement of which I am resolved to bear silently all criticisms, abuses, and even praises for bad pantomimes never composed by me,—without even a contradictory aspect. I suppose the root of this report is my loan to the manager of my Turkish drawings for his dresses, to which he was more welcome than to my name. I suppose the real author will soon own it, as it has succeeded; if not, Job be my model, and Lethe my beverage!

" * * * * has received the portrait safe; and, in answer, the only remark she makes upon it is, ' indeed it is like'—and again, ' indeed it is like.' * * * With her the likeness ' covered a multitude of sins;' for I happen to know that this portrait was not a flatterer, but dark and stern,—even black as the mood in which my mind was scorching last July, when I sate for it. All the others of me—like most portraits whatsoever—are, of course, more agreeable than nature.

" Redde the Ed. Review of Rogers. He is ranked highly,—but where he should be. There is a summary view of us all—*Moore* and *me* among the rest; and both (the *first* justly) praised—though, by implication (justly again) placed beneath our memorable friend. Mackintosh is the writer, and also of the critique on the Staël. His grand essay on Burke, I hear, is for the next number. But I know nothing of the Edinburgh, or of any other Review, but from rumour; and I have long ceased—indeed, I could not, in justice, complain of any, even though I were to rate poetry in general, and my rhymes in particular, more highly than I really do. To withdraw *myself* from *myself* (oh that cursed selfishness!)

has ever been my sole, my entire, my sincere motive in scribbling at all; and publishing is also the continuance of the same object, by the action it affords to the mind, which else recoils upon itself. If I valued fame, I should flatter received opinions, which have gathered strength by time, and will yet wear longer than any living works to the contrary. But, for the soul of me, I cannot and will not give the lie to my own thoughts and doubts, come what may. If I am a fool, it is, at least, a doubting one; and I envy no one the certainty of his self-approved wisdom.

" All are inclined to believe what they covet, from a lottery-ticket up to a passport to Paradise,—in which, from description, I see nothing very tempting. My restlessness tells me I have something within that ' passeth show.' It is for Him, who made it, to prolong that spark of celestial fire which illuminates, yet burns, this frail tenement; but I see no such horror in a ' dreamless sleep,' and I have no conception of any existence which duration would not render tiresome. How else ' fell the angels,' even according to your creed? They were immortal, heavenly, and happy as their *apostate Abdiel* is now by his treachery. Time must decide; and eternity won't be the less agreeable or more horrible because one did not expect it. In the mean time, I am grateful for some good, and tolerably patient under certain evils—grace à Dieu et mon bon tempérament.

" Sunday, 28th.

" Monday, 29th.

" Tuesday, 30th.

" Two days missed in my log-book;—hiatus *haud* deflendus. They were as little worth recollection as the rest; and, luckily, laziness or society prevented me from *notching* them.

" Sunday, I dined with the Lord Holland in St. James's-square. Large party—among them Sir S. Romilly and Lady R.ʸ—General Sir Somebody Bentham, a man of science and talent, I am told.—Horner— —*the* Horner, an Edinburgh Reviewer, an excellent speaker in the ' Honourable House,' very pleasing, too, and gentlemanly in company, as far as I have seen—Sharpe—Phillips of Lancashire—Lord John Russell, and others, ' good men and true.' Holland's society is very good you always see some one or other in it worth knowing. Stuffed myself with sturgeon, and exceeded in champagne and wine in general, but not to confusion of head. When I *do* dine, I gorge like an Arab or a Boa snake, on fish and vegetables, but no meat. I am always better, however, on my tea and biscuit than any other regimen,—and even *that* sparingly.

" Why does Lady H. always have that damned screen between the whole room and the fire? I, who bear cold no better than an antelope, and never yet found a sun quite *done* to my taste, was absolutely petrified, and could not even shiver. All the rest, too, looked as if they were just unpacked, like salmon from an ice-basket, and set down to table for that day only. When she retired, I watched their looks as I dismissed the screen, and every cheek thawed, and every nose reddened with the anticipated glow.

" Saturday, I went with Harry Fox to Nourjahad; and, I believe, convinced him, by incessant yawning, that it was not mine. I wish the precious author would own it, and release me from his fame. The dresses are pretty, but not in costume;—Mrs. Horne's, all but the turban, and the want of a small dagger (if she is a Sultana), *perfect*. I never saw a Turkish woman with a turban in my life—nor did any one else. The Sultanas have a small poniard at the waist. The dialogue is drowsy—the action heavy—the scenery fine—the actors tolerable. I can't say much for their seraglio—Teresa, Phannio, or * * * * were worth them all.

" Sunday, a very handsome note from Mackintosh, who is a rare instance of the union of very transcendent talent and great good-nature. To-day (Tuesday), a very pretty billet from M. la Baronne de Staël Holstein. She is pleased to be much pleased with my mention of her and her last work in my notes. I spoke as I thought. Her works are my delight, and so is she herself, for—half an hour. I don't like her politics—at least, her *having changed* them; had she been *qualis ab incepto*, it were nothing. But she is a woman by herself, and has done more than all the rest of them together, intellectually;—she ought to have been a man. She *flatters* me very prettily in her note;—but I *know* it. The reason that adulation is not displeasing is, that, though untrue, it shows one to be of consequence enough, in one way or other, to induce people to lie, to make us their friend:—that is their concern.

"* * is, I hear, thriving on the repute of a *pun* (which was *mine* at Mackintosh's dinner some time back), on Ward, who was asking 'how much it would take to *re-whig* him?' I answered that, probably, he 'must first, before he was *re-whigged*, be re-*warded*.' This foolish quibble, before the Staël and Mackintosh and a number of conversationers, has been mouthed about, and at last settled on the head of * *, where long may it remain!

"George* is returned from afloat to get a new ship. He looks thin, but better than I expected. I like George much more than most people like their heirs. He is a fine fellow, and every inch a sailor. I would do any thing, *but apostatize*, to get him on in his profession.

"Lewis called. It is a good and good-humoured man, but pestilently prolix and paradoxical and *personal*. If he would but talk half, and reduce his visits to an hour, he would add to his popularity. As an author, he is very good, and his vanity is *ouverte*, like Erskine's, and yet not offending.

"Yesterday, a very pretty letter from Annabella†, which I answered. What an odd situation and friendship is ours!—without one spark of love on either side, and produced by circumstances which in general lead to coldness on one side, and aversion on the other. She is a very superior woman, and very little spoiled, which is strange in an heiress—a girl of twenty—a peeress that is to be, in her own right—an only child, and a *savante*, who has always had her own way. She is a poetess—a mathematician—a metaphysician, and yet, withal, very kind, generous, and gentle, with very little pretension. Any other head would be turned with half her acquisitions, and a tenth of her advantages.

* His cousin, the present Lord Byron.
† Miss Milbanke, afterwards Lady Byron.

"Wednesday, December 1st, 1813.

"To-day responded to La Baronne de Staël Holstein, and sent to Leigh Hunt (an acquisition to my acquaintance—through Moore—or last summer) a copy of the two Turkish Tales. Hunt is an extraordinary character, and not exactly of the present age. He reminds me more of the Pym and Hampden times—much talent, great independence of spirit, and an austere, yet not repulsive, aspect. If he goes on *qualis ab incepto*, I know few men who will deserve more praise or obtain it. I must go and see him again;—the rapid succession of adventure since last summer, added to some serious uneasiness and business, have interrupted our acquaintance; but he is a man worth knowing; and though, for his own sake, I wish him out of prison, I like to study character in such situations. He has been unshaken, and will continue so. I don't think him deeply versed in life;—he is the bigot of virtue (not religion), and enamoured of the beauty of that 'empty name,' as the last breath of Brutus pronounced, and every day proves it. He is, perhaps, a little opiniated, as all men who are the *centre* of *circles*, wide or narrow—the Sir Oracles, in whose name two or three are gathered together—must be, and as even Johnson was; but, withal, a valuable man, and less vain than success and even the consciousness of preferring 'the right to the expedient' might excuse.

"To-morrow there is a party of *purple* at the 'blue' Miss * * *'s. Shall I go? um!—I don't much affect your blue-bottles;—but one ought to be civil. There will be, 'I guess now' (as the Americans say), the Staëls and Mackintoshes—good—the * * *s and * * *s—not so good—the * * *s, &c. &c.—good for nothing. Perhaps that blue-winged Kashmirian butterfly of book-learning, Lady * * * *, will be there. I hope so; it is a pleasure to look upon that most beautiful of faces.

"Wrote to H.—he has been telling that I——*. I am sure, at least, *I* did not mention it, and I wish he had not. He is a good fellow,

---

* Two or three words are here scratched out in the manuscript, but the import of the sentence evidently is, that Mr. Hodgson (to whom the passage refers) had been revealing to some friends the secret of Lord Byron's kindness to him.

and I obliged myself ten times more by being of use than I did him,—
and there's an end on't.

"Baldwin is boring me to present their King's Bench petition. I
presented Cartwright's last year; and Stanhope and I stood against the
whole House, and mouthed it valiantly—and had some fun and a little
abuse for our opposition. But 'I am not i' th' vein' for this business.
Now, had * * been here, she would have *made* me do it. *There* is a
woman, who, amid all her fascination, always urged a man to usefulness
or glory. Had she remained, she had been my tutelar genius. * * *

"Baldwin is very importunate—but, poor fellow, 'I can't get out,
I can't get out—said the starling.'—Ah, I am as bad as that dog Sterne,
who preferred whining over 'a dead ass to relieving a living mother'—
villain—hypocrite—slave—sycophant! but *I* am no better. Here I cannot
stimulate myself to a speech for the sake of these unfortunates, and three
words and half a smile of * *, had she been here to urge it (and urge it
she infallibly would—at least, she always pressed me on senatorial duties,
and particularly in the cause of weakness), would have made me an
advocate, if not an orator. Curse on Rochefoucault for being always
right! In him a lie were virtue,—or, at least, a comfort to his readers.

"George Byron has not called to-day; I hope he will be an admiral,
and, perhaps, Lord Byron into the bargain. If he would but marry, I
would engage never to marry, myself, or cut him out of the heirship.
He would be happier, and I should like nephews better than sons.

"I shall soon be six-and-twenty (January 22d, 1814). Is there any
thing in the future that can possibly console us for not being always
twenty-five?

> Oh Gioventu!
> Oh Primavera! gioventu dell' anno.
> Oh Gioventu! primavera della vita.'

> * * * * *

"Sunday, December 5th.

"Dallas's nephew (son to the American Attorney-general) is arrived
in this country, and tells Dallas that my rhymes are very popular in the
United States. These are the first tidings that have ever sounded like

Fame to my ears—to be redde on the banks of the Ohio! The greatest pleasure I ever derived, of this kind, was from an extract, in Cooke the actor's Life, from his Journal, stating that in the reading-room of Albany near Washington, he perused English Bards and Scotch Reviewers. To be popular in a rising and far country has a kind of *posthumous feel*, very different from the ephemeral *éclat* and fête-ing, buzzing and party-ing compliments of the well-dressed multitude. I can safely say that, during my *reign* in the spring of 1812, I regretted nothing but its duration of six weeks instead of a fortnight, and was heartily glad to resign.

"Last night I supped with Lewis;—and, as usual, though I neither exceeded in solids nor fluids, have been half dead ever since. My stomach is entirely destroyed by long abstinence, and the rest will probably follow. Let it—I only wish the *pain* over. The 'leap in the dark' is the least to be dreaded.

"The Duke of * * called. I have told them forty times that, except to half-a-dozen old and specified acquaintances, I am invisible. His grace is a good, noble, ducal person; but I am content to think so at a distance, and so—I was not at home.

"Galt called.—Mem.—to ask some one to speak to Raymond in favour of his play We are old fellow-travellers, and, with all his eccentricities, he has much strong sense, experience of the world, and is, as far as I have seen, a good-natured philosophical fellow. I showed him Sligo's letter on the reports of the Turkish girl's *aventure* at Athens soon after it happened. He and Lord Holland, Lewis, and Moore, and Rogers, and Lady Melbourne have seen it. Murray has a copy. I thought it had been *unknown*, and wish it were; but Sligo arrived only some days after, and the *rumours* are the subject of his letter. That I shall preserve,—*it is as well.* Lewis and Galt were both *horrified*; and L. wondered I did not introduce the situation into ' the Giaour.' He *may* wonder;—he might wonder more at that production's being written at all. But to describe the *feelings* of *that situation* were impossible—it is *icy* even to recollect them.

"The Bride of Abydos was published on Thursday the second of December; but how it is liked or disliked, I know not. Whether it succeeds or not is no fault of the public, against whom I can have no complaint. But I am much more indebted to the tale than I can ever be to the most partial reader; as it wrung my thoughts from reality to imagination—from selfish regrets to vivid recollections—and recalled me to a country replete with the *brightest* and *darkest*, but always most *lively* colours of my memory. Sharpe called, but was not let in,—which I regret.

*   *   *   *   *   *   *

"Saw * * yesterday. I have not kept my appointment at Middleton, which has not pleased him, perhaps; and my projected voyage with * * will, perhaps, please him less. But I wish to keep well with both. They are instruments that don't do, in concert; but, surely, their separate tones are very musical, and I won't give up either.

"It is well if I don't jar between these great discords. At present, I stand tolerably well with all, but I cannot adopt their *dislikes ;*—so many *sets*. Holland's is the first;—every thing *distingué* is welcome there, and certainly the *ton* of his society is the best. Then there is M^{de.} de Staël's—there I never go, though I might, had I courted it. It is composed of the * *s and the * * family, with a strange sprinkling,—orators, dandies, and all kinds of *Blue*, from the regular Grub-street uniform, down to the azure jacket of the *Littérateur*. To see * * and * * sitting together, at dinner, always reminds me of the grave, where all distinctions of friend and foe are levelled; and they—the Reviewer and Reviewée—the Rhinoceros and Elephant—the Mammoth and Megalonyx —all will lie quietly together. They now *sit* together, as silent, but not so quiet, as if they were already immured.

*   *   *   *   *   *   *

"I did not go to the Berrys' the other night. The elder is a woman of much talent, and both are handsome, and must have been beautiful. To-night asked to Lord H.'s—shall I go? um!—perhaps.

"Morning, two o'clock.

"Went to Lord H.'s,—party numerous—*mi*lady in perfect good-humour, and consequently *perfect*. No one more agreeable, or perhaps so much so, when she will. Asked for Wednesday to dine and meet the Staël—asked particularly, I believe, out of mischief, to see the first interview after the *note*, with which Corinne professes herself to be so much taken. I don't much like it;—she always talks of *my*self or *her*self, and I am not (except in soliloquy, as now) much enamoured of either subject—especially one's Works. What the devil shall I say about 'De l'Allemagne?' I like it prodigiously; but unless I can twist my admiration into some fantastical expression, she won't believe me; and I know, by experience, I shall be overwhelmed with fine things about rhyme, &c. &c. The lover, Mr. * *, was there to-night, and C * * said ' it was the only proof *he* had seen of her good taste.' Monsieur L'Amant is remarkably handsome; but *I* don't think more so than her book.

" C * * looks well,—seemed pleased, and dressed to *sprucery*. A blue coat becomes him —so does his new wig. He really looked as if Apollo had sent him a birthday suit, or a wedding-garment, and was witty and lively. * * * He abused Corinne's book, which I regret; because, firstly, he understands German, and is consequently a fair judge; and, secondly, he is *first-rate*, and, consequently, the best of judges. I reverence and admire him; but I won't give up my opinion —why should I? I read *her* again and again, and there can be no affectation in this. I cannot be mistaken (except in taste) in a book I read and lay down, and take up again; and no book can be totally bad, which finds *one*, even *one* reader, who can say as much sincerely.

" C. talks of lecturing next spring; his last lectures were eminently successful. Moore thought of it, but gave it up,—I don't know why. * * had been prating *dignity* to him, and such stuff; as if a man disgraced himself by instructing and pleasing at the same time.

" Introduced to Marquis Buckingham—saw Lord Gower—he is going to Holland;—Sir J. and Lady Mackintosh and Horner, G. Lamb, with I know not how many (R. Wellesley, one—a clever man) grouped about the room. Little Henry Fox, a very fine boy, and very promising in mind and manner,—he went away to bed, before I had time to talk to him. I am sure I had rather hear him than all the *savans*.

" Monday, December 6th.

" Murray tells me that C——r asked him why the thing was called the *Bride* of Abydos? It is a cursed awkward question, being unanswerable. *She* is not a *bride*, only about to be one; but for, &c. &c. &c.

" I don't wonder at his finding out the *Bull;* but the detection * * * is too late to do any good. I was a great fool to make it, and am ashamed of not being an Irishman. 　　*　　*　　*　　*　　*

" C——l last night seemed a little nettled at something or other— I know not what. We were standing in the ante-saloon, when Lord H. brought out of the other room a vessel of some composition similar to that which is used in catholic churches, and, seeing us, he exclaimed, ' Here is some *incense* for you.' C——l answered—' Carry it to Lord Byron—*he is used to it.*' *　　*　　*

" Now, this comes of ' bearing no brother near the throne.' I, who have no throne, nor wish to have one *now*—whatever I may have done —am at perfect peace with all the poetical fraternity;—or, at least, if I dislike any, it is not *poetically*, but *personally*. Surely the field of thought is infinite;—what does it signify who is before or behind in a race where there is no *goal?* The temple of Fame is like that of the Persians, the Universe;—our altar, the tops of mountains. I should be equally content with Mount Caucasus or Mount Anything; and those who like it may have Mont Blanc or Chimborazo, without my envy of their elevation.

" I think I may *now* speak thus; for I have just published a Poem, and am quite ignorant whether it is *likely* to be *liked* or not. I have hitherto heard little in its commendation, and no one can *downright* abuse it to one's face, except in print. It can't be good, or I should not have stumbled over the threshold, and blundered in my very title. But I begun it with my heart full of * * *, and my head of orient*alities* (I can't call them *isms*), and wrote on rapidly, 　*　　*　　*　　*　　*

" This journal is a relief. When I am tired—as I generally am— out comes this, and down goes every thing. But I can't read it over;— and God knows what contradictions it may contain. If I am sincere with myself (but I fear one lies more to one's self than to any one else), every page should confute, refute, and utterly abjure its predecessor.

" Another scribble from Martin Baldwin the petitioner: I have

neither head nor nerves to present it. That confounded supper at
Lewis's has spoiled my digestion and my philanthropy. I have no more
charity than a cruet of vinegar. Would I were an ostrich and dieted on
fire-irons,—or any thing that my gizzard could get the better of.

"To-day saw W. His uncle is dying, and W don't much affect
our Dutch determinations. I dine with him on Thursday, provided
l'oncle is not dined upon, or peremptorily bespoke by the posthumous
epicures, before that day. I wish he may recover—not for *our* dinner's
sake, but to disappoint the undertaker, and the rascally reptiles that may
well wait, since they *will* dine at last.

"Gell called—he of Troy—after I was out. Mem.—to return his
visit. But my Mems. are the very land-marks of forgetfulness;—something like a lighthouse, with a ship wrecked under the nose of its
lantern. I never look at a Mem. without seeing that I have remembered
to forget. Mem.—I have forgotten to pay Pitt's taxes, and suppose I
shall be surcharged. 'An I do not turn rebel when thou art king'—
oons! I believe my very biscuit is leavened with that Impostor's
imposts.

"L^y. M^e. returns from Jersey's to-morrow;—I must call. A Mr.
Thomson has sent a song, which I must applaud. I hate annoying them
with censure or silence;—and yet I hate *lettering*.

"Saw Lord Glenbervie and his Prospectus, at Murray's, of a new
Treatise on Timber. Now here is a man more useful than all the
historians and rhymers ever planted. For by preserving our woods and
forests, he furnishes materials for all the history of Britain worth reading,
and all the odes worth nothing.

"Redde a good deal, but desultorily. My head is crammed with
the most useless lumber. It is odd that when I do read, I can only bear
the chicken broth of—*any thing* but Novels. It is many a year since I
have looked into one (though they are sometimes ordered, by way of
experiment, but never taken) till I looked yesterday at the worst parts
of the Monk. These descriptions ought to have been written by Tiberius
at Caprea—they are forced—the *philtred* ideas of a jaded voluptuary. It
is to me inconceivable how they could have been composed by a man of
only twenty—his age when he wrote them. They have no nature—all

the sour cream of cantharides. I should have suspected Buffon of writing them on the deathbed of his detestable dotage. I had never redde this edition, and merely looked at them from curiosity and recollection of the noise they made, and the name they have left to Lewis. But they could do no harm, except *   *   *   *.

"Called this evening on my agent—my business as usual. Our strange adventures are the only inheritances of our family that have not diminished. *   *   *   *

"I shall now smoke two cigars, and get me to bed. The cigars don't keep well here. They get as old as a *donna di quaranti anni* in the sun of Africa. The Havannah are the best;—but neither are so pleasant as a hooka or chibouque. The Turkish tobacco is mild, and their horses entire—two things as they should be. I am so far obliged to this Journal, that it preserves me from verse,—at least from keeping it. I have just thrown a Poem into the fire (which it has relighted to my great comfort), and have smoked out of my head the plan of another. I wish I could as easily get rid of thinking, or, at least, the confusion of thought.

"Tuesday, December 7.

"Went to bed, and slept dreamlessly, but not refreshingly. Awoke, and up an hour before being called; but dawdled three hours in dressing. When one subtracts from life infancy (which is vegetation),—sleep, eating, and swilling—buttoning and unbuttoning—how much remains of downright existence? The summer of a dormouse. *   *   *

"Redde the papers and *tea*-ed and soda-watered, and found out that the fire was badly lighted. Ld. Glenbervie wants me to go to Brighton —um!

"This morning, a very pretty billet from the Staël about meeting her at Ld. H.'s to-morrow. She has written, I dare say, twenty such this morning to different people, all equally flattering to each. So much the better for her and those who believe all she wishes them, or they wish to believe. She has been pleased to be pleased with my slight eulogy in the note annexed to the 'Bride.' This is to be accounted for in several ways:—firstly, all women like all, or any, praise; secondly, this was unexpected, because I have never courted her; and thirdly, as Scrub says, those who have been all their lives regularly praised, by regular critics, like a little variety, and are glad when any one goes out of his way to say a civil thing; and fourthly, she is a very good-natured creature, which is the best reason, after all, and, perhaps, the only one.

"A knock—knocks single and double. Bland called.—He says Dutch society (he has been in Holland) is second-hand French; but the women are like women every where else. This is a bore; I should like to see them a little *un*like; but that can't be expected.

"Went out—came home—this, that, and the other—and 'all is vanity, saith the preacher,' and so say I, as part of his congregation. Talking of vanity—whose praise do I prefer? Why, Mrs. Inchbald's, and that of the Americans. The first, because her 'Simple Story' and 'Nature and Art' are, to me, *true* to their *titles*; and, consequently, her short note to Rogers about the 'Giaour' delighted me more than any thing, except the Edinburgh Review. I like the Americans, because *I* happened to be in *Asia*, while the English Bards and Scotch Reviewers were redde in *America*. If I could have had a speech against the *Slave Trade, in Africa*, and an Epitaph on a Dog, in *Europe*, (i. e. in the Morning Post), my *vertex sublimis* would certainly have displaced stars enough to overthrow the Newtonian system.

"Friday, December 10th, 1813.

"I am *ennuyé* beyond my usual tense of that yawning verb, which I am always conjugating; and I don't find that society much mends the matter. I am too lazy to shoot myself—and it would annoy Augusta, and perhaps * *; but it would be a good thing for George, on the other side, and no bad one for me; but I won't be tempted.

"I have had the kindest letter from M * * e. I *do* think that man is the best-hearted, the only *hearted* being I ever encountered; and then, his talents are equal to his feelings.

"Dined on Wednesday at Lord H.'s—the Staffords, Staëls, Cowpers, Ossulstones, Melbournes, Mackintoshes, &c. &c.—and was introduced to the Marquis and Marchioness of Stafford,—an unexpected event. My quarrel with Lord Carlisle (their or his brother-in-law) having rendered it improper, I suppose, brought it about. But, if it was to happen at all, I wonder it did not occur before. She is handsome, and must have been beautiful—and her manners are *princessly*. 　*　　*　　*

"The Staël was at the other end of the table, and less loquacious than heretofore. We are now very good friends; though she asked Lady Melbourne whether I had really any *bonhommie*. She might as well have asked that question before she told C. L. 'c'est un démon.' True enough, but rather premature, for *she* could not have found it out, and so—she wants me to dine there next Sunday.

"Murray prospers, as far as circulation. For my part, I adhere (in liking) to my Fragment. It is no wonder that I wrote one—my mind is a fragment.

"Saw Lord Gower, Tierney, &c. in the square. Took leave of Lord Gr. who is going to Holland and Germany. He tells me, that he carries with him a parcel of 'Harolds' and 'Giaours,' &c. for the readers of Berlin, who, it seems, read English, and have taken a caprice for mine. Um!—have I been *German* all this time, when I thought myself *oriental*? 　*　　*　　*

"Lent Tierney my box for to-morrow; and received a new Comedy sent by Lady C. A.—but *not hers*. I must read it, and endeavour not to displease the author. I hate annoying them with cavil; but a comedy I take to be the most difficult of compositions, more so than tragedy.

"G—t says there is a coincidence between the first part of 'the Bride' and some story of his—whether published or not, I know not, never having seen it. He is almost the last person on whom any one would commit literary larceny, and I am not conscious of any *witting* thefts on any of the genus. As to originality, all pretensions are ludicrous,—'there is nothing new under the sun.'

"Went last night to the play. 　*　　*　　*　　* Invited out to a party, but did not go;—right. Refused to go to Lady * *'s on Monday;—right again. If I must fritter away my life, I would rather do it alone. I was much tempted;—C * * looked so Turkish with her red turban, and her regular dark and clear features. Not that *she* and *I* ever were, or could be, any thing; but I love any aspect that reminds me of the 'children of the sun.'

" To dine to-day with Rogers and Sharpe, for which I have some
appetite, not having tasted food for the preceding forty-eight hours.   I
wish I could leave off eating altogether.

" Saturday, December 11.
" Sunday, December 12.

" By G—t's answer, I find it is some story in *real life*, and not any
work with which my late composition coincides.   It is still more singular,
for mine is drawn from *existence* also.

" I have sent an excuse to M. de Staël.   I do not feel sociable enough
for dinner to-day ;—and I will not go to Sheridan's on Wednesday.   Not
that I do not admire and prefer his unequalled conversation ; but—that
' *but*' must only be intelligible to thoughts I cannot write.   Sheridan was
in good talk at Rogers's the other night, but I only staid till *nine*.   All
the world are to be at the Staël's to-night, and I am not sorry to escape
any part of it.   I only go out to get me a fresh appetite for being alone.
Went out—did not go to the Staël's, but to Ld. Holland's.   Party
numerous—conversation general.   Staid late—made a blunder—got over
it—came home and went to bed, not having eaten.   Rather empty, but
fresco, which is the great point with me.

" Monday, December 13, 1813.

" Called at three places—read, and got ready to leave town to-
morrow.   Murray has had a letter from his brother Bibliopole of
Edinburgh, who says ' he is lucky in having such a *poet*'—something as
if one was a pack-horse, or ' ass, or any thing that is his :' or, like Mrs.
Packwood, who replied to some inquiry after the Odes on Razors,
' Laws, sir, we keeps a Poet.'   The same illustrious Edinburgh bookseller once sent an order for books, poesy, and cookery, with this agreeable postscript—' The *Harold* and *Cookery* are much wanted.'   Such is
fame, and, after all, quite as good as any other ' life in other's breath.'
'Tis much the same to divide purchasers with Hannah Glasse or Hannah
More.

" Some editor of some Magazine has *announced* to Murray his intention of abusing the thing '*without reading it.*' So much the better; if he redde it first, he would abuse it more.

" Allen (Lord Holland's Allen—the best informed and one of the ablest men I know —a perfect Magliabecchi—a devourer, a Helluo of books, and an observer of men) has lent me a quantity of Burns's unpublished, and never-to-be published, Letters. They are full of oaths and obscene songs. What an antithetical mind !—tenderness, roughness—delicacy, coarseness—sentiment, sensuality—soaring and grovelling, dirt and deity—all mixed up in that one compound of inspired clay !

" It seems strange; a true voluptuary will never abandon his mind to the grossness of reality. It is by exalting the earthly, the material, the *physique* of our pleasures, by veiling these ideas, by forgetting them altogether, or, at least, never naming them hardly to one's self, that we alone can prevent them from disgusting.

*　　*　　*　　*　　*　　*　　*

" December 14, 15, 16.

" Much done, but nothing to record. It is quite enough to set down my thoughts,—my actions will rarely bear retrospection.

" December 17, 18.

" Lord Holland told me a curious piece of sentimentality in Sheridan* The other night we were all delivering our respective and various opinions on him and other *hommes marquans*, and mine was this. ' Whatever Sheridan has done or chosen to do has been, *par excellence*, always the *best* of its kind. He has written the *best* comedy (School for Scandal), the *best* drama (in my mind, far before that St. Giles's lampoon, the Beggar's Opera), the best farce (the Critic—it is only too good for a farce), and the best Address (Monologue on Garrick), and, to crown all, delivered the very best Oration (the famous Begum Speech) ever conceived or heard in this country ' Somebody told S. this the next day, and on hearing it, he burst into tears !

---

* This passage of the Journal has already appeared in my Life of Sheridan.

" Poor Brinsley! if they were tears of pleasure, I would rather have said these few, but most sincere, words than have written the Iliad or made his own celebrated Philippic. Nay, his own comedy never gratified me more than to hear that he had derived a moment's gratification from any praise of mine, humble as it must appear to ' my elders and my betters.'

" Went to my box at Covent-garden to-night; and my delicacy felt a little shocked at seeing S * * *'s mistress (who, to my certain knowledge, was actually educated, from her birth, for her profession) sitting with her mother, 'a three-piled b——d, b——d-Major to the army,' in a private box opposite. I felt rather indignant; but, casting my eyes round the house, in the next box to me, and the next, and the next, were the most distinguished old and young Babylonians of quality;—so I burst out a laughing. It was really odd; Lady * * divorced—Lady * * and her daughter, Lady * *, both divorceable—Mrs. * * †, in the next, the like, and still nearer * * * * * *! What an assemblage to me, who know all their histories. It was as if the house had been divided between your public and your understood courtesans;—but the Intriguantes much outnumbered the regular mercenaries. On the other side were only Pauline and her mother, and, next box to her, three of inferior note. Now, where lay the difference between her and mamma, and Lady * * and daughter? except that the two last may enter Carleton and any other house, and the two first are limited to the opera and b—— house. How I do delight in observing life as it really is!—and myself, after all, the worst of any. But, no matter—I must avoid egotism, which, just now, would be no vanity.

" I have lately written a wild, rambling, unfinished rhapsody, called ' The Devil's Drive‡,' the notion of which I took from Porson's ' Devil's Walk.'

" Redde some Italian, and wrote two Sonnets on * * *. I never wrote but one sonnet before, and that was not in earnest, and many

† These names are all left blank in the original.

‡ Of this strange, wild Poem, which extends to about 250 lines, the only copy that Lord Byron, I believe, ever wrote, he presented to Lord Holland. Though with a good deal of vigour and imagination, it is, for the most part, rather clumsily executed, wanting the point and

years ago, as an exercise—and I will never write another. They are the most puling, petrifying, stupidly platonic compositions. I detest the Petrarch so much*, that I would not be the man even to have obtained his Laura, which the metaphysical, whining dotard never could.

*   *   *   *   *   *

condensation of those clever verses of Mr. Coleridge which Lord Byron, adopting a notion long prevalent, has attributed to Professor Porson. There are, however, some of the stanzas of " The Devil's Drive" well worth preserving.

1.

" The Devil return'd to hell by two,
     And he staid at home till five ;
When he dined on some homicides done in *ragoût*,
     And a rebel or so in an *Irish* stew,
And sausages made of a self-slain Jew,
And bethought himself what next to do,
     ' And,' quoth he, ' I 'll take a drive.
I walk'd in the morning, I 'll ride to-night ;
In darkness my children take most delight,
     And I 'll see how my favourites thrive.

2.

" ' And what shall I ride in?' quoth Lucifer, then—
     ' If I follow'd my taste, indeed,
I should mount in a waggon of wounded men,
     And smile to see them bleed.
But these will be furnish'd again and again,
     And at present my purpose is speed ;
To see my manor as much as I may,
And watch that no souls shall be poach'd away.

3.

" ' I have a state-coach at C——— House,
     A chariot in Seymour-place ;
But they 're lent to two friends, who make me amends
     By driving my favourite pace :
And they handle their reins with such a grace,
I have something for both at the end of their race.

4.

" ' So now for the earth to take my chance.'
     Then up to the earth sprung he ;

---

* He learned to think more reverently of " the Petrarch" afterwards.

" January 16, 1814.

* * * * * *

" To-morrow I leave town for a few days.   I saw Lewis to-day, who is just returned from Oatlands, where he has been squabbling with Mad. de Staël about himself, Clarissa Harlowe, Mackintosh, and me.   My homage has never been paid in that quarter, or we would have agreed still worse.   I don't talk—I can't flatter, and won't listen, except to a pretty or a foolish woman.   She bored Lewis with praises of himself till he sickened—found out that Clarissa was perfection, and Mackintosh the first man in England.   There I agree, at least, *one* of the first—but Lewis did not.   As to Clarissa, I leave to those who can read it to judge

And making a jump from Moscow to France,
 He stepp'd across the sea,
And rested his hoof on a turnpike road,
No very great way from a bishop's abode.

5
" But first as he flew, I forgot to say,
That he hover'd a moment upon his way
 To look upon Leipsic plain ;
And so sweet to his eye was its sulphury glare,
And so soft to his ear was the cry of despair,
 That he perch'd on a mountain of slain ;
And he gazed with delight from its growing height,
Nor often on earth had he seen such a sight,
 Nor his work done half as well :
For the field ran so red with the blood of the dead,
 That it blush'd like the waves of Hell !
Then loudly, and wildly, and long laugh'd he:
' Methinks they have here little need of *me!*'

* * * * * *

8.
" But the softest note that sooth'd his ear
 Was the sound of a widow sighing;
And the sweetest sight was the icy tear,
Which Horror froze in the blue eye clear
 Of a maid by her lover lying—
As round her fell her long fair hair;
And she look'd to Heaven with that frenzied air
Which seem'd to ask if a God were there!

and dispute. I could not do the one, and am, consequently, not qualified for the other. She told Lewis wisely, he being my friend, that I was affected, in the first place, and that, in the next place, I committed the heinous offence of sitting at dinner with my *eyes* shut, or half shut. * * * I wonder if I really have this trick. I must cure myself of it, if true. One insensibly acquires awkward habits, which should be broken in time If this is one, I wish I had been told of it before. It would not so much signify if one was always to be checkmated by a plain woman, but one may as well see some of one's neighbours, as well as the plate upon the table.

" I should like, of all things, to have heard the Amabæan eclogue

And, stretch'd by the wall of a ruin'd hut,
With its hollow cheek, and eyes half shut,
　A child of famine dying:
And the carnage begun, when resistance is done,
　And the fall of the vainly flying!
*　　*　　*　　*　　*　　*

10.
" But the Devil has reach'd our cliffs so white,
　And what did he there, I pray?
If his eyes were good, he but saw by night
　What we see every day;
But he made a tour, and kept a journal
Of all the wondrous sights nocturnal,
And he sold it in shares to the *Men* of the *Row*,
Who bid pretty well—but they *cheated* him, though!

11.
" The Devil first saw, as he thought, the *Mail*,
　Its coachman and his coat;
So instead of a pistol he cock'd his tail,
　And seized him by the throat:
Aha,' quoth he, ' what have we here?
'Tis a new barouche, and an ancient peer!'

12.
" So he sat him on his box again,
　And bade him have no fear,
But be true to his club, and stanch to his rein,
　His brothel, and his beer;

between her and Lewis—both obstinate, clever, odd, garrulous, and shrill. In fact, one could have heard nothing else. But they fell out, alas!—and now they will never quarrel again. Could not one reconcile them for the 'nonce?' Poor Corinne—she will find that some of her fine sayings won't suit our fine ladies and gentlemen.

"I am getting rather into admiration of * *, the youngest sister of * *. A wife would be my salvation. I am sure the wives of my acquaintances have hitherto done me little good. * * is beautiful, but very young, and, I think, a fool. But I have not seen enough to judge; besides, I hate an *esprit* in petticoats. That she won't love me is very probable, nor shall I love her. But, on my system, and the modern system in general, that don't signify. The business (if it came to business) would probably be arranged between papa and me. She

> ' Next to seeing a lord at the council board,
>   I would rather see him here.'
> *   *   *   *   *

17.

" The Devil gat next to Westminster,
    And he turn'd to ' the room' of the Commons;
But he heard, as he purposed to enter in there,
    That ' the Lords' had received a summons;
And he thought, as a ' *quondam* Aristocrat,'
He might peep at the peers, though to *hear* them were flat;
And he walk'd up the house so like one of our own,
That they say that he stood pretty near the throne.

18.

" He saw the Lord L————l seemingly wise,
    The Lord W————d certainly silly,
And Johnny of Norfolk—a man of some size—
    And Chatham, so like his friend Billy;
And he saw the tears in Lord E—n's eyes,
    Because the Catholics would *not* rise,
    In spite of his prayers and his prophecies;
And he heard—which set Satan himself a staring—
A certain Chief Justice say something like *swearing*.
And the Devil was shock'd—and quoth he, ' I must go,
For I find we have much better manners below.
If thus he harangues when he passes my border,
I shall hint to friend Moloch to call him to order.' "

would have her own way; I am good-humoured to women, and docile; and, if I did not fall in love with her, which I should try to prevent, we should be a very comfortable couple. As to conduct, *that* she must look to. * * * * * But *if* I love, I shall be jealous;—and for that reason I will not be in love. Though, after all, I doubt my temper, and fear I should not be so patient as becomes the *bienséance* of a married man in my station. * * * * * Divorce ruins the poor *femme*, and damages are a paltry compensation. I do fear my temper would lead me into some of our oriental tricks of vengeance, or, at any rate, into a summary appeal to the court of twelve paces. So 'I'll none on 't,' but e'en remain single and solitary;—though I should like to have somebody now and then, to yawn with one.

"W. and, after him, * *, has stolen one of my buffooneries about Mde. de Staël's Metaphysics and the Fog, and passed it, by speech and letter, as their own. As Gibbet says, 'they are the most of a gentleman of any on the road.' W. is in sad enmity with the Whigs about this Review of Fox (if he *did* review him);—all the epigrammatists and essayists are at him. I hate *odds*, and wish he may beat them. As for me, by the blessing of indifference, I have simplified my politics into an utter detestation of all existing governments; and, as it is the shortest and most agreeable and summary feeling imaginable, the first moment of an universal republic would convert me into an advocate for single and uncontradicted despotism. The fact is, riches are power, and poverty is slavery, all over the earth, and one sort of establishment is no better, nor worse, for a *people* than another. I shall adhere to my party, because it would not be honourable to act otherwise; but, as to *opinions*, I don't think politics *worth* an *opinion*. *Conduct* is another thing:—if you begin with a party, go on with them. I have no consistency, except in politics; and *that* probably arises from my indifference on the subject altogether."

I must here be permitted to interrupt, for a while, the progress of this Journal,—which extends through some months of the succeeding year,—for the purpose of noticing, without infringement of chronological order, such parts of the poet's literary history and correspondence as belong properly to the date of the year 1813.

At the beginning, as we have seen, of the month of December, the

Bride of Abydos was published,—having been struck off, like its pre
decessor, the Giaour, in one of those paroxysms of passion and imagina
tion, which adventures such as the poet was now engaged in were, in a
temperament like his, calculated to excite. As the mathematician of old
required but a spot to stand upon, to be able, as he boasted, to move the
world, so a certain degree of foundation in *fact* seemed necessary to
Byron, before that lever which he knew how to apply to the world of
the passions could be wielded by him. So small, however, was, in many
instances, the connexion with reality which satisfied him, that to aim at
tracing through his stories these links with his own fate and fortunes,
which were, after all, perhaps, visible but to his own fancy, would be a
task as uncertain as unsafe;—and this remark applies not only to the
Bride of Abydos, but to the Corsair, Lara, and all the other beautiful
fictions that followed, in which, though the emotions expressed by the poet
may be, in general, regarded as vivid recollections of what had, at different
times, agitated his own bosom, there are but little grounds,—however he
might himself, occasionally, encourage such a supposition,—for connecting
him personally with the groundwork or incidents of the stories.

While yet uncertain about the fate of his own new poem, the fol
lowing observations on the work of an ingenious follower in the same
track were written.

LETTER CXLIII.

TO MR. MURRAY.

" December 4th, 1813.

" I have redde through your Persian Tales*, and have taken the
liberty of making some remarks on the *blank* pages. There are many
beautiful passages, and an interesting story; and I cannot give you a
stronger proof that such is my opinion than by the *date* of the *hour—two
o'clock*, till which it has kept me awake *without a yawn*. The conclusion
is not quite correct in *costume:* there is no *Mussulman suicide* on record
—at least for *love*. But this matters not. The tale must have been
written by some one who has been on the spot, and I wish him, and he

---

* Poems by Mr. Galley Knight, of which Mr. Murray had transmitted the MS. to Lord
Byron, without, however, communicating the name of the author.

deserves, success. Will you apologise to the author for the liberties I have taken with his MS.? Had I been less awake to, and interested in, his theme, I had been less obtrusive; but you know *I* always take this in good part, and I hope he will. It is difficult to say what *will* succeed, and still more to pronounce what *will not*. *I* am at this moment in *that uncertainty* (on our *own* score), and it is no small proof of the author's powers to be able to *charm* and *fix* a *mind's* attention on similar subjects and climates in such a predicament. That he may have the same effect upon all his readers is very sincerely the wish, and hardly the *doubt*, of yours truly,　　　　　　　　　　　　　　　　　　　　　　　　" B."

To the Bride of Abydos he made additions, in the course of printing, amounting altogether to near two hundred lines; and, as usual, among the passages thus added were some of the happiest and most brilliant in the whole Poem. The opening lines, " Know ye the land," &c.—supposed to have been suggested to him by a song of Goëthe's*—were among the number of these new insertions, as were also those fine verses, " Who hath not proved how feebly words essay," &c. Of one of the most popular lines in this latter passage, it is not only curious, but instructive, to trace the progress to its present state of finish. Having, at first, written—

" Mind on her lip and music in her face,"

he afterwards altered it to

" The mind of music breathing in her face."

But, this not satisfying him, the next step of correction brought the line to what it is at present—

" The mind, the music breathing from her face †."

---

* " Kennst du das Land wo die Citronen blühn," &c.

† Among the imputed plagiarisms so industriously hunted out in his writings, this line has been, with somewhat more plausibility than is·frequent in such charges, included,—the lyric poet Lovelace having, it seems, written,

" The melody and music of her face."

Sir Thomas Brown, too, in his Religio Medici, says—" There is music even in beauty," &c. The coincidence, no doubt, is worth observing, and the task of " tracking" thus a favourite writer

But the longest, as well as most splendid, of those passages, with which the perusal of his own strains, during revision, inspired him, was that rich flow of eloquent feeling which follows the couplet, " Thou my Zuleika, share and bless my bark," &c.—a strain of poetry which, for energy and tenderness of thought, for music of versification, and select- ness of diction, has, throughout the greater portion of it, but few rivals in either ancient or modern song. All this passage was sent, in successive scraps, to the printer,—correction following correction, and thought reinforced by thought. We have here, too, another example of that retouching process, by which some of his most exquisite effects were attained. Every reader remembers the four beautiful lines—

> " Or, since that hope denied in worlds of strife,
> Be thou the rainbow to the storms of life !
> The evening beam that smiles the clouds away,
> And tints to-morrow with prophetic ray !"

In the first copy of this passage sent to the publisher, the last line was written thus—

$$\text{" And tints to-morrow with } \begin{Bmatrix} \textit{an airy} \\ \text{a fancied} \end{Bmatrix} \text{ ray."}$$

The following note being annexed:—" Mr. Murray,—Choose which of the two epithets, ' fancied,' or ' airy,' may be the best; or, if neither will do, tell me, and I will dream another." The poet's dream was, it must be owned, lucky,—" prophetic" being the word, of all others, for his purpose*.

I shall select but one more example, from the additions to this

---

" in the snow (as Dryden expresses it) of others" is sometimes not unamusing; but to those who found upon such resemblances a general charge of plagiarism, we may apply what Sir Walter Scott says, in that most agreeable work, his Lives of the Novelists :—" It is a favourite theme of laborious dulness to trace such coincidences, because they appear to reduce genius of the higher order to the usual standard of humanity, and of course to bring the author nearer to a level with his critics."

* It will be seen, however, from a subsequent letter to Mr. Murray, that he himself was at first unaware of the peculiar felicity of this epithet; and it is, therefore, probable, that, after all, the merit of the choice may have belonged to Mr. Gifford.

Poem, as a proof that his eagerness and facility, in producing, was sometimes almost equalled by his anxious care in correcting. In the long passage, just referred to, the six lines beginning " Blest as the Muezzin's strain," &c., having been despatched to the printer too late for insertion, were, by his desire, added in an errata page; the first couplet, in its original form, being as follows :—

> " Soft as the Mecca-Muezzin's strains invite
> Him who hath journey'd far to join the rite."

In a few hours after, another scrap was sent off, containing the lines thus—

> " Blest as the Muezzin's strain from Mecca's dome,
> Which welcomes Faith to view her Prophet's tomb."

With the following note to Mr. Murray:—

" December 3d, 1813.

" Look out in the Encyclopedia, article *Mecca*, whether it is there or at *Medina* the Prophet is entombed. If at Medina, the first lines of my alteration must run—

> " Blest as the call which from Medina's dome
> Invites Devotion to her Prophet's tomb," &c.

If at Mecca, the lines may stand as before. Page 45, canto 2d, Bride of Abydos. 　　　　　　　　　　　　　 " Yours,
　　　　　　　　　　　　　　　　　　　　　 " B.

" You will find this out either by article *Mecca*, *Medina*, or *Mohammed*. I have no book of reference by me."

Immediately after succeeded another note:—

" Did you look out? Is it *Medina* or *Mecca* that contains the *Holy* Sepulchre? Don't make me blaspheme by your negligence. I have no book of reference, or I would save you the trouble. I *blush*, as a good Mussulman, to have confused the point. "Yours,

"B."

Notwithstanding all these various changes, the couplet in question stands, at present, thus :—

" Blest as the Muezzin's strain from Mecca's wall
To pilgrims pure and prostrate at his call."

In addition to his own watchfulness over the birth of his new Poem, he also, as will be seen from the following letter, invoked the veteran taste of Mr. Gifford on the occasion.

LETTER CXLIV.

TO MR. GIFFORD.

" November 12th, 1813.

" MY DEAR SIR,

" I hope you will consider, when I venture on any request, that it is the reverse of a certain Dedication, and is addressed, *not* to ' The Editor of the Quarterly Review,' but to Mr. Gifford. You will understand this, and on that point I need trouble you no farther.

" You have been good enough to look at a thing of mine in MS.— a Turkish story, and I should feel gratified if you would do it the same favour in its probationary state of printing. It was written, I cannot say for amusement, nor ' obliged by hunger and request of friends,' but in a state of mind, from circumstances which occasionally occur to ' us youth,' that rendered it necessary for me to apply my mind to something, any thing but reality; and under this not very brilliant inspiration it was composed. Being done, and having at least diverted me from myself, I thought you would not perhaps be offended if Mr. Murray forwarded it to you. He has done so, and to apologise for his doing so a second time is the object of my present letter.

" I beg you will *not* send me any answer. I assure you very sincerely I know your time to be occupied, and it is enough, more than enough, if you read; you are not to be bored with the fatigue of answers.

"A word to Mr. Murray will be sufficient, and send it either to the flames, or

> ' A hundred hawkers' load,
> On wings of winds to fly or fall abroad.'

It deserves no better than the first, as the work of a week, and scribbled ' stans pede in uno (by the by, the only foot I have to stand on); and I promise never to trouble you again under forty Cantos, and a voyage between each.

"Believe me ever
"your obliged and affectionate servant,
"BYRON."

The following letters and notes, addressed to Mr. Murray at this time, cannot fail, I think, to gratify all those to whom the history of the labours of Genius is interesting.

LETTER CXLV.

TO MR. MURRAY.

"Nov. 12th, 1813.

"Two friends of mine (Mr. Rogers and Mr. Sharpe) have advised me not to risk at present any single publication separately, for various reasons. As they have not seen the one in question, they can have no bias for or against the merits (if it has any) or the faults of the present subject of our conversation. You say all the last of the ' Giaour' are gone—at least out of your hands. Now, if you think of publishing any new edition with the last additions which have not yet been before the reader (I mean distinct from the two-volume publication), we can add the ' Bride of Abydos,' which will thus steal quietly into the world: if liked, we can then throw off some copies for the purchasers of former ' Giaours;' and, if not, I can omit it in any future publication. What think you? I really am no judge of those things, and with all my natural partiality for one's own productions, I would rather follow any one's judgment than my own.

"P.S. Pray let me have the proofs I sent *all* to-night. I have some alterations that I have thought of that I wish to make speedily. I hope the proof will be on separate pages, and not all huddled together on a mile-long ballad-singing sheet, as those of the Giaour sometimes are; for then I can't read them distinctly."

TO MR. MURRAY.

"Nov. 13, 1813.

"Will you forward the letter to Mr. Gifford with the proof? There is an alteration I may make in Zuleika's speech, in second Canto (the only one of *hers* in that Canto). It is now thus:

"And curse, if I could curse, the day.

It must be—

"And mourn—I dare not curse—the day
That saw my solitary birth, &c. &c.

"Ever yours,

"B.

"In the last MS. lines sent, instead of 'living heart,' convert to 'quivering heart.' It is in line 9th of the MS. passage.

"Ever yours again,

"B."

TO MR. MURRAY.

"Alteration of a line in Canto second.

Instead of—

"And tints to-morrow with a *fancied* ray,

Print—

"And tints to-morrow with *prophetic* ray.

"The evening beam that smiles the clouds away,
And tints to-morrow with prophetic ray;

Or,

"And $\begin{Bmatrix} gilds \\ tints \end{Bmatrix}$ the hope of morning with its ray;

Or,

"And gilds to-morrow's hope with heavenly ray.

" I wish you would ask Mr. Gifford which of them is best, or rather *not worst.*

" Ever, &c.

" You can send the request contained in this at the same time with the *revise, after* I have seen the *said revise.*"

TO MR. MURRAY.

" Nov. 13, 1813.

" Certainly.   Do you suppose that no one but the Galileans are acquainted with *Adam*, and *Eve*, and *Cain**, and *Noah?*—Surely, I might have had Solomon, and Abraham, and David, and even Moses.   When you know that *Zuleika* is the *Persian poetical* name for *Potiphar*'s wife, on whom and Joseph there is a long poem, in the Persian, this will not surprise you.   If you want authority, look at Jones, D'Herbelot, Vathek, or the notes to the Arabian Nights; and, if you think it necessary, model this into a note.

" Alter, in the inscription, ' the most affectionate respect,' to ' with every sentiment of regard and respect.' "

TO MR. MURRAY.

" Nov. 14, 1813.

" I send you a note for the *ignorant*, but I really wonder at finding *you* among them.   I don't care one lump of sugar for my *poetry*; but for my *costume* and my *correctness* on those points (of which I think the *funeral* was a proof), I will combat lustily.

" Yours, &c."

" Nov. 14, 1813.

" Let the revise which I sent just now (and *not* the proof in Mr.

---

* Some doubt had been expressed by Mr. Murray as to the propriety of his putting the name of Cain into the mouth of a Mussulman.

Gifford's possession) be returned to the printer, as there are several additional corrections, and two new lines in it.

"Yours, &c."

LETTER CXLVI.

TO MR. MURRAY.

"November 15th, 1813.

"Mr. Hodgson has looked over and *stopped*, or rather *pointed*, this revise, which must be the one to print from. He has also made some suggestions, with most of which I have complied, as he has always, for these ten years, been a very sincere, and by no means (at times) flattering, intimate of mine. *He* likes it (you will think *flatteringly*, in this instance) better than the Giaour, but doubts (and so do I) its being so popular; but, contrary to some others, advises a separate publication. On this we can easily decide. I confess I like the *double* form better. Hodgson says, it is *better versified* than any of the others; which is odd, if true, as it has cost me less time (though more hours at a time) than any attempt I ever made.

"P.S. Do attend to the punctuation: I can't, for I don't know a comma—at least where to place one.

"That tory of a printer has omitted two lines of the opening, and *perhaps more*, which were in the MS. Will you, pray, give him a hint of accuracy? I have reinserted the *two*, but they were in the manuscript, I can swear."

LETTER CXLVII.

TO MR. MURRAY.

"November 17th, 1813.

"That you and I may distinctly understand each other on a subject, which, like 'the dreadful reckoning when men smile no more,' makes conversation not very pleasant, I think it as well to *write* a few lines on the topic.—Before I left town for Yorkshire, you said that you were ready and willing to give five hundred guineas for the copyright of 'The Giaour;' and my answer was—from which I do not mean to recede—that we would discuss the point at Christmas. The new story may or may not succeed; the probability, under present circumstances, seems to be, that it may at least pay its expenses—but even that remains to be proved, and till it is proved one way or another, we will say nothing about it. Thus then be it: I will postpone all arrangement about it, and the Giaour also, till Easter, 1814; and you shall then, according to your own notions of fairness, make your own offer for the two. At the same time, I do not rate the last in my own estimation at half the Giaour; and according to your own notions of its worth and its success within the time mentioned, be the addition or deduction to or from whatever sum may be your proposal for the first, which has already had its success.

" The pictures of Phillips I consider as *mine*, all three; and the one (not the Arnaout) of the two best is much at *your service,* if you will accept it as a present.

" P.S. The expense of engraving from the miniature send me in my account, as it was destroyed by my desire; and have the goodness to burn that detestable print from it immediately.

" To make you some amends for eternally pestering you with alterations, I send you Cobbett, to confirm your orthodoxy.

" One more alteration of *a* into *the* in the MS.; it must be—' The *heart whose softness,*' &c.

" Remember—and in the inscription ' to the Right Honourable Lord Holland,' *without* the previous names, Henry, &c."

TO MR. MURRAY.

" November 20, 1813.

" More work for the *Row.* I am doing my best to beat the 'Giaour' —*no* difficult task for any one but the author."

TO MR. MURRAY.

"November 22, 1813.

"I have no time to *cross*-investigate, but I believe and hope all is right. I care less than you will believe about its success, but I can't survive a single *misprint*: it *chokes* me to see words misused by the printers. Pray look over, in case of some eyesore escaping me.

"P.S. Send the earliest copies to Mr. Frere, Mr. Canning, Mr. Heber, Mr. Gifford, Lord Holland, Lord Melbourne (Whitehall), Lady Caroline Lamb (Brocket), Mr. Hodgson (Cambridge), Mr. Merivale, Mr. Ward, from the author."

TO MR. MURRAY.

"November 23, 1813.

"You wanted some reflections, and I send you *per Selim* (see his speech in Canto 2d, page 46), eighteen lines in decent couplets, of a pensive, if not an *ethical*, tendency. One more revise—positively the last, if decently done—at any rate the *pen*ultimate. Mr. Canning's approbation (*if* he did approve) I need not say makes me proud*. As to printing, print as you will and how you will—by itself, if you like; but let me have a few copies in *sheets*.

"November 24th, 1813.

"You must pardon me once more, as it is all for your good: it must be thus—

"He makes a solitude, and calls it peace.

'*Makes*' is closer to the passage of Tacitus, from which the line is taken, and is, besides, a stronger word than '*leaves*.'

"Mark where his carnage and his conquests cease,
    He makes a solitude, and calls it—peace."

---

* Mr. Canning's note was as follows:—"I received the books and, among them, the Bride of Abydos. It is very, very beautiful. Lord Byron (when I met him, one day, at dinner at Mr. Ward's) was so kind as to promise to give me a copy of it. I mention this, not to save my purchase, but because I should be really flattered by the present."

LETTER CXLVIII.

TO MR. MURRAY.

" November 27th, 1813.

" If you look over this carefully by the *last proof* with my corrections, it is probably right; this *you* can *do* as well or better;—I have not now time.　The copies I mentioned to be sent to different friends last night, I should wish to be made up with the new Giaours, if it also is ready.　If not, send the Giaour afterwards.

" The Morning Post says *I* am the author of Nourjahad!!　This comes of lending the drawings for their dresses; but it is not worth a *formal contradiction*.　Besides, the criticisms on the *supposition* will, some of them, be quite amusing and furious.　The *Orientalism*—which I hear is very splendid—of the melodrame (whosoever it is, and I am sure I don't know) is as good as an advertisement for your Eastern Stories, by filling their heads with glitter.

" P.S. You will of course *say* the truth, that I am *not* the melodramatist—if any one charges me in your presence with the performance."

LETTER CXLIX.

TO MR. MURRAY.

" November 28th, 1813.

" Send another copy (if not too much of a request) to Lady Holland of the *Journal**, in my name, when you receive this; it is for *Earl Grey* —and I will relinquish my *own*.　Also to Mr. Sharpe, and Lady Holland, and Lady Caroline Lamb, copies of ' The Bride,' as soon as convenient.

" P.S. Mr. Ward and myself still continue our purpose; but I shall not trouble you on any arrangement on the score of the Giaour and the Bride till our return—or, at any rate, before *May*, 1814—that is, six months from hence: and before that time you will be able to ascertain

---

* Penrose's Journal, a book published by Mr. Murray at this time.

how far your offer may be a losing one; if so, you can deduct proportionably; and if not, I shall not at any rate allow you to go higher than your present proposal, which is very handsome and more than fair*.

"I have had,—but this must be *entre nous*,—a very kind note, on the subject of 'the Bride,' from Sir James Mackintosh, and an invitation to go there this evening, which it is now too late to accept."

TO MR. MURRAY.

" November 29, 1813.
" Sunday—Monday morning—3 o'clock—in
my doublet and hose, *swearing*.

"I send you in time an errata page, containing an omission of mine, which must be thus added, as it is too late for insertion in the text. The passage is an imitation altogether from Medea in Ovid, and is incomplete without these two lines. Pray let this be done, and directly; it is necessary, will add one page to your book (*making*), and can do no harm, and is yet in time for the *public*. Answer me, thou oracle, in the affirmative. You can send the loose pages to those who have copies already, if they like; but certainly to all the *critical* copy-holders.

"P.S. I have got out of my bed (in which, however, I could not sleep, whether I had amended this or not), and so good morning. I am trying whether De L'Allemagne will act as an opiate, but I doubt it."

TO MR. MURRAY.

" November 29th, 1813.

" '*You have looked at it!*' to much purpose, to allow so stupid a blunder to stand; it is *not* '*courage*,' but '*carnage*;' and if you don't want me to cut my own throat, see it altered.

"I am very sorry to hear of the fall of Dresden."

---

* Mr. Murray had offered him a thousand guineas for the two Poems.

LETTER CL.

TO MR. MURRAY.

" Nov. 29th, 1813, Monday.

" You will act as you please upon that point; but whether I go or stay, I shall not say another word on the subject till May—nor then, unless quite convenient to yourself. I have many things I wish to leave to your care, principally papers. The *vases* need not be now sent, as Mr. Ward is gone to Scotland. You are right about the errata page; place it at the beginning. Mr. Perry is a little premature in his compliments: these may do harm by exciting expectation, and I think we ought to be above it—though I see the next paragraph is on the *Journal**, which makes me suspect *you* as the author of both.

" Would it not have been as well to have said ' in Two Cantos' in the advertisement? they will else think of *fragments*, a species of composition very well for *once*, like *one ruin* in a *view;* but one would not build a town of them. The Bride, such as it is, is my first *entire* composition of any length (except the Satire, and be d—d to it), for the Giaour is but a string of passages, and Childe Harold is, and I rather think always will be, unconcluded. I return Mr. Hay's note, with thanks to him and you.

" There have been some epigrams on Mr. Ward: one I see to-day. The first I did not see, but heard yesterday. The second seems very bad. I only hope that Mr. Ward does not believe that I had any connexion with either. I like and value him too well to allow my politics to contract into spleen, or to admire any thing intended to annoy him or his. You need not take the trouble to answer this, as I shall see you in the course of the afternoon.

" P.S. I have said this much about the epigrams, because I lived so much in the *opposite camp*, and, from my post as an engineer, might be suspected as the flinger of these hand-grenadoes; but with a worthy foe, I am all for open war, and not this bush-fighting, and have had, nor will have, any thing to do with it. I do not know the author."

* Penrose's Journal.

TO MR. MURRAY.

" Nov. 30th, 1813.

" Print this at the end of *all that is of the ' Bride of Abydos,'* as an errata page.

" BN.

" Omitted, canto 2d, page 47, after line 449,

" So that those arms cling closer round my neck.

Read,

" Then if my lip once murmur, it must be
No sigh for safety, but a prayer for thee."

TO MR. MURRAY.

" Tuesday evening, Nov. 30th, 1813.

" For the sake of correctness, particularly in an errata page, the alteration of the couplet I have just sent (half an hour ago) must take place, in spite of delay or cancel; let me see the *proof* early to-morrow. I found out *murmur* to be a neuter *verb*, and have been obliged to alter the line so as to make it a substantive, thus—

" The deepest murmur of this lip shall be
No sigh for safety, but a prayer for thee !

Don't send the copies to the *country* till this is all right."

TO MR. MURRAY.

" Dec. 2d, 1813.

" When you can, let the couplet enclosed be inserted either in the page, or in the errata page. I trust it is in time for some of the copies. This alteration is in the same part—the page *but one* before the last correction sent.

" P.S. I am afraid, from all I hear, that people are rather inordinate in their expectations, which is very unlucky, but cannot now be helped. This comes of Mr. Perry and one's wise friends; but do not *you* wind *your* hopes of success to the same pitch, for fear of accidents, and I can assure you that my philosophy will stand the test very fairly; and I have done every thing to ensure you, at all events, from positive loss, which will be some satisfaction to both."

TO MR. MURRAY.

" Dec. 3d, 1813.

" I send you a *scratch* or *two*, the which *heal*. The Christian Observer is very savage, but certainly well written—and quite uncomfortable at the naughtiness of book and author. I rather suspect you won't much like the *present* to be more moral, if it is to share also the usual fate of your virtuous volumes.

" Let me see a proof of the *six* before incorporation."

TO MR. MURRAY.

" Monday evening, Dec. 6th, 1813.

" It is all very well, except that the lines are not numbered properly, and a diabolical mistake, page 67, which *must* be corrected with the *pen*, if no other way remains; it is the omission of ' *not*' before ' *disagreeable*,' in the *note* on the *amber* rosary. This is really horrible, and nearly as bad as the stumble of mine at the threshold—I mean the *misnomer* of Bride. Pray do not let a copy go without the ' *not*;' it is nonsense and worse than nonsense as it now stands. I wish the printer was saddled with a vampire.

" P.S. It is still *hath* instead of *have* in page 20; never was any one so *misused* as I am by your devils of printers.

" P.S. I hope and trust the ' *not*' was inserted in the first edition. We must have something—any thing—to set it right. It is enough to answer for one's own bulls, without other people's."

LETTER CLI.

TO MR. MURRAY.

"December 27th, 1813.

"Lord Holland is laid up with the gout, and would feel very much obliged if you could obtain, and send as soon as possible, Madame D'Arblay's (or even Miss Edgeworth's) new work. I know they are not out; but it is perhaps possible for your *Majesty* to command what we cannot with much suing purchase, as yet. I need not say that when you are able or willing to confer the same favour on me, I shall be obliged. I would almost fall sick myself to get at Madame D'Arblay's writings.

"P.S. You were talking to-day of the American edition of a certain unquenchable memorial of my younger days. As it can't be helped now, I own I have some curiosity to see a copy of Transatlantic typography. This you will perhaps obtain, and one for yourself; but I must beg that you will not *import more*, because, *seriously*, I *do wish* to have that thing forgotten as much as it has been forgiven.

"If you send to the Globe editor, say that I want neither excuse nor contradiction, but merely a discontinuance of a most ill-grounded charge. I never was consistent in any thing but my politics; and as my redemption depends on that solitary virtue, it is murder to carry away my last anchor."

Of these hasty and characteristic missives with which he despatched off his "still-breeding thoughts," there yet remain a few more that might be presented to the reader; but enough has here been given to show the fastidiousness of his self-criticism, as well as the restless and unsatisfied ardour with which he pressed on in pursuit of perfection,—still seeing, according to the usual doom of genius, much farther than he could reach.

An appeal was, about this time, made to his generosity, which the reputation of the person from whom it proceeded would, in most minds, have justified him in treating with disregard, but which a more enlarged feeling of humanity led him to view in a very different light; for, when expostulated with by Mr. Murray on his generous intentions towards one " whom nobody else would give a single farthing to," he answered, " it is for that very reason *I* give it, because nobody else will." The person in question was Mr. Thomas Ashe, author of a certain notorious publication called " The Book," which, from the delicate mysteries discussed in its pages, attracted far more notice than its talent, or even mischief, deserved. In a fit, it is to be hoped, of sincere penitence, this man wrote to Lord Byron, alleging poverty as his excuse for the vile uses to which he had hitherto prostituted his pen, and soliciting his lordship's aid towards enabling him to exist, in future, more reputably. To this application the following answer, marked, in the highest degree, by good sense, humanity, and honourable sentiment, was returned by Lord Byron.

LETTER CLII.

TO MR. ASHE.

" 4, Bennet-street, St. James's, Dec. 14th, 1813.

" SIR,

" I leave town for a few days to-morrow: on my return, I will answer your letter more at length. Whatever may be your situation, I cannot but commend your resolution to abjure and abandon the publication and composition of works such as those to which you have alluded. Depend upon it, they amuse *few*, disgrace both *reader* and *writer*, and benefit *none*. It will be my wish to assist you, as far as my limited means will admit, to break such a bondage. In your answer, inform me what sum you think would enable you to extricate yourself from the hands of your employers, and to regain at least temporary independence, and I shall be glad to contribute my mite towards it. At present, I must conclude. Your name is not unknown to me, and I regret, for your own sake, that you have ever lent it to the works you mention. In saying this, I merely repeat your *own words* in your letter to me, and have no wish whatever to say a single syllable that may appear to insult your misfortunes. If I have, excuse me; it is unintentional.

" Yours, &c.

" BYRON."

In answer to this letter, Ashe mentioned, as the sum necessary to extricate him from his difficulties, £150—to be advanced at the rate of ten pounds per month; and, some short delay having occurred in the reply to this demand, the modest applicant, in renewing his suit, complained, it appears, of neglect: on which Lord Byron, with a good temper which few, in a similar case, could imitate, answered him as follows.

LETTER CLIII.

TO MR. ASHE.

" January 5th, 1814.

" SIR,

" When you accuse a stranger of neglect, you forget that it is possible business or absence from London may have interfered to delay his answer, as has actually occurred in the present instance. But to the point. I am willing to do what I can to extricate you from your situation. Your first scheme * I was considering; but your own impatience appears to have rendered it abortive, if not irretrievable. I will deposit in Mr. Murray's hands (with his consent) the sum you mentioned, to be advanced for the time at ten pounds per month.

" P.S. I write in the greatest hurry, which may make my letter a little abrupt; but, as I said before, I have no wish to distress your feelings."

The service thus humanely proffered was no less punctually performed; and the following is one of the many acknowledgments of payment which I find in Ashe's letters to Mr. Murray:—" I have the honour to enclose you another memorandum for the sum of ten pounds, in compliance with the munificent instructions of Lord Byron†."

---

* His first intention had been to go out, as a settler, to Botany Bay.

† When these monthly disbursements had amounted to £70, Ashe wrote to beg that the whole remaining sum of £80 might be advanced to him at one payment, in order to enable him, as he said, to avail himself of a passage to New South Wales, which had been again offered to him. The sum was, accordingly, by Lord Byron's orders, paid into his hands.

His friend, Mr. Merivale, one of the translators of those Selections from the Anthology which we have seen he regretted so much not having taken with him on his travels, published a Poem about this time, which he thus honours with his praise.

LETTER CLIV.

TO MR. MERIVALE.

"January, 1814.

" MY DEAR MERIVALE,

" I have redde Roncesvaux with very great pleasure, and (if I were so disposed) see very little room for criticism.   There is a choice of two lines in one of the last Cantos,—I think ' Live and protect' better, because ' Oh who?' implies a doubt of Roland's power or inclination.   I would allow the—but that point you yourself must determine on—I mean the doubt as to where to place a part of the Poem, whether between the actions or no.   Only if you wish to have all the success you deserve, *never listen to friends*, and—as I am not the least troublesome of the number—least of all, to me.

" I hope you will be out soon.   *March*, sir, *March* is the month for the *trade*, and they must be considered.   You have written a very noble Poem, and nothing but the detestable taste of the day can do you harm, —but I think you will beat it.   Your measure is uncommonly well chosen and wielded †."

*   *   *   *   *   *

In the extracts from his Journal, just given, there is a passage that cannot fail to have been remarked, where, in speaking of his admiration of some lady, whose name he has himself left blank, the noble writer says—" a wife would be the salvation of me."   It was under this conviction, which not only himself but some of his friends entertained, of the prudence of his taking timely refuge in matrimony from those perplexities

† This letter is but a fragment,—the remainder being lost.

which form the sequel of all less regular ties, that he had been induced about a year before, to turn his thoughts seriously to marriage,—at least as seriously as his thoughts were ever capable of being so turned,—and chiefly, I believe, by the advice and intervention of his friend Lady Melbourne, to become a suitor for the hand of a relative of that lady, Miss Milbanke. Though his proposal was not then accepted, every assurance of friendship and regard accompanied the refusal; a wish was ever expressed that they should continue to write to each other, and a correspondence,—somewhat singular between two young persons of different sexes, inasmuch as love was not the subject of it,—ensued between them. We have seen how highly Lord Byron estimated as well the virtues as the accomplishments of the young lady, but it is evident that on neither side, at this period, was love either felt or professed *.

In the mean time, new entanglements, in which his heart was the willing dupe of his fancy and vanity, came to engross the young poet; and still, as the usual penalties of such pursuits followed, he again found himself sighing for the sober yoke of wedlock, as some security against their recurrence. There were, indeed, in the interval between Miss Milbanke's refusal and acceptance of him, two or three other young women of rank who, at different times, formed the subject of his matrimonial dreams. In the society of one of these, whose family had long honoured me with their friendship, he and I passed much of our time, during this and the preceding spring; and it will be found that, in a subsequent part of his correspondence, he represents me as having entertained an anxious wish that he should so far cultivate my fair friend's favour as to give a chance, at least, of matrimony being the result.

That I, more than once, expressed some such feeling is undoubtedly true. Fully concurring with the opinion, not only of himself but of others of his friends, that in marriage lay his only chance of salvation from the sort of perplexing attachments into which he was now constantly tempted, I saw in none of those whom he admired with more

---

* The reader has already seen what Lord Byron himself says, in his Journal, on this subject:—" What an odd situation and friendship is ours!—without one spark of love on either side," &c. &c.

legitimate views so many requisites for the difficult task of winning him into fidelity and happiness as in the lady in question. Combining beauty of the highest order with a mind intelligent and ingenuous,—having just learning enough to give refinement to her taste, and far too much taste to make pretensions to learning,—with a patrician spirit proud as his own, but showing it only in a delicate generosity of spirit, a feminine high-mindedness, which would have led her to tolerate his defects in consideration of his noble qualities and his glory, and even to sacrifice silently some of her own happiness rather than violate the responsibility in which she stood pledged to the world for his;—such was, from long experience, my impression of the character of this lady; and perceiving Lord Byron to be attracted by her more obvious claims to admiration, I felt a pleasure no less in rendering justice to the still rarer qualities which she possessed, than in endeavouring to raise my noble friend's mind to the contemplation of a higher model of female character than he had, unluckily for himself, been much in the habit of studying.

To this extent do I confess myself to have been influenced by the sort of feeling which he attributes to me. But in taking for granted (as it will appear he did from one of his letters) that I entertained any very decided or definite wishes on the subject, he gave me more credit for seriousness in my suggestions than I deserved. If even the lady herself, the unconscious object of these speculations, by whom he was regarded in no other light than that of a distinguished acquaintance, could have consented to undertake the perilous,—but still possible and glorious,—achievement of attaching Byron to virtue, I own that, sanguinely as, in theory, I might have looked to the result, I should have seen, not without trembling, the happiness of one whom I had known and valued from her childhood risked in the experiment.

I shall now proceed to resume the thread of the Journal, which I had broken off, and of which, it will be perceived, the noble author himself had for some weeks, at this time, interrupted the progress.

" JOURNAL, 1814.

" February 18.

" Better than a month since I last journalized:—most of it out of London, and at Notts., but a busy one and a pleasant, at least three weeks of it.   On my return, I find all the newspapers in hysterics *, and town in an uproar, on the avowal and republication of two stanzas on Princess Charlotte's weeping at Regency's speech to Lauderdale in 1812.   They are daily at it still;—some of the abuse good, all of it hearty.   They talk of a motion in our House upon it—be it so.

" Got up—redde the Morning Post, containing the battle of Buonaparte, the destruction of the Custom-house, and a paragraph on me as long as my pedigree, and vituperative, as usual.   *   *   *

" Hobhouse is returned to England.   He is my best friend, the most lively, and a man of the most sterling talents extant.

" 'The Corsair' has been conceived, written, published, &c. since I last took up this Journal.   They tell me it has great success;—it was written *con amore*, and much from *existence*.   Murray is satisfied with its

---

* Immediately on the appearance of the Corsair (with those obnoxious verses, " Weep, daughter of a royal line," appended to it), a series of attacks, not confined to Lord Byron himself, but aimed also at all those who had lately become his friends, was commenced in the Courier and Morning Post, and carried on through the greater part of the months of February and March.   The point selected by these writers, as a ground of censure on the poet, was one which *now*, perhaps, even themselves would agree to class among his claims to praise,—namely, the atonement which he had endeavoured to make for the youthful violence of his Satire by a measure of justice, amiable even in its overflowings, to every one whom he conceived he had wronged.

Notwithstanding the careless tone in which, here and elsewhere, he speaks of these assaults, it is evident that they annoyed him;—an effect which, in reading them over now, we should be apt to wonder they could produce, did we not recollect the property which Dryden attributes to " small wits," in common with certain other small animals:—

" We scarce could know they live, but that they *bite*."

The following is a specimen of the terms in which these party scribes could then speak of one of the masters of English song:—" They might have slept in oblivion with Lord Carlisle's Dramas and Lord Byron's Poems."—" Some certainly extol Lord Byron's Poems much, but most of the best judges place his lordship rather low in the list of our minor poets."

progress; and if the public are equally so with the perusal, there's an end of the matter.

" Nine o'clock.

" Been to Hanson's on business. Saw Rogers, and had a note from Lady Melbourne, who says, it is said that I am 'much out of spirits.' I wonder if I really am or not? I have certainly enough of 'that perilous stuff which weighs upon the heart,' and it is better they should believe it to be the result of these attacks than of the real cause; but— ay, ay, always *but*, to the end of the chapter.   *   *   *   *

" Hobhouse has told me ten thousand anecdotes of Napoleon, all good and true. My friend H. is the most entertaining of companions, and a fine fellow to boot.

" Redde a little—wrote notes and letters, and am alone, which, Locke says, is bad company. 'Be not solitary, be not idle'—Um!—the idleness is troublesome; but I can't see so much to regret in the solitude. The more I see of men, the less I like them. If I could but say so of women too, all would be well. Why can't I? I am now six-and-twenty; my passions have had enough to cool them; my affections more than enough to wither them,—and yet—and yet—always *yet* and *but*—' Excellent well, you are a fishmonger—get thee to a nunnery.' 'They fool me to the top of my bent.'

" Midnight.

" Began a letter, which I threw into the fire. Redde—but to little purpose. Did not visit Hobhouse, as I promised and ought. No matter, the loss is mine. Smoked cigars.

" Napoleon!—this week will decide his fate. All seems against him; but I believe and hope he will win—at least, beat back the Invaders. What right have we to prescribe sovereigns to France? Oh for a Republic! 'Brutus, thou sleepest.' Hobhouse abounds in continental anecdotes of this extraordinary man; all in favour of his intellect and courage, but against his *bonhommie*. No wonder;—how should he, who knows mankind well, do other than despise and abhor them.

3 s 2

" The greater the equality, the more impartially evil is distributed and becomes lighter by the division among so many—therefore, a Republic!

" More notes from Mad. de * * unanswered—and so they shall remain. I admire her abilities, but really her society is overwhelming —an avalanche that buries one in glittering nonsense—all snow and sophistry.

" Shall I go to Mackintosh's on Tuesday? um!—I did not go to Marquis Lansdowne's, nor to Miss Berry's, though both are pleasant. So is Sir James's,—but I don't know—I believe one is not the better for parties; at least, unless some *regnante* is there.

" I wonder how the deuce any body could make such a world; for what purpose dandies, for instance, were ordained—and kings—and fellows of colleges—and women of ' a certain age'—and many men of any age—and myself, most of all!

> ' Divesne prisco et natus ab Inacho,
>   Nil interest, an pauper, et infimâ
>   De gente, sub dio moreris,
>   Victima nil miserantis Orci.
>   *   *   *   *
>   Omnes eodem cogimur.'

" Is there any thing beyond?—*who* knows? *He* that can't tell. Who tells that there *is*? He who don't know. And when shall he know? perhaps, when he don't expect, and, generally, when he don't wish it. In this last respect, however, all are not alike: it depends a good deal upon education,—something upon nerves and habits—but most upon digestion.

" Saturday, Feb. 19th.

" Just returned from seeing Kean in Richard. By Jove, he is a soul! Life—nature—truth—without exaggeration or diminution. Kemble's Hamlet is perfect;—but Hamlet is not Nature. Richard is a man; and Kean is Richard. Now to my own concerns.

*　*　*　*　*　*

" Went to Waite's. Teeth all right and white; but he says that
I grind them in my sleep and chip the edges. That same sleep is no
friend of mine, though I court him sometimes for half the 24.

" February 20th.

" Got up and tore out two leaves of this Journal—I don't know why.
Hodgson just called and gone. He has much *bonhommie* with his other
good qualities, and more talent than he has yet had credit for beyond
his circle.

" An invitation to dine at Holland-house to meet Kean. He is
worth meeting; and I hope, by getting into good society, he will be
prevented from falling like Cooke. He is greater now on the stage, and
off he should never be less. There is a stupid and under-rating criticism
upon him in one of the newspapers. I thought that, last night, though
great, he rather under-acted more than the first time. This may be the
effect of these cavils; but I hope he has more sense than to mind them.
He cannot expect to maintain his present eminence, or to advance still
higher, without the envy of his green-room fellows, and the nibbling of
their admirers. But, if he don't beat them all, why, then—merit hath
no purchase in ' these coster-monger days.'

" I wish that I had a talent for the drama; I would write a tragedy
now. But no,—it is gone. Hodgson talks of one,—he will do it well;—
and I think M—e should try. He has wonderful powers, and much
variety; besides, he has lived and felt. To write so as to bring home to
the heart, the heart must have been tried,—but, perhaps, ceased to be so.
While you are under the influence of passions, you only feel, but cannot
describe them,—any more than, when in action, you could turn round
and tell the story to your next neighbour! When all is over,—all, all,
and irrevocable,—trust to memory—she is then but too faithful.

" Went out, and answered some letters, yawned now and then, and
redde the Robbers. Fine,—but Fiesco is better; and Alfieri and Monti's
Aristodemo *best*. They are more equal than the Tedeschi dramatists.

" Answered—or, rather, acknowledged—the receipt of young Reynolds's Poem, Safie. The lad is clever, but much of his thoughts are

borrowed,—*whence*, the Reviewers may find out. I hate discouraging a young one; and I think,—though wild, and more oriental than he would be, had he seen the scenes where he has placed his tale,—that he has much talent, and, certainly, fire enough.

" Received a very singular epistle; and the mode of its conveyance, through Lord H.'s hands, as curious as the letter itself. But it was gratifying and pretty.

" Sunday, Feb. 27th.

" Here I am, alone, instead of dining at Lord H.'s, where I was asked,—but not inclined to go any where. Hobhouse says I am growing a *loup garou*,—a solitary hobgoblin. True;—' I am myself alone.' The last week has been passed in reading—seeing plays—now and then, visitors—sometimes yawning and sometimes sighing, but no writing,— save of letters. If I could always read, I should never feel the want of society. Do I regret it?—um!—' Man delights not me,' and only one woman—at a time.

" There is something to me very softening in the presence of a woman,—some strange influence, even if one is not in love with them, —which I cannot at all account for, having no very high opinion of the sex. But yet,—I always feel in better humour with myself and every thing else, if there is a woman within ken. Even Mrs. Mule *, my fire-lighter,—the most ancient and withered of her kind,—and (except

---

* This ancient housemaid, of whose gaunt and witch-like appearance it would be impossible to convey any idea but by the pencil, furnished one among the numerous instances of Lord Byron's proneness to attach himself to any thing, however homely, that had once inlisted his good-nature in its behalf, and become associated with his thoughts. He first found this old woman at his lodgings in Bennet-street, where, for a whole season, she was the perpetual scare-crow of his visitors. When, next year, he took chambers in Albany, one of the great advantages which his friends looked to in the change was, that they should get rid of this phantom. But, no,—there she was again—he had actually brought her with him from Bennet-street. The following year saw him married, and, with a regular establishment of servants, in Piccadilly; and here,—as Mrs. Mule had not appeared to any of the visitors,—it was concluded, rashly, that the witch had vanished. One of those friends, however, who had most fondly indulged in this persuasion, happening to call one day when all the male part of the establishment were abroad, saw, to his dismay, the door opened by the same grim personage, improved considerably in point of habiliments since he last saw her, and keeping pace with the increased scale of her master's

to myself) not the best-tempered—always makes me laugh,—no difficult task when I am 'i' the vein.'

"Heigho! I would I were in mine island!—I am not well; and yet I look in good health. At times, I fear, 'I am not in my perfect mind;' —and yet my heart and head have stood many a crash, and what should ail them now? They prey upon themselves, and I am sick—sick— 'Prithee, undo this button—why should a cat, a rat, a dog, have life— and *thou* no life at all?' Six-and-twenty years, as they call them,—why, I might and should have been a Pasha by this time. 'I 'gin to be a weary of the sun.'

"Buonaparte is not yet beaten; but has rebutted Blucher, and repiqued Swartzenburg. This it is to have a head. If he again wins, 'Væ victis!'

> "Sunday, March 6th.

"On Tuesday last dined with Rogers,—Madᵉ. de Staël, Mackintosh, Sheridan, Erskine, and Payne Knight, Lady Donegall and Miss R. there. Sheridan told a very good story of himself and Mᵉ. de Recamier's handkerchief; Erskine a few stories of himself only. *She* is going to write a big book about England, she says;—I believe her. Asked by her how I liked Miss * *'s thing, called * *, and answered (very sincerely) that I thought it very bad for *her*, and worse than any of the others. Afterwards thought it possible Lady Donegall, being Irish, might be a Patroness of * *, and was rather sorry for my opinion, as I hate putting people into fusses, either with themselves, or their favourites; it looks as if one did it on purpose. The party went off very well, and the fish was very much to my gusto. But we got up too soon after the women; and Mrs. Corinne always lingers so long after dinner, that we wish her in— the drawing-room.

"To-day C. called, and, while sitting here, in came Merivale. During our colloquy, C. (ignorant that M. was the writer) abused the

household, as a new peruke, and other symptoms of promotion, testified. When asked "how he came to carry this old woman about with him from place to place," Lord Byron's only answer was, "the poor old devil was so kind to me."

' mawkishness of the Quarterly Review of Grimm's Correspondence.
I (knowing the secret) changed the conversation as soon as I could; and
C. went away, quite convinced of having made the most favourable
impression on his new acquaintance.   Merivale is luckily a very good-
natured fellow, or, God he knows what might have been engendered
from such a malaprop.   I did not look at him while this was going on,
but I felt like a coal,—for I like Merivale, as well as the article in
question.   *   *   *   *   *   *   *

"Asked to Lady Keith's to-morrow evening—I think I will go;
but it is the first party invitation I have accepted this ' season,' as the
learned Fletcher called it, when that youngest brat of Lady * *'s cut my
eye and cheek open with a misdirected pebble—' Never mind, my lord,
the scar will be gone before the *season;*' as if one's eye was of no
importance in the mean time.

"Lord Erskine called, and gave me his famous pamphlet, with a
marginal note and corrections in his handwriting.   Sent it to be bound
superbly, and shall treasure it.

"Sent my fine print of Napoleon to be framed.   It *is* framed; and
the emperor becomes his robes as if he had been hatched in them.

" March 7th.

"Rose at seven—ready by half past eight—went to Mr. Hanson's,
Berkeley-square—went to church with his eldest daughter, Mary Anne
(a good girl), and gave her away to the Earl of Portsmouth.   Saw her
fairly a countess—congratulated the family and groom (bride)—drank a
bumper of wine (wholesome sherris) to their felicity, and all that,—and
came home.   Asked to stay to dinner, but could not.   At three sat to
Phillips for faces.   Called on Lady M.—I like her so well, that I always
stay too long.   (Mem. to mend of that.)

"Passed the evening with Hobhouse, who has begun a Poem, which
promises highly;—wish he would go on with it.   Heard some curious
extracts from a life of Morosini, the blundering Venetian, who blew up
the Acropolis at Athens with a bomb, and be d—d to him!   Waxed
sleepy—just come home—must go to bed, and am engaged to meet
Sheridan to-morrow at Rogers's.

" Queer ceremony that same of marriage—saw many abroad, Greek and Catholic—one, at *home*, many years ago. There be some strange phrases in the prologue (the exhortation), which made me turn away, not to laugh in the face of the surpliceman. Made one blunder, when I joined the hands of the happy—rammed their left hands, by mistake, into one another. Corrected it—bustled back to the altar-rail, and said ' Amen.' Portsmouth responded as if he had got the whole by heart; and, if any thing, was rather before the priest. It is now midnight, and
*   *   *   *   *   *   *   *.

" March 10th, Thor's Day.

" On Tuesday dined with Rogers,—Mackintosh, Sheridan, Sharpe, —much talk, and good,—all, except my own little prattlement. Much of old times—Horne Tooke—the Trials—evidence of Sheridan, and anecdotes of those times, when *I*, alas! was an infant. If I had been a man, I would have made an English Lord Edward Fitzgerald.

" Set down Sheridan at Brookes's,—where, by the by, he could not have well set down himself, as he and I were the only drinkers. Sherry means to stand for Westminster, as Cochrane (the stock-jobbing hoaxer) must vacate. Brougham is a candidate. I fear for poor dear Sherry. Both have talents of the highest order, but the youngster has *yet* a character. We shall see, if he lives to Sherry's age, how he will pass over the red-hot ploughshares of public life. I don't know why, but I hate to see the *old* ones lose; particularly Sheridan, notwithstanding all his *méchanceté*.

" Received many, and the kindest, thanks from Lady Portsmouth, *père* and *mère*, for my match-making. I don't regret it, as she looks the countess well, and is a very good girl. It is odd how well she carries her new honours. She looks a different woman, and high-bred, too. I had no idea that I could make so good a peeress.

" Went to the play with Hobhouse. Mrs. Jordan superlative in Hoyden, and Jones well enough in Foppington. *What plays!* what wit!—helas! Congreve and Vanbrugh are your only comedy. Our society is too insipid now for the like copy. Would *not* go to Lady Keith's. Hobhouse thought it odd. I wonder *he* should like parties. If one is in love, and wants to break a commandment and covet any thing that is there, they do very well. But to go out amongst the mere herd, without a motive, pleasure, or pursuit—'sdeath! 'I'll none of it.' He told me an odd report,—that *I* am the actual Conrad, the veritable Corsair, and that part of my travels are supposed to have passed in privacy. Um!—people sometimes hit near the truth; but never the whole truth. H. don't know what I was about the year after he left the Levant; nor does any one—nor—nor—nor—however, it is a lie— but, 'I doubt the equivocation of the fiend that lies like truth!'

"I shall have letters of importance to-morrow. Which, * *, * *, or * *? heigho!—* * is in my heart, * * in my head, * * in my eye, and the *single* one, Heaven knows where. All write, and will be answered. 'Since I have crept in favour with myself, I must maintain it;' but *I* never 'mistook my person,' though I think others have.

"* * called to-day in great despair about his mistress, who has taken a freak of * * *. He began a letter to her, but was obliged to stop short —I finished it for him, and he copied and sent it. If *he* holds out and keeps to my instructions of affected indifference, she will lower her colours. If she don't, he will, at least, get rid of her, and she don't seem much worth keeping. But the poor lad is in love—if that is the case, she will win. When they once discover their power, *finita è la musica.*

"Sleepy, and must go to bed.

"Tuesday, March 15th.

"Dined yesterday with R., Mackintosh, and Sharpe. Sheridan could not come. Sharpe told several very amusing anecdotes of Henderson, the actor. Staid till late, and came home, having drank so much *tea*, that I did not get to sleep till six this morning. R. says I am to be in *this* Quarterly—cut up, I presume, as they 'hate us youth.' *N'importe.* As Sharpe was passing by the doors of some Debating Society (the Westminster Forum) in his way to dinner, he saw rubricked on the walls, *Scott's* name and *mine*—'Which the best poet?' being the question of the evening; and I suppose all the Templars and *would bes* took our rhymes in vain, in the course of the controversy. Which had the greater show of hands, I neither know nor care; but I feel the coupling of the names as a compliment,—though I think Scott deserves better company.

*   *   *   *   *

" W. W. called—Lord Erskine, Lord Holland, &c. &c. Wrote to * * the Corsair report. She says she don't wonder, since 'Conrad is so *like*.' It is odd that one, who knows me so thoroughly, should tell me this to my face. However, if she don't know, nobody can.

" Mackintosh is, it seems, the writer of the defensive letter in the Morning Chronicle. If so, it is very kind, and more than I did for myself.

*   *   *   *   *

" Told Murray to secure for me Bandello's Italian Novels at the sale to-morrow. To me they will be *nuts*. Redde a satire on myself, called ' Anti-Byron,' and told Murray to publish it if he liked. The object of the author is to prove me an Atheist and a systematic conspirator against law and government. Some of the verse is good; the prose I don't quite understand. He asserts that my ' deleterious works' have had ' an effect upon civil society, which requires, &c. &c. &c.' and his own poetry. It is a lengthy poem, and a long preface, with a harmonious title-page. Like the fly in the fable, I seem to have got upon a wheel which makes much dust; but, unlike the said fly, I do not take it all for my own raising.

" A letter from *Bella*, which I answered. I shall be in love with her again, if I don't take care.

*   *   *   *   *

" I shall begin a more regular system of reading soon.

" Thursday, March 17th.

" I have been sparring with Jackson for exercise this morning; and mean to continue and renew my acquaintance with the muffles. My chest, and arms, and wind are in very good plight, and I am not in flesh. I used to be a hard hitter, and my arms are very long for my height (5 feet 8½ inches). At any rate, exercise is good, and this the severest of all; fencing and the broad-sword never fatigued me half so much.

" Redde the ' Quarrels of Authors' (another sort of *sparring*)—a

new work, by that most entertaining and researching writer, Israeli
They seem to be an irritable set, and I wish myself well out of it
'I'll not march through Coventry with them, that's flat.' What th
devil had I to do with scribbling? It is too late to inquire, and al
regret is useless. But, an' it were to do again,—I should write again,
suppose. Such is human nature, at least my share of it;—though I shal
think better of myself, if I have sense to stop now. If I have a wife
and that wife has a son—by any body—I will bring up mine heir in th
most anti-poetical way—make him a lawyer, or a pirate, or—any thing
But if he writes too, I shall be sure he is none of mine, and cut him of
with a Bank token. Must write a letter—three o'clock.

> " Sunday, March 20th.

"I intended to go to Lady Hardwicke's, but won't. I always begin
the day with a bias towards going to parties; but, as the evening
advances, my stimulus fails, and I hardly ever go out—and, when I do,
always regret it. This might have been a pleasant one;—at least the
hostess is a very superior woman. Lady Lansdowne's to-morrow— Lady
Heathcote's, Wednesday. Um!—I must spur myself into going to some
of them, or it will look like rudeness, and it is better to do as other
people do—confound them!

"Redde Machiavel, parts of Chardin, and Sismondi, and Bandello,
—by starts. Redde the Edinburgh, 44, just come out. In the beginning
of the article on 'Edgeworth's Patronage,' I have gotten a high compliment, I perceive. Whether this is creditable to me, I know not; but
it does honour to the editor, because he once abused me. Many a man
will retract praise; none but a high-spirited mind will revoke its censure,
or *can* praise the man it has once attacked. I have often, since my
return to England, heard Jeffrey most highly commended by those who
know him for things independent of his talents. I admire him for *this*
—not because he has *praised me* (I have been so praised elsewhere and
abused, alternately, that mere habit has rendered me as indifferent to
both as a man at twenty-six can be to any thing), but because he is,
perhaps, the *only man* who, under the relations in which he and I stand,
or stood, with regard to each other, would have had the liberality to act

thus; none but a great soul dared hazard it. The height on which he stands has not made him giddy;—a little scribbler would have gone on cavilling to the end of the chapter. As to the justice of his panegyric, that is matter of taste. There are plenty to question it, and glad, too, of the opportunity.

"Lord Erskine called to-day. He means to carry down his reflections on the war—or rather wars—to the present day. I trust that he will. Must send to Mr. Murray to get the binding of my copy of his pamphlet finished, as Lord E. has promised me to correct it, and add some marginal notes to it. Any thing in his handwriting will be a treasure, which will gather compound interest from years. Erskine has high expectations of Mackintosh's promised History. Undoubtedly it must be a classic, when finished.

"Sparred with Jackson again yesterday morning, and shall to-morrow. I feel all the better for it, in spirits, though my arms and shoulders are very stiff from it. Mem. to attend the pugilistic dinner—Marquis Huntley is in the chair.

*　　　*　　　*　　　*　　　*

"Lord Erskine thinks that ministers must be in peril of going out. So much the better for him. To me it is the same who are in or out;—we want something more than a change of ministers, and some day we will have it.

"I remember *, in riding from Chrisso to Castri (Delphos) along the sides of Parnassus, I saw six eagles in the air. It is uncommon to see so many together; and it was the number—not the species, which is common enough—that excited my attention.

"The last bird I ever fired at was an *eaglet*, on the shore of the Gulf of Lepanto, near Vostitza. It was only wounded, and I tried to save it, the eye was so bright; but it pined, and died in a few days; and I never did since, and never will, attempt the death of another bird. I wonder what put these two things into my head just now? I have been reading Sismondi, and there is nothing there that could induce the recollection.

"I am mightily taken with Braccio di Montone, Giovanni Galeazzo,

---

* Part of this passage has been already extracted, but I have allowed it to remain here in its original position, on account of the singularly sudden manner in which it is introduced.

and Eccelino. But the last is *not* Bracciaferro (of the same name), Count of Ravenna, whose history I want to trace. There is a fine engraving in Lavater, from a picture by Fuseli, of *that* Ezzelin, over the body of Meduna, punished by him for a *hitch* in her constancy during his absence in the Crusades. He was right—but I want to know the story.

*   *   *   *   *

" Tuesday, March 22d.

" Last night, *party* at Lansdowne-house. To-night, *party* at Lady Charlotte Greville's—deplorable waste of time, and something of temper. Nothing imparted—nothing acquired—talking without ideas—if any thing like *thought* in my mind, it was not on the subjects on which we were gabbling. Heigho!—and in this way half London pass what is called life. To-morrow there is Lady Heathcote's—shall I go? yes—to punish myself for not having a pursuit.

" Let me see—what did I see? The only person who much struck me was Lady S** d's eldest daughter, Lady C. L. They say she is *not* pretty. I don't know—every thing is pretty that pleases; but there is an air of *soul* about her—and her colour changes—and there is that shyness of the antelope (which I delight in) in her manner so much, that I observed her more than I did any other woman in the rooms, and only looked at any thing else when I thought she might perceive and feel embarrassed by my scrutiny. After all, there may be something of association in this. She is a friend of Augusta's, and whatever she loves, I can't help liking.

" Her mother, the marchioness, talked to me a little; and I was twenty times on the point of asking her to introduce me to *sa fille*, but I stopped short. This comes of that affray with the Carlisles.

" Earl Grey told me, laughingly, of a paragraph in the last *Moniteur*, which has stated, among other symptoms of rebellion, some particulars of the *sensation* occasioned in all our government gazettes by the ' tear' lines,—*only* amplifying, in its re-statement, an epigram (by the by, no epigram except in the *Greek* acceptation of the word) into a *roman*. I wonder the Couriers, &c.&c. have not translated that part of the Moniteur, with additional comments.

" The Princess of Wales has requested Fuseli to paint from ' the Corsair,'—leaving to him the choice of any passage for the subject: so Mr. Locke tells me. Tired—jaded—selfish and supine—must go to bed.

" *Roman*, at least *Romance*, means a song sometimes, as in the Spanish. I suppose this is the Moniteur's meaning—unless he has confused it with ' the Corsair.'

" Albany, March 28.

" This night got into my new apartments, rented of Lord Althorpe, on a lease of seven years. Spacious, and room for my books and sabres. *In* the *house*, too, another advantage. The last few days, or whole week, have been very abstemious, regular in exercise, and yet very *un*well.

" Yesterday, dined *tête-à-tête* at the Cocoa with Scrope Davies— sate from six till midnight—drank between us one bottle of champagne and six of claret, neither of which wines ever affect me. Offered to take Scrope home in my carriage; but he was tipsy and pious, and I was obliged to leave him on his knees, praying to I know not what purpose or pagod. No headache, nor sickness, that night nor to-day. Got up, if any thing, earlier than usual—sparred with Jackson *ad sudorem*, and have been much better in health than for many days. I have heard nothing more from Scrope. Yesterday paid him four thousand eight hundred pounds, a debt of some standing, and which I wished to have paid before. My mind is much relieved by the removal of that *debit*.

" Augusta wants me to make it up with Carlisle. I have refused *every* body else, but I can't deny her any thing;—so I must e'en do it, though I had as lief ' drink up Eisel—eat a crocodile.' Let me see— Ward, the Hollands, the Lambs, Rogers, &c. &c.—every body, more or less, have been trying for the last two years to accommodate this *couplet* quarrel to no purpose. I shall laugh if Augusta succeeds.

" Redde a little of many things—shall get in all my books to-morrow. Luckily this room will hold them—with ' ample room and verge, &c. the characters of hell to trace.' I must set about some employment soon; my heart begins to eat *itself* again.

" Out of town six days. On my return, find my poor little pagod
Napoleon, pushed off his pedestal;—the thieves are in Paris. It is his
own fault. Like Milo, he would rend the oak*; but it closed again,
wedged his hands, and now the beasts—lion, bear, down to the dirtiest
jackall—may all tear him. That Muscovite winter *wedged* his arms;—
ever since, he has fought with his feet and teeth. The last may still leave
their marks; and ' I guess now' (as the Yankies say) that he will yet
play them a pass. He is in their rear—between them and their homes.
Query—will they ever reach them ?

" I mark this day!

" Napoleon Buonaparte has abdicated the throne of the world.
' Excellent well.' Methinks Sylla did better; for he revenged, and
resigned in the height of his sway, red with the slaughter of his foes—
the finest instance of glorious contempt of the rascals upon record.
Dioclesian did well too—Amurath not amiss, had he become aught
except a dervise—Charles the Fifth but so, so—but Napoleon, worst of
all. What! wait till they were in his capital, and then talk of his
readiness to give up what is already gone!! ' What whining monk art
thou—what holy cheat?' 'Sdeath !—Dionysius at Corinth was yet a king
to this. The ' Isle of Elba' to retire to!—Well—if it had been Caprea,
I should have marvelled less. ' I see men's minds are but a parcel of
their fortunes.' I am utterly bewildered and confounded.

" I don't know—but I think *I*, even *I* (an insect compared with this
creature), have set my life on casts not a millionth part of this man's.
But, after all, a crown may be not worth dying for. Yet, to outlive
Lodi for this!!! Oh that Juvenal or Johnson could rise from the dead !
' Expende—quot libras in duce summo invenies?' I knew they were
light in the balance of mortality; but I thought their living dust weighed
more *carats*. Alas! this imperial diamond hath a flaw in it, and is now

---

* He adopted this thought afterwards in his Ode to Napoleon, as well as most of the
historical examples in the following paragraph.

hardly fit to stick in a glazier's pencil:—the pen of the historian won't rate it worth a ducat.

" Psha! ' something too much of this.' But I won't give him up even now; though all his admirers have, ' like the Thanes, fall'n from him.'

" April 10th.

" I do not know that I am happiest when alone; but this I am sure of, that I never am long in the society even of *her* I love (God knows too well, and the Devil probably too), without a yearning for the company of my lamp and my utterly confused and tumbled-over library*. Even in the day, I send away my carriage oftener than I use or abuse it. *Per esempio,*—I have not stirred out of these rooms for these four days past: but I have sparred for exercise (windows open) with Jackson an hour daily, to attenuate and keep up the ethereal part of me. The more violent the fatigue, the better my spirits for the rest of the day; and then, my evenings have that calm nothingness of languor, which I most delight in. To-day I have boxed one hour—written an ode to Napoleon Buonaparte —copied it—eaten six biscuits—drunk four bottles of soda water—redde away the rest of my time—besides giving poor * * a world of advice about this mistress of his who is plaguing him into a phthisic and intolerable tediousness. I am a pretty fellow truly to lecture about ' the sect.' No matter, my counsels are all thrown away.

" April 19th, 1814.

" There is ice at both poles, north and south—all extremes are the same—misery belongs to the highest and the lowest only,—to the emperor and the beggar, when unsixpenced and unthroned. There is, to be sure, a damned insipid medium—an equinoctial line—no one knows where, except upon maps and measurement.

　　' And all our *yesterdays* have lighted fools
　　　The way to dusty death.'

---

　* " As much company," says Pope, " as I have kept, and as much as I love it, I love reading better, and would rather be employed in reading than in the most agreeable conversation."

I will keep no further journal of that same hesternal torch-light; and, to prevent me from returning, like a dog, to the vomit of memory, I tear out the remaining leaves of this volume, and write, in *Ipecacuanha*,— ' that the Bourbons are restored!!!' 'Hang up philosophy.' To be sure, I have long despised myself and man, but I never spat in the face of my species before—' O fool! I shall go mad.' "

The perusal of this singular Journal having made the reader acquainted with the chief occurrences that marked the present period of his history—the publication of the Corsair, the attacks upon him in the newspapers, &c.—there only remains for me to add his correspondence at the same period, by which the moods and movements of his mind, during these events, will be still further illustrated.

TO MR. MURRAY.

" Sunday, Jan. 2, 1814.

" Excuse this dirty paper—it is the *pen*ultimate half-sheet of a quire. Thanks for your book and the Ln. Chron. which I return. The Corsair is copied, and now at Lord Holland's; but I wish Mr. Gifford to have it to-night.

" Mr. Dallas is very *perverse;* so that I have offended both him and you, when I really meant to do good, at least to one, and certainly not to annoy either*. But I shall manage him, I hope.—I am pretty con-

---

* He had made a present of the copyright of " The Corsair" to Mr. Dallas, who thus describes the manner in which the gift was bestowed:—" On the 28th of December, I called in the morning on Lord Byron, whom I found composing ' The Corsair.' He had been working upon it but a few days, and he read me the portion he had written. After some observations, he said, ' I have a great mind—I will.' He then added that he should finish it soon, and asked me to accept of the copyright. I was much surprised. He had, before he was aware of the value of his works, declared that he never would take money for them, and that I should have the whole advantage of all he wrote. This declaration became morally void when the question was about thousands, instead of a few hundreds; and I perfectly agree with the admired and admirable Author of Waverley, that ' the wise and good accept not gifts which are made in heat of blood, and which may be after repented of.'—I felt this on the sale of ' Childe Harold,' and observed it to him. The copyright of ' The Giaour' and ' The Bride of Abydos' remained undisposed of, though the poems were selling rapidly, nor had I the slightest notion that he

fident of the *Tale* itself; but one cannot be sure. If I get it from Lord Holland, it shall be sent. Yours, &c."

TO MR. MURRAY.

"[Jan. 1814.]

"I will answer your letter this evening: in the mean time, it may be sufficient to say, that there was no intention on my part to annoy you, but merely to *serve* Dallas, and also to rescue myself from a possible imputation that *I* had other objects than fame in writing so frequently. Whenever I avail myself of any profit arising from my pen, depend upon it, it is not for my own convenience; at least it never has been so, and I hope never will.

"P.S. I shall answer this evening, and will set all right about Dallas. I thank you for your expressions of personal regard, which I can assure you I do not lightly value."

LETTER CLV.

TO MR. MOORE.

"January 6, 1814.

"I have got a devil of a long story in the press, entitled 'The Corsair,' in the regular heroic measure. It is a pirate's isle, peopled with my own creatures, and you may easily suppose they do a world of mischief through the three Cantos. Now for your Dedication—if you will accept it. This is positively my last experiment on public *literary* opinion, till I turn my thirtieth year,—if so be I flourish until that downhill period. I have a confidence for you—a perplexing one to me,

would ever again give me a copyright. But as he continued in the resolution of not appropriating the sale of his works to his own use, I did not scruple to accept that of 'The Corsair,' and I thanked him. He asked me to call and hear the portions read as he wrote them. I went every morning, and was astonished at the rapidity of his composition. He gave me the Poem complete on new-year's day, 1814, saying, that my acceptance of it gave him great pleasure, and that I was fully at liberty to publish it with any bookseller I pleased, independent of the profit."

Out of this last-mentioned permission arose the momentary embarrassment between the noble poet and his publisher, to which the above notes allude.

and, just at present, in a state of abeyance in itself.   *   *   *
*   *   *   *   *   *   *   *   *   *   *   *
However, we shall see.   In the mean time, you may amuse yourself wit
my suspense, and put all the justices of peace in requisition, in case
come into your county with   hack but bent.'

"Seriously, whether I am to hear from her or him, it is a *paus*
which I shall fill up with as few thoughts of my own as I can borrow
from other people.   Any thing is better than stagnation; and now, i
the interregnum of my autumn and a strange summer adventure, whicl
I don't like to think of (I don't mean * *'s, however, which is laughabl
only), the antithetical state of my lucubrations makes me alive, and
Macbeth can 'sleep no more:'—he was lucky in getting rid of the drows
sensation of waking again.

"Pray write to me.   I must send you a copy of the letter o
Dedication.   When do you come out?   I am sure we don't *clash* thi
time, for I am all at sea, and in action,—and a wife, and a mistress, &c. &c

"Thomas, thou art a happy fellow; but if you wish us to be so, you
must come up to town, as you did last year; and we shall have a worl
to say, and to see, and to hear.   Let me hear from you.

"P.S. Of course you will keep my secret, and don't even talk in
your sleep of it.   Happen what may, your Dedication is ensured, being
already written; and I shall copy it out fair to-night, in case business
or amusement—*Amant alterna Camœnæ.*"

TO MR. MURRAY.

"Jan. 7, 1814.

"You don't like the Dedication—very well; there is another: but
you will send the other to Mr. Moore, that he may know I *had* written
it.   I send also mottos for the Cantos.   I think you will allow that an
elephant may be more sagacious, but cannot be more docile.

"Yours,

"Bn.

"The *name* is again altered to *Medora**."

* It had been at first Genevra,—not Francesca, as Mr. Dallas asserts.

LETTER CLVI.

TO MR. MOORE.

" January 8th, 1814.

" As it would not be fair to press you into a Dedication, without previous notice, I send you *two*, and I will tell you *why two*. The first, Mr. M., who sometimes takes upon him the critic (and I bear it from *astonishment*), says, may do you *harm*—God forbid!—this alone makes me listen to him. The fact is, he is a damned Tory, and has, I dare swear, something of *self*, which I cannot divine, at the bottom of his objection, as it is the allusion to Ireland to which he objects. But he be d—d— though a good fellow enough (your sinner would not be worth a d—n).

" Take your choice;—no one, save he and Mr. Dallas, has seen either, and D. is quite on my side, and for the first*. If I can but testify to you and the world how truly I admire and esteem you, I shall be quite satisfied. As to *prose*, I don't know Addison's from Johnson's; but I will try to mend my cacology. Pray perpend, pronounce, and don't be offended with either.

" My last epistle would probably put you in a fidget. But the devil, who *ought* to be civil on such occasions, proved so, and took my letter to the right place.

*　　*　　*　　*　　*.　　*　　*

" Is it not odd?—the very fate I said she had escaped from * *, she

---

* The first was, of course, the one that I preferred. The other ran as follows:—

" MY DEAR MOORE, " January 7th, 1814.

" I had written to you a long letter of dedication, which I suppress, because, though it contained something relating to you which every one had been glad to hear, yet there was too much about politics, and poesy, and all things whatsoever, ending with that topic on which most men are fluent, and none very amusing—*one's self*. It might have been re-written—but to what purpose? My praise could add nothing to your well-earned and firmly-established fame: and with my most hearty admiration of your talents, and delight in your conversation, you are already acquainted. In availing myself of your friendly permission to inscribe this Poem to you, I can only wish the offering were as worthy your acceptance as your regard is dear to,

" Yours, most affectionately and faithfully,

" BYRON."

has now undergone from the worthy * *. Like Mr. Fitzgerald, shall
not lay claim to the character of 'Vates?'—as he did in the Mornin·
Herald for prophesying the fall of Buonaparte,—who, by the by, I don'
think is yet fallen. I wish he would rally and rout your legitimat·
sovereigns, having a mortal hate to all royal entails.—But I am scrawlin,
a treatise. Good night. Ever, &c."

TO MR. MURRAY.

" Jan. 11th, 1814.

"Correct this proof by Mr. Gifford's (and from the MSS.), particu·
larly as to the *pointing*. I have added a section for *Gulnare*, to fil·
up the parting, and dismiss her more ceremoniously. If Mr. Gifford o·
you dislike, 'tis but a *sponge* and another midnight better employed thar
in yawning over Miss * *; who, by the by, may soon return th·
compliment.

" Wednesday or Thursday.

"P.S. I have redde * *. It is full of praises of Lord Ellen-
borough!!! (from which I infer near and dear relations at the bar), and
*   *   *   *

"I do not love Madame de Staël, but, depend upon it, she beats all
your natives hollow as an authoress, in my opinion; and I would not
say this if I could help it.

"P.S. Pray report my best acknowledgments to Mr. Gifford in
any words that may best express how truly his kindness obliges me. I
won't bore him with *lip* thanks or *notes*."

TO MR. MOORE.

" January 13, 1814.

"I have but a moment to write, but all is as it should be. I have
said really far short of my opinion, but if you think enough, I am content.
Will you return the proof by the post, as I leave town on Sunday, and
have no other corrected copy. I put 'servant,' as being less familiar
before the public; because I don't like presuming upon our friendship

to infringe upon forms.   As to the other *word*, you may be sure it is one I cannot hear or repeat too often.

"I write in an agony of haste and confusion.—Perdonate."

LETTER CLVII.

TO MR. MURRAY.

"Jan. 15, 1814.

"Before any proof goes to Mr. Gifford, it may be as well to revise this, where there are *words omitted*, faults committed, and the devil knows what.   As to the Dedication, I cut out the parenthesis of *Mr.* *, but not another word shall move unless for a better.   Mr. Moore has seen, and decidedly preferred the part your Tory bile sickens at.   If every syllable were a rattle-snake, or every letter a pestilence, they should not be expunged.   Let those who cannot swallow chew the expressions on Ireland; or should even Mr. Croker array himself in all his terrors against them, I care for none of you, except Gifford; and he won't abuse me, except I deserve it—which will at least reconcile me to his justice.   As to the poems in Hobhouse's volume, the translation from the Romaic is well enough; but the best of the other volume (of *mine*, I mean) have been already printed.   But do as you please—only, as I shall be absent when you come out, *do, pray*, let Mr. *Dallas* and *you* have a care of the *press*.   "Yours, &c."

TO MR. MURRAY.

["1814, Jan. 16]

"I do believe that the devil never created or perverted such a fiend as the fool of a printer †.   I am obliged to enclose you, *luckily* for me,

---

* He had, at first, after the words "Scott alone," inserted, in a parenthesis,—"He will excuse the *Mr.*—'we do not say *Mr.* Cæsar.'"

† The amusing rages into which he was thrown by the printer were vented not only in these notes, but frequently on the proof-sheets themselves.   Thus, a passage in the Dedication having been printed "the first of her bands in estimation," he writes in the margin, "*bards*, not *bands*—was there ever such a stupid misprint?" and, in correcting a line that had been curtailed of its due number of syllables, he says, "*Do not* omit words—it is quite enough to alter or mis-spell them."

this *second* proof, *corrected*, because there is an ingenuity in his blunder peculiar to himself. Let the press be guided by the present sheet.

"Yours, &c.

"*Burn the other*.

"Correct *this also* by the other in some things which I may have forgotten. There is one mistake he made, which, if it had stood, would most certainly have broken his neck."

LETTER CLVIII.

TO MR MURRAY.

"Newstead Abbey, January 22d, 1814.

"You will be glad to hear of my safe arrival here. The time of my return will depend upon the weather, which is so impracticable that this letter has to advance through more snows than ever opposed the emperor's retreat. The roads are impassable, and return impossible for the present; which I do not regret, as I am much at my ease, and *six-and-twenty* complete this day—a very pretty age, if it would always last. Our coals are excellent, our fireplaces large, my cellar full, and my head empty; and I have not yet recovered my joy at leaving London. If any unexpected turn occurred with my purchasers, I believe I should hardly quit the place at all; but shut my door, and let my beard grow.

"I forgot to mention (and I hope it is unnecessary) that the lines beginning—*Remember him*, &c. must *not* appear with the *Corsair*. You may slip them in with the smaller pieces newly annexed to *Childe Harold;* but on *no* account permit them to be appended to the Corsair. Have the goodness to recollect this particularly.

"The books I have brought with me are a great consolation for the confinement, and I bought more as we came along. In short, I never consult the thermometer, and shall not put up prayers for a *thaw*, unless I thought it would sweep away the rascally invaders of France. Was ever such a thing as Blucher's proclamation?

"Just before I left town, Kemble paid me the compliment of desiring me to write a *tragedy;* I wish I could, but I find my scribbling mood subsiding—not before it was time; but it is lucky to check it at all. If I lengthen my letter, you will think it is coming on again; so, good bye.

"Yours alway,

"B.

"P.S. If you hear any news of battle or retreat on the part of the Allies (as they call them), pray send it. He has my best wishes to manure the fields of France with an *invading* army. I hate invaders of all countries, and have no patience with the cowardly cry of exultation over him, at whose name you all turned whiter than the snow to which you are indebted for your triumphs.

"I open my letter to thank you for yours just received. The 'Lines to a Lady Weeping' must go with the Corsair. I care nothing for consequence, on this point. My politics are to me like a young mistress to an old man—the worse they grow, the fonder I become of them. As Mr. Gifford likes the 'Portuguese Translation*,' pray insert it as an addition to the Corsair.

"In all points of difference between Mr. Gifford and Mr. Dallas, let the first keep his place; and in all points of difference between Mr. Gifford and Mr. Anybody-else, I shall abide by the former; if I am wrong, I can't help it. But I would rather not be right with any other person. So there is an end of that matter. After all the trouble he has taken about me and mine, I should be very ungrateful to feel or act otherwise. Besides, in point of judgment, he is not to be lowered by a comparison. In *politics*, he may be right too; but that with me is a *feeling*, and I can't *torify* my nature."

---

* His translation of the pretty Portuguese song, "Tu mi chamas." He was tempted to try another version of this ingenious thought, which is, perhaps, still more happy, and has never, I believe, appeared in print.

> "You call me still your *life*—ah! change the word—
> Life is as transient as th' inconstant's sigh;
> Say rather I'm your *soul*, more just that name,
> For, like the soul, my love can never die."

LETTER CLIX.

TO MR. MURRAY.

"Newstead Abbey, February 4th, 1814.

" I need not say that your obliging letter was very welcome, and not the less so for being unexpected.

" It doubtless gratifies me much that our *finale* has pleased, and that the curtain drops gracefully* *You* deserve it should, for your promptitude and good nature in arranging immediately with Mr. Dallas; and I can assure you that I esteem your entering so warmly into the subject, and writing to me so soon upon it, as a personal obligation. We shall now part, I hope, satisfied with each other. I *was* and *am* quite in earnest in my prefatory promise not to intrude any more; and this not from any affectation, but a thorough conviction that it is the best policy, and is at least respectful to my readers, as it shows that I would not willingly run the risk of forfeiting their favour in future. Besides, I have other views and objects, and think that I shall keep this resolution; for, since I left London, though shut up, *snow*-bound, *thaw*-bound, and tempted with all kinds of paper, the dirtiest of ink, and the bluntest of pens, I have not even been haunted by a wish to put them to their combined uses, except in letters of business. My rhyming propensity is quite gone, and I feel much as I did at Patras on recovering from my fever—weak, but in health, and only afraid of a relapse. I do most fervently hope I never shall.

" I see by the Morning Chronicle there hath been discussion in the *Courier;* and I read in the Morning Post a wrathful letter about Mr. Moore, in which some Protestant Reader has made a sad confusion about *India* and Ireland.

" You are to do as you please about the smaller poems; but I think removing them *now* from the Corsair looks like *fear;* and if so, you must allow me not to be pleased. I should also suppose that, after the *fuss* of these newspaper esquires, they would materially assist the circulation of

---

* It will be recollected that he had announced the Corsair as " the last production with which he should trespass on public patience for some years."

the Corsair; an object I should imagine at *present* of more importance to *yourself* than Childe Harold's seventh appearance. Do as you like; but don't allow the withdrawing that *poem* to draw any imputation of *dismay* upon me.

" Pray make my respects to Mr. Ward, whose praise I value most highly, as you well know; it is in the approbation of such men that fame becomes worth having. To Mr. Gifford I am always grateful, and surely not less so now than ever. And so good night to my authorship.

" I have been sauntering and dozing here very quietly, and not unhappily. You will be happy to hear that I have completely established my title-deeds as marketable, and that the purchaser has succumbed to the terms, and fulfils them, or is to fulfil them forthwith. He is now here, and we go on very amicably together—one in each *wing* of the Abbey. We set off on Sunday—I for town, he for Cheshire.

" Mrs. Leigh is with me—much pleased with the place, and less so with me for parting with it, to which not even the price can reconcile her. Your parcel has not yet arrived—at least the *Mags.* &c.; but I have received Childe Harold and the Corsair. I believe both are very correctly printed, which is a great satisfaction.

" I thank you for wishing me in town; but I think one's success is most felt at a distance, and I enjoy my solitary self-importance in an agreeable sulky way of my own, upon the strength of your letter—for which I once more thank you, and am, very truly, &c.

" P.S. Don't you think Buonaparte's next *publication* will be rather expensive to the Allies? Perry's Paris letter of yesterday looks very reviving. What a Hydra and Briareus it is! I wish they would pacify: there is no end to this campaigning."

LETTER CLX.

TO MR. MURRAY.

" Newstead Abbey, February 5th, 1814.

" I quite forgot, in my answer of yesterday, to mention that I have no means of ascertaining whether the Newark *Pirate* has been doing what you say *. If so, he is a rascal, and a *shabby* rascal too; and if his offence is punishable by law or pugilism, he shall be fined or buffeted. Do you try and discover, and I will make some inquiry here. Perhaps some *other* in town may have gone on printing, and used the same deception.

"The *fac-simile* is omitted in Childe Harold, which is very awkward, as there is a *note* expressly on the subject. Pray *replace* it as *usual*.

"On second and third thoughts, the withdrawing the small poems from the Corsair (even to add to Childe Harold) looks like shrinking and shuffling, after the fuss made upon one of them by the Tories. Pray replace them in the Corsair's appendix. I am sorry that Childe Harold requires some and such abetments to make him move off: but, if you remember, I told you his popularity would not be permanent. It is very lucky for the author that he had made up his mind to a temporary reputation in time. The truth is, I do not think that any of the present day (and least of all, one who has not consulted the flattering side of human nature) have much to hope from posterity; and you may think it affectation very probably, but to me, my present and past success has appeared very singular, since it was in the teeth of so many prejudices. I almost think people like to be contradicted. If Childe Harold flags, it will hardly be worth while to go on with the engravings: but do as you please; I have done with the whole concern; and the enclosed lines written years ago, and copied from my skull-cup, are among the last with which you will be troubled. If you like, add them to Childe Harold, if only for the sake of another outcry. You received so long an answer yesterday, that I will not intrude on you further than to repeat myself,

"Yours, &c.

"P.S. Of course, in reprinting (if you have occasion), you will take great care to be correct. The present editions seem very much so, except in the last note of Childe Harold, where the word *responsible* occurs twice nearly together; correct the second into *answerable*."

---

* Reprinting the " Hours of Idleness."

TO MR. MURRAY.

"Newark, February 6th, 1814.

"I am thus far on my way to town. Master Ridge * I have seen, and he owns to having *reprinted* some *sheets*, to make up a few complete remaining copies! I have now given him fair warning, and if he plays such tricks again, I must either get an injunction, or call for an account of profits (as I never have parted with the copyright), or, in short, any thing vexatious to repay him in his own way. If the weather does not relapse, I hope to be in town in a day or two.

"Yours, &c."

TO MR. MURRAY.

"February 7th, 1814.

*   *   *   *   *   *   *

"I see all the papers in a sad commotion with those eight lines; and the Morning Post, in particular, has found out that I am a sort of Richard III.,—deformed in mind and *body*. The *last* piece of information is not very new to a man who passed five years at a public school.

"I am very sorry you cut out those lines for Childe Harold. Pray reinsert them in their old place in 'The Corsair.'"

LETTER CLXI.

TO MR. HODGSON.

"February 28th, 1814.

"There is a youngster—and a clever one, named Reynolds, who has just published a poem called 'Safie,' published by Cawthorne. He is in the most natural and fearful apprehension of the Reviewers—and as you and I both know by experience the effect of such things upon a *young* mind, I wish *you* would take his production into dissection and do it *gently*. *I* cannot, because it is inscribed to me; but I assure you this is not my motive for wishing him to be tenderly entreated, but because

---

* The printer at Newark.

I know the misery, at his time of life, of untoward remarks upon first appearance.

"Now for *self.* Pray thank your *cousin*—it is just as it should be, to my liking, and probably *more* than will suit any one else's. I hope and trust that you are well and well doing. Peace be with you. Ever yours, my dear friend."

LETTER CLXII.

TO MR. MOORE.

"February 10th, 1814.

"I arrived in town late yesterday evening, having been absent three weeks, which I passed in Notts. quietly and pleasantly. You can have no conception of the uproar the eight lines on the little Royalty's weeping in 1812 (now republished) have occasioned. The R**, who had always thought them *yours*, chose—God knows why—on discovering them to be mine, to be *affected* 'in sorrow rather than anger.' The Morning Post, Sun, Herald, Courier, have all been in hysterics ever since. M. is in a fright, and wanted to shuffle—and the abuse against me in all directions is vehement, unceasing, loud—some of it good, and all of it hearty. I feel a little compunctious as to the R**'s *regret;*—'would he had been only angry! but I fear him not.'

"Some of these same assailments you have probably seen. My person (which is excellent for 'the nonce') has been denounced in verses, the more like the subject, inasmuch as they halt exceedingly. Then, in another, I am an *atheist*—a *rebel*—and, at last, the *Devil* (*boiteux*, I presume). My demonism seems to be a female's conjecture: if so, perhaps, I could convince her that I am but a mere mortal,—if a queen of the Amazons may be believed, who says αριϛον χολος οιφει. I quote from memory, so my Greek is probably deficient; but the passage is *meant* to mean * * * * * *

"Seriously, I am in, what the learned call, a dilemma, and the vulgar, a scrape; and my friends desire me not to be in a passion, and like Sir Fretful, I assure them that I am 'quite calm,'—but I am nevertheless in a fury.

" Since I wrote thus far, a friend has come in, and we have been talking and buffooning, till I have quite lost the thread of my thoughts; and, as I won't send them unstrung to you, good morning, and

" Believe me ever, &c.

" P.S. Murray, during my absence, *omitted* the Tears in several of the copies. I have made him replace them, and am very wroth with his qualms ;—' as the wine is poured out, let it be drunk to the dregs.' "

TO MR. MURRAY.

" February 10th, 1814.

" I am much better, and indeed quite well this morning. I have received *two*, but I presume there are more of the *Ana*, subsequently, and also something previous, to which the Morning Chronicle replied. You also mentioned a parody on the *Skull*. I wish to see them all, because there may be things that require notice either by pen or person.

" Yours, &c.

" You need not trouble yourself to answer this; but send me the things when you get them."

TO MR. MURRAY.

" February 12th, 1814.

" If you have copies of the ' Intercepted Letters,' Lady Holland would be glad of a volume, and when you have served others, have the goodness to think of your humble servant.

" You have played the devil by that injudicious *suppression,* which you did totally without my consent. Some of the papers have exactly said what might be expected. Now I *do* not, and *will* not be supposed to shrink, although myself and every thing belonging to me were to perish with my memory.

" Yours, &c.

" Bn.

" P.S. Pray attend to what I stated yesterday on *technical* topics."

LETTER CLXIII.

TO MR. MURRAY.

" Monday, February 14th, 1814.

" Before I left town yesterday, I wrote you a note, which I presume you received. I have heard so many different accounts of *your* proceedings, or rather of those of others towards *you*, in consequence of the publication of these everlasting lines, that I am anxious to hear from yourself the real state of the case. Whatever responsibility, obloquy, or effect is to arise from the publication should surely *not* fall upon you in any degree; and I can have no objection to your stating, as distinctly and publicly as you please, *your* unwillingness to publish them, and my own obstinacy upon the subject. Take any course you please to vindicate *yourself*, but leave me to fight my own way, and, as I before said, do not *compromise* me by any thing which may look like *shrinking* on *my* part; as for your own, make the best of it.

" Yours,

" BN."

LETTER CLXIV.

TO MR. ROGERS.

" February 16th, 1814.

" MY DEAR ROGERS,

" I wrote to Lord Holland briefly, but I hope distinctly, on the subject which has lately occupied much of my conversation with him and you*. As things now stand, upon that topic my determination must be unalterable.

" I declare to you most sincerely that there is no human being on whose regard and esteem I set a higher value than on Lord Holland's; and, as far as concerns himself, I would concede even to humiliation without any view to the future, and solely from my sense of his conduct

* Relative to a proposed reconciliation between Lord Carlisle and himself.

as to the past. For the rest, I conceive that I have already done all in my power by the suppression *. If that is not enough, they must act as they please; but I will not ' teach my tongue a most inherent baseness,' come what may. You will probably be at the Marquis Lansdowne's to-night. I am asked, but I am not sure that I shall be able to go. Hobhouse will be there. I think, if you knew him well, you would like him.

" Believe me always yours very affectionately,

" B."

LETTER CLXV.

TO MR. ROGERS.

" February 16th, 1814.

" If Lord Holland is satisfied, as far as regards himself and Lady Hd., and as this letter expresses him to be, it is enough.

" As for any impression the public may receive from the revival of the lines on Lord Carlisle, let them keep it,—the more favourable for him, and the worse for me—better for all.

" All the sayings and doings in the world shall not make me utter another word of conciliation to any thing that breathes. I shall bear what I can, and what I cannot, I shall resist. The worst they could do would be to exclude me from society. I have never courted it, nor, I may add, in the general sense of the word, enjoyed it—and ' there is a world elsewhere !'

" Any thing remarkably injurious, I have the same means of repaying as other men, with such interest as circumstances may annex to it.

" Nothing but the necessity of adhering to regimen prevents me from dining with you to-morrow.

" I am yours most truly,

" Bn."

* Of the Satire.

LETTER CLXVI.

TO MR. MOORE.

"February 16th, 1814.

"You may be assured that the only prickles that sting from the
Royal hedgehog are those which possess a torpedo property, and may
benumb some of my friends. *I* am quite silent, and 'hush'd in grim
repose.' The frequency of the assaults has weakened their effects,—if
ever they had any;—and, if they had had much, I should hardly have
held my tongue, or withheld my fingers. It is something quite new to
attack a man for abandoning his resentments. I have heard that previous praise and subsequent vituperation were rather ungrateful, but I
did not know that it was wrong to endeavour to do justice to those who
did not wait till I had made some amends for former and boyish prejudices, but received me into their friendship, when I might still have
been their enemy.

"You perceive justly that I must *intentionally* have made my fortune,
like Sir Francis Wronghead. It were better if there were more merit
in my independence, but it really is something nowadays to be independent at all, and the *less* temptation to be otherwise, the more uncommon the case, in these times of paradoxical servility. I believe that
most of our hates and likings have been hitherto nearly the same; but
from henceforth, they must, of necessity, be one and indivisible,—and
now for it! I am for any weapon,—the pen, till one can find something
sharper, will do for a beginning.

"You can have no conception of the ludicrous solemnity with
which these two stanzas have been treated. The Morning Post gave
notice of an intended motion in the House of my brethren on the subject,
and God he knows what proceedings besides;—and all this, as Bedreddin
in the 'Nights' says, 'for making a cream tart without pepper.' This last
piece of intelligence is, I presume, too laughable to be true; and the
destruction of the Custom-house appears to have, in some degree, interfered with mine;—added to which, the last battle of Buonaparte has
usurped the column hitherto devoted to my bulletin.

" I send you from this day's Morning Post the best which have hitherto appeared on this 'impudent doggerel,' as the Courier calls it. There was another about my *diet*, when a boy—not at all bad—some time ago; but the rest are but indifferent.

" I shall think about your *oratorical* hint*;—but I have never set much upon ' that cast,' and am grown as tired as Solomon of every thing, and of myself more than any thing. This is being what the learned call philosophical, and the vulgar, lack-a-daisical. I am, however, always glad of a blessing†; pray, repeat yours soon,—at least your letter, and I shall think the benediction included.

" Ever, &c."

LETTER CLXVII.

TO MR. DALLAS.

" February 17th, 1814.

" The Courier of this evening accuses me of having 'received and pocketed' large sums for my works. I have never yet received, nor wished to receive, a farthing for any. Mr. Murray offered a thousand for the Giaour and Bride of Abydos, which I said was too much, and that if he could afford it at the end of six months, I would then direct how it might be disposed of; but neither then, nor at any other period, have I ever availed myself of the profits on my own account. For the republication of the Satire, I refused four hundred guineas; and for the previous editions I never asked nor received a *sous*, nor for any writing whatever. I do not wish you to do any thing disagreeable to yourself; there never was nor shall be any conditions nor stipulations with regard to any accommodation that I could afford you; and, on your part, I can see nothing derogatory in receiving the copyright. It was only assistance afforded to a worthy man, by one not quite so worthy.

---

* I had endeavoured to persuade him to take a part in parliamentary affairs, and to exercise his talent for oratory more frequently.

† In concluding my letter, having said " God bless you !" I added—" that is, if you have no objection."

" Mr. Murray is going to contradict this*; but your *name* will not
be mentioned: for your own part, you are a free agent, and are to do as
you please. I only hope that now, as always, you will think that I wish
to take no unfair advantage of the accidental opportunity which cir
cumstances permitted me of being of use to you.

" Ever, &c."

In consequence of this letter, Mr. Dallas addressed an explanation
to one of the newspapers, of which the following is a part;—the remainder
being occupied with a rather clumsily managed defence of his noble
benefactor on the subject of the Stanzas.

TO THE EDITOR OF THE MORNING POST.

" SIR,

" I have seen the paragraph in an evening paper, in which Lord
Byron is *accused* of ' receiving and pocketing' large sums for his works.
I believe no one who knows him has the slightest suspicion of this kind;
but the assertion being public, I think it a justice I owe to Lord Byron
to contradict it publicly. I address this letter to you for that purpose,
and I am happy that it gives me an opportunity at this moment to make
some observations which I have for several days been anxious to do
publicly, but from which I have been restrained by an apprehension that
I should be suspected of being prompted by his lordship.

" I take upon me to affirm that Lord Byron never received a
shilling for any of his works. To my certain knowledge, the profits of
the Satire were left entirely to the publisher of it. The gift of the copyright of Childe Harold's Pilgrimage, I have already publicly acknowledged
in the dedication of the new edition of my novels; and I now add my
acknowledgment for that of the Corsair, not only for the profitable part
of it, but for the delicate and delightful manner of bestowing it while
yet unpublished. With respect to his two other poems, the Giaour and

---

* The statement of the Courier, &c.

the Bride of Abydos, Mr. Murray, the publisher of them, can truly attest that no part of the sale of them has ever touched his hands, or been disposed of for his use. Having said thus much as to facts, I cannot but express my surprise that it should ever be deemed a matter of reproach that he should appropriate the pecuniary returns of his works. Neither rank nor fortune seems to me to place any man above this; for what difference does it make in honour and noble feelings, whether a copyright be bestowed, or its value employed in beneficent purposes? I differ with my Lord Byron on this subject, as well as some others; and he has constantly, both by word and action, shown his aversion to receiving money for his productions."

LETTER CLXVIII.

TO MR. MOORE.

" Feb. 26th, 1814.

" Dallas had, perhaps, have better kept silence;—but that was *his* concern, and, as his facts are correct, and his motive not dishonourable to himself, I wished him well through it. As for his interpretations of the lines, he and any one else may interpret them as they please. I have and shall adhere to my taciturnity, unless something very particular occurs to render this impossible. Do *not you* say a word. If any one is to speak, it is the person principally concerned. The most amusing thing is, that every one (to me) attributes the abuse to the *man they personally most dislike!*—some say C**r, some C**e, others F**d, &c. &c. &c. I do not know, and have no clue but conjecture. If discovered, and he turns out a hireling, he must be left to his wages; if a cavalier, he must ' wink, and hold out his iron.'

" I had some thoughts of putting the question to C**r, but H., who, I am sure, would not dissuade me, if it were right, advised me by all means *not;*—' that I had no right to take it upon suspicion,' &c. &c. Whether H. is correct, I am not aware, but he believes himself so, and says there can be but one opinion on that subject. This I am, at least, sure of, that he would never prevent me from doing what he deemed the duty of a *preux* chevalier. In such cases—at least, in this country—we

must act according to usages. In considering this instance, I dismiss m
own personal feelings. Any man will and must fight, when necessary
—even without a motive. *Here*, I should take it up really withou
much resentment; for, unless a woman one likes is in the way, it is som
years since I felt a *long* anger. But, undoubtedly, could I, or may I
trace it to a man of station, I should and shall do what is proper.

"* * was angerly, but tried to conceal it. *You* are not called upo
to avow the ' Twopenny,' and would only gratify them by so doing. D
you not see the great object of all these fooleries is to set him, and you
and me, and all persons whatsoever, by the ears?—more especially thos
who are on good terms,—and nearly succeeded. Lord H. wished me t
concede to Lord Carlisle—concede to the devil!—to a man who used m
ill? I told him, in answer, that I would neither concede, nor recede o
the subject, but be silent altogether; unless any thing more could be sai
about Lady H. and himself, who had been since my very good friends
—and there it ended. This was no time for concessions to Lord C.

" I have been interrupted, but shall write again soon. Believe me
ever, my dear Moore, &c."

Another of his friends having expressed, soon after, some intention
of volunteering publicly in his defence, he lost no time in repressing him
by the following sensible letter.

LETTER CLXIX.

TO W * * W * *, ESQ.

" February 28th, 1814.

" MY DEAR W.,

" I have but a few moments to write to you. *Silence* is the only
answer to the things you mention; nor should I regard that man as my
friend who said a word more on the subject. I care little for attacks,
but I will not submit to *defences;* and I do hope and trust that *you* have
never entertained a serious thought of engaging in so foolish a controversy. Dallas's letter was, to his credit, merely as to facts which he
had a right to state; *I* neither have nor shall take the least *public* notice,

nor permit any one else to do so.   If I discover the writer, then I may act in a different manner; but it will not be in writing.

"An expression in your letter has induced me to write this to you, to entreat you not to interfere in any way in such a business,—it is now nearly over, and depend upon it *they* are much more chagrined by my silence than they could be by the best defence in the world.   I do not know any thing that would vex me more than any further reply to these things.   Ever yours, in haste,

"B."

LETTER CLXX.

TO MR. MOORE.

"March 3, 1814.

"MY DEAR FRIEND,

"I have a great mind to tell you that I *am* 'uncomfortable,' if only to make you come to town; where no one ever more delighted in seeing you, nor is there any one to whom I would sooner turn for consolation in my most vapourish moments.   The truth is, I have 'no lack of argument' to ponder upon of the most gloomy description, but this arises from *other* causes.   Some day or other, when we are *veterans*, I may tell you a tale of present and past times; and it is not from want of confidence that I do not now;—but—but—always a *but* to the end of the chapter.

"There is nothing, however, upon the *spot* either to love or hate;—but I certainly have subjects for both at no very great distance, and am besides embarrassed between *three* whom I know, and one (whose name, at least) I do not know.   All this would be very well, if I had no heart; but, unluckily, I have found that there is such a thing still about me, though in no very good repair, and, also, that it has a habit of attaching itself to *one*, whether I will or no.   'Divide et impera,' I begin to think, will only do for politics.

"If I discover the 'toad,' as you call him, I shall 'tread,'—and put spikes in my shoes to do it more effectually.   The effect of all these fine things, I do not inquire much nor perceive.   I believe * * felt them

more than either of us. People are civil enough, and I have had r
dearth of invitations,—none of which, however, I have accepted. I wer
out very little last year, and mean to go about still less. I have n
passion for circles, and have long regretted that I ever gave way to wh:
is called a town life;—which, of all the lives I ever saw (and they ar
nearly as many as Plutarch's), seems to me to leave the least for the pas
and future.

"How proceeds the Poem? Do not neglect it, and I have no fear
I need not say to you that your fame is dear to me,—I really might sa
dearer than my own; for I have lately begun to think my things hav
been strangely overrated; and, at any rate, whether or not, I have don
with them for ever. I may say to you, what I would not say to ever;
body, that the last two were written, the Bride in four, and the Corsai
in ten days*,—which I take to be a most humiliating confession, as i
proves my own want of judgment in publishing, and the public's ir
reading things, which cannot have stamina for permanent attention
'So much for Buckingham.'

"I have no dread of your being too hasty, and I have still less o.
your failing. But I think a *year* a very fair allotment of time to a com
position which is not to be Epic; and even Horace's 'Nonum prematur
must have been intended for the Millenium, or some longer-lived generation than ours. I wonder how much we should have had of *him*, had h
observed his own doctrines to the letter. Peace be with you! Remembe:
that I am always and most truly yours, &c.

"P.S. I never heard the 'report' you mention, nor, I dare say
many others. But, in course, you, as well as others, have 'damned good-

---

* In asserting that he devoted but four days to the composition of the Bride, he must b
understood to refer only to the first sketch of that poem,—the successive additions by which it
was increased to its present length having occupied, as we have seen, a much longer period
The Corsair, on the contrary, was, from beginning to end, struck off at a heat—there being but
little alteration or addition afterwards,—and the rapidity with which it was produced (being at
the rate of nearly two hundred lines a day) would be altogether incredible, had we not his own
as well as his publisher's, testimony to the fact. Such an achievement,—taking into account
the surpassing beauty of the work,—is, perhaps, wholly without a parallel in the history o:
Genius, and shows that " écrire *par passion*," as Rousseau expresses it, may be sometimes a
shorter road to perfection than any that Art has ever struck out.

natured friends,' who do their duty in the usual way. One thing will make you laugh   *   *   *   *   *   * "

LETTER CLXXI.

TO MR. MOORE.

" March 12th, 1814.

" Guess darkly, and you will seldom err. At present, I shall say no more, and, perhaps—but no matter. I hope we shall some day meet, and whatever years may precede or succeed it, I shall mark it with the ' white stone' in my calendar. I am not sure that I shall not soon be in your neighbourhood again. If so, and I am alone (as will probably be the case), I shall invade and carry you off, and endeavour to atone for sorry fare by a sincere welcome. I don't know the person absent (barring ' the sect') I should be so glad to see again.

" I have nothing of the sort you mention but *the lines* (the Weepers), if you like to have them in the Bag. I wish to give them all possible circulation. The *Vault* reflection is downright actionable, and to print it would be peril to the publisher; but I think the Tears have a natural right to be bagged, and the editor (whoever he may be) might supply a facetious note or not, as he pleased.

" I cannot conceive how the *Vault** has got about,—but so it is. It is too *farouche;* but, truth to say, my satires are not very playful. I have the plan of an epistle in my head, *at* him and *to* him; and, if they are not a little quieter, I shall imbody it. I should say little or nothing of *myself.* As to mirth and ridicule, that is out of my way; but I have a tolerable fund of sternness and contempt, and, with Juvenal before me, I shall perhaps read him a lecture he has not lately heard in the C——t. From particular circumstances, which came to my knowledge almost by accident, I could ' tell him what he is—I know him well.'

" I meant, my dear M., to write to you a long letter, but I am hurried, and time clips my inclination down to yours, &c.

---

* Those bitter and powerful lines which he wrote on the opening of the vault that contained the remains of Henry VIII. and Charles I.

" P.S. *Think again* before you *shelf* your Poem. There is a youngster (older than me, by the by, but a younger poet), Mr. G Knight, with a vol. of Eastern Tales, written since his return,—for he has been in the countries. He sent to me last summer, and I advised him to write one in *each measure*, without any intention, at that time of doing the same thing. Since that, from a habit of writing in a fever, I have anticipated him in the variety of measures, but quite unintentionally. Of the stories, I know nothing, not having seen them*; but *he* has some lady in a sack, too, like the Giaour:—he told me at the time.

" The best way to make the public ' forget' me is to remind them of yourself. You cannot suppose that *I* would ask you or advise you to publish, if I thought you would *fail*. I really have *no* literary envy; and I do not believe a friend's success ever sat nearer another than yours do to my best wishes. It is for *elderly gentlemen* to ' bear no brother near,' and cannot become our disease for more years than we may perhaps number. I wish you to be out before Eastern subjects are again before the public."

LETTER CLXXII.

TO MR. MURRAY.

" March 12th, 1814.

" I have not time to read the whole MS.†, but what I have seen seems very well written (both *prose* and *verse*), and though I am and can be no judge (at least a *fair* one on this subject), containing nothing which you *ought* to hesitate publishing upon *my* account. If the author is not Dr. *Busby* himself, I think it a pity, on his *own* account, that he should dedicate it to his subscribers ; nor can I perceive what Dr. Busby has to do with the matter, except as a translator of Lucretius, for whose doctrines he is surely not responsible. I tell you openly, and really most

* He was not yet aware, it appears, that the anonymous manuscript sent to him by his publisher was from the pen of Mr. Knight.

† The manuscript of a long grave satire, entitled " Anti-Byron," which had been sent to Mr. Murray, and by him forwarded to Lord Byron, with a request—not meant, I believe, seriously—that he would give his opinion as to the propriety of publishing it.

sincerely, that, if published at all, there is no earthly reason why you should *not;* on the contrary, I should receive it as the greatest compliment *you* could pay to your good opinion of my candour, to print and circulate that, or any other work, attacking me in a manly manner, and without any malicious intention, from which, as far as I have seen, I must exonerate this writer.

"He is wrong in one thing,—*I* am no *atheist;* but if he thinks I have published principles tending to such opinions, he has a perfect right to controvert them. Pray publish it; I shall never forgive myself if I think that I have prevented you.

"Make my compliments to the author, and tell him I wish him success; his verse is very deserving of it; and I shall be the last person to suspect his motives. Yours, &c.

"P.S. If *you* do not publish it, some one else will. You cannot suppose me so narrow-minded as to shrink from discussion. I repeat once for all, that I think it a good Poem (as far as I have redde); and that is the only point *you* should consider. How odd that *eight lines* should have given birth, I really think, to *eight thousand,* including *all* that has been said, and will be, on the subject!"

LETTER CLXXIII.

TO MR. MURRAY.

"April 9th, 1814.

"All these news are very fine; but nevertheless I want my books, if you can find, or cause them to be found for me,—if only to lend them to Napoleon in 'the island of Elba,' during his retirement. I also (if convenient, and you have no party with you) should be glad to speak with you for a few minutes this evening, as I have had a letter from Mr. Moore, and wish to ask you, as the best judge, of the best time for him to publish the work he has composed. I need not say, that I have his success much at heart; not only because he is my friend, but something much better—a man of great talent, of which he is less sensible than I believe any even of his enemies. If you can so far oblige me as to step

down, do so; and if you are otherwise occupied, say nothing about i
I shall find you at home in the course of next week.

"P.S. I see Sotheby's Tragedies advertised. The Death of Darnle
is a famous subject—one of the best, I should think, for the drama. Pra
let me have a copy, when ready.

"Mrs. Leigh was very much pleased with her books, and desired m
to thank you; she means, I believe, to write to you her acknowledgments.

LETTER CLXXIV.

TO MR. MOORE.

"2, Albany, April 9th, 1814.

"Viscount Althorpe is about to be married, and I have gotten hi
spacious bachelor apartments in Albany, to which you will, I hope
address a speedy answer to this mine epistle.

"I am but just returned to town, from which you may infer that
I have been out of it; and I have been boxing, for exercise, with
Jackson for this last month daily. I have also been drinking,—and, on
one occasion, with three other friends at the Cocoa Tree, from six till
four, yea, unto five in the matin. We clareted and champagned till
two—then supped, and finished with a kind of regency punch composed
of madeira, brandy, and *green* tea, no *real* water being admitted therein.
There was a night for you!—without once quitting the table, except to
ambulate home, which I did alone, and in utter contempt of a hackney-
coach and my own *vis*, both of which were deemed necessary for our
conveyance. And so,—I am very well, and they say it will hurt my
constitution.

"I have also, more or less, been breaking a few of the favourite
commandments; but I mean to pull up and marry,—if any one will have
me. In the mean time, the other day I nearly killed myself with a
collar of brawn, which I swallowed for supper, and *in*digested for I don't
know how long;—but that is by the by. All this gourmandise was in
honour of Lent; for I am forbidden meat all the rest of the year,—but
it is strictly enjoined me during your solemn fast. I have been, and am,
in very tolerable love;—but of that hereafter, as it may be.

" My dear Moore, say what you will in your Preface ; and quiz any thing, or any body,—me, if you like it. Oons dost thou think me of the *old*, or rather *elderly*, school? If one can't jest with one's friends, with whom can we be facetious? You have nothing to fear from * *, whom I have not seen, being out of town when he called. He will be very correct, smooth, and all that, but I doubt whether there will be any ' grace beyond the reach of art;'—and, whether there is or not, how long will you be so d—d modest? As for Jeffrey, it is a very handsome thing of him to speak well of an old antagonist,—and what a mean mind dared not do. Any one will revoke praise ; but—were it not partly my own case—I should say that very few have strength of mind to unsay their censure, or follow it up with praise of other things.

" What think you of the review of *Levis?* It beats the Bag and my hand-grenade hollow, as an invective, and hath thrown the Court into hysterics, as I hear from very good authority. Have you heard from　　*　　*　　*　　*　　*　　*　　*　　*

" No more rhyme for—or rather, *from*—me. I have taken my leave of that stage, and henceforth will mountebank it no longer. I have had my day, and there's an end. The utmost I expect, or even wish, is to have it said in the Biographia Britannica, that I might perhaps have been a poet, had I gone on and amended. My great comfort is, that the temporary celebrity I have wrung from the world has been in the very teeth of all opinions and prejudices. I have flattered no ruling powers ; I have never concealed a single thought that tempted me. They can't say I have truckled to the times, nor to popular topics (as Johnson, or somebody, said of Cleveland), and whatever I have gained has been at the expenditure of as much *personal* favour as possible ; for I do believe never was a bard more unpopular, *quoad homo*, than myself. And now I have done ;—' ludite nunc alios.' Every body may be d—d, as they seem fond of it, and resolved to stickle lustily for endless brimstone.

" Oh—by the by, I had nearly forgot. There is a long Poem, an ' Anti-Byron,' coming out, to prove that I have formed a conspiracy to overthrow, by *rhyme*, all religion and government, and have already made great progress ! It is not very scurrilous, but serious and ethereal. I never felt myself important, till I saw and heard of my being such a

little Voltaire as to induce such a production. Murray would not publish
it, for which he was a fool, and so I told him; but some one else will
doubtless. 'Something too much of this.'

"Your French scheme is good, but let it be *Italian*; all the Angles
will be at Paris. Let it be Rome, Milan, Naples, Florence, Turin,
Venice, or Switzerland, and 'egad!' (as Bayes saith), I will connubiate
and join you; and we will write a new 'Inferno' in our Paradise. Pray
think of this—and I will really buy a wife and a ring, and say the
ceremony, and settle near you in a summer-house upon the Arno, or the
Po, or the Adriatic.

"Ah! my poor little pagod, Napoleon, has walked off his pedestal.
He has abdicated, they say. This would draw molten brass from the
eyes of Zatanai. What! 'kiss the ground before young Malcolm's feet,
and then be baited by the rabble's curse!' I cannot bear such a crouching
catastrophe. I must stick to Sylla, for my modern favourites don't do,—
their resignations are of a different kind. All health and prosperity, my
dear Moore. Excuse this lengthy letter. Ever, &c.

"P.S. The Quarterly quotes you frequently in an article on
America; and every body I know asks perpetually after you and yours.
When will you answer them in person?"

He did not long persevere in his resolution against writing, as will
be seen from the following notes to his publisher.

TO MR. MURRAY.

"April 10th, 1814.

"I have written an Ode on the fall of Napoleon, which, if you like,
I will copy out, and make you a present of. Mr. Merivale has seen part
of it, and likes it. You may show it to Mr. Gifford, and print it, or not,
as you please—it is of no consequence. It contains nothing in *his* favour,
and no allusion whatever to our own government or the Bourbons.
Yours, &c.

"P.S. It is in the measure of my stanzas at the end of Childe
Harold, which were much liked, beginning 'And thou art dead,' &c. &c.
There are ten stanzas of it—ninety lines in all."

TO MR. MURRAY.

"April 11th, 1814.

" I enclose you a letter*et* from Mrs. Leigh.

" It will be best *not* to put my name to our *Ode;* but you may *say* as openly as you like that it is mine, and I can inscribe it to Mr. Hobhouse, from the *author,* which will mark it sufficiently. After the resolution of not publishing, though it is a thing of little length and less consequence, it will be better altogether that it is anonymous; but we will incorporate it in the first *tome* of ours that you find time or the wish to publish.   " Yours alway,

" B.

" P.S. I hope you got a note of alterations, sent this matin?

" P.S. Oh my books! my books! will you never find my books?

" Alter '*potent* spell' to '*quickening* spell:' the first (as Polonius says) ' is a vile phrase,' and means nothing, besides being common-place and *Rosa-Matildaish.*"

TO MR. MURRAY.

"April 12th, 1814.

" I send you a few notes and trifling alterations, and an additional motto from Gibbon, which you will find *singularly appropriate.* A ' Good-natured Friend' tells me there is a most scurrilous attack on *us* in the Antijacobin Review, which you have *not* sent. Send it, as I am in that state of languor which 'will derive benefit from getting into a passion. Ever, &c."

LETTER CLXXV.

TO MR. MOORE.

"Albany, April 20th, 1814.

" I *am* very glad to hear that you are to be transient from Mayfield so very soon, and was taken in by the first part of your letter*. Indeed,

---

* I had begun my letter in the following manner:—" Have you seen the 'Ode to Napoleon Buonaparte?'—I suspect it to be either F—g—d's or Rosa Matilda's. Those rapid and

for aught I know, you may be treating me, as Slipslop says, wit
' ironing' even now.   I shall say nothing of the *shock*, which had nothin,
of *humeur* in it; as I am apt to take even a critic, and still more a friend
at his word, and never to doubt that I have been writing cursed nonsense
if they say so.   There was a mental reservation in my pact with th
public*, in behalf of *anonymes;* and, even had there not, the provocatio
was such as to make it physically impossible to pass over this damnabl
epoch of triumphant tameness.   'Tis a cursed business; and, after all
I shall think higher of rhyme and reason, and very humbly of you
heroic people, till—Elba becomes a volcano, and sends him out again.
can't think it all over yet.

"My departure for the continent depends, in some measure, on th
*in*continent.   I have two country invitations at home, and don't know
what to say or do.   In the mean time, I have bought a macaw and a
parrot, and have got up my books; and I box and fence daily, and g
out very little.

"At this present writing, Louis the Gouty is wheeling in triumph
into Piccadilly, in all the pomp and rabblement of royalty.   I had an
offer of seats to see them pass; but, as I have seen a Sultan going to
mosque, and been at *his* reception of an ambassador, the most Christian
King ' hath no attractions for me :'—though in some coming year of the
Hegira, I should not dislike to see the place where he *had* reigned,
shortly after the second revolution, and a happy sovereignty of two
months, the last six weeks being civil war.

"Pray write, and deem me ever, &c."

masterly portraits of all the tyrants that preceded Napoleon have a vigour in them which would
incline me to say that Rosa Matilda is the person—but then, on the other hand, that powerful
grasp of history," &c. &c.   After a little more of this mock parallel, the letter went on thus :—
" I should like to know what *you* think of the matter?   Some friends of mine here *will* insist
that it is the work of the author of Childe Harold,—but then they are not so well read in
F—g—d and Rosa Matilda as I am ; and, besides, they seem to forget that *you* promised,
about a month or two ago, not to write any more for years.   Seriously," &c. &c.

I quote this foolish banter merely to show how safely, even on his most sensitive points, one
might venture to jest with him.

* We find D'Argenson thus encouraging Voltaire to break a similar vow :—" Continue to
write without fear for five-and-twenty years longer, but write poetry, notwithstanding your
oath in the Preface to Newton."

LETTER CLXXVI.

TO MR. MURRAY.

" April 21st, 1814.

" Many thanks with the letters which I return. You know I am a jacobin, and could not wear white, nor see the installation of Louis the Gouty.

" This is sad news, and very hard upon the sufferers at any, but more at *such* a time—I mean the Bayonne sortie.

" You should urge Moore to come *out*.

" P.S. I want *Moreri* to purchase for good and all. I have a Bayle, but want Moreri too.

" P.S. Perry hath a piece of compliment to-day ; but I think the *name* might have been as well omitted. No matter ; they can but throw the old story of inconsistency in my teeth—let them,—I mean, as to not publishing. However, *now* I will keep my word. Nothing but the occasion, which was *physically* irresistible, made me swerve ; and I thought an *anonyme* within my *pact* with the public. It is the only thing I have or shall set about."

LETTER CLXXVII.

TO MR. MURRAY.

" April 25th, 1814.

" Let Mr. Gifford have the letter and return it at his leisure. I would have offered it, had I thought that he liked things of the kind.

" Do you want the last page *immediately?* I have doubts about the lines being worth printing ; at any rate, I must see them again and alter some passages, before they go forth in any shape into the *ocean* of circulation ;—a very conceited phrase, by the by : well then—*channel* of publication will do.

" ' I am not i' the vein,' or I could knock off a stanza or three for

the Ode, that might answer the purpose better*.   At all events, I *mus*
see the lines again *first*, as there be two I have altered in my mind
manuscript already.   Has any one seen and judged of them? that is th◄

* Mr. Murray had requested of him to make some additions to the Ode, so as to save th◄
Stamp Duty imposed upon publications not exceeding a single sheet, and the lines he sent hir
for this purpose were, I believe, those beginning "We do not curse thee, Waterloo."   To th
Ode itself, he afterwards added, in successive editions, five or six stanzas, the original numbe◄
being but eleven.   There were also three more stanzas which he never printed, but which, fo◄
the just tribute they contain to Washington, are worthy of being preserved.

17.

"There was a day—there was an hour,
   While earth was Gaul's—Gaul thine—
When that immeasurable power
   Unsated to resign
Had been an act of purer fame
Than gathers round Marengo's name
   And gilded thy decline,
Through the long twilight of all time,
Despite some passing clouds of crime.

18.

"But thou forsooth must be a king
   And don the purple vest,
As if that foolish robe could wring
   Remembrance from thy breast.
Where is that faded garment? where
The gewgaws thou wert fond to wear,
   The star—the string—the crest?
Vain froward child of empire! say
Are all thy playthings snatch'd away?

19.

"Where may the wearied eye repose
   When gazing on the great;
Where neither guilty glory glows,
   Nor despicable state?
Yes—one—the first—the last—the best—
The Cincinnatus of the West,
   Whom envy dared not hate,
Bequeath'd the name of Washington,
To make man blush there was but One!"

criterion by which I will abide—only give me a *fair* report, and 'nothing extenuate,' as I will in that case do something else.

" Ever, &c.

" I want *Moreri*, and an *Athenæus*."

LETTER CLXXVIII.

TO MR. MURRAY.

" April 26th, 1814.

" I have been thinking that it might be as well to publish no more of the Ode separately, but incorporate it with any of the other things, and include the smaller Poem too (in that case)—which I must previously correct, nevertheless. I can't, for the head of me, add a line worth scribbling; my 'vein' is quite gone, and my present occupations are of the gymnastic order—boxing and fencing—and my principal conversation is with my macaw and Bayle. I want my Moreri, and I want Athenæus.

" P.S. I hope you sent back that poetical packet to the address which I forwarded to you on Sunday: if not, pray do; or I shall have the author screaming after his Epic."

LETTER CLXXIX.

TO MR. MURRAY.

" April 26th, 1814.

" I have no guess at your author,—but it is a noble Poem *, and worth a thousand Odes of any body's. I suppose I may keep this copy; —after reading it, I really regret having written my own. I say this very sincerely, albeit unused to think humbly of myself.

" I don't like the additional stanzas *at all*, and they had better be left out. The fact is, I can't do any thing I am asked to do, however

---

* A Poem by Mr. Stratford Canning, full of spirit and power, entitled " Buonaparte." In a subsequent note to Mr. Murray, Lord Byron says:—" I do not think less highly of ' Buonaparte' for knowing the author. I was aware that he was a man of talent, but did not suspect him of possessing *all* the *family* talents in such perfection."

gladly I *would;* and at the end of a week my interest in a compositio
goes off. This will account to you for my doing no better for you
' Stamp Duty' Postscript.

" The S. R. is very civil—but what do they mean by Childe Harol
resembling Marmion? and the next two, Giaour and Bride, *not* resem
bling Scott? I certainly never intended to copy him; but, if there b
any copyism, it must be in the two Poems, where the same versificatio
is adopted. However, they exempt the Corsair from all resemblance t
any thing,—though I rather wonder at his escape.

" If ever I did any thing original, it was in Childe Harold, which
prefer to the other things always, after the first week. Yesterday
re-read English Bards;—bating the *malice,* it is the *best.*

" Ever, &c."

A resolution was, about this time, adopted by him, which, how
ever strange and precipitate it appeared, a knowledge of the previou
state of his mind may enable us to account for satisfactorily. He
had now, for two years, been drawing upon the admiration of the
public with a rapidity and success which seemed to defy exhaustion
—having crowded, indeed, into that brief interval the materials of
a long life of fame. But admiration is a sort of impost from which
most minds are but too willing to relieve themselves. The eye
grows weary of looking up to the same object of wonder, and begins
to exchange, at last, the delight of observing its elevation for the less
generous pleasure of watching and speculating on its fall. The reputation of Lord Byron had already begun to experience some of these
consequences of its own prolonged and constantly renewed splendour.
Even among that host of admirers who would have been the last to
find fault, there were some not unwilling to repose from praise; while
they, who had been from the first reluctant eulogists, took advantage of
these apparent symptoms of satiety to indulge in blame *.

* It was the fear of this sort of back-water current to which so rapid a flow of fame seeme
liable that led some even of his warmest admirers, ignorant as they were yet of the boundless
ness of his resources, to tremble a little at the frequency of his appearances before the public
In one of my own letters to him, I find this apprehension thus expressed:—" If you did no

The loud outcry raised, at the beginning of the present year, by his verses to the Princess Charlotte, had afforded a vent for much of this reserved venom; and the tone of disparagement in which some of his assailants now affected to speak of his poetry was, however absurd and contemptible in itself, precisely that sort of attack which was the most calculated to wound his, at once, proud and diffident spirit. As long as they confined themselves to blackening his moral and social character, so far from offending, their libels rather fell in with his own shadowy style of self-portraiture, and gratified the strange inverted ambition that possessed him. But the slighting opinion which they ventured to express of his genius,—seconded as it was by that inward dissatisfaction with his own powers, which they whose standard of excellence is highest are always the surest to feel,—mortified and disturbed him; and, being the first sounds of ill augury that had come across his triumphal career, startled him, as we have seen, into serious doubts of its continuance.

Had he been occupying himself, at the time, with any new task, that confidence in his own energies, which he never truly felt but while in the actual exercise of them, would have enabled him to forget these humiliations of the moment in the glow and excitement of anticipated success. But he had just pledged himself to the world to take a long farewell of poesy,—had sealed up that only fountain from which his heart ever drew refreshment or strength,—and thus was left, idly and helplessly, to brood over the daily taunts of his enemies, without the power of avenging

write so well,—as the Royal wit observed,—I should say you write too much; at least, too much in the same strain. The Pythagoreans, you know, were of opinion that the reason why we do not hear or heed the music of the heavenly bodies is that they are always sounding in our ears; and I fear that even the influence of *your* song may be diminished by falling upon the world's dull ear too constantly."

The opinion, however, which a great writer of our day (himself one of the few to whom his remark applies) had the generosity, as well as sagacity, to pronounce on this point, at a time when Lord Byron was indulging in the fullest lavishment of his powers, must be regarded, after all, as the most judicious and wise:—"But they cater ill for the public," says Sir Walter Scott, "and give indifferent advice to the poet, supposing him possessed of the highest qualities of his art, who do not advise him to labour while the laurel around his brows yet retains its freshness. Sketches from Lord Byron are more valuable than finished pictures from others; nor are we at all sure that any labour which he might bestow in revisal would not rather efface than refine those outlines of striking and powerful originality, which they exhibit when flung rough from the hand of a master."—*Biographical Memoirs, by* SIR W. SCOTT.

himself when they insulted his person, and but too much disposed to agree with them when they made light of his genius. " I am afraid (he says, in noticing these attacks in one of his letters) what you call *trash* is plaguily to the purpose, and very good sense into the bargain ; and, to tell the truth, for some little time past, I have been myself much of the same opinion."

In this sensitive state of mind,—which he but ill disguised or relieved by an exterior of gay defiance or philosophic contempt,—we can hardly feel surprised that he should have, all at once, come to the resolution, not only of persevering in his determination to write no more in future, but of purchasing back the whole of his past copyrights and suppressing every page and line he had ever written. On his first mention of this design, Mr. Murray naturally doubted as to his serious-ness ; but the arrival of the following letter, enclosing a draft for the amount of the copyrights, put his intentions beyond question.

LETTER CLXXX.

TO MR. MURRAY.

"2, Albany, April 29th, 1814.

" DEAR SIR,

" I enclose a draft for the money; when paid, send the copyright. I release you from the thousand pounds agreed on for the Giaour and Bride, and there's an end.

" If any accident occurs to me, you may do then as you please ; but, with the exception of two copies of each for *yourself* only, I expect and request that the advertisements be withdrawn, and the remaining copies of *all* destroyed ; and any expense so incurred, I will be glad to defray.

" For all this, it might be as well to assign some reason. I have none to give, except my own caprice, and I do not consider the circum-stance of consequence enough to require explanation.

" In course, I need hardly assure you that they never shall be pub-lished with my consent, directly or indirectly, by any other person what-soever,—that I am perfectly satisfied, and have every reason so to be, with your conduct in all transactions between us as publisher and author.

" It will give me great pleasure to preserve your acquaintance, and to consider you as my friend. Believe me very truly, and for much attention,

" Your obliged
" and very obedient servant,
" Byron.

" P.S. I do not think that I have overdrawn at Hammersley's; but if *that* be the case, I can draw for the superflux on Hoares'. The draft is £5 short, but that I will make up. On payment—*not* before—return the copyright papers."

In such a conjuncture, an appeal to his good-nature and considerateness was, as Mr. Murray well judged, his best resource; and the following prompt reply will show how easily, and at once, it succeeded.

LETTER CLXXXI.

TO MR. MURRAY.

" May 1, 1814.

" DEAR SIR,

" If your present note is serious, and it really would be inconvenient, there is an end of the matter: tear my draft, and go on as usual: in that case, we will recur to our former basis. That *I* was perfectly *serious*, in wishing to suppress all future publication, is true; but certainly not to interfere with the convenience of others, and more particularly your own. Some day, I will tell you the reason of this apparently strange resolution. At present, it may be enough to say that I recall it at your suggestion; and as it appears to have annoyed you, I lose no time in saying so.   " Yours truly,

" B."

During my stay in town this year, we were almost daily together; and it is in no spirit of flattery to the dead I say, that the more intimately

I became acquainted with his disposition and character, the more warmly I felt disposed to take an interest in every thing that concerned him Not that, in the opportunities thus afforded me of observing more closely his defects, I did not discover much to lament, and not a little to condemn But there was still, in the neighbourhood of even his worst faults, some atoning good quality, which was always sure, if brought kindly and with management into play, to neutralize their ill effects. The very frank ness, indeed, with which he avowed his errors seemed to imply a con fidence in his own power of redeeming them,—a consciousness that he could afford to be sincere. There was also, in such entire unreserve a pledge that nothing worse remained behind; and the same quality that laid open the blemishes of his nature gave security for its honesty " The cleanness and purity of one's mind," says Pope, " is never better proved than in discovering its own faults, at first view; as when a stream shows the dirt at its bottom, it shows also the transparency of the water."

The theatre was, at this time, his favourite place of resort. We have seen how enthusiastically he expresses himself on the subject of Mr. Kean's acting, and it was frequently my good fortune, during this season, to share in his enjoyment of it,—the orchestra being, more than once, the place where, for a nearer view of the actor's countenance, we took our station. For Kean's benefit, on the 25th of May, a large party had been made by Lady J * *, to which we both belonged; but Lord Byron having also taken a box for the occasion, so anxious was he to enjoy the representation uninterrupted, that, by rather an unsocial arrangement, only himself and I occupied his box during the play, while every other in the house was crowded almost to suffocation; nor did we join the remainder of our friends till supper. Between the two parties, however, Mr. Kean had no reason to complain of a want of homage to his talents; as Lord J * *, on that occasion, presented him with a hundred pound share in the theatre; while Lord Byron sent him, next day, the sum of fifty guineas*; and, not long after, on seeing him act

---

* To such lengths did he, at this time, carry his enthusiasm for Kean, that when Miss O'Neil soon after appeared, and, by her matchless representation of feminine tenderness, attracted all eyes and hearts, he was not only a little jealous of her reputation, as interfering with that of his favourite, but, in order to guard himself against the risk of becoming a convert, refused to go to see her act. I endeavoured sometimes to persuade him into witnessing, at least, one of her

some of his favourite parts, made him presents of a handsome snuff-box and a costly Turkish sword.

Such effect had the passionate energy of Kean's acting on his mind, that, once, in seeing him play Sir Giles Overreach, he was so affected as to be seized with a sort of convulsive fit; and we shall find him, some years after, in Italy, when the representation of Alfieri's tragedy of Mirra had agitated him in the same violent manner, comparing the two instances as the only ones in his life when " any thing under reality" had been able to move him so powerfully.

The following are a few of the notes which I received from him during this visit to town.

TO MR. MOORE.

" May 4th, 1814.

" Last night we supp'd at R——fe's board, &c. *

*   *   *   *   *   *

" I wish people would not shirk their *dinners*—ought it not to have been a dinner†?—and that d—d anchovy sandwich!

" That plaguy voice of yours made me sentimental, and almost fall in love with a girl who was recommending herself, during your song, by *hating* music. But the song is past, and my passion can wait, till the *pucelle* is more harmonious.

" Do you go to Lady Jersey's to-night? It is a large party, and

---

performances; but his answer was (punning upon Shakspeare's word, " unanealed,") " No—I 'm resolved to continue *un-Oneiled.*"

To the great queen of all actresses, however, it will be seen, by the following extract from one of his Journals, he rendered due justice.

" Of actors, Cooke was the most natural, Kemble the most supernatural,—Kean the medium between the two. But Mrs. Siddons was worth them all put together."—*Detached Thoughts.*

* An epigram here followed which, as founded on a scriptural allusion, I thought it better to omit.

† We had been invited by Lord R. to dine *after* the play,—an arrangement which, from its novelty, delighted Lord Byron exceedingly. The dinner, however, afterwards dwindled into a mere supper, and this change was long a subject of jocular resentment with him.

you won't be bored into 'softening rocks,' and all that. Othello is
to-morrow and Saturday too. Which day shall we go? when shall I
see you? If you call, let it be after three and as near four as you
please. Ever, &c."

TO MR. MOORE.

" May 4th, 1814.

" DEAR TOM,

    " Thou hast asked me for a song, and I enclose you an experiment,
which has cost me something more than trouble, and is, therefore, less
likely to be worth your taking any in your proposed setting*. Now,
if it be so, throw it into the fire without *phrase*.

" Ever yours,
" BYRON.

1.

" I speak not, I trace not, I breathe not thy name,
  There is grief in the sound, there is guilt in the fame;
  But the tear which now burns on my cheek may impart
  The deep thoughts that dwell in that silence of heart.

2.

" Too brief for our passion, too long for our peace
  Were those hours—can their joy or their bitterness cease?
  We repent—we abjure—we will break from our chain,—
  We will part,—we will fly to—unite it again!

3.

" Oh! thine be the gladness, and mine be the guilt!
  Forgive me, adored one!—forsake, if thou wilt;—
  But the heart which is thine shall expire undebased,
  And *man* shall not break it—whatever *thou* mayst.

---

* I had begged of him to write something for me to set to music. The above verses
have lately found their way into print, but through a channel not very likely to bring
them into circulation. I shall, therefore, leave them here, undisturbed, in their natural
position.

4.

" And stern to the haughty, but humble to thee,
　This soul, in its bitterest blackness, shall be;
　And our days seem as swift, and our moments more sweet,
　With thee by my side, than with worlds at our feet.

5.

" One sigh of thy sorrow, one look of thy love,
　Shall turn me or fix, shall reward or reprove;
　And the heartless may wonder at all I resign—
　Thy lip shall reply, not to them, but to *mine*."

TO MR. MOORE.

" Will you and Rogers come to my box at Covent, then? I shall be there, and none else—or I won't be there, if you *twain* would like to go without me. You will not get so good a place hustling among the publican *boxers*, with damnable apprentices (six feet high) on a back row. Will you both oblige me and come—or one—or neither—or, what you will?

" P.S. An' you will, I will call for you at half-past six, or any time of your own dial."

TO MR. MOORE.

" I have gotten a box for Othello to-night, and send the ticket for your friends the R—fes. I seriously recommend to you to recommend to them to go for half an hour, if only to see the third act—they will not easily have another opportunity. We—at least, I—cannot be there, so there will be no one in their way. Will you give or send it to them? it will come with a better grace from you than me.

" I am in no good plight, but will dine at * *'s with you, if I can. There is music and Covent-g.—Will you go, at all events, to my box there afterwards, to see a *début* of a young 16* in the ' Child of Nature?' "

---

* Miss Foote's first appearance, which we witnessed together.

TO MR. MOORE.

"Sunday matin.

"Was not Iago perfection? particularly the last look. I was *close* to him (in the orchestra), and never saw an English countenance half so expressive. I am acquainted with no *im*material sensuality so delightful as good acting; and, as it is fitting there should be good plays, now and then, besides Shakspeare's, I wish you or Campbell would write one:— the rest of 'us youth' have not heart enough.

"You were cut up in the Champion—is it not so? this day, so am I —even to *shocking* the editor. The critic writes well; and as, at present, poesy is not my passion predominant, and my snake of Aaron has swallowed up all the other serpents, I don't feel fractious. I send you the paper, which I mean to take in for the future. We go to M." together. Perhaps I shall see you before, but don't let me *bore* you, now nor ever.

"Ever, as now, truly and affectionately, &c."

TO MR. MOORE.

"May 5th, 1814.

"Do you go to the Lady Cahir's this even? If you do—and whenever we are bound to the same follies—let us embark in the same 'Shippe of Fooles.' I have been up till five, and up at nine; and feel heavy with only winking for the last three or four nights.

"I lost my party and place at supper trying to keep out of the way of * * * * I would have gone away altogether, but that would have appeared a worse affectation than t'other. You are of course engaged to dinner, or we may go quietly together to my box at Covent-garden, and afterwards to this assemblage. Why did you go away so soon?

"Ever, &c.

"P.S. *Ought not* R * * * fe's supper to have been a dinner? Jackson is here, and I must fatigue myself into spirits."

TO MR. MOORE.

"May 18th, 1814.

"Thanks—and punctuality. *What* has passed at * * * * House? I suppose that *I* am to know, and 'pars fui' of the conference. I regret that your * * * *s will detain you so late, but I suppose you will be at Lady Jersey's. I am going earlier with Hobhouse. You recollect that to-morrow we sup and see Kean.

"P.S. *Two* to-morrow is the hour of pugilism."

The supper, to which he here looks forward, took place at Watier's, of which club he had lately become a member; and, as it may convey some idea of his irregular mode of diet, and thus account, in part, for the frequent derangement of his health, I shall here attempt, from recollection, a description of his supper on this occasion. We were to have been joined by Lord R * *, who however did not arrive, and the party accordingly consisted but of ourselves. Having taken upon me to order the repast, and knowing that Lord Byron, for the last two days, had done nothing towards sustenance, beyond eating a few biscuits and (to appease appetite) chewing mastic, I desired that we should have a good supply of, at least, two kinds of fish. My companion, however, confined himself to lobsters, and of these finished two or three, to his own share,—interposing, sometimes, a small liqueur-glass of strong white brandy, sometimes a tumbler of very hot water, and then pure brandy again, to the amount of near half a dozen small glasses of the latter, without which, alternately with the hot water, he appeared to think the lobster could not be digested. After this, we had claret, of which having despatched two bottles between us, at about four o'clock in the morning we parted.

As Pope has thought his " delicious lobster-nights" worth commemorating, these particulars of one in which Lord Byron was concerned may also have some interest.

Among other nights of the same description which I had the happiness of passing with him, I remember once, in returning home from some assembly at rather a late hour, we saw lights in the windows

of his old haunt Stevens's, in Bond-street, and agreed to stop there and su]
On entering, we found an old friend of his, Sir G * * W * *, who joine
our party, and the lobsters and brandy and water being put in requisition
it was (as usual on such occasions) broad daylight before we separated.

LETTER CLXXXII.

TO MR. MOORE.

" May 23d, 1814.

" I must send you the Java government gazette of July 3d, 1813
just sent to me by Murray. Only think of *our* (for it is you and I
setting paper warriors in array in the Indian seas. Does not this soun.
like fame—something almost like *posterity?* It is something to have
scribblers squabbling about us 5000 miles off, while we are agreeing s.
well at home. Bring it with you in your pocket;—it will make you
laugh, as it hath me.

" Ever yours,

" B."

" P.S. Oh the anecdote!   *   *   *   *   *   *   *
*   *   *   *   *   *   *   *   *."

To the circumstance mentioned in this letter he recurs more than
once in the Journals which he kept abroad; as thus, in a passage of his
" Detached Thoughts,"—where it will be perceived that, by a trifling lapse
of memory, he represents himself as having produced this gazette, for
the first time, on our way to dinner.

" In the year 1814, as Moore and I were going to dine with Lord
Grey in Portman-square, I pulled out a ' Java Gazette' (which Murray
had sent to me), in which there was a controversy on our respective
merits as poets. It was amusing enough that we should be proceeding
peaceably to the same table while they were squabbling about us in the
Indian seas (to be sure, the paper was dated six months before), and
filling columns with Batavian criticism. But this is fame, I presume."

The following Poem, written about this time and, apparently, for the purpose of being recited at the Caledonian Meeting, I insert principally on account of the warm feeling which it breathes towards Scotland and her sons :—

" Who hath not glow'd above the page where Fame
Hath fix'd high Caledon's unconquer'd name ;
The mountain-land which spurn'd the Roman chain,
And baffled back the fiery-crested Dane,
Whose bright claymore and hardihood of hand
No foe could tame—no tyrant could command.

" That race is gone—but still their children breathe,
And glory crowns them with redoubled wreath :
O'er Gael and Saxon mingling banners shine,
And, England ! add their stubborn strength to thine.
The blood which flow'd with Wallace flows as free,
But now 'tis only shed for Fame and thee !
Oh ! pass not by the Northern veteran's claim,
But give support—the world hath given him fame !

" The humbler ranks, the lowly brave, who bled
While cheerly following where the mighty led—
Who sleep beneath the undistinguish'd sod
Where happier comrades in their triumph trod,
To us bequeath—'tis all their fate allows—
The sireless offspring and the lonely spouse :
She on high Albyn's dusky hills may raise
The tearful eye in melancholy gaze,
Or view, while shadowy auguries disclose
The Highland seer's anticipated woes,
The bleeding phantom of each martial form
Dim in the cloud, or darkling in the storm ;
While sad, she chants the solitary song,
The soft lament for him who tarries long—
For him, whose distant relics vainly crave
The Coronach's wild requiem to the brave !

" 'Tis Heaven—not man—must charm away the woe
Which bursts when Nature's feelings newly flow ;
Yet tenderness and time may rob the tear
Of half its bitterness for one so dear :

> A nation's gratitude perchance may spread
> A thornless pillow for the widow'd head;
> May lighten well her hearts maternal care,
> And wean from penury the soldier's heir."

LETTER CLXXXIII.

TO MR. MOORE.

" May 31st, 1814.

"As I shall probably not see you here to-day, I write to request that if not inconvenient to yourself, you will stay in town till *Sunday*; if not to gratify me, yet to please a great many others, who will be very sorry to lose you. As for myself, I can only repeat that I wish you would either remain a long time with us, or not come at all; for these *snatches* of society make the subsequent separations bitterer than ever.

"I believe you think that I have not been quite fair with that Alpha and Omega of beauty, &c. with whom you would willingly have united me. But if you consider what her sister said on the subject, you will less wonder that my pride should have taken the alarm; particularly as nothing but the every-day flirtation of every-day people ever occurred between your heroine and myself. Had Lady ** appeared to wish it—or even *not* to oppose it—I would have gone on, and very possibly married (that is, *if* the other had been equally accordant) with the same indifference which has frozen over the ' Black Sea' of almost all my passions. It is that very indifference which makes me so uncertain and apparently capricious. It is not eagerness of new pursuits, but that nothing impresses me sufficiently to *fix*; neither do I feel disgusted, but simply indifferent to almost all excitements. The proof of this is, that obstacles, the slightest even, *stop* me. This can hardly be *timidity*, for I have done some impudent things too, in my time; and in almost all cases, opposition is a stimulus. In mine, it is not; if a straw were in my way, I could not stoop to pick it up.

"I have sent this long tirade, because I would not have you suppose that I have been *trifling* designedly with you or others. If you think so, in the name of St. Hubert (the patron of antlers and hunters) let me be married out of hand—I don't care to whom, so that it amuses any body else, and don't interfere with me much in the daytime.

" Ever, &c."

LETTER CLXXXIV.

TO MR. MOORE.

" June 14th, 1814.

" I *could* be very sentimental now, but I won't. The truth is, that I have been all my life trying to harden my heart, and have not yet quite succeeded—though there are great hopes—and you do not know how it sunk with your departure. What adds to my regret is having seen so little of you during your stay in this crowded desert, where one ought to be able to bear thirst like a camel,—the springs are so few, and most of them so muddy.

" The newspapers will tell you all that is to be told of emperors, &c.* They have dined, and supped, and shown their flat faces in all

---

* In a few days after this, he sent me a long rhyming Epistle full of jokes and pleasantries upon every thing and every one around him, of which the following are the only parts producible.

> " ' What say *I*?'—not a syllable further in prose ;
> I 'm your man ' of all measures,' dear Tom,—so, here goes !
> Here goes, for a swim on the stream of old Time,
> On those buoyant supporters, the bladders of rhyme.
> If our weight breaks them down, and we sink in the flood,
> We are smother'd, at least, in respectable mud,
> Where the Divers of Bathos lie drown'd in a heap,
> And S * *'s last Pæan has pillow'd his sleep ;—
> That ' Felo de se' who, half drunk with his malmsey,
> Walk'd out of his depth and was lost in a calm sea,
> Singing ' Glory to God' in a spick and span stanza,
> The like (since Tom Sternhold was choked) never man saw.

> " The papers have told you, no doubt, of the fusses,
> The fêtes, and the gapings to get at these Russes,—
> Of his Majesty's suite, up from coachman to Hetman,—
> And what dignity decks the flat face of the great man.

thoroughfares, and several saloons.   Their uniforms are very becoming but rather short in the skirts; and their conversation is a catechism, fo which and the answers I refer you to those who have heard it.

  " I think of leaving town for Newstead soon.   If so, I shall not b remote from your recess, and (unless Mrs. M. detains you at home ove the caudle-cup and a new cradle) we will meet.   You shall come to me or I to you, as you like it;—but *meet* we will.   An invitation from Aston has reached me, but I do not think I shall go.   I have also heard of * * *—I should like to see her again, for I have not met her fo years; and though ' the light that ne'er can shine again' is set, I do not know that ' one dear smile like those of old' might not make me for a moment forget the ' dulness' of ' life's stream.'

  " I am going to R * *'s to-night—to one of those suppers which ' *ought* to be dinners.'   I have hardly seen her, and never *him*, since you set out.   I told you, you were the last link of that chain.   As for * *, we have not syllabled one another's names since.   The post will not permit me to continue my scrawl.   More anon.

" Ever, dear Moore, &c.

  " P.S. Keep the Journal*, I care not what becomes of it, and if it has amused you, I am glad that I kept it.   ' Lara' is finished, and I am copying him for my third vol., now collecting;—but *no separate* publication."

I saw him, last week, at two balls and a party,—
For a prince, his demeanour was rather too hearty.
You know, *we* are used to quite different graces,
*   *   *   *   *

" The Czar's look, I own, was much brighter and brisker,
But then he is sadly deficient in whisker;
And wore but a starless blue coat, and in kersey-
-mere breeches whisk'd round, in a waltz with the J * *,
Who, lovely as ever, seem'd just as delighted
With majesty's presence as those she invited."
*   *   *   *   *
*   *   *   *   *

  * The Journal from which I have given extracts in the preceding pages.

TO MR. MURRAY.

" June 14th, 1814.

" I return your packet of this morning. Have you heard that Bertrand has returned to Paris with the account of Napoleon's having lost his senses? It is a *report;* but, if true, I must, like Mr. Fitzgerald and Jeremiah (of lamentable memory) lay claim to prophecy; that is to say, of saying, that he *ought* to go out of his senses, in the penultimate stanza of a certain Ode,—the which, having been pronounced *nonsense* by several profound critics, has a still further pretension, by its unintelligibility, to inspiration.

" Ever, &c."

LETTER CLXXXV.

TO MR. ROGERS.

" June 19th, 1814.

" I am always obliged to trouble you with my awkwardnesses, and now I have a fresh one. Mr. W.* called on me several times, and I have missed the honour of making his acquaintance, which I regret, but which *you,* who know my desultory and uncertain habits, will not wonder at, and will, I am sure, attribute to any thing but a wish to offend a person who has shown me much kindness, and possesses character and talents entitled to general respect. My mornings are late, and passed in fencing and boxing, and a variety of most unpoetical exercises, very wholesome, &c. but would be very disagreeable to my friends, whom I am obliged to exclude during their operation. I never go out till the evening, and I have not been fortunate enough to meet Mr. W. at Lord Lansdowne's or Lord Jersey's, where I had hoped to pay him my respects.

" I would have written to him, but a few words from you will go further than all the apologetical sesquipedalities I could muster on the

* Mr. Wrangham.

4 c 2

occasion. It is only to say that, without intending it, I contrive to behave very ill to every body, and am very sorry for it.

" Ever, dear R., &c."

The following undated notes to Mr. Rogers must have been written about the same time.

" Sunday.

" Your non-attendance at Corinne's is very *apropos*, as I was on the eve of sending you an excuse. I do not feel well enough to go there this evening, and have been obliged to despatch an apology. I believe I need not add one for not accepting Mr. Sheridan's invitation on Wednesday which I fancy both you and I understood in the same sense :—with him the saying of Mirabeau, that ' *words* are *things*,' is not to be taken literally.

" Ever, &c."

" I will call for you at a quarter before *seven*, if that will suit you. I return you Sir Proteus*, and shall merely add in return, as Johnson said of, and to, somebody or other, ' Are we alive after all this censure?'

" Believe me, &c."

" Tuesday.

" Sheridan was yesterday, at first, too sober to remember your invitation, but in the dregs of the third bottle he fished up his memory. The Staël out-talked Whitbread, was *ironed* by Sheridan, confounded Sir Humphry, and utterly perplexed your slave. The rest (great names in the red book, nevertheless) were mere segments of the circle. Ma'mselle danced a Russ saraband with great vigour, grace, and expression.

" Ever, &c."

---

* A satirical pamphlet, in which all the writers of the day were attacked.

TO MR. MURRAY.

"June 21st, 1814.

"I suppose 'Lara' is gone to the devil,—which is no great matter, only let me know, that I may be saved the trouble of copying the rest, and put the first part into the fire. I really have no anxiety about it, and shall not be sorry to be saved the copying, which goes on very slowly, and may prove to you that you may *speak out*—or I should be less sluggish.   "Yours, &c."

LETTER CLXXXVI.

TO MR. ROGERS.

"June 27th, 1814.

"You could not have made me a more acceptable present than Jacqueline,—she is all grace, and softness, and poetry; there is so much of the last, that we do not feel the want of story, which is simple, yet *enough*. I wonder that you do not oftener unbend to more of the same kind. I have some sympathy with the *softer* affections, though very little in *my* way, and no one can depict them so truly and successfully as yourself. I have half a mind to pay you in kind, or rather *un*kind, for I have just 'supped full of horror' in two Cantos of darkness and dismay.

"Do you go to Lord Essex's to-night? if so, will you let me call for you at your own hour? I dined with Holland-house yesterday at Lord Cowper's; my lady very gracious, which she can be more than any one when she likes. I was not sorry to see them again, for I can't forget that they have been very kind to me.

"Ever yours most truly,
"BN.

"P.S. Is there any chance or possibility of making it up with Lord Carlisle, as I feel disposed to do any thing reasonable or unreasonable to effect it? I would before, but for the Courier,' and the possible misconstructions at such a time. Perpend, pronounce."

On my return to London, for a short time, at the beginning of July I found his Poem of "Lara," which he had begun at the latter end of May, in the hands of the printer, and nearly ready for publication. He had, before I left town, repeated to me, as we were on our way to some evening party, the first hundred and twenty lines of the Poem, which he had written the day before,—at the same time giving me a general sketch of the characters and the story.

His short notes to Mr. Murray, during the printing of this work, are of the same impatient and whimsical character as those, of which I have already given specimens, in my account of his preceding publications: but, as matter of more interest now presses upon us, I shall forbear from transcribing them at length. In one of them he says, " I have just corrected some of the most horrible blunders that ever crept into a proof:"—in another, " I hope the next proof will be better; this was one which would have consoled Job, if it had been of his ' enemy's book:' "— a third contains only the following words: " Dear sir, you demanded more *battle*—there it is. Yours, &c."

The two letters that immediately follow were addressed to me, at this time, in town.

LETTER CLXXXVII.

TO MR. MOORE.

" July 8th, 1814.

" I returned to town last night, and had some hopes of seeing you to-day, and would have called,—but I have been (though in exceeding distempered good health) a little head-achy with free living, as it is called, and am now at the freezing point of returning soberness. Of course, I should be sorry that our parallel lines did not deviate into intersection before you return to the country,—after that same nonsuit* whereof the papers have told us,—but, as you must be much occupied

* He alludes to an action for piracy brought by Mr. Power (the publisher of my musical works), to the trial of which I had been summoned as a witness.

I won't be affronted, should your time and business militate against our meeting.

" Rogers and I have almost coalesced into a joint invasion of the public. Whether it will take place or not, I do not yet know, and I am afraid Jacqueline (which is very beautiful) will be in bad company*. But, in this case, the lady will not be the sufferer.

" I am going to the sea, and then to Scotland; and I have been doing nothing,—that is, no good,—and am very truly, &c."

LETTER CLXXXVIII.

TO MR. MOORE.

" I suppose, by your non-appearance, that the philosophy of my note, and the previous silence of the writer, have put or kept you in *humeur*. Never mind—it is hardly worth while.

" This day have I received information from my man of law of the *non*—and never likely to be—performance of purchase by Mr. Claughton, of *im*pecuniary memory. He don't know what to do, or when to pay; and so all my hopes and worldly projects and prospects are gone to the devil. He (the purchaser, and the devil too, for aught I care) and I, and my legal advisers, are to meet to-morrow,—the said purchaser having first taken special care to inquire ' whether I would meet him with temper?'—Certainly. The question is this—I shall either have the estate back, which is as good as ruin, or I shall go on with him dawdling, which is rather worse. I have brought my pigs to a Mussulman market. If I had but a wife now, and children, of whose paternity I entertained doubts, I should be happy, or rather fortunate, as Candide or Scarmentado. In the mean time, if you don't come and see me, I shall think that Sam.'s bank is broke too; and that you, having assets there, are despairing of more than a piastre in the pound for your dividend.

" Ever, &c."

* Lord Byron afterwards proposed that I should make a third in this publication; but the honour was a perilous one, and I begged leave to decline it.

TO MR. MURRAY.

" July 11, 1814.

" You shall have one of the pictures.   I wish you to send the proof of 'Lara' to Mr. Moore, 33, Bury-street, *to-night*, as he leaves town to-morrow, and wishes to see it before he goes *; and I am also willing to have the benefit of his remarks.

" Yours, &c."

TO MR. MURRAY.

" July 18th, 1814.

" I think *you* will be satisfied even to *repletion* with our northern friends †, and I won't deprive you longer of what I think will give you pleasure: for my own part, my modesty, or my vanity, must be silent.

" P.S. If you could spare it for an hour in the evening, I wish you to send it up to Mrs. Leigh, your neighbour, at the London Hotel, Albemarle-street."

LETTER CLXXXIX.

TO MR. MURRAY.

" July 23, 1814.

" I am sorry to say that the print ‡ is by no means approved of by those who have seen it, who are pretty conversant with the original, as well as the picture from whence it is taken.   I rather suspect that it is

---

* In a note which I wrote to him, before starting, next day, I find the following:—" I got Lara at three o'clock this morning—read him before I slept, and was enraptured.   I take the proofs with me."

† He here refers to an article in the number of the Edinburgh Review, just then published (No. 45), on the Corsair and Bride of Abydos.

‡ An engraving by Agar from Phillips's portrait of him.

from the *copy*, and not the *exhibited* portrait, and in this dilemma would recommend a suspension, if not an abandonment, of the *prefixion* to the volumes which you purpose inflicting upon the public.

" With regard to *Lara*, don't be in any hurry. I have not yet made up my mind on the subject, nor know what to think or do till I hear from you; and Mr. Moore appeared to me in a similar state of indetermination. I do not know that it may not be better to *reserve* it for the *entire* publication you proposed, and not adventure in hardy singleness, or even backed by the fairy Jacqueline. I have been seized with all kinds of doubts, &c. &c. since I left London.

" Pray let me hear from you, and believe me, &c."

LETTER CXC.

TO MR. MURRAY.

" July 24th, 1814.

" The minority must, in this case, carry it, so pray let it be so, for I don't care sixpence for any of the opinions you mention, on such a subject; and P * * must be a dunce to agree with them. For my own part, I have no objection at all; but Mrs. Leigh and my cousin must be better judges of the likeness than others; and they hate it; and so I won't have it at all.

" Mr. Hobhouse is right as for his conclusion; but I deny the premises. The name only is Spanish*; the country is not Spain, but the Morea.

" Waverley is the best and most interesting novel I have redde since—I don't know when. I like it as much as I hate * *, and * *, and * *, and all the feminine trash of the last four months. Besides, it is all easy to me, I have been in Scotland so much (though then young enough too), and feel at home with the people, Lowland and Gael.

" A note will correct what Mr. Hobhouse thinks an error (about the feudal system in Spain);—it is *not* Spain. If he puts a few words of prose any where, it will set all right.

* Alluding to Lara.

" I have been ordered to town to vote. I shall disobey. There is no good in so much prating, since ' certain issues strokes should arbitrate.' If you have any thing to say, let me hear from you.

" Yours, &c."

LETTER CXCI.

TO MR. MURRAY.

" August 3d, 1814.

" It is certainly a little extraordinary that you have not sent the Edinburgh Review, as I requested, and hoped it would not require a note a day to remind you. I see *advertisements* of Lara and Jacqueline; pray, *why?* when I requested you to postpone publication till my return to town.

" I have a most amusing epistle from the Ettrick bard—Hogg; in which, speaking of his bookseller, whom he denominates the ' shabbiest' of the *trade* for not ' lifting his bills,' he adds, in so many words, ' G—d d—n him and them both.' This is a pretty prelude to asking you to adopt him (the said Hogg); but this he wishes; and if you please, you and I will talk it over. He has a poem ready for the press (and your *bills* too, if ' *lift*able'), and bestows some benedictions on Mr. Moore for his abduction of Lara from the forthcoming Miscellany *.

" P.S. Sincerely, I think Mr. Hogg would suit you very well; and surely he is a man of great powers, and deserving of encouragement. I must knock out a Tale for him, and you should at all events consider before you reject his suit. Scott is gone to the Orkneys in a gale of wind, and Hogg says that, during the said gale, ' he is sure that Scott is not quite at his ease, to say the best of it.' Ah! I wish these home-keeping bards could taste a Mediterranean white squall, or the Gut in a gale of wind, or even the Bay of Biscay with no wind at all."

---

* Mr. Hogg had been led to hope that he should be permitted to insert this Poem in a Miscellany which he had at this time some thoughts of publishing; and whatever advice I may have given against such a mode of disposing of the work arose certainly not from any ill-will to this ingenious and remarkable man, but from a consideration of what I thought most advantageous to the fame of Lord Byron.

LETTER CXCII.

TO MR. MOORE.

"Hastings, August 3d, 1814.

"By the time this reaches your dwelling, I shall (God wot) be in town again probably. I have been here renewing my acquaintance with my old friend Ocean; and I find his bosom as pleasant a pillow for an hour in the morning as his daughter's of Paphos could be in the twilight. I have been swimming and eating turbot, and smuggling neat brandies and silk handkerchiefs,—and listening to my friend Hodgson's raptures about a pretty wife-elect of his,—and walking on cliffs, and tumbling down hills, and making the most of the 'dolce far-niente' for the last fortnight. I met a son of Lord Erskine's, who says he has been married a year, and is the 'happiest of men;' and I have met the aforesaid H., who is also the 'happiest of men;' so, it is worth while being here, if only to witness the superlative felicity of these foxes, who have cut off their tails, and would persuade the rest to part with their brushes to keep them in countenance.

"It rejoiceth me that you like 'Lara.' Jeffrey is out with his 45th Number, which I suppose you have got. He is only too kind to me, in my share of it, and I begin to fancy myself a golden pheasant, upon the strength of the plumage wherewith he hath bedecked me. But then, 'surgit amari,' &c.—the gentlemen of the Champion, and Perry, have got hold (I know not how) of the condolatory address to Lady J. on the picture-abduction by our R***, and have published them—with my name, too, smack—without even asking leave, or inquiring whether or no! D—n their impudence, and d—n every thing. It has put me out of patience, and so, I shall say no more about it.

"You shall have Lara and Jacque (both with some additions) when out; but I am still demurring and delaying, and in a fuss, and so is R. in his way.

"Newstead is to be mine again. Claughton forfeits twenty-five thousand pounds; but that don't prevent me from being very prettily ruined.   I mean to bury myself there—and let my beard grow—and hat⸱ you all.

"Oh! I have had the most amusing letter from Hogg, the Ettric⸱ minstrel and shepherd.   He wants me to recommend him to Murray and, speaking of his present bookseller, whose 'bills' are never 'lifted⸱ he adds, *totidem verbis*, 'God d—n him and them both.'   I laughed, an⸱ so would you too, at the way in which this execration is introduced⸱ The said Hogg is a strange being, but of great, though uncouth, powers I think very highly of him, as a poet; but he, and half of these Scotc⸱ and Lake troubadours, are spoilt by living in little circles and petty societies.   London and the world is the only place to take the conceit ou⸱ of a man—in the milling phrase.   Scott, he says, is gone to the Orkney⸱ in a gale of wind;—during which wind, he affirms, the said Scott, 'he i⸱ sure, is not at his ease,—to say the best of it.'   Lord, Lord, if these home⸱ keeping minstrels had crossed your Atlantic or my Mediterranean, and tasted a little open boating in a white squall—or a gale in 'the Gut'—o⸱ the 'Bay of Biscay,' with no gale at all—how it would enliven and introduce them to a few of the sensations!—to say nothing of an illici⸱ amour or two upon shore, in the way of essay upon the Passions, beginning with simple adultery, and compounding it as they went along.

"I have forwarded your letter to Murray,—by the way, you had addressed it to *Miller*.   Pray write to me, and say what art thou doing? 'Not finished!'—Oons! how is this?—these 'flaws and starts' must be 'authorised by your grandam,' and are unbecoming of any other author⸱ I was sorry to hear of your discrepancy with the ** s, or rather, your abjuration of agreement.   I don't want to be impertinent, or buffoon on a serious subject, and am therefore at a loss what to say.

"I hope nothing will induce you to abate from the proper price of your poem, as long as there is a prospect of getting it.   For my own part, I have, *seriously*, and *not whiningly* (for that is not my way—at least, it used not to be), neither hopes, nor prospects, and scarcely even wishes.   I am, in some respects, happy, but not in a manner that can or ought to last,— but enough of that.   The worst of it is, I feel quite enervated and indifferent.   I really do not know, if Jupiter were to offer me my choice of the contents of his benevolent cask, what I would pick out of it. If I was born, as the nurses say, with a 'silver spoon in my mouth,' it has stuck in my throat, and spoiled my palate, so that nothing put into it is swallowed with much relish,—unless it be cayenne. However, I have grievances enough to occupy me that way too;—but for fear of adding to yours by this pestilent long diatribe, I postpone the reading them, *sine die*. Ever, dear M., yours, &c.

" P.S. Don't forget my godson. You could not have fixed on a fitter porter for his sins than me, being used to carry double without inconvenience." *　　*　　*　　*　　*　　*　　*

LETTER CXCIII.

TO MR. MURRAY.

" August 4th, 1814.

" Not having received the slightest answer to my last three letters, nor the book (the last number of the Edinburgh Review) which they requested, I presume that you were the unfortunate person who perished in the pagoda on Monday last, and address this rather to your executors than yourself, regretting that you should have had the ill-luck to be the sole victim on that joyous occasion.

" I beg leave then to inform these gentlemen (whoever they may be) that I am a little surprised at the previous neglect of the deceased, and also at observing an advertisement of an approaching publication on Saturday next, against the which I protested, and do protest, for the present.

" Yours (or theirs), &c.

" B."

LETTER CXCIV.

TO MR. MURRAY.

" August 5th, 1814.

"The Edinburgh Review is arrived—thanks. I enclose Mr. Hobhouse's letter, from which you will perceive the work you have made. However, I have done: you must send my rhymes to the devil your own way. It seems also that the 'faithful and spirited likeness' is another of your publications. I wish you joy of it; but it is no likeness—that is the point. Seriously, if I have delayed your journey to Scotland, I am sorry that you carried your complaisance so far; particularly as upon trifles you have a more summary method;—witness the grammar of Hobhouse's 'bit of prose,' which has put him and me into a fever.

"Hogg must translate his own words: '*lifting*' is a quotation from his letter, together with 'God d—n,' &c., which I suppose requires no translation.

"I was unaware of the contents of Mr. Moore's letter; I think your offer very handsome, but of that you and he must judge. If he can get more, you won't wonder that he should accept it.

"Out with Lara, since it must be. The tome looks pretty enough —on the outside. I shall be in town next week, and in the mean time wish you a pleasant journey.

"Yours, &c."

LETTER CXCV.

TO MR. MOORE.

"August 12th, 1814.

"I was *not* alone, nor will be while I can help it. Newstead is not yet decided. Claughton is to make a grand effort by Saturday week to complete,—if not, he must give up twenty-five thousand pounds, and the estate, with expenses, &c. &c. If I resume the Abbacy, you shall have due notice, and a cell set apart for your reception, with a pious welcome. Rogers, I have not seen, but Larry and Jacky came out a few days ago. Of their effect, I know nothing.

*　　*　　*　　*　　*　　*

"There is something very amusing in *your* being an Edinburgh Reviewer. You know, I suppose, that T * * is none of the placidest, and may possibly enact some tragedy on being told that he is only a fool. If, now, Jeffrey were to be slain on account of an article of yours, there would be a fine conclusion. For my part, as Mrs. Winifred Jenkins says, 'he has done the handsome thing by me,' particularly in his last number; so, he is the best of men and the ablest of critics, and I won't have him killed,—though I dare say many wish he were, for being so good-humoured.

"Before I left Hastings, I got in a passion with an ink-bottle, which I flung out of the window one night with a vengeance;—and what then? why, next morning I was horrified by seeing that it had struck, and split upon, the petticoat of Euterpe's graven image in the garden, and grimed her as if it were on purpose*. Only think of my distress,—and the epigrams that might be engendered on the Muse and her misadventure.

"I had an adventure, almost as ridiculous, at some private theatricals near Cambridge—though of a different description—since I saw you last. I quarrelled with a man in the dark for asking me who I was (insolently enough, to be sure), and followed him into the green-room (a *stable*) in a rage, amongst a set of people I never saw before. He turned out to be a low comedian, engaged to act with the amateurs, and to be a civil-spoken man enough, when he found out that nothing very pleasant was to be got by rudeness. But you would have been amused with the row, and the dialogue, and the dress—or rather the undress—of the party, where I had introduced myself in a devil of a hurry, and the astonishment that ensued. I had gone out of the theatre, for coolness, into the garden;—there I had tumbled over some dogs, and, coming away from them in very ill-humour, encountered the man in a worse, which produced all this confusion.

"Well—and why don't you 'launch?'—Now is your time. The people are tolerably tired with me, and not very much enamoured of * *, who has just spawned a quarto of metaphysical blank verse, which is nevertheless only a part of a poem.

"Murray talks of divorcing Larry and Jacky—a bad sign for the authors, who, I suppose, will be divorced too, and throw the blame upon one another. Seriously, I don't care a cigar about it, and I don't see why Sam should.

* His servant had brought him up a large jar of ink, into which, not supposing it to be full, he had thrust his pen down to the very bottom. Enraged, on finding it come out all smeared with ink, he flung the bottle out of the window into the garden, where it lighted, as here described, upon one of eight leaden Muses, that had been imported, some time before, from Holland, —the ninth having been, by some accident, left behind.

" Let me hear from and of you and my godson. If a daughter the name will do quite as well.   *   *   *   *

"Ever, &c."

LETTER CXCVI.

TO MR. MOORE.

"August 13th, 1814.

" I wrote yesterday to Mayfield, and have just now enfranked your letter to mamma. My stay in town is so uncertain (not later than next week) that your packets for the north may not reach me; and as I know not exactly where I am going—however, *Newstead* is my most probable destination, and if you send your despatches before Tuesday, I can forward them to our new ally. But, after that day, you had better not trust to their arrival in time.

" * * has been exiled from Paris, *on dit*, for saying the Bourbons were old women. The Bourbons might have been content, I think, with returning the compliment.   *   *   *   *

" I told you all about Jacky and Larry yesterday;—they are to be separated,—at least, so says the grand M., and I know no more of the matter. Jeffrey has done me more than 'justice;' but as to tragedy—um!—I have no time for fiction at present. A man cannot paint a storm with the vessel under bare poles, on a lee-shore. When I get to land, I will try what is to be done, and, if I founder, there be plenty of mine elders and betters to console Melpomene.

" When at Newstead, you must come over, if only for a day—should Mrs. M. be *exigeante* of your presence. The place is worth seeing, as a ruin, and I can assure you there *was* some fun there, even in my time; but that is past. The ghosts*, however, and the gothics, and the waters, and the desolation, make it very lively still.

"Ever, dear Tom, yours, &c."

---

* It was, if I mistake not, during his recent visit to Newstead, that he himself actually fancied he saw the ghost of the Black Friar, which was supposed to have haunted the Abbey from the time of the dissolution of the monasteries, and which he thus describes, from the recollection perhaps of his own fantasy, in Don Juan :—

" It was no mouse, but, lo! a monk, array'd
    In cowl and beads and dusky garb, appear'd,

LETTER CXCVII.

TO MR. MURRAY.

" Newstead Abbey, September 2d, 1814.

" I am obliged by what you have sent, but would rather not see any thing of the kind*; we have had enough of these things already, good and bad, and next month you need not trouble yourself to collect even the *higher* generation—on my account. It gives me much pleasure to hear of Mr. Hobhouse's and Mr. Merivale's good entreatment by the journals you mention.

" I still think Mr. Hogg and yourself might make out an alliance. *Dodsley's* was, I believe, the last decent thing of the kind, and *his* had great success in its day, and lasted several years; but then he had the double advantage of editing and publishing. The Spleen, and several of *Gray's* odes, much of *Shenstone*, and many others of good repute, made their first appearance in his collection. Now, with the support of Scott, Wordsworth, Southey, &c., I see little reason why you should not do as well; and if once fairly established, you would have assistance from the youngsters, I dare say. Stratford Canning (whose ' Buonaparte' is excellent), and many others, and Moore, and Hobhouse, and I, would try a fall now and then (if permitted), and you might coax Campbell, too, into it. By the by, *he* has an unpublished (though printed) poem on a scene in Germany (Bavaria, I think), which I saw last year, that is perfectly magnificent, and equal to himself. I wonder he don't publish it.

" Oh!—do you recollect S * *, the engraver's, mad letter about not

> Now in the moonlight, and now lapsed in shade,
>   With steps that trod as heavy, yet unheard:
> His garments only a slight murmur made;
>   He moved as shadowy as the sisters weird,
> But slowly; and as he pass'd Juan by,
> Glanced, without pausing, on him a bright eye."

It is said, that the Newstead ghost appeared, also, to Lord Byron's cousin, Miss Fanny Parkins, and that she made a sketch of him from memory.

* The reviews and magazines of the month.

engraving Phillip's picture of Lord *Foley?* (as he blundered it); well, have traced it, I think. It seems, by the papers, a preacher of Johanna Southcote's is named *Foley;* and I can no way account for the said S * *'s confusion of words and ideas, but by that of his head's running on Johanna and her apostles. It was a mercy he did not say Lord *Tozer*. You know, of course, that S * * is a believer in this new (old) virgin of spiritual impregnation.

"I long to know what she will produce*: her being with child at sixty-five is indeed a miracle, but her getting any one to beget it, a greater.

"If you were not going to Paris or Scotland, I could send you some game: if you remain, let me know.

"P.S. A word or two of 'Lara,' which your enclosure brings before me. It is of no great promise separately; but, as connected with the other tales, it will do very well for the volumes you mean to publish. I would recommend this arrangement—Childe Harold, the smaller Poems, Giaour, Bride, Corsair, Lara; the last completes the series, and its very likeness renders it necessary to the others. Cawthorne writes that they are publishing *English Bards* in *Ireland:* pray inquire into this; because *it must* be stopped."

LETTER CXCVIII.

TO MR. MURRAY.

"Newstead Abbey, Sept. 7th, 1814.

"I should think Mr. Hogg, for his own sake as well as yours, would be 'critical' as Iago himself in his editorial capacity; and that such a publication would answer his purpose, and yours too, with tolerable management. You should, however, have a good number to start with—I mean, *good* in quality; in these days, there can be little fear of not coming up to the mark in quantity. There must be many 'fine

---

* The following characteristic note, in reference to this passage, appears, in Mr. Gifford's handwriting, on the copy of the above letter:—" It is a pity that Lord B. was ignorant of Jonson. The old poet has a Satire on the Court Pucelle that would have supplied him with some pleasantry on Joanna's pregnancy."

things' in Wordsworth; but I should think it difficult to make *six* quartos (the amount of the whole) all fine, particularly the pedlar's portion of the poem; but there can be no doubt of his powers to do almost any thing.

"I *am* 'very idle.' I have read the few books I had with me, and been forced to fish, for lack of argument. I have caught a great many perch and some carp, which is a comfort, as one would not lose one's labour willingly.

"Pray, who corrects the press of your volumes? I hope 'The Corsair' is printed from the copy I corrected with the additional lines in the first Canto, and some *notes* from Sismondi and Lavater, which I gave you to add thereto. The arrangement is very well.

"My cursed people have not sent my papers since Sunday, and I have lost Johanna's divorce from Jupiter. Who hath gotten her with prophet? Is it Sharpe? and how?　 *　 *　 *　 *　 *　 * I should like to buy one of her seals: if salvation can be had at half-a-guinea a head, the landlord of the Crown and Anchor should be ashamed of himself for charging double for tickets to a mere terrestrial banquet. I am afraid, seriously, that these matters will lend a sad handle to your profane scoffers, and give a loose to much damnable laughter.

"I have not seen Hunt's Sonnets nor Descent of Liberty: he has chosen a pretty place wherein to compose the last. Let me hear from you before you embark. Ever, &c."

LETTER CXCIX.

TO MR. MOORE.

"Newstead Abbey, September 15, 1814.

"This is the fourth letter I have begun to you within the month. Whether I shall finish or not, or burn it like the rest, I know not. When we meet, I will explain *why* I have not written—*why* I have not asked you here, as I wished—with a great many other *whys* and where-fores, which will keep cold. In short, you must excuse all my seeming omissions and commissions, and grant me more *remission* than St. Athanasius will to yourself, if you lop off a single shred of mystery from

his pious puzzle. It is my creed (and it may be St. Athanasius's too
that your article on T * * will get somebody killed, and *that*, on th
Saints, get him d—d afterwards, which will be quite enow for on
number. Oons, Tom! you must not meddle just now with the incom
prehensible; for if Johanna Southcote turns out to be   *   *

    * * * * * . *

 " Now for a little egotism. My affairs stand thus. To-morrow,
shall know whether a circumstance of importance enough to chang
many of my plans will occur or not. If it does not, I am off for Italy
next month, and London, in the mean time, next week. I have go
back Newstead and twenty-five thousand pounds (out of twenty-eigh
paid already),—as a ' sacrifice,' the late purchaser calls it, and he may
choose his own name. I have paid some of my debts, and contracted
others; but I have a few thousand pounds, which I can't spend after my
own heart in this climate, and so, I shall go back to the south. Hob
house, I think and hope, will go with me; but, whether he will or not
I shall. I want to see Venice, and the Alps, and Parmesan cheeses, and
look at the coast of Greece, or rather Epirus, from Italy, as I once did—
or fancied I did—that of Italy, when off Corfu. All this, however
depends upon an event, which may, or may not, happen. Whether it
will, I shall know probably to-morrow, and, if it does, I can't well go
abroad at present.

 " Pray pardon this parenthetical scrawl. You shall hear from me
again soon;—I don't call this an answer.

       " Ever most affectionately, &c."

 The " circumstance of importance," to which he alludes in this letter,
was his second proposal for Miss Milbanke, of which he was now waiting
the result. His own account, in his Memoranda, of the circumstances
that led to this step is, in substance, as far as I can trust my recollection,
as follows. A person, who had for some time stood high in his affection
and confidence, observing how cheerless and unsettled was the state both
of his mind and prospects, advised him strenuously to marry; and, after
much discussion, he consented. The next point for consideration was—
who was to be the object of his choice; and while his friend mentioned

one lady, he himself named Miss Milbanke. To this, however, his adviser strongly objected,—remarking to him, that Miss Milbanke had at present no fortune, and that his embarrassed affairs would not allow him to marry without one; that she was, moreover, a learned lady, which would not at all suit him. In consequence of these representations, he agreed that his friend should write a proposal for him to the other lady named, which was accordingly done;—and an answer, containing a refusal, arrived as they were, one morning, sitting together. "You see," said Lord Byron, "that, after all, Miss Milbanke is to be the person;—I will write to her." He accordingly wrote on the moment, and, as soon as he had finished, his friend, remonstrating still strongly against his choice, took up the letter,—but, on reading it over, observed, "Well, really, this is a very pretty letter;—it is a pity it should not go. I never read a prettier one." "Then it *shall* go," said Lord Byron, and in so saying, sealed and sent off, on the instant, this fiat of his fate.

LETTER CC.

TO MR. MOORE.

"Nd., September 15th, 1814.

"I have written to you one letter to-night, but must send you this much more, as I have not franked my number, to say that I rejoice in my god-daughter, and will send her a coral and bells, which I hope she will accept, the moment I get back to London.

"My head is at this moment in a state of confusion, from various causes, which I can neither describe nor explain—but let that pass. My employments have been very rural—fishing, shooting, bathing, and boating. Books I have but few here, and those I have read ten times over, till sick of them. So, I have taken to breaking soda water bottles with my pistols, and jumping into the water, and rowing over it, and firing at the fowls of the air. But why should I 'monster my nothings' to you, who are well employed, and happily too, I should hope. For my part, I am happy too, in my way—but, as usual, have contrived to get into three or four perplexities, which I do not see my way through. But a few days, perhaps a day, will determine one of them.

" You do not say a word to me of your Poem. I wish I could see or hear it. I neither could, nor would, do it or its author any harm. I believe I told you of Larry and Jacquy. A friend of mine was reading—at least a friend of his was reading—said Larry and Jacquy in a Brighton coach. A passenger took up the book and queried as to the author. The proprietor said ' there were *two*'—to which the answer of the unknown was, ' Ay, ay—a joint concern, I suppose, *summot* like Sternhold and Hopkins.'

" Is not this excellent? I would not have missed the ' vile comparison' to have scaped being one of the 'Arcades ambo et cantare pares.' Good night. Again yours."

LETTER CCI.

TO MR. MOORE.

" Newstead Abbey, Sept. 20th, 1814.

" Here 's to her who long
    Hath waked the poet's sigh!
The girl who gave to song
    What gold could never buy.—My dear Moore, I am going to be married—that is, I am accepted*, and one usually hopes the rest will follow. My mother of the Gracchi (that *are* to be) *you* think too strait-laced for me, although the paragon of only children, and invested with ' golden opinions of all sorts of men,' and full of 'most blest conditions' as Desdemona herself. Miss Milbanke is the lady, and I have her father's invitation to proceed there in my elect capacity,—which, however, I cannot do till I have settled some business in London, and got a blue coat.

---

* On the day of the arrival of the lady's answer, he was sitting at dinner, when his gardener came in and presented him with his mother's wedding ring, which she had lost many years before, and which the gardener had just found in digging up the mould under her window. Almost at the same moment, the letter from Miss Milbanke arrived, and Lord Byron exclaimed, " If it contains a consent, I will be married with this very ring " It *did* contain a very flattering acceptance of his proposal, and a duplicate of the letter had been sent to London, in case this should have missed him.—*Memoranda.*

" She is said to be an heiress, but of that I really know nothing certainly, and shall not inquire. But I do know, that she has talents and excellent qualities, and you will not deny her judgment, after having refused six suitors and taken me.

" Now, if you have any thing to say against this, pray do; my mind's made up, positively fixed, determined, and therefore I will listen to reason, because now it can do no harm. Things may occur to break it off, but I will hope not. In the mean time, I tell you (a *secret*, by the by,—at least, till I know she wishes it to be public) that I have proposed and am accepted. You need not be in a hurry to wish me joy, for one mayn't be married for months. I am going to town to-morrow; but expect to be here, on my way there, within a fortnight.

" If this had not happened, I should have gone to Italy. In my way down, perhaps, you will meet me at Nottingham, and come over with me here. I need not say that nothing will give me greater pleasure. I must, of course, reform thoroughly; and, seriously, if I can contribute to her happiness, I shall secure my own. She is so good a person, that —that—in short, I wish I was a better.

" Ever, &c."

LETTER CCII.

TO THE COUNTESS OF * * *.

" Albany, October 5th, 1814.

" DEAR LADY * *,

" Your recollection and invitation do me great honour; but I am going to be 'married, and can't come.' My intended is two hundred miles off, and the moment my business here is arranged, I must set out in a great hurry to be happy. Miss Milbanke is the good-natured person who has undertaken me, and, of course, I am very much in love, and as silly as all single gentlemen must be in that sentimental situation. I have been accepted these three weeks; but when the event will take place, I don't exactly know. It depends partly upon lawyers, who are never in a hurry. One can be sure of nothing; but, at present, there appears no other interruption to this intention, which seems as

mutual as possible, and now no secret, though I did not tell first,—an
all our relatives are congratulating away to right and left in the mos
fatiguing manner.

"You perhaps know the lady. She is niece to Lady Melbourn
and cousin to Lady Cowper and others of your acquaintance, and has n
fault, except being a great deal too good for me, and that *I* must pardor
if nobody else should. It might have been *two* years ago, and, if it had
would have saved me a world of trouble. She has employed the interva
in refusing about half a dozen of my particular friends (as she did m
once, by the way), and has taken me at last, for which I am very mucl
obliged to her. I wish it was well over, for I do hate bustle, and ther
is no marrying without some;—and then, I must not marry in a blacl
coat, they tell me, and I can't bear a blue one.

"Pray forgive me for scribbling all this nonsense. You know I
must be serious all the rest of my life, and this is a parting piece o:
buffoonery, which I write with tears in my eyes, expecting to be agitated
Believe me most seriously and sincerely your obliged servant,

"BYRON.

"P. S. My best rems. to Lord * * on his return."

LETTER CCIII.

TO MR. MOORE.

"October 7th, 1814.

"Notwithstanding the contradictory paragraph in the Morning
Chronicle, which must have been sent by **, or perhaps—I know not
why I should suspect Claughton of such a thing, and yet I partly do,
because it might interrupt his renewal of purchase, if so disposed; in
short, it matters not, but we are all in the road to matrimony—lawyer:
settling, relations congratulating, my intended as kind as heart could
wish, and every one, whose opinion I value, very glad of it. All her
relatives, and all mine too, seem equally pleased.

"Perry was very sorry, and has *re*-contradicted, as you will perceiv
by this day's paper. It was, to be sure, a devil of an insertion, since the
first paragraph came from Sir Ralph's own County Journal, and this in

the teeth of it would appear to him and his as *my* denial. But I have written to do away that, enclosing Perry's letter, which was very polite and kind.

" Nobody hates bustle so much as I do; but there seems a fatality over every scene of my drama, always a row of some sort or other. No matter—Fortune is my best friend, and as I acknowledge my obligations to her, I hope she will treat me better than she treated the Athenian, who took some merit to *himself* on some occasion, but (after that) took no more towns. In fact, *she*, that exquisite goddess, has hitherto carried me through every thing, and will, I hope, now; since I own it will be all *her* doing.

" Well, now for thee. Your article on ** is perfection itself. You must not leave off reviewing. By Jove, I believe you can do any thing. There is wit, and taste, and learning, and good-humour (though not a whit less severe for that) in every line of that critique.

*   *   *   *   *   *   *

" Next to *your* being an E. Reviewer, *my* being of the same kidney, and Jeffrey's being such a friend to both, are amongst the events which I conceive were not calculated upon in Mr.—what's his name? 's—' Essay on Probabilities.'

" But, Tom, I say—Oons! Scott menaces the ' Lord of the Isles.' Do you mean to compete? or lay by, till this wave has broke upon the *shelves* (of booksellers, not rocks—a *broken* metaphor, by the way). You *ought* to be afraid of nobody; but your modesty is really as provoking and unnecessary as a * *'s. I am very merry, and have just been writing some elegiac stanzas on the death of Sir P. Parker. He was my first cousin, but never met since boyhood. Our relations desired me, and I have scribbled and given it to Perry, who will chronicle it to-morrow. I am as sorry for him as one could be for one I never saw since I was a child; but should not have wept melodiously, except ' at the request of friends.'

" I hope to get out of town and be married, but I shall take Newstead in my way, and you must meet me at Nottingham and accompany me to mine Abbey. I will tell you the day when I know it.

" Ever, &c.

"P. S. By the way, my wife elect is perfection, and I hear of nothing but her merits and her wonders, and that she is 'very pretty.' Her expectations, I am told, are great; but *what*, I have not asked. have not seen her these ten months."

LETTER CCIV.

TO MR. MOORE.

"October 15th, 1814.

"An' there were any thing in marriage that would make a difference between my friends and me, particularly in your case, I would 'non on't.' My agent sets off for Durham next week, and I shall follow him, taking Newstead and you in my way. I certainly did not address Miss Milbanke with these views, but it is likely she may prove a considerable *parti*. All her father can give, or leave her, he will; and from her childless uncle, Lord Wentworth, whose barony, it is supposed, will devolve on Ly. Milbanke (his sister), she has expectations. But these will depend upon his own disposition, which seems very partial towards her. She is an only child, and Sir R.'s estates, though dipped by electioneering, are considerable. Part of them are settled on her; but whether *that* will be *dowered* now, I do not know,—though, from what has been intimated to me, it probably will. The lawyers are to settle this among them, and I am getting my property into matrimonial array, and myself ready for the journey to Seaham, which I must make in a week or ten days.

"I certainly did not dream that she was attached to me, which it seems she has been for some time. I also thought her of a very cold disposition, in which I was also mistaken—it is a long story, and I won't trouble you with it. As to her virtues, &c. &c. you will hear enough of them (for she is a kind of *pattern* in the north), without my running into a display on the subject. It is well that *one* of us is of such fame, since there is a sad deficit in the *morale* of that article upon my part,—all owing to my 'bitch of a star,' as Captain Tranchemont says of his planet.

"Don't think you have not said enough of me in your article on T**; what more could or need be said?

*   *   *   *   *   *   *

" Your long-delayed and expected work—I suppose you will take fright at ' The Lord of the Isles' and Scott now. You must do as you like,—I have said my say. You ought to fear comparison with none, and any one would stare, who heard you were so tremulous,—though, after all, I believe it is the surest sign of talent. Good morning. I hope we shall meet soon, but I will write again, and perhaps you will meet me at Nottingham. Pray say so.

" P. S. If this union is productive, you shall name the first fruits."

LETTER CCV.

TO MR. HENRY DRURY.

" October 18th, 1814.

" MY DEAR DRURY,

" Many thanks for your hitherto unacknowledged ' Anecdotes.' Now for one of mine—I am going to be married, and have been engaged this month. It is a long story, and therefore, I won't tell it,—an old and (though I did not know it till lately) a *mutual* attachment. The very sad life I have led since I was your pupil must partly account for the offs and *ons* in this now to be arranged business. We are only waiting for the lawyers and settlements, &c., and next week, or the week after, I shall go down to Seaham in the new character of a regular suitor for a wife of mine own.

*   *   *   *   *   *

" I hope Hodgson is in a fair way on the same voyage—I saw him and his idol at Hastings. I wish he would be married at the same time. I should like to make a party,—like people electrified in a row, by (or rather through) the same chain, holding one another's hands, and all feeling the shock at once. I have not yet apprized him of this. He makes such a serious matter of all these things, and is so ' melancholy and gentlemanlike,' that it is quite overcoming to us choice spirits.

*   *   *   *   *   *

" They say one shouldn't be married in a black coat. I won't have a blue one,—that's flat. I hate it.

" Yours, &c."

4 F 2

LETTER CCVI.

TO MR. COWELL.

" October 22d, 1814.

" MY DEAR COWELL,

" Many and sincere thanks for your kind letter—the bet, or rather forfeit, was one hundred to Hawke, and fifty to Hay (nothing to Kelly, for a guinea received from each of the two former*. I shall feel much obliged by your setting me right if I am incorrect in this statement in any way, and have reasons for wishing you to recollect as much as possible of what passed, and state it to Hodgson. My reason is this: some time ago Mr. * * * required a bet of me which I never made, and of course refused to pay, and have heard no more of it; to prevent similar mistakes is my object in wishing you to remember well what passed, and to put Hodgson in possession of your memory on the subject.

" I hope to see you soon in my way through Cambridge. Remember me to H., and believe me ever and truly, &c."

Soon after the date of this letter, Lord Byron had to pay a visit to Cambridge for the purpose of voting for Mr. Clarke, who had been started by Trinity College as one of the candidates for Sir Busick Harwood's Professorship. On this occasion, a circumstance occurred which could not but be gratifying to him. As he was delivering in his vote to the Vice-Chancellor, in the Senate House, the under-graduates in the gallery ventured to testify their admiration of him by a general murmur of applause and stamping of the feet. For this breach of order, the gallery was immediately cleared by order of the Vice-Chancellor.

At the beginning of the month of December, being called up to town by business, I had opportunities, from being a good deal in my noble friend's society, of observing the state of his mind and feelings under the prospect of the important change he was now about to undergo

---

* He had agreed to forfeit these sums to the persons mentioned, should he ever marry.

and it was with pain I found that those sanguine hopes* with which I had sometimes looked forward to the happy influence of marriage, in winning him over to the brighter and better side of life, were, by a view of all the circumstances of his present destiny, considerably diminished; while, at the same time, not a few doubts and misgivings, which had never before so strongly occurred to me, with regard to his own fitness, under any circumstances, for the matrimonial tie, filled me altogether with a degree of foreboding anxiety as to his fate, which the unfortunate events that followed but too fully justified.

The truth is, I fear, that rarely, if ever, have men of the higher order of genius shown themselves fitted for the calm affections and comforts that form the cement of domestic life. " One misfortune (says Pope) of extraordinary geniuses is, that their very friends are more apt to admire than love them." To this remark there have, no doubt, been exceptions,—and I should pronounce Lord Byron, from my own experience, to be one of them,—but it would not be difficult, perhaps, to show, from the very nature and pursuits of genius, that such must generally be the lot of all pre-eminently gifted with it; and that the same qualities which enable them to command admiration are also those that too often incapacitate them from conciliating love.

The very habits, indeed, of abstraction and self-study to which the occupations of men of genius lead, are, in themselves, necessarily, of an unsocial and detaching tendency, and require a large portion of allowance and tolerance not to be set down as unamiable. One of the chief sources, too, of sympathy and society between ordinary mortals being their dependence on each other's intellectual resources, the operation of this social principle must naturally be weakest in those, whose own mental stores are most abundant and self-sufficing, and who, rich in such mate-

---

* I had frequently, both in earnest and in jest, expressed these hopes to him ; and, in one of my letters, after touching upon some matters relative to my own little domestic circle, I added, " This will all be unintelligible to you ;—though I sometimes cannot help thinking it within the range of possibility, that even *you*, volcano as you are, may, one day, cool down into something of the same *habitable* state. Indeed, when one thinks of lava having been converted into buttons for Isaac Hawkins Browne, there is no saying what such .fiery things may be brought to at last."

rials for thinking within themselves, are rendered so far independent of the external world. It was this solitary luxury (which Plato called " banqueting his own thoughts") that led Pope, as well as Lord Byron to prefer the silence and seclusion of his library to the most agreeable conversation.—And not only, too, is the necessity of commerce with other minds less felt by such persons, but, from that fastidiousness which the opulence of their own resources generates, the society of those less gifted with intellectual means than themselves becomes often a restraint and burden, to which not all the charms of friendship, or even love, can reconcile them. " Nothing is so tiresome (says the poet of Vaucluse, in assigning a reason for not living with some of his dearest friends) as to converse with persons who have not the same information as oneself."

But it is the cultivation and exercise of the imaginative faculty that, more than any thing, tends to wean the man of genius from actual life, and, by substituting the sensibilities of the imagination for those of the heart, to render, at last, the medium through which he feels no less unreal than that through which he thinks. Those images of ideal good and beauty that surround him in his musings soon accustom him to consider all that is beneath this high standard unworthy of his care till, at length, the heart becoming chilled as the fancy warms, it too often happens that, in proportion as he has refined and elevated his theory of all the social affections, he has unfitted himself for the practice of them* Hence so frequently it arises that, in persons of this temperament, we see some bright but artificial idol of the brain usurp the place of all real and natural objects of tenderness. The poet Dante, a wanderer away from wife and children, passed the whole of a restless and detached life in nursing his immortal dream of Beatrice; while Petrarch, who would not suffer his only daughter to reside beneath his roof, expended thirty-two years of poetry and passion on an idealized love.

---

* Of the lamentable contrast between sentiments and conduct, which this transfer of the seat of sensibility from the heart to the fancy produces, the annals of literary men afford unluckily too many examples. Alfieri, though he could write a sonnet full of tenderness to his mother never saw her (says Mr W. Rose) but once after their early separation, though he frequently passed within a few miles of her residence. The poet Young, with all his parade of domestic sorrows, was, it appears, a neglectful husband and harsh father; and Sterne (to use the words already employed by Lord Byron) preferred " whining over a dead ass to relieving a living mother."

It is, indeed, in the very nature and essence of genius to be for ever occupied intensely with Self, as the great centre and source of its strength. Like the sister Rachel, in Dante, sitting all day before her mirror,

> " mai non si smaga
> Del suo ammiraglio, e siede tutto giorno."

To this power of self-concentration, by which alone all the other powers of genius are made available, there is, of course, no such disturbing and fatal enemy as those sympathies and affections that draw the mind out actively towards others*; and, accordingly, it will be found that, among those who have felt within themselves a call to immortality, the greater number have, by a sort of instinct, kept aloof from such ties, and, instead of the softer duties and rewards of being amiable, reserved themselves for the high, hazardous chances of being great. In looking back through the lives of the most illustrious poets,—the class of intellect in which the characteristic features of genius are, perhaps, most strongly marked,—we shall find that, with scarcely one exception, from Homer down to Lord Byron, they have been, in their several degrees, restless and solitary spirits, with minds wrapped up, like silk-worms, in their own tasks, either strangers, or rebels, to domestic ties, and bearing about with them a deposite for Posterity in their souls, to the jealous watching and enriching of which almost all other thoughts and considerations have been sacrificed.

" To follow poetry as one ought (says the authority† I have already quoted), one must forget father and mother and cleave to it alone." In these few words is pointed out the sole path that leads genius to greatness. On such terms alone are the high places of fame to be won; —nothing less than the sacrifice of the entire man can achieve them. However delightful, therefore, may be the spectacle of a man of genius tamed and domesticated in society, taking docilely upon him the yoke of

---

* It is the opinion of Diderot, in his Treatise on Acting, that not only in the art of which he treats, but in all those which are called Imitative, the possession of real sensibility is a bar to eminence;—sensibility being, according to his view, " le caractère de la bonté de l'ame et de la médiocrité du génie."

† Pope.

the social ties, and enlightening without disturbing the sphere in which l
moves, we must nevertheless, in the midst of our admiration, bear i
mind that it is not thus smoothly or amiably immortality has been ev
struggled for, or won. The poet thus circumstanced may be popula
may be loved; for the happiness of himself and those linked with hi
he is in the right road,—but not for greatness. The marks by whic
Fame has always separated her great martyrs from the rest of mankin
are not upon him, and the crown cannot be his. He may dazzle, ma
captivate the circle, and even the times in which he lives, but he is no
for hereafter.

To the general description here given of that high class of huma
intelligences to which he belonged, the character of Lord Byron was, i
many respects, a signal exception. Born with strong affections an
ardent passions, the world had, from first to last, too firm a hold o
his sympathies to let imagination altogether usurp the place of reality
either in his feelings, or in the objects of them. His life, indeed
was one continued struggle between that instinct of genius, which
was for ever drawing him back into the lonely laboratory of Self, an
those impulses of passion, ambition, and vanity, which again hurried hin
off into the crowd, and entangled him in its interests; and though i
may be granted that he would have been more purely and abstractedly
the *poet*, had he been less thoroughly, in all his pursuits and propensities
the *man*, yet from this very mixture and alloy has it arisen that his page
bear so deeply the stamp of real life, and that in the works of no poet
with the exception of Shakspeare, can every various mood of the mind—
whether solemn or gay, whether inclined to the ludicrous or the sublime
whether seeking to divert itself with the follies of society or panting
after the grandeur of solitary nature—find so readily a strain of sentimen
in accordance with its every passing tone.

But while the naturally warm cast of his affections and temperamen
gave thus a substance and truth to his social feelings which those of to
many of his fellow votaries of Genius have wanted, it was not to b
expected that an imagination of such range and power should have been
so early developed and unrestrainedly indulged without producing, a
last, some of those effects upon the heart which have invariably bee

found attendant on such a predominance of this faculty. It must have been observed, indeed, that the period when his natural affections flourished most healthily was before he had yet arrived at the full consciousness of his genius,—before Imagination had yet accustomed him to those glowing pictures, after gazing upon which all else appeared cold and colourless. From the moment of this initiation into the wonders of his own mind, a distaste for the realities of life began to grow upon him. Not even that intense craving after affection, which nature had implanted in him, could keep his ardour still alive in a pursuit whose results fell so short of his " imaginings ;" and though, from time to time, the combined warmth of his fancy and temperament was able to call up a feeling which to his eyes wore the semblance of love, it may be questioned whether his heart had ever much share in such passions, or whether, after his first launch into the boundless sea of imagination, he could ever have been brought back and fixed by any lasting attachment. Actual objects there were, in but too great number, who, as long as the illusion continued, kindled up his thoughts and were the themes of his song. But they were, after all, little more than mere dreams of the hour;—the qualities with which he invested them were almost all ideal, nor could have stood the test of a month's, or even week's, cohabitation. It was but the reflection of his own bright conceptions that he saw in each new object; and while persuading himself that they furnished the models of his heroines, he was, on the contrary, but fancying that he beheld his heroines in them.

There needs no stronger proof of the predominance of imagination in these attachments than his own serious avowal, in the Journal already given, that often, when in the company of the woman he most loved, he found himself secretly wishing for the solitude of his own study. It was *there*, indeed,—in the silence and abstraction of that study,—that the chief scene of his mistress's empire and glory lay. It was there that, unchecked by reality, and without any fear of the disenchantments of truth, he could view her through the medium of his own fervid fancy, enamour himself of an idol of his own creating, and out of a brief delirium of a few days or weeks send forth a dream of beauty and passion through all ages.

While such appears to have been the imaginative character of his loves (of all, except the one that lived unquenched through all his friendships, though, of course, far less subject to the influence of fancy, could not fail to exhibit also some features characteristic of the peculiar mind in which they sprung. It was a usual saying of his own, and will be found repeated in some of his letters, that he had "no genius for friendship," and that whatever capacity he might once have possessed for that sentiment had vanished with his youth. If in saying thus he shaped his notions of friendship according to the romantic standard of his boyhood, the fact must be admitted; but as far as the assertion was meant to imply that he had become incapable of a warm, manly, and lasting friendship, such a charge against himself was unjust, and I am not the only living testimony of its injustice.

To a certain degree, however, even in his friendships, the effects of a too vivid imagination, in disqualifying the mind for the cold contact of reality, were visible. We are told that Petrarch (who, in this respect, as in most others, may be regarded as a genuine representative of the poetic character) abstained purposely from a too frequent intercourse with his nearest friends, lest, from the sensitiveness he was so aware of in himself, there should occur any thing that might chill his regard for them*; and though Lord Byron was of a nature too full of social and kindly impulses ever to think of such a precaution, it is a fact confirmatory, at least, of the principle on which his brother poet, Petrarch, acted, that the friends, whether of his youth or manhood, of whom he had seen least, through life, were those of whom he always thought and spoke with the most warmth and fondness. Being brought less often to the touchstone of familiar intercourse, they stood naturally a better chance of being adopted as the favourites of his imagination, and of sharing, in consequence, a portion of that bright colouring reserved for all that gave it interest and pleasure. Next to the dead, therefore, whose hold upon his fancy had been placed beyond all risk of severance, those friends whom he but saw occasionally, and by such favourable glimpses as only

* See Foscolo's Essay on Petrarch. On the same principle, Orrery says, in speaking of Swift, " I am persuaded that his distance from his English friends proved a strong incitement to their mutual affection."

renewed the first kindly impression they had made, were the surest to live unchangingly, and without shadow, in his memory.

To the same cause, there is little doubt, his love for his sister owed much of its devotedness and fervour. In a mind sensitive and versatile as his, long habits of family intercourse might have estranged, or at least dulled, his natural affection for her;—but their separation, during youth, left this feeling fresh and untried*. His very inexperience in such ties made the smile of a sister no less a novelty than a charm to him, and before the first gloss of this newly awakened sentiment had time to wear off, they were again separated, and for ever.

If the portrait which I have here attempted of the general character of those gifted with high genius be allowed to bear, in any of its features, a resemblance to the originals, it can no longer, I think, be matter of question whether a class so set apart from the track of ordinary life, so removed, by their very elevation, out of the influences of our common atmosphere, are at all likely to furnish tractable subjects for that most trying of all social experiments, matrimony. In reviewing the great names of philosophy and science, we shall find that all who have most distinguished themselves in those walks have, at least, virtually admitted their own unfitness for the marriage tie by remaining in celibacy;—Bacon†, Newton, Gassendi, Galileo, Descartes, Bayle, Locke, Leibnitz, Boyle, Hume, and a long list of other illustrious sages, having all led single lives.

The poetic race, it is true, from the greater susceptibility of their imaginations, have more frequently fallen into the ever ready snare. But the fate of the poets in matrimony has but justified the caution of the philosophers. While the latter have given warning to genius by keeping free of the yoke, the others have still more effectually done so by their misery under it;—the annals of this sensitive race having, at all times,

---

* That he was himself fully aware of this appears from a passage in one of his letters already given:—" My sister is in town, which is a great comfort; for, never having been much together, we are naturally more attached to each other."

† This great philosopher threw not only his example but his precepts into the scale of celibacy. Wife and children, he tells us in one of his Essays, are " impediments to great enterprises;" and adds, " Certainly, the best works, and of greatest merit for the public, have proceeded from the unmarried or childless men." See, with reference to this subject, chapter xviii. of Mr. D'Israeli's work on " The Literary Character."

abounded with proofs, that genius ranks but low among the elements of social happiness,—that, in general, the brighter the gift, the more disturbing its influence, and that in the married life particularly, it effects have been too often like that of the " Wormwood Star," whose light filled the waters on which it fell with bitterness.

Besides the causes already enumerated as leading naturally to such a result, from the peculiarities by which, in most instances, these great labourers in the field of thought are characterized, there is also much no doubt, to be attributed to an unluckiness in the choice of help mates,—dictated, as that choice frequently must be, by an imagination accustomed to deceive itself. But from whatever causes it may have arisen, the coincidence is no less striking than saddening that, on the list of married poets who have been unhappy in their homes, there should already be found four such illustrious names as Dante, Milton* Shakspeare†, and Dryden; and that we should now have to add, as a partner in their destiny, a name worthy of being placed beside the greatest of them,—Lord Byron.

I have already mentioned my having been called up to town in the December of this year. The opportunities I had of seeing Lord Byron during my stay were frequent; and, among them, not the least memorable

---

* Milton's first wife, it is well known, ran away from him, within a month after their marriage, disgusted, says Phillips, " with his spare diet and hard study;" and it is difficult to conceive a more melancholy picture of domestic life than is disclosed in his Nuncupative Will one of the witnesses to which deposes to having heard the great Poet himself complain, that his children " were careless of him, being blind, and made nothing of deserting him."

† By whatever austerity of temper or habits the poets Dante and Milton may have drawn upon themselves such a fate, it might be expected that, at least, the " gentle Shakspeare" would have stood exempt from the common calamity of his brethren. But, among the very few facts of his life that have been transmitted to us, there is none more clearly proved than the unhappiness of his marriage. The dates of the birth of his children, compared with that of his removal from Stratford,—the total omission of his wife's name in the first draft of his will, and the bitter sarcasm of the bequest by which he remembers her afterwards,—all prove beyond a doubt both his separation from the lady early in life, and his unfriendly feeling towards her at the close of it.

In endeavouring to argue against the conclusion naturally to be deduced from this will Boswell, with a strange ignorance of human nature, remarks:—" If he had taken offence at any part of his wife's conduct, I cannot believe that he would have taken this petty mode of expressing it."

or agreeable were those evenings we passed together at the house of his
banker, Mr. Douglas Kinnaird, where music,—followed by its accustomed
sequel of supper, brandy and water, and not a little laughter,—kept us
together, usually, till rather a late hour. Besides those songs of mine which
he has himself somewhere recorded as his favourites, there was also one, to
a Portuguese air, " The song of war shall echo through our mountains,"
which seemed especially to please him;—the national character of the
music, and the recurrence of the words " sunny mountains," bringing
back freshly to his memory the impressions of all he had seen in
Portugal.   I have, indeed, known few persons more alive to the charms
of simple music; and not unfrequently have seen the tears in his eyes
while listening to the Irish Melodies. Among those that thus affected him
was one, beginning " When first I met thee warm and young," the words
of which, besides the obvious feeling which they express, were intended
also to admit of a political application. He, however, discarded the latter
sense wholly from his mind, and gave himself up to the more natural
sentiment of the song with evident emotion

On one or two of these evenings, his favourite actor, Mr. Kean, was
of the party; and on another occasion, we had at dinner his early instructor
in pugilism, Mr. Jackson, in conversing with whom, all his boyish tastes
seemed to revive;—and it was not a little amusing to observe how
perfectly familiar with the annals of " the Ring*," and with all the most
recondite phraseology of " the Fancy," was the sublime poet of Childe
Harold.

The following note is the only one, of those I received from him at
this time, worth transcribing.

" December 14, 1814.

" MY DEAREST TOM,

" I will send the pattern to-morrow, and since you don't go to our
friend (' of the *keeping* part of the town') this evening, I shall e'en sulk
at home over a solitary potation. My self-opinion rises much by your
eulogy of my social qualities. As my friend Scrope is pleased to say, I

* In a small book which I have in my possession, containing a sort of chronological History
of the Ring, I find the name of Lord Byron, more than once, recorded among the " backers."

believe I am very well for a ' holiday drinker.' Where the devil ar you? with Woolridge *, I conjecture—for which you deserve anothe abscess. Hoping that the American war will last for many years, an that all the prizes may be registered at Bermoothes, believe me, &c.

" P. S. I have just been composing an epistle to the archbishop fc an especial licence. Oons! it looks serious. Murray is impatient to se you, and would call, if you will give him audience. Your new coat!— I wonder you like the colour, and don't go about, like Dives, in purple.

LETTER CCVII.

TO MR. MURRAY.

" Dec. 31st, 1814.

" A thousand thanks for Gibbon: all the additions are very great improvements.

" At last, I must be *most* peremptory with you about the *print* from Phillips's picture: it is pronounced on all hands the most stupid and disagreeable possible; so do, pray, have a new engraving, and let me see it first; there really must be no more from the same plate. I don't much care, myself; but every one I honour torments me to death about it, and abuses it to a degree beyond repeating. Now, don't answer with excuses; but, for my sake, have it destroyed: I never shall have peace till it is. I write in the greatest haste.

" P.S. I have written this most illegibly; but it is to beg you to destroy the print, and have another 'by particular desire.' It must be d—d bad, to be sure, since every body says so but the original; and he don't know what to say. But do *do* it: that is, burn the plate, and employ a new *etcher* from the other picture. This is stupid and sulky."

On his arrival in town, he had, upon inquiring into the state of his affairs, found them in so utterly embarrassed a condition as to fill him with some alarm, and even to suggest to his mind the prudence of deferring his marriage. The die was, however, cast, and he had now no

---

* Doctor Woolriche, an old and valued friend of mine, to whose skill, on the occasion here alluded to, I was indebted for my life.

alternative but to proceed. Accordingly, at the end of December, accompanied by his friend, Mr. Hobhouse, he set out for Seaham, the seat
of Sir Ralph Milbanke, the lady's father, in the county of Durham, and
on the 2d of January, 1815, was married.

> " I saw him stand
> Before an altar with a gentle bride;
> Her face was fair, but was not that which made
> The Starlight of his Boyhood;—as he stood
> Even at the altar, o'er his brow there came
> The self-same aspect, and the quivering shock
> That in the antique Oratory shook
> His bosom in its solitude; and then—
> As in that hour—a moment o'er his face
> The tablet of unutterable thoughts
> Was traced,—and then it faded as it came,
> And he stood calm and quiet, and he spoke
> The fitting vows, but heard not his own words,
> And all things reel'd around him; he could see
> Not that which was, nor that which should have been—
> But the old mansion, and the accustom'd hall,
> And the remember'd chambers, and the place,
> The day, the hour, the sunshine, and the shade,
> All things pertaining to that place and hour,
> And her, who was his destiny, came back,
> And thrust themselves between him and the light:—
> What business had they there at such a time*?"

This touching picture agrees so closely, in many of its circumstances,
with his own prose account of the wedding in his Memoranda, that I
feel justified in introducing it, historically, here. In that Memoir, he
described himself as waking, on the morning of his marriage, with the
most melancholy reflections, on seeing his wedding-suit spread out before
him. In the same mood, he wandered about the grounds alone, till he
was summoned for the ceremony, and joined, for the first time on that
day, his bride and her family. He knelt down,—he repeated the words
after the clergyman; but a mist was before his eyes,—his thoughts were

---

* The Dream

elsewhere; and he was but awakened by the congratulations of the by standers, to find that he was—married.

The same morning the wedded pair left Seaham for Halnaby, anothe seat of Sir Ralph Milbanke, in the same county. When about to depar Lord Byron said to the bride, "Miss Milbanke, are you ready?"— mistake which the lady's confidential attendant pronounced to be " bad omen."

It is right to add, that I quote these slight details from memory and am alone answerable for any inaccuracy there may be found in them

LETTER CCVIII

TO MR. MURRAY.

" Kirkby, January 6th, 1815.

" *The* marriage took place on the 2d instant; so pray make haste and congratulate away.

" Thanks for the Edinburgh Review and the abolition of the print Let the next be from the *other* of Phillips—I mean (*not* the Albanian but) the original one in the exhibition; the last was from the copy. I should wish my sister and Lady Byron to decide upon the next, as they found fault with the last. *I* have no opinion of my own upon the subject.

" Mr. Kinnaird will, I dare say, have the goodness to furnish copies of the Melodies*, if you state my wish upon the subject. You may have them, if you think them worth inserting. The volumes in their collected state must be inscribed to Mr. Hobhouse, but I have not yet mustered the expressions of my inscription; but will supply them in time.

" With many thanks for your good wishes, which have all been realized, I remain very truly,

" Yours,

" BYRON."

* The Hebrew Melodies which he had employed himself in writing, during his recent stay in London.

LETTER CCIX.

TO MR. MOORE.

"Halnaby, Darlington, January 10th, 1815.

"I was married this day week. The parson has pronounced it—Perry has announced it—and the Morning Post, also, under the head of 'Lord Byron's Marriage'—as if it were a fabrication, or the puff-direct of a new stay-maker.

"Now for thine affairs. I have redde thee upon the Fathers, and it is excellent well. Positively, you must not leave off reviewing. You shine in it—you kill in it; and this article has been taken for Sydney Smith's (as I heard in town), which proves not only your proficiency in parsonology, but that you have all the airs of a veteran critic at your first onset. So, prithee, go on and prosper.

"Scott's 'Lord of the Isles' is out—'the mail-coach copy' I have, by special licence of Murray.

*　　*　　*　　*　　*　　*

"Now is *your* time;—you will come upon them newly and freshly. It is impossible to read what you have lately done (verse or prose) without seeing that you have trained on tenfold. * * has floundered; * * has foundered. *I* have tired the rascals (i. e. the public) with my Harrys and Larrys, Pilgrims and Pirates. Nobody but S * * * *y has done any thing worth a slice of bookseller's pudding; and *he* has not luck enough to be found out in doing a good thing. Now, Tom, is thy time—'Oh joyful day!—I would not take a knighthood for thy fortune.' Let me hear from you soon, and believe me ever, &c.

"P.S. Lady Byron is vastly well. How are Mrs. Moore and Joe Atkinson's 'Graces?' We must present our women to one another."

LETTER CCX.

TO MR. MOORE.

"January 19th, 1815.

"Egad! I don't think he is 'down;' and my prophecy—like mos▮ auguries, sacred and profane—is not annulled, but inverted.   *   *

*   *   *   *   *   *

"To your question about the 'dog *'—Umph!—my 'mother,' ▮ won't say any thing against—that is, about her; but how long a 'mis▮ tress' or friend may recollect paramours or competitors (lust and thirs▮ being the two great and only bonds between the amatory or the amicable) I can't say,—or, rather, you know as well as I could tell you.   But a▮ for canine recollections, as far as I could judge by a cur of mine own (always bating Boatswain, the dearest and, alas! the maddest of dogs), ▮ had one (half a *wolf* by the she side) that doted on me at ten years old, and very nearly ate me at twenty.   When I thought he was going to enact Argus, he bit away the backside of my breeches, and never would consent to any kind of recognition, in despite of all kinds of bones which I offered him.   So, let Southey blush and Homer too, as far as I can decide upon quadruped memories.

"I humbly take it, the mother knows the son that pays her jointure —a mistress her mate, till he * * and refuses salary—a friend his fellow, till he loses cash and character, and a dog his master, till he changes him.

"So, you want to know about milady and me?   But let me not, as Roderick Random says, 'profane the chaste mysteries of Hymen †'—

---

* I had just been reading Mr. Southey's fine Poem of " Roderick," and with reference to an incident in it, had put the following question to Lord Byron—" I should like to know from *you*, who are one of the Philocynic sect, whether it is at all probable, that any dog (out of a melodrame) could recognise a master, whom neither his own mother or mistress was able to find out.   I don't care about Ulysses's dog, &c.—all I want is to know from *you* (who are renown'd as ' friend of the dog, companion of the bear,') whether such a thing is probable."

† The letter H. is blotted in the MS.

damn the word, I had nearly spelt it with a small *h*. I like Bell as well as you do (or did, you villain!) Bessy—and that is (or was) saying a great deal.

"Address your next to Seaham, Stockton-on-Tees, where we are going on Saturday (a bore, by the way) to see father-in-law, Sir Jacob, and my lady's lady-mother. Write—and write more.at length—both to the public and

"Yours ever most affectionately,
"B."

LETTER CCXI.

TO MR. MOORE.

" Seaham, Stockton-on-Tees, February 2d, 1815.

" I have heard from London that you have left Chatsworth and all the women full of ' entusymusy *' about you, personally and poetically; and, in particular, that ' When first I met thee' has been quite overwhelming in its effect. I told you it was one of the best things you ever wrote, though that dog Power wanted you to omit part of it. They are all regretting your absence at Chatsworth, according to my informant— ' all the ladies quite, &c. &c. &c.' Stap my vitals!

" Well, now you have got home again—which I dare say is as agreeable as a ' draught of cool small beer to the scorched palate of a waking sot'—now you have got home again, I say, probably I shall hear from you. Since I wrote last, I have been transferred to my father-in-law's, with my lady and my lady's maid, &c. &c. &c. and the treacle-moon is over, and I am awake, and find myself married. My spouse and I agree to—and in—admiration. Swift says ' no *wise* man ever married;' but, for a fool, I think it the most ambrosial of all possible future states. I still think one ought to marry upon *lease;* but am very sure I should renew mine at the expiration, though next term were for ninety and nine years.

" I wish you would respond, for I am here ' oblitusque meorum

---

* It was thus that, according to his account, a certain celebrated singer and actor used frequently to pronounce the word " enthusiasm."

4 H 2

obliviscendus et illis.' Pray tell me what is going on in the way of intriguery, and how the w——s and rogues of the upper Beggar's Oper go on—or rather go off—in or after marriage; or who are goin to break any particular commandment. Upon this dreary coast, we hav nothing but county meetings and shipwrecks; and I have this day dine upon fish, which probably dined upon the crews of several colliers los in the late gales. But I saw the sea once more in all the glories of sur and foam,—almost equal to the Bay of Biscay, and the interesting whit squalls and short seas of Archipelago memory.

"My papa, Sir Ralpho, hath recently made a speech at a Durhan tax-meeting; and not only at Durham, but here, several times since after dinner. He is now, I believe, speaking it to himself (I left him i the middle) over various decanters, which can neither interrupt him no fall asleep,—as might possibly have been the case with some of hi audience.

"Ever thine,

"B.

"I must go to tea—damn tea. I wish it was Kinnaird's brandy, and with you to lecture me about it."

LETTER CCXII.

TO MR. MURRAY.

"Seaham, Stockton-upon-Tees, February 2d, 1815.

"You will oblige me very much by making an occasional inquiry at Albany, at my chambers, whether my books, &c. are kept in tolerable order, and how far my old woman * continues in health and industry as keeper of my old den. Your parcels have been duly received and perused; but I had hoped to receive 'Guy Mannering' before this time. I won't intrude further for the present on your avocations professional or plea-surable, but am, as usual,

" Very truly, &c."

* Mrs. Mule.

LETTER CCXIII.

TO MR. MOORE.

"February 4th, 1815.

" I enclose you half a letter from * * which will explain itself—at least the latter part—the former refers to private business of mine own. If Jeffrey will take such an article, and you will undertake the revision, or, indeed, any portion of the article itself (for unless *you do*, by Phœbus, I will have nothing to do with it), we can cook up, between us three, as pretty a dish of sour-crout as ever tipped over the tongue of a book-maker.　　*　　*　　*　　*

" You can, at any rate, try Jeffrey's inclination. Your late proposal from him made me hint this to * *, who is a much better proser and scholar than I am, and a very superior man indeed. Excuse haste—answer this.

" Ever yours most,

" B.

" P.S. All is well at home. I wrote to you yesterday."

LETTER CCXIV.

TO MR. MOORE.

"February 10th, 1815.

" MY DEAR THOM,

" Jeffrey has been so very kind about me and my damnable works, that I would not be indirect or equivocal with him, even for a friend. So, it may be as well to tell him that it is not mine; but that, if I did not firmly and truly believe it to be much better than I could offer, I would never have troubled him or you about it. You can judge between you how far it is admissible, and reject it, if not of the right sort. For my own part, I have no interest in the article one way or the other, further than to oblige * *, and should the composition be a good one, it can hurt neither party,—nor, indeed, any one, saving and excepting Mr. * * * *.

*   *   *   *   *   *   *

" Curse catch me if I know what H * * means or meaned about th demonstrative pronoun *, but I admire your fear of being inoculate with the same. Have you never found out that you have a particula style of your own, which is as distinct from all other people, as Hafiz o Shiraz from Hafiz of the Morning Post?

" So you allowed B * * and such like to hum and haw you, o rather, Lady J * * out of her compliment, and *me* out of mine †. Sun burn me but this was pitiful-hearted. However, I will tell her all abou it when I see her.

" Bell desires me to say all kinds of civilities, and assure you of he recognition and high consideration. I will tell you of our movement south, which may be in about three weeks from this present writing By the way, don't engage yourself in any travelling expedition, as I have a plan of travel into Italy, which we will discuss. And then, think of the poesy wherewithal we should overflow, from Venice to Vesuvius to say nothing of Greece, through all which—God willing—we might perambulate in one twelve-months. If I take my wife, you can take yours; and if I leave mine, you may do the same. ' Mind you stand by me, in either case, Brother Bruin.'

> " And believe me inveterately yours,
>> " B."

LETTER CCXV.

TO MR. MOORE.

" February 22d, 1815.

" Yesterday I sent off the packet and letter to Edinburgh. It consisted of forty-one pages, so that I have not added a line; but in my letter, I mentioned what passed between you and me in autumn, as my inducement for presuming to trouble him either with my own or * *'s

---

* Some remark which he told me had been made with respect to the frequent use of the demonstrative pronoun both by himself and by Sir W. Scott.

† Verses to Lady J * * (containing an allusion to Lord Byron) which I had written, while at Chatsworth, but consigned afterwards to the flames.

ucubrations. I am any thing but sure that it will do; but I have told J. that if there is any decent raw material in it, he may cut it into what shape he pleases, and warp it to his liking.

"So you *won't* go abroad, then, with *me,*—but alone. I fully purpose starting much about the time you mention, and alone, too.

*   *   *   *   *   *

"I hope J. won't think me very impudent in sending * * only; here was not room for a syllable. I have avowed * * as the author, and said that you thought or said, when I met you last, that he (J.) would not be angry at the coalition (though, alas! we have not coalesced), and so, if I have got into a scrape, I must get out of it—Heaven knows how.

"Your Anacreon * is come, and with it I sealed (its first impression) the packet and epistle to our patron.

"Curse the Melodies and the Tribes, to boot †. Braham is to assist —or hath assisted—but will do no more good than a second physician. I merely interfered to oblige a whim of K.'s, and all I have got by it was ' a speech' and a receipt for stewed oysters.

" ' Not meet'—pray don't say so. We must meet somewhere or somehow. Newstead is out of the question, being nearly sold again, or, if not, it is uninhabitable for my spouse. Pray write again. I will soon.

"P.S. Pray when do you come out? ever, or never? I hope I have made no blunder; but I certainly think you said to me (after W * *th, whom I first pondered upon, was given up) that * * and I might attempt * * * *. *His* length alone prevented me from trying my part, though I should have been less severe upon the Reviewée.

"Your seal is the best and prettiest of my set, and I thank you very much therefor. I have just been—or, rather, ought to be—very much shocked by the death of the Duke of Dorset. We were at school together, and there I was passionately attached to him. Since, we have

---

* A seal, with the head of Anacreon, which I had given him.

† I had taken the liberty of laughing a little at the manner in which some of his Hebrew Melodies had been set to music.

never met—but once, I think, since 1805—and it would be a paltry affect
tion to pretend that I had any feeling for him worth the name.   Bu
there was a time in my life when this event would have broken m
heart; and all I can say for it now is that—it is not worth breaking.

" Adieu—it is all a farce."

LETTER CCXVI.

TO MR. MOORE.

" March 2d, 1815.

" MY DEAR THOM,

" Jeffrey has sent me the most friendly of all possible letters, an
has accepted * *'s article.   He says he has long liked not only, &c. &
but my 'character.'   This must be *your* doing, you dog—ar'n't yo
ashamed of yourself, knowing me so well?   This is what one gets fo
having you for a father confessor.

" I feel merry enough to send you a sad song *.   You once aske
me for some words which you would set.   Now you may set or not, a
you like,—but there they are, in a legible hand †, and not in mine, bu
of my own scribbling; so you may say of them what you please.   Wh
don't you write to me?   I shall make you 'a speech ‡' if you don'
respond quickly.

" I am in such a state of sameness and stagnation, and so totall
occupied in consuming the fruits—and sauntering—and playing dul
games at cards—and yawning—and trying to read old Annual Register
and the daily papers—and gathering shells on the shore—and watchin

---

* The verses enclosed were those melancholy ones, now printed in his works, " There 's no
a joy the world can give like those it takes away."

† The MS. was in the handwriting of Lady Byron.

‡ These allusions to " a speech" are connected with a little incident, not worth mention
ing, which had amused us both when I was in town.   He was rather fond (and had bee
always so, as may be seen in his early letters) of thus harping on some conventional phrase o
joke.

the growth of stunted gooseberry bushes in the garden—that I have neither time nor sense to say more than

"Yours ever,

"B.

"P.S. I open my letter again to put a question to you. What would Lady C——k, or any other fashionable Pidcock, give to collect you and Jeffrey and me to *one* party? I have been answering his letter, which suggested this dainty query. I can't help laughing at the thoughts of your face and mine; and our anxiety to keep the Aristarch in good humour during the *early* part of a compotation, till we got drunk enough to make him 'a speech.' I think the critic would have much the best of us—of one, at least—for I don't think diffidence (I mean social) is a disease of yours."

LETTER CCXVII.

TO MR. MOORE.

"March 8th, 1815.

"An event—the death of poor Dorset—and the recollection of what I once felt, and ought to have felt now, but could not—set me pondering, and finally into the train of thought which you have in your hands. I am very glad you like them, for I flatter myself they will pass as an imitation of your style. If I could imitate it well, I should have no great ambition of originality—I wish I could make you exclaim with Dennis, 'That's my thunder, by G—d!' I wrote them with a view to your setting them, and as a present to Power, if he would accept the words, and *you* did not think yourself degraded, for once in a way, by marrying them to music.

"Sunburn N * *!—why do you always twit me with his vile Ebrew nasalities? Have I not told you it was all K.'s doing, and my own ex-quisite facility of temper? But thou wilt be a wag, Thomas; and see what you get for it. Now for my revenge.

"Depend—and perpend—upon it that your opinion of * *'s Poem

will travel through one or other of the quintuple correspondents, till i
reaches the ear and the liver of the author*. Your adventure, howeve
is truly laughable—but how could you be such a potatoe? You, '
brother' (of the quill) too, 'near the throne,' to confide to a man's *ow
publisher* (who has ' bought,' or rather sold, 'golden opinions' about him
such a damnatory parenthesis! ' Between you and me,' quotha—i
reminds me of a passage in the Heir at Law—' Tête-à-tête with Lad
Duberly, I suppose'—' No—tête-à-tête with *five hundred people*;' an
your confidential communication will doubtless be in circulation to tha
amount, in a short time, with several additions, and in several letters, al
signed L. H. R. O. B., &c. &c. &c.

"We leave this place to-morrow, and shall stop on our way to tow
(in the interval of taking a house there) at Col. Leigh's, near Newmarket
where any epistle of yours will find its welcome way.

"I have been very comfortable here,—listening to that d—d mono
logue, which elderly gentlemen call conversation, and in which my piou
father-in-law repeats himself every evening—save one, when he playe
upon the fiddle. However, they have been very kind and hospitable
and I like them and the place vastly, and I hope they will live many
happy months. Bell is in health, and unvaried good-humour and
behaviour. But we are all in the agonies of packing and parting; and
I suppose by this time to-morrow I shall be stuck in the chariot with
my chin upon a band-box. I have prepared, however, another carriage
for the abigail, and all the trumpery which our wives drag along with
them. 　　　　　　　　 " Ever thine, most affectionately,

　　　　　　　　　　　　　　　　　　　　　　 " B."

---

* He here alludes to a circumstance which I had communicated to him in a preceding
letter. In writing to one of the numerous partners of a well-known publishing establishmen
(with which I have since been lucky enough to form a more intimate connexion), I had said con-
fidentially (as I thought), in reference to a Poem that had just appeared,—"Between you and
me, I do not much admire Mr. * *'s Poem." The letter being chiefly upon business, was answered
through the regular business channel, and, to my dismay, concluded with the following words
—"We are very sorry that you do not approve of Mr. * *'s new Poem, and are your obedient,
&c. &c. L. H. R. O., &c. &c."

LETTER CCXVIII.

TO MR. MOORE.

" March 27th, 1815.

" I meaned to write to you before on the subject of your loss*; but the recollection of the uselessness and worthlessness of any observations on such events prevented me. I shall only now add, that I rejoice to see you bear it so well, and that I trust time will enable Mrs. M. to sustain it better. Every thing should be done to divert and occupy her with other thoughts and cares, and I am sure all that can be done will.

" Now to your letter. Napoleon—but the papers will have told you all. I quite think with you upon the subject, and for my *real* thoughts this time last year, I would refer you to the last pages of the Journal I gave you. I can forgive the rogue for utterly falsifying every line of mine Ode—which I take to be the last and uttermost stretch of human magnanimity. Do you remember the story of a certain abbé, who wrote a Treatise on the Swedish Constitution, and proved it indissoluble and eternal? Just as he had corrected the last sheet, news came that Gustavus III. had destroyed this immortal government. ' Sir,' quoth the abbé, ' the King of Sweden may overthrow the *constitution,* but not *my book!!*' I think *of* the abbé, but not *with* him.

" Making every allowance for talent and most consummate daring, there is, after all, a good deal in luck or destiny. He might have been stopped by our frigates—or wrecked in the Gulf of Lyons, which is particularly tempestuous—or—a thousand things. But he is certainly Fortune's favourite, and

> Once fairly set out on his party of pleasure,
> Taking towns at his liking and crowns at his leisure,
> From Elba to Lyons and Paris he goes,
> Making *balls for* the ladies, and *bows to* his foes.

You must have seen the account of his driving into the middle of the

---

* The death of his infant god-daughter, Olivia Byron Moore.

royal army, and the immediate effect of his pretty speeches.   And nov
if he don't drub the allies, there is 'no purchase in money.'   If he ca
take France by himself, the devil's in't if he don't repulse the invade
when backed by those celebrated sworders—those boys of the blade, tl
Imperial Guard, and the old and new army.   It is impossible not to I
dazzled and overwhelmed by his character and career.   Nothing ever s
disappointed me as his abdication, and nothing could have reconciled m
to him but some such revival as his recent exploit; though no one coul
anticipate such a complete and brilliant renovation.

"To your question, I can only answer that there have been som
symptoms which look a little gestatory.   It is a subject upon which
am not particularly anxious, except that I think it would please he
uncle, Lord Wentworth, and her father and mother.   The former (Lor
W.) is now in town, and in very indifferent health.   You perhaps knov
that his property, amounting to seven or eight thousand a year, wil
eventually devolve upon Bell.   But the old gentleman has been so ver
kind to her and me, that I hardly know how to wish him in heaver
if he can be comfortable on earth.   Her father is still in the country.

"We mean to metropolize to-morrow, and you will address you
next to Piccadilly.   We have got the Duchess of Devon's house there
she being in France.

"I don't care what Power says to secure the property of the Song
so that it is *not* complimentary to me, nor any thing about 'condescending
or '*noble* author'—both 'vile phrases,' as Polonius says.

*   *   *   *   *

"Pray, let me hear from you, and when you mean to be in town
Your continental scheme is impracticable for the present.   I have t
thank you for a longer letter than usual, which I hope will induce yor
to tax my gratitude still further in the same way.

"You never told me about 'Longman' and 'next winter,' and I an
not a 'mile-stone*.'"

---

* I had accused him of having entirely forgot that, in a preceding letter, I had informe
him of my intention to publish with the Messrs. Longman in the ensuing winter, and adde
that, in giving him this information, I found I had been,—to use an elegant Irish metaphor,—
"whistling jigs to a mile-stone."

LETTER CCXIX.

TO MR. COLERIDGE.

"Piccadilly, March 31st, 1815.

"DEAR SIR,

"It will give me great pleasure to comply with your request, though I hope there is still taste enough left amongst us to render it almost unnecessary, sordid and interested as, it must be admitted, many of 'the trade' are, where circumstances give them an advantage. I trust you do not permit yourself to be depressed by the temporary partiality of what is called 'the public' for the favourites of the moment; all experience is against the permanency of such impressions. You must have lived to see many of these pass away, and will survive many more —I mean personally, for *poetically*, I would not insult you by a comparison.

"If I may be permitted, I would suggest that there never was such an opening for tragedy. In Kean, there is an actor worthy of expressing the thoughts of the characters which you have every power of imbodying; and I cannot but regret that the part of Ordonio was disposed of before his appearance at Drury-lane. We have had nothing to be mentioned in the same breath with 'Remorse' for very many years; and I should think that the reception of that play was sufficient to encourage the highest hopes of author and audience. It is to be hoped that you are proceeding in a career which could not but be successful. With my best respects to Mr. Bowles, I have the honour to be

"Your obliged
"and very obedient servant,
"BYRON.

"P. S. You mention my 'Satire,' lampoon, or whatever you or others please to call it. I can only say, that it was written when I was very young and very angry, and has been a thorn in my side ever since; more particularly as almost all the persons animadverted upon became subsequently my acquaintances, and some of them my friends, which is 'heaping fire upon an enemy's head,' and forgiving me too readily to

permit me to forgive myself. The part applied to you is pert, an
petulant, and shallow enough; but, although I have long done ever
thing in my power to suppress the circulation of the whole thing,
shall always regret the wantonness or generality of many of its attempte
attacks."

It was in the course of this spring that Lord Byron and Sir Walte
Scott became, for the first time, personally acquainted with each othe
Mr. Murray, having been previously on a visit to the latter gentlemar
had been intrusted by him with a superb Turkish dagger, as a present t
Lord Byron; and the noble poet, on their meeting this year, in Londor
—the only time when these two great men had ever an opportunity o
enjoying each other's society,—presented to Sir Walter, in return, a vase
containing some human bones that had been dug up from under a part o
the old walls of Athens. The reader, however, will be much better pleased
to have these particulars in the words of Sir Walter Scott himself, who
with that good-nature which renders him no less amiable than he i
admirable, has found time, in the midst of all his marvellous labours fo
the world, to favour me with the following interesting communication*

* A few passages at the beginning of these recollections have been omitted, as containin
particulars relative to Lord Byron's mother, which have already been mentioned in the earl
part of this work. Among these, however, there is one anecdote, the repetition of which wil
be easily pardoned, on account of the infinitely greater interest and authenticity imparted to it
details by coming from such an eye-witness as Sir Walter Scott:—" I remember," he says
" having seen Lord Byron's mother before she was married, and a certain coincidence rendere
the circumstance rather remarkable. It was during Mrs. Siddons's first or second visit to Edin
burgh, when the music of that wonderful actress's voice, looks, manner, and person, produce
the strongest effect which could possibly be exerted by a human being upon her fellow-creature
Nothing of the kind that I ever witnessed approached it by a hundred degrees. The high state c
excitation was aided by the difficulties of obtaining entrance, and the exhausting length of tim
that the audience were contented to wait until the piece commenced. When the curtain fell, a
large proportion of the ladies were generally in hysterics.

" I remember Miss Gordon of Ghight, in particular, harrowing the house by the desperat
and wild way in which she shrieked out Mrs. Siddons's exclamation, in the character of Isabella
' Oh my Byron! Oh my Byron!' A well-known medical gentleman, the benevolent Dr
Alexander Wood, tendered his assistance; but the thick-pressed audience could not for a lon
time make way for the doctor to approach his patient, or the patient the physician. Th
remarkable circumstance was, that the lady had not then seen Captain Byron, who, like Si
Toby, made her conclude with ' Oh !' as she had begun with it."

*   *   *   *   *   *   *

" My first acquaintance with Byron began in a manner rather doubtful. I was so far from having any thing to do with the offensive criticism in the Edinburgh, that I remember remonstrating against it with our friend, the editor, because I thought the ' Hours of Idleness' treated with undue severity. They were written, like all juvenile poetry, rather from the recollection of what had pleased the author in others than what had been suggested by his own imagination: but, nevertheless, I thought they contained some passages of noble promise. I was so much impressed with this, that I had thoughts of writing to the author; but some exaggerated reports concerning his peculiarities, and a natural unwillingness to intrude an opinion which was uncalled for, induced me to relinquish the idea.

" When Byron wrote his famous Satire, I had my share of flagellation among my betters. My crime was having written a poem (Marmion, I think) for a thousand pounds; which was no otherwise true than that I sold the copyright for that sum. Now, not to mention that an author can hardly be censured for accepting such a sum as the booksellers are willing to give him, especially as the gentlemen of the trade made no complaints of their bargain, I thought the interference with my private affairs was rather beyond the limits of literary satire. On the other hand, Lord Byron paid me, in several passages, so much more praise than I deserved, that I must have been more irritable than I have ever felt upon such subjects, not to sit down contented and think no more about the matter.

" I was very much struck, with all the rest of the world, at the vigour and force of imagination displayed in the first Cantos of Childe Harold, and the other splendid productions which Lord Byron flung from him to the public with a promptitude that savoured of profusion. My own popularity, as a poet, was then on the wane, and I was unaffectedly pleased to see an author of so much power and energy taking the field. Mr. John Murray happened to be in Scotland that season, and as I mentioned to him the pleasure I should have in making Lord Byron's acquaintance, he had the kindness to mention my wish to his lordship, which led to some correspondence.

"It was in the spring of 1815 that, chancing to be in London, I ha
the advantage of a personal introduction to Lord Byron. Report ha
prepared me to meet a man of peculiar habits and a quick temper, and
had some doubts whether we were likely to suit each other in society.
was most agreeably disappointed in this respect. I found Lord Byrc
in the highest degree courteous, and even kind. We met, for an hou
or two almost daily, in Mr. Murray's drawing-room, and found a gre
deal to say to each other. We also met frequently in parties and evenin
society, so that for about two months I had the advantage of considerabl
intimacy with this distinguished individual. Our sentiments agreed
good deal, except upon the subjects of religion and politics, upon neithe
of which I was inclined to believe that Lord Byron entertained ver
fixed opinions. I remember saying to him, that I really thought, that i
he lived a few years he would alter his sentiments. He answered, rathe
sharply, 'I suppose you are one of those who prophesy I will tur
Methodist.' I replied, 'No—I don't expect your conversion to be o
such an ordinary kind. I would rather look to see you retreat upon th
Catholic faith, and distinguish yourself by the austerity of your penance:
The species of religion to which you must, or may, one day attac
yourself must exercise a strong power on the imagination.' He smile
gravely, and seemed to allow I might be right.

"On politics, he used sometimes to express a high strain of what i
now called Liberalism; but it appeared to me that the pleasure it afforde
him as a vehicle of displaying his wit and satire against individuals i
office was at the bottom of this habit of thinking, rather than any rea
conviction of the political principles on which he talked. He was certainl
proud of his rank and ancient family, and, in that respect, as much a
aristocrat as was consistent with good sense and good breeding. Som
disgusts, how adopted I know not, seemed to me to have given thi
peculiar and, as it appeared to me, contradictory cast of mind; but, a
heart, I would have termed Byron a patrician on principle.

"Lord Byron's reading did not seem to me to have been ver
extensive either in poetry or history. Having the advantage of him i
that respect, and possessing a good competent share of such reading as i
little read, I was sometimes able to put under his eye objects which ha

for him the interest of novelty. I remember particularly repeating to him the fine poem of Hardyknute, an imitation of the old Scottish Ballad, with which he was so much affected, that some one who was in the same apartment asked me what I could possibly have been telling Byron by which he was so much agitated.

" I saw Byron, for the last time, in 1815, after I returned from France. He dined, or lunched, with me' at Long's, in Bond-street. I never saw him so full of gaiety and good-humour, to which the presence of Mr. Matthews, the comedian, added not a little. Poor Terry was also present. After one of the gayest parties I ever was present at, my fellow-traveller, Mr. Scott, of Gala, and I, set off for Scotland, and I never saw Lord Byron again. Several letters passed between us—one perhaps every half year. Like the old heroes in Homer, we exchanged gifts;— I gave Byron a beautiful dagger mounted with gold, which had been the property of the redoubted Elfi Bey. But I was to play the part of Diomed, in the Iliad, for Byron sent me, some time after, a large sepulchral vase of silver. It was full of dead men's bones, and had inscriptions on two sides of the base. One ran thus—' The bones contained in this urn were found in certain ancient sepulchres within the land walls of Athens, in the month of February, 1811.' The other face bears the lines of Juvenal:

> ' Expende—quot libras in duce summo invenies.
> —Mors sola fatetur quantula hominum corpuscula.'
>
> JUV. X.

" To these I have added a third inscription, in these words—' The gift of Lord Byron to Walter Scott*.' There was a letter with this vase more valuable to me than the gift itself, from the kindness with which

---

* Mr. Murray had, at the time of giving the vase, suggested to Lord Byron, that it would increase the value of the gift to add some such inscription; but the feeling of the noble poet on this subject will be understood from the following answer which he returned.

" April 9th, 1815.

" Thanks for the books. I have great objection to your proposition about inscribing the vase,—which is, that it would appear *ostentatious* on my part; and of course I must send it as it is, without any alteration.

" Yours, &c."

the donor expressed himself towards me. I left it naturally in the ur
with the bones,—but it is now missing. As the theft was not of a natur
to be practised by a mere domestic, I am compelled to suspect the ir
hospitality of some individual of higher station,—most gratuitousl
exercised certainly, since, after what I have here said, no one wi
probably choose to boast of possessing this literary curiosity.

" We had a good deal of laughing, I remember, on what the publi
might be supposed to think, or say, concerning the gloomy and ominou
nature of our mutual gifts.

" I think I can add little more to my recollections of Byron. H
was often melancholy,—almost gloomy. When I observed him in thi
humour, I used either to wait till it went off of its own accord, or til
some natural and easy mode occurred of leading him into conversation
when the shadows almost always left his countenance, like the mist rising
from a landscape. In conversation, he was very animated.

" I met with him very frequently in society; our mutual acquaint
ances doing me the honour to think that he liked to meet with me
Some very agreeable parties I can recollect,—particularly one at Sir
George Beaumont's, where the amiable landlord had assembled some
persons distinguished for talent. Of these I need only mention the late
Sir Humphry Davy, whose talents for literature were as remarkable a
his empire over science. Mr. Richard Sharpe and Mr. Rogers were also
present.

" I think I also remarked in Byron's temper starts of suspicion
when he seemed to pause and consider whether there had not been a
secret, and perhaps offensive, meaning in something casually said to him
In this case, I also judged it best to let his mind, like a troubled spring
work itself clear, which it did in a minute or two. I was considerably
older, you will recollect, than my noble friend, and had no reason to fear
his misconstruing my sentiments towards him, nor had I ever the
slightest reason to doubt that they were kindly returned on his part. I
I had occasion to be mortified by the display of genius which threw
into the shade such pretensions as I was then supposed to possess, I migh
console myself that, in my own case, the materials of mental happines
had been mingled in a greater proportion.

"I rummage my brains in vain for what often rushes into my head unbidden,—little traits and sayings which recall his looks, manner, tone, and gestures; and I have always continued to think that a crisis of life was arrived in which a new career of fame was opened to him, and that had he been permitted to start upon it, he would have obliterated the memory of such parts of his life as friends would wish to forget."

LETTER CCXX.

TO MR. MOORE.

"April 23d, 1815.

"Lord Wentworth died last week. The bulk of his property (from seven to eight thousand per ann.) is entailed on Lady Milbanke and Lady Byron. The first is gone to take possession in Leicestershire, and attend the funeral, &c. this day.

*   *   *   *   *

"I have mentioned the facts of the settlement of Lord W.'s property, because the newspapers, with their usual accuracy, have been making all kinds of blunders in their statement. His will is just as expected—the principal part settled on Lady Milbanke (now Noel) and Bell, and a separate estate left for sale to pay debts (which are not great) and legacies to his natural son and daughter.

"Mrs. * *'s tragedy was last night damned. They may bring it on again, and probably will; but damned it was,—not a word of the last act audible. I went (*malgré* that I ought to have staid at home in sackcloth for unc., but I could not resist the *first* night of any thing) to a private and quiet nook of my private box, and witnessed the whole process. The first three acts, with transient gushes of applause, oozed patiently but heavily on. I must say it was badly acted, particularly by * *, who was groaned upon in the third act,—something about ' horror—such a horror' was the cause. Well, the fourth act became as muddy and turbid as need be; but the fifth—what Garrick used to call (like a fool) the *concoction* of a play—the fifth act stuck fast at the King's prayer. You know he says ' he never went to bed without saying them, and did not like to omit them now.' But he was no sooner upon his knees, than the

audience got upon their legs—the damnable pit—and roared, and groane
and hissed, and whistled. Well, that was choked a little; but the ruffia
scene—the penitent peasantry—and killing the Bishop and the Prince
—oh, it was all over. The curtain fell upon unheard actors, and th
announcement attempted by Kean for Monday was equally ineffectua
Mrs. Bartley was so frightened, that, though the people were tolerabl
quiet, the Epilogue was quite inaudible to half the house. In short,—
you know all. I clapped till my hands were skinless, and so did S
James Mackintosh, who was with me in the box. All the world wer
in the house, from the Jerseys, Greys, &c. &c. downwards. But it woul
not do. It is, after all, not an *acting* play; good language, but no powe

*   *   *   *   *   *   *   *   *

Women (saving Joanna Baillie) cannot write tragedy; they have no
seen enough nor felt enough of life for it. I think Semiramis c
Catherine II. might have written (could they have been unqueened)
rare play.

*   *   *   *   *

   " It is, however, a good warning not to risk or write tragedies.
never had much bent that way; but, if I had, this would have cured me

                              " Ever, carissime Thom.,

                                        " thine, B."

LETTER CCXXI.

TO MR. MURRAY.

                                        " May 21st, 1815.

   " You must have thought it very odd, not to say ungrateful, that
made no mention of the drawings *, &c. when I had the pleasure o
seeing you this morning. The fact is, that till this moment I had no
seen them, nor heard of their arrival: they were carried up into th
library, where I have not been till just now, and no intimation given t
me of their coming. The present is so very magnificent, that—in short

---

   * Mr. Murray had presented Lady Byron with twelve drawings, by Stothard, from Lor
Byron's Poems.

I leave Lady Byron to thank you for it herself, and merely send this to apologise for a piece of apparent and unintentional neglect on my own part.

" Yours, &c."

LETTER CCXXII.

TO MR. MOORE *.

" 13, Piccadilly Terrace, June 12th, 1815.

" I have nothing to offer in behalf of my late silence, except the most inveterate and ineffable laziness; but I am too supine to invent a lie, or I *certainly* should, being ashamed of the truth. K * *, I hope, has appeased your magnanimous indignation at his blunders. I wished and wish you were in the Committee, with all my heart †. It seems so hopeless a business, that the company of a friend would be quite consoling,—but more of this when we meet. In the mean time, you are entreated to prevail upon Mrs. Esterre to engage herself. I believe she has been written to, but your influence, in person, or proxy, would probably go farther than our proposals. What they are, I know not; all *my* new function consists in listening to the despair of Cavendish Bradshaw, the hopes of Kinnaird, the wishes of Lord Essex, the complaints of Whitbread, and the calculations of Peter Moore,—all of which, and whom, seem totally at variance. C. Bradshaw wants to light the theatre with *gas*, which may, perhaps (if the vulgar be believed) poison half the audience, and all the *Dramatis Personæ*. Essex has endeavoured to persuade K * * not to get drunk, the consequence of which is, that he has never been sober since. Kinnaird, with equal success, would have convinced Raymond that he, the said Raymond, had too much salary. Whitbread wants us to assess the pit another sixpence,—a d—d insidious

* This and the following letter were addressed to me in Ireland, whither I had gone about the middle of the preceding month.

† He had lately become one of the members of the Sub-Committee (consisting, besides himself, of the persons mentioned in this letter), who had taken upon themselves the management of Drury-lane Theatre; and it had been his wish, on the first construction of the Committee, that I should be one of his colleagues. To some mistake in the mode of conveying this proposal to me, he alludes in the preceding sentence.

proposition,—which will end in an O. P. combustion. To crown al
R * *, the auctioneer, has the impudence to be displeased, because he ha
no dividend. The villain is a proprietor of shares, and a long-lunge
orator in the meetings. I hear he has prophesied our incapacity,—'
foregone conclusion,' whereof I hope to give him signal proofs before w
are done.

"Will you give us an Opera? no, I'll be sworn, but I wish yo
would.   *   *   *   *   *   *   *   *

          *   *   *   *   *   *

"To go on with the poetical world, Walter Scott has gone back to
Scotland. Murray, the bookseller, has been cruelly cudgelled of mis
begotten knaves, 'in Kendal green,' at Newington Butts, in his way
home from a purlieu dinner—and robbed,—would you believe it?—o
three or four bonds of forty pound apiece, and a seal-ring of his grand
father's, worth a million! This is his version,—but others opine tha
D'Israeli, with whom he dined, knocked him down with his last pub
lication, 'the Quarrels of Authors,' in a dispute about copyright. B
that as it may, the newspapers have teemed with his 'injuria formæ,
and he has been embrocated and invisible to all but the apothecary eve
since.

"Lady B. is better than three months advanced in her progres.
towards maternity, and, we hope, likely to go well through with it. W
have been very little out this season, as I wish to keep her quiet in he
present situation. Her father and mother have changed their names to
Noel, in compliance with Lord Wentworth's will, and in complaisance
to the property bequeathed by him.

"I hear that you have been gloriously received by the Irish,—an
so you ought. But don't let them kill you with claret and kindness a
the national dinner in your honour, which, I hear and hope, is in con
templation. If you will tell me the day, I'll get drunk myself on thi
side of the water, and waft you an applauding hiccup over the Channel

"Of politics, we have nothing but the yell for war; and C * * h i
preparing his head for the pike, on which we shall see it carried befor
he has done. The loan has made every body sulky. I hear often from
Paris, but in direct contradiction to the home statements of our hire

ings. Of domestic doings, there has been nothing since Lady D * *. Not a divorce stirring,—but a good many in embryo, in the shape of marriages.

" I enclose you an epistle received this morning from I know not whom; but I think it will amuse you. The writer must be a rare fellow*.

" P.S. A gentleman named D'Alton (not your Dalton) has sent me National Poem called ' Dermid.' The same cause which prevented my writing to you operated against my wish to write to him an epistle of thanks. If you see him, will you make all kinds of fine speeches for me, and tell him that I am the laziest and most ungrateful of mortals?

" A word more ;—don't let Sir John Stevenson (as an evidence on trials for copyright, &c.) talk about the price of your next Poem, or they will come upon you for the *Property Tax* for it. I am serious, and have just heard a long story of the rascally tax-men making Scott pay for his. So, take care. Three hundred is a devil of a deduction out of three thousand."

LETTER CCXXIII.

TO MR. MOORE.

" July 7th, 1815.

" ' Grata superveniet,' &c. &c. I had written to you again, but burnt the letter, because I began to think you seriously hurt at my

---

* The following is the enclosure here referred to.

" Darlington, June 3, 1815.

" MY LORD,

" I have lately purchased a set of your works, and am quite vexed that you have not can-celled the Ode to Buonaparte. It certainly was prematurely written, without thought or reflection. Providence has now brought him to reign over millions again, while the same Pro-vidence keeps as it were in a garrison another potentate, who, in the language of Mr. Burke, he hurled from his throne.' See if you cannot make amends for your folly, and consider that, in almost every respect, human nature is the same, in every clime and in every period, and don't act the part of a *foolish boy*. Let not Englishmen talk of the stretch of tyrants, while the torrents of blood shed in the East Indies cry aloud to Heaven for retaliation. Learn, good sir, not to cast the first stone. I remain your lordship's servant,

" J. R * *."

indolence, and did not know how the buffoonery it contained might taken. In the mean time, I have yours, and all is well.

"I had given over all hopes of yours. By the by, my 'gra superveniet' should be in the present tense; for I perceive it looks no as if it applied to this present scrawl reaching you, whereas it is to t receipt of thy Kilkenny epistle that I have tacked that venerab sentiment.

"Poor Whitbread died yesterday morning,—a sudden and seve loss. His health had been wavering, but so fatal an attack was n apprehended. He dropped down and, I believe, never spoke afterward I perceive Perry attributes his death to Drury-lane,—a consolatory e couragement to the new Committee. I have no doubt that * *, who of a plethoric habit, will be bled immediately; and as I have, since m marriage, lost much of my paleness, and,—' horresco referens' (for I ha even *moderate* fat)—that happy slenderness, to which, when I first kne you, I had attained, I by no means sit easy under this dispensation of t Morning Chronicle. Every one must regret the loss of Whitbread; h was surely a great and very good man.

"Paris is taken for the second time. I presume it, for the futur will have an anniversary capture. In the late battles, like all the worl I have lost a connexion,—poor Frederick Howard, the best of his rac I had little intercourse, of late years, with his family, but I never saw c heard but good of him. Hobhouse's brother is killed. In short, th havoc has not left a family out of its tender mercies.

"Every hope of a republic is over, and we must go on under th old system. But I am sick at heart of politics and slaughters; and th luck which Providence is pleased to lavish on Lord * * is only a proc of the little value the gods set upon prosperity, when they permit suc * * *s as he and that drunken corporal, old Blucher, to bully thei betters. From this, however, Wellington should be excepted. He *is* man,—and the Scipio of our Hannibal. However, he may thank th Russian frosts, which destroyed the *real élite* of the French army, for th successes of Waterloo.

"La! Moore—how you blasphemes about 'Parnassus' and 'Moses

I am ashamed for you. Won't you do any thing for the drama? We beseech an Opera. Kinnaird's blunder was partly mine. I wanted you of all things in the Committee, and so did he. But we are now glad you were wiser; for it is, I doubt, a bitter business.

"When shall we see you in England? Sir Ralph Noel (*late* Milbanke—he don't promise to be *late* Noel in a hurry) finding that one man can't inhabit two houses, has given his place in the north to me for a habitation; and there Lady B. threatens to be brought to bed in November. Sir R. and my Lady Mother are to quarter at Kirby—Lord Wentworth's that was. Perhaps you and Mrs. Moore will pay us a visit at Seaham in the course of the autumn. If so, you and I (*without* our *wives*) will take a *lark* to Edinburgh and embrace Jeffrey. It is not much above one hundred miles from us. But all this, and other high matters, we will discuss at meeting, which I hope will be on your return. We don't leave town till August.

"Ever, &c."

LETTER CCXXIV.

TO MR. SOTHEBY.

"Sept. 15, 1815. Piccadilly Terrace.

"DEAR SIR,

"'Ivan' is accepted, and will be put in progress on Kean's arrival.

"The theatrical gentlemen have a confident hope of its success. I know not that any alterations for the stage will be necessary; if any, they will be trifling, and you shall be duly apprized. I would suggest that you should not attend any except the latter rehearsals—the managers have requested me to state this to you. You can see them, viz., Dibdin and Rae, whenever you please, and I will do any thing you wish to be done on your suggestion, in the mean time.

"Mrs. Mardyn is not yet out, and nothing can be determined till she has made her appearance—I mean as to her capacity for the part you

mention, which I take it for granted is not in Ivan—as I think Ivan ma
be performed very well without her.　But of that hereafter.

"Ever yours, very truly,

"Byron.

"P.S. You will be glad to hear that the season has begun uncon
monly well—great and constant houses—the performers in much ha
mony with the Committee and one another, and as much good-humou
as can be preserved in such complicated and extensive interests as th
Drury-lane proprietary."

TO MR. SOTHEBY.

"September 25th, 1815.

"Dear Sir,

"I think it would be advisable for you to see the acting-manager
when convenient, as these must be points on which you will want t
confer ; the objection I stated was merely on the part of the performer
and is *general* and not *particular* to this instance.　I thought it as we
to mention it at once—and some of the rehearsals you will doubtless se
notwithstanding.

"Rae, I rather think, has his eye on Naritzin for himself.　He is
more popular performer than Bartley, and certainly the cast will b
stronger with him in it ; besides, he is one of the managers, and will fee
doubly interested if he can act in both capacities.　Mrs. Bartley will b
Petrowna ;—as to the Empress, I know not what to say or think.　Th
truth is, we are not amply furnished with tragic women ; but make th
best of those we have, you can take your choice of them.　We have a
great hopes of the success—on which, setting aside other considerations
we are particularly anxious, as being the first tragedy to be brought ou
since the old Committee.

"By the way—I have a charge against you.　As the great M
Dennis roared out on a similar occasion—'By G—d, *that* is *my* thunder
so do I exclaim ' *This* is *my* lightning !'　I allude to a speech of Ivan's
in the scene with Petrowna and the Empress, where the thought an

lmost expression are similar to Conrad's in the 3d Canto of the 'Corsair.' , however, do not say this to accuse you, but to exempt myself from uspicion*, as there is a priority of six months' publication, on my part, etween the appearance of that composition and of your tragedies.

"George Lambe meant to have written to you. If you don't like o confer with the managers at present, I will attend to your wishes—so tate them.

" Yours very truly,

" BYRON."

LETTER CCXXV.

TO MR. TAYLOR.

" 13, Terrace, Piccadilly, September 25th, 1815.

" DEAR SIR,

" I am sorry you should feel uneasy at what has by no means troubled me†. If your Editor, his correspondents, and readers, are amused, I have no objection to be the theme of all the ballads he can find room for,—provided his lucubrations are confined to *me* only.

" It is a long time since things of this kind have ceased to ' fright me from my propriety;' nor do I know any similar attack which would

---

* Notwithstanding this precaution of the poet, the coincidence in question was, but a few years after, triumphantly cited in support of the sweeping charge of plagiarism brought against him by some scribblers. The following are Mr. Sotheby's lines.

> " And I have leapt
> In transport from my flinty couch, to welcome
> The thunder as it burst upon my roof,
> And beckon'd to the lightning, as it flash'd
> And sparkled on these fetters."

† Mr. Taylor having inserted in the Sun newspaper (of which he was then chief proprietor) a sonnet to Lord Byron, in return for a present which his lordship had sent him of a handsomely bound copy of all his works, there appeared in the same journal, on the following day (from the pen of some person who had acquired a control over the paper), a parody upon this sonnet, containing some disrespectful allusion to Lady Byron; and it is to this circumstance, which Mr. Taylor had written to explain, that the above letter, so creditable to the feelings of the noble husband, refers.

4 L 2

induce me to turn again,—unless it involved those connected with m
whose qualities, I hope, are such as to exempt them in the eyes of tho
who bear no good-will to myself.   In such a case, supposing it to occ
—to *reverse* the saying of Dr. Johnson,—' what the law could not do f
me, I would do for myself,' be the consequences what they might.

"I return you, with many thanks, Colman and the letters.   Th
Poems, I hope, you intended me to keep;—at least, I shall do so, till
hear the contrary.

" Very truly yours."

TO MR. MURRAY.

" Sept. 25, 1815.

"Will you publish the Drury-lane ' Magpye?' or, what is mor
will you give fifty, or even forty, pounds for the copyright of the said
I have undertaken to ask you this question on behalf of the translato
and wish you would.   We can't get so much for him by ten poun
from any body else, and I, knowing your magnificence, would be gla
of an answer.   " Ever, &c."

LETTER CCXXVI.

TO MR. MURRAY.

" September 27th, 1815.

" That's right, and splendid, and becoming a publisher of hig
degree.   Mr. Concanen (the translator) will be delighted, and pay h
washerwoman; and in reward for your bountiful behaviour in th
instance, I won't ask you to publish any more for Drury-lane, or an
lane whatever again.   You will have no tragedy or any thing else fror
me, I assure you, and may think yourself lucky in having got rid of m
for good and all, without more damage.   But I'll tell you what we wi
do for you,—act Sotheby's Ivan, which will succeed; and then you
present and next impression of the dramas of that dramatic gentlema
will be expedited to your heart's content; and if there is any thin

very good, you shall have the refusal; but you sha'n't have any more requests.

"Sotheby has got a thought, and almost the words, from the Third Canto of the Corsair, which, you know, was published six months before his tragedy. It is from the storm in Conrad's cell. I have written to Mr. Sotheby to claim it; and, as Dennis roared out of the pit, 'By G—d, *that's my* thunder!' so do I, and will I, exclaim, 'By G—d, that's *my lightning!*' that electrical fluid being, in fact, the subject of the said passage.

"You will have a print of Fanny Kelly, in the Maid, to prefix, which is honestly worth twice the money you have given for the MS. Pray what did you do with the note I gave you about Mungo Park?

"Ever, &c."

LETTER CCXXVII.

TO MR. MOORE.

"13, Terrace, Piccadilly, October 28, 1815.

"You are, it seems, in England again, as I am to hear from every body but yourself; and I suppose you punctilious, because I did not answer your last Irish letter. When did you leave the 'swate country?' Never mind, I forgive you;—a strong proof of—I know not what—to give the lie to—

'He never pardons who hath done the wrong.'

"You have written to * *. You have also written to Perry, who intimates hope of an Opera from you. Coleridge has promised a Tragedy. Now, if you keep Perry's word, and Coleridge keeps his own, Drury-lane will be set up;—and, sooth to say, it is in grievous want of such a lift. We began at speed, and are blown already. When I say 'we,' I mean Kinnaird, who is the 'all in all sufficient,' and can count, which none of the rest of the Committee can.

"It is really very good fun, as far as the daily and nightly stir of these strutters and fretters go; and, if the concern could be brought to

pay a shilling in the pound, would do much credit to the managemen
Mr. —— has an accepted tragedy, * * * * *, whose first scene is in his slee
(I don't mean the author's). It was forwarded to us as a prodigiou
favourite of Kean's; but the said Kean, upon interrogation, denies h
eulogy, and protests against his part. How it will end, I know not.

"I say so much about the theatre, because there is nothing els
alive in London at this season. All the world are out of it, except u
who remain to lie in,—in December, or perhaps earlier. Lady B.
very ponderous and prosperous, apparently, and I wish it well over.

"There is a play before me from a personage who signs himsel
'Hibernicus.' The hero is Malachi, the Irishman and king; and th
villain and usurper, Turgesius, the Dane. The conclusion is fine
Turgesius is chained by the leg (*vide* stage direction) to a pillar on th
stage; and King Malachi makes him a speech, not unlike Lord Castle
reagh's about the balance of power and the lawfulness of legitimacy
which puts Turgesius into a frenzy—as Castlereagh's would, if hi
audience was chained by the leg. He draws a dagger and rushes at th
orator; but, finding himself at the end of his tether, he sticks it into hi
own carcass, and dies, saying, he has fulfilled a prophecy.

"Now, this is *serious, downright matter of fact*, and the gravest par
of a tragedy which is not intended for burlesque. I tell it you for th
honour of Ireland. The writer hopes it will be represented:—but wha
is Hope? nothing but the paint on the face of Existence; the least touc
of truth rubs it off, and then we see what a hollow-cheeked harlot w
have got hold of. I am not sure.that I have not said this last superfin
reflection before. But never mind;—it will do for the tragedy o
Turgesius, to which I can append it.

"Well, but how dost thou do? thou bard, not of a thousand, bu
three thousand! I wish your friend, Sir John Piano-forte, had kept tha
to himself, and not made it public at the trial of the song-seller i
Dublin. I tell you why; it is a liberal thing for Longman to do, an
honourable for you to obtain; but it will set all the 'hungry and dinner
less, lank-jawed judges' upon the fortunate author. But they be d—d
—the 'Jeffrey and the Moore together are confident against the worl
in ink!' By the way, if poor C * * e—who is a man of wonderful talent

nd in distress*, and about to publish two vols. of Poesy and Biography,
nd who has been worse used by the critics than ever we were—will you,
f he comes out, promise me to review him favourably in the E. R.?
Praise him, I think you must, but you will also praise him *well*,—of all
hings the most difficult.   It will be the making of him.

"This must be a secret between you and me, as Jeffrey might not
ike such a project;—nor, indeed, might C. himself like it.   But I do
hink he only wants a pioneer and a sparkle or two to explode most
gloriously.

"Ever yours most affectionately,

"B.

"P.S.   This is a sad scribbler's letter; but the next shall be 'more
of this world.'"

As, after this letter, there occur but few allusions to his connexion
with the Drury-lane Management, I shall here avail myself of the opportunity to give some extracts from his "Detached Thoughts," containing
recollections of his short acquaintance with the interior of the theatre.

"When I belonged to the Drury-lane Committee, and was one of
the Sub-Committee of Management, the number of *plays* upon the shelves
were about *five* hundred.   Conceiving that amongst these there must be
some of merit, in person and by proxy I caused an investigation.   I do
not think that of those which I saw there was one which could be conscientiously tolerated.   There never were such things as most of them!
Mathurin was very kindly recommended to me by Walter Scott, to
whom I had recourse, firstly, in the hope that he would do something
for us himself, and secondly, in my despair, that he would point out to
us any young (or old) writer of promise.   Mathurin sent his Bertram and
a letter *without* his address, so that at first I could give him no answer.

---

* It is but justice both to "him that gave and him that took" to mention that the noble
poet, at this time, with a delicacy which enhanced the kindness, advanced to the eminent person
here spoken of, on the credit of some work he was about to produce, one hundred pounds.

When I at last hit upon his residence, I sent him a favourable answ
and something more substantial. His play succeeded; but I was at th
time absent from England.

"I tried Coleridge too; but he had nothing feasible in hand at t
time. Mr. Sotheby obligingly offered *all* his tragedies, and I pledg
myself, and notwithstanding many squabbles with my Committed Br
thren, did get 'Ivan' accepted, read, and the parts distributed. But, l
in the very heart of the matter, upon some *tepid*ness on the part of Kea
or warmth on that of the author, Sotheby withdrew his play. Sir J.
Burgess did also present four tragedies and a farce, and I moved gree
room and Sub-Committee, but they would not.

"Then the scenes I had to go through!—the authors, and tl
authoresses, and the milliners, and the wild Irishmen,—the people fro
Brighton, from Blackwall, from Chatham, from Cheltenham, from Du
lin, from Dundee,—who came in upon me! to all of whom it was prop
to give a civil answer, and a hearing, and a reading. Mrs. * * * *'s fathe
an Irish dancing-master of sixty years, called upon me to request to pla
Archer, dressed in silk stockings on a frosty morning to show his le
(which were certainly good and Irish for his age, and had been still bette
—Miss Emma Somebody with a play entitled 'The Bandit of Bohemi
or some such title or production,—Mr. O'Higgins, then resident at Ricl
mond, with an Irish tragedy, in which the unities could not fail to l
observed, for the protagonist was chained by the leg to a pillar durin
the chief part of the performance. He was a wild man, of a salvag
appearance, and the difficulty of *not* laughing at him was only to be g
over by reflecting upon the probable consequences of such cachinnation

"As I am really a civil and polite person, and *do* hate giving pai
when it can be avoided, I sent them up to Douglas Kinnaird,—who is
man of business, and sufficiently ready with a negative,—and left the
to settle with him; and as the beginning of next year I went abroad,
have since been little aware of the progress of the theatres.

                *   *   *   *   *   *

"Players are said to be an impracticable people. They are so; bu
I managed to steer clear of any disputes with them, and excepting on

lebate* with the elder Byrne about Miss Smith's *pas de*—(something—I forget the technicals),—I do not remember any litigation of my own. I used to protect Miss Smith, because she was like Lady Jane Harley in the face, and likenesses go a great way with me. Indeed, in general, I left such things to my more bustling colleagues, who used to reprove me seriously for not being able to take such things in hand without buffooning with the histrions, or throwing things into confusion by treating light matters with levity.

*   *   *   *   *   *

" Then the Committee!—then the Sub-committee!—we were but few, but never agreed. There was Peter Moore who contradicted Kinnaird, and Kinnaird who contradicted every body: then our two managers, Rae and Dibdin; and our secretary, Ward! and yet we were all very zealous and in earnest to do good and so forth. * * * * furnished us with prologues to our revived old English plays; but was not pleased with me for complimenting him as ' the *Upton*' of our theatre (Mr. Upton is or was the poet who writes the songs for Astley's), and almost gave up prologuing in consequence.

*   *   *   *   *   *

" In the pantomime of 1815-16, there was a representation of the masquerade of 1814 given by ' us youth' of Watier's Club to Wellington and Co. Douglas Kinnaird and one or two others, with myself, put on masques, and went on the stage with the *οἱ πολλοί*, to see the effect of

---

* A correspondent of one of the monthly Miscellanies gives the following account of this incident.

" During Lord Byron's administration, a ballet was invented by the elder Byrne, in which Miss Smith (since Mrs. Oscar Byrne) had a *pas seul*. This the lady wished to remove to a later period in the ballet. The ballet-master refused, and the lady swore she would not dance it at all. The music incidental to the dance began to play, and the lady walked off the stage. Both parties flounced into the green-room to lay the case before Lord Byron who happened to be the only person in that apartment. The noble committee-man made an award in favour of Miss Smith, and both complainants rushed angrily out of the room at the instant of my entering it. ' If you had come a minute sooner,' said Lord Byron, ' you would have heard a curious matter decided on by me: a question of dancing!—by me,' added he, looking down at the lame limb, ' whom Nature from my birth has prohibited from taking a single step.' His countenance fell after he had uttered this, as if he had said too much ; and for a moment there was an embarrassing silence on both sides."

a theatre from the stage :—it is very grand. Douglas danced among tl figuranti too, and they were puzzled to find out who we were, as beir more than their number. It was odd enough that Douglas Kinnaird ar I should have been both at the *real* masquerade, and afterwards in tl mimic one of the same, on the stage of Drury-lane theatre."

LETTER CCXXVIII.

TO MR. MOORE.

" Terrace, Piccadilly, October 31, 1815.

" I have not been able to ascertain precisely the time of duration the stock market; but I believe it is a good time for selling out, and hope so. First, because I shall see you; and, next, because I shall receiv certain monies on behalf of Lady B., the which will materially conduc to my comfort,—I wanting (as the duns say) ' to make up a sum.'

" Yesterday, I dined out with a largeish party, where were Sherida and Colman, Harry Harris of C. G. and his brother, Sir Gilbert Heatl cote, Dᵉ. Kinnaird, and others, of note and notoriety. Like other partie of the kind, it was first silent, then talky, then argumentative, then dis putatious, then unintelligible, then altogethery, then inarticulate, an then drunk. When we had reached the last step of this glorious laddel it was difficult to get down again without stumbling;—and, to crown al Kinnaird and I had to conduct Sheridan down a d—d corkscrew staircase which had certainly been constructed before the discovery of fermente liquors, and to which no legs, however crooked, could possibly accom modate themselves. We deposited him safe at home, where his mar evidently used to the business, waited to receive him in the hall.

" Both he and Colman were, as usual, very good; but I carried awa much wine, and the wine had previously carried away my memory; s that all was hiccup and happiness for the last hour or so, and I am no impregnated with any of the conversation. Perhaps you heard of a lat answer of Sheridan to the watchman who found him bereft of tha ' divine particle of air,' called reason, * * * * * *
* * *. He, the watchman, found Sherry in the street, fuddle and bewildered, and almost insensible. ' Who are *you*, sir ?'—no answer

What's your name?'—a hiccup. 'What's your name?'—Answer, in a slow, deliberate, and impassive tone—'Wilberforce!!!' Is not that Sherry all over?—and, to my mind, excellent. Poor fellow, *his* very dregs are better than the 'first sprightly runnings' of others.

" My paper is full, and I have a grievous headache.

" P.S. Lady B. is in full progress. Next month will bring to light (with the aid of 'Juno Lucina, *fer opem*,' or rather *opes*, for the last are most wanted), the tenth wonder of the world—Gil Blas being the eighth, and he (my son's father) the ninth."

LETTER CCXXIX.

TO MR. MOORE.

" November 4th, 1815.

" Had you not bewildered my head with the 'stocks,' your letter would have been answered directly. Hadn't I to go to the city? and hadn't I to remember what to ask when I got there? and hadn't I forgotten it?

" I should be undoubtedly delighted to see you; but I don't like to urge against your reasons my own inclinations. Come you must soon, for stay you *won't*. I know you of old;—you have been too much leavened with London to keep long out of it.

" Lewis is going to Jamaica to suck his sugar-canes. He sails in two days; I enclose you his farewell note. I saw him last night at D. L. T. for the last time previous to his voyage. Poor fellow! he is really a good man—an excellent man—he left me his walking-stick and a pot of preserved ginger. I shall never eat the last without tears in my eyes, it is so *hot*. We have had a devil of a row among our ballerinas: Miss Smith has been wronged about a hornpipe. The Committee have interfered; but Byrne, the d—d ballet-master, won't budge a step. *I* am furious, so is George Lamb. Kinnaird is very glad, because—he don't know why; and I am very sorry, for the same reason. To-day I dine with Kd.—we are to have Sheridan and Colman again; and to-morrow, once more, at Sir Gilbert Heathcote's.

*　　　*　　　*　　　*　　　*

" Leigh Hunt has written a *real good* and *very original Poem,* whi
I think will be a great hit.　You can have no notion how very well it
written, nor should I, had I not redde it.　As to us, Tom—eh, when a
thou out?　If you think the verses worth it, I would rather they we
embalmed in the Irish Melodies, than scattered abroad in a separate sor
—much rather.　But when are thy great things out?　I mean the Po
Pos—thy Shah Nameh.　It is very kind in Jeffrey to like the Hebre
Melodies.　Some of the fellows here preferred Sternhold and Hopkin
and said so ;—' the fiend receive their souls therefor !'

" I must go and dress for dinner.　Poor, dear Murat, what an end
You know, I suppose, that his white plume used to be a rallying poin
in battle, like Henry Fourth's.　He refused a confessor and a bandage
—so would neither suffer his soul or body to be bandaged.　You sha
have more to-morrow or next day.

" Ever, &c."

LETTER CCXXX.

TO MR. MURRAY.

" November 4th, 1815.

" When you have been enabled to form an opinion on Mr. Cole
ridge's MS. * you will oblige me by returning it, as, in fact, I have n
authority to let it out of my hands.　I think most highly of it, and fee
anxious that you should be the publisher; but if you are not, I do no
despair of finding those who will.

" I have written to Mr. Leigh Hunt, stating your willingness t
treat with him, which, when I saw you, I understood you to be.　Term
and time, I leave to his pleasure and your discernment; but this I wil
say, that I think it the *safest* thing you ever engaged in.　I speak to yo
as a man of business: were I to talk to you as a reader or a critic,
should say, it was a very wonderful and beautiful performance, with jus
enough of fault to make its beauties more remarked and remarkable.

" And now to the last—my own, which I feel ashamed of after th

---

* A Tragedy entitled, I think, Zopolia.

others:—publish or not as you like, I don't care *one damn*. If *you* don't, no one else shall, and I never thought or dreamed of it, except as one in the collection. If it is worth being in the fourth volume, put it there and nowhere else; and if not, put it in the fire.

" Yours,

" N."

Those embarrassments which, from a review of his affairs previous to the marriage, he had clearly foreseen would, before long, overtake him, were not slow in realizing his worst omens. The increased expenses induced by his new mode of life, with but very little increase of means to meet them,—the long arrears of early pecuniary obligations, as well as the claims which had been, gradually, since then, accumulating, all pressed upon him now with collected force, and reduced him to some of the worst humiliations of poverty. He had been even driven, by the necessity of encountering such demands, to the trying expedient of parting with his books,—which circumstance coming to Mr. Murray's ears, that gentleman instantly forwarded to him £1500, with an assurance that another sum of the same amount should be at his service in a few weeks, and that if such assistance should not be sufficient, Mr. Murray was most ready to dispose of the copyrights of all his past works for his use.

This very liberal offer, Lord Byron acknowledged in the following letter.

LETTER CCXXXI.

TO MR. MURRAY.

" November 14, 1815.

" I return you your bills not accepted, but certainly not *unhonoured*. Your present offer is a favour which I would accept from you, if I accepted such from any man. Had such been my intention, I can assure you I would have asked you fairly, and as freely as you would give; and I cannot say more of my confidence or your conduct.

" The circumstances which induce me to part with my books, though sufficiently, are not *immediately*, pressing. I have made up my mind to them, and there's an end.

" Had I been disposed to trespass on your kindness in this way,
would have been before now ; but I am not sorry to have an opportunit
of declining it, as it sets my opinion of you, and indeed of huma
nature, in a different light from that in which I have been accustome
to consider it.

" Believe me very truly, &c."

TO MR. MURRAY.

" December 25th, 1815.

" I send some lines, written some time ago, and intended as a
opening to the ' Siege of Corinth.' I had forgotten them, and am no
sure that they had not better be left out now :—on that, you and you
Synod can determine.

" Yours, &c."

The following are the lines alluded to in this note. They ar
written in the loosest form of that rambling style of metre which hi
admiration of Mr. Coleridge's " Christabel" led him, at this time, t
adopt ; and he judged rightly, perhaps, in omitting them as the opening
of his Poem. They are, however, too full of spirit and character to b
lost. Though breathing the thick atmosphere of Piccadilly when he wrot
them, it is plain that his fancy was far away, among the sunny hills an
vales of Greece ; and their contrast with the tame life he was leading a
the moment but gave to his recollections a fresher spring and force.

> " In the year since Jesus died for men,
> Eighteen hundred years and ten,
> We were a gallant company,
> Riding o'er land, and sailing o'er sea.
> Oh ! but we went merrily !
> We forded the river, and clomb the high hill,
> Never our steeds for a day stood still ;
> Whether we lay in the cave or the shed,
> Our sleep fell soft on the hardest bed ;
> Whether we couch'd in our rough capote,
> On the rougher plank of our gliding boat,

Or stretch'd on the beach, or our saddles spread
As a pillow beneath the resting head,
Fresh we woke upon the morrow:
   All our thoughts and words had scope,
   We had health, and we had hope,
Toil and travel, but no sorrow.
We were of all tongues and creeds;—
Some were those who counted beads,
Some of mosque, and some of church,
   And some, or I mis-say, of neither;
Yet through the wide world might ye search
   Nor find a motlier crew nor blither.

But some are dead, and some are gone,
And some are scatter'd and alone,
And some are rebels on the hills *
   That look along Epirus' valleys
   Where Freedom still at moments rallies,
And pays in blood Oppression's ills;
   And some are in a far countree,
And some all restlessly at home;
   But never more, oh! never, we
Shall meet to revel and to roam.

But those hardy days flew cheerily,
And when they now fall drearily,
My thoughts, like swallows, skim the main,
And bear my spirit back again
Over the earth, and through the air,
A wild bird, and a wanderer.
'Tis this that ever wakes my strain,
And oft, too oft, implores again
The few who may endure my lay,
To follow me so far away.

Stranger—wilt thou follow now,
And sit with me on Acro-Corinth's brow?"

---

* " The last tidings recently heard of Dervish (one of the Arnaouts who followed me)
state him to be in revolt upon the mountains, at the head of some of the bands common in that
country in times of trouble."

LETTER CCXXXII.

TO MR. MOORE.

" January 5th, 1816.

" I hope Mrs. M. is quite re-established. The little girl was bor
on the 10th of December last: her name is Augusta *Ada* (the second
very antique family name,—I believe not used since the reign of Kin
John). She was, and is, very flourishing and fat, and reckoned ver
large for her days—squalls and sucks incessantly. Are you answered
Her mother is doing very well, and up again.

" I have now been married a year on the second of this month—
heigh-ho! I have seen nobody lately much worth noting, except S *
and another general of the Gauls, once or twice at dinners out of door
S * * is a fine, foreign, villanous-looking, intelligent, and very agreeabl
man; his compatriot is more of the *petit-maître*, and younger, but
should think not at all of the same intellectual calibre with the Corsica
—which S * *, you know, is, and a cousin of Napoleon's.

" Are you never to be expected in town again? To be sure, there i
no one here of the 1500 fillers of hot rooms, called the fashionable worl
My approaching papa-ship detained us for advice, &c. &c.—though
would as soon be here as any where else on this side of the straits o
Gibraltar.

" I would gladly—or, rather, sorrowfully—comply with your reques
of a dirge for the poor girl you mention *   But how can I write on on
I have never seen or known? Besides, you will do it much bette
yourself. I could not write upon any thing, without some persona
experience and foundation; far less on a theme so peculiar. Now, yo
have both in this case; and, if you had neither, you have mor
imagination, and would never fail.

" This is but a dull scrawl, and I am but a dull fellow. Just a
present, I am absorbed in 500 contradictory contemplations, though wit

---

* I had mentioned to him, as a subject worthy of his best powers of pathos, a melancho
event which had just occurred in my neighbourhood, and to which I have myself made allusic
in one of the Sacred Melodies—" Weep not for her."

but one object in view—which will probably end in nothing, as most things we wish do.   But never mind—as somebody says, ' for the blue sky bends over all.'   I only could be glad, if it bent over me where it is a little bluer; like the ' skyish top of blue Olympus,' which, by the way, looked very white when I last saw it.   Ever, &c."

On reading over the foregoing letter, I was much struck by the tone of melancholy that pervaded it; and well knowing it to be the habit of the writer's mind to seek relief, when under the pressure of any disquiet or disgust, in that sense of freedom which told him that there were homes for him elsewhere, I could perceive, I thought, in his recollections of the " blue Olympus," some return of this restless and roving spirit, which unhappiness or impatience always called up in his mind.   I had, indeed, at the time when he sent me those melancholy verses, " There's not a joy this world can give," &c. felt some vague apprehensions as to the mood into which his spirits were then sinking, and, in acknowledging the receipt of the verses, thus tried to banter him out of it:—" But why thus on your stool of melancholy again, Master Stephen?—This will never do—it plays the deuce with all the matter-of-fact duties of life, and you must bid adieu to it.   Youth is the only time when one can be melancholy with impunity.   As life itself grows sad and serious, we have nothing for it but——to be, as much as possible, the contrary."

My absence from London during the whole of this year had deprived me of all opportunities of judging for myself how far the appearances of his domestic state gave promise of happiness; nor had any rumours reached me which at all inclined me to think that the course of his married life hitherto exhibited less smoothness than such unions,— on the surface, at least,—generally wear.   The strong and affectionate terms in which, soon after the marriage, he had, in some of the letters I have given, declared his own happiness—a declaration which his known frankness left me no room to question—had, in no small degree, tended to still those apprehensions which my first view of the lot he had chosen for himself awakened.   I could not, however, but observe that these indications of a contented heart soon ceased.   His mention of the partner of his home became more rare and formal, and there was ob-

servable, I thought, through some of his letters a feeling of unqui
and weariness that brought back all those gloomy anticipations wit
which I had, from the first, regarded his fate. This last letter of his, i
particular, struck me as full of sad omen, and, in the course of m
answer, I thus noticed to him the impression it had made on me :—
" And so, you are a whole year married !—

> ' It was last year I vow'd to thee
>   That fond impossibility.'

Do you know, my dear B., there was a something in your last letter—
sort of unquiet mystery, as well as a want of your usual elasticity o
spirits—which has hung upon my mind unpleasantly ever since. I lon
to be near you, that I might know how you really look and feel
for these letters tell nothing, and one word, *a quattr'occhi*, is worth whol
reams of correspondence. But only *do* tell me you are happier than tha
letter has led me to fear, and I shall be satisfied."

It was in a few weeks after this latter communication between u
that Lady Byron adopted the resolution of parting from him. She ha
left London at the latter end of January, on a visit to her father's house
in Leicestershire, and Lord Byron was, in a short time after, to follow her
They had parted in the utmost kindness,—she wrote him a letter, full o
playfulness and affection, on the road, and, immediately on her arrival a
Kirkby Mallory, her father wrote to acquaint Lord Byron that she woul
return to him no more. At the time when he had to stand this un
expected shock, his pecuniary embarrassments, which had been fast gather
ing around him during the whole of the last year (there having been n
less than eight or nine executions in his house within that period), ha
arrived at their utmost; and at a moment when, to use his own stron
expressions, he was " standing alone on his hearth, with his househol
gods shivered around him," he was also doomed to receive the startlin
intelligence that the wife who had just parted with him in kindness ha
parted with him—for ever.

About this time the following note was written.

TO MR. ROGERS.

" Feb. 8, 1816.

" Do not mistake me—I really returned your book for the reason assigned, and no other. It is too good for so careless a fellow. I have parted with all my own books, and positively won't deprive you of so valuable ' a drop of that immortal man.'

" I shall be very glad to see you, if you like to call, though I am at present contending with ' the slings and arrows of outrageous fortune,' some of which have struck at me from a quarter whence I did not indeed expect them.—But, no matter, ' there is a world elsewhere,' and I will cut my way through this as I can.

" If you write to Moore, will you tell him that I shall answer his letter the moment I can muster time and spirits ?

" Ever yours,
" Bn."

The rumours of the separation did not reach me till more than a week afterwards, when I immediately wrote to him thus :—" I am most anxious to hear from you, though I doubt whether I ought to mention the subject on which I am so anxious. If, however, what I heard last night, in a letter from town, be true, you will know immediately what I allude to, and just communicate as much or as little upon the subject as you think proper ;—only *something* I should like to know, as soon as possible, from yourself, in order to set my mind at rest with respect to the truth or falsehood of the report." The following is his answer.

LETTER CCXXXIII.

TO MR. MOORE.

" Feb. 29th, 1816.

" I have not answered your letter for a time ; and, at present, the reply to part of it might extend to such a length, that I shall delay it till it can be made in person, and then I will shorten it as much as I can.

" In the mean time, I am at war ' with all the world and his wife ;' or rather, ' all the world and *my* wife' are at war with me, and have not yet crushed me,—whatever they *may* do. I don't know that in the

course of a hair-breadth existence I was ever, at home or abroad, in
situation so completely uprooting of present pleasure, or rational ho
for the future, as this same. I say this, because I think so, and feel
But I shall not sink under it the more for that mode of considering t]
question.—I have made up my mind.

" By the way, however, you must not believe all you hear on t]
subject; and don't attempt to defend me. If you succeeded in that,
would be a mortal, or an immortal, offence—who can bear refutation?
have but a very short answer for those whom it concerns; and all t]
activity of myself and some vigorous friends have not yet fixed on ar
tangible ground or personage, on which or with whom I can discu
matters, in a summary way, with a fair pretext;—though I nearly ha
nailed one yesterday, but he evaded by—what was judged by others—
satisfactory explanation. I speak of *circulators*—against whom I have r
enmity, though I must act according to the common code of usage, whe
I hit upon those of the serious order.

" Now for other matters—Poesy, for instance. Leigh Hunt's poer
is a devilish good one—quaint, here and there, but with the substratu
of originality, and with poetry about it, that will stand the test. I d
not say this because he has inscribed it to me, which I am sorry for, as
should otherwise have begged you to review it in the Edinburgh*.]
is really deserving of much praise, and a favourable critique in the E. I
would but do it justice, and set it up before the public eye where :
ought to be.

" How are you? and where? I have not the most distant idea whe
I am going to do myself, or with myself—or where—or what. I hae
a few weeks ago, some things to say, that would have made you laugh
but they tell me now that I must not laugh, and so I have been ver
serious—and am.

" I have not been very well—with a *liver* complaint—but am muc
better within the last fortnight, though still under Iatrical advice.

---

* My reply to this part of his letter was, I find, as follows: " With respect to Hunt
Poem, though it is, I own, full of beauties, and though I like himself sincerely, I really coul
not undertake to praise it *seriously*. There is so much of the *quizzible* in all he writes, that
never can put on the proper pathetic face in reading him."

have latterly seen a little of   *   *   *   *   *   *   *   *
*   *   *   *   *   *   *.

" I must go and dress to dine. My little girl is in the country, and, they tell me, is a very fine child, and now nearly three months old. Lady Noel (my mother-in-law, or, rather, *at* law) is at present overlooking it. Her daughter (Miss Milbanke that was) is, I believe, in London with her father. A Mrs. C. (now a kind of housekeeper and spy of Lady N.") who, in her better days, was a washerwoman, is supposed to be—by the learned—very much the occult cause of our late domestic discrepancies.

" In all this business, I am the sorriest for Sir Ralph. He and I are equally punished, though *magis pares quem similes* in our affliction. Yet it is hard for both to suffer for the fault of one, and so it is—I shall be separated from my wife; he will retain his.

" Ever, &c."

In my reply to this letter, written a few days after, there is a passage which (though containing an opinion it might have been more prudent, perhaps, to conceal) I feel myself called upon to extract, on account of the singularly generous avowal,—honourable alike to both the parties in this unhappy affair,—which it was the means of drawing from Lord Byron. The following are my words:—" I am much in the same state as yourself with respect to the subject of your letter, my mind being so full of things which I don't know how to write about, that *I* too must defer the greater part of them till we meet in May, when I shall put you fairly on your trial for all crimes and misdemeanors. In the mean time, you will not be at a loss for judges,—nor executioners either, if they could have their will. The world, in their generous ardour to take what they call the weaker side, soon contrive to make it most formidably the strongest. Most sincerely do I grieve at what has happened. It has upset all my wishes and theories as to the influence of marriage on your life; for, instead of bringing you, as I expected, into something like a regular orbit, it has only cast you off again into infinite space, and left you, I fear, in a far worse state than it found you. As to defending you, the only person with whom I have yet attempted this task is myself; and, considering the little I know upon the subject (or

rather, perhaps, *owing* to this cause), I have hitherto done it with ver
tolerable success. After all, your *choice* was the misfortune. I neve
liked,—but I'm here wandering into the απορρητα, and so must chang
the subject for a far pleasanter one, your last new Poems, which
&c. &c."

The return of post brought me the following answer, which, whi
it raises our admiration of the generous candour of the writer, but add
to the sadness and strangeness of the whole transaction.

LETTER CCXXXIV.

TO MR. MOORE.

" March 8th, 1816.

" I rejoice in your promotion as Chairman and Charitable Steward
&c. &c. These be dignities which await only the virtuous. But then
recollect you are *six* and *thirty* (I speak this enviously—not of your age
but the 'honour—love—obedience—troops of friends,' which accompan
it), and I have eight years good to run before I arrive at such hoar
perfection; by which time,—if I *am* at all*,—it will probably be in
state of grace or progressing merits.

" I must set you right in one point, however. The fault was *not*—
no, nor even the misfortune—in my 'choice' (unless in *choosing at all*)—
for I do not believe—and I must say it, in the very dregs of all thi
bitter business—that there ever was a better, or even a brighter, a kinder
or a more amiable and agreeable being than Lady B. I never had, no
can have, any reproach to make her, while with me. Where there i
blame, it belongs to myself, and, if I cannot redeem, I must bear it.

" Her nearest relatives are a * * * *—my circumstances have beer
and are in a state of great confusion—my health has been a good dea
disordered, and my mind ill at ease for a considerable period. Such ar
the causes (I do not name them as excuses) which have frequently driver
me into excess, and disqualified my temper for comfort. Something als

---

* This sad doubt,—" if I *am* at all,"—becomes no less singular than sad when we recollec
that six and thirty was actually the age when he ceased to " be," and at a moment, too, whe
(as even the least friendly to him allow) he was in that state of " progressing merits" whic
he here jestingly anticipates.

may be attributed to the strange and desultory habits which, becoming my own master at an early age, and scrambling about, over and through the world, may have induced. I still, however, think that, if I had had a fair chance, by being placed in even a tolerable situation, I might have gone on fairly. But that seems hopeless,—and there is nothing more to be said. At present—except my health, which is better (it is odd, but agitation or contest of any kind gives a rebound to my spirits and sets me up for the time)—I have to battle with all kinds of unpleasantnesses, including private and pecuniary difficulties, &c. &c.

" I believe I may have said this before to you,—but I risk repeating it. It is nothing to bear the *privations* of adversity, or, more properly, ill fortune; but my pride recoils from its *indignities*. However, I have no quarrel with that same pride, which will, I think, buckler me through every thing. If my heart could have been broken, it would have been so years ago, and by events more afflicting than these.

" I agree with you (to turn from this topic to our shop) that I have written too much. The last things were, however, published very reluctantly by me, and for reasons I will explain when we meet. I know not why I have dwelt so much on the same scenes, except that I find them fading, or *confusing* (if such a word may be) in my memory, in the midst of present turbulence and pressure, and I felt anxious to stamp before the die was worn out. I now break it. With those countries, and events connected with them, all my really poetical feelings begin and end. Were I to try, I could make nothing of any other subject,— and that I have apparently exhausted. 'Woe to him,' says Voltaire, 'who says all he could say on any subject.' There are some on which, perhaps, I could have said still more: but I leave them all, and not too soon.

" Do you remember the lines I sent you early last year, which you still have? I don't wish (like Mr. Fitzgerald, in the Morning Post) to claim the character of 'Vates' in all its translations, but were they not a little prophetic? I mean those beginning 'There's not a joy the world can,' &c. &c. on which I rather pique myself as being the truest, though the most melancholy, I ever wrote.

" What a scrawl have I sent you! You say nothing of yourself,

except that you are a Lancasterian churchwarden, and an encourager
mendicants. When are you out? and how is your family? My chi
is very well and flourishing, I hear; but I must see also. I feel
disposition to resign it to the contagion of its grandmother's societ
though I am unwilling to take it from the mother. It is weane
however, and something about it must be decided.

" Ever, &c."

Having already gone so far in laying open to my readers some
the sentiments which I entertained, respecting Lord Byron's marriage,
a time when, little foreseeing that I should ever become his biographe
I was, of course, uninfluenced by the peculiar bias supposed to belon
to that task, it may still further, perhaps, be permitted me to extrac
from my reply to the foregoing letter some sentences of explanatio
which its contents seemed to me to require.

" I had certainly no right to say any thing about the unluckiness o
your choice,—though I rejoice that now I did, as it has drawn fron
you a tribute which, however unaccountable and mysterious it render
the whole affair, is highly honourable to both parties. What I mean
in hinting a doubt with respect to the object of your selection did no
imply the least impeachment of that perfect amiableness which th
world, I find, by common consent, allows to her. I only feared tha
she might have been too perfect—too *precisely* excellent—too matter-of
fact a paragon for you to coalesce with comfortably; and that a person
whose perfection hung in more easy folds about her, whose brightnes
was softened down by some of ' those fair defects which best conciliat
love,' would, by appealing more dependently to your protection, hav
stood a much better chance with your good-nature. All these suppo
sitions, however, I have been led into by my intense anxiety to acqui
you of any thing like a capricious abandonment of such a woman*
and. totally in the dark as I am with respect to all but the fact of you
separation, you cannot conceive the solicitude, the fearful solicitude, wit
which I look forward to a history of the transaction from your own lip

* It will be perceived from this that I was as yet unacquainted with the true circumstanc
of the transaction

when we meet,—a history in which I am sure of, at least, *one* virtue—manly candour."

With respect to the causes that may be supposed to have led to this separation, it seems needless, with the characters of both parties before our eyes, to go in quest of any very remote or mysterious reasons to account for it. I have already, in some observations on the general character of men of genius, endeavoured to point out those peculiarities, both in disposition and habitudes, by which, in the far greater number of instances, they have been found unfitted for domestic happiness. Of these defects (which are, as it were, the shadow that genius casts, and too generally, it is to be feared, in proportion to its stature,) Lord Byron could not, of course, fail to have inherited his share, in common with all the painfully-gifted class to which he belonged. How thoroughly, with respect to one attribute of this temperament which he possessed,—one, that "sicklies o'er" the face of happiness itself,—he was understood by the person most interested in observing him, will appear from the following anecdote, as related by himself*.

"People have wondered at the melancholy which runs through my writings. Others have wondered at my personal gaiety. But I recollect once, after an hour in which I had been sincerely and particularly gay and rather brilliant, in company, my wife replying to me when I said (upon her remarking my high spirits), ' And yet, Bell, I have been called and mis-called melancholy—you must have seen how falsely, frequently?' —' No, Byron,' she answered, ' it is not so: at heart you are the most melancholy of mankind; and often when apparently gayest.' "

To these faults and sources of faults, inherent in his own sensitive nature, he added also many of those which a long indulgence of self-will generates,—the least compatible, of all others (if not softened down, as they were in him, by good-nature), with that system of mutual concession and sacrifice by which the balance of domestic peace is maintained. When we look back, indeed, to the unbridled career, of which this marriage was meant to be the goal,—to the rapid and restless course in which his life had run along, like a burning train, through a series of wanderings, adventures, successes, and passions, the fever of all which

---

* MS.—"Detached Thoughts."

was still upon him, when, with the same headlong recklessness, he rushe
into this marriage,—it can but little surprise us that, in the space of on
short year, he should not have been able to recover all at once from hi
bewilderment, or to settle down into that tame level of conduct whic
the officious spies of his privacy required. As well might it be expecte
that a steed like his own Mazeppa's,

> " Wild as the wild deer and untaught,
> With spur and bridle undefiled—
> 'Twas but a day he had been caught,"

should stand still, when reined, without chafing or champing the bit.

Even had the new condition of life into which he passed been on
of prosperity and smoothness, some time, as well as tolerance, mus
still have been allowed for the subsiding of so excited a spirit int
rest. But, on the contrary, his marriage (from the reputation, no doubt
of the lady, as an heiress) was, at once, a signal for all the arrears an
claims of a long-accumulating state of embarrassment to explode upon
him;—his door was almost daily beset by duns, and his house nine time
during that year in possession of bailiffs*; while, in addition to these
anxieties and—what he felt still more—indignities of poverty, he had
also the pain of fancying, whether rightly or wrongly, that the eyes of
enemies and spies were upon him, even under his own roof, and that hi
every hasty word and look were interpreted in the most perverting light.

As, from the state of their means, his lady and he saw but little

---

* An anecdote connected with one of these occasions is thus related in the Journal just
referred to.

" When the bailiff (for I have seen most kinds of life) came upon me in 1815 to seize my
chattels (being a peer of parliament, my person was beyond him), being curious (as is my habit),
I first asked him 'what extents elsewhere he had for government?' upon which he showed me
one upon *one house only* for *seventy thousand pounds!* Next I asked him if he had nothing
for Sheridan? 'Oh—Sheridan!' said he; 'ay, I have this' (pulling out a pocket-book, &c.)
' but, my lord, I have been in Sheridan's house a twelvemonth at a time—a civil gentleman—
knows how to deal with *us*,' &c. &c. &c. Our own business was then discussed, which wa
none of the easiest for me at that time. But the man was civil, and (what I valued more
communicative. I had met many of his brethren, years before, in affairs of my friends (com
moners, that is), but this was the first (or second) on my own account.—A civil man; fee
accordingly: probably he anticipated as much."

ciety, his only relief from the thoughts which a life of such embar-
ssment brought with it was in those avocations which his duty, as a
member of the Drury-lane Committee, imposed upon him.   And here,
-in this most unlucky connexion with the theatre,—one of the fatalities
f his short year of trial, as husband, lay.   From the reputation which he
ad previously acquired for gallantries, and the sort of reckless and boyish
evity to which—often in very " bitterness of soul"—he gave way, it was
ot difficult to bring suspicion upon some of those acquaintances which
is frequent intercourse with the green-room induced him to form, or
ven (as, in one instance, was the case) to connect with his name inju-
iously that of a person to whom he had scarcely ever addressed a single
ord.

Notwithstanding, however, this ill-starred concurrence of circum-
tances, which might have palliated any excesses either of temper or
onduct into which they drove him, it was, after all, I am persuaded, to
o such serious causes that the unfortunate alienation, which so soon
nded in disunion, is to be traced.   " In all the marriages I have ever
een," says Steele, " most of which have been unhappy ones, the great
ause of evil has proceeded from slight occasions;" and to this remark
he marriage at present under our consideration would not be found,
 think, on inquiry, to furnish much exception.   Lord Byron himself,
ndeed, when at Cephalonia, a short time before his death, seems to have
xpressed, in a few words, the whole pith of the mystery.   An English
entleman with whom he was conversing on the subject of Lady Byron,
aving ventured to enumerate to him the various causes he had heard
lleged for the separation, the noble poet, who had seemed much amused
vith their absurdity and falsehood, said, after listening to them all,—
 the causes, my dear sir, were too simple to be easily found out."

In truth, the circumstances, so unexampled, that attended their
eparation,—the last words of the parting wife to the husband being
hose of the most playful affection, while the language of the deserted
usband towards the wife was in a strain, as the world knows, of tenderest
ulogy,—are in themselves a sufficient proof that, at the time of their
arting, there could have been no very deep sense of injury on either
ide.   It was not till afterwards that, in both bosoms, the repulsive force
ame into operation,—when, to the party which had taken the first

decisive step in the strife, it became naturally a point of pride to p
severe in it with dignity, and this unbendingness provoked, as naturall
in the haughty spirit of the other, a strong feeling of resentment whi
overflowed, at last, in acrimony and scorn. If there be any trut
however, in the principle that they " never pardon who have done tl
wrong," Lord Byron, who was, to the last, disposed to reconciliatio
proved so far, at least, his conscience to have been unhaunted by an
very disturbing consciousness of aggression.

But though it would have been difficult, perhaps, for the victin
of this strife, themselves, to have pointed out any single, or definit
cause for their disunion,—beyond that general incompatibility which
the canker of all such marriages,—the public, which seldom allows itse
to be at a fault on these occasions, was, as usual, ready with an amp
supply of reasons for the breach,—all tending to blacken the alread
darkly painted character of the poet, and representing him, in short, as
finished monster of cruelty and depravity. The reputation of the obje
of his choice for every possible virtue (a reputation which had been,
doubt not, one of his own chief incentives to the marriage, from tl
vanity, reprobate as he knew he was deemed, of being able to win such
paragon), was now turned against him by his assailants, not only in tl
way of contrast with his own character, but as if the excellences of tl
wife were proof positive of every enormity they chose to charge upc
the husband.

Meanwhile, the unmoved silence of the lady herself (from motive
it is but fair to suppose, of generosity and delicacy), under the repeate
demands made for a specification of her charges against him, left
malice and imagination the fullest range for their combined industr
It was accordingly stated, and almost universally believed, that the nob
lord's second proposal to Miss Milbanke had been but with a view
revenge himself for the slight inflicted by her refusal of the first, an
that he himself had confessed so much to her, on their way from churc
At the time when, as the reader has seen from his own honey-moo
letters, he was, with all the good-will in the world, imagining himse
into happiness, and even boasting, in the pride of his fancy, that
marriage were to be upon *lease*, he would gladly renew his own for
term of ninety-nine years,—at this very time, according to these ver

ious chroniclers, he was employed in darkly following up the aforesaid
scheme of revenge, and tormenting his lady by all sorts of unmanly
cruelties,—such as firing off pistols, to frighten her as she lay in bed *,
and other such freaks.

To the falsehoods concerning his green-room intimacies, and particularly with respect to one beautiful actress, with whom, in reality, he
had hardly ever exchanged a single word, I have already adverted; and
the extreme confidence with which this tale was circulated and believed
affords no unfair specimen of the sort of evidence with which the public,
in all such fits of moral wrath, is satisfied. It is, at the same time, very
far from my intention to allege that, in the course of the noble poet's
intercourse with the theatre, he was not sometimes led into a line of
acquaintance and converse, unbefitting, if not dangerous to, the steadiness
of married life. But the imputations against him on this head were (as
far as affected his conjugal character) not the less unfounded,—as the
sole case, in which he afforded any thing like *real* grounds for such an
accusation did not take place till *after* the period of the separation.

Not content with such ordinary and tangible charges, the tongue of
rumour was imboldened to proceed still further; and, presuming upon
the mysterious silence maintained by one of the parties, ventured to
throw out dark hints and vague insinuations, of which the fancy of every
hearer was left to fill up the outline as he pleased. In consequence of all
this exaggeration, such an outcry was now raised against Lord Byron as,
in no case of private life, perhaps, was ever before witnessed; nor had the
whole amount of fame which he had gathered, in the course of the last
four years, much exceeded in proportion the reproach and obloquy that

---

* For this story, however, there was so far a foundation that the practice to which he had
accustomed himself from boyhood, of having loaded pistols always near him at night, was considered so strange a propensity as to be included in that list of symptoms (sixteen, I believe, in
number) which were submitted to medical opinion, in proof of his insanity. Another symptom
was the emotion, almost to hysterics, which he had exhibited on seeing Kean act Sir Giles
Overreach. But the most plausible of all the grounds, as he himself used to allow, on which
these articles of impeachment against his sanity were drawn up, was an act of violence committed by him on a favourite old watch that had been his companion from boyhood, and had gone
with him to Greece. In a fit of vexation and rage, brought on by some of those humiliating
embarrassments to which he was now almost daily a prey, he furiously dashed this watch upon
the hearth, and ground it to pieces among the ashes with the poker.

were now, within the space of a few weeks, showered upon him.
addition to the many who conscientiously believed and reprobated wh
they had but too much right to consider credible excesses, whether viewi
him as poet or man of fashion, there were also actively on the alert th
large class of persons who seem to hold violence against the vices
others to be equivalent to virtue in themselves, together with all tho
natural haters of success who, having long sickened under the splendo
of the *poet*, were now able, in the guise of champions for innocence,
wreak their spite on the *man*. In every various form of paragrap
pamphlet, and caricature, both his character and person were held up
odium*;—hardly a voice was raised, or at least listened to, in his beha
and though a few faithful friends remained unshaken by his side, tl
utter hopelessness of stemming the torrent was felt as well by them as h
himself, and, after an effort or two to gain a fair hearing, they submitte
in silence. Among the few attempts made by himself towards confutir
his calumniators was an appeal (such as the following short letter contain
to some of those persons with whom he had been in the habit of livir
familiarly.

* Of the abuse lavished upon him, the following extract from a Poem, published at tl
time, will give some idea.

> " From native England, that endured too long
>   The ceaseless burden of his impious song;
>   His mad career of crimes and follies run,
>   And gray in vice, when life was scarce begun;
>   He goes, in foreign lands prepared to find
>   A life more suited to his guilty mind;
>   Where other climes new pleasures may supply
>   For that pall'd taste, and that unhallow'd eye;—
>   Wisely he seeks some yet untrodden shore,
>   For those who know him less may prize him more."

In a rhyming pamphlet, too, entitled " A Poetical Epistle from Delia, addressed to Lo
Byron," the writer thus charitably expresses herself.

> " Hopeless of peace below, and, shuddering thought!
>   Far from that Heav'n, denied, if never sought,
>   Thy light a beacon—a reproach thy name—
>   Thy memory ' damn'd to everlasting fame,'
>   Shunn'd by the wise, admired by fools alone—
>   The good shall mourn thee—and the Muse disown."

LETTER CCXXXV.

TO MR. ROGERS.

" March 25th, 1816.

" You are one of the few persons with whom I have lived in what called intimacy, and have heard me at times conversing on the unto-ard topic of my recent family disquietudes. Will you have the goodness ɔ say to me at once, whether you ever heard me speak of her with isrespect, with unkindness, or defending myself at *her* expense by any erious imputation of any description against *her?* Did you never heaf ɪe say ' that when there was a right or a wrong, she had the *right?'*— 'he reason I put these questions to you or others of my friends is, ecause I am said, by her and hers, to have resorted to such means of xculpation. Ever very truly yours,

" B."

In those Memoirs (or, more properly, Memoranda) of the noble poet, ʋhich it was thought expedient, for various reasons, to sacrifice, he gave detailed account of all the circumstances connected with his marriage, ɾom the first proposal to the lady till his own departure, after the breach, ɾom England. In truth, though the title of " Memoirs," which he him-elf sometimes gave to that manuscript, conveys the idea of a complete nd regular piece of biography, it was to this particular portion of his ife that the work was principally devoted; while the anecdotes, having eference to other parts of his career, not only occupied a very dispropor-ionate space in its pages, but were most of them such as are found epeated in the various Journals and other MSS. he left behind. The hief charm, indeed, of that narrative was the melancholy playfulness— ɪelancholy, from the wounded feeling so visible through its pleasantry —with which events unimportant and persons uninteresting, in almost ʋery respect but their connexion with such a man's destiny, were detailed nd described in it. Frank, as usual, throughout, in his avowal of his ʋwn errors, and generously just towards her who was his fellow-sufferer ɪ the strife, the impression his recital left on the minds of all who

perused it was, to say the least, favourable to him;—though, upon t
whole, leading to a persuasion, which I have already intimated to be n
own, that, neither in kind or degree, did the causes of disunion betwe
the parties much differ from those that loosen the links of most su
marriages.

With respect to the details themselves, though all important in I
own eyes at the time, as being connected with the subject that supersed
most others in his thoughts, the interest they would possess for othe
now that their first zest as a subject of scandal is gone by, and the great
number of the persons to whom they relate forgotten, would be to
slight to justify me in entering upon them more particularly, or runnin
the risk of any offence that might be inflicted by their disclosure. *
far as the character of the illustrious subject of these pages is concerne
I feel that Time and Justice are doing far more in its favour than cou
be effected by any such gossiping details. During the lifetime of a ma
of genius, the world is but too much inclined to judge of him rather k
what he wants than by what he possesses, and even where conscious, as i
the present case, that his defects are among the sources of his greatnes
to require of him unreasonably the one without the other. If Pope ha
not been splenetic and irritable, we should have wanted his Satires; an
an impetuous temperament, and passions untamed, were indispensable t
the conformation of a poet like Byron. It is by posterity only that fu
justice is rendered to those who have paid such hard penalties to reac
it. The dross that had once hung about the ore drops away, and th
infirmities, and even miseries, of genius are forgotten in its greatnes
Who now asks whether Dante was right or wrong in his matrimoni
differences? or by how many of those whose fancies dwell fondly on h
Beatrice is even the name of his Gemma Donati remembered?

Already, short as has been the interval since Lord Byron's death, th
charitable influence of time in softening, if not rescinding, the harsh judg
ments of the world against genius is visible. The utter unreasonablene
of trying such a character by ordinary standards, or of expecting to fin
the materials of order and happiness in a bosom constantly heaving fort
from its depths such " lava floods," is—now that his spirit has passed from
among us—felt and acknowledged. In reviewing the circumstances e

is marriage, a more even scale of justice is held; and while every tribute
f sympathy and commiseration is accorded to her, who, unluckily for
.er own peace, became involved in such a destiny,—who, with virtues
nd attainments that would have made the home of a more ordinary man
appy, undertook, in evil hour, to " turn and wind a fiery Pegasus," and
ut failed where it may be doubted whether even the fittest for such a
ask would have succeeded,—full allowance is, at the same time, made
or the great martyr of genius himself, whom so many other causes,
eside that restless fire within him, concurred to unsettle in mind and
as he himself feelingly expresses it) " disqualify for comfort;"—whose
loom it was to be either thus or less great, and whom to have tamed
night have been to extinguish; there never, perhaps, having existed an
ndividual to whom, whether as author or man, the following line was
more applicable,—

> " Si non errâsset, fecerat ille minus *."

While these events were going on,—events, of which his memory
nd heart bore painfully the traces through the remainder of his short
ife,—some occurrences took place, connected with his literary history,
o which it is a relief to divert the attention of the reader from the
listressing subject that has now so long detained us.

The letter that follows was in answer to one received from Mr.
Murray, in which that gentleman had enclosed him a draft for a thousand
;uineas for the copyright of his two Poems, the Siege of Corinth and
Parisina.

LETTER CCXXXVI.

TO MR. MURRAY.

" January 2d, 1816.

" Your offer is *liberal* in the extreme (you see I use the word *to* you
and *of* you, though I would not consent to your using it of yourself to
Mr. * * * *), and much more than the two poems can possibly be worth;

---

* Had he not *erred*, he had far less achieved.

but I cannot accept it, nor will not.   You are most welcome to them
additions to the collected volumes, without any demand or expectati
on my part whatever.   But I cannot consent to their separate publicatio
I do not like to risk any fame (whether merited or not), which I ha
been favoured with, upon compositions which I do not feel to be at a
equal to my own notions of what they should be (and as I flatter myse
some *have been*, here and there), though they may do very well as thing
without pretension, to add to the publication with the lighter pieces.

"I am very glad that the handwriting was a favourable omen of th
morale of the piece: but you must not trust to that, for my copyist wou
write out any thing I desired in all the ignorance of innocence—I hop
however, in this instance, with no great peril to either.

"P.S.   I have enclosed your draft *torn*, for fear of accidents by th
way—I wish you would not throw temptation in mine.   It is not fro
a disdain of the universal idol, nor from a present superfluity of his tre
sures, I can assure you, that I refuse to worship him; but what is rigl
is right, and must not yield to circumstances."

Notwithstanding the ruinous state of his pecuniary affairs, th
resolution which the poet had formed not to avail himself of the profit
of his works still continued to be held sacred by him, and the sum thu
offered for the copyright of the Siege of Corinth and Parisina was, a
we see, refused and left untouched in the publisher's hands.   It hap
pened that, at this time, a well-known and eminent writer on politica
science had been, by some misfortune, reduced to pecuniary em
barrassment; and the circumstance having become known to Mr. Roger
and Sir James Mackintosh, it occurred to them that a part of the sur
thus unappropriated by Lord Byron could not be better bestowed tha
in relieving the necessities of this gentleman.   The suggestion was n
sooner conveyed to the noble poet than he proceeded to act upon it, an
the following letter to Mr. Rogers refers to his intentions.

LETTER CCXXXVII.

TO MR. ROGERS.

" February 20th, 1816.

" I wrote to you hastily this morning by Murray, to say that I was lad to do as Mackintosh and you suggested about Mr. * * It occurs o me now, that as I have never seen Mr. * * but once, and consequently ave no claim to his acquaintance, that you or Sir J. had better arrange : with him in such a manner as may be least offensive to his feelings, nd so as not to have the appearance of officiousness nor obtrusion on y part. I hope you will be able to do this, as I should be very sorry o do any thing by him that may be deemed indelicate. The sum Murray offered and offers was and is one thousand and fifty pounds:— his I refused before, because I thought it more than the two things vere worth to Murray, and from other objections, which are of no con- equence. I have, however, closed with M. in consequence of Sir J.'s nd your suggestion, and propose the sum of six hundred pounds to be ransferred to Mr. * * in such manner as may seem best to your friend, —the remainder I think of for other purposes.

" As Murray has offered the money down for the copyrights, it may e done directly. I am ready to sign and seal immediately, and perhaps t had better not be delayed. I shall feel very glad if it can be of any se to * *; only don't let him be plagued, nor think himself obliged and ll that, which makes people hate one another, &c.

" Yours, very truly,

" B."

In his mention here of other " purposes," he refers to an intention vhich he had of dividing the residue of the sum between two other entlemen of literary celebrity, equally in want of such aid, Mr. Maturin nd Mr. * *. The whole design, however, though entered into with the tmost sincerity on the part of the noble poet, ultimately failed. Mr. Murray, who was well acquainted with the straits to which Lord Byron imself had been reduced, and foresaw that a time might come when

even money thus gained would be welcome to him, on learning the u
to which the sum was to be applied, demurred in advancing it,
alleging that, though bound not only by his word but his will to p
the amount to Lord Byron, he did not conceive himself called upon
part with it to others. How earnestly the noble poet himself, thou
with executions, at the time, impending over his head, endeavoured
urge the point, will appear from the following letter.

LETTER CCXXXVIII.

TO MR. MURRAY.

" February 22d, 1816.

" When the sum offered by you, and even *pressed* by you, wa
declined, it was with reference to a separate publication, as you kno
and I know. That it was large, I admitted and admit; and *that* mad
part of my consideration in refusing it, till I knew better what you wer
likely to make of it. With regard to what is past, or is to pass, abou
Mr. * *, the case is in no respect different from the transfer of forme
copyrights to Mr. Dallas. Had I taken you at your word, that is, take
your money, I might have used it as I pleased; and it could be in n
respect different to you whether I paid it to a w—, or a hospital, c
assisted a man of talent in distress. The truth of the matter seems this
you offered more than the poems are worth. I *said* so, and I *think* so
but you know, or at least ought to know, your own business best; an
when you recollect what passed between you and me upon pecuniar
subjects before this occurred, you will acquit me of any wish to tak
advantage of your imprudence.

" The things in question shall not be published at all, and there i
an end of the matter.

" Yours, &c."

The letter that follows will give some idea of those embarrassmen
in his own affairs, under the pressure of which he could be thus co
siderate of the wants of others.

LETTER CCXXXIX.

TO MR. MURRAY.

" March 6th, 1816.

*   *   *   *   *   *   *

" I sent to you to-day for this reason—the books you purchased
re again seized, and, as matters stand, had much better be sold at once
by public auction*. I wish to see you to return your bill for them,
which, thank God, is neither due nor paid. *That* part, as far as *you* are
concerned, being settled (which it can be, and shall be, when I see you
o-morrow), I have no further delicacy about the matter. This is about
he tenth execution in as many months; so I am pretty well hardened;
but it is fit I should pay the forfeit of my forefathers' extravagance and
my own; and whatever my faults may be, I suppose they will be pretty
well expiated in time—or eternity.

" Ever, &c.

" P.S. I need hardly say that I knew nothing till this *day* of the
new *seizure*. I had released them from former ones, and thought, when
you took them, that they were yours.

" You shall have your bill again to-morrow."

During the month of January and part of February, his Poems of
he Siege of Corinth and Parisina were in the hands of the printers, and

---

* The sale of these books took place the following month, and they were described in the
catalogue as the property of " a Nobleman about to leave England on a tour."

From a note to Mr. Murray, it would appear that he had been first announced as going to
he Morea.

" I hope that the catalogue of the books, &c., has not been published without my seeing it.
I must reserve several, and many ought not to be printed. The advertisement is a very bad one.
I am not going to the *Morea ;* and if I was, you might as well advertise a man in Russia as
going to *Yorkshire.*   " Ever, &c."

Together with the books was sold an article of furniture, which is now in the possession of
Mr. Murray, namely, " a large screen covered with portraits of actors, pugilists, representations
of boxing-matches," &c.

about the end of the latter month made their appearance. The followi
letters are the only ones I find connected with their publication.

LETTER CCXL.

TO MR. MURRAY.

" February 3d, 1816.

" I sent for ' Marmion,' which I return, because it occurred to m
there might be a resemblance between part of ' Parisina' and a simila
scene in Canto 2nd of ' Marmion.' I fear there is, though I neve
thought of it before, and could hardly wish to imitate that which i
inimitable. I wish you would ask Mr. Gifford whether I ought to sa
any thing upon it;—I had completed the story on the passage fror
Gibbon, which indeed leads to a like scene naturally, without a though
of the kind: but it comes upon me not very comfortably.

" There are a few words and phrases I want to alter in the MS
and should like to do it before you print, and will return it in an hour.

" Yours ever."

LETTER CCXLI.

TO MR. MURRAY.

" February 20th, 1816.

*   *   *   *   *   *

" To return to *our* business—your epistles are vastly agreeable
With regard to the observations on carelessness, &c. I think, with al
humility, that the gentle reader has considered a rather uncommon, an
designedly irregular, versification for haste and negligence. The measur
is not that of any of the other poems, which (I believe) were allowed t
be tolerably correct, according to Byshe and the fingers—or ears—b
which bards write, and readers reckon. Great part of the ' Siege' is i
(I think) what the learned call Anapests (though I am not sure, bein
heinously forgetful of my metres and my ' Gradus'), and many of th
lines intentionally longer or shorter than its rhyming companion; an

hyme also occurring at greater or less intervals of caprice or con-
enience.

"I mean not to say that this is right or good, but merely that I
ould have been smoother, had it appeared to me of advantage; and that
was not otherwise without being aware of the deviation, though I now
eel sorry for it, as I would undoubtedly rather please than not. My
vish has been to try at something different from my former efforts; as
endeavoured to make them differ from each other. The versification
f the 'Corsair' is not that of 'Lara;' nor the 'Giaour' that of the
Bride:' Childe Harold is again varied from these; and I strove to vary
he last somewhat from *all* of the others.

"Excuse all this d—d nonsense and egotism. The fact is, that I
m rather trying to think on the subject of this note, than really thinking
n it.—I did not know you had called: you are always admitted and
velcome when you choose.   "Yours, &c. &c.

"P.S. You need not be in any apprehension or grief on my account:
vere I to be beaten down by the world and its inheritors, I should have
uccumbed to many things, years ago. You must not mistake my *not*
ullying for dejection; nor imagine that because I feel, I am to faint:—
ut enough for the present.

"I am sorry for Sotheby's row. What the devil is it about? I
hought it all settled; and if I can do any thing about him or Ivan still,
 am ready and willing. I do not think it proper for me just now to be
nuch behind the scenes, but I will see the committee and move upon it,
f Sotheby likes.

"If you see Mr. Sotheby, will you tell him that I wrote to Mr.
Coleridge, on getting Mr. Sotheby's note, and have, I hope, done what
Mr. S. wished on that subject?"

It was about the middle of April that his two celebrated copies of
verses, "Fare thee well," and "a Sketch," made their appearance in the
newspapers:—and while the latter poem was generally and, it must be
owned, justly condemned, as a sort of literary assault on an obscure
emale, whose situation ought to have placed her as much *beneath* his

satire as the undignified mode of his attack certainly raised her *above*
with regard to the other poem, opinions were a good deal more divid
To many it appeared a strain of true conjugal tenderness, a kind of appe
which no woman with a heart could resist; while by others, on the co
trary, it was considered to be a mere showy effusion of sentiment,
difficult for real feeling to have produced as it was easy for fancy and a
and altogether unworthy of the deep interests involved in the subje
To this latter opinion, I confess my own to have, at first, strongly incline
and suspicious as I could not help thinking the sentiment that could,
such a moment, indulge in such verses, the taste that prompted or san
tioned their publication appeared to me even still more questionab
On reading, however, his own account of all the circumstances in t
Memoranda, I found that on both points I had, in common with a lar
portion of the public, done him injustice. He there described, and in
manner whose sincerity there was no doubting, the swell of tend
recollections under the influence of which, as he sat one night musing
his study, these stanzas were produced,—the tears, as he said, falling fa
over the paper as he wrote them. Neither did it appear, from th
account, to have been from any wish or intention of his own, b
through the injudicious zeal of a friend whom he had suffered to tal
a copy, that the verses met the public eye.

The appearance of these Poems gave additional violence to the ang
and inquisitorial feeling now abroad against him; and the title under whi
both pieces were immediately announced by various publishers, as " Poer
by Lord Byron on his domestic circumstances," carried with it a sufficie
exposure of the utter unfitness of such themes for rhyme. It is, indee
only in those emotions and passions, of which imagination forms
predominant ingredient,—such as love, in its first dreams, before reali
has come to imbody or dispel them, or sorrow, in its wane, whe
beginning to pass away from the heart into the fancy,—that poet
ought ever to be employed as an interpreter of feeling. For the e
pression of all those immediate affections and disquietudes that have the
root in the actual realities of life, the art of the poet, from the ve
circumstance of its being an art, as well as from the coloured form

which it is accustomed to transmit impressions, cannot be otherwise than a medium as false as it is feeble.

To so very low an ebb had the industry of his assailants now succeeded in reducing his private character, that it required no small degree of courage, even among that class who are supposed to be the most tolerant of domestic irregularities, to invite him into their society One distinguished lady of fashion, however, ventured so far as, on the eve of his departure from England, to make a party for him expressly; and nothing short, perhaps, of that high station in society which a life as blameless as it is brilliant has secured to her, could have placed beyond all reach of misrepresentation, at that moment, such a compliment to one marked with the world's censure so deeply. At this assembly of Lady J**'s he made his last appearance, publicly, in England, and the amusing account given of some of the company in his Memoranda,—of the various and characteristic ways in which the temperature of their manner towards him was affected by the cloud under which he now appeared,—was one of the passages of that Memoir it would have been most desirable, perhaps, to have preserved; though, from being a gallery of sketches, all personal and many satirical, but a small portion of it, if any, could have been presented to the public till the originals had long left the scene, and any interest they might once have excited was gone with themselves. Besides the noble hostess herself, whose kindness to him, on this occasion, he never forgot, there was also one other person (then Miss M**, now Lady K**) whose frank and fearless cordiality to him on that evening he most gratefully commemorated,—adding, in acknowledgment of a still more generous service, " She is a high-minded woman, and showed me more friendship than I deserved from her. I heard also of her having defended me in a large company, which *at that time* required more courage and firmness than most women possess."

As we are now approaching so near the close of his London life, I shall here throw together the few remaining recollections of that period with which the gleanings of his Memorandum-book, so often referred to, furnish me.

"I liked the Dandies; they were always very civil to *me*, thou[g]
in general they disliked literary people, and persecuted and mystifi[ed]
Madame de Staël, Lewis, * * **, and the like, damnably. They p[er]
suaded Madame de Staël that A * * had a hundred thousand a ye[ar]
&c. &c. till she praised him to his *face* for his *beauty!* and made a set [at]
him for * *, and a hundred fooleries besides. The truth is, that, thou[gh]
I gave up the business early, I had a tinge of dandyism* in my minorit[y]
and probably retained enough of it to conciliate the great ones at fiv[e]
and-twenty. I had gamed, and drank, and taken my degrees in mo[st]
dissipations, and having no pedantry, and not being overbearing, we r[an]
quietly together. I knew them all more or less, and they made me [a]
member of Watier's (a superb club at that time), being, I take it, t[he]
only literary man (except *two others*, both men of the world, Moore a[nd]
Spenser) in it. Our masquerade† was a grand one; so was the dand[y]
ball too, at the Argyle, but *that* (the latter) was given by the four chief[s]
B., M., A., and P., if I err not.

"I was a member of the Alfred, too, being elected while in Greec[e.]
It was pleasant; a little too sober and literary, and bored with * * an[d]
Sir Francis D'Ivernois; but one met Peel, and Ward, and Valentia, an[d]
many other pleasant or known people; and it was, upon the whole, [a]
decent resource in a rainy day, in a dearth of parties, or parliament, or i[n]
an empty season.

"I belonged, or belong, to the following clubs or societies:—to th[e]
Alfred; to the Cocoa Tree; to Watier's; to the Union; to Racket's ([at]
Brighton); to the Pugilistic; to the Owls, or 'Fly-by-night;' to th[e]
Cambridge Whig Club; to the Harrow Club, Cambridge; and to one [or]
two private clubs; to the Hampden (political) Club; and to the Itali[an]
Carbonari, &c. &c. &c. 'though last, *not least.*' I got into all these, an[d]

---

* Petrarch was, it appears, also, in his youth, a Dandy. "Recollect," he says, in a letter [to]
his brother, "the time, when we wore white habits, on which the least spot, or a plait i[ll]
placed, would have been a subject of grief; when our shoes were so tight we suffered ma[r]
tyrdom, &c."

† To this masquerade he went in the habit of a Caloyer, or Eastern monk,—a dress part[i]
cularly well calculated to set off the beauty of his fine countenance, which was according[ly]
that night, the subject of general admiration.

ever stood for any other—at least to my own knowledge. I declined
being proposed to several others, though pressed to stand candidate.

"When I met H * * L * *, the jailor, at Lord Holland's, before he
sailed for St. Helena, the discourse turned on the battle of Waterloo.
I asked him whether the dispositions of Napoleon were those of a great
general? He answered, disparagingly, ' that they were very *simple.*' I
had always thought that a degree of simplicity was an ingredient of
greatness.

"I was much struck with the simplicity of Grattan's manners in
private life: they were odd, but they were natural. Curran used to
take him off, bowing to the very ground, and ' thanking God that he
had no peculiarities of gesture or appearance,' in a way irresistibly
ludicrous; and * * used to call him a ' Sentimental harlequin.'

"Curran! Curran 's the man who struck me most*. Such imagination! there never was any thing like it that ever I saw or heard of. His
published life—his published speeches, give you *no* idea of the man—
none at all. He was a *machine* of imagination, as some one said that
Piron was an epigrammatic machine.

"I did not see a great deal of Curran—only in 1813; but I met
him at home (for he used to call on me), and in society, at Mackintosh's,

---

* In his Memoranda there were equally enthusiastic praises of Curran. " The riches,"
said he, " of his Irish imagination were exhaustless. I have heard that man speak more poetry
than I have ever seen written,—though I saw him seldom and but occasionally. I saw him presented to Madame de Staël at Mackintosh's;—it was the grand confluence between the Rhone
and the Saone, and they were both so d—d ugly, that I could not help wondering how the best
intellects of France and Ireland could have taken up respectively such residences." * * * *
   In another part, however, he was somewhat more fair to Madame de Stael's personal appearance:—" Her figure was not bad; her legs tolerable; her arms good. Altogether, I can
conceive her having been a desirable woman, allowing a little imagination for her soul, and so
forth. She would have made a great man."

Holland House, &c. &c. and he was wonderful even to me, who had se
many remarkable men of the time.

" * * * (commonly called *long* * * *, a very clever man, but od
complained to our friend Scrope B. Davies, in riding, that he had a *stit*
in his side. ' I don't wonder at it,' said Scrope, ' for you ride *like*
tailor.' Whoever had seen * * * on horseback, with his very tall figu
on a small nag, would not deny the justice of the repartee.

" When B * * was obliged (by that affair of poor M * *, wl
thence acquired the name of ' Dick the Dandy-killer'—it was abo
money, and debt, and all that) to retire to France, he knew no Frenc
and having obtained a grammar for the purpose of study, our frien
Scrope Davies was asked what progress Brummell had made in Frencl
he responded, ' that Brummell had been stopped, like Buonaparte i
Russia, by the *Elements.*'

" I have put this pun into Beppo, which is ' a fair exchange and n
robbery,' for Scrope made his fortune at several dinners (as he owne
himself) by repeating occasionally, as his own, some of the buffoonerie
with which I had encountered him in the morning.

" * * * is a good man, rhymes well (if not wisely), but is a bor
He seizes you by the button. One night of a rout, at Mrs. Hope's, l
had fastened upon me, notwithstanding my symptoms of manifest distre
(for I was in love, and had just nicked a minute when neither mother
nor husbands, nor rivals, nor gossips, were near my then idol, who wa
beautiful as the statues of the gallery where we stood at the time)-
* * *, I say, had seized upon me by the button and the heart-string
and spared neither. W. Spencer, who likes fun, and don't dislike mi
chief, saw my case, and coming up to us both, took me by the hand, an
pathetically bade me farewell; ' for,' said he, ' I see it is all over wit
you.' * * * then went away. *Sic me servavit Apollo.*

" I remember seeing Blucher in the London assemblies, and never saw any thing of his age less venerable. With the voice and manners of a recruiting serjeant, he pretended to the honours of a hero,—just as if a stone could be worshipped because a man had stumbled over it."

We now approach the close of this eventful period of his history. In a note to Mr. Rogers, written a short time before his departure for Ostend*, he says:—" My sister is now with me, and leaves town to-morrow; we shall not meet again for some time, at all events—if ever; and, under these circumstances, I trust to stand excused to you and Mr. Sheridan for being unable to wait upon him this evening."

This was his last interview with his sister,—almost the only person from whom he now parted with regret; it being, as he said, doubtful *which* had given him most pain, the enemies who attacked or the friends who condoled with him. Those beautiful and most tender verses, " Though the day of my destiny's over," were now his parting tribute to her† who, through all this bitter trial, had been his sole consolation; and, though known to most readers, so expressive are they of his wounded feelings at this crisis, that there are few, I think, who will object to seeing some stanzas of them here.

*   *   *   *   *

" Though the rock of my last hope is shiver'd,
    And its fragments are sunk in the wave,
Though I feel that my soul is deliver'd
    To pain—it shall not be its slave.
There is many a pang to pursue me:
    They may crush, but they shall not contemn—
They may torture, but shall not subdue me—
    'Tis of *thee* that I think—not of them.

---

* Dated April 16th.

† It will be seen, from a subsequent letter, that the first stanza of that most cordial of Fare-wells, " My boat is on the shore," was also written at this time.

" Though human, thou didst not deceive me,
  Though woman, thou didst not forsake,
Though loved, thou forborest to grieve me,
  Though slander'd, thou never couldst shake.
Though trusted, thou didst not disclaim me,
  Though parted, it was not to fly,
Though watchful, 'twas not to defame me,
  Nor mute, that the world might belie.

" From the wreck of the past, which hath perish'd,
  Thus much I at least may recall,
It hath taught me that what I most cherish'd,
  Deserved to be dearest of all:
In the desert a fountain is springing,
  In the wide waste there still is a tree,
And a bird in the solitude singing,
  Which speaks to my spirit of *thee*."

On a scrap of paper, in his handwriting, dated April 14th, 1816, I
find the following list of his attendants, with an annexed outline of hi
projected tour:—" *Servants*, —— Berger, a Swiss, William Fletche
and Robert Rushton.——John William Polidori, M.D.——Swisserland
Flanders, Italy, and (perhaps) France." The two English servants, i
will be observed, were the same " yeoman" and " page" who had set ou
with him on his youthful travels in 1809; and now,—for the second an
last time taking leave of his country,—on the 25th of April he saile
for Ostend.

END OF VOL. I.

LONDON:

PRINTED BY THOMAS DAVISON, WHITEFRIARS.

Milton Keynes UK
Ingram Content Group UK Ltd.
UKHW051358100624
444000UK00022B/218